The Creation

*Pan-African Chronology III: A Comprehensive Reference
to the Black Quest for Freedom in Africa,
the Americas, Europe and Asia, 1914–1929* (2001)

*The Muslim Diaspora: A Comprehensive Reference
to the Spread of Islam in Asia, Africa,
Europe and the Americas, Volume 2, 1500–1799* (2000)

*The Muslim Diaspora: A Comprehensive Reference
to the Spread of Islam in Asia, Africa,
Europe and the Americas, Volume 1, 570–1500* (1999)

*Pan-African Chronology II: A Comprehensive Reference
to the Black Quest for Freedom in Africa,
the Americas, Europe and Asia, 1865–1915* (1998)

*Pan-African Chronology I: A Comprehensive Reference
to the Black Quest for Freedom in Africa,
the Americas, Europe and Asia, 1400–1865* (1996)

The Creation

Secular, Jewish,
Catholic, Protestant and
Muslim Perspectives Analyzed

by Everett Jenkins, Jr.

McFarland & Company, Inc., Publishers
Jefferson, North Carolina, and London

Library of Congress Cataloguing-in-Publication Data

Jenkins, Everett, Jr., 1953–
The creation : secular, Jewish, Catholic, Protestant and Muslim
perspectives analyzed / by Everett Jenkins, Jr.
p. cm.
Includes bibliographical references and index.

ISBN 0-7864-1042-6 (library binding : 50# alkaline paper) ∞

1. Creation. I. Title.
BL227 .J46 2003   291.2'4—dc21   2002006494

British Library cataloguing data are available

Manufactured in the United States of America

McFarland & Company, Inc., Publishers
Box 611, Jefferson, North Carolina 28640
www.mcfarlandpub.com

To God,
for the days
in heaven
that I have been allowed
to spend here on earth

Acknowledgments

This book would not have been possible without the contributions made by my mother, Lillie Bell (Ingram) Jenkins. It was Lillie who gave birth to both my physical and spiritual life. In taking me to church (usually the First Missionary Baptist Church of Victorville, California), Lillie provided me with my first introduction to the wonders of God. And it was Lillie whose prayers have sustained and protected me for all of my life. For all of these reasons, and for so very many more, I acknowledge Lillie Bell—I acknowledge Mom—as being the primary "human" source of inspiration for this book.

Contents

Before our beginning, there was God...

One of the great unifying ideas that permeates all of the Abrahamic religions—the religions derived from the biblical patriarch Abraham—is the notion that there is an eternal God who created the universe. For some three billion people—for half of the world's population in the year 2000—one key idea is that before there was a universe, before there was even time itself, there was God.

This great unifying idea of the Abrahamic religions is humbling because it suggests that mankind can never understand God. God is, after all, beyond the physical universe, beyond time, and beyond the laws of nature. God is simply beyond understanding, not only for now but for all time to come.

Nevertheless, during most of our existence we humans have struggled to know God. Indeed, for many theologians, philosophers, historians, and even scientists, it is this struggle to know God which is the great story—the great quest—of humankind. What follows is a retelling of the beginnings of this great quest.

Introduction

A few years ago, I began a series of books which were collectively entitled *The Muslim Diaspora*. In the Introduction to *The Muslim Diaspora* I wrote a few passages which bear repeating now. I wrote:

I am not a Muslim. I am simply a man in search of truth—the truth about myself, my people, my country, my world and God. In my search for truth, I have discovered that there is much that I once believed to be true that is certainly not the total truth and, indeed, may not be true at all.

I once believed that I am only an "African American." However, in my search for truth, I discovered that such a label is not entirely true. I discovered that, like myself, most persons of African descent who live in the United States also have European and Indigenous American blood. By labeling such individuals as being only "African American," society may be denying essential elements of their being.

As a so-called "African American," I once believed that American slavery defined my past and impacted my present. But once I escaped the confines of the label, I learned that my triple heritage—my African, European and Indigenous American heritage—is far richer than I could ever have imagined. With a triple heritage, African slavery is not an overriding historical theme. With a triple heritage, the self-evident fact is that for people like me the overriding historical theme concerns the creation of a new people and the beginning of a new experiment with fascinating possibilities for the future history of man.

Another consequence of discovering the nature of a triple heritage is the realization that one of the defining labels that is currently en vogue in American society simply does not fit. On almost any day of the week, in schools, churches, and the halls of power throughout the land, one can hear pronouncements being made concerning the "Judeo-Christian" heritage of America. However, as a person with a triple heritage, there are other religious traditions which have obviously had some bearing on the individual that I am today. In addition to my "Judeo-Christian" heritage, there is also a lingering influence of the tribal religions of the African and Indigenous American peoples and, perhaps more significantly, there is the ongoing influence of Islam.

In discovering the truth about my

African heritage, I was frequently confronted by the role that Islam played in developing African society and in initiating the African diaspora. After all, it was the Muslim Arab merchants who took African slaves and companions with them as they traversed the then known world. China, Malaysia, India, and Spain all came to be the home of Africans because of the peripatetic Arabs. It was the Muslims who spread their religion to both the West and East coasts of Africa and through persuasion and intermarriage converted the African people to the Islamic faith. And it was African Muslims from the West coast of Africa who frequently were the slave cargo of the European ships that came to the Americas, speaking such Muslim languages as Hausa, Mandingo, and Fulfulde. It was these forefathers who played such an integral part in the bold experiment which eventually made me what I am.

Yes, Islam has, undoubtedly, had an historical role in defining what it means to be an African American. But, for me, there is even more.

For me, there are moments and times in my life which are indelibly etched in my psyche. There was the time while living in Glasgow, Montana, that I became aware of the sport of boxing when a brash young boxer by the name of Cassius Clay defeated the "invincible bear" known as Sonny Liston. Cassius Clay would soon become the legendary Muhammad Ali—a Muslim who became the dominant sports figure of my generation.

There was the time in high school when I first began to explore my African heritage by reading a story about a small time hoodlum who underwent two Islamic conversions—first as the Nation of Islam leader known as Malcolm X and later as the more orthodox Muslim, El Hajj Malik Shabazz.

Then there was the crucial period of my life when during my first two years of college I served as the "Minister of Information" of the Amherst Afro-American Society under the leadership of the Umar Zaid Muhammad.

No, I am not a Muslim. But my personal heritage, and my personal experiences, compel me to say that here too I have a triple heritage. I have not just a Judeo-Christian heritage, but rather a heritage that is a combination of Judaism, Christianity *and* Islam.

The book which you now hold in your hands is a product of my continuing exploration of my heritage—my continuing exploration of my roots. In this exploration, I have been drawn back in time to the beginning—the genesis—of all that is. In doing so, I believe that I have been allowed to taste a bit of the fruit from the tree of knowledge but, unlike Adam, I have not come away filled with shame, but rather I have come away filled with awe.

My words cannot adequately express the feelings that I have had during the course of this exploration. It seems that with each new day my eyes have encountered another new aspect of God. In exploring our creation from not only a multi-religious but also from a multi-disciplinary and multi-cultural approach, I believe I have discovered facets of the divine which may not be readily apparent to everyone, not unless they are willing to venture out on a similar exploration of their own. Indeed, for me, in studying the various religions, disciplines and cultures of our world, it often seems that people are so focused on one particular facet of God that they fail to see the extraordinary beauty associated with the many facets of God. Although no words can hope to fully convey the extent of the facets of God and no words can do full justice to the beauty, as one who has seen some of the other facets and who has been overwhelmed by their beauty, I do feel a sense of obligation to attempt to convey to others the beauty that I have seen.

This book is the first volume of my exploration into our creation. In this volume, I have attempted to present a number of perspectives on the Creation. The perspectives which are the focus of this volume are the Secular, Jewish, Catholic, Protestant, Fundamentalist Protestant, and Muslim perspectives on the Creation. In the manner in which these items are presented, and in the scope in which they are presented, I believe that there is simply no other reference work to compare. Even so, this work is incomplete. There are many more perspectives, many more facets, to explore and, God willing, in future volumes, I shall attempt to explore them. However, for this volume—for this beginning—I believe that the perspectives that are provided here can form the starting point from which one can begin a personal quest for understanding ourselves and understanding our relationship to God.

In reading this book, you the reader may discover the use of some terminology with which you may be unfamiliar. The first noticeable difference from other history books is that in this book a new designation is used to indicate time according to the Christian calendar. Instead of using "A.D." or "C.E.," I have used "C.C." "C.C." stands for Christian calendar. "C.C." is used here because "A.D." stands for the Latin phrase "anno Domini" which means "in the year of our Lord." For a Muslim, there is no God but God and the use of "A.D." may be deemed to be an heretical affront to one of the basic tenets of the Islamic faith.

As for not using "C.E.," "C.E." can stand for "Common Era" but is frequently designated as "Christian Era." The term "Christian Era" seems to imply a religious supremacy which is objectionable not only from a Muslim perspective but from an historical perspective. A review of history reveals that Christianity, while a powerful global force, has never predominated throughout the world and, arguably, does not predominate now. To assert that time as determined by the perceived birth of Christ should govern the history of the world (as well as the fate of mankind) is an assertion which, from the perspective of many non–Christians, is simply erroneous.

With regards to time before the birth of Christ, I have used the abbreviation "B.C.T." "B.C.T." stands for "before Christian time" and corresponds to the phrase referred to as "B.C.E." [before Common (Christian) Era] or "B.C." (before Christ) in most Western time schemes.

Additionally, in contrast to most anthropological treatises, the beliefs and folktales of various peoples are referred to in this book as "beliefs" and "folktales." The use of the words "myth" or "myths" has been avoided because of the pejorative connotation associated with such words. As the author of this work, I am well aware that anthropologists are quite correct in pointing out that the primary definition of the word "myth," according to Webster's Dictionary, is "a usually traditional story of ostensibly historical events that serves to unfold part of the world view of a people or explain, a practice, belief, or natural phenomena." However, in my experience, the term myth has become all too identified with its alternative, subordinate definition, namely "an ill-founded belief held uncritically especially by an interested group." As such, in the interest of developing avenues of dialogue instead of erecting emotionally charged linguistic barriers, this text uses words which, hopefully, will prove to be more conducive to understanding and discourse.

While reading this book, you will notice that occasionally there is a bracketed phrase instructing the reader to see another year, page or section in this book. These bracketed references are provided to assist the reader to find another reference in this book which may be more explanatory than the reference currently being read.

With regard to the sources of the information contained within this book, the information has been primarily compiled using secondary sources such as other commentaries and chronologies. Without meaning any disrespect to the sources I have relied upon, I must admit that there have been a number of errors or outdated information which I have encountered in compiling the information contained in this book. To the best of my ability, I have attempted to correct the errors and to update the information. However, it is inevitable that errors and outdated information continue to exist within this text.

For any errors or outdated information which may appear in this book, I, as the author, take full responsibility. However, as the author, I do make a special request of you, the reader. If you find errors, I would greatly appreciate your informing me of them by writing to me in care of the publisher of this book. As I envision the life of this book, it will be subject to additional editions and revisions. Therefore, your assistance as a critical reader would be most appreciated in correcting any deficiencies that may exist in this edition so that the same deficiencies will not exist in future.

Furthermore, in the course of reading this book you will find certain interpretations of scientific, historical and biblical events which I have provided. From the outset, it must be noted that these interpretations are based upon my own particular perspective which may not necessarily comport with the perspective which has historically been placed on the

same event. After all, given the complexity of science and history, the uncertainty of numbers, and the contestability of facts, it is quite understandable that differing viewpoints may arise concerning the same scientific, historical or biblical event. The comments I have made simply set forth my particular opinion with regards to the significance of the event. You, as an independent reader, are encouraged to read and develop opinions of your own.

Nevertheless, while saying this, there is one area of concern which I do wish to address. While I fully expect disagreement with my interpretations or opinions, the one criticism I am particularly sensitive to is a criticism that my interpretations are unfair or are not based on facts. Having lived in a country where the history of African American people has largely been ignored, where even today, erroneous facts and historical interpretations, are presented as the truth, I am loathe to perpetuate an evil that I am endeavoring to cure.

If, during the course of reading this book, you find that a certain unfair or unwarranted bias has interfered with the presentation of the truth, I implore you to convey that criticism to me. As the author of this book, I want it to be as accurate as it can be. Only by hearing from you the reader will I be able correct what may be wrong.

Finally, as a student of history, the most important lesson I have learned is that history is not written in stone. After all, even some of the more basic facts are often contested, numbers are frequently merely estimates, and the historical records almost invariably reflect the interests and biases of the historian.

Given all this, the study of history, and the corollary study of our origins, must be an evolving process which, if done appropriately, is approached from different perspectives as well as from different times. The study of our origins must be a never ending search which examines the ramifications of historical and religious events not only for the conquerors but also for the conquered, not only for the believers but also for those who do not so believe.

In this book, I have endeavored to present a study of the Creation as I believe it should be done. However, I know all too well, that this book is not finished, that my work is incomplete. What I have ultimately discovered in compiling and writing this book is that the impassioned quest of this writer as an intrepid explorer has become synonymous with a never ending quest for truth in a never ending search for God.

Everett Jenkins
Fairfield, California
December 2002

PART ONE.
A SECULAR
PERSPECTIVE

In our beginning, God created this universe...

One of the inescapable realities of our existence, is that in our corporeal form—in our mode as physical beings—we appear to be confined to the physical space that surrounds us. This physical space is part of a physical universe and it is this physical universe which, for the most part, has been the focus of the work of scientists, in general, and of modern astrophysicists, in particular.

However, even with all the advances that have been made in the realm of astrophysics, a world of questions about our universe continues to abound. And one of the key questions is: Is this the only universe that is?

In recent years the discussion of multiple universes (and even multiple dimensions) has become almost a religious exercise with many of its advocates forwarding the notion that there are an infinite number of universes and that the central driving force of our own universe is nothing. Such concepts defy our human ability of conceptualization and go far beyond the realm of concise discussion. For most of us, and for the purposes of this book, simplicity is what is most wanted and anything beyond a factor of three becomes troublesome.

With this self-imposed limitation in mind, it is notable that one of the earliest theories concerning the creation of multiple universes was advanced by J. Richard Gott III. Gott's model proposed that not one but three universes sprang from the Creation. The Gott model attempts to account for two odd facts about our universe that trouble many cosmologists. One of these is that while the basic equations of physics are time-symmetrical—that is, they can be run forward or backward in time with equal efficacy—in the real universe, time, it seems, moves in one direction only. The second oddity confronted by Gott is the scarcity of anti-matter in our universe. For every sort of sub-atomic particle of matter, it is possible to conceive of a particle with the same mass but with opposite charge—an anti-particle. Yet only mere traces of anti-matter have been found in nature. Why should nature be so asymmetrical, favoring matter over anti-matter, running time in one direction but not the other?

Building on a theory offered by certain physicists that anti-matter can be thought of as ordinary matter moving in reverse time, Gott constructed a three-universe cosmology. In Gott's three universe cosmology, the Creation generated not only our universe, but also a second universe composed of anti-matter and evolving in reverse time, as well as a third universe made up exclusively of particles that travel faster than light. The fleet particles of this ghostly third universe, called tachyons, are permissible under Einstein's relativity theory, which requires only that nothing in our universe can be accelerated to the velocity of light. Tachyons need not worry about this provision, for they have always been going faster than the speed of light. The tacyhon particles occupy a mirror universe where everything travels faster than light and nothing can be reined in to a velocity as slow as that of light. The Gott cosmology is a masterpiece of symmetry without being dictatorial about it. The theory predicts, for instance, that there should be traces of contamination of our universe by anti-matter (as has been verified by observation) and by tachyons (as has not).

Ultimately, the cosmological theories of today, including Gott's theory, may be looked upon by our descendants with respect, bemusement, scorn or even hilarity. After all, even though cosmological inquiries need no longer be purely speculative in nature, and even though, mankind has learned how to test such inquiries against the real universe, the universe continues to surprise and to tease, and to escape human comprehension. For inexplicable reasons which cause all to wonder, just when our universe appears to be a lucid, intelligible, observable, and evolving entity, along comes some disconcerting fact or theory which causes us to pause, to reevaluate, to be confused and, usually, to be humbled by the primitiveness of our former understanding. To be sure, our universe will continue to invite inquiry—and man does appear to be destined to respond to the invitation. Nevertheless, as the physical world has shown over and over again, just when man becomes arrogantly certain concerning the knowledge that has been

achieved, along comes a surprise which shakes the confidence that was based on all that had been. It is this continuing uncertainty which makes the study of both science and religion so compelling. Ideally, both should be a search for truth but, ultimately, both seem to wind up being tests of our faith.

15 BILLION B.C.T.

At the beginning of the third millenium of the Christian calendar—at the beginning of the 21st century—it was believed by most of the scientific community that our universe began some 15 billion years ago with the "big bang."

The commonly accepted model of the universe suggests that it began in an infinitely compact and singular state, enclosing a space even smaller than an atomic particle. The beginning of our universe then occurred when the compact particle—the singularity—grew not in a violent explosion (a "big bang") but rather through an incredibly rapid expansion—a "creation."

While today scientists may feel relatively secure with the notion that the incredible expansion did occur, what they are not so secure about are some of the more troubling aspects of the "scientific" belief in creation. Although the basic framework of the incredible expansion model has achieved wide acceptance, along with this acceptance has come an increased sophistication with regards to its shortcomings. As the potential for actually obtaining answers has improved, the questions have evolved from the "whats" and "wheres" to the "hows" and "whys." For instance, how did the universe go from a smooth expansion of particles to being so lumpy and complex and why was the universe so perfectly balanced gravitationally that it neither flew apart nor crunched back together before the first star or galaxy could form?

Indeed, the balance exhibited even by today's universe is so improbable that it is likened to the balance exhibited by a pencil that is able to stand upright on its own on its point. Any tipping at all and the universe would immediately fall all the way over in one direction or another. But for billions of years no such tipping has occurred. Why not?

Time, as we know it, began.

The universe inflated at a rate faster than the speed of light.

The creative expansion was not an explosion in the classic sense. In our human experience with explosions, shrapnel like objects fly through a pre-existing space. However, with the expansion of the initial singularity, space itself was being created at the same time that time, matter and even gravity were being formed. Indeed, at its beginning, the expansion of the singularity caused space to expand at speeds that, at times, exceeded the speed of light. This was possible because while light, energy and matter cannot exceed the speed of light, the expansion (the "creation") of space itself was not so restricted.

Gravity separated from the three other forces: electromagnetic, strong nuclear, and weak interaction.

Three forces began operating: electromagnetic, strong nuclear, and gravitational.

Weak interaction and electromagnetic force separated.

Quarks combined to form particles.

The nuclei of atoms formed.

The first true, complex atoms formed.

14.5 BILLION B.C.T.

The galaxies began to form out of gaseous clouds of hydrogen and helium.

14 BILLION B.C.T.

The Cosmic Dark Ages came to an end as the first stars were formed. After a billion years of darkness, there was light.

The "habitable areas" of the first galaxies began to be formed.

The Earth occupies a privileged position within the solar system. If the Earth had been located much closer to the Sun, then, like Venus, it would have been too hot to support life. If the Earth had been located slightly farther from the Sun, then, like Mars, the Earth would have been too cold to sustain life. Our Earth sits in a so-called "habitable zone," a ring around the Sun within which liquid water can exist on a planet. Without liquid water, any kind of life as we know it is highly unlikely.

Scientists now posit that just as our solar system has a "habitable zone" so too do entire galaxies. Although most galaxies contain millions of stars, many of these stars appear to be located in uninhabitable zones. Scientists theorize that the habitable zone of a spiral galaxy (like our own Milky Way) may encircle its center, just as the habitable zone of the solar system encircles the Sun. Inside or outside this band, the galaxy is sterile and life cannot exist.

The question that arises is why? It is easy enough to understand why a single star should have a habitable zone, but it is not so easy to understand why a galaxy should have a habitable zone.

In response, scientists note that it is a delicate matter to make a planet like our Earth. To make an Earth, you need the right materials: heavy, rock-forming elements like silicon and aluminum, and iron for the core. At our location in the Milky Way, these elements are fairly abundant, but farther out, these elements become scarcer, and corollarily any existing rocky planets would tend to be smaller. These planets would also be cooler because there would be less of the heavy radioactive elements, that in the case of Earth, warm up the interior by radioactive decay.

Without a warm interior, an Earth-like planet cannot have plate tectonics—the gradual movement of the planet crust. This means that the planet can not keep water circulating through its atmosphere, and so it is likely to run down to a frozen state. That is what happened to Mars. Mars is actually within the solar system's habitable zone, but Mars froze because, being smaller than Earth, it cooled down too quickly and lost the ability to maintain plate tectonics.

In contrast, further in towards the center of a spiral galaxy—of our Milky Way—other factors frustrate the development of life. Stars are more densely crowded together, and so conditions would be stormier. Exploding stars—"supernovae," for instance—may bathe nearby planetary systems in hazardous radiation. And planets are likely to suffer heavier bombardment by comets, which are sent charging through a star's planetary system by the gravitational pull of other stars. On Earth, the deadly effects of gigantic comet collisions may have choked life several times on the young planet, and so delayed the evolution of complex organisms. If this bombardment had been more frequent, life might never have taken hold at all, or it may have been constantly prevented from evolving into complex forms.

Based on these observations and conjectures, scientists suggest that most galaxies might have only limited regions where Earth-like planets could both form at all and be able to support life. Indeed, it may be that because many galaxies have less heavy elements than the Milky Way, their habitable zones might shrink out of existence, leaving no room for life.

In the final analysis, it may be that all that glitters is not gold—that the Universe is likely filled with millions of galaxies with billions of solar systems all of which are as sterile as our Moon.

8 BILLION B.C.T.

The expansion of the universe began to speed up.

5 BILLION B.C.T.

The solar system began to take shape.

One of the great beauties of all creation—one of the great beauties of the universe—is the solar system in which we live. At the end of the second millennium of the Christian calendar, scientists had begun to marvel at the unique quality of our solar system. Although other worlds had been discovered and, although at least one other solar system had been detected, none of the planets or solar systems matches the delicate machinery that is associated with our solar system.

What makes our solar system so unique is that instead of having the planets orbit the sun in egg-shaped orbits much like the comets do, the planets of our system orbit the sun in neatly stacked, circular orbits. Scientists generally acknowledge that the presence of a circular orbit made possible the existence of life, as we know it, on this earth. The relatively circular orbit of our earth provided nearly equal temperatures all year-round. In other words, it was the unique circular orbit of our earth which created a stable temperature and climate which facilitated the development of life.

Temperatures and climate would be much more volatile and life as we know it could not have survived if the earth had had an elliptical orbit. Indeed, if the Jupiter of our solar system did not itself have a relatively circular orbit, it is doubtful that our earth itself would even exist.

As the new millennium begins, there is

much, so very much to be thankful for, not the least of which is the fact that, on any given night, we can view the beauty of the planets of our solar system, we can marvel at the mystery of how it came to be; and we can feel blessed that the planets and their unique motion continue to watch over us.

4.6 BILLION B.C.T.

The solar system was formed.

Solar systems elsewhere in the galaxy appeared.

The Kuiper Belt was formed.

The Kuiper Belt extends from just beyond the orbit of Neptune to a distance of about 30 billion kilometers (19 billion miles) from the sun. The Kuiper Belt is named for a Dutch-American astronomer, Gerald Kuiper, who predicted its existence in 1951, and it is the Kuiper Belt which has begun to provide the clues to answering the riddle of the solar system.

Astronomers had long theorized that many icy bodies orbit the sun beyond the planets. Astronomers predicted the existence of such objects based on a widely accepted theory that the planets in our solar system were formed from a rotating disk of gas and dust surrounding the infant sun. Theoretical models of solar system formation showed that beyond Neptune, small bodies, representing debris from the formation of the main planets, should exist. In addition, the motions of comets indicated that these small icy bodies originate far beyond the known planets.

Many astronomers now think that Pluto, the ninth planet, may be more closely related to the Kuiper Belt objects than to the other planets. Pluto is far smaller than any other planet, and physically it is much more like a Kuiper Belt object or a large moon than a planet. Additionally, the orbit of Pluto is different from the other planets but is similar to other Kuiper Belt objects. Finally, Pluto is firmly within the Kuiper Belt. Accordingly, many astronomers view Pluto as the largest known Kuiper Belt object rather than a planet in its own right.

Astronomers are fascinated by Kuiper Belt objects because they are cosmic leftovers, material that is virtually unchanged from the time when the sun and planets formed, about 4.6 billion years ago. By studying the Kuiper Belt, astronomers expect to learn much about the early solar system.

4.56 BILLION B.C.T.

The Hadeon Eon began. During this period the Earth-Moon system would be formed.

Although the moon itself is devoid of air, water and life, its creation and existence has proven to be essential to the origin of life on Earth. It is, after all, our unusually large moon which exerts a stabilizing influence on Earth's spin axis that has prevented the planet from wobbling like an out-of-control top—and has thereby saved it from wild climate fluctuations that would have been hostile to life. Indeed, it is generally conceded that we, the inhabitants of Earth, are in an exceptional state. We owe our very existence to the terrestrial stability caused by the nightly present moon.

The tilt of the Earth's spin axis, called the obliquity, is what gives us seasons. If the Earth were spinning like a perfectly upright top, perpendicular to the plane of its orbit around the sun (an obliquity of zero), there would hardly be any seasons at all because every point on the planet would receive a constant amount of sunlight all year long. However, if the Earth were rolling on its side (an obliquity of 90 degrees), each pole would swing between extreme heat and total darkness every year. Because the Earth's spin axis is only slightly tilted, by about 23.5 degrees, the planet enjoys moderate seasonal variations.

This slight tilt has been the case for eons and it has been so because of the moon. Because the Earth spins, the planet bulges at the equator. The sun and the other planets exert a gravitational pull on this bulge, causing the Earth's axis to rock slowly. As the planets move in their orbits—and as they deform one another's orbits through their gravitational interactions—the overall strength of the various forces acting on the Earth's bulge fluctuates erratically. If left unchecked these gravitational forces would cause the Earth's spin axis to oscillate in an inherently unpredictable, chaotic way. Computer modeling indicates that the oscillation could vary anywhere from 0 to 85 degrees—an amount which would make the possibility of life on earth very unlikely.

However, with the moon, chaos is averted and stability is imposed. The moon packs enough gravitational pull to effectively cancel most of the other forces on Earth's spin axis. With just a little help from the sun, the moon makes the Earth's axis settle into a regular motion, causing it to precess in a small circle every 26,000 years. The tilt of the axis does change over time, but only by 1.3 degrees instead of 85.

It is important to note that a mere one degree change in obliquity is not entirely harmless. Indeed, many scientists think that such a degree change can trigger an ice age. Given that such a traumatic climatic change can accompany only a minor oscillation, an obliquity that fluctuated by tens of degrees would have played havoc with the world's environment. The climate would have swung between epochs with extreme seasonal variations and epochs with none at all. Eco-systems would not have been able to stabilize long enough for advanced life-forms such as humans to evolve.

It is now a generally accepted theory that the stability of the Earth's spin axis is a key to life. And as further proof of the validity of this theory, scientists point to Mars. Even though Mars currently tilts at a comfortable 25 degrees, that situation is probably temporary. Mars has only two Manhattan-size satellites. Even together, these moons exert a puny gravitational force—hardly enough to counteract other planetary influences.

It is estimated that the obliquity of Mars has probably varied between 0 and 60 degrees. That suggests a Martian history (and future) of wild climate fluctuations. Indeed, photographs of Mars' polar regions from the twin *Viking* orbiters reveal layers of ice and dust stacked unevenly like hotcakes—a possible geologic record of the advance and retreat of the polar ice caps over hundreds of millions of years.

There are two implications of the association of the Moon with life on earth which are quite profound. While planets like the Earth may well be abundant in the universe, astronomers now concede that Earth-size planets with moons as large as ours are likely to be extremely rare. Thus, if a large moon is a prerequisite for the evolution of life, beings like us might turn out to be exceedingly rare as well.

The other implication is that the Earth can count on its stable climate only as long as it has a large moon nearby. But the moon, as a result of its gravitational interaction with the Earth, is gradually being accelerated to a higher orbit. The moon is receding from the Earth at a rate of about one inch per year. In about one billion years, the pull of the moon will be so weak that the Earth's obliquity will begin to fluctuate chaotically. When that happens the Earth's climate will surely undergo wild variations making life on the planet extremely difficult and probably impossible—at least based upon our current perspective and upon the currently known abilities of the beings known as *Homo sapiens.*

4.0 BILLION B.C.T.

Conditions for the creation of life on Earth began to be maximized.

A meteor struck Mars.

When a meteor perhaps as large as a hundred miles in diameter crashed into Mars four billion years ago, the force of the impact re-contoured much of the southern Martian hemisphere. The collision punched a hole in the surface 1,300 miles across and 5 miles deep. The fallout of debris, enough to theoretically deposit a mile-thick layer across the continental United States, stretched 2,500 miles from the basin's center.

The Martian meteor impact of four billion years ago has a bearing on life on Earth because the debris from such impacts wound up landing on Earth and possibly contributing to the organic chemistry that came to exist.

By 1996, scientists had collected more than 16,000 meteorites in Antarctica, as many as in the rest of the world combined. Some are previously unknown types, including fragments believed to have come from Mars. Some planetary scientists think that the impact of asteroids and comets on Mars sent chunks of Martian rock hurtling into space, where they orbited the sun for millions of years. Finally, some of these bits of Mars came crashing down in Antarctica and in other places on Earth.

3.8 BILLION B.C.T.

The Archaen Eon began.

3.6 BILLION B.C.T.

A meteorite from Mars landed on earth.

3.5 BILLION B.C.T.

The first primitive life forms emerged on Earth. The fossil record shows prokaryotes (cells without nuclei) up to 3.5 billion years old, and eukaryotes (cells with nuclei) dating back to 1.75 billion years ago.

Sexual reproduction began.

All sexual reproduction, no matter how large or small the organisms may be, is a performance of single cells. Only at the level of single cells can the essential genetic recombinations be accomplished. So in every generation new life begins with the egg, which is a single cell, however large it may be. Egg and sperm unite at fertilization, but the fertilized egg is as much a single cell as before.

When it is asked, "When did sexual reproduction begin?" The answer invariably is that the fundamental, or molecular, basis of sexuality is an ancient evolutionary development that goes back almost to the beginning of life on earth, several billion years ago, for it is evident among the vast world of single-celled organisms, including bacteria.

It is believed that photosynthesis may have begun at this time.

2.5 BILLION B.C.T.

The Proterozoic Eon began.

2 BILLION B.C.T.

About two billion years ago, rising levels of oxygen in the atmosphere provided an environment in which eukaryotes flourished.

1 BILLION B.C.T.

A billion years of geological stability on Earth came to an end.

700 MILLION B.C.T.

The Earth became an iceball.

During the 1960s, geologists discovered rocks about 700 million years old all over the world bore the signature of rough treatment from glaciers. The Soviet scientist, M. I. Budyko, proposed one possible cause: runaway global cooling. According to the theory, bright, white polar ice sheets reflect more of the sun's heat and light back into space than do darker land masses or open water. So as the ice sheets grow during an Ice Age, they exert a feedback effect that further cools the world. The bigger they get, the more cooling they cause and so the more the ice sheets grow. Budyko's theoretical models of the Earth's climate suggested that this feedback could pass a point of no return, leaving the planet to freeze over.

On the resulting Iceball Earth, ice was everywhere: even the oceans were frozen. Except for a few organisms clinging on or around volcanoes, no life could survive. The temperature around the world was an average minus 40 degrees centigrade. It was extremely cold.

How then could Iceball Earth have shaken off its Arctic glaze and returned to being the liquid blue planet that we know today? The answer may lie in the volcanoes. Volcanoes thrusting through the ice would have continued to disgorge gases, mostly carbon dioxide. Carbon dioxide is a greenhouse gas which causes global warming. Today, volcanic carbon dioxide is kept in check by natural processes such as chemical weathering of rocks, which removes the gas from the atmosphere in the form of carbonate minerals. However, on Iceball Earth, weathering would be suppressed because there would be no rain to wash the carbon dioxide from the skies, and no exposed rocks to react with it. So volcanic carbon dioxide would accumulate gradually in the atmosphere and warm the planet.

At some point, there would be enough of it to break the reign of ice, and the seas would thaw. Calculations suggest that a huge amount of carbon dioxide is needed to do this: about 350 times the amount in today's atmosphere. So once melting began, temperatures would soar and the planet would gravitate toward becoming a hothouse.

570 MILLION B.C.T.

The Phanerozoic Eon; the Paleozoic Era; and the Cambrian Period began. During the Cambrian Period, there appears in the fossil record hard-bodied animals and plants. This period also saw the advent of mollusks, arthropods, chordates, foraminifera, dinomastigotes, radiolarians, and red algae.

Multicellular animals appeared in the sea only in the very late Precambrian era. During the Cambrian Period (570 to 510 million years ago), invertebrates with hard fossilized skeletons increased in number and variety. Fish, the first vertebrates, date to the Ordovician Period (510 to 440 million years ago) but are far outnumbered in the fossil record by corals and other invertebrates that inhabited the sea bed.

543 MILLION B.C.T.

The Cambrian Explosion began.

The Cambrian Explosion—Earth's evolutionary equivalent of the "Big Bang"—began some 543 million years ago. Within the span of a mere 5 million years, the ancestors of almost all animals suddenly appeared on Earth. There have been a number of theories advanced concerning the reasons for this explosion. Some have said that an increase in the Earth's oxygen supply fueled the outburst. Others say that a decrease in carbon dioxide in the Earth's atmosphere led to mass "creation."

One of the more intriguing theories for the species explosion is that the evolution of eyes sparked the Cambrian "Big Bang." According to this theory, before the eye came along, there were just simple animals—essentially just worms and jellyfish. However, once the evolution of the eye came along, massive natural selection pressures began to exert themselves forcing these simple life forms to alter themselves for purposes of protection and reproduction. These alterations led to life forms learning how to swim, burrow, hide, have armored body parts or reflect warning colors. And it was these adaptations which eventually led to our diversity of life.

At least, that is the theory.

During the Cambrian period, invertebrates with hard external skeletons, such as mollusks and trilobites (arthropods which grew by molting their old skeletons to form new ones), diversified. Most of the earliest fossils with hard skeletons were composed of calcium phosphate, but forms with skeletons of calcium carbonate minerals later became dominant.

530 MILLION B.C.T.

The first fish appeared.

510 MILLION B.C.T.

The Cambrian Period came to an end.

During the Cambrian Period, an explosion of life populated the seas, but the land areas remained barren. Animal life was wholly invertebrate, and the commonest animals were arthropods called trilobites with species numbering in the thousands.

The Ordovician Period began.

During the Ordovician Period, the predecessor of today's Atlantic Ocean began to shrink as the continents of that time drifted closer together. Trilobites were still abundant; important groups making their first appearance included the corals, crinoids, bryozoans, and pelecypods. Armored, jawless fishes—the oldest known vertebrates—made their appearance as well. Primitive fish fossils came to be found in ancient estuary beds in North America.

500 MILLION B.C.T.

It is believed that, 500 million years ago, land masses, including North America and what is now Siberia, were laid along the equator. Below the equator, South America, India, Australia, Antarctica, and Africa were all melded into a single supercontinent, Gondwana.

The name "Gondwana" came from the Austrian geologist Edward Suess, a contemporary of Alfred Wegener, a visionary pioneer of the modern study of plate tectonics. Suess derived the name from an ancient tribe of India, the Gonds.

Throughout geological history, the continents have moved and fragmented as new oceans opened, and coalesced with other continents as old oceans closed. It is not precisely known how the continents were distributed in the earliest Precambrian era. However, about 500 million years ago, the large continent known as Gondwana was situated over the southern polar region while smaller areas of land existed around the equator and in the Northern Hemisphere.

Around this time, the colonization of land surfaces by algae and insects began.

440 MILLION B.C.T.

The Ordovician Period came to an end.

The Ordovician Period was a period of relative stability in the Earth's history, which may have been an important factor in the substantial growth of biological diversity which took place. However, as the period drew to a close, 440 million years ago, there was a huge extinction event with some animal groups losing more than half their species.

The extinction seems to have been the result of a period of glaciation—an ice age, the seas retreated as more and more water was taken up into ice sheets, and the marine habitats (which harbored the vast majority of life in the Ordovician Period) changed drastically, destroying ecosystems and reducing the number of ecological riches.

There seem to have been two peak periods of extinction—one at the beginning of the glaciation, and another at the end of the extinction, between 500 thousand and 1 million years later, when sea levels rose rapidly. Echinoderms, trilobites, nautiloids and many other groups suffered significant losses, although the overall effect was less drastic than that of most other major extinctions.

The Silurian Period began. During this period, the first terrestrial plants appeared. This period also saw the beginning of the widespread dispersal of life on land.

During the Silurian Period, life ventured onto land in the form of simple plants called psilophytes, with a vascular system for circulating water, and scorpion-like animals akin to now extinct marine arthropods called eurypterids. Trilobites decreased in number and variety, but the seas teemed with reef corals, cephalopods, and jawed fishes.

410 MILLION B.C.T.

The Silurian Period came to an end while the Devonian Period began. During this period, armored fish and invertebrate marine animals came to be. Additionally, plants

with seeds made their first appearance on Earth.

The Devonian Period is known as the "Age of Fishes" because of the abundance of fish life as evidenced by the fossil record in Devonian rocks. During the Devonian Period, fishes also became adapted to fresh water as well as to salt water. These fishes included a diversity of both jawless and jawed armored fishes, early sharks, and bony fishes, from the last of which amphibians evolved. Indeed, one subdivision of the sharks of that time is still extant.

400 MILLION B.C.T.

Gondwana, the supercontinent, became the south pole. While there, Africa was covered with glaciers, its ice cap was as thick as Antarctica's is today. Indeed, the region which is today known as the Sahara—a region which is today one of the hottest places on Earth—bears traces of the time when the desert was an iceland.

360 MILLION B.C.T.

The Devonian Period came to an end.

Although it is clear that there was a massive loss of biodiversity towards the end of the Devonian Period, it is not clear over how long a period these extinctions took place, with estimates varying from 500 thousand to 15 million years. Neither is it clear whether it was a single mass extinction or a series of several smaller ones one after the other. Nevertheless, the balance of evidence suggests that the extinctions took place over a period of some 3 million years, about 365 million years ago.

During the late Devonian extinction, as many as 70 percent of all species vanished. Marine species were more severely affected than those in freshwater. Brachiopods, ammonites, and many other invertebrates suffered heavily, as did Agnathan and Placoderm fish. On land, where plants were diversifying and amphibians were beginning their evolution, there seem to have been far fewer losses.

The causes of the Devonian extinction are unclear. The disproportionate losses amongst warm water species suggest that the Earth's climate changed—most likely for the cooler. The global cooling was an important factor and it has been suggested that this was associated with (or may have even caused) a drop in the oxygen levels of the shallower waters.

The Carboniferous (Mississippian) Period began. This period saw the widespread occurrence of fish and amphibian vertebrates in fossil record.

During the Carboniferous Period, trilobites almost became extinct, but corals, crinoids, and brachiopods were abundant, as were all groups of the mollusks. Warm, humid climates fostered lush forests in swamplands, where the major coal beds of today were formed. Dominant plants included treelike lycopods, horsetails, ferns, and (now extinct) plants called pteridosperms, or seed ferns. Amphibians spread and gave rise to reptiles, the first vertebrates to live entirely on land; and winged insects such as the dragonfly appeared.

320 MILLION B.C.T.

The Pennsylvanian Period began. This period saw the widespread dispersal of large trees in swamps. It was the abundance of these trees which became the source of the coal deposits utilized by modern man.

290 MILLION B.C.T.

The Carboniferous Period came to an end while the Permian Period began. This period saw the appearance of the first archosaurs.

During the Permian Period, the Earth's land areas became welded into a single landmass that geologists call Pangaea, and in the North American region the Appalachians were formed. Cycadlike plants and true conifers appeared in the northern hemisphere, replacing the coal forests. Trilobites and many fishes and corals died out as the Paleozoic era came to an end.

Twin impact craters were created by an object striking Quebec, Canada. The resulting Clearwater Lake West has a diameter of 32 kilometers (20 miles) and Clearwater Lake East has a diameter of 22 kilometers (13.7 miles). These two impact craters form a rare pairing of meteorite impacts.

245 MILLION B.C.T.

The Permian Period came to an end. The end of the Permian Period saw the largest extinction event in the history of life on earth.

Life flourished during the Carboniferous and Permian Periods. Crinoids, ammonites, corals and fish diversified and flourished in the seas, while amphibians and reptiles continued their invasion of the land. However, after more than a 100 million years of relative stability, the end of the Permian (245 million years ago) saw the largest extinction event in the history of the Earth. Indeed, the Permian extinction was far more devastating than the much more famous Cretaceous extinction—the extinction which brought to an end the reign of the dinosaurs.

It has been estimated that as many as

96 percent of all marine species were lost during the Permian extinction. Additionally, on land, more than three quarters of all vertebrate families became extinct. Many causes have been proposed for the Permian extinctions. Some have said it was fluctuations in the sea level; others have said it was the change in the salinity of the oceans; and some have posited that there was increased volcanic activity. However, most seem to agree that the major factor was a dramatic, cataclysmic climate change.

A primary candidate for the cataclysmic climate change which brought about the Permian mass extinction is volcanic activity. In 1783, the Laki volcano in Iceland erupted, spitting out three cubic miles of lava. Floods, ash, and fumes wiped out 9,000 people and 80 percent of the livestock. The ensuing starvation killed a quarter of Iceland's population. Atmospheric dust caused winter temperatures to plunge by 9 degrees in the newly independent United States.

As catastrophic as the Iceland volcanic eruption was, it was merely a baby burp compared to the two great volcanic eruptions in the history of life on Earth. Sixty-five million years ago, a plume of hot rock from the mantle burst through the crust in what is now India. Eruptions raged century after century, ultimately unleashing a quarter million cubic miles of lava—the Laki eruption multiplied 100,000 times over. Some scientists have argued that it was the Indian volcanic eruption, not an asteroid, which caused the demise of the dinosaurs. But even this monumental, mind boggling eruption pales in comparison to the volcanic eruptions which marked the end of the Permian period.

Centered in what is today Siberia, the Permian period volcanic eruption produced huge quantities of sulfurous volcanic gases. These sulfurous volcanic gases in turn produced acid rains. Chlorine bearing compounds presented yet another threat to the fragile ozone layer—a noxious brew all around.

The conditions created by the Permian volcanic eruptions undoubtedly contributed to the most thorough extermination known to paleontology. It was most likely the volcanoes that exterminated 95 percent of all the species on the Earth. And it is the volcanoes which could pose the most imminent threat life on earth, including the life that is known as human.

The Mesozoic Era began. It would last until 65 Million B.C.T.

Whatever the causes of the Permian disaster, new life forms began to emerge after the Permian mass extinction. Mollusks, corals, and sea lilies diversified, and the first turtles and ichthyosaurs (fish-like reptiles) date to this period.

Of all the reptiles of the Mesozoic Era (245-65 Million B.C.T.), the dinosaurs are the most dominant. However, mammal-like therapsids, flying pterosaurs, and early lizards and crocodiles also evolved. Mammals and birds first appeared in the Triassic and Jurassic respectively. Dinosaurs died out in the mass extinction at the end of the Cretaceous Period (146-65 Million B.C.T.).

The Triassic Period began. During the Triassic Period, the Pangaea supercontinent broke up into two distinct portions named Laurasia and Gondwana.

The Mesozoic Era (and Triassic Period) opened with Pangaea splitting into a northern landmass called Laurasia and a southern one called Gondwanaland. Forms of life changed considerably in the Mesozoic, also known as the Age of Reptiles. New pteridosperm families appeared, and conifers and cycads became major floral groups, along with ginkgos and other genera. Such reptiles as dinosaurs and turtles appeared, as did mammals.

235 Million B.C.T.

The first true mammals appeared.

230 Million B.C.T.

By 230 million years ago, scientists believe that some amphibians had become reptiles. These reptiles became the first dinosaur and the first pterosaur.

212 Million B.C.T.

Around 212 million years ago, an object struck near Manicouagan, Quebec, Canada, creating an impact crater 100 kilometers (62 miles) wide. The Manicouagan impact crater is today one of the largest impact craters still preserved on the surface of the Earth.

208 Million B.C.T.

The Triassic Period came to an end.

Although it has been viewed as one of the less significant extinctions, some studies suggest that almost a quarter of all families became extinct during the late Triassic Period, making this extinction comparable in importance to the late Cretaceous extinction—the one that killed the dinosaurs.

The causes of the Triassic extinction are poorly known, perhaps because it has attracted relatively little study. However, once again, severe climate change seems to be important with an increase in rainfall being the most prominent factor.

The Jurassic Period began.

As Gondwanaland rifted apart during the Jurassic Period, the North Atlantic Ocean widened and the South Atlantic was born. Giant dinosaurs ruled on land, while marine reptiles such as ichthyosaurs and plesiosaurs increased in number. Primitive

birds appeared, and modern reef-building corals grew in coastal shallows. Crablike and lobsterlike animals evolved among the arthropods.

200 Million B.C.T.

Around 200 Million B.C.T., much of what is now North America, Europe, Africa, and South America drifted together, whole oceans closing between them. The Appalachians were heaved up, first north, then south, by the collisions. The supercontinent Pangaea placed North America and Western Europe next to each other along the equator, where grew lush tropical forests that we are now harvesting as coal in Pennsylvania and Wales.

An asteroid or a comet struck the region which is today in the country of Chad, Africa. The crater—the Aorounga crater—left in the Sahara Desert by the object is 17 kilometers wide and may be one of a string of impact craters created by multiple impacts from an object which broke up before impacting the Earth.

180 Million B.C.T.

Around 180 Million B.C.T., the northern group of continents which today comprise Asia, Europe and North America, but which scientists have collectively named Laurasia, split away from the southern group of continents. The southern group comprised the continents of Africa, Antarctica, Australia and South America along with the subcontinent of India and scientists have named this supercontinent Gondwana.

150 Million B.C.T.

Between 150 and 100 Million B.C.T., a meteor hit Saskatchewan, Canada, creating Deep Bay a near circular bay about

5 kilometers (3 miles) wide and 220 meter (720 feet) deep.

146 MILLION B.C.T.

The Cretaceous Period began.

During the Cretaceous Period, marine life continued the diversification that marked the Mesozoic Era (245-65 Million B.C.T.). The ancestors of many modern groups can be traced back to this period. Mosasaurs (giant lizards), rudists (coral-shaped bivalves), and other exotic animals inhabited Cretaceous seas. Bony fish proliferated during this time. These fish are today the most abundant group of freshwater and marine fish and include such popular species as salmon, cod, herring, plaice, and pike.

It was also during the Cretaceous Period that the Rocky Mountains began to rise in North America. Dinosaurs flourished and evolved into highly specialized forms, but they abruptly disappeared at the end of the period, along with many other kinds of life. (Theories to account for these mass extinctions are currently of great scientific interest.) The floral changes that took place in the Cretaceous were the most marked of all alterations in the organic world known to have occurred in the history of the earth. Gymnosperms were widespread, but in the later part of the period angiosperms (flowering plants) appeared.

142 MILLION B.C.T.

An object struck Gosses Bluff in the Northern Territory in Australia. The object created a 22 kilometer (13.7 mile) crater.

140 MILLION B.C.T.

The first birds appeared.

135 MILLION B.C.T.

South America and Africa split along a rift that would become the southern portion of the Atlantic Ocean.

122 MILLION B.C.T.

Flowering plants (angiosperms) appeared.

84 MILLION B.C.T.

About 84 million years ago, the Earth's rotational axis began a shift which resulted in a shift of 16 to 21 degrees in just 2 million years. Scientists believe that the shift may have been caused by the movement of rock masses within the Earth's mantle, the region below the outer crust.

65 MILLION B.C.T.

The Cretaceous Period came to an end. The end of this period saw a mass extinction of non-avian dinosaurs, pterosaurs, marine reptiles, and many other kinds of animals and plants.

The extinction at the boundary of the Cretaceous and the Tertiary Periods, some 65 million years ago, is the most famous of all mass extinctions. Its fame comes not from its magnitude (the Permian extinction was far larger) but rather from the victims of this extinction—the dinosaurs.

The Cretaceous-Tertiary (or "K-T") extinction wiped out around 85 percent of all species. The dinosaurs were not the only victims. Pterosaurs (flying reptiles), mosasaurs and other marine reptiles, fish, brachiopods, plankton and many plants either died out completely or suffered heavy losses. Even the ammonites, who had survived four previous extinctions finally disappeared.

For some reason, however, some species seem to have been almost entirely unaffected by the K-T extinction. Crocodiles, turtles and lizards, mammals and birds all made it through the K-T extinction relatively unscathed.

The cause of the K-T extinction event has been the subject of intensive scientific research, with many hundreds of research papers published since 1980 when Luis Alvarez reawakened interest in the subject, almost overnight, by suggesting that the death of the dinosaurs was due to a giant meteorite crashing into the earth, severely disrupting the Earth's ecosystem. While other theories suggest volcanic activity, climate change, environmental pollution or even cosmic radiation as causes, the meteorite (comet or asteroid) impact theory remains the most probable cause—at least for now.

An asteroid hit the earth ending the Age of Dinosaurs.

Large terrestrial impacts are of great importance for the history of life on the planet Earth. Recent studies of the Cretaceous/Tertiary boundary period—a period which saw the abrupt demise of a large number of biological species including dinosaurs—revealed unusual enrichments of elements which are associated with meteorite impact events.

Most researchers now believe that a large asteroid hit the Earth at the end of the Cretaceous Period around 65 million years ago. The collision of the asteroid triggered an environmental crisis which contributed to the mass extinctions of a vast quantity of life.

Recent satellite observations of the Earth's surface have revealed that a likely candidate site for the impact crater for the object which created the K-T extinction level event is at Chicxulub on the Yucatan Peninsula in Mexico.

Although, today the impact basin is buried under several hundred feet of sediment which hide it from easy view, maps which depict local gravity and magnetic field variations show a multi-ringed structure some 170 kilometers (about 102 miles) wide. In comparison, the famous Meteor Crater in Arizona is only a little over one (1) kilometer wide.

NASA scientists believe that an asteroid 10 to 20 kilometers (6 to 12 miles) in diameter produced the impact basin. The asteroid hit a geologically, unique, sulfur-rich region of the Yucatan Peninsula and kicked up billions of tons of sulfur and other materials into the atmosphere. Darkness prevailed over the earth for about half a year. This darkening caused global temperatures to plunge near freezing. Half of the species on Earth at the time became extinct, including the dinosaurs.

It is important to understand that the asteroid that struck the Earth 65 million years ago quite literally created a Hell on Earth. Scientists say that the impact blackened skies; created poisonous, acidic rain, caused wildfires to rage; initiated monster floods and windstorms; and literally tore the Earth apart. The impact was the greatest environmental disaster experienced by this planet in the last 250 million years.

Many scientists believe that the great disaster of 65 million years ago was caused by a 6 to 12 mile wide asteroid that slammed into the Gulf of Mexico. The impact crater of this monstrous asteroid has been identified by researchers as being the 100 mile wide crater which is today buried under a half-mile of sediment in what is now the Yucatan Peninsula of Mexico. The crater is known as Chicxulub (pronounced "chick-shoo-loob") for the small village located at its center.

Scientists now have pieced together evidence from around the world of the devastation wrought by the asteroid of Chicxulub. It is estimated that the energy of the Chicxulub impact was equivalent to the explosive energy of 100 trillion (100,000,000,000,000) tons of dynamite.

This explosive force is 10 billion times more powerful than the atom bomb that destroyed Hiroshima in 1945 and is 6 million times more powerful than the earthquake that ravaged San Francisco in 1906.

The Chicxulub asteroid smashed into Earth at a speed estimated as high as 150,000 mph. The shock of the impact raised the temperature at ground zero to thousands of degrees. The surrounding sea erupted in steam, and a fireball consumed everything for hundreds of miles around.

The blast of the Chicxulub asteroid excavated 25 trillion tons of debris from the seabed. Some of it rocketed halfway to the moon. Indeed, a fraction of this debris material achieved escape velocity and left Earth's orbit. However, most of the debris ultimately fell back to Earth, pummeling oceans and continents with a secondary barrage of flaming rock.

The asteroid impact also set off an earthquake measuring 12 to 13 on the Richter scale—at least 1,000 times greater than any humans have ever experienced. The quake heaved the land upward by hundreds of yards as far as 600 miles from ground zero.

Underwater landslides generated an enormous tidal wave that surged across the oceans and blanketed coastal areas throughout North and South America. Scientists have found evidence of the huge wave in traces of wood from highland trees that they say were swept down by the wave from the mountains of Mexico.

After its mind-boggling initial impact, the asteroid's long term impact produced effects which were even more profound. After all, the sea floor at Chicxulub consisted mostly of limestone, a compound of calcium and carbon. When the limestone was vaporized, it released 600 billion tons of carbon dioxide, a "greenhouse gas" that trapped the sun's heat on Earth. This great gas cloud produced a greenhouse effect that lasted for a thousand years or more.

The Chicxulub sediments were laced with sulfur, causing a global rain of sulfuric acid. Nitric acid created as a byproduct of the shock wave also helped to poison rivers, lakes and shallow seas for years. The protective ozone layer of the atmosphere was destroyed, exposing the Earth to lethal ultraviolet radiation.

Dust from the explosion lingered in the sky for months. Thick black clouds hid the sun, halting photosynthesis, the basis for the Earth's food supply. For months on end, it was too dark to see. Additionally, entire ecosystems were destroyed by the collapse of food chains and the loss of wildlife habitat.

Most scientists now agree that the great dinosaurs, along with anywhere from 50 to 70 percent of all other living species, met a swift end from this boulder being tossed from the Heavens to create a Hell on Earth.

The earth was ravaged by a series of major volcanic eruptions.

In 1993, researchers found trapped helium inside old volcanic rock in the Deccan Traps in west India. The presence of helium in these rocks was a sign of ancient volcanic eruptions. The researchers believe that the eruptions may have occurred between 68.5 and 65 million years ago, and may have coincided with, and contributed to, the extinction of the dinosaurs.

Sixty-five million years ago, the vast bulk of the Deccan Traps lavas erupted onto the Earth's surface. One of the greatest episodes of volcanism in the history of the Earth, the Deccan Traps lava flow flooded over a million square miles of India and surrounding areas with layer after layer of basaltic lava. These lava flows formed a vast lava pile. Today, after 65 million years of erosion, the Deccan Traps lava pile is still about one and one-half miles thick in western India, near the city of Bombay.

By the end of the Cretaceous period, the South Atlantic had widened into a major ocean. A new rift had carved Madagascar away from Africa. The rift in the North Atlantic had switched from the west side to the east side of Greenland. The Mediterranean Sea was clearly recognizable. Australia was still attached to Antarctica. An extensive north-south trench must also have existed in the Pacific to absorb the westward drift of the North American and South American plates.

The Cenozoic Era, the Tertiary Period and the Paleocene epoch began.

The world as we know it today was produced in the past 65 million years in the Cenozoic Era. Nearly half of the ocean floor was created in this geologically brief period. During these 65 million years, India completed its northward journey and collided with Asia. Also during this period, a rift developed which separated Australia from Antarctica. The North Atlantic rift finally entered the Arctic Ocean, splitting North America from Eurasia. The widening gap between South America and Africa was closely traced by the thread ridges produced by the Walvis thermal center.

If the Earth continues to exist in the universe as it does today, fifty million years from now, the geography of the world will be much different than it is today. Scientists speculate that Antarctica will remain essentially fixed at the South Pole, although it may be rotated slightly clockwise. The Atlantic (particularly the South Atlantic) and the Indian Ocean will continue to grow at the expense of the Pacific. Australia will drift northward and begin rubbing against the Eurasian plate. The eastern portion of Africa will split off along the Rift Valley, while its northward drift will close the Bay of Biscay and virtually collapse the Mediterranean. Due to compressional uplift, the islands of the Caribbean will cease to be islands and instead become part of the same land mass jutting out from what is today known as Central America. Baja California and a sliver of California west of the San Andreas fault will be severed from North America and begin drifting northwest. Indeed, a mere ten million years from now Los Angeles will be next to Sacramento and sixty million years from Los Angeles will suffer its ultimate fate. Los Angeles shall quietly slide into the Aleutian Trench of Alaska.

58 MILLION B.C.T.

The first true primates appeared.

From a secular perspective, the human story begins with that of the apes. Apes are primates, an ancient group of animals that also includes, among others, monkeys and humans. Early primate fossils, dating to about 55 million years ago, are of creatures resembling today's small nocturnal primates, such as galagos. By 36 million years ago, primitive ancestors of monkeys and apes had appeared. The first apes, emerging around 25 million years ago, established the primate superfamily Hominoidea, which today includes humans, gorillas, chimps, orangutans, and gibbons. For 10 million years the early apes were confined to Africa. By around 15 million years ago, apes had reached Turkey; then, around 12 million years ago, India and Pakistan. Over the next 6 or 7 million years the first hominids were to evolve through the natural process of diversification and development among the apes.

56.5 MILLION B.C.T.

The Eocene epoch began.

During the Eocene Period (56.5–35.4 Million B.C.T.), angiosperms (flowering plants that protect their seeds in a fruit) formed the dominant group of land plants. Many angiosperm species thrive today, including roses. Grasses first evolved in the earliest Eocene, but grasslands appeared much later.

The majority of modern mammals had evolved by the Eocene, including primates, rodents, carnivores, and bats. However, other groups of mammals became extinct at the end of the Eocene, during a period of global cooling and initial growth of the Antarctic icecap.

Large, primitive whales evolved in the Eocene period. Squid flourished, but were seldom fossilized. There was diversification among gastropod (snail-like) mollusks and bivalves (those with a shell made up of two hinged valves).

50 MILLION B.C.T.

Fifty millions years ago, the Earth looked almost as it does now. However, India was still an island and was headed on a collision course with Asia. The island of India was just within hailing distance off the southeast coast of Asia. Australia, meanwhile, was parting from Antarctica, and the ocean between them was still a narrow strait. Along the west coast of North America, Baja California was snug against Mexico, and the Gulf of California had not yet opened. Additionally, the famous San Andreas fault of California did not yet exist.

45 MILLION B.C.T.

The Himalayan Mountains began to rise as India crashed into Asia.

38 MILLION B.C.T.

A meteor struck at what is today Mistastin Lake, in Newfoundland and Labrador,

Canada, creating a 28 kilometer (17.4 mile) wide crater.

35.4 MILLION B.C.T.

The Oligocene epoch began.

Mammals that survived the late Eocene extinction evolved significantly during the Oligocene. Huge rhinos were abundant, including Indricotherium, which stood over 15 feet tall and weighed as much as four modern day elephants.

25 MILLION B.C.T.

The first apes emerged, establishing the primate superfamily, Hominoidea, which today includes humans, gorillas, chimps, orangutans, and gibbons.

23.3 MILLION B.C.T.

The Miocene epoch began.

Mammals continued to diversify during the Miocene. They included species of deer, antelope, cattle, and sheep. Songbirds, snakes, and rodents became more common as spreading grasslands provided suitable habitats. The development of *Proconsul*, a species of ape, and its fellow primates set the scene for the first hominids to appear. Out of the many species of apes that existed in the Miocene Period only chimpanzees, gorillas, gibbons and orangutans survive today.

19 MILLION B.C.T.

Monkeys became fossilized.

Fossil monkeys date to around 19 million years ago. Light, agile tree-dwellers, today's monkeys are divided into two groups: those living in Africa (the group *Cercopithecoidea*) and those in South America (*Ceboidea*).

17 Million B.C.T.

A tremendous pulse of flood basalt volcanism occurred in the Western Hemisphere. The Columbia River plateau was the result.

15 Million B.C.T.

Kenyapithecus *evolved.*

The appearance of *Kenyapithecus* in East Africa around 15 million years ago marked the first major shift in the course of ape evolution. Thick tooth enamel enabled *Kenyapithecus* to eat hard fruits and thus move into more seasonal and varied habitats. The development of thick enamel had begun about 17 million years ago in *Afropithecus,* a possible ancestor of *Kenyapithecus*, in Africa. Thick-enameled teeth appear in *Griphopithecus*, another possible descendant of *Afropithecus* first found in Turkey. Some 14 million year old *Kenyapithecus* jaw fragments have been found at Fort Ternan, Kenya.

11 Million B.C.T.

Sivapithecus *appeared.*

Possibly a descendant of *Kenyapithecus* {see 15 Million B.C.T.}, dating from 11 to 7 million years ago, the ape *Sivapithecus* emerged. Found in India and Pakistan, *Sivapithecus* had thick-enameled teeth and showed many of the specializations of the modern orangutan. Indeed, it is generally recognized that *Sivapithecus* was the ancestor of the modern orangutan.

Today apes are found only in tropical Africa and Asia. However, fossil ape finds indicate that at one time apes were common not only in the tropical regions of today, but also in parts of southern Europe, Southwest Asia, and Pakistan. The development of thick-enameled teeth, enabling a more varied diet, was crucial to the early migration of apes from Africa.

10 Million B.C.T.

A meteor struck Kara-Kul, Tajikistan, creating a 45 kilometer (28 mile) wide crater. Partly filled by the 25 kilometer (16 mile) diameter Kara-Kul Lake, the impact crater is located at almost 6,000 meters (20,000 feet above sea level in the Pamir Mountain Range near the Afghan border with Tajikistan.

6 Million B.C.T.

While no fossils had been found by the end of the twentieth century, most paleontologists theorize that human and ape lines diverged from a common ancestor around six million years ago.

The divergence of the earliest human ancestors from the lineage leading to the modern apes began between 8 million years ago, a time that has yielded such fossil evidence as the ape *Sivapithecus*, and 4 million years ago, the date of the earliest hominid fossils. The dearth of fossil finds from this period inhibits our understanding of the human story and makes it difficult to trace the ancestral patterns of all of today's higher primates. The fragmentary discoveries that have been made give rise to many questions. While it is possible to chart the chronological stages in development from early primate to modern human over the millennia, the links between the stages cannot be firmly established until more evidence comes to light.

5.2 Million B.C.T.

The Pliocene epoch began. This period saw the diversification of Miocene apes and the arise of Proconsul, Ramapithecus *and the* australopithecines.

During the Pliocene Period, marine animals were similar to those of the present day, with a large number of species still surviving, especially among sea bed dwellers such as bivalves and gastropods. One notable species of Pliocene marine life was the Carcharadon, *a species of giant sharks. The teeth of the* Carcharadon *can be four inches long which suggests that some* Carcharadon *may have been over 39 feet long.*

An object struck the Earth in South West Africa (Namibia) at what is today known as Roter Kamm. The crater created by this object is 2.5 kilometers (1.55 miles) wide and, as much as, 700 feet deep.

4.4 MILLION B.C.T.

Ardipithecus ramidus *lived in or around the lands which today comprise Aramis, Ethiopia.*

The name *Ardipithecus ramidus* comes from the word *ardi* which means ground or floor in the local Afar language and the word *ramid* which means root. The importance of the find was that *Ardipithecus ramidus* may have been the first primate descended creature to develop bi-pedalism.

Paleoanthropologists believe that bipedalism was the first significant modification separating the theorized ancestors of man from the great apes. By studying the bones and fossil footprints of *Australopithecus afarensis* as well as those of half a dozen other australopithecine species, scientists have long known that the theorized ancestors of man walked upright long before they acquired other human traits—and that bipedalism gave the theorized ancestors of man a huge edge.

According to conventional wisdom, this evolutionary breakthrough came at a time when climate change was transforming eastern and southern Africa from dense forest into open grassland. Standing upright in such an environment could have offered the theorized ancestors of man many advantages. Standing upright would

have let the theorized ancestors to scan the horizon for predators, exposed less body surface to the scorching equatorial sun or freed the hands of the theorized ancestors for carrying food.

However, the conventional wisdom which was held by paleontologists for a significant portion of the twentieth century was seriously challenged by the discovery of *Ardipithecus ramidus*, because *Ardipithecus ramidus* lived before the African landscape had changed. Fossilized seeds, petrified wood and animal bones found near the village of Aramis indicate that the Africa of *Ardipithecus ramidus* was a densely wooded terrain. If so, why would *Ardipithecus ramidus* ever need to stand up? This is the question which will puzzle paleontologists well into the new millennium.

4.2 MILLION B.C.T.

From 4.2 million years ago to about 3.9 million years ago Australopithecus anamensis *roamed the earth near what is today Kanapoi, Kenya.*

Australopithecus anamensis demonstrated that the theorized ancestors of man walked upright at least 500,000 years earlier than had been believed. Discovered in 1995 at two sites near Lake Turkana, Kenya, by a team led by Meave Leakey (wife of well-known fossil hunter Richard Leakey) and Alan Walker, *Australopithecus anamensis* was clearly bipedal although its form of bipedal locomotion would not be recognized as "walking."

4 MILLION B.C.T.

By 4 million years ago, it is believed my most in the secular scientific community that the fossil evidence shows that the human evolutionary line had become distinct from those of the other primates.

Hominid development between 4 and 1 million years ago falls into what can be called a "pre-human" (*Australopithecus*) and a human (*Homo habilis* and *Homo erectus*) stage. *Australopithecus* was the name coined for a fossil find in South Africa: an ape-like child's skull with human looking teeth. Its discoverer, anatomist Raymond Dart, believed that *Australopithecus* represented an early stage of human evolution, but it took many more discoveries of australopithecines and members of the *Homo* species before his views were taken seriously. It is not known how *Australopithecus*, *Homo habilis*, and *Homo erectus* were related to each other, but they may be taken to represent successive stages in human development.

3.9 Million B.C.T.

In East Africa (around Laetoli, Tanzania), from 3.9 million years ago to 2.9 million years ago, Australopithecus afarensis *(the southern ape of the Afar) lived.*

The most famous example of *Australopithecus afarensis* is the 3.2 million year old skeleton known around the world as "Lucy." It is widely believed that *Australopithecus afarensis* eventually gave rise to the genus *Homo*—the genus of man. The australopithecines like Lucy were mainly herbivores. Their upright stance, manual dexterity, and hard teeth enabled them to live on a varied vegetarian diet. Australopithecines may have used convenient rocks, sticks, and other debris for various tasks, such as cracking nuts.

In 1974 of the Christian calendar, the archaeologist Carl Johanson found the half-complete fossil of a teenaged female at Hadar, Ethiopia. It was this female fossil that Johanson named "Lucy." Paleontologists would later conjecture that, unlike a quadruped, which is sexually receptive to males only during limited periods of estrus,

the erect ape-woman could conceive and bear children at any time of year. The pelvic canal of the australopithecines narrowed as they evolved, and natural selection favored those individuals who bore premature infants small enough to emerge from the narrowed pelvic canals. Because such infants could not stand on their feet immediately after birth and required longer postnatal care, female australopithecines became increasingly dependent on males for food and protection while they nursed their babies.

3.6 Million B.C.T.

Australopithecus *walked.*

The long-suspected fact that the australopithecines could stand and walk was dramatically confirmed by the discovery, in 1978, of footprints preserved in hardened ash from a then active East African volcano. The prints showed that one day around 3.6 million years ago, three australopithecines walked across the ash.

Kenyanthropus platyops *lived.*

Early in 2001, the origins of humankind were thrown into question when scientists released research announcing that a new species of hominids had been discovered in Kenya. Named *Kenyanthropus platyops*—the flat-faced man of Kenya—the new species cast doubt on the origins of man because it provided an alternative to the *australopithecines*.

With its tiny teeth, distinctive jaw structure and relatively modern face, *Kenyanthropus platyops* is set apart from the *Australopithecus afarensis* species, the best known example of which is the 3.2 million year old skeleton called Lucy. *Kenyanthropus platyops* had a much flatter face than Lucy, as well as particularly small molar teeth, leading the researchers to believe that it fed on a mixture of fruit, berries, grubs, and small animals and birds.

The discovery of *Kenyanthropus platyops* is evidence that instead of evolving from a straight line of hominids, humanity may have emerged from an evolutionary maze of false starts, dead ends and competing adaptations. Indeed, some scientists now speculate that other hominid species may have existed at this time and that any or all of the species which existed may have contributed to making the hominids which eventually led to the creation of the forefathers of us.

3.4 MILLION B.C.T.

The Isthmus of Panama developed as a land bridge linking the Americas.

3 MILLION B.C.T.

From 3 million years ago to 2.3 million years ago, around Taung, South Africa, Australopithecus africanus *roamed. The first of the theorized human ancestors,* Australopithecus africanus *was once thought to be the missing link between apes and humans.*

Australopithecus africanus was an upright-walking ape-man with thumb-opposed hands in place of forefeet, permitting him and his female counterpart to use tools.

2.8 MILLION B.C.T.

Around the Omo Basin in Ethiopia, from 2.8 million years ago to 2.3 million years ago, Australopithecus aethiopicus *thrived.* Australopithecus aethiopicus *may be an ancestor of* Australopithecus boisei *and* Australopithecus robustus. *A fossil of* Australopithecus aethiopicus *found by Richard Leakey's team is called the Black Skull.*

2.5 MILLION B.C.T.

Around Bouri, Ethiopia, Australopithecus garhi *lived.* Australopithecus garhi *may have been the first to use stone tools and to eat meat.*

2.4 MILLION B.C.T.

Around 2.4 million years ago to 1.8 million years ago, Homo rudolfensis *came to be near or around what is today Koobi Fora, Kenya.*

Homo rudolfensis may be an early form of *Homo habilis.* However, if it is a distinct species, *Homo rudolfensis* is the earliest known member of the *homo* genus.

2.3 MILLION B.C.T.

The first ancient hominid found by the Leakeys, from 2.3 million years ago to 1.4 million years ago, Australopithecus boisei *roamed the Olduvai Gorge in Tanzania. A skull found by the Leakeys possessed such large molars that it earned the nickname "Nutcracker Man."*

In 1959, Dr. Mary Leakey discovered the first hominid of great antiquity to be found in East Africa and named it *Zinjanthropus.* Once later discoveries had established and defined *Australopithecus,* "Zinj"—the 1.75 million year old skull found by Dr. Leakey—was classified as a robust australopithecine, and was renamed *Australopithecus boisei* after the Leakeys' benefactor, Charles Boise.

2.0 MILLION B.C.T.

Hominids appeared.

Most anthropologists believe that the first people evolved from an australopithecine about 2 million years B.C.T. The oldest tools scientists have found date from about that time. But because no hominid fossils were found with these tools, scientists do not know whether an australopithecine or an early member of the *Homo* genus made them.

The first members of the *Homo* genus lived in Africa about 2 million B.C.T. Anthropologists have found important fossils of these people near the shores of Lake Turkana in Kenya and in Olduvai Gorge in Tanzania. Many scientists divide these people into three species—*Homo habilis, Homo rudolfensis,* and *Homo erectus.*

Homo habilis had a brain larger than an australopithecine brain but only about half the size of a modern human brain. *Homo habilis* also had similar molars and a less protruding face than the australopithecines had. The Latin word *Homo* means *human being. Habilis* means *handy* or *skillful. Homo rudolfensis* had a brain larger than that of *Homo habilis.* It also had large molars, like those of the australopithecines. The name *rudolfensis* comes from Lake Rudolph, an old name for Lake Turkana. Fossils of *Homo rudolfensis* have been discovered near the lake.

Some anthropologists are uncertain whether *Homo habilis* and *Homo rudolfensis* were two different species or whether they represent, respectively, the females and males of one species. Such a difference in size between the sexes is known as sexual dimorphism. This type of difference appears among many modern apes and was present among the australopithecines. Sexual dimorphism is less extreme in modern human beings.

Another species of the early *Homo* genus, *Homo erectus,* lived at the same time as *Homo habilis* and *Homo rudolfensis.* The *erectus* refers to the upright posture of these creatures. Most scientists believe *Homo erectus* was the species that evolved into modern people.

Homo erectus had a brain slightly larger than that of *Homo rudolfensis,* but it

also had a smaller back molars. During the course of *Homo erectus'* evolution, brain size increased, eventually reaching a size just slightly smaller than that of a modern human brain. *Homo erectus* individuals had thick skulls, sloping foreheads, and large, chinless jaws. Their skulls had a brow ridge, a raised strip of bone across the lower forehead. *Homo erectus* also had a smaller and less protruding face than *Homo habilis* and *Homo rudolfensis* had. Fossils indicate that the *Homo erectus* males were larger than the females.

The earliest *Homo erectus* fossils have been found in Africa. They date from more than 1.75 million years ago. One of the best known examples of *Homo erectus* is a nearly complete fossil skeleton of a boy who was probably eleven or twelve years old when he died. The skeleton, which is over 1.5 million years old, was found near Lake Turkana. The boy had already reached 5 feet 3 inches (160 centimeters) in height and might have grown to 6 feet 1 inch (185 centimeters) if he had lived to adulthood.

Members of *Homo erectus* eventually migrated from Africa to Asia and Europe. The species reached the island of Java, in Indonesia, by 1.2 million years ago, and perhaps, as early as 1.6 million years ago. *Homo erectus* reached Europe more than 700,000 years ago. By 600,000 years ago, the species had spread into northern Asia.

Homo erectus was probably the first human-like creature to master the use of fire. These beings may also have been the first to wear clothing. Scientists believe that as *Homo erectus* moved into northern areas and faced cold winters, fire and clothing became necessary. Archaeologists have not found any traces of early clothing, but it was probably made from animal hides. The oldest evidence of the use of fire was found in a cave that *Homo erectus* occupied about 600,000 years ago near what is now Beijing, in northern China. Stone tools and the remains of more than 40 *Homo erectus* individuals were found in the cave, along with burned animal bones.

1.9 MILLION B.C.T.

From 1.9 million years ago to 1.5 million years ago, Australopithecus robustus *lived in and around Kromdraai, South Africa.*

Discovered by Robert Broom in 1938, *Australopithecus robustus* was found only in southern Africa and was determined not to be a direct human ancestor.

From 1.9 million years ago to 1.6 million years ago, Homo habilis *could be found near Olduvai Gorge in Tanzania. Unearthed by the Leakeys in the early 1960s, "Handy Man" was once thought to be the earliest tool user.*

The first habilines (*Homo habilis*) lived around 2 million years ago. There are many reasons for supposing that *Homo habilis,* or "handy man" (so-called because of its dexterity and toolmaking ability), was an intermediary between australopithecines and later humans. *Homo habilis* had a relatively large brain and possessed new skills, including the ability to make stone tools.

Homo habilis used tools to make tools, a crucial innovation. It was also probably the first hominid to eat meat regularly. The two developments went hand in hand: stone tools were essential to detach meat from animal carcasses. The slightly built habilines were largely scavengers rather than hunters who killed their prey.

Some archaeological sites in the Olduvai Gorge in Tanzania from around this time until about 1.6 million B.C.T. are thought to be living floors—to be home bases or campsites. At these sites, tools and hominid remains seem to concentrate. Some paleoanthropologists believe that such concentrations are caused by agencies other than use as home bases.

The oldest known stone tool "industry" is characterized by remains that started about this time at the Olduvai Gorge in northern Tanzania, accounting for the name Oldowan. The choppers and scrappers are simple chips of stone and are sometimes classed as pebble tools.

1.8 MILLION B.C.T.

By 1.8 million years ago, snakes had evolved.

1.75 MILLION B.C.T.

Anthropoids began using patterned tools.

1.7 MILLION B.C.T.

From 1.7 million years ago to 1.5 million years ago, Homo ergaster *inhabited the area around Koobi Fora in Kenya.* Homo ergaster *may have been an early form of* Homo erectus. Homo ergaster *was found only in Africa and its designation as a separate species has been debated.*

From 1.7 million years ago to 250,000 years ago, Homo erectus *spread over much of Africa and Asia. Discovered in Trinil, Indonesia, in 1891,* Homo erectus *may have been the first hominid to use fire and the first to migrate out of Africa.*

About 1.7 million years ago, while the last of the habilines and robust australopithecines still lived in Africa, a new species appeared—*Homo erectus,* or "upright man." *Homo erectus* walked fully erect and was larger brained, with a tall, long-legged, narrow hipped physique. Compared with earlier forms, the skull of *Homo erectus* was quite distinctive: longer and thicker walled, it had a strong brow ridge of bone jutting out over the eyes. By around 1 million years ago, *Homo erectus* had spread from Africa to Asia, Southeast Asia, and probably to Europe as well.

The key feature that *Homo habilis* and *Homo erectus* share with modern humans is a larger brain capacity, for their size, than that of the apes. The human cranium, or vault of the skull, is fully rounded. The human skull sits atop the spine, indicating an upright stance, whereas apes, although they can stand upright, cannot do so for long. Human teeth are directly below the brow, rather than protruding in front, possibly a result of a change to gathering by hand rather than with the teeth.

Fossilized hominid braincases record the increasing size of the brains of the hominids. While hominid body size and weight were also increasing, the accompanying increases in brain size exceed what would be expected from a simple incremental progression. At present, it is unknown why such extraordinary brain growth occurred.

For the australopithecines, the skull capacity was 21 to 37 cubic inches. For *Homo erectus*, the skull capacity averaged between 43 and 76 cubic inches. For modern man, the skull capacity ranges between 73 to 98 cubic inches.

With a brain twice the size of an australopithecine, *Homo erectus* was skillful and enterprising, making innovations that were to enable hominids to migrate from their tropical homelands. *Homo erectus* invented the hand ax, which was to be the most versatile and most widely used tool for the following million years, and by 1 million years ago may already have made one of the greatest human discoveries—how to make and control fire.

1.65 MILLION B.C.T.

The Tertiary Period came to an end.

In the Tertiary Period, North America's land link to Europe was broken, but its ties to South America were forged toward the end of the period. During Cenozoic times (the times from 65 million years ago to the present), life forms both on land and in the sea became more like those of today. Grasses became more prominent, leading to marked changes in the dentition of plant-eating animals. With most of the dominant reptile forms having vanished at the end of the Cretaceous, the Cenozoic became the Age of Mammals. Thus, in the Eocene epoch (the period from 54 to 38 million years ago), new mammal groups developed such as small, horselike animals, rhinoceroses, tapirs, ruminants, whales, and the ancestors of elephants. Members of the cat and dog families appeared in the Oligocene epoch (the period from 38 to 26 million years ago) as did species of monkeys. In Miocene times (the times from 26 to 12 million years ago), marsupials were numerous, and anthropoid (humanlike) apes first appeared. Placental mammals reached their zenith, in numbers and variety of species, in Pliocene times (12 to 2.5 million years ago) and early Pleistocene times (2.5 million years ago).

The Quaternary Period and the Pleistocene epoch began. During this period, Homo erectus *and* Homo neanderthalensis *appeared in the Middle East, Africa, and Europe.*

During the Quaternary Period, intermittent continental ice sheets covered much of the northern hemisphere. Fossil remains show that many primitive prehuman types existed in south-central Africa, China, and Java by Lower and Middle Pleistocene times. However, modern humans (*Homo sapiens*) did not appear until the later Pleistocene. Late in the period, humans crossed over into the New World by means of the Bering land bridge. The ice sheets finally retreated, and the modern age began.

1.5 MILLION B.C.T.

Although still unverified, patches of baked earth near hominid sites at Koobi Fora and Chesowanja in Kenya suggest that hominids were using fire. {**See also 1,000,000 B.C.T.**}

Acheulean artifact assemblies, which would continue to be produced until 200,000 B.C.T., were first left behind in Africa, probably by Homo erectus. *This toolkit was characterized by bifaces (hand axes, cleavers, and picks), typically large, ovoid stones from which flakes have been removed by hammerstones and whose exact purpose is unknown.*

1.3 MILLION B.C.T.

An object struck Bosumtwi, Ghana, creating a 10.5 kilometer (6.5 mile) wide crater.

1,000,000 B.C.T.

Around one million years ago, the australopithecines became extinct as the human species became more developed.

Homo erectus *populations began to move out of Africa into Asia and from there ultimately to Europe.*

Homo erectus erectus proved to be quite unique among primates in having a diet with a high proportion of meat relative to dietary plant foods. However, like other primates, *Homo erectus erectus* was omnivorous, a scavenger who competed with hyenas and other scavengers while eluding meat-eating predators such as lions and leopards.

Ancient hearths found in the Swartkrans cave in South Africa indicate that Homo erectus, *believed by scientists to be the immediate predecessor of modern human beings, used fire.* {**See also 1.5 Million B.C.T. and 600,000 B.C.T.**}

A few fossils suggest that some form of archaic Homo sapiens *developed this early, although fully modern humans are far in the future.*

950,000 B.C.T.

Evidence from the Vallonnet Cave on the Mediterranean coast of France indicates that it was occupied by hominids as early as 950,000 B.C.T.

800,000 B.C.T.

A meteorite struck Vietnam.

Around 800,000 B.C.T., a meteorite blasted into what is now Vietnam severely altering the ecology of southeast Asia. However, within a relatively short period of time afterwards, hominids could be found in the region. These hominids found a freshly exposed outcropping of rock which proved to be perfect for making stone tools. It was these stone tools, the oldest stone tools ever found in China, which are these exploring hominids great legacy.

The blast area for the meteorite is well documented. Tektites—little pieces of broken stone associated with meteorites—have been found scattered across southeast Asia and as far south as Australia. No one knows whether the meteorite hit the ground and broke up, or exploded just above ground level, throwing up earth and broken rocks. However, whatever may have become of the meteorite, its impact was simply devastating.

Into this devastated land came *Homo erectus*. In an area near Guangxi Zhuang Autonomous Province, near the Chinese border with Vietnam in southern China, a rich collection of stone tools was found. Surprisingly, these stone tools were found in layers which also contained microscopic pieces of plant fragments, burned wood, and charcoal.

The presence of the Chinese stone tools from 800,000 years ago indicates that the Asian *Homo erectus* was as culturally advanced as the contemporary *Homo erectus* of Africa.

Sophisticated stone tools were utilized in China.

By 800,000 years ago, Homo antecessor had spread to Europe. With remains found in Gran Dolina, Spain, Homo antecessor may be the last common ancestor of both Neanderthals and modern humans. However, the exact species designation has been debated.

780,000 B.C.T.

The Earth's magnetic field flipped.

Every few hundred thousand years Earth's magnetic field dwindles almost to nothing for perhaps a century. Then, gradually, the magnetic field reappears with the north and south poles flipped. The last such reversal was 780,000 years ago.

The significance of the reversal of the magnetic field is that the magnetic field deflects particle storms and cosmic rays from the sun, as well as even more energetic subatomic particles from deep space. Without magnetic protection, these particles would strike Earth's atmosphere, eroding the already beleaguered ozone layer. Additionally, many creatures navigate by magnetic reckoning. A magnetic reversal might cause serious ecological mischief.

Given the fact that the last magnetic field flip occurred 780,000 years ago, and the fact that the strength of our magnetic field has decreased about five percent in the past century, it appears that the Earth may be overdue for a magnetic field reversal. When it comes, it undoubtedly will have vast ramifications for the well-being of humankind.

700,000 B.C.T.

Europe

At Torralba and Ambrona, two large lakeside sites in central Spain dating to between 700,000 and 300,000 years ago, stone tools were found with many partially dismembered animals, especially straight-tusked elephants and horses. Many bones were transported there by the action of rivers, but it is possible that bone implements were brought there by hominids to kill or butcher some of the animals.

600,000 B.C.T.

Europe

A thick ash layer formed between this time and 400,000 B.C.T. in L'Escale Cave in southeastern France. This layer has sometimes been viewed as the earliest known evidence of fire made by hominids in Europe, although it cannot be definitely established that it was not the result of naturally caused fires. {See also 1.5 Million B.C.T. and 40,000 B.C.T.}

Homo heidelbergensis *inhabited Europe.* Homo heidelbergensis *may be an early form of* Homo neanderthalensis.

500,000 B.C.T.

Asia

Homo erectus *discovered the use of fire. The earliest firm evidence of the use of fire was found at Zhoukoudian, near Beijing, China. {See 13,000 B.C.T.}*

460,000 B.C.T.

Asia

Evidence from the Zhoukoudian caves in northern China indicates that the cave occupants controlled fire around 460,000 years ago.

Early hominids in Africa may have learned to control fire more than one million years ago, but the first definite evidence of using fire is found in the Zhoukoudian Cave in northern China and dates to around 460,000 years ago. The fires that were lit in the cave left ash layers up to 20 feet deep, along with large quantities of charred bones and stones. Fire would have been invaluable both for warmth and for the protection it gave from wild animals.

400,000 B.C.T.

Homo erectus *developed the spear.*

The burin, thought to be the primary tool for engraving and carving such materials as bone, antler, ivory, and wood became common, as did endscrapers (grattoirs), *tools thought to have been used for hide scraping or wood working.*

Asia

Homo erectus hominid—*Peking Man— may have used fire to cook venison which served to supplement the species' diet of berries, roots, nuts, acorns, legumes, and grains. By conserving energy,* Homo erectus hominid *could track down swifter but less intelligent animals (although the species does continue to split bones to get at the marrow because it does not yet use fire effectively to make the marrow easily available).*

Around 400,000 years ago, the inhabitants of the Zhoukoudian Cave in northern China lived on a mixed diet of meat, nuts, and berries. This is indicated by remains of food discovered in the cave, which included wild fruit, especially hackberries, together with shoots and tubers, insects and reptiles, birds and eggs, rats, and large mammals.

Evidence from China is used to support the theory of multi-regionalism—the theory of parallel human development in many different areas of the world. The Lower Cave at Zhoukoudian near Peking is famous as the home of a *Homo erectus* community some 450,000 years ago. The skulls of these *Homo erectus* individuals are somewhat different from those found in Africa and other regions. Some of these differences are claimed to reappear in a modern human skull found in the Upper Cave, suggesting that there may have been some continuity between ancient indigenous *Homo erectus* and modern populations in China—meaning that these fully modern humans evolved directly from their local predecessors.

Europe

Evidence at Terra Amata, a site near Nice, France, suggests that Homo erectus *occupied oval huts that were 15 meters (50 feet) by 6 meters (20 feet). This is the first evidence of housing construction.*

380,000 B.C.T.

Europe

The world's earliest known artificial shelter was erected.

Although early hominids moved around in search of food, they still built simple shelters. At Terra Amata in southern France, there is evidence of a succession of 15 brief stays, around 380,000 years ago, by hominids who built small hearths and erected oval huts or tent-like structures on the beach dunes. This was a seasonal camp, occupied in late spring or early summer.

The early hominids probably followed the advance and retreat of plants and animals. The quest for food was rivaled only by the constant necessity to keep warm, a key problem of the early hominids who migrated from the tropics to less hospitable regions. The cold was combated not by slow adaptation to the new environment through biological changes, but by the peculiarly human urge to experiment with materials to find out about their characteristics, and by the ability to make things, notably shelters and clothing.

300,000 B.C.T.

Europe

By around 300,000 B.C.T., very early Neanderthals were living in what is now Spain. {See also 200,000 B.C.T.}

The earliest known example of a wooden spear, the tip of a yew spear, was left in a site at Clacton-on-Sea in England. {See also 120,000 B.C.T.}

Australia

A meteor struck Australia at Wolfe Creek creating a 0.875 kilometer (0.544 mile) wide crater.

250,000 B.C.T.

Evidence of archaic Homo sapiens, *appeared in Africa, Asia, and Europe.*

By around 250,000 years ago, humans had become very different from their early ancestors. Although physical forms varied, their intellectual advancement grouped them as a new species, *Homo sapiens—* "thinking man."

Africa

Simple shelters were probably built by early hominids throughout Africa by this time, but few remains survive. At Orangia in southern Africa, six stone semicircles, each 2 to 3 yards in diameter, may have been the bases of structures for sleeping or sheltering in during the hunting season. They were all open to the west, and the ground inside was slightly sunken. It is possible

that up to 12 of these structures existed originally, providing shelter for between 20 and 30 individuals at any one time.

Asia

The earliest campsites in South Asia date from around 250,000 years ago, and include both rock shelters and open sites. Bhimbetka, located in central India, is a typical large rock shelter, which was occupied for many thousands of years. In contrast, the open campsites at Hunsgi, in southern India, were probably occupied for only a very short period, some perhaps on just a single occasion.

Europe

Numerous oval and heart shaped hand axes made during this period have been found at Hoxne in eastern England. Some have wear patterns that suggest they were used for cutting meat. Wooden spears with fire-hardened tips may have been made for hunting, although game was more likely caught using traps and pits.

At Becov in Bohemia, a quartzite rubbing stone and a lump of red ocher dating to 250,000 years ago were found at a site used by early hominids. Ocher powder found on a floor nearby may have been mixed with blood and fat to make red paint, although there is no evidence to indicate how it was used.

240,000 B.C.T.

Asia

Wood was probably used by early hominids for making tools and implements, but little is known of early wood technology because remains rarely survive. A wooden plank over 240,000 years old from Gesher Benot Ya'aqov in the Jordan Valley in Israel is a remarkable exception. Made of willow, the plank is ten inches long, 5 inches wide, and 1½ inches thick. One side is flat and polished.

200,000 B.C.T.

Well made side scrapers became common, suggesting that Homo erectus *was manufacturing clothing by 200,000 B.C.T.*

Although characteristic of the much later Middle Paleolithic industries, the first Levallois prepared core flake tools began to appear. In Levallois technology, the core was carefully shaped into a regular block of stone from which very large, thin, nearly uniform flakes that could be used without further shaping were struck. {See also 400,000 B.C.T.}

Africa

Many stone tools made by early hominids in Africa were multipurpose implements. The earliest found tools were made around 200,000 years ago.

Asia

By 200,000 years ago, the whole of mainland East Asia (China, Mongolia and Siberia) had been colonized by populations of Homo erectus. *Many of their sites, including caves, rock shelters, and open encampments on river terraces, have been identified. These early hunter gatherers moved from place to place throughout the year, exploiting different seasonal resources.*

Europe

From 200,000 years ago to about 30,000 years ago, Homo neanderthalensis *walked upon the earth (especially in the Neander Valley of Germany). The duration of* Homo neanderthalensis *overlapped the beginning of* Homo sapiens— *the beginning of modern man.*

Homo neanderthalensis— the Neanderthals—became common in Europe around 200,000 B.C.T. These puzzling hominids are clearly in the genus *Homo*, but scientists differ on whether they can be classified as a subspecies of *Homo sapiens* or whether they are a different species that arose separately from *Homo erectus* or possibly from archaic *Homo sapiens*. Neanderthals had a technology all their own,—one that is more diverse and advanced than that of *Homo erectus*, but much more stable and unchanging that that of fully modern *Homo sapiens*. Neanderthal technology changed very little over periods as long as 100,000 years.

On a more physical level, the Neanderthals had large front teeth which were used as tools. Less than half of the Neanderthal offspring reached age 20. 9 out of 10 of all Neanderthals died before the age of 40.

150,000 B.C.T.

Europe

The earliest known Mousterian tool industries began at such sites as Biache in northwestern France. This toolmaking tradition, associated with Neanderthals, was characterized by Levallois and discoidal core manufacturing of side-scrappers, backed knives, hand axes, and points. {See also 400,000 B.C.T. and 200,000 B.C.T.}

130,000 B.C.T.

Africa

A site in the Orange River Valley of Namibia was first occupied. It would remain so until 4000 B.C.T. {See also 40,000 B.C.T.}

Asia

Prehistoric beings reached Siberia.

By 130,000 years ago, human beings had spread to the cold, harsh plains of western Siberia, but not until later did people move into the eastern part of the region. At that time, because so much water had been frozen as glacial ice, the level of the oceans and seas was lower than it is today. As a result, the Bering Strait was dry and formed a land bridge between northeast Asia and North America. Most scientists believe prehistoric people crossed this bridge and were living in North America by about 15,000 to 20,000 years ago. Eventually, early modern people populated all of North and South America.

120,000 B.C.T.

The first Neanderthals appeared in Europe and Southwest Asia.

The Neanderthals (*Homo sapiens neanderthalensis*), so called because the first skull cap of their type was recognized in the Neander Valley in Germany, lived in Europe and Southwest Asia from around 120,000 years ago. Although in physical appearance the archetypal "caveman" of popular imagination, Neanderthals had brains at least the size of modern humans and were far from brutish, with a way of life that may have included cultural rituals and expression. Like modern human groups at Qafzeh in Israel and other sites Neanderthals sometimes buried their dead, decorating the graves. Meat and tools found in Neanderthal graves suggest that the Neanderthals had a belief in the afterlife. One man buried at Shanidar Cave in Iraq some 60,000 years ago had been badly injured at some point in his life. He had lost an arm and probably an eye, and was crippled in both legs. To have survived until his comparatively advanced age of 40, he must have been supported by his community. If so, such actions suggest that Neanderthal groups possessed a degree of social solidarity and practiced a form of communal welfare.

Despite many similarities, the Neanderthals were significantly different in skeleton and physique from fully modern humans—heavily muscled, with great physical strength and a compact body shape, ideally adapted to a harsh, cold environment.

Neanderthals were stocky and extremely powerfully built, with stout, sometimes bowed limb bones. Their skulls have a low, flattened crown with a bulging bun at the back. The neck muscles that attached there helped brace the head against any force generated in using the strong jaw. The face is large and forward-thrusting, with large teeth, no chin, a large nose, and characteristic brow ridges. The modern human skeleton is taller and less powerful, with a higher skull crown, smaller teeth, a prominent chin, a shorter and flatter face, and almost no brow ridge.

Although the Neanderthals may have behaved like fully modern humans in certain respects, their language skills were probably not as highly developed. A command of language would have enabled fully modern humans to talk about the past, and to plan ahead—which gave them a formidable advantage over the Neanderthals. Fully modern humans also possessed a new capacity for abstract expression. Fragments of engraved animal bone and traces of red ocher (a natural pigment) testify to emergent artistic activity in many regions.

The discovery of a Neanderthal skull in 1856 provided crucial evidence for the theory of human evolution that scientists were beginning to piece together. At the time when the skull was found, many people still interpreted the Bible as saying that modern humans similar to ourselves had been created by a special act of God less than 6,000 years ago. The Neanderthal skull, however, showed clearly that other types of hominids had once existed and had since become extinct. The discovery gave scientific support to Darwin's *Origin of Species*, published in 1859, which claimed that all living things today are the result of millions of years of evolution.

Africa

Some of the oldest evidence in the world for hominid use of coastal resources comes from South Africa. Marine resources such as limpets and mussels were systematically exploited by the inhabitants of the Klasies River Mouth Cave on the coast of South Africa around 120,000 years ago. Fur seals and penguins were occasionally caught and killed, but there is no evidence of fishing.

Caves and rock shelters, many of which looked out over wide plains rich in game, continued to be important habitation sites for African hunter-gatherers during this period. They offered protection from lions and other predators and shelter in wet weather. Most groups used convenient shelters for short periods of the year, returning for generations to the same location—perhaps when local plants were ripe or shellfish abundant. The coast of southeastern Africa was home to many hunter-gatherers who used caves as base camps for hunting game and sea mammals for several months of the year. One of the inhabited caves was at Klasies River Mouth in South Africa. First occupied 120,000 years ago, it was used as a shelter by visiting groups until 1,000 years ago.

Europe

The earliest known example of a charred wooden spear was made. This spear was found with an elephant carcass at a site called Lehringen in Germany. {See 300,000 B.C.T.}

110,000 B.C.T.

The last Ice Age began.

Today, the polar ice caps cover one-tenth of the earth's surface. However, a drop of only 8 degrees Fahrenheit in the world's average temperature would result in one-third of the globe being covered in ice. Such regular climatic changes have

been occurring at intervals for at least the last 2.5 million years, resulting in the cycle known as the Ice Ages. The advance and retreat of glaciers and ice sheets has had profound effects on the earth's surface. Erosion caused by glaciation diversifies the landscape, creating deep valleys and lakes, jagged peaks, and mountain ridges. As the ice melts, rivers and waterfalls form, and the drowning of glacial valleys creates fjords and deep-cut estuarine inlets. Glaciation depletes the amount of available water on earth, resulting in falling sea levels and reduced rainfall. The reverse occurs during an interglacial episode. The alternate locking up and release of vast quantities of water has had far-reaching implications for earth's flora and fauna—including humankind.

The cycle of repeated glaciation began around 2.5 million years ago. Warmer periods, known as interglacials, have punctuated the Ice Ages, but have rarely lasted more than 20,000 years. The last Ice Age began about 110,000 years ago. Its climatic fluctuations have been traced through evidence from sediments and pollen on land, and from geological core samples drilled from the ocean bed. At the height of the last Ice Age, between around 25,000 and 15,000 years ago, global temperatures reached their lowest levels, ice sheets were at their maximum extent, and sea levels were dramatically lower than they are now. The latest interglacial began about 10,000 years ago and continues today.

Europe

A carved mammoth tooth and other incised bone objects from the Tata site in Hungary became among the earliest carvings and incised objects known. Ground pigments are also found at the site.

The earliest known ornament, a decorative amulet, was made from a piece of mammoth's tooth by a Neanderthal. The amulet was found in what is today Hungary.

100,000 B.C.T.

Africa

Homo sapiens sapiens *ventured out of Africa.*

The spread of *Homo sapiens sapiens,* anatomically modern humans, across the Eastern Hemisphere and into the Americas is a highly controversial issue in archaeology. There are two schools of thought. One believes that all modern humans evolved in tropical Africa before 100,000 years ago, and then spread across the Sahara Desert into Southwest Asia by 100,000 years ago. After more than 50,000 years, much later modern human groups spread into southern and eastern Asia, and into northern latitudes, crossing into the Americas either during or after the Late Ice Age, by at least 15,000 years ago.

Another group of scholars argues that modern humans evolved in several parts of the Eastern Hemisphere after 250,000 years ago, and that anatomically modern people enjoyed considerable biological diversity from their first appearance.

The earliest known fossils of Homo sapiens—*of modern people—date to about 100,000 B.C.T.*

By 100,000 years ago, Saharan communities were using smaller, more specialized flaked tools, known as Aterian after the site of Bir el Ater in Tunisia. These included triangular points that may have been used as spearheads mounted on wooden shafts, and sharp-edged scraping tools, perhaps for chopping plant foods or preparing animal hides.

Language continued to evolve.

The evolution of human language and cognitive ability apparently resulted from a generally slow and gradual succession of minute anatomical and neural modifications transfiguring and improving upon earlier properties, structures, forms and functions. The evolution of human language, therefore, can only fruitfully be considered within a general matrix of human evolution, so that the "origin of language" is itself to be seen as but one emergent stage in a general ongoing biological process.

The central questions concerning the evolution of human language which continue to bedevil scientists are: (1) "Why is it that human language, as we know it today, evolved at all?" and (2) "Why is it that language developed in humans and not in any other species?"

While scientists do not know the answers to these questions, they do have a possible, maybe even plausible, theory for the evolution of language. Under this theory, the elements of language began with a select certain group of individuals. These individuals were from the common ancestral stock of modern man and by an evolutionary process of divergent adaptive modification developed a capacity for language.

Scientists believe that, due to extreme selective pressures, gradual genetic transformations ensued amongst a select group of individuals. Over time, these transformations generated fateful structural changes. These structural changes may, for instance, have been triggered by fortuitous local natural conditions of isolation and a changing environment. Within the matrix of such a scenario, human language as an ongoing process evolved from a biological substrate harking back millions of years.

Interestingly, in recent years, many scholars have independently come to a number of nearly congruent conclusions. This observation concerns the phenomenon of what appear to be silent, though not less forceful and salient witnesses to chronological milestones in the "origin" and development of human "language."

It may be that the transition to upright posture and bipedal locomotion, with a subsequent freeing of the hands, and an ensuing descending of the larynx (coupled with diminution of canine dentition), led to the morphing of hominids into verbal beings.

Scientists also believe that it can be said with reasonably justified confidence that the toolmaking of man was when and where hominids began their ascent to true *Homo sapiens*. Judging by the long trail of bones and stones they left behind them, the hominids before long started radiating or spreading out over the world, out of curiosity, or wanderlust as nomads will do, or simply, being as yet but humble scavengers—hunter-gatherers, in search of food, which had become too scarce locally for the rapidly expanding tribe.

Another milestone the current scientific consensus focuses upon is the acute and profound changes noted in finds dated to around 200,000 years ago in the increase in size and intricacy of brain cases, especially those attesting to more complex convolution patterns of the frontal lobe, as well as the sophistication of the accompanying tool-kits. All of these indicia are silent but no less solid witnesses to yet another quantum leap up the human pyramid, and they all may possibly be associated with the ascent of *Homo sapiens sapiens,* however slow and painful.

A final milestone concerns the find made in the 1990s of a well-preserved 60,000 year old human hyoid bone, the only one of its kind in the world, in the Kebara Cave on Mount Carmel, Haifa, Israel. The size and morphology of the hyoid from Kebara and its relations to other anatomical components are almost identical to those in modern humans, suggesting that Middle Paleolithic populations were anatomically capable of fully modern speech.

Whatever the milestones may be, it now appears evident that human language was not only a product of evolution but also a cause of evolution as one can see by the ongoing communication process which is so prevalent amongst the humans of today.

Asia

The world's first known burials occurred in Southwest Asia.

The first known human burials were found in the Qafzeh Cave in Israel. Four individuals of fully modern type were buried in the cave around 100,000 years ago. The most remarkable burial was that of a young woman, around 20 years of age, with the body of a six-year-old child at her feet. The two bodies had been placed in a rectangular pit cut into the accumulated deposits on the cave floor. Nearby was another pit containing the burial of a 13 year old male, with a fallow-deer antler placed across the hands and upper chest.

Communities of hunter-gatherers spread wherever there were sufficient food sources, and the changing climate played a significant part in their movements. Until about 100,000 years ago, the Thar Desert region of northwestern India was sparsely populated, owing to the aridity of the area. About 100,000 years ago, however, the climate became wetter and the desert was transformed into an open grassland, which was ideal territory for early hunters.

Homo erectus *reached Japan.*

The first proof that is known to exist of ancient man crossing a substantial body of water is the stone tools found in Japan from about 100,000 B.C.T. Not much is known about the makers of the tools, but the mainland at that time was probably inhabited by a late population of *Homo erectus*. Japan is about 150 kilometers (90 miles) from Korea, but there are several lands along the route. Japan is not thought to have been linked by land to Asia as the

British Isles were linked to Europe during the most recent Ice Age.

The earliest evidence of *Homo sapiens* crossing a substantial body of water is found in the desert of central Australia, where traces of human occupation have been dated at 60,000 B.C.T. Probably, early people paddled across the Indian Ocean in short hops from one island to another, although during the periods of low sea level (around 16,000 B.C.T.), when the oceans were about 130 meters (425 feet) lower than at present, the early explorers could have walked most of the way across what is now Indonesia.

80,000 B.C.T.

Stone tools became more specialized.

Europe

As evidenced by the Regourdou site in southwestern France, Neanderthals began to bury their dead in graves with symbolic use of red ocher dyes.

79,000 B.C.T.

Simple forms of stone lamps, probably fueled with animal fat and using grass or moss for a wick, were in use.

75,000 B.C.T.

Ice sheets began to advance in the Northern Hemisphere.

In response to the harsh climate, cave dwellings between 100,000 and 50,000 B.C.T. were sometimes improved by building structures at the entrance to give added protection from bad weather. These windbreaks or fences were probably supported by stakes driven into the ground. A small hole at the mouth of a cave at Combe-Grenal in France may have held a stake that supported one of these structures. A cast taken of the hole was shaped like the pointed end of a stake.

Around 75,000 years ago, Homo neanderthalensis— Neanderthal man— became a skilled hunter, able to bring down large, hairy elephant-like mammals, saber toothed tigers, and other creatures that would also become extinct.

Neanderthal man cared for his sick and aged but was also known to engage in cannibalism.

Neanderthal man communicated by a rudimentary form of speech, setting the species apart from other mammals.

69,000 B.C.T.

Mount Toba erupted. It was the largest volcanic eruption in more than 400 million years.

When geneticists examine the genetic makeup of the people of the earth, they are often startled by the fact that the people of today are amazingly similar. Some geneticists believe that this genetic homogeneity is the result of "population bottleneck"—a time in history when the population of the world was greatly reduced thereby reducing the genetic variation of man.

Based upon the estimates of mutation rates, the geneticists believe that the "population bottleneck" occurred sometime after modern humans left Africa 100,000 years ago and before a population increase spurred by the advent of better stone tools around 50,000 years ago. If so, what could conceivably have caused the bottleneck to occur?

One possible answer may be found in the eruption of Mount Toba. 71,000 years ago, Mount Toba in Sumatra erupted spewing 800 cubic kilometers of ash into the atmosphere. The amount of ash spewed forth was more than 4,000 times as much as was ejected by Mount St. Helens in 1980.

The ash from Mount Toba buried most of India and darkened the skies over a third of the hemisphere for weeks.

Climatologists speculate that a six-year global volcanic winter ensued after the eruption of Mount Toba. This volcanic winter was caused by the light reflecting sulfur particles which lingered in the atmosphere. During this volcanic winter, average summer temperatures dropped by 21 degrees at high latitudes and 75 percent of the Northern Hemisphere's plants may have died.

This six year global volcanic winter was followed by a thousand year ice age ostensibly caused by an increasing amount of snow failing to melt during the summer. The snow cover would have reflected more sunlight off Earth's surface, making the world colder. The effect on humans, who had been enjoying a relatively warm period, must have been devastating. After 60,000 years of basking in relatively balmy temperatures, all of humanity was suddenly thrown into the proverbial freezer.

It is conjectured that only a few thousand people, living in isolated pockets in Africa, Europe, and Asia, survived. For a thousand years, our genetic ancestors were forced to huddle together in a desperate struggle to exist.

When, around 70,000 years ago, the climate warmed again, humanity emerged and began to disperse and to grow. However, the piece of humanity that remained was a far cry from the genetically diverse humanity that once was. {**See and compare with Genesis 5-11.**}

68,000 B.C.T.

Asia

Woodworking began in East Asia.

The oldest evidence of woodworking in East Asia is a plank from Nishiyagi, Japan, which dates to between 50,000 and 70,000 years ago. The evidence is a thin, narrow board of mulberry wood which is 10½ inches long, 2 inches wide, and up to ¼ inch thick. Cut across the tree rings, probably by splitting a trunk with wedges, the plank displays the scars of whittling, although what it was used for is unknown.

60,000 B.C.T.

The Races of Man

While it is unknown when man developed into discernible races, by the beginning of the twenty-first century of the Christian calendar, scientists had concluded that the variations in human skin color are most likely the result of adaptations to the amount of ultraviolet light from the sun falling on different regions of the Earth. Scientists posit that people's bodies change their skin color over time to let in just the right amount of ultraviolet light, which is the key to having healthy babies.

Ultraviolet light affects the skin's production of folate, part of the B vitamin complex, and vitamin D-3, both of which are essential for having healthy children. Folate is necessary for the proper development of the nervous system in fetuses and for sperm production in adult males. Vitamin D-3 helps build and maintain strong bones and a healthy immune system. However, too much solar ultraviolet light can not only cause skin cancer, it can also damage those chemicals, thereby hurting a person's chances for reproductive success.

This finding may also explain why women tend to be lighter-skinned than men. Lighter skin lets in more solar ultraviolet light, increasing a woman's vitamin D-3 production, which helps the fetus grow during pregnancy and helps nourish newborns through breast feeding.

Ultraviolet light from the sun varies from region to region for reasons including latitude, humidity and cloudiness. Scientists have found that the variations in human skin color was directly linked to the amount of ultraviolet light from the sun which falls on the different regions of the Earth.

Skin color is based on the level of melanin, an organic molecule with an undetermined chemical structure. Those with more melanin have darker skin, and melanin levels are genetic. But the variations in skin color are adaptations to solar ultraviolet light, not biological differences among people.

The essential finding of these recent discoveries and theories is that skin coloration is an environmental adaptation and that over the passage of time, in differing locales, those who are white would begin producing offspring who would become progressively darker until, over time, they would become black, while, in a similar reversal of locales, those who are black would produce offspring that would eventually become white. Ultimately, it is in our ability to adapt that we are all the same under the skin.

Africa

The huge cave at Haua Fteah, on the Libyan coast of North Africa, was occupied continuously from at least 60,000 years ago. It was probably a seasonal camp used by people exploiting coastal resources during the dry summer months. During the wet winter season, the occupants moved inland to areas of open grassland where there were abundant equine animals and gazelles.

Around 60,000 years ago, the eland became abundant in what is now Cape Province, South Africa. A natural herd animal, it was probably killed in mass drives. The ferocious Cape buffalo was more difficult to kill, and only the most vulnerable individuals would have been hunted. Meat must have been scavenged from animals that were already dead. Eland and buffalo bones have been found in South African caves that were occupied during this period.

Asia

Neanderthals occupied the Kebara Cave in what is today Israel.

The limestone cave at Kebara in Israel was occupied by Neanderthals around 60,000 years ago. Hearths and layers of ash show that the Kebara Cave was used as a dwelling. Caves were particularly favored as shelters in which to survive the rigors of the last Ice Age. Where caves were not available, groups of humans may have built shelters of wooden frames covered in animal hides.

A Neanderthal man was buried at Shanidar Cave in Iraq.

Some Neanderthals buried their dead, marking and seemingly mourning the loss of a community member—a characteristic that they shared with fully modern humans. Evidence of ceremonies has been found in both Europe and Southwest Asia. Some graves appear to contain items to equip the deceased for an afterlife. At some sites, burned or charred bones, showing evidence of butchering, suggest that cooked joints of meat were placed in the grave. At Shanidar in Iraq, flowers seem to have been placed in one grave. Children's burials were often a focus for such activity. At La Ferrassie in France, an infant's skull was found beneath a patterned slab in what appears to have been a family cemetery in a rock shelter.

As for the Shanidar Cave, one man buried at Shanidar Cave in Iraq some 60,000 years ago had been badly injured at some point in his life. He had lost an arm and probably an eye, and was crippled in both legs. To have survived until his comparatively advanced age of 40, he must have been supported by his community. If so, such actions suggest that Neanderthal groups possessed a degree of social solidarity and practiced a form of communal welfare.

Europe

The use of flint was revolutionized by the Neanderthals.

Around 60,000 years ago, a new technique of working flint was developed in Southwest Asia and Europe. Flint nodules were carefully shaped so that large flakes of predetermined size and form could be removed. This new method is known as the Levallois technique, after the site of Levallois in France.

The Neanderthals revolutionized toolmaking with the prepared core technique, in which several sharp flakes were split from a single flint. Their simple but effective implements included scrapers and piercing tools to make warm clothing from hides. Tools made by fully modern humans—single-edged knives and leaf-shaped blades—show more refined stoneworking techniques.

Australia

Based on the dating of bone fragments from Central Australia, early humans reached Australia around 60,000 B.C.T.

Australian Aborigines lived as hunter-gatherers for perhaps 60,000 years. However, their earliest days may have had the most impact on the continent and holds implications for mankind today.

When the Aborigines arrived, Australia was populated by a group of megafauna—super large animals—such as the diprotodon (a wombat the size of a rhinoceros) and the giant kangaroo, a roo that was taller than modern man. However, after the Aborigines arrived in Australia, these mega-animals became extinct,—most likely at the hands of the Aborigines.

Like the mass extinctions that would accompany the arrival of the Indigenous Americans to the Americas {see 9000 B.C.T.}, the extinctions which accompanied the Aborigines of Australia should cause us to pause. Both incursions diminished the land's bounty, forcing the new immigrants in the Americas and in Australia to adapt to harsher conditions to survive. This should cause us to pause because the ecological devastation caused by primitive man continues at an increasingly rapid pace today and, ultimately, it is this continuing devastation which may pose the gravest threat to the continued existence of man.

55,000 B.C.T.

Australia

When modern humans first reached Australia between 60,000 and 55,000 years ago, the continent was inhabited by a variety of large marsupials, including giant kangaroos and wallabies and the wombat-like diprotodon, a plant-eater that weighed up to 2 tons. These animals became extinct mainly because they were hunted by humans.

Among the few carnivorous predators encountered by Australia's first settlers was the Tasmanian tiger, a marsupial that became extinct on the mainland around 3,000 years ago owing to competition from the more efficient dingo. The Tasmanian tiger survived until much more recently in Tasmania, where there were no dingoes.

The oldest campsites in Australia are the sandstone rock shelters at Malakunaja and Malangangerr. These lie at the foot of the Arnheim Land plateau, near the northern coast of the continent. The modern humans who set up camp here around 55,000 years ago were probably the near descendants of the first humans to cross the open sea to Australia from Southeast Asia.

50,000 B.C.T.

The first culturally modern, cave-painting humans appeared.

Date palms flourished in parts of Africa and Asia where they would become an important food source.

Asia

The climate of Southwest Asia in 50,000 B.C.T. was much like it is today.

Pollen found in Shanidar Cave in northern Iraq shows that the climate around 50,000 years ago was much as it is now. Plants existing at that time still grow in the area today: yarrow, St. John's wort, hollyhocks, St. Barnaby's thistle, groundsel, grape hyacinth, and woody horsetail. Some have medicinal properties, but whether they were used medicinally at this date is unknown.

The Shanidar Cave was occupied around 50,000 years ago by a group of Neanderthals. Located in the foothills of the Zagros mountains, in Anatolia (modern Turkey), the cave was used as a seasonal base from which to hunt bezoar goats in the surrounding mountains, and to gather local food plants. The occupants probably spent the rest of the year in lower terrain.

Like the Neanderthals who occupied Kebara Cave in Palestine some 10,000 years before, the Neanderthals living in Shanidar Cave buried their dead. Some may have been victims of a rock fall, but others were intentionally buried. Remains of pollen suggest that one adult may have been laid on a bed of woody branches with a variety of small, brightly colored flowers placed around the body.

The bezoar goat was hunted in western Asia.

The bezoar goat, the wild ancestor of the modern goat, was one of the staple resources exploited by modern human groups living around 50,000 years ago in the mountains of western Asia. Like most wild goats, the bezoar goat was probably hunted most effectively by ambushing the herbs or by driving them into natural cul-de-sacs for slaughter.

By 50,000 B.C.T., hunting had become more sophisticated.

The appearance of specialized open-air slaughter camps in southern France indicates the development of more effective hunting methods. At these camps, large animals such as the steppe bison and the aurochs (wild ox) were killed and butchered en masse. In a camp at Mauran, in the Pyrenees, thousands of bone fragments from over 100 animals were found, representing hundreds of tons of meat.

Europe

Around 50,000 B.C.T., the decoration of bones may have begun. A bone fragment from a cave at Bacho Kiro in central Bulgaria bears zigzag markings that seem to be deliberate engravings rather than the result of damage caused by chopping strokes.

The Americas

It is theorized that Neanderthal man may have reached the west coast of the Western Hemisphere.

49,000 B.C.T.

The Americas

A meteor struck the Earth at what is today known as Arizona, creating the 1.186 kilometer (.737 mile) wide Barringer Meteor Crater.

45,000 B.C.T.

A perforated part of the bone of an antelope or other bovine animal dated at

45,000 B.C.T. is believed by some to be the oldest known musical instrument, a form of whistle. Indisputable whistles appeared more than 15,000 years later. {**See also 30,000 B.C.T.**}

44,000 B.C.T.

Africa

Humans or the ancestors at the Orange River Valley settlement in Namibia painted slabs. This is the oldest known "art" found in Africa. {**See also 20,000 B.C.T.**}

43,000 B.C.T.

Africa

Jewelry was created.

Humans in Eurasia wore beads, bracelets, pins, rings, pendants, diadems, and pectorals, although the earliest recognizable jewelry of any type consists of ostrich-shell beads from the Border Cave in South Africa which may date from as early as 43,000 B.C.T.

Around 43,000 B.C.T., the Sahara was much wetter that it is today, with types of Mediterranean like evergreen vegetation in the highlands, and rivers crossing the dry grassland plains below. At Bir Tarfawi in southwestern Egypt, settlers on the shore of a shallow lake were able to hunt gazelles, warthogs, and ostriches. This way of life changed around 38,000 years ago when the Sahara entered an arid phase, and human communities were forced to withdraw to its margins.

Asia

In Southwest Asia, the production of flint tools was modified.

Around 45,000 years ago, human communities in Southwest Asia began to produce smaller flint tools, which were suitable for setting into wooden or bone handles. Many tools of this kind have been found in the Mount Carmel Caves on the coast of Israel. Known as Aurignacian, the new technology was later adopted by communities across the whole of southern Europe.

Europe

The cave bear and a cave culture reigned in Europe.

The cave bear, which is now extinct, was so named because it hibernated in caves and often died there. It was a huge animal, twice the size of a brown bear. Its teeth and the chemistry of its bones show that it was a vegetarian. Cave bear bones are often found in caves mixed with stone tools and other traces of human settlement. Some archaeologists believe that humans hunted the bears.

Australia

The world's first known rock art was created.

By 60,000 years ago fully modern humans must have been established in Southeast Asia. Armed with the capacity to plan and the ability to coordinate activities, humans began to colonize areas that had previously been beyond human reach. Seagoing boats were needed to make the crossing from Southeast Asia to Australia, as there would have been at least 37 miles of open sea to cross at any given time. Indeed, by 55,000 years ago, the first human settlements had been established in northern Australia. It is here that some of the oldest human creative expressions are seen. The petroglyphs (rock engravings) found at Panaramitee, around 45,000 years old, are the earliest known examples of rock art in the world.

The petroglyphs of Panaramitee, the oldest rock engravings in the world, are simple non-figurative designs that were etched into rocks in Australia from around 45,000 years ago. These engravings come in a variety of patterns: mazes, circles, dots, and arcs. The Panaramitee petroglyphs represent the earliest stage in a long and varied tradition of Australian rock art.

The petroglyphs of Panaramitee marked the start of a rock art tradition of the same name that continued into the 20th century. Many petroglyphs discovered on rock slabs are covered with "desert varnish," a natural coating that gives them a dark sheen and takes many millennia to build up. Petroglyph motifs are linear and abstract in design, often representing kangaroo tracks, bird tracks, spirals, crescents and circles. Tracks and human footprints may symbolize creatures as seen by an imaginary eye looking up from beneath the earth's surface.

There is no comparison between the simple, non-utilitarian markings that distinguish the few Neanderthal art objects that have been discovered and the mass of art—engravings, rock paintings, figures—that is found at the later *Homo sapiens sapiens* sites such as Panaramitee, Australia. Nevertheless, the existing Neanderthal objects—burial slabs, engraved bones, or the very early objects from Tata, Hungary, testify to an emerging appreciation of decorative artifacts that may have had some symbolic function.

42,000 B.C.T.

Australia

By 42,000 B.C.T., the continent that would come to be called Australia was populated by the earth's first seafaring people. These intrepid colonists arrived from the Asian mainland. {But see also 100,000 and 60,000 B.C.T.}

40,000 B.C.T.

Simple forms of stone lamps fueled with animal fat and using lichens, moss, or juniper for a wick, began to be utilized.

In cold climates, large dwellings were constructed of mammoth bones. Some houses covered as much as 30 square meters (300 square feet).

Around 40,000 B.C.T., construc-tion of hearths in the northern latitudes began to improve noticeably. Stone borders were arranged for heat retention and to direct air flow. {See also 600,000 B.C.T.}

Some hearths were enclosed in clay walls and may have been used as kilns for ceramic production, although they may also have been used for baking food or other purposes.

Europe

The earliest blade stone tool industry in Europe was known from the Bacho Kiro site in what is now Bulgaria.

38,000 B.C.T.

Homo sapiens *emerged from the shadow of the Neanderthals. While physically less powerful,* Homo sapiens—*modern man—possessed a more prominent chin, a much larger brain volume, and superior intelligence.* Homo sapiens' *control of fire, development of new, lightweight bone and horn tools, weapons, and fishhooks, and superior intelligence permitted* Homo sapiens *to obtain food more easily and to preserve it longer.* Homo sapiens *hunters provided early tribes with meat from bison and tigers, while other tribespeople fished and collected honey, fruits, and nuts.*

Around 40,000 years ago, the increased availability of food would lead to an increase in human populations. Of these humanoid populations, the Cro-Magnon people *Homo sapiens* would appear in

Europe, the Middle East, and North Africa. These anatomically modern humans would replace the Neanderthal populations. Along with other modern human populations in places as far apart as Australia and southern Africa, *Homo sapiens* would develop art and specialized tools, and would exhibit physical and cultural differences over place and time.

It is believed that modern human language began.

Defined as the production and perception of speech, language evolved as the human species evolved. As a communication system, it can be related to the communication systems of other animals. However, human language has a creative and interpretive aspect that appears to mark it as distinctive. The understanding of human speech is believed to involve specialization of part of the left hemisphere of the brain (Broca's area). It is possible that human language may not have been distinct from animal communication until this physiological specialization occurred. The production of human language is believed to have occurred first in the Neanderthals (100,000 to 30,000 years ago). It is also speculated that about 40,000 to 30,000 years ago, the emergence of modern *Homo sapiens* (with an increased skull capacity and improved vocal tract) was accompanied by significant linguistic development. Modern human language, then, may be only 30,000 to 40,000 years old. The immense diversity of languages spoken in the world indicates an incredible acceleration in the rate of change of human language, once it emerged. If there was in fact a first language, its sounds, grammar, and vocabulary cannot be definitely known. Historical linguists, focusing on finding out and describing how, why, and in what form languages occur, can only suggest hypotheses to account for language change.

In the 18th century of the Christian calendar, the German philosopher Gottfried Wilhelm Leibniz suggested that all ancient and modern languages diverged from a single proto-language. This idea is referred to as monogenesis. Most scholars believe that such a language can, at best, be posited only as a set of hypothetical formulas from which one can derive the world's languages. However, it is unlikely that such a reconstruction reflects a real first language as it was actually spoken.

Although many modern languages do indeed derive from a single ancestral tongue, it is possible that the diversity that exists today is attributable to the fact that human language arose or evolved simultaneously at many different places on earth and that today's languages do not, in fact, have a single common ancestor.

The notion that the present families of languages are derived from many original ancestral languages is called polygenesis. However, today it would seem that any great debate concerning whether human language was ultimately monogenetic or polygenetic is counterproductive. What may be most important to recognize is that, although many humans find it difficult to learn a second language, and although languages such as Chinese, English, and Swahili may seem to have little in common, the differences among languages are not nearly so great as the similarities between them. The sounds and sound combinations of the world's languages, despite the ways in which they differ from language to language, are believed to have been selected from a universal set of possible sounds and sound combinations available to, and common with, all human languages. Human languages likewise have individual structural properties that are selected from a common pool of possible structures. That is, no human language utilizes any sounds that cannot be produced by any human being, or any grammatical categories that cannot be learned by any human—whether or not the native language of a given person makes use of those sounds and structures. In other words, the range of possible language changes appears to be limited by the universal—the universally human—structural properties of language.

Africa
Composite tools were developed in Africa.

Asia
Portable art was crafted.

The earliest examples of portable art in South Asia are engravings on ostrich eggshells, carved between 40,000 and 25,000 years ago. One of the best examples is a fragment from Patne in central India, which is decorated with a crosshatched pattern. The complete eggshells may have been used as containers.

The Niah caves of Sarawak, Borneo were first occupied.

A network of huge limestone caves at Niah in Sarawak, Borneo, has the longest record of human occupation on any island in Southeast Asia. The Great Cave, an enormous cavern 800 feet wide at the mouth and nearly 200 feet high inside, is the most important. Its floor area covers approximately 64 acres. This splendid natural shelter was first occupied by modern humans around 40,000 years ago.

By 38,000 B.C.T. humans had reached New Guinea.

Heavy stone axes with flaked cutting edges are among the earliest traces of human presence on the island of New Guinea. These axes had notches cut into either side, creating a narrow waist where a wooden handle would have been attached. On the Huon Peninsula in northeastern New Guinea, such waisted axes were in use 40,000 years ago.

36,000 B.C.T.

Africa
The Sahara entered an arid phase.

As the Sahara became increasingly dry with the onset of an arid phase around 38,000 years ago, new types of settlements and tools developed. Dabban tools, named after the site of ed-Dabba in Libya, are characterized by smaller flint blades mounted in wooden or bone hafts. These tools are restricted to coastal North Africa, because the interior was by then too dry for permanent habitation.

The Americas
It is theorized that Homo sapiens *reached the northern continent of the Western Hemisphere, where the Neanderthals had probably preceded them.*

35,000 B.C.T.

About this time there is plentiful evidence of fully modern Homo sapiens *as the only member of the* Homo *genus left on Earth. The Neanderthals had mysteriously disappeared. From this time onward, technological change became increasingly swift.*

Africa
Around 35,000 B.C.T., the Sehonghong rock shelter of Lesotho and the Kalemba rock shelter of Zambia were founded.

Rock shelters provided convenient temporary camps for early African hunter-gatherers. Many of these shelters would have been used as stopovers by small groups moving about the landscape collecting wild fruit and hunting game.

Rudimentary counting devices may have been made in Africa as long as 37,000 years ago. Among engraved pieces of wood and bone from Border Cave in South Africa was a baboon fibula with 29 parallel incised notches. This resembles the wooden calendar sticks that are still used today by some Bushman clans in southwestern Africa.

Australia

People crossed a land bridge from Australia into Tasmania. The changing sea levels eventually made Tasmania an isolated island, with its last land connection to Australia submerged around 8,000 B.C.T.

34,000 B.C.T.

Australia

Between 34,000 and 29,000 B.C.T. substantial middens (mounds of discarded shells) were created by the Aborigines at the Willandra Lakes.

The Willandra Lakes, located in a now arid part of New South Wales, Australia, were frequented by Aboriginal groups. Their dietary staple was shellfish, including mussels. On the shores of one of these lakes, substantial middens were created by the Aborigines.

The campsites on the shores of Lake Mungo, one of the Willandra Lakes in New South Wales, Australia, were used repeatedly by Aboriginal groups for several thousand years. The clearest remains are of hearths containing fish, bird, and mammal bones. In addition to the hearths, shallow scoops in the ground have been identified at some of the campsites. Heated lumps of clay may have been placed in these scoops to cook food. The Aboriginal groups spent the remainder of the year at other sites with different kinds of resources.

33,000 B.C.T.

By 35,000 years ago, Homo sapiens had become the dominate species on the earth, with no serious rivals.

What occurred some 100,000 years ago, when Homo sapiens first met their Ne-

anderthal cousins—the only other hominid species that had not dwindled into extinction—is a matter of much speculation. Homo sapiens—the species of modern man—would be the only hominid species to survive but whatever happened to the Neanderthals did not happen quickly. Archaeological evidence proves that Homo sapiens and Homo neanderthalensis inhabited the same general area turf in many parts of Europe and Southwest Asia for thousands of years. That did not prove, however, that they lived as peaceable neighbors. Populations were so sparse that run-ins probably would have been rare.

A romantic notion of how the Neanderthals disappeared has been around for a long time. It has been suggested that perhaps the Neanderthals were eliminated by interbreeding with Homo sapiens. However, in 1997, molecular biologists tested that hypothesis by extracting some DNA from a Neanderthal fossil and comparing it with that of modern humans. The conclusion the biologists reached was that the differences between the Neanderthals and modern man are so great that wide spread interbreeding would have been infeasible, although some sporadic interbreeding was biologically possible.

However, whatever the cause may have been the Neanderthals disappeared some 30,000 years ago and their exit paved the way to the dominance of man.

Africa

Microlith stone points were developed in Africa.

In northeastern Zaire, hunter-gatherers began to make tiny stone blades from local quartz. These blades are known as microliths, and were mounted in handles of wood or bone to make composite tools. Often of standardized shapes, microliths later became widespread in Africa, Europe, western Asia, and China.

Advanced tool traditions developed in different parts of the world, characterized by ever-smaller stone points and blades, and by the first extensive use of bone and antler. The development of microliths in Africa around 33,000 B.C.T. was a critical improvement. These tiny stone blades could be mounted in wooden or bone handles to produce tools whose damaged blades could be replaced. New, more refined toolmaking techniques also became the standard technology throughout Europe and Southwest Asia.

Asia

At Patna, India, and other sites in South Asia, ostrich eggshells, perhaps used as containers, were engraved with decorative, non-representational patterns.

Europe

Early Europeans made body ornamentation such as beads and pendants, the first known form of art.

In France and other sites in Europe, beads, pendants, and other body ornamentation were fashioned from bone fragments and animal teeth.

The earliest remains of bone, antler, and ivory objects, especially tubular beads, were found in central and southwestern France and northeastern Spain. The tool industry of this time and place would become known as the Chatelperronian.

The Neanderthals became extinct.

Between 45,000 and 35,000 years ago, fully modern humans had spread throughout Europe. Contact with the indigenous Neanderthals is evident from the way the newcomers' improved toolmaking techniques influenced the Neanderthals' tool industry. However, ultimately the Neanderthals would not benefit from this contact. By 35,000 years ago, for reasons that are still unclear, modern humans completely replaced the Neanderthals. In contrast to the hundreds of millennia during which early hominid types had co-existed, the demise of the Neanderthals was swift and decisive. As temperatures fell still further and the Ice Age entered its coldest phase, modern humans found themselves the only hominid species left on what was then an increasingly hostile Earth.

It should be noted that at the extent of their existence Neanderthals appear to have ranged from Western Europe to Iraq. During the coldest phase of the Ice Age, ice sheets would have isolated the Neanderthals of Europe from those of the Middle East.

The last Neanderthals in western Europe produced flint tools similar to those of contemporary groups of modern humans further east. The tools were smaller than any previously known and were set into handles. This style, known as Chatelperronian because the first examples were found at Chatelperron in France, is exemplified by small flint points that were probably set obliquely into handles of bone or wood.

It is theorized that near the end, late Neanderthals began to modify their toolmaking techniques, perhaps through contact with communities of modern humans.

It is unknown whether the extinction of the Neanderthals holds any lessons for the future of mankind. If the Neanderthals simply died out from disease, then such an act of God could arise anytime and little could be learned. However, if Neanderthals died out from being outsmarted by *Homo sapiens*, then *Homo sapiens* may find their own future in the history of the Neanderthals. After all, if the theory of Darwinism is correct, evolution is a continuing process and the species known as *Homo sapiens* is not the ultimate in creation but rather just a phase. Indeed, it may be argued that the heavens are not promised to

man but rather to the future superior beings that man may one day become. If such
is the case, then the tale of the Neanderthals
may be quite instructive. Perhaps one day,
we too shall be confronted by a superior
species and face the realization that the best
course for the future of life on earth is for
Homo sapiens to go gently into the night.
{But see also 22,500 B.C.T.}

*The horses that abounded in Europe
around this time resembled the modern
Przewalski or Mongolian wild horse. Living
in areas of open grassland, these horses
were of great importance to prehistoric people as a source of meat. Horse bones are
commonly found at habitation sites, and
horses were frequently depicted in the rock
art of the period.*

32,000 B.C.T.

Asia

*Around 32,000 B.C.T., the El Wad Cave at
Mount Carmel, Palestine, provided shelter
for a group of modern humans who hunted
fallow deer on the hills above. The cave inhabitants probably spent several months
each year at the site, moving inland during
the winter.*

Europe

*In Europe, a toolmaking industry termed
the Aurignacian produced the characteristic
toolmaking industry of the Upper Paleolithic Era. The toolmaking industry featured blades, points, scrapers, and burins of
stone as well as tools worked from bone and
antler.*

30,000 B.C.T.

Africa

*At caves in South Africa, traces of charcoal
and pollen show that the local environment
at this time was made up of shrubs and
grass, with few fruits. The fauna was domi-*

*nated by grazing animals such as a giant
species of buffalo, horse, and hartebeest.
These species later became extinct as the
climate and vegetation changed. The horse
was only reintroduced into South Africa in
the 17th century.*

*Around 30,000 B.C.T., in South Africa, few
caves were permanently inhabited. Most
were used only occasionally as convenient
bases for specific activities such as tool
manufacture or, at coastal sites, collecting
shellfish. Some caves like Boomplaas in
South Africa, located near open grasslands
rich in game, were occupied repeatedly
throughout this period, and until relatively
recent times.*

Asia

*Between 30,000 and 16,000 B.C.T., human
groups in Iraq and Iran began to broaden
their range of stone tools, making slender
leaf-shaped points, which may have been
used as spear points. These smaller, finer
tools, called Baradostian after the caves in
Mount Baradost in southern Kurdistan, are
part of a trend also occurring in Africa and
Europe at this time.*

Europe

*Between 30,000 B.C.T. and 17,000 B.C.T.,
new stone tools were made by human
groups in western Europe. These stone
tools were known as Aurignacian, after
the site of Aurignac in southern France.
The tool tradition includes flint blades,
smaller and more finely worked than those
of the Neanderthals, as well as bone and
antler tools, particularly split-based bone
points.*

*In Europe, the sculpting of portable art ob-
jects began over 30,000 years ago. A carved
ivory statuette from the cave at Hohlen-
stein-Stadel in Germany depicts a human
with a feline head. Found inside the cave
near the entrance to a dwelling and dating
from around 30,000 B.C.T., the statuette is*

one of the earliest known figurines in the world.

In Germany and elsewhere in Europe, sculptures were made from stone, bone, ivory, antler, and horn. Some of these sculptures depict animals, some exaggerated female shapes called "Venuses," such as the four-inch Venus of Willendorf.

From very early on we know that *Homo sapiens* developed a picture of the universe based on religion. Ancient burials provide the earliest evidence. In later times, statues, shrines, and, most likely, cave paintings attest to these early beliefs, even if evidence does not tell much about the specific beliefs.

Paleolithic peoples in central Europe and France used tallies on the bones of animals, ivory, and stone to record numbers. For example, a wolf bone from this period shows 55 cuts arranged in groups of five.

In what is now Germany, the earliest recovered animal images were made. These are detailed and sophisticated three-dimensional carvings of lions, horses, bison, and mammoths.

Beads, bracelets, and pendants began to be worn by humans.

Australia

The oldest known edge-ground ax, from Sandy Creek in Queensland, was created.

Aboriginal stoneworkers in Australia developed the technique of grinding the edges of stones to make axes over 30,000 years ago. Edge-ground axes were often traded over hundreds of miles and were probably used for cutting branches off trees.

28,500 B.C.T.

Asia

The island that would be called New Guinea was populated by colonists who arrived either from Australia or from the Asian mainland. {See 42,000 B.C.T.}

28,000 B.C.T.

Asia

At Pushkar in northwestern India, a series of lakes in an otherwise arid region attracted groups of hunter-gatherers who first settled there around 28,000 B.C.T. Increasingly dry conditions from this time onward made these lakes a vital source of water and game, such as the spotted deer. Campsites, marked by scatters of stone tools and debris, were clustered around the shores of the lakes.

Europe

In Europe, flutes, the earliest musical instruments, began to be regularly used. These early instruments were made from bones.

The earliest known unequivocally identified musical instruments were flutes and whistles made from bird or bear bones or from reindeer antlers that date from 28,000 B.C.T. forward. The instruments have been found from France deep into central Europe and the Russian Plain. {See also 45,000 B.C.T.}

The earliest fired ceramics, found at sites in the Pavlov Hills of Moravia (the Czech Republic) and made from the local loess, were manufactured, a development that continued for the next 6000 years. One theory is that the small statues and variously shaped blobs were intended to explode on refiring, since most were found shattered, with the shards used in divination. Animal statuettes were nearly all of predators, while human statuettes occurred later. {See also 25,000 B.C.T.}

In France, people carved and engraved vulvas and, more rarely, phalluses.

27,000 B.C.T.

Africa

At Kisese in central Tanzania, ocher fragments and ocher stained palettes dating back to 27,000 B.C.T. were left in decorated rock shelters and evidenced the presence of the art of painting.

Some of the most striking records of human achievement during the last Ice Age are provided by the decorated cave sites. The vast majority are caves and rock shelters, although open-air surfaces were sometimes decorated. Between 35,000 and 20,000 years ago, most decoration was limited to areas exposed to daylight, and much of the detail has therefore weathered away. Most surviving cave art dates to between 20,000 and 10,000 years ago, when the darker depths of large caves were decorated.

The late Ice Age cave art encompasses an astonishing variety of subjects and techniques, from hand stencils, outline drawings, and polychrome paintings to engravings, bas-relief sculptures, and clay figures. The artists applied pigments with fingers, brushes of animal hair, pads (perhaps of animal fur), or spitting techniques.

Some of the art is clearly visible, while some is carefully hidden in crevices, possibly indicating that the act of producing an image, rather than the image itself, was an important factor.

Early attempts at interpretation involved notions of artistic expression, hunting magic, or fertility magic. It is now generally accepted that complex religious beliefs underlie the content and distribution of cave art.

As for the cave art materials utilized, cave artists made pigments from a variety of minerals ground to a powder, then mixed with water. Red pigment was produced from hematite (iron oxide, or red ocher) white came from kaolin or chalk, while black was either manganese dioxide or charcoal. Some communities heated minerals to produce new colors. Most minerals used for pigments were readily available and could be collected locally, although some must have been mined. In Africa, ocher mines have been discovered that were first worked around 42,000 years ago.

Asia

Homo sapiens *reached the islands that would be called Japan and may have arrived on the islands as early as 5,000 years earlier. Access to the islands was provided by ice sheets or land bridges.*

26,000 B.C.T.

Africa

At Kisese, Tanzania, human artists began to paint.

The world's oldest known rock paintings come not from Europe but from southern Africa. In the Apollo 11 cave in Namibia, archaeologists have found slabs painted in black and red, dating from 26,000 to 19,000 years ago, portraying animals such as the zebra and black rhinoceros. Rock painting was also practiced in central East Africa. At Kisese, Tanzania, the remnants of painters' tools, ocher fragments, and palettes stained with ocher, have been found dating to 29,000 years ago.

Other paintings would later appear in the caves of Europe. At Lascaux, France

(17,000 years old) and Altamira, Spain (14,000 years old), there are cave paintings which are among the first examples of prehistoric European art.

By 13,000 years ago, rock painting was being practiced in such distant places as India and Australia. By 9,000 years ago, it was also taking place in the Sahara plateaus of North Africa. {See 24,000 B.C.T.}

Europe

Single-backed points and burins characterize the Gravettian tool assemblage found throughout much of Europe around 26,000 B.C.T.

25,000 B.C.T.

Around 25,000 B.C.T. the last Ice Age entered its coldest phase.

At the height of the last Ice Age, ice covered huge areas of Europe, Asia, and North America. A drop of more than 330 feet in sea levels exposed newly dry land around the world's coastlines and uncovered bridges between landmasses formerly separated by water. The Bering land bridge between Siberia and Alaska was over 620 miles wide; Australia, Tasmania, and New Guinea were one huge continent; Britain was joined to Europe; and Indonesia was all part of mainland Southeast Asia.

As temperatures dropped during this glacial episode, the ice sheets advanced and forests were replaced by open vegetation. Animals either became extinct, adapted their diet and way of life, or followed the retreating wooded areas. Animals from cold latitudes, such as the musk ox and reindeer, spread into what are now very warm areas of Europe. Reindeer even lived in northern Spain, as shown in Ice Age rock art such as is present in a Basque cave.

In northern latitudes, bulky, thick-coated, cold tolerant animals such as the woolly mammoth and woolly rhinoceros prevailed during the glacial periods. In tundra areas, where wood was scarce, mammoth bones were used for the framework and supports of skin-covered huts. At the end of the last Ice Age, deprived of their natural environment and habitat, many of these species became extinct.

Glacial episodes associated with the peak of the last Ice Age initiated long periods of dry climate. Because so much water was locked up in the glaciers and thus so much less water was available, deserts became even more arid than they are today and covered larger areas. Fossil sand dunes discovered in the Sahel of north-central Africa show that the Sahara once extended much farther south, and the Zaire rainforest was much smaller. The release of water at the end of a glacial period was not the only encouragement to new vegetation. Huge quantities of rock dust, shattered and ground by the ice, combined with impacted earth to produce loess, a fertile, loamy soil more amenable to plant growth.

The dramatic landscape changes of the Ice Ages in the tropics can be seen in Africa where lake levels and fossil pollen show fluctuations in the distribution of forest, savanna, and desert during the last glacial cycle. When the last Ice Age was at its coldest, rainforests and lakes contracted while deserts reached their maximum extent. Once the Ice Age was over, lakes and forests expanded again, and were in fact more extensive 6,000 years ago than today.

The fossil record of tiny lake organisms and evidence of changing shorelines over the past million years reveal that lake levels oscillated widely. The accompanying shifts in vegetation and the landscape probably affected the survival of early humans and other species. The end of the last Ice

Age affected lake levels in every continent. The Great Lakes of North America, for example, were created by meltwater.

During the peak of the last Ice Age, *Homo sapiens sapiens* was the sole surviving species of the genus *Homo*. Although physically less robust than the Neanderthals who had inhabited northerly latitudes, these fully modern humans were able to use their skills and ingenuity to combat the increasing cold. Resourceful and inventive, they used natural materials fully, employing not only stone but also bone, hide, and antler in new ways. Innovations included weapons that could be thrown or aimed accurately over long distances—spear-throwers, bows and arrows, boomerangs, and barbed harpoons; improved clothing technology—thong-softeners, toggles, and needles with eyes; and sturdier shelters to protect them from the harsh climate.

Larger, more durable shelters were built during the Last Ice Age in many regions of the world. The most common form was a superstructure of wooden posts covered with animal hides. Some of these huts had sunken floors and hearths. Most notable were the mammoth-bone dwellings known to have been built in eastern Europe, which demonstrate an ability to use whatever materials were available for building. Meanwhile, caves continued to provide convenient, ready-made shelters in many regions of the world.

In the harsh Ice Age conditions, the resilience of modern humans was fully tested. Scattered groups of hunter-gatherers managed to survive, and some even migrated northward into the frozen steppes of Siberia. Superior hunting skills, improved weaponry, and a command of language—combined with a detailed knowledge of the habits, diets, and movements of animals—resulted in a seemingly never-ending search for fresh hunting territory.

Asia

Rock engravings were made in Arabia and India.

Europe

Fishermen in Europe's Dordogne Valley developed short, baited toggles that became wedged at an angle in fishes' jaws when the line, made of plant fibers was pulled taut.

Homo sapiens *used small pits lined with hot embers or pebbles preheated in fires to cook food that was covered with layers of leaves or wrapped in seaweed to prevent scorching.*

Gravettian cultures in Europe burned bone in deep pit hearths for heat and probably for cooking.

Perigordian sites in southwestern France showed complex arrangements of hearths, slabs, and postholes, implying complex living or storage structures.

Gravettian cultures at sites such as Pavlov and Dolni Vestronice, in the Czech Republic, and Kostenki, in Russia, constructed huts that used mammoth bone for support when wood was not available.

In the Pyrenees and Spain, spears were decorated with grouped incisions and simplified animal carvings.

Music was produced by humans in what is now France. Archaelogical evidence includes cave paintings, footprints in caves that appear to be those of dancers, and carved bones that appear to be wind and percussion instruments.

People made artifacts with primitive geometrical designs.

24,000 B.C.T.

Africa

The first rock paintings were created in Africa.

The oldest rock paintings in Africa, found on the walls of Apollo II Cave in Namibia, are between 24,000 B.C.T. and 17,000 B.C.T. The cave art is painted on to slabs on rock that were buried among the occupation layers (accumulations of debris left by successive inhabitants. These layers can be dated very accurately. The paintings are in black or red and include figures of animals such as a black rhinoceros and zebras.

Evidenced by the migration to the Western Hemisphere that would occur during this period, the last Ice Age was a period of great change. However, it was also a period of great cultural expression, which is most vividly reflected in the rock paintings of Africa, Europe, and Australia.

Examples in Africa and Europe were being produced around 24,000 B.C.T. In Australia, the first rock paintings, as opposed to the earlier petroglyphs (rock engravings), are more than 18,000 years old. The rich tradition of African rock art began to take shape during this period; some of the oldest examples can be seen in the Apollo II Cave in Namibia. Other noted African cave art objects include terra-cotta figurines from Afalou Bou Rhummel in Algeria, incised and engraved objects from the Border Cave in South Africa, and a perforated stone from Zaire which is decorated with incised lines and dated to around 18,000 B.C.T.

The most famous European sites of polychrome rock art dating to this period are in caves at Lascaux and Pech-Merle in France and Altamira in Spain. Simple outline drawings of animals were more common, however.

The rock art of European cave sites is particularly instructive. Typically, horse, bison, and wild cattle dominate the cave walls, but non-figurative signs such as dots, rectangles, and lines often appear to be of equal importance. At Lascaux, wooden scaffolding was used to enable the artists to reach high walls and ceilings. One Lascaux cave passage even has sockets for a platform of posts. The interior of the European caves would have been lit by burning animal fat placed on flat or dished stones. Cave paintings by adults are in some cases accompanied by finger-tracings and simple figures that may be the work of children. Most footprints in caves appear to be those of children.

Cave art is by no means restricted to the painted figures of Lascaux or Altamira. Engraving was by far the most common means of creating images on cave walls. The artists were also highly skilled at working in three dimensions, incorporating natural rock shapes ingeniously into their compositions to give them volume, or carving bas-relief sculptures and clay statues.

As for bas-relief sculptures, these sculptures were limited to western and central France where the local limestone was easy to carve. Such work is always found in areas exposed to daylight, and many of the earliest sculptures were on large blocks rather than on walls. Most sculptures were also painted, but few traces of pigment survive.

In addition to cave sculptures, there are also cave engravings. Almost any sharp flint could be used for such work. Fine engravings are almost invisible when lit from the front, so cave artists must have positioned their light source to one side while they worked, to prevent the shadows of their hands from falling on the image.

The lighting of the caves was most commonly achieved by the use of flaming torches and simple lamps made from flat stones holding burning lumps of animal fat. However, at Lascaux, in France, specially carved stone bowl lamps were utilized.

Europe

By 24,000 B.C.T. European hunter-gatherers had become adept at building permanent dwellings. One of the huts at Dolni Vestonice in Moravia had a low outer wall of clay and limestone, and a few shallow postholes that would have supported a basic timber superstructure with a skin and brushwood roof. In the center of the hut was a hearth modeled from clay and stone.

The use of sewing needles made of bone and antlers began in Spain and France.

The sewing needle was in use in southwestern France and tailored clothing was known from what is now Russia.

The fish hook and fishing line were developed.

In Europe, humans made huts as long-term dwellings. One example from Moravia probably consisted of a low outer wall of clay and limestone with a timber superstructure and a roof of animal skins and brushwood.

Pits dug at sites in the East European Plain around 24,000 B.C.T. constituted the first unequivocal evidence of food storage over winter. The same pits were apparently used during summer for storage of such non-food items as fuel and raw materials for manufacture of tools and jewelry.

Australia
The earliest known cremation occurred.

In many parts of the world, human communities were producing sculpted forms and engraved objects in bone, stone, and ivory, and clay figurines. The few examples that survive only hint at a wealth of artistic and symbolic expression that may well have taken many other forms, including decoration on perishable materials such as wood, animal hides, and the human body.

Oral traditions such as myth and storytelling may also have existed. Burial was common to many groups during this period, although the beliefs held about death are unknown. The earliest cremation, near ancient Lake Mungo in southeastern Australia, dates to around 24,000 B.C.T. Together with sophisticated rock painting and engraving, this cremation testifies to the complexity of Aboriginal ceremonial life.

Cremation was not the only funerary rite practiced by the Aboriginal community, as indicated by the discovery of a burial of a male adult, sprinkled with red ocher.

23,000 B.C.T.

Africa
The progenitors of modern Europeans emerged from Africa.

In April 2001, it was reported that modern Europeans, and perhaps populations in other parts of the world, were descended from no more than a few hundred Africans who left Africa as recently as 25,000 years ago. The findings were reported at a conference of the Human Genome Organization, the international collaboration of scientists researching the genetic makeup of the human race. The findings are important because they provide the first estimate of how many people actually founded modern Europe and because the findings undermine the commonly held notion that modern humans evolved simultaneously in Africa, Europe and Asia from multiple early humans.

The genetic study involved comparing about 300 chromosomes from people in Sweden, central Europe and Nigeria. The differences in the genetic pattern between the European and African chromosomes revealed how long ago Europeans left Africa and about how many there must have been. The pattern showed that the

Europeans were descended from fewer ancestors than the Africans. The Nigerian chromosomes had been well shuffled around indicating that the Nigerians came from a wide and diversified gene pool with a long breeding history. On the other hand, the European chromosomes had long stretches of unshuffled genetic material, indicating fewer chromosome types entering the mix. In essence, the European people were the product of a relatively recent evolutionary bottleneck.

Europe

The world's earliest known clay figurines were made.

An ivory Venus figurine's skirt of intertwined fibers, from the cave of Lespugue, France, evidenced the beginnings of weaving.

The Venus figurines, small statues of faceless pregnant women with large breasts and buttocks, were made in Europe. These Venus figurines would continue to be manufactured for the next 2000 years. Venus figurines are among the oldest ceramic objects known to be made by humans. Other fired ceramic figures of animals or of unknown blobs, nearly all shattered, were also found in sites in the Pavlov Hills of Moravia (the Czech Republic). {**See also 28,000 B.C.T.**}

Sites in the Pavlov Hills of Moravia in the Czech Republic showed that round, oval, and oblong surface and semi-subterranean dwellings were constructed around 23,000 B.C.T.

22,500 B.C.T.

Europe

A Neanderthal-human child died in what is today known as Portugal's Lapedo Valley at a site known as Abrigo do Lagar Velho.

In June 1999, scientists announced the discovery of the skeleton of a child with anatomical characteristics of both Neanderthals and modern humans. While this evidence supported the theory that Neanderthals and humans were closely related, contrary evidence was reported in March 2000 when a genetic analysis of Neanderthal remains indicated that Neanderthals and modern humans were only distantly related.

The Neanderthal-human child skeleton was of a child about four years in age. The child, according to radiocarbon dating of charcoal and animal bones associated with the skeleton, died about 24,500 years ago. (Radiocarbon dating involves measuring the amount of naturally occurring radioactive carbon 14 remaining in materials that were once alive to determine how long ago they died and stopped absorbing the element.)

Some of the features of the Lagar Velho child, such as the size of teeth and the proportions of the pubic bone, look like those of a modern human. Other features, such as the proportions of the limbs and the shape of the lower jaw, are more like those of a Neanderthal.

These observations contributed to an ongoing debate about the relationship between Neanderthals and modern humans. Some anthropologists believe that modern humans completely replaced the Neanderthals, who lived in Europe and western Asia from about 200,000 to about 30,000 years ago. Researchers supporting this theory claim that Neanderthals contributed few if any genes to modern human populations.

Other anthropologists argue that modern humans and Neanderthals interbred. The existence of the Lagar Velho child would seem to support this theory, especially in light of the fact that Portugal is a logical place to find such a mixture because the Iberian Peninsula was home to many of the last Neanderthal populations.

While the existence of the Lagar Velho child clearly demonstrated the "possibility" of the interbreeding of humans and Neanderthals, the March 2000 genetic study seems to indicate that such pairings were rare and not the norm.

In March 2000, a team of scientists from Russia, Scotland, and Sweden announced that they had determined the molecular sequence of DNA (deoxyribonucleic acid, the molecule that genes are made of) obtained from an adult Neanderthal skeleton discovered in 1999 in Mezmaiskaya Cave in the Northern Caucasus region of Russia. According to radiocarbon dating, the Mezsmaiskaya Neanderthal died about 29,000 years ago, making it one of the last surviving Neanderthals in Europe.

The Mezmaiskaya Neanderthal DNA analysis was the second of such studies. In 1997, German scientists reported that they had successfully extracted DNA from a Neanderthal skeleton from Feldhofer Cave in Germany. The researchers found that the Neanderthal DNA was significantly different from that of modern humans, leading them to conclude that Neanderthals were not the ancestors of modern humans.

The scientists studying the Mezmaiskaya DNA compared it to both the Feldhofer DNA and to the DNA of modern humans. The researchers found that the Mezmaiskaya DNA is very similar to the Feldhofer DNA and very different from that of modern humans. The 2000 study was especially important to anthropologists because it confirmed the 1997 study, adding credibility to the argument that Neanderthals were only distantly related to modern humans.

21,000 B.C.T.

Europe

The boomerang was developed in Europe.

Among the thousands of carved art objects that date to the height of the last Ice Age in Europe, one of the most remarkable is a curved piece of mammoth tusk from a cave at Oblazowa in Poland. It is about 21,000 years old and thought to be the oldest boomerang in the world. Its flattened ends and span of 27 inches would have made it a formidable hunting weapon, which could be thrown with accuracy from a distance of 650 feet—a distance far greater than that of any spear. Together with the carved antler spear-throwers found in southwestern France at sites such as Mas d'Azil and Bruniquel, and other finds of portable art in Europe, they testify to the ingenuity and sophistication of the Ice Age hunter-gatherer communities.

20,000 B.C.T.

Asia

People inhabiting caves in what are now Israel and Jordan used notches in bones to record sequences of numbers. The devices are thought to function primarily as lunar calendars.

Europe

The bow and arrow were developed and used in Spain and North Africa.

The bow and arrow were invented around 20,000 B.C.T., according to evidence from sites at Parpallo (Spain) and the Sahara. Stone points from Parpallo appear to be tips of arrows. Drawings were found at the North African site. Other evidence, however, suggests a later origin perhaps as late as 8000 B.C.T.

Primitive oil lamps were developed. These lamps were probably fueled by animal fat in hollowed-out stones, with wicks of plant fiber.

The first cave paintings in Europe were created.

In France and Spain, paintings were made on cave walls. Images include horses, bison, cattle, and non-representational designs such as dots and lines, along with stenciled silhouettes of hands. Along with the paintings, the pre-historic people of France and Spain also decorated their caves with realistic and abstract engravings and lifelike bas-relief animal sculptures.

The earliest animal engravings were made in the Altamira Cave in northwestern Spain, although the famous red-and-black paintings in the cave were from a later date. {See 12,000 B.C.T.}

Animal sculpture became much more common in central and eastern Europe as artists carved ivory statuettes of felines, horses and bison.

19,000 B.C.T.

Europe

In western Europe between 19,000 B.C.T. and 16,000 B.C.T., the Solutrean tool tradition was developed. Named after Solutre in eastern France, this technique involved the knapping of tiny flakes off a flint core, which was sometimes heated to make the final flaking more precise. Tools made in this way included elegant laurel-leaf points, carefully worked on both faces.

The Solutrean toolmaking industry in France and Spain began around 19,000 B.C.T. The Solutrean toolmaking industry was characterized by large symmetrical flint tools known as laurel-leaf points. The exact purpose of these points is unknown, as they are too thin and well-made to be used for normal tasks; some archaeologists have suggested that they were made for their aesthetic value. A Solutrean technological innovation was treating the flint with heat, giving Solutrean laurel-leaf blades a sheen like porcelain and also making the stone easier to work. {See also 16,000 B.C.T.}

18,000 B.C.T.

The Epipaleolithic era began.

The coldest point was reached in the last Ice Age.

At the coldest phase of the last Ice Age, the North American mainland was connected to the Siberian land mass by the Bering land bridge. Groups of hunters from Siberia settled the land bridge itself, and arrived on the North American mainland around 13,000 B.C.T. These were tundra hunters who relied on larger animals such as mammoths, bison, caribou, and camels for their survival.

Africa

Eland's Bay Cave on the southwestern coast of South Africa was re-occupied.

Eland's Bay Cave, on the southwestern coast of South Africa, had been abandoned for thousands of years before it was reoccupied by groups of hunter-gatherers some 20,000 years ago. Although the cave was probably used for only a few weeks or months each year, occupation debris accumulated to a depth of 10 feet.

At Ishango, on the shores of Lake Edward in Zaire, a mound of accumulated debris dating to around 20,000 years ago contains evidence of a long sequence of settlement by hunter-gatherer groups. Together with fish and animal remains, the debris includes crude quartz microliths (tiny blades), and an abundance of bone implements, notably harpoon heads. The earlier harpoons were barbed on both sides, later ones were barbed on one side only.

People began to make smaller and smaller stone blades, called micro-blades in Central Africa and Eurasia. It is believed that the micro-blades and equally small micro-points were combined with each other by hafting several to the same piece of wood or bone to form more complex tools, such as saws.

Asia

The Kebaran tool tradition began.

In Southwest Asia, two important tool traditions were the Baradostian (circa 32,000–18,000 B.C.T. and named after the caves in the Baradost Mountains in southern Kurdistan) and the Kebaran (circa 18,000 B.C.T.–12,500 B.C.T. and named after the Kebara Cave in Palestine). The Kebaran tool industry included flint microliths, which were probably used in implements such as reaping knives, and a variety of grinding stones, since the hunter-gatherer groups who developed the Kebaran tradition also gathered wild grains and other seeds as part of their diet. These people were the predecessors of Natufian communities (named after the site of Wadi en-Natuf in Palestine) who, by the end of this period, are known to have been harvesting wild grains intensively in the Levant—the coastal strip of Syria, Lebanon and Palestine.

The Yafteh Cave in the Zagros Mountains region of Southwest Asia was occupied.

At the Yafteh Cave there is evidence of a heavy dependence on wild sheep and goats.

A pebble was carved in Aq Kupruk, Afghanistan.

Rock art in central Arabia and at Bhimbetka, India, was probably first produced during the coldest phase of the last Ice Age. Rare finds of "portable" art include an engraved pebble from Urkan e-Rub, Israel, an engraved ostrich eggshell from Patne in central India, and a carved limestone pebble from Aq Kupruk, Afghanistan, showing a human head. The pebble from Aq Kupruk dates from around 20,000 years ago and is 2¼ inches tall, has circles for eyes, a concave nose, an ear, and a strangely shaped mouth. Such pieces are evidence of artistic activity throughout the region during this period.

Europe

For many hunter-gatherer communities in Europe at this time, reindeer were an important resource. Their very presence in southern Europe indicates how the Ice Age conditions forced northern species to migrate southward. Reindeer were hunted not only for meat, but also for their hides, sinews, bones, and antlers, which were important raw materials used for making tools, clothing, and portable art objects.

In areas of central and eastern Europe where wood was scarce, hunter-gatherer groups used mammoth bones and tusks to construct huts. Those at Mezhirich in the Ukraine, the remains of which are between 18,000 and 12,000 years old, were 13 to 26 feet in diameter, and were probably covered in animal hides.

By 20,000 years ago, hunter-gatherer communities in western Europe were producing a wide range of portable art objects, from simple engravings on stone slabs or plaques, to carved ivory sculptures such as an ivory reindeer from Bruniquel in southwestern France. The reindeer was one of the most common subjects depicted in portable art.

Genetic evidence suggests that the domesticated cat diverged from the wild cats of Europe around 18,000 B.C.T.

Australia

The Kutikina cave was first occupied.

The world's southernmost Ice Age

dwelling site is a huge cave at Kutikina in southwestern Tasmania, which extends more than 550 feet back into the limestone cliff. The cave is situated near the banks of the lower reaches of the Franklin River, in a remote and heavily forested part of the island. It has extraordinarily rich remains sealed beneath a stalagmite layer. The cave was occupied by 20 to 30 people for a few weeks each year between 20,000 and 15,000 years ago. These people were highly specialized hunters whose principal prey was the wallaby. Hearths were built on the cave floor, and openings in the roof of the cave provided patches of light. Below each of these openings was a mass of debris left from the manufacture of stone tools, such as scrapers, choppers, and blades.

17,000 B.C.T.

Asia

Wild grain gathering was practiced in Southwest Asia.

The earliest evidence for the harvesting of wild grains comes from Ohalo, a large winter base camp on the shore of Lake Galilee in Palestine. Wild barley and wheat grains dating to around 17,000 B.C.T. were found there. The camp inhabitants also relied heavily on fish, fruit, and other plant foods.

The winter base camp at Ohalo on the shores of Lake Galilee covered roughly 1,800 square yards. The remains of a hut, two other structures, a cooking area, a circle of stones, and hearths have been found there. The hut, built of wood, was 15 feet wide and was occupied during at least three distinct periods.

16,550 B.C.T.

Australia

In Australia, bone tools were used for working animal hides and plant fibers.

Among the tools found at Cave Bay Cave, on an island off the coast of Tasmania, was a small, sharp bone point 3½ inches long that is around 18,550 years old. It was made from the shin bone of a wallaby and was probably used as an awl for making fur clothing or as a needle for making nets and baskets.

16,000 B.C.T.

Africa

Bone harpoons were left at the Ishango site in Zaire, dated as being from around 16,000 B.C.T. are the earliest known examples of harpoons.

Asia

Grinding stones found in Southwest Asia were probably used around 16,000 B.C.T. for processing the seeds of wild grasses, prelude to plant domestication.

Europe

People in the Perigord region of France around 16,000 B.C.T. made pendants that have what appear to be allegorical scenes carved into them, such as a bison's head surrounded by a schematic representation of six or more people (found at Raymonden-Chancelade).

Australia

The rock paintings of Australia reflected a changing Australian coastline.

Evidence for the changing coastline of Australia is provided by rock paintings located near what is now the Australian continent's northern coast. The paintings, some of which are over 18,000 years old, are the earliest examples of their kind in Australia. The fact that they depict only land animals such as the now extinct long-beaked echidna suggests that the coastline was much farther north than it is today.

The Americas

It is theorized that the Solutreans—a people from the Iberian peninsula—traveled to and settled in North America.

In 1999, a radical new view of prehistory was forwarded. Two prominent archaeologists posited that North America's first inhabitants may have crossed the Atlantic Ocean some 18,000 years ago from Europe's Iberian Peninsula.

Standard theory on the populating of the Western Hemisphere holds that the hemisphere's first settlers came across a land bridge from Asia. According to this theory, some Asiatic nomads made their way into Alaska and found an ice-free way into the continent some time around 13,500 years ago. As the theory develops, these Asiatic people found their way to New Mexico and established the Clovis culture. This Clovis culture was distinctive in that it produced projectile point weapons.

However, two of the problems with the Asia to Alaska land bridge theory is that the presence of human beings have been documented in places throughout the Western Hemisphere at a time that far precedes the time of the land bridge. Researchers who believe that the Clovis and Bering Sea land bridge theory is outdated point to sites at Monte Verde, Chile, as well as Pennsylvania, Virginia, and South Carolina as being settled from 16,000 B.C.T. to 12,500 B.C.T. Additionally, recent years have revealed that there have been a number of skeletons found in pre-historic America which do not fit the Asiatic pattern.

The new theory that was forwarded in 1999 may provide some explanation for the discrepancies with the Asia-Alaska land bridge theory. According to the new theory, the hemispheres first inhabitants crossed the Atlantic more than 18,000 years ago from Europe's Iberian Peninsula—the area that is now Spain, Portugal and southwestern France.

Belonging to a group known as the Solutreans, these pre-modern explorers are believed to have originally settled the Eastern seaboard, according to the researchers. Over the next six thousand years, the Solutreans' hunter-gatherer culture may have spread as far as the American deserts and the Canadian tundra, and even perhaps as far south as southern South America.

The theory was forwarded by Dennis Stanford and Bruce Bradley. Stanford and Bradley concede that the Solutreans may not have been the only paleo-explorers to reach the Western Hemisphere. However, judging by the Solutreans' distinctive style of projectile points and other clues in the archaelogical record, Stanford and Bradley came to the conclusion that the Solutreans may have been the first settlers who brought to North America what, until 1999, had been considered the Clovis culture.

In examining the blades fashioned by the Solutreans and the Clovis people, Stanford and Bradley found them to be virtually indistinguishable. However, the Stanford and Bradley theory presently rests solely on these comparisons. No unequivocal Solutrean settlement remains have been found.

Nevertheless, it is noteworthy that only two places in the world at only two times in history have a people produced the unique projectile points found at Clovis and in Spain. Only the older Solutrean projectile points from Europe and the more recent Clovis points from the Americas closely resemble each other.

How seafaring Solutreans could have arrived in North America is, at present, unknown. However, it is conceivable that the Solutreans reached American shores in the same manner that modern Arctic Circle peoples have managed to navigate the frigid waters of the North. Utilizing skin boats, Solutreans may have reached American shores some four thousand years before their Asiatic brothers did so.

15,000 B.C.T.

Europe

In Europe, pierced staffs began to feature finely engraved animal decorations.

Throwing sticks made of reindeer horn were frequently decorated with animal carvings or reliefs.

A tool made of antler (usually from reindeer), known today as the baton de commandement, a part of the main body and two major branches of the antler with a hole bored near their junction, became common around 15,000 B.C.T. It is not clear today what the baton was used for, although shaft straighteners for spears and softeners for leather thongs are among the uses that have been suggested. Often designs or illustrations are carved into the baton. The name "baton de commandement" comes from the idea that the tool may have been a symbol of authority.

Artists in the Lascaux Cave in southern France painted lifelike animals on cave walls, using earth pigments such as ocher. Paint is applied with bundled grasses, reeds, or hands, or blown through hollow bones.

The Magdalenian culture, which ranged from northeastern Spain deep into central Europe, produced, in addition to the famous cave paintings of its southern portion, such as at Lascaux, France, many engravings on bone, antler, and slate, including animal figures and abstracted female human figures.

The Magdalenian tool industry in Europe over the next 3500 years produced fine harpoons with both single and double rows of barbs, needles, awls, spear throwers, and points, all made from bone or antler, as well as microliths and unretouched flake points.

Two bison were modeled in clay in the cave of the Le Tuc d'Audoubert, France.

The first known artifact with a map on it is made on bone at what is now Mezhirich, Russia. The map appears to show the region immediately around the site at which it was found.

According to evidence at Lascaux, France, rope began to be used.

13,600 B.C.T.

A Great Flood inundated much of the world following a sudden 130 foot rise in sea levels as a result of runoff from a rapid melting of a glacial ice sheet covering much of the northern continent of the Western Hemisphere.

13,000 B.C.T.

The ice sheets began to recede.

As the ice sheets began to recede from Eurasia and North America, the world was transformed radically. Global temperatures, which had been rising since the coldest point of the last Ice Age (c. 18,000 B.C.T.) had almost reached their present level by 8000 B.C.T. As the ice sheets melted, trapped water was released, causing sea levels to rise by around 325 feet. This inundated what had previously been dry lowland areas such as the Bering land bridge, the Gulf of Siam, the North Sea, and the Sahul Shelf—the land between Australia and New Guinea. More water was available to fall as rain, so the extensive deserts that had formed in parts of the tropics began to shrink.

Although gradual, these climatic

changes offered new opportunities to the human populations whose survival strategies became so highly developed under the harsh conditions of the Ice Age. As the climate improved, plants and animals colonized larger areas of the world, including previously uninhabitable parts of Africa, Europe, and North America. The abundant resources in these territories more than compensated for the lands lost beneath the rising seas. Indeed, the availability of new food supplies catalyzed a steady growth in human populations, which has continued almost unbroken to the present day.

During these more benign climatic conditions, the Americas were fully colonized as groups of hunter-gatherers penetrated south of the retreating ice sheets and began to establish themselves throughout North America. By 11,000 B.C.T., humans were present in South America, as shown by the well-established settlement at Monte Verde in central Chile, where remains of hearths and shelters have been found. By at least 9000 B.C.T., they had reached Patagonia, at the continent's southern tip.

By 13,000 B.C.T., the worst of the Ice Age was over, and communities throughout the inhabited world began to consolidate their gains. The total human population was still sparse, but well adapted to a variety of environments. The skills and adaptability built up in climatic adversity would soon prevail in the more favorable conditions following the retreat of the northern ice sheets. As the milder climate precipitated an expansion of new vegetation on fertile soils, the grain-gatherers of Southwest Asia pioneered the next major development in the human story.

Africa

Around 13,000 B.C.T., rising sea levels began to submerge coastal areas of Africa. When the sea was still 7 miles away, the cave dwellers at Nelson Bay and Eland's Bay in South Africa mainly exploited the large game animals, such as the Cape buffalo, which grazed the open grasslands nearby. As the sea encroached and the grasslands were submerged, buffalo became extremely rare and marine foods became the cave dwellers' dietary staples.

In the southern continents of Africa and Australasia, the wetter climate at the end of the last Ice Age turned some desert areas to grassland, making them more attractive to hunter-gatherers. In resource rich areas of Africa such as the Nile Valley, groups began burying their dead in cemeteries, sometimes consisting of many dozens of graves. In both Africa and Australia, the tradition of rock art established in previous centuries continued to flourish. Rock art provides insights into everyday activities in South Asia during this period; the scenes that depict hunting and fishing in the rock shelters at Bhimbetka in central India are particularly vivid.

Evidence for the beginnings of portable art in Africa is supported by finds in the north of simple terra-cotta figurines such as a small hand-modeled head of a horned animal from Afalou Bou Rhummel in eastern Algeria.

Shelters were erected at a site near Midrand, South Africa.

In January 2000, it was announced that a shelter from about 10,000 to 15,000 years ago was discovered near Midrand, South Africa. The early people of South Africa, who had lived there for hundreds of thousands of years, commonly used rock shelters or caves for dwellings. The people hunted animals and collected plants, and they did not stay in any one place for very long.

Archaeologists found a site with boulders about the size of watermelons arranged in a semi-circle. The rocks had apparently been carried from a field of boulders located about 90 meters (100 yards) away. Around the arrangement of stones, stone knives and adzes (axlike tools for shaping wooden structures) were found.

It is theorized that the people had wedged tree limbs into the earth and held them in place with the boulders. The limbs were then lashed together to create a roof.

Remains of several such dwellings have been found in other parts of the world, and some of them date as far back as 350,000 years ago, but the January 1999 discovery was the first to be discovered in sub-Saharan Africa where the temperate climate would tend not to have compelled people to build shelters. It is speculated that the dwelling in South Africa may have been the "home base" of an organized group of hunter-gatherers.

Asia

The Natufian culture flourished.

The people of the Natufian culture, named after the site of Wadi en-Natuf in Israel, began living in villages in the Levant (the coastal strip of Syria, Lebanon, and Israel) around 13,000 B.C.T. They began to manufacture a wide variety of tools made from bone. These included awls and needles for working animal hides, fish hooks, spatulae, and reaping knives with grooves into which small flint cutting blades were set. Some of these implements were decorated with incised geometric patterns. The handles of reaping knives were occasionally carved into the form of animal heads, such as deer heads.

Around 13,000 B.C.T., the hunter-gatherer communities of the Levant (the coastal strip of Syria, Lebanon, and Palestine) produced few decorative objects that have survived. Only one portable object, an engraved limestone pebble with "ladder" motifs and parallel lines carved into it, has been found. It comes from Urkan e-Rub in Palestine. These hunter-gatherer communities buried their dead as burials found beneath the floors of cave dwellings and artificial shelters indicate.

Europe

The spear thrower (sometimes called the atlatl, its Aztec name) and the harpoon were developed.

Simple machines are devices that do nothing but change the direction, duration, or size of a force; duration or size is changed as a result of an inverse relationship between amount and distance traveled. The single pulley is the dullest simple machine, changing only the direction of a force. Most of the other simple machines are variations on the lever or the inclined plane. For example, the wheel and axle (or crank handle) is a rotary lever, while the screw is a helical inclined plane. Perhaps the most sophisticated simple machine is the compound pulley, in which mechanical advantage is cleverly applied. The pulley appears to have been invented in Hellenistic times, about 200 B.C.T.

Which simple machines were used by early humans? Almost any large creature climbing a hill uses a form of inclined plane to avoid the force required in going straight up, so that hardly counts. It is also easy to believe, although difficult to prove, that early humans used levers to turn or lift heavy objects. Similarly, wedges undoubtedly go back to early times, but we have better evidence for these, since many early wedges were made from rock (early levers would have been made of biodegradable wood). The earliest stone tool is a form of wedge, as are most stone tools. The handle of an axe or hammer is a form of lever, so hafted axe heads (in use by the middle of the Old Stone Age) qualify as simple machines. Other early evidence of thoughtful use of simple machines before Neolithic times is hard to come by.

An important application of the lever from about 13,000 B.C.T. is the spear thrower, or *atlatl*, an extension of the human arm used to translate a small motion near the shoulder into a large motion near the end of the spear thrower. Since the time of the motion does not change while the length of the motion increases, the result is a higher velocity for the spear thrown with such a device. The higher velocity gives the spear greater momentum, useful either for distance or for penetrating power.

Huts built from mammoth bones and a map drawn on bone appeared in Mezhirich in eastern Europe (the Ukraine). The map appears to show the region immediately around the site where it was found.

At Mezhirich, storage pits near mammoth bone dwellings were distributed unequally, suggesting that some family units had more resources than others. This was the first known evidence of a social hierarchy.

Also at Mezhirich, the huts made from the mammoth bones used specific bones for particular parts of the dwellings. Hundreds of bones were used to make the frame and the weight of the bones alone was estimated at 22 tons. In 1992, workers found that a hut had been constructed with an underground entrance about 3000 to 5000 years prior to any other known underground entrances.

At Mezhirich, marine shells from the Black Sea, some 580 kilometers (360 miles) to the south, demonstrate that the people who lived there were part of an extensive trade network.

At Mezhirich in Ukraine, as at other sites of the same region around 13,000 B.C.T., pits were dug into permafrost to store food, offering up the first known form of cold storage.

Humans began making their own fires. Previously they had relied on "found" fires,

which they carefully carried and maintained. {See also 500,000 B.C.T.}

Figurines from around 13,000 B.C.T. were sometimes made wearing such clothing as skirts, aprons, headdresses, or parkas.

Australia

The first Australian hand stencils were created in the Wargata Mina Cave.

Stencils of hands are quite common and sometimes dominate certain areas of a cave. They were produced by placing the hand flat on the wall and spraying or spitting pigment at it. In some caves, particularly at Gargas in France, the hands are incomplete, with various combinations of fingers or finger segments missing. It is unclear whether the joints had actually been lost through frostbite or some other condition, or whether the fingers were bent in some kind of signaling system.

Some of the silhouettes of hands on the walls of the Wargata Mina Cave in southwestern Tasmania are 15,000 years old. There are 16 stencils of the left and right hands of five people, made by blowing a spray of powdered pigment mixed with water over the hands. Located in the pitch-black interior of the cave, the stencils might have been associated with initiation rituals or visits by initiates and elders.

The Americas

The first tundra hunters arrived in North America.

The first tundra hunters to arrive in mainland North America around 13,000 B.C.T. sheltered from the harsh arctic climate in caves. Stone and bone artifacts, similar to those found in Siberia, along with the remains of Ice Age animals dating to this time, together testify to the occupation by tundra hunter groups of the Bluefish Caves in the western Yukon territory of Canada.

The stone tools found in the Bluefish Caves in western Yukon included microliths (tiny stone blades), a wedge-shaped core, and other tools. These tools would have been used for hunting, and for the processing of animal carcasses and hides.

The first tundra hunters, isolated from their Siberian homeland by the Bering Sea, ventured south in search of new hunting grounds. Traveling in small bands, they followed game over vast expanses of new territory. These scattered groups developed a common stoneworking technology. Although stone points from the Monte Verde site attest to earlier styles, the best known of the Paleoindian (earliest people in the Americas) weapon types was the large Clovis point, capable of piercing mammoth hide; the later Folsom points were used to kill bison. Both technologies are named after towns in New Mexico where the first examples were found. The wide distribution of tools indicates that band territories incorporated vast areas.

It is likely that tundra hunters migrated south into the plains of North America only when an ice-free corridor of land existed between the Cordilleran and Laurentide ice masses. Alternatively, when this corridor was blocked, it is possible that humans ventured south along the Pacific coast in boats. The earliest possible human habitation sites in the Americas are known as Pre-Clovis sites, but these are not accepted by all archaeologists. The first sites that archaeologists agree were definitely inhabited by humans are those that have yielded finds of Clovis stone tool technology—for example, Murray Springs and Blackwater Draw.

Throughout the Americas, finds of butchering tools dating to this period are widespread, confirming that meat was an important dietary staple.

At a site in Virginia called Cactus Hill, stone tools were utilized.

In 1999 and 2000, several reports expanded the ongoing debate over when and how people first came to the Americas. A growing body of evidence that challenges a long-accepted theory continued to gain wide acceptance from archaeologists and anthropologists.

The traditional theory traces the peopling of the Americas to a single cultural group known as the Clovis culture. The name comes from a site near Clovis, New Mexico, where researchers in the 1930's first found distinct tools and other archaeological evidence of these big-game hunters, who lived in North America about 11,200 years ago. According to the standard explanation, the Clovis people originally migrated to the Americas by crossing a land bridge between present day Siberia and Alaska that was exposed during the last Ice Age, when sea levels were lower than they are today. About 12,000 years ago, they began migrating down North America through an ice-free corridor in present-day Canada and then spread throughout the Americas.

Evidence challenging this theory did not gain much recognition until the 1990's. By 1997, however, most archaeologists had accepted evidence showing that Monte Verde, a site in southern Chile, is about 12,500 years old. The research at Monte Verde and other pre-Clovis sites has led to new theories for the peopling of the Americas.

In December 1999, researchers reported the discovery of pre-Clovis tools at the Topper Site, an excavation near Allendale, South Carolina. The artifacts were found below an earlier excavation in which many Clovis tools were found.

The primitive tools were found in sandy soils, with no surviving organic materials that were suitable for radiocarbon dating. (Radiocarbon dating involves measuring the amount of naturally occurring radioactive carbon 14 remaining in materials that were once alive to determine how long ago they died and stopped absorbing the element.) Alternative dating tests were not completed at the time that this text was written, but it was estimated that the tools were 12,000 to 20,000 years old, based on their location at a depth considerably below that of the Clovis artifacts.

A similar age was announced in April 2000 for artifacts discovered at a site in Virginia known as Cactus Hill. There it was reported that stone tools found at the site were at least 15,000 years old, according to radiocarbon tests of organic material found near the tools. The Cactus Hill site revealed two layers of artifacts, indicating two distinct periods of occupation. The upper layer contained Clovis tools, while the lower level contained more primitive bladelike tools for butchering animals and scrapping hides.

In October 1999, reports from Brazil announced that the skull and partial skeleton of a woman found in a central Brazilian rock shelter in 1975 was about 11,500 years old. The date was based on radiocarbon tests of organic material found at the site.

The Brazilian skeleton, referred to as Luzia, became important for two reasons. First, Luzia is from the same time period as the North American Clovis sites, but the Luzia site is located significantly farther south. Secondly, it appears that the features of the skull resembled those of people native to Southeast Asia and Australia, rather than the features of modern Indigenous Americans or people native to Siberia. These conclusions suggest that migrations, possibly by water, predated the migration of the Clovis people.

Other researchers working in South America reported on skulls older than the Clovis culture that have features similar to those of Luzia. In the near future it is anticipated that genetic testing will be done on these remains to provide a clearer picture of the peopling of the Americas.

12,000 B.C.T.

Asia

The dog was domesticated from the Asian wolf and used for tracking game.

The dog was domesticated in Mesopotamia (Iraqi Kurdistan) and in the Levant in the first example of animal domestication. The earliest known remains of domestic dogs are from the Zarzian site at Palegawra, Iraq.

Europe

The famous polychrome red and black paintings of standing and lying bison were made on the ceiling of the Altamira Cave in northwestern Spain. {See also 20,000 B.C.T.}

Crosshatching and shaded applications of color began to enhance the modeling of cave engravings.

The Americas

The earliest evidence for constructed dwellings in the Americas is from the site of Monte Verde in Chile, which dates to the 12th millennium B.C.T. The remains of 10 huts were found. They were originally joined together in two parallel rows. Each dwelling consisted of a square wooden frame covered with animal skins. Small clay-lined pits located inside the dwellings were used for cooking or heating. The large hearths outside the huts suggest a high degree of group cooperation.

11,000 B.C.T.

Africa

Microliths appeared in the eastern Rift Valley.

For tens of thousands of years, African hunters relied on stone-tipped spears. The tips were microliths (tiny blades), often of obsidian (black volcanic glass), which were mounted on wooden shafts. Such blades were in use in central and western Africa 35,000 years ago, but appeared in the eastern Rift Valley only 13,000 years ago.

Edible plant foods became increasingly important in tropical Africa in the period leading up to the end of the Ice Age. The bauhinia tree was favored by hunter-gatherers for its fruit and roots, especially during the summer. It is still a staple today for the San people of southern Africa and many other hunter-gatherer groups.

In the Nile and Niger river valleys, African hunter-gatherers spent much of the year in permanent base camps, living on fish, wild grains, and tubers.

The quantity of fish in the Nile River is greatest in the autumn, when the annual floods recede. The fishing communities that settled on the river banks at this time lived in temporary huts made of grass and matting. These were abandoned when rising waters forced the people to higher ground.

The Saharan highlands were home to highly mobile hunter-gatherers, whose staple diet included gazelles.

The forest regions of western and central Africa supported foraging groups who relied on plants and small tree-living game, including monkeys.

Nomadic hunter-gatherers lived in the savanna and semiarid lands of eastern and southern Africa, including the modern Kalahari Desert, hunting and foraging for seasonal plants.

Asia

The world's first known domesticated dogs appeared in Southwest Asia.

Dogs were the first animals to be domesticated. Their wild ancestors were probably wolves rather than jackals. The earliest evidence for domesticated dogs in the world comes from Israel and dates to around 11,000 B.C.T., but it is possible that wolves were tamed and trained at an earlier date to help in hunting.

The tradition of rock painting flourished in Bhimbetka, India.

The tradition of rock painting in the shelters at Bhimbetka in central India began well before 11,000 B.C.T. and was still flourishing at this time. Some of the paintings are abstract outlines, others are colorfully filled in. They depict animals (such as deer, antelope, and bison), fishermen, hunters, expeditions to gather honey, scenes of family life, and dances.

The earliest known portable art object from China dates to around 13,000 years ago. Found at Longgu Cave, it is a red deer antler engraved with three distinct patterns: a wavy line, several inches long, with parallel grooves, and regularly spaced oblique strokes. The antler was originally coated with red ocher pigment and the precision of the engraving is fairly sophisticated.

Vast fields of wild grain appeared in parts of Southwestern Asia (the Middle East) as the glaciers began to retreat.

Europe

Greek sailors were able to import obsidian from the island of Melos to the mainland around 11,000 B.C.T.

As early as 11,000 B.C.T., the inhabitants of the Franchthi Cave in southern Greece were sailing over 80 miles in simple boats to gather obsidian from the Cycladic island of Melos in the Aegean Sea.

High-quality stone for tool-making was of vital importance to human communities throughout the world at this time. One of the best materials was obsidian (black volcanic glass), which produced a razor-sharp edge when flaked and one of the prime locations for such obsidian was Melos, Greece.

The Americas

By 11,000 B.C.T., Monte Verde, in Chile, had been inhabited for a long period of time.

Wild plant remains found at Monte Verde, in the Andean region of central Chile, include tubers and sugarcane. These were gathered from distant areas and brought back to the settlement for processing. Herbal remedies made from such plants are still used by indigenous Andeans today. This knowledge of the medicinal properties of plants could only have evolved over many years of experimentation and familiarity with their sources, which suggests a well-established human occupation of the area by 11,000 B.C.T.

Stone points chipped on both faces were produced at Monte Verde in Chile. They date to 11,000 B.C.T. This bifacial technology is also known from sites over 20,000 years old in northeastern Asia. This technological link is evidence of the probable connection between Asia and the first Americans.

10,900 B.C.T.

Europe

Bison were painted in the cave of El Castillo in Spain and at the Black Room of Niaux.

10,500 B.C.T.

Africa

During this period of time, in the Nile and Niger river valleys, African hunter-gatherers spent much of the year in permanent base camps, living on fish, wild grains, and tubers. The Saharan highlands were home to highly mobile hunter gatherers, whose

staple diet included gazelles. The forest regions of western and central Africa supported foraging groups who relied on plants and small tree-living game, including monkeys. Nomadic hunter-gatherers also lived in the savanna and semi-arid lands of eastern and southern Africa, including the modern Kalahari Desert, hunting and foraging for seasonal plants.

Asia

The world's first known pottery vessels appeared in Japan.

The earliest pottery vessels in the world were produced by hunter-gatherers in Japan over 12,000 years ago.

The earliest populations of Japan survived on seafood and the hunting of forest animals such as deer and wild pigs. Those living near the coast gathered shellfish. Favored locations along the east coast of Honshu, where fish and other marine resources proliferated in the warm Pacific currents during spring and early summer, were probably visited each year. Large middens (mounds of discarded fish bones and shell debris) built up at these seasonal campsites. Inland resources were important in the autumn. Hunters used stone arrowheads to kill their prey and stone scrapers for working the hides.

In Japan, caves were popular dwellings for hunter-gatherer groups, and some were occupied for many thousands of years. The earliest occupation of the Fukui Cave, near Nagasaki in southern Japan, began around 13,000 years ago and remains from this period include some of the earliest pottery in the world. The cave was probably used by groups exploiting the resources of the coastal lowlands nearby, but only for short periods at specific times of the year.

The Americas

Red ocher, a powder pigment derived from grinding iron ores such as hematite, was used by early North Americans in a variety of ways: to make red paint to protect the skin from insects and sunburn; in the processing of animal hides; and for ceremonial purposes. Its use is considered to be a cultural link between the earliest Americans and Eurasia (and indeed Australia), where similar evidence is commonly found.

Human habitations appeared even at the southernmost parts of the Western Hemisphere where cavemen pursued guanaco and hunted a horse species that would become extinct.

During the twentieth century, one of the attributes assigned to the indigenous peoples of the Americas was that they, more so than the Europeans, lived in harmony with nature. Perhaps such an attribute was true for the nineteenth century and twentieth century Indigenous Americans, but it was not always so. Indeed, not unlike their European counterparts of the nineteenth and twentieth centuries, the first Indigenous Americans—the Indigenous Americans of some thirteen thousand years ago—were immigrants to the Western Hemisphere who ultimately had a devastating impact on the environment of this land.

The first known people in the Americas—the ancestors of today's Indigenous Americans—are today associated with the Clovis culture. The Clovis culture is named for stone tools first discovered in 1952 at a site near Clovis, New Mexico, that dates from 11,000 B.C.T. to 9,500 B.C.T. Similar tools dating from about the same time have since been found across North America.

The Clovis people are widely believed to have been the original discoverers of America, although some archaeologists place the date for the earliest human migration into the Americas as early as 35,000 years ago. The Clovis people migrated from Siberia into Alaska across the land bridge that then existed across the Bering Strait. By about 10,500 years ago the Clovis descendants reached the southern tip of South America.

The arrival of the Clovis people coincided with a remarkable wave of species extinctions. Just before the Clovis people arrived, the American wilderness was abundant with big mammals: mammoths, mastodons, giant ground sloths, giant beavers, saber-toothed cats, camels, horses. By about 9000 B.C.T., shortly after the Clovis people's arrival, all these species became extinct. Within the span of a few centuries, North America lost 73 percent of its genera of large mammals, South America about 80 percent.

While a number of theories were posited for the disappearance of so many species, the most likely culprit was the appearance of the Clovis people. It is now generally recognized that the most likely cause of the mass extinctions was the hunting practices of the Clovis people. Never having seen humans, the animals of the Western Hemisphere would not have feared them, and the humans, having no reason to hold back, allowed the slaughter to begin.

Sadly, the arrival of the first Americans may well have been marked by an environmental disaster as great as any other in human history. Perhaps, the forefathers of the Indigenous Americans only came to appreciate nature after they had destroyed it.

10,000 B.C.T.

The Holocene epoch began. This epoch would see the appearance of agricultural urban centers based on the cultivation of grasses (wheat, rice, etc.).

The rise of agriculture, according to most scientists, began in Southwest Asia about 10,000 years ago, or around 8,000 B.C.T. The first farmers lived in a region called the Fertile Crescent, which covers what is now Lebanon and parts of Iran, Iraq, Israel, Jordan, Syria and Turkey. At first, these people probably did not depend entirely on the crops they raised. But as they improved their methods, farming became their most important source of food. The earliest plants grown in the Middle East were probably barley and wheat. Early farmers in Southwest Asia eventually raised cattle, goats, and sheep.

The first farmers originated in areas where there were enough wild plants and animals to provide food for large populations. As a result, people often settled in permanent villages for years at a time. At the end of the Ice Age, the climate became warmer and affected the food supply. New plants, such as grains, replaced older plants. Scientists believe that Upper Paleolithic people could live in permanent settlements because they discovered how to control these new plants and increase the amount of food in their area. They learned that they could plant seeds from the plants they ate. They also learned that they could domesticate animals, perhaps by capturing young ones from the wild and raising them. In time, people began to depend on these planted crops and domestic animals for a steady supply of food.

People were herding cattle and growing grain in northern Africa by 6000 B.C.T. By about 5000 to 4000 B.C.T., agriculture had developed independently in Asia. In the Yangtze Valley of China, and perhaps in what is now Thailand, farmers grew rice and millet. By the same time, people had begun to farm in the Indus River Valley of what is now Pakistan.

Between about 4500 B.C.T. and 4000 B.C.T., farming peoples spread from southeastern Europe into the dense forests of central and western Europe. These people brought wheat and cattle with them.

Foraging people in Scandinavia learned how to farm from these newcomers.

Agriculture began to develop in southern Africa by about 3000 B.C.T. By 1500 B.C.T., people had begun to cultivate corn and beans in what is now Mexico. By 1000 B.C.T., peoples in what became the eastern United States were raising gourds and sunflowers. Farming began later in other parts of North America.

Prehistoric farmers, called *Neolithic* people, had a way of life that differed from that of Upper Paleolithic people. In some ways, farming made life easier. It provided a steady supply of food and enabled people to live in one place for a long time. But farmers had to work more than hunters and gatherers.

Prehistoric farmers set up villages near their fields and lived there as long as their crops grew well. Most fields produced good crops for a few years. The land then became unproductive because the crops used up nutrients in the soil. The farmers did not know about fertilizers. They shifted their crops to new fields until none of the land near their village was fertile. Then they moved to a new area and built another village. In this way, farmers settled many new areas.

Prehistoric farmers built larger, longer-lasting settlements than the camps that Paleolithic people had built. In the Middle East, for example, early farmers constructed their houses of solid, sun-dried mud, sometimes on stone foundations. Dried mud was much more resistant to weather than the materials earlier people used, such as skins and bark. The early farmers also learned to build fences to confine and protect their livestock.

The world wide population of Homo sapiens *increased in number to roughly three million.*

By 10,000 B.C.T., across much of the inhabited world, in Europe, Asia, Africa, and the Americas, the art of building tents and huts from such materials as timber, animal bones, hides, and brushwood had become widespread. In some sites, notably in Australia, simple windbreaks made of branches were used as shelters.

Africa

From around 10,000 B.C.T., African hunting and foraging methods became increasingly sophisticated, as more lightweight and specialized weaponry was developed. Many groups of people settled near rivers and lakes, exploiting their rich resources of fish and mollusks, while sea mammals were of greater importance for coastal settlements. The ability to extract these resources from rivers, lakes, and the sea enabled many groups to remain in the same place for most the year. At this time, much of the Sahara was covered with semi-arid grassland and shallow lakes, which attracted small groups of hunters as they ranged over large hunting territories. Elsewhere, Africans became increasingly localized, living off the abundant resources that were available within limited areas.

Ostrich eggshell was an invaluable raw material for making beads. Small pieces of shell were carefully pierced through the center with a fine, stone-tipped drill. The perforated fragments were then strung on a suitable fiber or thong, and ground into uniform, round beads that were used to make necklaces and amulets. Sometimes the shell beads were used to adorn caps or skins, or were worn in the hair. Fragmentary remains of such decorated ostrich eggshell have been found in graves at a rock shelter in Taforalt, Algeria, and date to around 12,000 years ago.

Asia

Around 12,000 years ago, round, stone-walled, sunken huts became common in the Levant (the coastal strip of Syria, Lebanon, and Israel). The inhabitants gathered wild grains that could be stored easily, so they could settle in one place all year round.

At Abu Hureyra in the Levant, there is evidence of a heavy dependence on wild grains. Additionally, gazelles and onagers (wild asses) were hunted.

By 10,000 B.C.T., people living in the hilly regions of the Fertile Crescent were relying increasingly on gathering wild grains and other seeds for their food. For harvesting, they may have used composite tools such as sickles made with microliths (tiny stone blades) set into wooden or bone handles. To grind the seeds into flour, a new technology of grindstones, mortars, and pestles gradually developed.

By 10,000 B.C.T., in Southwest Asia, burials under the floors of huts and in cemeteries were common. Personal ornaments such as necklaces, bracelets, and anklets were often buried with the dead.

At Zawi Chemi Shanidar, an open air site in the Zagros Mountain region of Southwest Asia, there is evidence of plant processing and evidence of a heavy dependence on wild sheep and goats. There is also some possible evidence of the early management (domestication) of sheep.

As sea levels continued to rise toward the end of the last Ice Age (around 10,000 years ago), large areas of coastal lowland were inundated in Southeast Asia. The islands of Borneo, Java, and Sumatra emerged. As temperatures, rose, forest vegetation became denser, creating new opportunities for hunter-gather communities. Coasts and estuaries—around the Gulf of Tongkin in modern Vietnam, for example—were good food sources, and occupation sites of the period can be identified from shell middens (mounds of discarded debris). Other groups of hunter-gatherers occupied upland caves and rock shelters.

Mainland occupation sites are characterized by finds of flaked cobble tools, called Hoabinhian after the cave at Hoa Binh in Vietnam. Island sites are characterized by finds of blades or flaked tools made of chert (a crystalline form of silica) or obsidian (black volcanic glass).

Goats were domesticated by Southwest Asian hunter-gatherer tribespeople who had earlier domesticated the dog. The dog had been earlier domesticated in Mesopotamia (Iraq) and in Canaan (Palestine) {See 12,000 B.C.T.}

Starting about 10,000 years B.C.T., people made the major technological advance of domesticating animals and plants. This occurred independently in Southwest Asia, Southeast Asia, East Asia, and in the Americas. At one time, historians assumed that the agricultural revolution was simply a form of progress. This interpretation is now in dispute. Some historians now hypothesized that people knew how to raise crops and keep animals much earlier, but were reluctant to do so until either rising population or reduced natural food supplies forced them into agriculture. This is partly supported by a rise in population preceding the adoption of agriculture, as indicated in the archaeological record. Another supporting element is that modern hunter-gatherers know about agriculture, but think it is too much work.

Another belief that has largely been discarded is that urban life began as a result of the agricultural revolution. Towns were forming before farming became a way of life. The principal purpose of pre-agricultural settlements was trade. Towns arose at the juncture of trade routes or near supplies of goods that could be traded. Jericho, for example, was founded well before the surrounding practice of agriculture began.

There is little evidence of the physical sciences around the time of the agricultural revolution, except for that implied by developing technology, such as the introduction of sun-dried bricks and mortar. Major developments of the period following the agricultural revolution were largely in astronomy, mathematics, and technology.

The forests of Southeast Asia provided abundant food resources for small bands of hunter-gatherers, such as the group that occupied the Spirit Cave in Thailand around 10,000 B.C.T. The Spirit Cave dwellers collected fish and shellfish from a nearby stream, as well as almonds and butternuts from the surrounding forest. The sap of poisonous plants was applied to arrowheads for hunting gibbons, macaques, and squirrels.

Hunters living in Siberia, where wood was scarce, constructed tents made from a framework of large animal bones covered with skins. These simple structures enabled them to survive the harsh climate and are similar in construction to the earlier mammoth-bone huts of the Ukraine. This indicates an eastward diffusion of tent-building techniques.

The first known pottery was made by the preagricultural Jomons, the second wave of immigrants to settle in Japan. {See also 7000 B.C.T.}

Neolithic farmers made inventions and discoveries at an even faster rate than did the people of the Upper Paleolithic. Early farmers developed a number of useful tools. These implements included sickles to cut grain, millstones to grind flour, and polished stone axeheads.

Perhaps as early as 9000 B.C.T. in Japan, and somewhat later in South West Asia, people discovered how to make pottery. Before then, they used animal skins or bark containers to hold water. To boil water, early cooks had to drop hot stones into the water because they could not hang animal skins or bark over a fire. Pottery containers enabled people to hold and boil water easily. Farmers also used pottery to store grain and other food.

No one knows when people made the first objects out of metal. But metals became important only after metalworkers learned to make bronze, a substance hard and durable enough to make lasting tools. People of Southwest Asia made bronze as early as 3500 B.C.T. The Bronze Age began when bronze replaced stone as the chief toolmaking material. In some areas, such as Southwest Asia, the Bronze Age began about 3000 B.C.T.

The development of farming was an important step toward the rise of civilization. As farming methods improved and food became more plentiful, many people were freed from the jobs of food production. These people developed new skills and trades. In addition, the abundant food supply enabled more people to live in each community. In time, some farming villages became cities. The first cities appeared by about 3500 B.C.T. These cities were the birthplaces of modern civilization.

Archaeologists believe writing was invented around 3500 B.C.T. in cities in the Tigris-Euphrates Valley in what is now Iraq. People then learned to record their history, and prehistoric times came to an end.

Eurasia

The retreating ice sheets in Eurasia brought significant environmental changes.

The retreat of the ice sheets altered the Eurasian environment dramatically. Mammoths and woolly rhinoceroses became extinct around 10,000 B.C.T., although dwarf mammoths may have survived until some 4,000 years ago on Wrangel Island, off the coast of Siberia. The cause of their extinction was most probably a combination of overhunting by humans and the gradual disappearance of their native habitat. De-

ciduous forests, which had been restricted to temperate areas in southernmost Europe, now spread northward, and with them came red deer, wild boar, and aurochs (wild ox).

Throughout Eurasia, human communities responded to the warmer conditions by increasing the range of plants and animals to their diet, notably seafood such as fish and shellfish. Large shell middens (mounds of discarded debris) found along the coast of northwestern Europe mark the campsites used by small groups of hunter-gatherers.

Seafood also played a major role in the diet of hunter-gatherers in East and Southeast Asia during this period. In Japan, the hunter-gatherer people of the Jomon culture exploited the abundant fish stocks along the east coast of Honshu island during the spring and early summer. The Jomon people were the first in the world to produce potter vessels, their culture being named after the *jomon* ("cord-marked") decorative patterns that characterize the pottery they made during the 10th millennium B.C.T.

Plants were also an important resource. Although evidence of particular species rarely survives, the remains of 22 plant types were found at the Spirit Cave in Thailand. The remains included some plants from which poison could have been extracted for use on arrows.

Europe

In Europe, the period between the coldest point of the last Ice Age (around 20,000 years ago) and 10,000 B.C.T. was marked by the gradual extinction of the large mammals that had previously flourished on the tundra. Among these were the woolly mammoth (an ancestor of the modern elephant that was protected against the harsh climate by a thick, warm coat), the woolly rhinoceros, and the giant deer. Changes in climate and forest cover were partly respon-

sible for their extinction, but many were tracked down and killed by human hunters with improved skills and hunting equipment.

In the summer months, late Ice Age hunters lived in wood framed tents covered in animal hides. At Pincevent, France, such tents once existed, but all that survives of those erected at the Pincevent campsite is a scattering of food remains, the ashes of a hearth, a few discarded flint tools, and a ring of stones that held the base of a tent in place.

Early rituals may have depended on observation of the seasons and measuring the passage of time. Found at the Grotte du Tai in France, a piece of bone about four inches long, dating to around 10,000 B.C.T., may be the oldest known solar calendar. Each of more than 1,000 marks engraved on the bone calendar may represent a day. The arrangement of the marks suggests they are grouped into years.

Flax was harvested, possibly for food, by people living near lakes in Switzerland. Domestic flax probably derived from the wild flax that grows around the Mediterranean several thousand years later.

Australia

Australian rock art began to flourish.

Australian rock art after the end of the last Ice Age (around 10,000 years ago) is distinguished by the development of figurative style and greater regional diversity. Simple figurative paintings and petroglyphs (rock engravings) are characterized by outline or filled in silhouettes of animals and humans. The prolific petroglyphs of the Pilbara include dynamic scenes of hunting, fighting, and lovemaking. The complex figurative style concentrated more on decoration, using fine polychrome linework. The so-called "X-ray" paintings in Arnhem Land depict the internal organs or bones of fish and other creatures. The Wandjina cloud-spirits in the Kimberley are portrayed with haloed heads, eyes, and noses, but with no mouths.

The Americas

Junin first became occupied.

Although global temperatures had risen virtually to present day levels by 8000 B.C.T., the high plateau of the Andes in South America remained cold, and hunter-gatherers lived in caves and rock shelters. Junin, a settlement high in Peru's central sierra over 13,000 feet above sea level, was one of the first places to domesticate llama and alpaca. Several caves were found to have been occupied continuously between 10,000 and 4000 B.C.T. These caves contain highly stylized depictions of llamas and alpacas, and hunting scenes.

9500 B.C.T.

Asia

The jomon *(meaning cord-marked) pottery vessels produced during the tenth millennium B.C.T. in Japan had pointed bases and were made by building up coils of clay into the desired shape. The cord-marked patterns that decorated the vessels were often complex. The vessels may have been intended for ritual or funerary use rather than for everyday purposes.*

Europe

People of the Azilian toolmakng industry in the Mesolithic (Middle Stone Age) in France painted geometric designs on pebbles, with no cave paintings, sculptures, jewelry, or other art forms.

Many anthropologists recognize that the end of the Old Stone Age was a significant transition period and label this era the Middle Stone Age. In any case, there is a dramatic change observable in stone tools, which in the modal system is labeled

Mode V. This tradition involves the reduction of points and other tools to such a small size that they are called microliths. This tendency actually began with the previous Magdalenian industry.

The first industry to be based largely on microliths, dated from about 9500 B.C.T. to about 7000 B.C.T. is known from its French manifestation as Azilian. There are clues that suggest that microlithic technology was inspired at least in part by the growing human population and its drain upon local resources, including good stone for tools. Similar to Azilian, although somewhat different in detail, microlithic industries that followed in France are called the Sauveterrian (to 5500 B.C.T.) and Tardenosian (to 4000 B.C.T.). Other parts of Europe as well as other continents had corresponding industries with different names. By the end of the Mode V tradition, there are so many individual names given that only specialists know them.

Co-existent with Mode V as well as following it, Mode VI involves a number of ground-stone tools, especially axes and adzes (an adz is essentially an axe with its blade turned 90 degrees, a tool used mainly to shape large pieces of wood). The modern re-creators of stone technology have shown that, although flaked tools are just as sharp as ground ones, ground edges hold up much better in hard use, in chopping down trees. Furthermore, if they lose their edge, ground tools are easily reground.

Around 5500 B.C.T., the Old Stone Age and the New Stone Age—the Neolithic Age—began. Indeed, the advent of the Neolithic Age is generally called the Neolithic Revolution because the advances in stone technology coincided with the advent of agriculture, a time anthropologists call the Agricultural Revolution. It is thought that Neolithic farmers replaced flaked stone edges with ground ones to have the kind of axes needed in clearing land.

One of the main differences between the New Stone Age and the Old is that the Neolithic people used stone as only one of a great variety of materials, even including native copper.

9200 B.C.T.

The Americas

Hunters in North America during the Clovis and Folsom periods (c. 9200–8900 B.C.T.) used projectile points with fluted bases. Clovis points have been found at mammoth kill sites, while smaller Folsom points were used to hunt bison. The sources of stone are widespread, indicating that early North Americans were highly mobile.

The first Americans were descendants of the big game hunters of the Siberian Arctic, possessing survival skills developed during the last Ice Age. As the Ice Age drew to a close, the first Americans ventured south beyond the retreating ice sheets in search of new game, armed with expertly made weapons, hunted mammoths, bison, and other North American animals such as the native camel and horse that had not developed a natural fear of humans. By 9000 B.C.T. the days of the large Ice Age mammals such as the mammoth were over, and the groups turned to other prey. The hunters of the vast American Plains were to focus their superb hunting and tracking skills on the bison.

9000 B.C.T.

By 9000 B.C.T., glaciers of the Ice Age had melted and receded and the New Stone Age had begun in Egypt and Mesopotamia.

Asia

At Mureybit, a village in the Levant, there is evidence of a heavy dependence on wild grain collecting and hunting gazelles and onagers.

Farming began to flourish in Southwest Asia.

It was in Southwest Asia that the most significant changes of early Post Ice Age occurred. Wild wheat and barley were native to the uplands of southern Turkey and the Fertile Crescent, a broad arc stretching from the southern Levant (coastal Israel) to the Zagros Mountains south of the Caspian Sea. People in the Levant had been gathering these wild grains since around 17,000 B.C.T. and had developed grinding stones to crush the grains into flour. By 13,000 B.C.T., their successors, the people of the Natufian communities (named after the site of Wadi en-Natuf in Israel) were harvesting wild grains even more intensively. From this point, it was only one further step to the intentional planting of some grains.

By this simple process, farming began in Southwest Asia around 9000 B.C.T. The long-term implications were enormous. Whole communities could be supported by cultivated crops, and storage of grain throughout the year made it easier for people to live in fixed settlements. The nomadic life of hunter-gatherer groups, their moving from place to place in order to use seasonal resources, gradually became more settled as dependence on different cultivated plants increased.

Around 9000 B.C.T., after millennia of harvesting wild grains and hunting, the inhabitants of Southwest Asia began cultivating wheat and barley and domesticating livestock. At first, the Asiatic mouflon and bezoar goat (the wild ancestors of sheep and goats) were simply herded. Later, they were bred selectively and changes in their size occurred. These changes have been observed in bones discovered at archaeological sites. Similarly, through selective harvesting and planting, new varieties of grains evolved. This change from hunting and gathering to farming ensured a supply of food throughout the year, and made it pos- *sible for people to develop a new, settled way of life in farming villages. This served as part of the basis from which all later civilizations would arise.*

Goats and sheep were domesticated in Persia (Iran) and Afghanistan. Emmer wheat and barley were cultivated in Canaan (Israel).

Houses of sun-dried brick held together without mortar were constructed in Jericho.

Tell el-Sultan, better known as the ancient site of Jericho, is situated north of Wadi el-Mafjar on a moderately sloping plain formed by the Late Pleistocene Lisan Lake. Rising as a mound some 26 to 39 feet (8 to 12 meters) above the current landscape, the site of Jericho covers an area of at least 30,000 square yards (25,000 square meters) and is oval shaped, with its long axis oriented along a north-south line.

Jericho appears to have been continually occupied into the Middle Bronze Age, indicated by the extensive cemetery, with vertical shaft tombs and underground burial chambers. In the Middle Bronze Age, the town was expanded with the construction of defensive fortifications. The elaborate burial offerings placed in some of the tombs of this period may reflect the emergence of local rulers. After destruction in the Late Bronze Age, Tell el-Sultan no longer served as an urban center.

Jericho was originally founded by sedentary foragers in the Natufian Period (10,800–8,500 B.C.T.), living in large semi-subterranean oval stone structures, although it is unclear how extensive this occupation was. With the introduction of domesticated plants between 8,300–7,300 B.C.T., Jericho mushroomed into a large regional agricultural community covering an area of some 30,000 square yards (25,000 square meters). Villagers lived year round in roofed, oval semi-subterranean dwellings, and engaged in long-distance trading of Anatolian obsidian and shells from the Mediterranean and Red Sea. Living on domesticated and wild plant crops as well as hunting on wild game, adult individuals were buried in single graves, almost always with their cranium later removed to secondary locations. The Jericho of this time had a spectacular large circular tower situated just inside of a 12 foot high (3.6 meter high) perimeter wall. Made of field stones, the tower was 28 feet (8.5 meters) in diameter, preserved to a height of 26.5 feet (8 meters), and had an internal staircase. Some believe that the tower and walls comprised an early defensive system. Others believe that the tower and the perimeter wall served as a water diversion system to protect the occupants from winter floods. It is also possible that the western wall, which does not totally surround Jericho, facilitated the ponding of water so as to support agriculture and a waterfowl habitat.

With the appearance of domesticated goat and sheep around 7,300–6,000 B.C.T., significant changes occurred at Jericho. The tower and perimeter walls of the earlier period were abandoned and villagers lived in rectangular thirteen-by-twenty-six-foot (four by eight meter) houses with painted red and white lime plaster floors. While displaying continuity with earlier burial practices, Jericho villagers of this time often cached multiple human skulls, up to nine at one time, beneath house floors. Evidence of these plastered human skulls, often with inset saltwater shells for eyes, and painted representations of hair and other facial features, clearly indicates the practice of a complex form of ancestor worship and the emergence of more complex social and ritual organizations.

As one of the earliest and most important agricultural villages in the Jordan Valley, Jericho existed as a regional focus for the trade of exotic goods and agricultural products. As the most extensively reported of Neolithic sites in the southern Levant, our knowledge of Jericho serves as the foundation for understanding Neolithic cultural chronology, the emergence of agriculture, and the development of complex social organizations in the Levantine Neolithic Period. Its continued cultural and economic development through the Bronze Age is testimony to its importance as a regional center.

Dwellers of what came to be known as northern Iraq began to domesticate sheep.

Herding would become the occupation ascribed by the Bible to the earliest Hebrews and to Abel, son of Adam and Eve. {**See Genesis 4:2**}

Einkorn wheat was domesticated by the Natufians, who lived at the north end of the Dead Sea in what is now Israel. {**See also 7000 B.C.T.**}

In Japan, jomon *(cord-marked) pottery vessels were made, notable for their pointed bases and cord-marked patterns.*

The Americas

The mammoths became extinct in North America.

The success of the early hunters may have played a part in the extinction, in North America, of the mammoth and other Ice Age fauna, which coincided with the end of the Clovis epoch. However, much debate surrounds this subject, changes in climate and vegetation patterns were probably equally important. By 8000 B.C.T., regional environments similar to those of the present day existed throughout North America. Groups began to settle and specialize in hunting the animals that characterized various habitats—caribou in the north; deer in the eastern woodlands; fish and sea mammals in coastal, lake and riverine territory; small game in the scrublands and arid mountains of the southwest; and, on the Great Plains, the bison.

By 9,000 B.C.T., mass extinctions of large animals in North and South America had occurred. {See 10,500 B.C.T.}

8750 B.C.T.

The Americas

Pumpkins and related squash were domesticated around 8750 B.C.T. in what is now Mexico and Central America.

8500 B.C.T.

The Neolithic era began.

Asia

Goats' milk became a food source in Southwestern Asia, where goats had been domesticated for at least 1,500 years since around 10,000 B.C.T.

Europe

Arrow shafts were left at a site at Stellmoor, Germany. These shafts are the earliest direct evidence of the bow and arrow known today. {But see also 20,000 B.C.T.}

The remains of animals occasionally bear the evidence of the work of early human hunters. The skeleton of an aurochs (wild ox) found in Denmark dating to this period had three flint arrowheads embedded in its chest. It must have been attacked on two occasions because the earlier wound had healed. The hunters might have been helped by trained domesticated dogs. The earliest skeletal evidence for the use of dogs in Europe dates to around 8500 B.C.T.

8400 B.C.T.

The Americas

According to evidence found in the Jaguar Cave (Idaho), around 8400 B.C.T., the dog became the first, and for a long time the only, domesticated animal in North America. This situation would persist until at least 1500 B.C.T.

Stone tools known as Folsom points, which were probably used as arrowheads, began to be manufactured in North America. Among the earliest examples known are those from Blackwater Draw, New Mexico, even though the points are named for the site of first discovery, Folsom, New Mexico.

8000 B.C.T.

Earth's human population soared to 5.3 million as agriculture provided a more reliable food source. Where it previously took 5,000 acres to support each member of a hunter-forager society, the same amount of land, with the application of agriculture, could feed 5,000 to 6,000 people.

Africa

In North Africa around 8000 B.C.T., hunter-gatherer groups represented humans and animals in a variety of media. In the rock shelter at Taforalt in Algeria, for example, there is a crude engraving of male and female genitalia. Other finds from the region include ostrich eggshells carved with intricate designs incorporating animal figures, and pebbles engraved with elephants. Stone pendants carved with human masks and phallic symbols have also been found.

Between 8000 and 5000 B.C.T., the wooded massifs, semiarid grasslands, and shallow lakes of what is now the Sahara Desert supported sparse bands of hunter-gatherers, whose staples were lake fish, edible plants, and such game as aurochs (wild oxen) and gazelles. After 6000 B.C.T., the Sahara gradually dried up. Drought forced humans and animals toward permanent but shrinking lakes and springs. Hunters domesticated wild cattle, then dispersed over their former hunting grounds as herders . This change is documented in Saharan rock art. The rock art dating to before 6000 B.C.T. depicts only wild animals. However, in the art from after 6000 B.C.T. domesticated animals were also portrayed. As the Sahara became drier, so the cattle herders withdrew to its margins where there were permanent water sources.

Floodwater agriculture was used in the Nile valley and in southwestern Asia.

By 8000 B.C.T., Africans began weaving matting from palm fronds and other fibrous materials for use in bedding and walls.

By 8000 B.C.T., microliths (tiny stone blades), which had first appeared in Zaire around 35,000 years ago, were being produced throughout most of the African continent. Hunter-gatherer groups developed tools for specific tasks, such as scrapers for woodworking and preparing animal hide cloaks that were worn by women when plant foraging.

A marked bone from this time or as late as 6500 B.C.T. which was found in Ishango (of Zaire [the Democratic Republic of the Congo]) was probably used as a record of months and lunar phases.

Asia

Around 8000 B.C.T., the first cities appeared in Southwest Asia, most notably Jericho in Palestine.

A farming culture established a permanent settlement, fortified in stone, at a site that would come to be known as Jericho. Elsewhere in the Land of the Prophets, people lived in caves and foraged, while at other sites the herding of animals was begun.

Nearly 10,000 years ago in Southwest Asia, a combination of environmental, biological, and cultural factors resulted in a dramatic change in the way people obtained food, and it was this dramatic change which would forever transform the relationship between humans and the world around them. The Fertile Crescent, an arc of land extending from the Zagros Mountains of Iran to the southern Levant (southern Israel and Jordan), was the region where plants and animals were first domesticated and the home of the first food-producing communities. Domestication involves control of the reproduction of a plant or animal to increase the yield of a resource produced by the species. Reliance on farming and herding need not immediately follow the initial domestication of plants and animals, however. In Southwest Asia, different species were domesticated in different places at different times, and fully-fledged farming communities were not established until more than 1,000 years after the first domesticates appeared.

Domestication often changes the physiology of a plant species, making it more attractive to humans and more dependent on them for its propagation. Cultivation also results in the spread of domestic plants into areas unsuitable for their wild progenitors. Wild wheat and barley have brittle stalks that ensure the seed head breaks on impact, allowing grains to reseed themselves, but making it difficult to harvest and transport ripe grain. Domestic grains have larger, plumper seeds and tough stalks, making them easier to harvest and carry from the fields for processing or storage.

The people living in Jericho constructed dome-shaped houses from sunbaked brick that was formed entirely by hand.

The oldest wall known to man was constructed in Jericho from boulders set in place without mortar. The wall was not more than 3.6 meters (12 feet) high and was 2 meters (6 feet 6 inches) thick at the base.

The place now known as Tell Mureybit in Syria had stone houses, although the

*villagers were hunters, not farmers. An-
thropologists believe that hunters normally
move from site to site and, therefore, do no
construct permanent dwellings.*

*Around 8000 B.C.T., agriculture began in
Southwestern Asia with women using digging sticks to plant the seeds of wild grasses,
including wheat and barley.*

When the seeds were seen to produce
crops of grain in the succeeding fall (or the
following spring), people would become
encouraged to give up their nomadic life
of hunting and gathering, live in one place,
raise families, and start communities. Settled agricultural communities would become the basis of civilization.

Beer was brewed in Mesopotamia.

*In Southwest Asia (Mesopotamia), clay to-
kens were used to tally shipments of grain
and animals. This system would become
the basis for the first system of numeration
and writing. {See 3500 B.C.T.}*

The first forms of fired clay tokens
were used by Neolithic people to record the
products of farming, such as jars of oil and
measures of grain, at sites in present-day
Syria and Iran. Tokens are believed to have
helped the separate ideas of number and
written word to evolve over the next 5000
years. At a few sites tokens continued to be
used until about 1500 B.C.T. {See also
30,000 B.C.T.}

*Although it is impossible to be certain, it
appears that copper was occasionally used
by this time. At this time, copper was
worked like a soft stone. It was not cast.
{See also 6400 B.C.T.}*

*Large farming settlements appeared in
Southwest Asia.*

An analysis of the world around 8000
B.C.T. would have shown that while farm-
ing was becoming established in parts of
Southwest Asia, hunting and gathering was

still the most widespread way of life in the
world as a whole. The same was true 3,000
years later (around 5000 B.C.T.) but by this
time communities in China, the Americas,
and perhaps also the Nile Valley and the
Sahara had, independently of each other,
adopted plant cultivation. Farming techniques spread to Europe from Southwest
Asia, possibly along trade routes. In Australia, on the other hand, the hunter-gatherer way of life continued to flourish. Aboriginal rock art at open-air sites and on the
walls of rock shelters, such as at Ingaladdi
in the Northern Territory, continued to depict the flora and fauna that were the basis
of the local diet.

The increased demand for food, created by an expanding human population,
was an important factor in the development of farming. After the end of the last
Ice Age around 10,000 years ago, abundant
plant and animal resources enabled communities to grow rapidly, requiring careful
management of resources. Domestication
of suitable wild species of plants and animals was the natural step toward securing
reliable food sources, first on a small scale,
then more intensively as communities grew
too large to be supported by hunting and
gathering alone.

The shift to more permanent settlements can be most clearly seen at Jericho in
the Jordan Valley, where a natural spring
provided a well-watered area of fertile soil
ideal for growing grain. By 8000 B.C.T. the
people farming this land had established a
flourishing settlement covering six acres.
Tiny by modern standards, but vast in comparison with anything that had gone before.

It is notable that early farming villages
in Southwest Asia had, at most, a few hundred inhabitants. Jericho, however, may
have had a population of more than 1,000.
As early as 8000 B.C.T., a ditch and stone
wall about 2,100 feet long surrounded it.
Inside the wall was a semi-circular tower
33 feet wide and at least 33 feet high.

At Asiah, an open air site in the Zagros Mountains of Southwest Asia, there is evidence that the people of Asiah relied heavily on adult male goats.

Farming, which began in the Fertile Crescent of Southwest Asia, was soon developed in China, Southeast Asia, Europe, and the Americas. It eventually became the mainstay of human existence, and remains so today. Whether the move away from the hunter-gatherer way of life was, in the long run, a good thing for humanity is, of course, debatable. But whatever the disadvantages of the farming way of life—such as the increased exposure to infectious diseases that was the corollary of a sedentary agricultural existence—there was no going back.

New farming practices developed after the end of the last Ice Age in Southwest Asia. The first farming villages appeared where rainfall alone provided water for the crops. In Mesopotamia, irrigation techniques enabled better use of fertile soils. An ample supply of water was available from the Tigris and Euphrates rivers and their tributaries. Toward the end of the 7th millennium B.C.T., farmers constructed canal systems to bring water to the fields. These were developed further by the farmers of the Ubaid period (c.5900–4300 B.C.T.), named after the site of Tell al-Ubaid in southern Mesopotamia. Ultimately, it was efficient irrigation systems that provided the economic basis for the first Mesopotamian cities.

The early farming villages of Southwest Asia were linked together by social ties, marriage alliances, and trade. The clearest evidence of trade at this period is provided by finds of obsidian (black volcanic glass), which was ideal for making sharp tools and was traded over extensive distances from sources in eastern Turkey. Trading contact between early Anatolian farmers and communities in southeastern Europe led to the adoption of farming in Europe around 6500 B.C.T.

Obsidian (black volcanic glass) was highly valued by the early farming communities of the Middle East for the sharp-edged cutting blades that could be made from obsidian flakes. Since the chemical composition of obsidian varies according to its origin, the sources of the obsidian found at settlement sites can be traced, and the tracing of the obsidian charts the contemporary trade routes along which it passed. The widespread distribution indicates that these trade routes were extensive, and that the early farming communities in the region were in regular contact with one another. The most highly prized, and therefore the most important, sources of obsidian were the extinct volcanoes of central and eastern Anatolia (modern Turkey). The unique chemical composition of this obsidian made it particularly good for creating the sharpest possible blades.

Ain Mallaha was founded in the Levant. Ain Mallaha was a large semi-permanent camp with evidence of grain storage and processing, burials, and art objects.

Mud bricks were used as a building material.

Mud is an exceptionally good material for building in dry climates. It has good structural and thermal qualities and is readily available wherever agriculture is practiced. Mud bricks had been invented in the 9th millennium B.C.T. The mud was molded by hand and dried in the sun, then built into walls using mud mortar. After 8000 B.C.T., mud bricks were mass-produced using wooden molds.

In mainland Southeast Asia around 8000 B.C.T., hunter-gatherers used simple tools made from beach or river pebbles, which were flaked along one side or all over to produce cutting edges. The tools were used for a wide range of tasks including butcher-

ing animals. Axes were made from larger stones, their regular, sharp cutting edges achieved by polishing. In addition to stone tools, bone points were used, probably for stitching animal hides.

Rice was cultivated in Indochina.

The woolly mammoth became extinct. {**See also 2000 B.C.T.**}

Europe

Europe's final post-glacial climatic improvements began. These improvements would produce a movement of people to the north of the continent, where the settlers would eat fish caught in nets of hair, thongs, and twisted fiber, along with shellfish, goose, and honey.

Toward the end of the last Ice Age, the milder climate and abundant deciduous forests provided an excellent environment for small groups of hunter-gatherers, who set up base camps in lowland valleys and on lake edges. These localities were often marshy, rich in edible roots and tubers; game and fish were plentiful, providing the impetus for the development of new hunting and fishing techniques and tools. The settlers at Star Carr, on the shores of ancient Lake Pickering in Yorkshire, England, were particularly adept at hunting red deer, aurochs (wild ox), elk and wild boar, making barbed points and harpoons of red-deer antler.

A typical European lowland settlement, Star Carr, situated on the shores of ancient Lake Pickering in Yorkshire, England, was a winter camp used by a group of hunter-gatherers. The inhabitants laid down birch brushwood to make dry platforms where they may have built simple shelters. The camp was probably one of several occupied by this particular group at various times of the year, as they moved from place to place exploiting different natural resources.

As well as stone, the early inhabitants of northern Europe made extensive use of organic materials, such as bone, antler, wood, and plant fibers, to make tools and equipment. The winter camp at Star Carr in England yielded a wide range of organic artifacts, such as wooden mattocks and barbed points of elk or deer antler. A wooden paddle indicates that canoes were in use.

Little is known of the religious practices in northern Europe, but at Star Carr in England a group of red deer frontlets (antlers still attached to the skull) were found. These may have been worn as headdresses in hunting or fertility rituals.

Oysters and other shellfish were an important source of protein for European coastal dwellers after the end of the last Ice Age around 10,000 years ago. Large shell middens (mounds of discarded debris) survive on Atlantic coasts from Iberia to Denmark, marking locations to which groups of hunter-gatherers returned year after year at certain seasons to gather and eat shellfish.

Flint microliths (tiny blades) are the hallmark of the European Mesolithic, the period between the end of the Ice Age (around 10,000 years ago) and the beginnings of farming (around 6500 B.C.T.). The blades were produced to standardized shapes and mounted on wooden hafts to form knives, spears, and arrowheads.

Australia

In Australia, rock paintings of animals were made.

Oceania

Polynesians in the East Indies and Australia began to spread out over the islands of the South Pacific.

The Americas

The Maya made astronomical inscriptions and constructions in Central America.

Potatoes and beans were cultivated in Peru.

Pumpkins were domesticated in Central America.

A dog died.

Although dogs were first domesticated in the Middle East and Europe, they are known to have accompanied the first settlers of North America. Dogs may have been used as pack animals and for pulling sleds. The earliest remains of a dog found in North America date to around 8000 B.C.T. and were found at the Jones-Miller site, a bison kill site in Colorado, which suggests that dogs may also have been used for hunting.

The earliest evidence for erected shelters in North America is identified by postholes. At the Hell Gap site in Wyoming, a small circular outline of postholes represents the remains of tents, which would have been covered either by animal hides or brushwood. The small size of the tents suggests that they were occupied by single families. In contrast, at the Thunderbird site in Virginia, posthole patterns appear to outline a large rectangular shelter, which was built as a dwelling for several families.

Decorative jewelry was developed in the Americas.

Beads from Wyoming which were made from clam shells and which date from around 8000 B.C.T. illustrate an emerging appreciation of decorative items. Sharp-tipped stone drills were used to pierce the shells, which were then strung on fine sinew cords to make necklaces. Earlier engraved bones and pebbles have been found, but they too are rare.

Deciduous forests, dominated by oaks and hickories, expanded across many areas of eastern North America during the climatic warming that followed the end of the last Ice Age (around 10,000 years ago). High in

starch and easily stored for later consumption, various species of acorn became an important food source for many thousands of years.

Located near a stone quarry in New Mexico, a shallow circular depression, ringed with a semi-circle of stones 6½ feet in diameter, outlines a hut used by a stoneworker. Broken tools at various stages of manufacture were found in the hut along with manufacturing equipment and discarded, worn-out tools.

Versatile weapons that could be adapted for use as tools were developed by hunters in North America. Weapon tips of chert (a crystalline form of silica) were mounted on a foreshaft (a short handle) and then hafted to a spear shaft. The spear was thrown with an atlatl, or spear-thrower, and when it was retrieved after a kill, the foreshaft and point could be removed and used simply as a hafted knife to butcher the animal.

Throughout the period dominated by hunter-gatherer societies in North America (c.8000–1000 B.C.T.), there was ongoing regional diversification in the variety of stone projectile points produced. In eastern Oklahoma, for example, some weapon tips became highly stylized. To achieve the razor sharp blade edges required skilled workmanship.

The early hunting societies of North America learned to adapt to the expansion of the forests that followed the end of the last Ice Age (around 10,000 years ago). Woodworking became important to these communities, and while wooden objects from this period are rarely preserved, the tools used are commonly found. Stone adzes with distinctive curved cutting edges are evidence of this type of craftsmanship.

As human population increased after the end of the last Ice Age (around 10,000 years ago), people living in the mountains and deserts of southern California found new ways of coping with their changing environment, including making a wider variety of tools to prepare foods in new ways. Stones for grinding nuts and seeds became more important as areas of forest increased.

7800 B.C.T.

Asia

At Tell Aswad in the Levant, there is the earliest evidence of fully domesticated emmer wheat, indicating that domestication had begun to occur by this time.

Wild einkorn (*Triticum boeticum*), the progenitor of one of the earliest forms of domestic wheat, is still found throughout Southwest Asia. Domestic einkorn (*Triticum monococcum*) is distinguished by its larger seeds and tough stalk, which requires threshing for seed dispersal. Like einkorn, emmer (another early domestic wheat) differs from its wild ancestral form in its plumper seeds and non-shattering stalk. Unlike einkorn, its distribution is largely restricted to the Levant where, even today, it can be found in dense stands.

7700 B.C.T.

Asia

By 7700 B.C.T., desert predominated over fertile lands in the arc extending from the head of the Persian Gulf through the Tigris-Euphrates Basin to the eastern Mediterranean and then south to the Nile Valley. Humans and animals were crowded in oases in the region that would ironically come to be called the "Fertile Crescent."

Ewes' milk became a food source and supplemented goats' milk and mothers' milk as lamb and mutton began to play a large role in human diets in Southwestern Asia, where sheep were domesticated.

7500 B.C.T.

Africa

Fishing communities arose in the southern Sahara.

The inhabitants of the Nile Valley relied heavily on river fish for their livelihood. Thousands of fish were stranded in the shallows when the Nile retreated after flooding each year in late summer. Nets made of reed and papyrus were used to trap fish throughout the year.

For the most part, Africans have generally utilized versatile local materials to build houses. From prehistoric times to the present day, they have employed matting woven from palm fronds and other fibrous materials. Sometimes richly decorated, these mats served not only as beds, but also as thin, airy walls for houses in hot climates. They could be easily removed or replaced as needed.

The African hunter depended on lightweight, composite spears and bows and arrows. These weapons had sharp points of bone or wood, often fitted with tiny stone barbs and smeared with poison. The head was mounted on a foreshaft (short handle), which broke off when the weapon struck an animal. Hunters carried quivers of spare points to replace heads that snapped off during the hunt.

A natural pigment, red ocher can be derived from any iron-bearing mineral, including brown clay. It was used as a paint by African hunters to adorn their bodies with intricate designs. In powdered form, it was scattered on the dead in their graves. Artists in southern Africa continued to use red ocher to paint animals and human figures on the walls of caves and rock shelters.

Asia

By 7500 B.C.T., sheep and goats had been domesticated in Southwest Asia.

From around 20,000 years ago, people in the rolling hills of the Levant relied increasingly on wild grains, and, by around 8000 B.C.T., on domestic crops. Hunting of wild game, especially gazelles, persisted until about 7000 B.C.T., when domestic sheep and goats first appear in the archaeological record. In the rugged Zagros Mountains, wild grains were restricted to less prolific varieties, and gazelles were less plentiful. Between 20,000 and 10,000 years ago, plants seem to have played a more limited role in the diet of people living in the region, and wild sheep and goats, which were more abundant than in the Levant, a more prominent one. Domestication of sheep and goats may have preceded the domestication of grains in the region, and is certain to have occurred by 7500 B.C.T., when the earliest evidence for domestic grains in the Zagros is found.

The earliest changes in the bodies and bones of domesticated animal species may have been side-effects of human selection—both conscious and unconscious—for certain behavioral characteristics, or the result of adaptations to the new conditions under which animals were kept. Sheep, goats, pigs, and cattle all show a reduction in size from the wild forms to the domestic—probably as a result of having a poorer diet, but also due to the selection of more docile, tractable, and smaller individuals for herding. In sheep, goats, and cattle, controlled breeding eliminated the need for the massive horns used in the wild for sexual display and combat, resulting in changes in horn size and shape. Additionally, as evidenced by the aurochs, the bones of the now extinct creature are larger than those of its domestic descendants. The diminutive size of the second phalanx (toe bone) of domestic cattle from the 5th millennium B.C.T. in northeastern Syria can be compared to that of wild cattle from the same region. The aurochs was hunted at the same time as this domestic specimen was being exploited for its milk, meat, or for use as a draft animal.

At Ganj Dareh in the Zagros Mountain region of Southwest Asia, there was evidence of domesticated grains and the exploitation of wild goats. Around 7500 B.C.T., Ganj Dareh was a transitory highland encampment.

At Ali Kosh in the Zagros Mountain region of Southwest Asia, there was evidence of the cultivation of domestic grains and a heavy emphasis on goats at a transitional stage between wild and domestic forms.

Hunter-gatherers in east and Southeast Asia relied on a range of wild plant and animal foods, including rice. Early remains of rice grains suggest that wild rice was native to Southeast Asia, southern China, and northern India. Carbonized grains of rice, broken husks and straws, and their imprints in clay have been found in coastal areas of southeastern China.

Stone tools are all that remain of the equipment used by hunter-gatherers in China. In the north, microliths (tiny stone blades) continued to be made as they had been for the last 4,000 years. In the south, people may have relied on larger tools and, in the southwest, on sharpened bamboo.

In northern China and Manchuria, the first personal ornaments were made around 7500 B.C.T. The hunters who made them worked the bones of tigers, leopards, bears, and deer into needles and picks, and engraved designs on antler pieces. The teeth of badgers and other game were perforated and strung together to make necklaces, pendants, or earrings.

The wild ancestors of pigs and cattle, the boar and the now extinct aurochs (wild ox), were domesticated after sheep and goats. Wild boar and aurochs were native to most of Europe and Asia. They were probably first domesticated in southern Turkey, and it is possible that they were domesticated independently in different regions. Pigs proved very useful, since they acted as scavengers in human settlements. It is difficult to see the benefits offered by domesticating cattle, however, as the animals were fierce and dangerous, and it was only later that they were kept for milk and as beasts of burden.

Europe

The Sauveterrian tool industry of inland France produced some of the smallest microliths, especially microblades with two sharpened edges.

The Maglemosian culture of the northern European plain, in addition to stone axes and microliths, used wooden canoes with paddles to engage in a fishing industry that involved both nets and fishhooks. Many of these organic items, including wooden fishhooks and harpoons, were preserved in bogs and other wet sites. {See also 4300 B.C.T.}

The earliest known houses in the British Isles were constructed around 7500 B.C.T. by a small community of hunter-gatherers on a low rise overlooking the Bann River in Northern Ireland. Flexible poles were sunk into the ground to form a circle, then bent inward to join at the center, creating a domed hut. Gaps were filled in with smaller branches and reeds. The huts were probably temporary shelters and were not intended to stand for long periods, although the site itself was reoccupied on several occasions over a period of 500 years.

Australia

In the Central Australian desert, the scarcity of building materials and food resources meant that nomadic groups moved frequently. In the absence of large trees or rock shelters, these groups erected simple windbreaks made with branches, which provided both privacy and shade. At night, when temperatures dropped below freezing, small fires were kept burning nearby, and people would huddle against dogs for warmth.

The Americas

The earliest known cemetery was created in North America.

The Sloan burial site in Arkansas, dating to 7500 B.C.T., is the earliest known cemetery in North America. Caches of unused projectile points, unfinished points, and other unused tools may have been placed as offerings in graves, hinting at a ritualized ceremony and a belief in an afterlife.

7400 B.C.T.

The Americas

Chilies (peppers) were grown in the Andean Highlands. Since they were originally a tropical plant, chilies were probably domesticated previously in the lowlands.

7300 B.C.T.

Europe

Dogs were domesticated by tribes in the British Isles.

7200 B.C.T.

Asia

Beginning around 7200 B.C.T., populations in Southwestern Asia (the Middle East) would increase over the next two millennia. More permanent camps would be established by people who had lived until this time in small groups that shifted camps every three or four months. Seed collection would become more important to the food supply.

Europe

Sheep were domesticated in Greece.

7000 B.C.T.

Africa

In the Saharan plateaus, which would begin to become a desert after 6000 B.C.T., animals were painted on rock walls, ushering in a long tradition of rock painting in the region.

In Africa, around 7000 B.C.T., the first pottery was manufactured by groups of hunters and fishermen living across a broad stretch of the southern Sahara, from Mali in the west to Khartoum in the Nile Valley to the east. The pottery was decorated with parallel wavy lines. In the Nile Valley, the pattern was made by dragging the spine of a fish across the clay while it was still soft, in the west, similar effects were achieved using wooden or bone points.

Asia

*In what is now southwestern Asia, farmers began to cultivate a new form of wheat and barley. {***See 8000 B.C.T.***}*

Around 7000 B.C.T., emmer wheat (*Triticum dicoccum*) a domesticated form of the wild grain, *Triticum dicoccoides*, was farmed in the Kurdistan area lying between what would become southeastern Turkey and northwestern Iran.

Barley (*Hordeum spolitalieum*), millet (*Panicum miliaceum*), and certain legumes, including lentils, were cultivated in Thessaly, where the Greeks may also have domesticated dogs and pigs.

Up to around 7000 B.C.T., the domestication of swine had been delayed because of the need of pigs for shade from the blazing desert sun; by the fact that pigs cannot be milked; and by the fact that the pigs cannot digest grass, leaves, or straw and, therefore, must be given food that humans themselves could eat, namely acorns, nuts, cooked grain, or meat scraps.

By 7000 B.C.T., neolithic Jericho evidenced a highly developed civilization, marked by animal domestication, cereal cultivation, toolmaking, and foreign trade.

By 7000 B.C.T., the town of Jericho, situated some 840 feet above sea level, had a population of 2,500. This populace was apparently attracted to the town by the area's perennial spring. Jericho would soon be walled to protect it from attack.

By 7000 B.C.T., mortar was being used with sun-dried brick in Jericho.

A group living in Jericho constructed rectangular houses from sunbaked brick and mortar formed by heating limestone and mixing the product with sand and water. The people of Jericho also used the transformed limestone (known as "burned lime" to archaeologists) to plaster walls and floors.

The faces of human skulls from Jericho were individually reconstructed in tinted plaster with pieces of seashells for the eyes. These Neolithic "sculptured heads" pointed the way to Mesopotamian portrait sculpture.

*Clay pottery was being made in Turkey and Southwest Asia. {***See also 10,000 B.C.T. and 6000 B.C.T.***}*

*Einkorn wheat was cultivated in Syria and durum (macaroni) wheat in Anatolia (Turkey). {***See also 9000 B.C.T.***}*

Woven cloth was developed in Anatolia.

The weaving of cloth became known in Anatolia (Turkey) and the first known samples of cloth were made in the early city Catal Huyuk.

The pig was domesticated, according to evidence found at a site called Cayonu in present day Turkey.

Cattle were domesticated in southeastern Anatolia (Turkey) and independently in Africa.

Flax was grown in Southwest Asia.

The oldest known woven mats were made in Beidha (Jordan). Basketry probably began much earlier.

At Beidha, in the Levant, there is evidence of the management of wild herds of goats.

Around this time, structures were small round self-contained houses. By 6500 B.C.T., the predominant houses would be larger rectangular structures, many of which showed signs of repeated remodeling and expansion.

At Jericho, in the Levant, there is evidence for the domestication of goats.

At Jericho, a large stone tower, storage facilities, and a wall on the western perimeter indicate that Jericho was a site of increasing communal activity.

Between 7000 and 5500 B.C.T., at Ain Ghazal, an early village in the Levant, there is evidence of the flowering and collapse of mixed farming and the pastoral way of life. A large cache of plaster figures in later levels indicates more elaborate forms of art and ritual.

Reliance on stored food that could be both shared and hoarded brought about profound social changes. Art forms such as the plaster figures found at Ain Ghazal may be tied to new forms of social relations, family organization, or ritual in these sedentary communities.

At Abu Hureyra, a village in the Levant, there was a shift from hunting and foraging to a more agricultural and pastoral economy around this time.

Around 7000 B.C.T. large Neolithic settlements appeared in Anatolia, Asia Minor. Some of the settlements were characterized by a technological innovation—pottery.

Before the development of pottery, vessels were made of unbaked, sun-dried mud or of white ware. White ware vessels, made from a mixture of lime and gray ash, were built up around a basket, which was removed just before firing. This kind of vessel was made and used at several villages in the Levant (the coastal strip of Syria, Lebanon, and Israel) and southern Turkey for several centuries around 7000 B.C.T.

Pottery first came into widespread use in the Middle East after 7000 B.C.T. The earliest vessels were crudely shaped and poorly fired, but progress was rapid. Within 1,000 years finely made pottery with elaborate painted and incised designs was being produced at village settlements from western Iran to Anatolia. In northern Mesopotamia, large domed kilns six feet in diameter generated high enough temperatures to fire exceptionally fine painted pottery, known as Hassuna ware after the site of Hassuna in central Mesopotamia. These kilns were also suited to the melting and smelting of copper, and it is no coincidence that the first experiments in copper metallurgy were made in northern Mesopotamia at this time.

Graves beneath the floors of houses in farming villages in the Levant often contained headless skeletons. The skulls may have been displayed in the houses or in a special hut. They sometimes had flesh modeled in plaster and shells in the eye sockets. It is thought that this was associated with ancestor worship.

At Cayonu, a village in Anatolia, there is evidence of domestic grains and possibly domestic sheep.

In coastal regions of China, early cultivation of tubers like taro and yam was

accompanied by the appearance of more sophisticated implements for digging and
planting. A spade, for example, would have
two holes drilled through one end, where a
wooden handle may have been attached.
Taro and yam fibers were used to make
fishing lines and nets, and for caulking canoes.

Throughout Southeast Asia, the adoption
of farming was a gradual process based on
such indigenous plants as wild rice and the
root crop taro, which were first domesticated in small plots adjacent to settlements.
A similar process of gradual adoption and
small scale cultivation took place in New
Guinea. As long ago as 7000 B.C.T., local
people endeavored to drain a marshy valley
floor in the highlands of the island so that
it could be cultivated. They dug a channel
to carry off excess water and created a system of tributary gutters draining into it.
This was replaced by an even more extensive network of drains 1,000 years later. The
prepared land was probably planted with
taro, and the scale of the drainage shows
that, although it grew wild in New Guinea,
taro also became an important cultivated
dietary staple.

The Yangshao people along the Huang He
(Yellow River) in China lived in underground, circular mud-and-timber huts.
Their communities featured large kilns for
making painted pottery.

Potters in southeast Asia (Burma to Vietnam) began to fire pottery in kilns. {See
also 10,000 B.C.T.}

From 7000 to 6000 B.C.T., the pig and the
water buffalo were domesticated in China
and East Asia, while the chicken was found
domesticated in South Asia.

Sugarcane was cultivated in New Guinea.

Yams, bananas, and coconuts were grown
in Indonesia.

Europe

In Denmark and southern Sweden, carvings of animals were first made around
7000 B.C.T. Most attractive were small
figurines of amber (a natural fossil resin),
including an elk's head and a bear or wild
boar. As well as these figurines, there are
engravings on tools and other objects of
bone and antler, including several stylized
humans and a detailed depiction of a red
deer.

Greek seafarers sailed to the Aegean island
of Milos, 75 miles from the mainland, to
obtain obsidian.

The first sledges came into use.

Australia

Rock shelters were sometimes occupied for
thousands of years. The one at Ingaladdi in
the Northern Territory of Australia, for example, was inhabited continuously from
before 7000 B.C.T. until the twentieth century. It provided welcome shade and protection from tropical downpours in the hot,
wet summer.

The Americas

Chilies and avocados added important variety to the Mesoamerican diet from as
early as 7000 B.C.T. While squash, maize,
and beans provided the staple complex car-
bohydrates and protein, chilies added
flavoring and essential vitamins, and avocados provided oils necessary for the break-
down of other nutrients.

Early hunter-gatherers in eastern North
America occupied small settlements for
short periods during a particular season,
often returning to the same place year after
year. They built temporary shelters, often
in river valleys, with a light frame of wood
covered in grass and an outdoor hearth.
The huts were renewed each time the site
was revisited.

In North America, early unfired clay figurines of humans were incised with stylized decoration, but had no details to indicate their gender. Complete figurines lack any facial features, although some fragments have noses formed by pinching a ridge, and holes for eyes. Their function is unknown, but they are found with objects that might have belonged to individuals rather than to a social group.

Glaciers receded in the northern continent of the Western Hemisphere.

Maize, squash, peppers, and beans were grown in the Tehuacan Valley of Mexico.

6800 B.C.T.

Asia

The Kurdistan village of Jarmo was founded with some 30 dwellings that covered three acres and housed 200 people. Jarmo became one of the first permanent agricultural settlements.

6700 B.C.T.

Asia

At Ali Kosh in the Zagros Mountain region of Southwestern Asia, a permanent village was established which relied upon the exploitation of domestic grains and fully domesticated goats and sheep, although wild hunted game continued to play a major role.

6500 B.C.T.

Africa

Around 6500 B.C.T., the borders of Africa's rainforests supported an exceptionally diverse population of edible plants. Among them was the wild African yam, which sustained people for millennia. Many groups exploited yams intensively, cutting off the tops and planting them so they would re-

germinate in the damp soil. Such a simple form of deliberate cultivation, sometimes called vegeculture, probably began thousands of years ago in some areas, and may be as old or older than the cultivation of wheat and barley in Europe and western Asia. Vegeculture was an effective and logical way to increase food supplies and is practiced to this day.

Around 6500 B.C.T., the first settlers at Nabta Playa, a village in semi-arid grasslands to the east of the Nile Valley, lived in oval huts that were dug into the ground and roofed with animal hides sometimes mixed with grass. This structure gave some protection during extremely hot days and bitterly cold nights and was widespread in northeastern Africa for many centuries.

Asia

At Bougras, a village in the Levant, there is evidence of both domestic grains and domestic goats, and, especially, domestic sheep.

At Catal Huyuk, a large settlement in Anatolia, was heavily involved in obsidian exploitation and trade, with evidence of cattle veneration and domestication of cattle.

The world's earliest known form of metallurgy was developed in Southwest Asia.

The earliest experiments with smelting copper took place in Southwest Asia around 6500 B.C.T. Although the first metallurgy was a milestone in human development, it did not revolutionize everyday activities to the same extent as the new food production methods had done. In its early stages, the use of metal was limited to making simple objects of copper, gold, and lead. These are all soft, easily worked metals that melt at relatively low temperatures. Beads and trinkets of copper and lead were made by the inhabitants of Catal Huyuk in Turkey by 6000 B.C.T., and 1000 years later the farming communities of southeastern

Europe were also experimenting with copper and gold.

Although copper was used to make axes and knives, it is likely that most early copper objects were intended to be impressive decorative items indicating the status of the owner rather than implements for daily use. Certainly, heavy tasks such as felling trees and woodworking became easier with the development of harder copper alloys such as bronze. Meanwhile, stone axes were also used for woodworking.

Catal Huyuk in southern Anatolia was perhaps the most spectacular of all early farming villages. It was one of the largest settlements of the 7th millennium B.C.T., covering some 32 acres. Mud-brick houses and shrines were built against each other, with occasional open yards but no intervening streets. Access was across flat rooftops, with ladders leading down into the buildings.

One third of the buildings at Catal Huyuk in southern Anatolia were decorated with wall paintings and figures of leopards, bulls' heads and horns, and female figures. These buildings have been identified as shrines. One wall painting that depicts scavenging birds attacking headless corpses may represent the practice of excarnation,—the practice of exposing the dead.

Farming began in South Asia.

In South Asia, farming began around 6500 B.C.T. at Mehrgarh, a village settlement in the hills west of the Indus Valley. The main crops, wheat and barley, were grown initially to supplement hunting and gathering. Sheep, goats, and cattle were also herded. The trade networks of the people of Mehrgarh were revealed by their burial goods of turquoise and lapis lazuli from Central Asia and Afghanistan.

Mehrgarh, in the hill country west of the Indus Valley, began as a seasonally occupied village of hunters and herders.

Around 6500 B.C.T., the people began to farm, cultivating wheat and barley, and raising sheep, goats, and cattle. The cattle (zebu) were probably indigenous to the area, but the grain and small stock may have originated elsewhere.

Between 6500 and 6300 B.C.T., the wheel was invented by Sumerians in the Tigris-Euphrates Basin. The wheel would radically transform transportation, travel, warfare, and industry. Other parts of the world, including the Western Hemisphere, would never develop the wheel on their own and would not enjoy its benefits until it was introduced by foreigners. The wheel would not only speed transportation, it would also facilitate construction and would lead to many technological advances.

Small lead beads were produced at Catal Huyuk (in Turkey), but most likely the smelter failed to recognize that lead is a specific metal.

Europe

Grain farming began in Europe.

Farming practices and pottery manufacture were first adopted in the Balkans shortly after 6500 B.C.T. through contact with farmers in Anatolia (modern Turkey). The new way of life, in permanent village settlements, spread through most of the rest of the continent, reaching the south of France and the Netherlands by 5000 B.C.T., although hunter-gatherer societies persisted in many areas. In the Mediterranean, plants, animals, and pottery were probably passed on and adopted by hunter-gatherer groups through contact with local sailors and fishermen. Typical early pottery from the Mediterranean is known as Cardial, after its distinctive *cardium* or "cockleshell" decoration. North of the Alps, farming was carried rapidly across Central Europe by groups of migrating Hungarian farmers, who developed the *Bandkeramik* pottery style, characterized by incised linear decoration. The distribution of Anatolian painted pottery also charts the locations of early farming communities.

Farming was first practiced in Europe around 6500 B.C.T., and was initially confined to the extreme southeast of the continent—Greece and the Balkans. These parts of Europe are closest to Southwest Asia, where farming had already been established for over 1,000 years, and it is clear that the early European farmers adopted the ideas and techniques of their Southwest Asian neighbors. These first European farmers grew barley and two varieties of wheat (emmer and einkorn), both of Southwest Asian origin. They herded sheep, goats, and cattle. Once established in the southeast, the new way of life soon began to spread north and west to adjacent parts of Europe.

The houses of the first farmers in southeastern Europe were small square or rectangular structures with walls of wattle and daub (interwoven twigs and sticks covered with clay), and a roof of reeds or thatch. The houses had only a single room, often with a raised hearth and a baking oven, and sometimes a clay storage bin to hold grain or flour.

The first European farmers were also the first people in Europe to produce pottery. Like farming, this was an innovation that had been developed in Southwest Asia, from where it spread to Europe. Early pottery in southeastern Europe was handmade without a potter's wheel, but was well-finished and painted with geometric designs in red or black.

The production of terra cotta figurines was another activity that the earliest farming communities of southeastern Europe copied from their neighbors in Southwest Asia. Female figurines with prominent buttocks are the most common type, and two were found together in a building at Nea Nikomedeia in Greece, which has been identified as a shrine.

Around 6500 B.C.T., the aurochs, an ancestor of domestic cattle, was domesticated. The fierce beast would be the last major food animal to be tamed for use as a source of milk, meat, power, and leather. The actual aurochs itself would become extinct in 1627.

Trepanning, the drilling of a hole in the skull as a treatment for head injuries, was practiced in Europe and Asia. In some regions, trepanning would continue through the Middle Ages and even into the beginning of the twentieth century.

In Russia, Europe and Southwest Asia, trepanation was practiced as long ago as the Neolithic period—the New Stone Age—of 9000–6000 B.C.T. In some places, trepanation would continue to be used up to the time of the Middle Ages. So globally diverse was the practice, that trepanned skulls have even been found associated with the Inca civilization of Peru of the thirteenth to sixteenth centuries of the Christian calendar.

Trepanation may have been done sometimes as a religious ritual, but in many cases it appears to have been a medical treatment for a blow to the cranium and the resulting hematoma, or swelling filled with blood. Trepanation was apparently intended to cure head injuries by allowing evil spirits to escape from the heads of the possessed. As late as the nineteenth century of the Christian calendar, trepanation was used to treat migraine headaches and epilepsy.

The art of cranial drilling varied by place and time. More than a dozen methods were developed for scraping and grooving the skull to remove bone without damaging the underlying dura—the underlying fibrous membrane that protects the brain. The Incas were trained to anesthetize the patient with herbs and nerve pressure, and there is evidence that some cultures successfully used primitive antibiotics to stave off infection.

Wooden sledges for travel over snow were in use in what is now Finland.

6400 B.C.T.

Asia

The first definitely known use of copper occurred in what is now Turkey. People learned that copper could be melted and cast.

The Americas

Haricot beans (common green and dried beans) and lima beans were grown in the Andean Highlands. Since they were tropical plants, they were probably domesticated previously in the lowlands.

6200 B.C.T.

The Americas

An ice dam blocking Lakes Agassiz and Ojibway in Canada melted and collapsed, causing the onset of a cold spell in the North Atlantic region.

Around 18,000 years ago, a North American ice sheet that extended south of the present day Great Lakes region began to recede. However, by about 8,200 years ago—around 6200 B.C.T.—the leading edge of the ice had moved so far north that an ice dam blocking Lakes Agassiz and Ojibway in Canada melted and collapsed, loosing a massive flood.

It is estimated that more than a hundred trillion cubic meters of frigid water poured into the Labrador Sea and on into the Atlantic Ocean. The consequences of the dam breach were dramatic. The influx of cold water caused the warm Gulf Stream to shift thereby wreaking havoc on the North Atlantic climate. The average air temperatures fell as much as 15 degrees Fahrenheit in Greenland and 6 degrees Fahrenheit in continental Europe and stayed down for more than two centuries.

6000 B.C.T.

Africa

Cattle were domesticated in the Sahara.

Cattle were first domesticated in the Sahara around 6000 B.C.T. and in the Nile Valley region sometime thereafter. It is not clear whether the idea developed independently, or as a result of influences from Southwest Asia. Cattle herding assumed great importance throughout the Sahara and the Sudan until the area became desert after 4000 B.C.T.

Rock paintings of the Saharan plateau reveal much about the life of the hunters who roamed the Saharan plateau before 6000 B.C.T. Paintings on the walls of caves and rock shelters depict wild animals long extinct in the region: Babalus antiquus *(an extinct buffalo), giraffe, elephant, rhinoceros, and hippopotamus. Only after 6000 B.C.T. were domestic cattle portrayed.*

Herds of domesticated humped cattle were featured prominently in Saharan rock art between 6000 and 4000 B.C.T. Many scenes show long and short-horned beasts, often accompanied by their herders and milkers. The people who painted these naturalistic scenes also produced startling depictions of supernatural beings and magical religious subjects.

Bulrush millet was cultivated in southern Algeria.

Finger millet was grown in Ethiopia.

Asia

In Southwest Asia, the first impressions of stamp seals on clay date to after 6000 B.C.T., and are thought to indicate ownership, suggesting the development of administrative practices and perhaps private property. No impressions have been found of earlier seals. The first seals had simple geometric designs; later ones had images of people and animals.

At Jarmo, a village located near the Zagros Mountain region of Southwest Asia, there was evidence of domestic grains, domestic sheep and goats, and early evidence of pig domestication.

One of the detrimental consequences of man's agricultural advances was the irreversible environmental changes which accompanied the initial success and eventual collapse of farming and herding in fragile Southwest Asian environments. Irrigation and an increasing reliance on pastoral products dramatically reduced biological diversity, changing the face of the landscape forever.

Burials dating to between 6000 and 5000 B.C.T. at Mehrgarh, in the hills west of the Indus Valley, show that the deceased were placed in pits beside mud-brick walls, together with funerary offerings. Among the offerings, the presence of beads of turquoise from Central Asia and lapis lazuli from Afghanistan suggests trade over long distances. A figurine reminiscent of those from the Zagros Mountains in Iran attests to contacts even farther afield. Even infants were sometimes buried with rich grave goods, which indicates that they inherited social status from their parents.

Around 6000 B.C.T., fertility goddesses made of baked clay began to appear in a number of religious shrines throughout Asia Minor.

Village culture, marked by painted pottery and craftsmaking, characterized Upper Mesopotamia.

Villages familiar with pottery emerged in Syria and along the Mediterranean coast. {See also 7000 B.C.T.}

The evolution of the first true pottery permitted new forms of cookery and cooking. Previously, food had been boiled in gourds, shells, and skin-lined pits into which hot stones were dropped.

Irrigation was developed in Mesopotamia.

Wine making began in northern Mesopotamia (now northern Iran and Iraq) or in the Levant.

Some buildings in Southwest Asia were rectilinear with several rooms, some with paintings on the walls. Internal furniture includes benches and platforms made from cattle horns and plaster.

People in what is now western Turkey began to make bricks in molds and then sun-dry the bricks. The same practice could be observed in Crete several hundred years later.

The weaving of cloth was known in Anatolia (Turkey). The first known samples of cloth were from the early city Catal Huyuk.

Modern style wheat for bread, along with lentils, were grown in Southwest Asia. {See also 7000 B.C.T.}

Citrus fruit was cultivated in Indonesia and Indochina.

Foxtail millet and peaches were grown in central China.

Millet farming began in China.

There were at least two centers of early plant domestication in East Asia, based on different types of grain. The earliest, dating to around 6000 B.C.T., was on the North China Plain, around the Yellow River and its tributaries, where the main domesticated plants were broomcorn and foxtail millet. In southern and central China, the crucial early domesticated plant was rice. Rice grew wild across a broad belt of territory stretching from northern India to the mountains of mainland Southeast Asia and into southern China. Rice cultivation was initially practiced by groups of hunter-gatherers, gradually spreading northward from one settlement to another. By around 5000 B.C.T., it was well established in the Yangtze River delta region.

The story of farming in China began in the fertile Yellow River Valley in the north around 6000 B.C.T. Here, the farmers lived in villages of small round or square houses, sometimes surrounded by a timber stockade. They grew millet and raised pigs, dogs and chickens. Rice was cultivated in southern and central China, and the practice spread northward to reach the Yellow River Valley around 5000 B.C.T.

During this time the Yellow River Valley was ideal for agriculture. Light rainfall meant that the forest was thin and easy to clear, while annual river floods enriched the soil. Grain was stored in pits and ground into flour.

It is noteworthy that perhaps the most far-reaching development of the period which lasted from 8000 to 5000 B.C.T. was the establishment of farming villages in many parts of the world. However, even with farming, wild food remained a significant part of the human diet, and the hunter-gatherer way of life survived not only in areas where the land was not suited to agriculture—the arctic wastes and arid deserts—but even in regions where the land could have been cultivated, but was not. The permanent settlements that resulted from the adoption of farming led to the building of large communal projects, such as irrigation systems. These in turn created larger, complex communities—the forerunners of all later civilizations.

Europe

Village farmers began to replace food-gathering tribespeople in much of Greece. {See also 7000 B.C.T.}

Around 6000 B.C.T., farming in Europe was still restricted to Greece and the Balkans. 1,000 years later it had spread as far as Iberia, where remains of cultivated grains have been found at cave settlements such as Coveta de l'Or on the southern coast of Spain. In the Mediterranean, the concept of plant and animal domestication which formed the basis of the new economy,—passed from one community to the next, eventually reaching Portugal. In Central Europe, however, groups of colonizing farmers advanced westward along the valley of the river Danube to the Rhineland and the Paris basin. These pioneer farmers preferred to plant their crops in the lighter soils that flanked the rivers, growing them in small fields or garden plots close to their dwellings.

The earliest farmers of Central Europe lived in a forested environment and were able to build substantial timber houses up to 150 feet long. A framework of load-bearing posts provided the basic structure. The outer walls were of wattle and daub (interwoven twigs and sticks covered with clay), and the roof, steeply pitched to keep out rain and snow, was thatched with reeds or straw. Each longhouse accommodated one or more families, plus their livestock and grain stores.

Pottery-making spread with farming along the Danube and the Rhine. The earliest pottery vessels of Central Europe, known as *Bandkeramik*, were decorated with incised lines infilled with dots or cross-hatching. Such pottery was found from France to Hungary and the Ukraine.

At Lepenski Vir on the banks of the Danube in Serbia, a flourishing community of hunters, fishers, and gatherers, who had not yet adopted settled farming, developed a distinctive style of stone carving. Their artistry is best represented by the fish sculptures placed next to the hearths in their houses, which may be representations of a local river deity.

People settled the island of Crete.

By 6000 B.C.T., inhabitants of the Swiss lake regions had domesticated dogs and plow oxen.

Swiss lake dwellers collected wild flax (Linum usitatissimum) or cultivated it and used its strong fibers to make lines and nets for fishing (and for animal traps and ropes and cords for building construction and navigational purposes).

Swiss lake dwellers made bread of crushed cereal grains and kept dried apples and legumes (including peas) in the houses they built on stilts.

Australia

A fragment of sandstone found in deposits dating to before 6000 B.C.T. at the Ingaladdi rock shelter in the Northern Territory of Australia was engraved with bird tracks and parallel lines. Similar marks appear on the walls of this and other shelters like Yiwarlarlay, and may have been symbols used in Aboriginal hunting magic.

The Americas

The American agave began to be utilized.

The American agave, or maguey, blooms once in 10 to 30 years. It was formerly thought to flower only every 100 years, which explains why it is also known as the century plant. A tropical plant native to Mesoamerica, the American agave was put to a variety of uses from earliest times. An important source of food and drink (some species can be used to make intoxicating beverages), the American agave also provided a fibrous material for making cords and clothing in the colder highland regions of Mexico and Guatemala.

Throughout the northern Amazon region of South America, groups of people carved thousands of images into rock outcrops. Some showed animals and the weapons and tools used in hunting and fishing. Others showed simple renderings of the human form along with symbols that may relate to the natural environment.

In Santarem on the floodplain of the Amazon in Brazil, people from a fishing culture made decorated red-brown pottery. The remains they left were the oldest known pottery fragments in the Americas. {See also 7000 B.C.T.}

Squash was grown in Mexico.

The Chinchorro, an indigenous people who lived on the coastline of Chile and Peru, produced human mummies which survived to modern times.

It is theorized that the process of mummification was developed independently in South America and Egypt, suggesting considerable practicable knowledge of biology in very disparate areas of the world.

5900 B.C.T.

Asia

In Mesopotamia, the Ubaid culture began to build temples consisting of a single mud-brick room with an altar and an offering temple.

By about 5900 B.C.T., a culture known as Ubaid (named after the site of Tell al-Ubaid) was flourishing in southern Mesopotamia. 500 years later it had spread to the whole of Mesopotamia, replacing the Halaf culture, which had dominated the north. Eridu, one of the earliest Ubaid settlements, had a series of temples, each built on the remains of the last. The oldest one consisted of a single mud-brick room with an altar and an offering table.

5600 B.C.T.

Asia

A Great Flood occurred in Asia Minor.

Scientists have never found traces of Noah or his ark, but they have found traces of a Flood which could have been the inspiration for the Genesis story.

Seven thousand, six hundred years ago (around 5600 B.C.T.), the Mediterranean Sea, swollen by melted glaciers, breached a natural dam separating it from the freshwater lake known by geologists as the New Euxine Lake but which we know of today as the Black Sea.

The intrusion of the saltwater of the Mediterranean into the New Euxine Lake was in many respects much worse that anything described in Genesis. While in Genesis, the Flood lasted for less than a year ostensibly covering every living thing on Earth. At the New Euxine Lake, the flood was much longer and indeed continues to this day.

Every day for two years, ten cubic miles of sea water from the Mediterranean cut through a narrow channel now known as the Bosporus and plunged into the New Euxine Lake. The flow through the Bosporus was more than 200 times the flow which we see today going over the Niagara Falls. Indeed, each and every day for two years, the lake level rose six inches.

Additionally, with each and every day the water of the lake marched outwards another mile. This encroachment forced people and animals to flee or to drown. The saltwater of the Mediterranean killed freshwater fish and plants by the ton, inundating forests and villages and entire cities. Pestilence and death spread for miles around.

As the deluge filled the lake, it transformed it into a sea, and, in the process, created an ecosystem which is unique in all the world.

Around 15,000 years ago (around 13,000 B.C.T.) the sea level worldwide began to rise as glaciers melted at the end of the last ice age. When the melt began, the Black Sea—the New Euxine Lake—was a freshwater lake fed by rivers, among them those known today as the Danube, the Dnieper and the Don.

On the lake's southern edge, a 360 foot natural dam held back the waters of what is now the Mediterranean Sea. However, by 7,600 years ago (around 5,600 B.C.T.) the sea level rose to within 15 feet of the lip of the Bosporus. And then it flooded.

What probably began as a trickle pierced the Bosporus valley. But when the trickle reached the Black Sea, it began to gouge out a channel. Within 60 days what began as a trickle had turned into a river— a river unlike any other river that has been encountered by man.

The flow of water associated with this flood was a one-of-a-kind event which produced a one-of-a-kind result. The incoming salt water, denser than the fresh water it displaced, plunged straight to the bottom of the lake bed. As the seawater rose, the fresh water floated on top, and being less dense, stayed on top, flowing in from the northern rivers and out via the Bosporus.

This bathtub phenomenon repressed the natural heat exchange that causes water to circulate and reoxygenate in seas and lakes throughout the world. Trapped on the bottom, the creatures that lived in the original floodwater used up the original oxygen, then died. The entire bottom of the Black Sea became anoxic—became devoid of oxygen—and, in the process, became wholly devoid of life.

Today, while the top 450 feet of the Black Sea are constantly renewed by the riverwater and support a vigorous marine life, the bottom of the sea—the abyss—lies like a cold blanket thousands of feet deep.

The abyss of the Black Sea is likely to contain a treasure of archaeological materials, because whatever existed on the ancient shores of the New Euxine Lake or whatever was sunk while floating on the Black Sea is likely to be pristinely preserved at the cold, oxygen free, sterile waters of the sea depths.

The prospect of finding ancient wooden ships which used the Black Sea as a commercial waterway for civilizations from ancient Greece to Byzantium as well as the Ottoman Empire is a tantalizing prospect which may produce some history altering finds in the 21st century.

After all, Greek folklore tells of a certain Jason whose quest for the Golden Fleece is believed to have made him the first of the ancient Greeks to enter the Black Sea. Today, modern archaeologists, while traversing and plumbing the depths of that same Black Sea, may succeed in finding a modern Golden Fleece—the truth about the history of the Great Flood.

The Americas

The grain quinoa was grown in the Andean Highlands.

5508 B.C.T.

Europe

Five thousand, five hundred eight B.C.T. was designated as the Year of Creation by the Eastern Orthodox Church of Constantinople in the seventh century of the Christian calendar. This date would be relied upon by the Eastern Orthodox Church and by secular authorities in Russia until early in the 18th century of the Christian calendar.

According to Sextus Julius Africanus, 5508 B.C.T. (or 5507 B.C.T.) was the Year of Creation. Sextus Julius Africanus (fl. 3rd century C.C.) was an early Christian historian and traveler. He was born in Libya. Sextus Julius Africanus is best known for estimating the date of the creation of the world in his *Chronographiae,* a history of the world from the creation to 221 C.C. He set the creation at 5499 years before the birth of Jesus and dated Jesus' birth three years earlier than the usual reckoning.

Africanus' calculations were adopted by most of the Eastern churches. Today, only fragments of the *Chronographiae* are extant.

5500 B.C.T.

Africa

Fishing implements were common finds at early settlement sites close to the shallows of the Nile and East African lakes, which supported vast populations of catfish and other sluggish, bottom-dwelling fish. The settlers who lived by such waters developed barbed bone harpoons and points mounted on wooden shafts to spear the fish, which were then dried.

Hunter-gatherers living on the edges of the great rainforests of Central Africa did not need permanent dwellings, because they were constantly on the move in search of game and wild plant foods, and because there was ample timber and brush for temporary shelters. They built low structures using branches and leaves, often tied together with long fibers, to house a family and provide shelter from wind and rain. Vegetable fibers were woven into clothing and matting for bedding and screens.

Asia

Copper was smelted from malachite (copper carbonate) by artisans in Persia. The smelted copper that was produced became the first metal that could be drawn, molded, and shaped. However, the metal was too soft to hold an edge.

Dates were harvested in Southwest Asia.

The date palm played an important role in the life of the earliest farming communities in southern Mesopotamia. Every part of the palm was used: the nutritious fruits were easily stored and transported, while the trunk and fronds provided valuable building materials. The fibers were twisted to make string and rope, and the leaves woven into mats and baskets.

Pottery was developed in China.

The earliest pottery in China was crafted in fishing settlements along the southern coast. Creamy buff and brown bowls and large globular jars were made from a thick gritty clay. The surface of the vessels, except for the rim, was decorated with marks made by fiber cords or stone knives.

The adoption of a settled way of life in Europe and Asia was accompanied by an important innovation—the widespread production of pottery containers for functional purposes. The first pottery containers were made by a community of hunter-gatherers in Japan more than 12,000 years ago, but the technique did not spread. It was not until the 7th millennium B.C.T. that communities in Africa, the Middle East, Europe, and South Asia independently developed the technique of using fired clay to produce containers. The spread of farming techniques throughout Europe was accompanied by a variety of decorated pottery styles. Terra-cotta figurines, probably used in cults or rituals, were also made, while in Southwest Asia, human figures were sculpted from lime plaster.

Heavy and fragile, pottery containers were useful only to peoples who remained in one place for long periods of time. Pottery containers dating to around 7000 B.C.T. from hunting and fishing communities in the Nile Valley and the southern Sahara demonstrate that the people in these regions had adopted a relatively settled life. Other fishing communities thrived by lakes in the Rift Valley of Kenya and Tanzania.

The first inkling that minerals could be transformed by heat into something with different properties probably came indirectly, from pottery production—perhaps through experiments with painted decoration. Early potters used a variety of ground minerals as pigments to make paint for their pots. They may have been attracted to brightly colored copper ores such as malachite or azurite as a source of pigment, only to find that the material with which they painted their vessels produced, when fired, not a blue or green coloring, but a few shiny droplets of copper.

The early farmers of the North China Plain built semi-permanent settlements, moving on when they needed new land, and returning when the soil had regained its fertility. Their houses were round or square with walls of wattle and daub (interwoven twigs and sticks covered with clay), and thatched roofs made of layers of millet stalks, reeds, and clay supported on beams.

In China, pure nephrite, the only jade known at the time, was imported as early as the 6th millennium B.C.T. from Central Asia or Lake Baikal in Siberia by people living in northern Manchuria. This indicates the existence of highly developed societies able to trade and support skilled craftsmen. From the earliest times, jade was associated with ritual or sacrifice, and its qualities of purity, hardness, luminescence, and varying color symbolized ideal virtues. Being too hard to be cut even with steel, jade must be worked with abrasives. It appeared indestructible and was, therefore, linked with immortality. Jade objects were buried with the dead and were used in rituals as a means of communicating with the spirits.

The Americas

Plants were domesticated in Mexico.

Cultivation in the Americas began with one or two crops grown as an adjunct to hunting and gathering. In Mexico,

chilies, squash, and avocados were cultivated at seasonal campsites from around
5500 B.C.T., over 1,000 years before maize,
which was to become the most important
crop, came into regular cultivation. In large
areas of the Americas, hunting and gathering continued to provide the everyday
foods, with human communities adapting
to changes in the food supply. Thus, when
bison began to leave the western part of the
Great Plains of North America around
5000 B.C.T., human groups responded by
moving with them.

5490 B.C.T.

Asia

*Five thousand, four hundred ninety B.C.T.
was the year designated as the Year of Creation by early Syrian Christians.*

5400 B.C.T.

Asia

*During the Late Ubaid period in Mesopo-
tamia, mud-brick houses were built on a
tripartite plan, consisting of a large rectangular room in the center with rows of
smaller rooms on either side.*

Throughout Mesopotamia during the
Late Ubaid period (c.5400–4300 B.C.T.)
mud-brick houses were arranged in a tripartite plan. A large rectangular or cross-
shaped room ran the full width of the
house, with rows of smaller rooms on each
side.

Also during the Late Ubaid period in
Mesopotamia, baked clay figurines of
human forms were sometimes deposited in
graves. Although their heads appear reptil-
ian, this seems to have been a stylistic con-
vention rather than an attempt to portray
hybrid beings. There is no indication that
they were intended as images of deities, but
the presence of offerings in the graves suggests a belief in an afterlife.

5300 B.C.T.

Europe

*A well was built of wood in northwest Ger-
many at the site now known as Kuckhoven.
Because of local conditions, it was preserved
and became the oldest known wooden
structure.*

The Americas

*The avocado was grown in Mexico and
Central America.*

5200 B.C.T.

Africa

*Egyptians began to practice agriculture in
the lower Nile Valley. Thousands of years
after the Agricultural Revolution came to
other peoples in Southwest Asia.*

5000 B.C.T.

By 5000 B.C.T., the physical outline of
the world had reached its present general
form, and temperatures were as high as those
of today, if not higher. Hunting and gathering were still the mainstay of life in many
parts of the world, but farming villages had
existed in northern China, southwest Asia,
Europe, the Nile Valley, and the hill country
west of the Indus Valley for 1,000 years or
more. Agriculture was also important in
Central and South America. After 5000
B.C.T., a number of factors, including
changes in social life, organization of craft
production, caused farming villages in Mesopotamia, Egypt, and the Indus Valley region
to develop into more complex societies, cul-
minating in the birth of cities and, ultimately,
in the creation of states and empires.

Africa

*Lands bordering the Nile River began to
dry out. The Egyptians constructed dikes
and canals for irrigation and started to develop a civilization in North Africa.*

The Sahara was too dry to allow the establishment of villages and towns, but groups of hunters and cattle herders roamed the semiarid grasslands around the high central Saharan plateaus and those of the Sahel strip bordering the southern edge of the desert. On the plateaus, these nomadic groups continued to leave a record of their presence in rock paintings. In certain areas, notably the wind-sculpted rock formations of the Sefar region, the subjects of the paintings included not only herds of cattle, but also white-painted depictions of mystical and fantastic creatures, perhaps spirits or demons. Spirit-beings were also a common subject in the Australian figurative rock art that proliferated throughout that continent after the end of the last Ice Age.

Grain farming began in Egypt.

Wheat and barley were first cultivated in the eastern Sahara and the Nile Valley around 5000 B.C.T. The new food source soon assumed great importance along the Nile, where domesticated crops quickly became a staple. Distinctive grindstones were used to prepare grain. These had developed from earlier types of grindstones made for the processing of wild seeds.

During the Pre-dynastic period in Egypt (c.5000–3100 B.C.T.), early farming communities like that at Nekhen, known for its distinctive pottery, flourished on the edges of the Nile floodplain as far as the First Cataract, including the Faiyum Basin. These villages gradually came together into increasingly large confederations headed by local rulers. At the same time, trading activity up and down the Nile increased. One confederation of villages was centered in Hieraconpolis in Upper Egypt, whose rulers prospered from trade, possibly mining gold deposits in the Eastern Desert. In around 3250 B.C.T., the first walled towns were built at Hieraconpolis and Naqada. One of the rulers of this region, Narmer,

unified Upper and Lower Egypt into a single kingdom in around 3100 B.C.T., establishing a new capital at Memphis. This heralded the start of the Early Dynastic period (3100–2685 B.C.T.).

From around 5000 B.C.T., nomadic cattle herders began to range widely over the semi-arid grasslands of the Sahara, Sahel, and Nubia, grazing their herds over enormous areas. They lived with their herds in small camps of dome-shaped huts protected by a thorn fence to keep out lions. The huts were made with a light framework of saplings and thatched with long grass. They were never permanent dwellings and were made from whatever materials were at hand, since the herders were constantly on the move, rotating their herds from one grazing ground to another, and making sure they were watered regularly.

The Badarian people (c.5000–4500 B.C.T.) of the Nile Valley were known for their finely made, semi-circular polished bowls. Some are red or black, while others, fired with their rims buried in sand, are red with black rims. Many were decorated with ripples produced by dragging a comb over the surface of the soft clay, and most were also highly burnished to give a smooth, polished surface.

A clay figurine of a female deity with a birdlike face may be a forerunner of the vulture goddess Nekhbet, the protective deity of the Pre-dynastic (c.5000–3100 B.C.T.) peoples of Lower Egypt.

Egyptians mined copper ores and smelted them.

In Egypt, weapons and implements made from native copper were occasionally deposited in graves. {See also 6500 B.C.T.}

Asia

At Mehrgarh, in the hill country west of the Indus Valley, a number of innovations in cultivation occurred during this period. Western Asiatic emmer wheat was crossed with local goatsface grass to produce breadwheat, and Indian dwarf wheat was also cultivated. Other domesticated crops at Mehrgarh included dates. Evidence of cotton plants suggest the beginnings of textile production.

Asia

The Sumerians entered Mesopotamia and started a civilization that would introduce cuneiform writing to the region.

The Sumerian city of Ur was founded in Mesopotamia (Iraq).

Ur lies near the modern city of An Nasiriya in southern Iraq, several kilometers west of the present bed of the Euphrates. From the presence of sherds it can be assumed that Ur was settled during an early phase of the Ubaid Period (late sixth millennium B.C.T.). The earliest excavated levels were from somewhat later in the Ubaid Period, when Ur appears to have been little more than a marsh village. These remains were covered by a deposit of about 10 feet (3 meters) of clean, water laid silt, in which some early archaeologists saw the universal flood of Noah. This interpretation has been rejected because flood deposits at other Mesopotamian sites do not occur at the same place in the archaeological sequence, which would have to be the case if the Ur flood were of more than local significance.

By about 3000 B.C.T. (in the Jamdat Nasr period), Ur occupied about 37 acres and at its center were cone-decorated buildings, apparently temples.

During the following Early Dynastic Period, Ur became one of the wealthiest cities of Sumer, approaching its maximum extent of 124 acres in the mid-third millennium. Ur's wealth was largely due to its role as a harbor town at the head of the Persian Gulf. Extensive trade contacts are suggested by burial goods from its Early Dynastic cemetery that were made of raw materials from the Arabian Peninsula, Iran, India, and Afghanistan.

Among 2,000 more modest burials in this mid-third millennium cemetery, there were found sixteen larger interments, each consisting of a built tomb at the bottom of a deep pit. The elite of the city—apparently its rulers—were buried in these graves with their attendants, between six and eighty willing victims, in a ritual that is attested only here in Mesopotamia. These graves yielded some of the most remarkable treasures from Ur: a golden dagger with a gold-studded hilt of lapis lazuli, the sounding box of a musical instrument decorated with inlaid scenes of war and peace, and two gold and lapis statues depicting a male goat with his forelegs resting on the limbs of a tree.

Most of the sixteen tombs were found looted, but that of Puabi, called "queen" on the seal buried with her, was untouched. A woman in her forties, Puabi was interred with twenty-three retainers, surrounded by the finery that had been a part of her privileged life, including a lyre adorned with a golden bull's head, gold and silver vessels, jewelry of precious metals and semiprecious stones, and a spectacular diadem of golden leaves and rosettes.

One of the simpler burials, a wooden coffin in a large hole, turned out to contain numerous vessels and weapons of copper, gold, and electrum, along with hundreds of gold and lapis beads. Most remarkable was a golden helmet in the form of a wig, representing the finest workmanship in the cemetery. The name Meskalamdug was engraved on three vessels from the burial, a name that appears with the title "king" on a seal from a female burial elsewhere in the cemetery. Whether this rich interment was the king's burial remains one of the numerous unanswered questions about the cemetery and the unique practices attested there.

The cult of the moon god Nanna at Ur

was one of the most venerable and prestigious in Sumer. Therefore, Sargon of Agade (2334–2279 B.C.T.) installed his daughter Enheduanna as high priestess of Nanna as part of his program for the unification of southern Mesopotamia. For centuries thereafter, this office was filled by the daughter or sister of the king.

After the fall of Agade, the rulers of Ur reunited southern Mesopotamia into a tightly organized kingdom for about a century (2112–2004 B.C.T.) and extended Sumerian rule to the plains of Assyria and the mountains of Iran. The founder of this dynasty, Ur-Nammu, and his successors completely rebuilt the center of their capital. Their most impressive architectural legacy is the ziggurat of Nanna, a massive three-stage tower, 205 by 142 feet (63 by 43 meters) at its base.

In the residential districts of Ur dating to the first quarter of the second millennium, the houses that lined the winding, irregular streets typically had a central courtyard off which the other rooms opened. Many of the houses seem to have had a second story. Some had private shrines and family burial vaults as well.

Ur became a minor city politically after 2000 B.C.T., although later kings continued to renovate its temples. The sixth century B.C.T., king Nabonidus reconstructed the ziggurat for the last time and installed his daughter as high priestess. In the fourth century B.C.T., Ur ceased to exist, probably because the Euphrates changed course.

Villages began to cluster together in the Fertile Crescent region. However, a common need for water sometimes led to savage warfare.

Sailing ships were developed in Mesopotamia.

Axes in Mesopotamia were made with stone heads inserted between the cleft ends of a stick and bound into place.

Domesticated cattle became common in the valleys of the Tigris and Euphrates rivers, and villagers often cooperated to build primitive irrigation canals and ditches.

Early farmers in the delta of the Euphrates, in present day Iraq, constructed houses of reeds that had been lashed together.

By 5000 B.C.T., nuggets of metal, including gold, silver, and copper, were being used as ornaments and for trade in Southwest Asia.

The earliest metallic objects known, small jewels and tools, were directly carved or cut from pieces of metal found in the native state. Gold, copper, and some silver were the first metals used in this way, since they are the only metals commonly found in their elemental form. As early as 7,000 years ago (approximately 5000 B.C.T.), especially in Southwestern Asia and Afghanistan, people found these metals, conspicuous by their luster, in mountains and rivers.

The next stage in the development of metallurgy was when people found that metals would become softer and more malleable when heated and could thus be given different shapes. The first forged and cast objects looked like real metal objects, not like the earlier ones that resembled stone tools.

In the vicinity of native metals one often finds colored minerals, such as malachite, turquoise, and the deep-blue lapis lazuli. The next important discovery was that when heated in a charcoal fire, those minerals yield copper. These ores were much more abundant than native metals, and thus larger amounts of metals became available. The Egyptians exploited mines in the Sinai peninsula, and produced thousands of tons of copper during the pre-dynastic period (about 3200 B.C.T.).

Bronze was the most important result of early attempts of rendering copper more resistant by adding different metals.

Bronze, a mixture of 90 percent copper and 10 percent tin, can easily be cast, and its use had a large influence on several civilizations. Indeed, bronze was the first metal technology that changed society.

The general use of iron appeared around 1000 B.C.T., about 2000 years after the appearance of bronze. Iron was probably introduced by the Hittites of Anatolia. The processing of iron requires higher temperatures only achievable with bellows, and it is known that quench hardening of iron became known early during the iron age.

Iron was occasionally used before the iron age in ornaments and ceremonial weapons. It was then very expensive. The Greek poet Homer mentions iron as a precious metal on a par with gold in the days of ancient Greece.

The influence of iron on ancient societies was great. Weapons made with hardened iron were superior to bronze ones. Tools and weapons were manufactured only by forging because temperatures high enough to melt iron were only achieved in Europe in the 14th century of the Christian calendar. In China, cast iron, which has a higher carbon content and melts at a lower temperature, was known around the third century B.C.T.

The Indo-European protolanguage began to evolve.

The best known language family is the Indo-European family. The Indo-European family of languages includes most of the languages of Europe and northern India and several languages of the region in between. Indo-European has the following subfamilies: Italic, Germanic, Celtic, Greek, Baltic, Slavic, Armenian, Albanian, Indo-Iranian, and the extinct Hittite and Tocharian. Further subclassifications exist within subfamilies. English, for example, belongs to the Anglo-Frisian group of the West Germanic branch of the Germanic family. The closest relative of English is Frisian, which is spoken today only in parts of Germany and the Netherlands.

By comparing Old English with Modern English one finds that over a relatively brief time, a language changes to a point where the older version is barely discernible by a modern speaker of the language. Similarly, over time the relationship of one language subfamily to another becomes less and less discernible. Thus, today the relationship of English to other Indo-European languages such as Swedish (North Germanic), Latin (Italic) and Sanskrit (Indo-Iranian) has become progressively more distant.

Date palms were cultivated in India.

In China, ritual jade objects were fashioned with abrasives.

Rice was cultivated in the Yangtze Delta of China.

In China, rice cultivation was well established in the Yangtze River delta by 5000 B.C.T. Large quantities of cultivated rice and bone tilling tools have been found at Hemudu in the delta. Rice was ideally suited to Monsoon Asia, and with time became the staple crop throughout the area. As well as being highly nutritious, rice is self-fertilizing, producing up to three crops a year. Wet rice farming, so called because the rice is grown in submerged paddy fields, had a decisive influence on rural society. The work was labor-intensive, but the need to build dikes, dams, and canals for irrigation led to organized cooperation on a scale unknown in other types of agricultural or pastoral societies.

The production of pottery became increasingly specialized in China during this period. Finely decorated wares were made for ritual purposes such as funerary offerings. Household pots like the self-filling water jar reflect sophisticated technology, when submerged in running water by a rope pulled through the handles, it automatically adjusted its own angle, allowing continuous filling.

The Chinese believed that earthly well being depended on achieving harmony with the heavenly sphere. From earliest times, the four cardinal points were symbolized by mythical creatures with supernatural powers. To ensure an easy passage into the next world, the corpse of the deceased had to be properly aligned. In one grave of this period, the corpse was placed on a north-south axis flanked by a stone dragon (a symbol of the east) and a stone tiger (symbol of the west).

Europe

Copperworking began in southeastern Europe.

Metallurgy was developed in southeastern Europe soon after 5000 B.C.T. Copper and gold were the first metals to be worked, and soon copper was being cast in molds to produce beads, daggers, and heavy tools such as axes with a shafthole for a wooden handle. Deposits of these metals were easily accessible in rivers and streams which flowed from the Balkan Mountains. Once these were exhausted, new supplies were sought, and by 4500 B.C.T., mining for metals had begun.

In the temperate regions of Europe, the early agriculturalists were forest-dwellers who cleared the forest or selected areas of open ground to cultivate their crops. Rings were cut through the bark and into the wood of trees that were too large to fell, such as oak or elm. This killed the tree, allowing light to reach crops underneath. Smaller trees and scrub were cleared by hand, using polished axes of flint or specially selected hard stone from upland regions such at the Alps and the English Lake District. These were some distance from the prime lowland farming areas, and a lively trade in axes developed from uplands to lowlands. In addition to its utilitarian role in forest clearance and woodworking, the axe became an important status symbol, and many examples were carefully finished to serve as attractive prestige goods.

The early farmers of western Europe developed a distinctive burial tradition involving the construction of megalithic (large standing stone) or dry-stone chambered tombs covered by a mound. The most famous of these are the passage graves, where a burial chamber within the mound was reached by a passage, allowing other corpses to be interred or bones from earlier burials to be removed, possibly for ceremonies outside the tomb.

Stone was used to construct buildings in Guernsey, an island in the English channel.

Influenced by the religious practices of Southwest Asia, baked clay fertility goddesses began to appear in the Balkans.

Agricultural peoples inhabited the plains of southeastern Europe.

The horse was domesticated in the Ukraine.

A cave painting in Zalavroug, near the White Sea (a large bay of the Arctic Ocean in Russia near Finland), depicted people walking on planks attached to their feet, an early form of skis.

Australia

The large, shady rock shelter at Garnawala in the Northern Territory of Australia was used by family groups who camped there during the wet season and decorated the walls with paintings of ancestors from the mythical past. The dry interior and soft earth floor made it ideal for use as sleeping quarters. Many stone tools used for chopping, cutting, scraping, and engraving were manufactured just outside the shelter.

The Americas

A period of reduced rainfall and warmer temperatures, which began before 5000 B.C.T., dominated much of the Great Plains of North America for the following 3,000 years. Grazing resources for bison declined and the herds moved eastward. Hunters dependent on bison for their survival were forced to follow the herds, leaving large regions thinly populated. The close relationship between humans and bison characterized life on the Great Plains for thousands of years, perhaps becoming even more intense after the introduction of the horse in the 1600s.

The colonization of the Caribbean islands began between 5000 B.C.T. and 4000 B.C.T. Settlers probably came from the Yucatan peninsula, crossing the sea in dug-out canoes. Stone tools at the Levisa rock shelter in Cuba and the Barrera-Mordan site in the Dominican Republic indicate the presence of a hunter-gatherer society, but there is no evidence of permanent architecture from this period. Some Caribbean settlers used a wide variety of stone tools called Casimiran after one find site. Such tools have only been found on the larger of the Greater Antilles (Cuba, Jamaica, Hispaniola, and Puerto Rico).

Corn (maize) and common beans grew under cultivation in the Western Hemisphere.

Avocados were grown in Mexico.

Cotton was grown in Mexico.

The llama and alpaca were domesticated in Peru.

4500 B.C.T.

Africa

The Egyptians mined copper ores and smelted them.

From 4500 to 3000 B.C.T., a flare for decoration on pottery appeared in Egypt. Predynastic vessels bore incised geometric designs, molded hippopotamuses and crocodiles, and painted motifs such as oared boats, ostriches, and dancers. Pottery was plentiful all over Egypt, and changes in its style through time give essential clues for dating ancient sites and artifacts.

Asia

The Chalcolithic era began. This era saw the early stages of urbanization in Southwestern Asia.

A material now known as "Egyptian faience," essentially an imitation lapis lazuli, was made in Mesopotamia by covering the surface of a talc stone or soapstone with a powder made from a copper ore such as azurite or malachite and then heating the combination to a high temperature. The result is a blue-coated glass. The faience was used for the manufacture of beads and other small ornaments. Later the talc substrate was replaced with a material made by fusing quartz sand and soda. Perhaps, the first artificial substance every made by humans.

Archaeological evidence suggests trade between Mesopotamia and port regions on the Indian Ocean. While this could have been overland trade, it seems more likely to have been conducted in boats.

Europe

Stone was used to construct buildings in Guernsey, an island in the English Channel.

Megalith tombs appeared in western Europe.

Substantial chamber tombs were built by agricultural communities in northern and western Europe around 4500 B.C.T. Bodies were placed together in the chambers, indicating that the tombs were designed as communal burial places, and the dynamics of the work required for tomb construction suggest increasing social organization. The most elaborate, such as Newgrange in Ireland, were decorated with complex designs engraved on the stones of the chamber or passage that led to it, or on the curb around the mound.

The Americas

The earliest cultivation of maize occurred in Mexico between 4500 and 3500 B.C.T. The domesticated plant was derived from teosinte, a native wild grass. Numerous and widespread archaeological finds indicate that several varieties of maize were experimented with and improved at this time throughout Mesoamerica.

Hunter-gatherers in northeastern California built small clusters of semi-subterranean dwellings, or pithouses, each with a single room and hearth. The superstructure consisted of a framework of pole covered with brush and a layer of soil.

The rivers of northwestern North America were fished intensively. Fishermen caught salmon and other migrating fish in gill nets (nets suspended vertically in the water) or speared them from platforms above rapids. River pebbles were chipped so that they could be more easily bound to the gill nets to weigh them down.

4400 B.C.T.

Asia

The simple tokens that had been used for keeping numerical records from about 8000 B.C.T. onward were first supplemented by complex tokens that had marks on them or that were in new and varied shapes. The earlier unmarked tokens were almost all simple geometric shapes or representations of jars or animals. {See also 8000 B.C.T.}

The Americas

The guinea pig was domesticated for food in Peru.

4350 B.C.T.

Europe

Around 4350 B.C.T., domesticated horses provided parts of Europe with a new source of power for transportation and agriculture.

4300 B.C.T.

Africa

In Egypt, the earliest known village culture appeared in the Fayyum area of the Nile Delta.

Asia

In Mesopotamia, during the Uruk period, elaborately decorated temples, raised on platforms, were built following the tripartite plan of houses of the Late Ubaid period. {See 5400 B.C.T.}

In Mesopotamia, during the Uruk period (c.4300–3100 B.C.T.) temples often followed the tripartite plan of houses from the Late Ubaid period (c.5400–4300 B.C.T.), but with much more elaborate wall decoration. The temples had complicated buttresses and niches and were raised on platforms. The labor invested in their construction and maintenance suggests that religion was a powerful force in the organization of society.

Although, in Mesopotamia, farming communities grew increasingly complex during the Late Ubaid period (c.5400–4300 B.C.T.), so called after the site of Tell al-Ubaid in southern Mesopotamia, the real urban revolution occurred during the Uruk period (c. 4300–3100 B.C.T.), named after Uruk, one of the first (perhaps the very first) city-states in Mesopotamia. The growth of this and other city-states was made possible by the exploitation of the natural fertility of the Mesopotamian Plain, larger areas of which were gradually brought into cultivation with more extensive canal systems. These canal systems transported water to the fields from the Tigris and Euphrates rivers. Tens of thousands of city-dwellers could then be supported on the abundant grain yields. The Mesopotamian Plain was deficient in many raw materials, however, including timber for building, hard stone for tools and weapons, and metals. These had to be imported from the upland regions of Lebanon, southern Anatolia in modern Turkey, and the western edge of the Iranian plateau. Extensive trading networks were established to carry these materials to the emerging Mesopotamian cities. Among the cities themselves, a system of accounting was developed to administer the lively trade in food and products, and this led to the invention of a pictographic system of writing around 3300 B.C.T.

Mass production was another development, and everyday objects such as beveled-rim bowls were made in large numbers to a highly standardized pattern. Temples played a major role in city life, acting as economic as well as religious institutions. Built of mud brick and colorfully decorated, they were raised on platforms that overlooked the cities, symbolizing the protective role of the deity or deities specific to each city.

Developments in Mesopotamia were paralleled in other parts of the world, where ample natural resources fueled population growth and the consequent development of modest farming villages into walled towns and cities. This was especially true in the Nile Valley, where farming settlements first arose after the adoption of Middle Eastern wheat and barley around 5000 B.C.T., and in the hill country west of the Indus Valley.

Europe

Oak canoes were used on the Seine at what is now Paris, France. Workers discovered three such canoes, the oldest wooden boats ever found in Europe, while digging foundations for a new building in Paris in 1992, the largest of the canoes was nearly 5 meters (16 feet) long. {See also 7500 B.C.T.}

The Americas

Cotton cultivation began in Mexico.

There were two species of domesticated cotton in the Americas, each with a different origin. One, *Gossypium hirsutum*, was domesticated in the Tehuacan Valley, Mexico, by 4300 B.C.T., and was later traded north into southwestern North America. The other, *Gossypium barbadense*, was domesticated in Peru and Ecuador between 3300–3100 B.C.T.

4200 B.C.T.

Africa

It is theorized that as early as 4200 B.C.T., Egyptians developed the first known calendar with a 365 day year broken into twelve thirty day months plus five days of festivals. This Egyptian calendar became the basis for the Roman and modern Gregorian calendars.

The first quantity that people could measure with any degree of accuracy, and on which all people could agree, was time, although only in fairly large units of time. Large amounts of time can be easily measured because the universe itself supplies "clockwork" in the daily and annual motion of the Earth and the moon. Even so, the measurement of time was not easy to work out. A day is one revolution of the Earth around its axis; a month is from one new moon to the next; but it is not so easy to measure a year. Even the day is not as easy to measure as it seems. It took a while to learn to measure the day from one noon to the next (noon is when the sun reaches its highest point in the sky).

Scientists believe that the ancient Egyptians were the first to establish a good length for the year, possibly because the Nile floods around the same time each year. This flooding generally coincides with the helical rising of the star Sirius,— when Sirius rises at about the same time as the sun. Although there are 365 days between such risings, the year is actually, 5 hours, 48 minutes, and 46 seconds long, or about a quarter of a day longer than 365 days.

The Egyptian calendar had 12 months with 30 days and a five (5) day festival. The five day festival started with the day that Sirius, the Dog Star, rose in line with the sun in the morning. The Egyptian calendar was possibly instituted (from astronomical evidence only) as early as 4241 B.C.T.

The Egyptian calendar is known to have accurately matched the seasons with dates in 139 C.C. Because the year is not exactly 365 days, the Egyptian calendar gradually went into and out of alignment with the seasons with a period of 1455 years. Knowing this, astronomers have speculated that the year of 365 days was instituted by either 4228 B.C.T. or 2773 B.C.T.

Hellenic astronomers added the missing quarter day to the Egyptian calendar by adding an extra (leap) day every four years, but most people ignored it. The calendar with a leap day was finally adopted by the Romans under Julius Caesar in 46 B.C.T. Since then, the calendar has had one major modification, when Pope Gregory, in 1582, on the advice of astronomers, dropped the leap day in years that end in two zeros.

Europe

The Danish village of Koln-Lindenthal, thought to be a typical northern European community of its time, was rebuilt for the last time around 4200 B.C.T. However, in this last reconstruction, it was, for the first time, constructed with a tall palisade and earth wall around it. Koln-Lindenthal was settled and abandoned at least seven times over a period of 370 years.

4004 B.C.T.

In 1650 C.C., the Irish theologian James Ussher, would calculate that Creation occurred on Sunday, October 23 of the year 4004 B.C.T. {**See Part Two: Scriptures: A Protestant Perspective.**}

THE USSHER CHRONOLOGY

The Ussher Chronology is based upon a history written by the Irish theologian James Ussher around 1650 C.C. While Ussher's chronology was considered for centuries to be an accurate and factual history, today the vast majority of historians and theologians consider Ussher's Chronology to be chronologically inaccurate and to be factually deficient. In this book, the Ussher Chronology is being used only for discussion and comparison purposes. Accordingly, the dates associated with the Ussher Chronology should not be relied upon as fact.

Nevertheless, because the "creation" date given by Bishop Ussher is the date which was long given for the beginning of creation, it seems appropriate at this point in our narrative to break from the secular perspective of creation and the ascent of man to present the scriptural perspectives. Accordingly, the scriptural perspectives of creation, the origin of life on earth, and the ascent of man follow.

PART TWO.
THE SCRIPTURES

A Jewish Perspective

THE TANAKH

In the world of Judaism, the Scriptures are known as the Tanakh. The title Tanakh is not really a word but an acronym "TNK." The acronym "TNK" consists of the first letters of the Hebrew names for the three principal parts of the Jewish Scriptures. The acronym consists of the first letters of the Hebrew words *Torah*, *Nevi'im*, and *Kethuvim*. *Torah* means the "Law" and the books to which it refers are also known as the "Pentateuch." *Nevi'im* means the "Prophets," and *Kethuvim* means the "Writings."

The *Torah*—the Pentateuch—is also commonly known as the Five Books of Moses since it comprises the books of Genesis, Exodus, Leviticus, Numbers and Deuteronomy. The *Nevi'im* (*Nebi'im*) includes several of the historical books (Joshua, Judges, I Samuel, II Samuel, I Kings, and II Kings), the three Major Prophets (Isaiah, Jeremiah, and Ezekiel), and the twelve Minor Prophets (Hosea, Joel, Amos, Obadiah, Jonah, Micah, Nahum, Habakkuk, Zephaniah, Haggai, Zechariah, and Malachi). The *Kethuvim* (*Ketubim*) consists of Psalms, Proverbs, Job, the Song of Songs, Ruth, Lamentations, Ecclesiastes, Esther, Daniel, Ezra, Nehemiah, I Chronicles, and II Chronicles.

It is notable that the sequence of the three segments of the Jewish "Bible" as set forth above differs significantly from the sequence in Christian Bibles. It is also notable that the use of the word "Scriptures" to describe the Tanakh is an accurate way to speak about what is in fact a collection of books, not a single book. Such a description is clear also from the origin of our term "Bible."

The word "Bible" comes from the Greek word *biblia* which means "books." However, Latin language users eventually construed the word as singular, and ultimately so did the users of the English language.

For Jews the Tanakh *is* the Bible. However, for Christians, the Tanakh is only the first, albeit the larger, portion of the Bible, identified as the "Old Testament." While for Muslims, the Tanakh is essentially a foundational document which was later clarified by the Qur'an.

The Tanakh covers many millennia of the human experience beginning with the creation of heaven and earth. The writing of the books of the Tanakh itself took something over a millennium. Most of the books of the Hebrew Scriptures bear the names of the writers to whom they have traditionally been ascribed—Isaiah, Solomon, or Nehemiah. In the case of the Book of Psalms, there are authors given for some individual psalms, such as Moses for Psalm 90 and above all King David for many of them, but no authors for others. By no means do all of the books carry any such identification: the historical narratives of Joshua, Judges, I Samuel, II Samuel, I Kings, II Kings, I Chronicles and II Chronicles are all anonymous. In some instances, most notably that of the Torah itself, the author's name does not appear in the body of the text but rather in the superscription—a superscription which may have been added later. In modern times, the question of authorship has engaged scholars, with various candidates being proposed for such anonymous works as the Book of Job. But it has been characteristic of biblical scholarship since the Enlightenment of the 1700s that all the traditional ascriptions of authorship have come under critical scrutiny. Indeed, the history of modern biblical criticism among both Jews and Christians in the seventeenth and eighteenth centuries may be said to have begun with the re-examination of the Mosaic authorship of the Torah, which most scholars today would regard as a composite work—the outcome of processes of compilation and revision that went on long after the time of Moses.

For the most part, the text of the Tanakh is written in Hebrew (with a smattering of Aramaic). Practically speaking, the Tanakh is the most important body of ancient Hebrew literature. Although it is, of course, impossible to pronounce any language without vowels or their equivalents, the authoritative Hebrew text itself consists only of consonants. Novices in the study of the Tanakh text learned, as they still do, which vowels to supply where; and around the end of the fifth century of the Christian calendar, a group of biblical scholars known as "Masoretes" provided a system of vowels written below the Hebrew consonants, resulting in what is now called the Masoretic Text.

The editorial work of the Masoretes stood in a long succession of scribes and scholars who copied and transmitted the sacred text and sometimes even restored it when it had suffered accidental neglect or deliberate destruction {see 2 Chronicles 34:14–18[1]}.

The discovery of the Dead Sea Scrolls has made available for the first time significant portions of the Hebrew Bible that antedate the work of the Masoretes by centuries and has made possible the clarification and correction of various problematical readings. Hebrew is only one of the ancient Semitic languages, and references to biblical words that appear in Ugaritic, Arabic, or other related languages may frequently illuminate individual passages of the Tanakh. Additionally, various ancient translations of the Tanakh have served as a source for critical enlightenment and conjecture concerning what the "unblemished" original might have been.

The three divisions of the Tanakh— the Torah, Nevi'im, and Kethuvim—correspond to the successive stages of the process by which the several books of the Jewish Scriptures acquired standing as a "canon." As the Five Books of Moses, the

---

[1] 2 Chronicles 34:14–18 reads:

> *14 As they took out the silver that had been brought to the House of the LORD, the priest Hilkiah found a scroll of the LORD's Teaching given by Moses. 15 Hilkiah spoke up and said to the scribe Shaphan, "I have found a scroll of the Teaching in the House of the LORD"; and Hilkiah gave the scroll to Shaphan. 16 Shaphan brought the scroll to the king and also reported to the king, "All that was entrusted to your servants is being done; 17 they have melted down the silver that was found in the House of the LORD and delivered it to those who were in charge, to the overseers." 18 The scribe Shaphan also told the king, "The priest Hilkiah has given me a scroll"; and Shaphan read from it to the king.*

Torah commanded the earliest, the highest, and the most universal respect, having evolved through the processes of editing and compiling. The Torah achieved its status as the foundation of the faith and life of the people of Israel by five centuries or so before the time of Jesus of Nazareth. The Torah held that status, moreover, in communities such as that of the Samaritans, who did not extend recognition to the other component parts of the Tanakh.

The assembling of the books of the Prophets (*Nevi'im*), or at any rate of many of them, into an authoritative collection seems to have been going on at the same time as the fixing of the Torah, but scholars tend to date the conclusion of the process after the definition of the Torah, with the rejection of their canonicity by the Samaritans being one argument in favor of a somewhat later date.

As the title Writings (*Kethuvim*) suggests, and as the character of the roster of books in this category confirms, these were works that seemed not to belong to either of the first two categories—works such as the Book of Psalms (Hebrew *Sefer Tehillim*—"book of praises"). In at least some cases, certain Kethuvim books seemed so problematic as perhaps not to belong in Scripture at all: for instance, the Book of Esther, in which the word "God" does not appear; Ecclesiates, which has a pervasive pessimism, despite the ascription to King Solomon but which does not seem to fit the tone of biblical religion; and, also attributed to Solomon, the Song of Songs, with its lush and erotic imagery. But eventually (traditionally, it was believed to have been around the end of the first century C.C.) all the books now identified as *Kethuvim* were officially accepted by normative Judaism.

The spiritual authority of the Tanakh is not confined to the first segment, but belongs directly also to the second as "Old Testament" and contributes to the third.

Ultimately, from a biblical perspective, Abraham is "the father of believers" and Moses is the bearer of divine revelation for Judaism in all its branches, for Christianity in all its denominations, and for Islam in all its varieties.

THE TORAH

The word "Torah" is the Hebrew term used for the first five books of Moses—the Pentateuch. The Book of Genesis is the first of these five books, as the Torah is the first part of the Bible. It is important for non–Jews and especially for Christians to understand that the term "Old Testament" is not used by Jews since the books which Christians call the "New Testament" are not recognized as such by Jews. Thus, when the word "Bible" is used amongst Jews and within the context of the following discussion, the term refers to the Hebrew Bible—a book which does not include Christian (New Testament) Scriptures.

Most modern Jewish scholars forward the premise that the Torah is a book which had its origin in the hearts and minds of the Jewish people. This thesis is in stark contrast to the belief held by many orthodox Jews that the Torah is "the word of God," given by direct inspiration by God to Moses. Some of the orthodox Jews may agree that the Torah in being transmitted from generation to generation may have been marred by certain scribal errors. Nevertheless, the orthodox insist that the Torah, as a whole, is the word of God and not of man.

From an orthodox perspective, the Torah being the word of God is indisputable fact. Thus, if the Torah says that "God created," then this is a fact because, by definition, the word of God is truth itself. Additionally, the orthodox perspective maintains that the Torah, being given by God, must carry meaning in every word and that not even one letter can be superfluous.

One may not understand everything, but that is a human shortcoming. If modern scientific knowledge appears to contradict the biblical word, then either our present day science will prove to be in error or we, being limited human beings, simply do not understand the Bible properly. This is the basic premise of not only Orthodox Judaism but also of fundamentalist Christianity and many of the commentators of the past.

Of course, most modern commentators do not share this perspective. Most modern commentators opine that the Torah—and indeed, the entire Bible—is the product of man and not necessarily of God. However, for such modern commentators two key questions arise: (1) Does God have anything to do with the Torah? and (2) How is the Torah different from any other significant literature of the past?

From the perspective of the modern commentators, while God is not perceived to be the author of the Torah in the fundamentalist sense, the Torah is a book about humanity's understanding of and experience with God. This understanding has varied over the centuries as have human experiences. Since the Torah tradition was at first repeated by word of mouth, and only after many generations set down in writing, the final text testifies to divergent ideas about God and the people. These divergent ideas stand side by side in the book and tell us of the Jewish ancestors' changing and developing beliefs.

In this sense, then, the Torah is not by God but rather is by a people. While individual authors had a hand in its composition, the "People of the Book" made the Torah their own and impressed their character upon it. In a very real sense, the Torah is often more a reflection of the Jewish people than it is a reflection of the word of God.

Ultimately, the Torah is ancient Israel's distinctive record of its search for God. The Torah attempts to record the meeting of the human and the Divine, and in doing so it often becomes infused with a presence which is of God.

As previously stated, contemporary scholars agree that God is not the author of the Torah but that the Jewish people are. Nevertheless, through the Jews' efforts to document their search for God, they found God and God's voice can still be heard through the scriptures which the Jews left behind.

While acknowledging that God's voice can be heard in the words of the Torah, the modern scholar is also conscious of the need not to abandon intellectual discernment when reading the Torah text. In reading the Torah, it is important not to treat all legend as fact. The modern scholar must especially take care to not gloss over those texts which represent God in anthropomorphic terms. Additionally, it must be warned that despite the enormous and imaginative scholarship which has been lavished on the Torah, the honest modern scholar must acknowledge that we still do not know how to interpret a word, or passage, and we still do not fully understand the original context in which a passage may appear.

For many of the scholars who perceive that the Torah is a people's search for and meeting with God, the Torah is deemed to be different from other literature of the past. The Jewish search for God and the meeting with God provide a record which by its very nature has something to say about the essentials of human existence. However, even for those who see the Torah only as a record of human quest, there is an aspect to the Torah which makes it special. For over 2500 years, the Torah has been the keystone of Jewish life, the starting point of Christendom, and the background of Islam. As such, the Torah has played and continues to play a significant role in the world. Western people especially are what they are in part because of the Torah. After all, it is what the Torah actually said or meant to say, along with what it was believed to have said and to have meant, that has become the foundation of what most Westerners point to as their Judeo-Christian heritage.

In reading the Torah, one should keep in mind that what the Torah authors said in their own time to their own contemporaries within their own intellectual framework may be entirely different from what later generations, including our own, would say about the same text. Accordingly, not everything that was of relevance in the past is of relevance today, while what may have seemed trivial in the past is today perceived as inspired prophecy. For example, the story of Babel was for many years seen as a parable of human arrogance. However, today the story of Babel has been given an added significance as being a warning about the dehumanizing effects of urban life.

The intellectual beauty of the Torah, and the Christian Bible and the Qur'an is that these great books are remarkably flexible documents. With regards to the Torah, one of its attractions is its open-endedness—its ability to raise issues without providing single answers that close the door to further inquiry. Thus, like a chameleon, portions of the Torah take on a different shade of significance from one generation to the next, thereby maintaining its living relevance throughout the passage of time.

Many contemporary readers shy away from a study of the Bible because they have been exposed to a method of biblical interpretation which understands the biblical text in a literal way. Thus, if Genesis says that God created woman out of the rib of man, or tells of a serpent speaking, or of ancient men living several hundred years, the literalist (fundamentalist) interprets the story to mean precisely what the words convey. Often this literal application reaches down to individual words and phrases and often such an application can lead to grave misconceptions.

It is important to note that even the ancient Jewish wise men—men who believed that the Torah was a divinely authored book—even these men did not take the text of the Torah in a literal sense. The sages of ancient Israel while taking the scriptures seriously, always looked behind the flat literal meaning. The ancient Jewish sages realized that the Torah incorporated numerous subtle metaphors and allusions. They also recognized that the Torah used word plays and other literary devices, that it sometimes spoke satirically rather than literally, and that its poetry could not be subjected to a simple literal approach. The Jewish sages agreed without embarrassment that one could disagree on what the Torah meant. Unfortunately, many modern day literalists (fundamentalists) are either ignorant of, have forgotten, or have chosen to disregard the wisdom of the ancient Jewish sages.

The Torah contains a great variety of material. Laws, narratives, history, folktales, songs, proverbial sayings, poetry, and especially, in the early parts of Genesis, creation stories and cultural folklore. From an historical perspective, it is important to note that what usually passes for history is not an accurate scientific recording of events but an interpretation of such events—assuming, of course, that one knows what the event "really" was.

It is generally believed that the best of modern historians is an interpreter, selective summarizer, commentator, and often philosopher who brings a point of view to the material. To a certain extent, this is what the writers of the Torah attempted to do. While the Torah admittedly contains material which consists of creation stories and folktales of questionable historical accuracy, nevertheless, these stories and folktales ultimately became incorporated into the consciousness of the Jewish people. After all, what a people believe their past to be often assumes a dynamism of its own and, whether true or not, becomes part of the people's psyche. Thus, while Abraham's vision of a God who promised Abraham the land of Canaan may not qualify as an historic "fact," this Torah tradition became an "accepted idealized reality" by generations of Abraham's descendants and, for them and the Jewish people as a whole, Abraham's vision validated the Jewish seizure and possession of the land.

In more contemporary times, one finds the adoption of an "accepted idealized reality" as being one of the principle foundations of American society. This can most readily be seen by the selective way in which Americans traditionally treat the lives of the old frontiersmen. For most of the 1900s, the frontiersmen of the 1800s were presented primarily as enterprising pioneers, courageous people whose love of independence was indelibly stamped on the nation they helped to build. Such a depiction is, of course, highly selective and even distorted. This "accepted idealized reality" ignores the fact that the pioneers independence was often purchased by the devastation of indigenous cultures which pre-existed on the frontier. This "accepted idealized reality" says little about the desire of the frontiersmen to get rich quickly or that the motivation for moving west was precipitated by the pioneers repeated failures in the east. No, for most of the 1900s, these negative aspects were rarely mentioned with regards to the "accepted idealized reality" of Americans, and subsequently, the resulting admiration of the values associated with the "accepted idealized reality" came to shape and be a part of the psychology of the nation even though the "accepted idealized reality" was not reality at all.

So to was this the case with the Torah.

The Torah may be said to mirror the collective "accepted idealized reality" of the Jewish people and, over the passage of centuries, the Torah became a source of "truth" for the Children of Abraham even though sometimes this "truth" was false. Thus, any reader of the Torah would do well to keep in mind that the Torah speaks not necessarily of "history" but rather of an "accepted idealized reality" which has come to be an integral part of Jewish heritage and, to a lesser extent, a part of the heritage of Christians and Muslims as well.

THE TORAH AUTHORS

Many fundamentalists contend that Moses was the sole author of the first five books of the Torah. However, doubts that the Torah was a book set down by one author began to develop centuries ago. By the nineteenth century, serious Bible scholars had concluded that the Torah had been written not by one person but by many.

Today the theory which predominates is called the Documentary Hypothesis. In substance, the Documentary Hypothesis states that there are four major sources or documents (called J, E, P, and D). The combination of these four sources, by the fifth century B.C.T., had resulted in the creation of a single source, the Torah. The Torah was declared a sacred text by official canonization around the year 400 C.C.

"J" is the name given by biblical critics to the author who used the divine name YHWH and probably lived in the Southern Kingdom some time after the death of Solomon. Scholars attribute most of Genesis to "J."

"E" uses the divine name of Elohim and is considered to be the author of the segments of Genesis dealing with the binding of Isaac (see Genesis 22) and other passages of Genesis, as well as much in Exodus and Numbers. It was "E" who was most likely a northern contemporary of "J."

"D" is the author of Deuteronomy. Deuteronomy is said to be the book found by King Josiah in 621 B.C.T. "D" is also reputed to be the author of Genesis 14.

"P" is the author of the first chapter of Genesis, the Book of Leviticus, and other sections characterized by interest in genealogies and priesthood.

Most contemporary scholars believe that the Torah was composed between 950 B.C.T. to 450 B.C.T. This time period covers the period of Jewish history from the days of the divided kingdoms of Israel and Judah to the destruction of the kingdoms and the time of the exile and return of the Jews. If the scholars are correct, then it is obvious that Moses, who lived in the 1200s B.C.T., had nothing to do with the writing of the complete Torah. Moses' name was attached to the Torah as its author only at the time of the Torah's canonization.

It has been theorized that the first four books of the Torah (Genesis, Exodus, Leviticus, Numbers) originally formed a four part unit called the Tetrateuch, while Deuteronomy, Joshua, Judges, Samuel, and Kings constituted another separate unit. It is also theorized that the major sources from which the Tetrateuch was formed were J, E, and P.

While it is generally accepted that different sources comprise, and different authors composed, the Torah, it is also accepted that various strands of tradition are very ancient—some of them are even older than the time of Moses while others are assignable to him. These strands of tradition were transmitted for many centuries by word of mouth. As the centuries wore on, all of these strands coalesced in popular telling, and in time, probably through the efforts of a literary genius of unknown name, these strands became a single story with many facets. Variants of the same story and even contradictions were left untouched because one did not tamper with sacred memories and also because the ancient era did not demand a single truth but rather that together both sides of the account represented the truth. Thus, if in one place it says that Israel spent 400 years in Egypt and in another 430, the ancient reader was satisfied that both 400 and 430 meant a long, long time.

Readers of the Torah are usually unaware that what they are reading is not "the" original version of the manuscript and that the translation they use is actually a kind of commentary on the Hebrew text which it attempts to render.

There is no original manuscript available which was written by any of the authors of the Bible. The oldest extant parchment scroll of the Torah dates from about 900 C.C. This is approximately 1,300 years after the scroll text's time of composition. Quite naturally, much happens to a text in the course of oral transmission and copying by hand, and one must not be astonished that a number of variants and versions arose. It is a great tribute to the care and devotion which were lavished on the text that the variants are relatively minor and that the scribal corruptions appear to be relatively few.

There are a number of versions of the Torah. The version employed for the Jewish Perspective segment of this book uses the Masoretic version. The Masoretes were so called because they transmitted the *Masorah*, the textural traditions. The Masoretes were scholars who over the centuries attempted to ascertain and preserve the best text. One of these versions, produced in Tiberias in the tenth century of the Christian calendar, found general acceptance and is the standard Hebrew text used in the synagogues of today.

With regards to the Hebrew language, it must be noted that languages, even sacred languages, have a history. Languages are born and they die. The Hebrew of the

Torah (and of the Tanakh) lived on as a language of worship and of scholarship, but in everyday life it was largely displaced, in Palestine, especially by Aramaic. Because the knowledge of classical Hebrew diminished or disappeared among many Jews after they returned from the Babylonian exile, the need for translations arose. Over the passage of time, there appeared translations in Aramaic (Targum) which was the popular language of post-exilic Jews, Greek (the Septuagint), Latin (the Vulgate), Syriac (the Peshitta), Arabic, and in modern times in every written language of man. The ancient translations often give the scholar significant clues about the original form in which they were translated, for there are differences between them. However, what is even more important is to recognize that every translator interprets the original text and from these interpretations variations will arise.

The nature of the variations becomes particularly apparent when one follows modern translations. For instance, there are great differences between the famous and beloved English King James Version (published in 1611) and later renditions such as the American version, or the German Luther Bible. Many of these differences are stylistic since the language of translation has itself undergone vast changes; others are due to new insights into the philology of ancient times and the political, social, and economic circumstances to which the text refers.

THE PEOPLE OF THE TORAH

The Torah was always the possession of the Jewish people. It was addressed to the entire people, who were to learn the contents of the Torah and teach them diligently to their children. A number of biblical passages, such as Psalms 19 and 119, testify to the love which the Torah evoked amongst the Jews and the widespread concern of the Jewish people with its teachings.

The Book of Nehemiah (chapters 8–10) reports a public reading of the Torah in Jerusalem, probably in the year 444 B.C.T. This reading was conducted by Ezra the Scribe, with the aid of assistants who were to make sure that all those present heard and understood what was read to them. A few days later, the entire people entered into a solemn undertaking to obey the Torah. It was this agreement which was ratified in writing by Jewish leaders. From the traditional standpoint, this incident was a reaffirmation of the covenant at Sinai. But many modern scholars explain the event as marking the completion of the written Torah in substantially its present form and its adoption as the official "constitution" of the Jewish community.

It is unknown exactly where, how and when the synagogue, the Jewish house of worship, came into existence. It is believed to have been some time between 500 B.C.T. and 200 B.C.T. However, what seems certain is that from the start, one of the principal activities of the synagogue was the public reading of the Torah.

A portion of the Torah was read every Sabbath. But there were farmers who lived in distant, scattered communities, too far from a synagogue to travel to it on the Sabbath. That they might not be deprived of hearing the Torah, a passage was read in the synagogues each Monday and Thursday—the market days when the country folk came to town to sell their produce. This custom survives to this day in the traditional synagogues.

The reading of the Torah in Hebrew was often followed by a translation, in Greek or Aramaic, for the benefit of those who did not understand the original. It is out of such translation or paraphrase, in all probability, that the practice which we know today as the "sermon" arose. This explains why the sermon was normally based on the Torah reading of the week.

From an early date, the instruction of children was associated with the synagogue. The effectiveness of its educational program, for young and old, was fully recognized by the enemies of Judaism. When the Syrian King Antiochus IV wished to break down Jewish solidarity and hasten the assimilation of the Jews into Hellenistic society, he not only prohibited the practice of Jewish ritual but he also forbade the reading and the teaching of the Torah. The penalty for violation of this prohibition was death. However, as history would prove over and over again, a people's love of God would prove to be stronger than their fear of death. Thus, the decrees of Antiochus went virtually unenforced.

Similarly, the Roman Emperor Hadrian, after he finally put down the Jewish revolt in 135 C.C., persecuted all those who persisted in teaching the Torah. It was then that the aged Rabbi Akiba defied the edict and suffered death by torture. The Torah, he declared in a famous parable, is the Jewish people's natural element, just as water is the natural element of the fish. While in the water, the fish may be exposed to many dangers, out of the water the fish is consigned to inevitable death.

THE ORAL TORAH

While the Torah soon became the "constitution" of the Jewish people. Like all statutory regulations, it was soon subject to interpretation. The Torah being a sacred text containing laws and commandments, needed to be interpreted and applied to the concrete situations of life. Those who proposed to make the Torah the rule of their life found many provisions which required more exact definition.

For example, the Torah prohibits work on the Sabbath. However, what precisely constitutes "work"? Similarly, the Torah speaks of divorce but does not make clear the grounds for divorce. On these and many other important subjects, the written Torah gives no guidance at all.

Such problems generated the concept of the oral Torah, in part explanation and elaboration of the written Torah, in part supplement to the latter. This oral Torah was not created consciously to meet the need of a certain time. Much of it was no doubt derived from established legal precedents and from popular custom and tradition. Once, however, the process of applying the law to new situations was undertaken in earnest, the material grew rapidly.

For a long time, the "oral Torah" was literally an oral Torah. It was deemed improper to put down in writing what Moses had not written down at God's command. Only much later, was it found necessary to compile this material in the Mishnah and other works of talmudic literature. However, despite its more recent composition, it was generally agreed that the entire body of oral Torah was also given to Moses at Sinai. Supposedly, it was to learn this vast corpus of teaching that Moses remained on the mountain forty days and nights.

The teachers of the oral Torah were chiefly laymen (that is, non-priests) who are known to us and history as the Pharisees. From about the year 100 C.C. on, accredited teachers bore the title of "rabbi." These teachers were opposed by a more conservative group, comprised mostly of priests, who came to be known as the Sadducees. It was the Sadducees who denied the validity of the oral tradition and regarded the written text alone as authoritative. The Sadducees interpreted the commandments in a strict literalist fashion. Perhaps it was this opposition which led the Pharisees to devise the method known as the "midrash" in an attempt to find some support in Scripture for the Pharisees' oral teachings. The term "midrash" refers to the "searching" of Scripture to discover divinely recorded meaning and the term, ultimately, came to refer to all classical rabbinic interpretation of the Bible and to the collections of such interpretations.

The Midrash uses a free, creative, and, at times, implausible method of biblical interpretation. In expounding legal passages—in expounding the "halachah"—the rabbis were subject to some rules and restrictions in the use of midrash. However, with regards to non-legal materials—to the ethical, theological, and folkloristic subject matter known as "aggadah" or "haggadah"—the Midrash was applied with virtually unlimited freedom.

Over time, the term "midrash" came to be used in three ways: (1) to apply to a method in general, (2) to apply to a single instance of the method, and (3) to apply to literary works in which the method is employed.

For most Jews, the written Torah was understood in accordance with the interpretation of the oral Torah, just as in modern law a written statute means what the courts interpret it to mean. The commandment "eye for eye, tooth for tooth" {see Exodus 21:24} meant that one who injures another must make restitution to his victim. "You shall not boil a kid in its mother's milk" {see Exodus 23:19} was taken to prohibit the cooking or eating of any kind of meat with milk or milk products. Similarly, people did not always differentiate between biblical stories and their aggadic elaborations.

Although the growth of the oral Torah, later written down in the Talmud, obscured the plain sense of Scripture in many instances, it was a force for progress which enriched Judaism. Beginning in the eighth century of the Christian calendar, a counter-trend emerged in Persia and spread widely. The rebels against talmudic Judaism were called Karaites—"Scripturalists." Returning to the position once held by the Sadducees, the Karaites proposed to live strictly by the simple word of the written Torah. However, the program of Karaites was much easier to talk about than it was to practice. Dissension amongst the Karaites arose as the Karaites disputed among themselves as to the proper interpretation of the many biblical commandments. Additionally, many rabbinic modifications of scriptural law were both reasonable and humane, and to reject them meant rejecting the accumulated wisdom and hard earned experience that the Jews had garnered over time. Such a retrogression would ultimately prove to be a futile undertaking.

The Christian apostle Paul, a Jew by birth, forwarded in his writings a new perspective of the Torah. Paul held that the Torah, with its innumerable commandments, constituted an overwhelming burden. No one could ever fulfill them properly. The "Law," in fact, was given by God to make us conscious of our sinfulness, that we may despair of attaining salvation by our own strivings.

Paul taught that salvation is available through faith in the crucified and risen Jesus. Thus, through Jesus, the "Law" served its purpose, and, for Christian believers, it is abrogated. This perspective has profoundly influenced Christian thought, even though the Christian churches rarely adopted Paul's teaching in its radical form and usually asserted the validity of the ethical laws of the Pentateuch.

In contrast to, and perhaps in response to, the Pauline doctrine, Jewish teachers insisted on the continuing authority of the Torah and on its beneficent character. For the Jews, God's gift of a voluminous Torah and its many commandments was a reflection of God's desire to confer a special benefit upon the Jewish people. And for the Jew, the failure to obey the Torah fully did not result in damnation but rather initiated a call for repentance and the creation of a new personal covenant with God.

Christian teachers, through the centuries, found in the Torah many passages which they interpreted as prophecies of the career and the messianic (or divine) character of Jesus of Nazareth. In the past, Jewish spokesmen had to devote a great deal of time and effort to refute such christological interpretations.

As for the Muslim perspective, Muhammad, the founder of Islam, the third monotheistic religion attributed to Abraham, recognized that the Jews were also "the people of the Book" because their religion was founded on Scripture. However, it is important to understand that Muhammad never personally read the Torah. Indeed, Muhammad never learned to read at all. It was only through his contacts with the Jews and Christians of Southwest Asia and Northeast Africa that Muhammad acquired knowledge of biblical narratives with their aggadic embellishments. It is to these biblical narratives that Muhammad occasionally alludes in the Qur'an. The Qur'an, which records the revelations received by the prophet, holds a position in Islam similar to that of the Torah in Judaism. And like the Torah, the Qur'an is supplemented by a tradition—the *hadith*—which is analogous to the oral Torah.

OTHER INFLUENCES

In the Judaic diaspora, Judaism encountered many new constellations of ideas. Sometimes these novelties were rejected by Jewish thinkers; but often they were accepted as compatible with Judaism. In such cases, an effort was made to show that these ideas were already suggested in Scripture.

The first exemplar using this method was Philo of Alexandria, who lived at the beginning of the Christian era. A devout Jew, Philo was deeply influenced by Plato and the Stoics. These influences led Philo to "discover" the ideas of the philosophers in the text of the Torah. For Philo, the biblical word veiled deeper meanings and had to be explained allegorically. For example, for Philo, the biblical Sarah symbolized divine wisdom, while her handmaiden Hagar typified secular learning.

The Jewish philosophers of the Middle Ages also employed allegorical interpretations, though with more restraint. They used this method to deal with Bible passages which appeared to contradict reason or morality, especially those describing God in anthropomorphic or human terms. Such Middle Age authors as Saadia, Maimonides (Ibn Maymun), and Ibn Ezra frequently found sophisticated philosophic concepts in the biblical text.

Still more extreme were the methods of the mystics. In general, such mystics as the Kabalists found cryptic meanings in the words and letters of Scripture, without any reference to the meaning of the text as a coherent whole. The Zohar, the chief work of the Kabalah, is a vast mystical midrash on the Torah. Indeed, many Kabalists, and later on the Chasidim, wrote their mystical treatises in the form of commentaries on the Pentateuch.

Ultimately, the view emerged that there are four ways to expound the Torah. Each way is deemed to be valid in its own manner. The four ways are (1) the rabbinic midrash, (2) the philosophical implication—the *remez*; (3) the mystical arcanum—the *sod*; and (4) the plain meaning—the *peshat*.

In the Middle Ages, many Jews returned to a literal interpretation of Scripture. This trend away from midrash to a simpler theology may have been stimulated by the Karaite revolt. The first great exponent of the plain meaning—the *peshat*—was Rav Saadia Gaon, the outstanding critic of Karaism. Gaon was followed by a distinguished school of grammarians and commentators in Muslim Spain, who developed a genuinely scientific approach to the Hebrew language and to textual studies. These scholars wrote chiefly in Arabic. The findings of these scholars were made accessible to the Hebrew reading public by Abraham ibn Ezra (Ibn Ezra), who came from northern (Christian) Spain.

Around this same time, another school of biblical scholars appeared independently in northern France. These scholars were more traditionalist, less systematic and philosophic than the Iberian Jews. However, they did display a keen sense for the niceties of language and for the spirit of the Bible. The outstanding production of this school is the Torah commentary of Rashi (Rabbi Solomon Itzchaki of Troyes). It would be Rashi's Torah commentary which would become the most popular commentary ever written in Hebrew. Its popularity was due both to the clarity of Rashi's style and to the fact that he combined the exposition of the *peshat* with a judicious selection of attractive *midrashim,* both legal and non-legal. Rashi's successors, however, concentrated more and more on the *peshat.*

The last of the great medieval Torah expositors was Moses ben Nachman. Despite his mystical tendencies, Moses ben Nachman also offered original and independent comments on the *peshat.* He and his predecessors had no difficulty with the fact that their simple exegesis—their simple process for drawing meaning out of a text—sometimes contradicted biblical interpretations given in talmudic literature. In non-legal matters there was no problem, since the aggadists—the folklorists—gave many diverse explanations of the same verse. On halachic (legal) matters, these same scholars accepted the talmudic explanations for practical legal purposes but noted that, according to the rules of grammar, a given verse might be understood differently.

These medieval expositors made a permanently valuable contribution to the understanding of the Torah. Although many other Hebrew commentaries on the Torah were written between the fourteenth and nineteenth centuries, they added little that was new. Only in the last two hundred years have new resources become available to broaden our contemporary—our modern—understanding of Scripture.

TORAH MANUSCRIPTS

From an early date in the Christian era, manuscripts, including Hebrew manuscripts, were written in the form of books, consisting of a number of pages fastened together along one edge. There are many manuscripts of the Hebrew Bible of this sort. These manuscripts are usually provided with vowel signs and with the punctuation indicating both sentence structure and the traditional chant. It is on such vocalized manuscripts that the contemporary printed Hebrew Bibles are based.

For ceremonial use in the synagogue, however, Jews have continued to employ Torah manuscripts in the more ancient scroll form. Each scroll is made up of numerous sheets of parchment, stitched together to make a continuous document. These sheets of parchment are then attached at either end to a wooden roller. The public reading of the Torah is from such resulting scrolls. A synagogue scroll (a *Sefer Torah*) contains only the consonantal text, without vowel points or punctuation, written on parchment with a vivid black ink. Tradition prescribes many details concerning the *Sefer Torah*—the beginning and end of paragraphs, the arrangement of certain poetic passages in broken instead of solid lines, the care of the scroll, the correction of mistakes, even the spiritual preparation of the scribe.

A synagogue usually possesses several scrolls. In ancient times, the synagogue scrolls were kept in a chest—a *tevah* or *aron*. The scroll chest was typically placed by the wall of the synagogue on the side nearest Jerusalem. In many early synagogues, this chest—this "ark"—stood in a niche, before which, in some cases, a curtain was hung. In modern synagogues the ark is usually a built-in recess, with a shelf for the scrolls. The ark is closed either by a curtain or by ornamental doors of wood or metal.

The removal of the scroll from the ark to the pulpit for reading and its return to the ark after the reading constitute a ceremony of considerable pomp, including the singing of processional melodies and demonstrations of respect and affection on the part of the congregants. When the ark is opened, and especially when the *Sefer Torah* is carried in procession, everyone stands.

The reverence and love evoked by the *Sefer Torah* is expressed in its outward adornments. Asian Jews generally keep the scroll in a hinged metal or wooden case, often handsomely painted or carved, from which the ends of the rollers project. The scroll remains in the case while it is open on the reading desk, and it may be rolled to a new passage without removing it from this receptacle. When it is closed, the upper rollers are often adorned with artistic metal finials (*rimonim*). In most European and American congregations, however, the *Sefer Torah*, after being fastened with a band of some woven material, is covered with a robe of silk or velvet, through which the top rollers protrude.

The *Sefer Torah* may be decorated with a silver (or other metal) breastplate (*tas*) as well as with *rimonim*. Sometimes a single finial—a single crowning ornament—covers both wooden uprights. Eastern and Western Jews alike use a pointer (a *yad,* literally a "hand"), most often of silver, with which the reader keeps his place in the scroll.

Some congregations, especially Sephardic congregations, attach a silk or other woven strip to the outside of the parchment, which is then rolled with the scroll to provide additional protection.

In contemporary synagogues, it is customary to read from the *Sefer Torah* scroll during every Sabbath and festival morning service, as well as on Monday and Thursday mornings. At the Saturday afternoon service—the *minchah*—part of the following week's scroll portion is read. There is no Torah reading on holy day afternoons, with the exception of the Day of Atonement and certain other fast days.

In the early centuries of the Christian calendar, the Jews of Palestine completed the reading of the entire Torah once in three years. We know, for the most part, how the text was divided into sections for this purpose; but scholars disagree as to when the triennial cycle began and ended—i.e., at what time in the first year of the cycle the first chapter of Genesis was read.

Babylonian congregations, however, read through the entire Torah each year, and their custom ultimately became standard. It was the Babylonian Jews who created the festival of Simchat Torah, rejoicing over the Torah. On this day, all the scrolls of the congregation are carried around the synagogue in joyous procession; the closing chapter of Deuteronomy is read from one *sefer*, and then the first chapter of Genesis is read from another.

For the annual cycle, the Torah is divided into fifty-four sections, called *sidrot*. They are read consecutively, starting with the Sabbath following Simchat Torah. To complete the reading in a year, two sections must be read on certain Sabbaths, except when the Jewish leap year adds an additional month. Each *sidrah* is known by its first (or first distinctive) Hebrew word. For each holiday, a suitable selection is designated, apart from the weekly series. On holidays and certain special Sabbaths, an additional passage is read from a second scroll.

Each *sidrah* is divided into seven subsections. It is customary to "call up" seven worshipers to take part in reading the several subsections. The number of participants varies on holidays, weekdays, etc.

Originally, each person called up was expected to read a passage with the correct chant. However, in practice, some of the participants who were selected were insufficiently familiar with the text and were limited to reciting benedictions while someone else read the Torah portion for them. This proved to be embarrassing to the uneducated, so long ago it became customary to assign the reading to one qualified person—to the *ba-al keriah*—and those "called up," no matter how learned, recited only the benedictions.

In many traditional congregations, the lengthy period of the Torah reading became a disorderly part of the service. Those who had the honor of participating were expected to make financial contributions, which were duly acknowledged in the prayer—the *Mi Sheberach*—recited on behalf of the donor or the donor's dear ones. Others present might also have recited special prayers of thanks or petition. On important holidays, moveover, the honors were sold at auction before the Torah service was conducted.

In reaction against such practices, Reform synagogues abolished the entire system of honors and limited participation to the ministry and to the congregational officers on the pulpit. More recently, some temples have reintroduced participation from the membership, but without the old abuses.

In order to shorten the weekly reading, some of the early Reformers proposed a return to the triennial cycle. However, this suggestion met with little favor and was not adopted. Thus, Reform congregations continue to follow the annual cycle,

but instead of reading the entire *sidrah*, they usually read only one subsection of each *sidrah*. The passage is most often read without the chant and the reader frequently translates it into the vernacular after reading it, or translates it sentence by sentence.

In the interest of relevance and inspiration, Reform Judaism made a number of changes in the readings for the holy days. Recently, a few Reform congregations have made changes also in the weekly reading, omitting *sidrot* (such as the opening sections of Leviticus) which seem to have no relevance for our time. In place of these *sidrot*, the Reform congregants substitute *sidrot* selections from other parts of the Torah.

THE TORAH TODAY

The last three centuries have seen a great upheaval in the religious thought of Western society, in general, and of the Jewish people, in particular. The development of natural science has undermined belief in the supernatural and miraculous and, consequently, has brought into question the authority of all sacred scriptures. Additionally, the proponents of religion can no longer rely on the method developed by Philo, who read into the Torah the ideas of Plato, or of Maimonides (Ibn Maymun), who understood the same texts in terms of Aristotelian thought. After all, most modern Bible scholars do tend to concede that the findings of Darwin or Einstein are not part of the Torah.

For the "modern," it is no longer possible to "explain away" errors of fact or to theologically dispute contravening scientific knowledge. Furthermore, the "modern" has developed a quite understandable scepticism towards unacceptable, or seemingly anachronistic, theological apprehensions and moral injunctions. Ultimately, for the "modern," a contemporary understanding of the Torah and its laws and commandments must be tempered by a thorough understanding of the context of time and place in which the Torah was written.

Finally, the rediscovery of the rich culture and literature of the ancient Southwest Asia and North Africa revealed many similarities between biblical and non–Israelite writings, and has led many to conclude that in some cases the biblical authors borrowed scriptural passages from their pagan neighbors. Such findings tended to undermine the "divinity" which for so long was attributed to the holy scripture known as the Torah.

The new perspectives and the new discoveries of the "modern" have raised some difficult questions which all three of the religions of Abraham must ultimately attempt to address. The most critical question is: Can any informed Jew, Christian or Muslim today regard the Torah as the word of God? After all, the word of God should be infallible, but the Torah, for all its greatness, is not.

On the other hand, if the Torah is not the word of God, then on what basis can any of the People of the Book make a claim to "superior," divinely guided righteousness?

For the "modern," the answers to these disturbing questions has become an uneasy quest. For now, the "modern" must attempt to discern not only the *extent* to which the Torah is the word of God but also the *sense* in which the Torah is the word of God.

It is not too surprising that many of the "modern" have abandoned this quest and have instead settled on the certain discernible tangibles associated with the Torah. Thus, for many of the "modern," the importance of the Torah is not so much that it is the infallible word of God but rather that in the Torah one finds how the Jewish people have historically understood their own character, their own destiny, and their own relationship with God.

THE BOOK OF GENESIS

The first book of the Torah is the Book of Genesis. The Book of Genesis tells a story which stretches from the creation of the world to the death of Joseph in Egypt. The first eleven chapters deal with a universal history, while the rest deals with the lives of Abraham, Isaac, Jacob, and their families. From the Jewish perspective, the total time elapsed from the beginning to the end of Genesis adds up to 1,946 (or 1,948) years.

The Book of Genesis is a tale of creations. In the beginning, God is described as creating heaven and earth and all they contain. The climax of creation is the creation of the human being who, originally, was created, in part, to help God in perfecting God's world. To achieve this, humanity is gifted with intellectual and moral freedom—a gift which humanity promptly used to disobey the injunction of God. The consequences of this disobedience are exile from the innocence of Eden and, ironically, the development of the human race.

The subsequent development of the human race proves to be a deep disappointment to God and God's disappointment leads the Creator to destroy the human race and to start anew with Noah and his family. But again, the result proves to be no better. Humanity's new existence starts with alcoholic abuse and sexual perversion. Once more God is disappointed, and, because God had sworn not to eradicate humanity again, God decides to work with it and within it in order to move it toward ultimate perfection. God chooses Abraham to begin this task by fathering a people who, in time, will become God's coworkers. The stories of the ancestors and their clan's descent into Egypt tell of the preparations which will lead to the creation, from a Jewish perspective, of God's chosen people—the Children of Israel.

Genesis then is the introduction to the Torah and to the rest of the Bible. In addition to its basic thrust, Genesis contains a number of sub-themes which are interwoven into the major story. Among these are the basic unity of all mankind, its propensity for evil, human rebellion, and the covenant between God and Abraham's people. Last but not least, there is the supposition that all human beings are descended from one common ancestor, which is to say that Genesis conceived of humanity as being of one kind, with no race or linguistic group superior to any other.

Genesis in its final form may be seen as a book of five parts. Part I is the prologue, and thereafter each part is introduced by the phrase, "These are the lines of" (*toledot*): the lines or genealogies of heaven, earth and primeval man (Part II); of Terah, Abraham's father (Part III); of Isaac and of Jacob (Parts IV and V).

The Book of Genesis consists of two distinct literary entities: the first eleven chapters, which relate stories of creation and ancient mankind, and the chapters that follow which speak of Abraham and Sarah and their descendants. The two parts are quite distinct from each other, held together only by a brief genealogical bridge. In the 39 later chapters of Genesis there is, indeed, no mention of the first eleven, not even an allusion, which suggests that the two parts were originally quite separate and were later on joined into one book.

While the first part may be distinct from the second, it seems evident that both parts come from the same traditions. The J, E, and P source materials apparently produced two sets of materials: one which dealt with pre-patriarchal traditions and were joined into one distinct "book" which

now comprises chapters 1–11, another which dealt with patriarchal traditions which now comprises chapters 12–50. In time, a redactor joined the two parts into what is now the Book of Genesis.

Biblical scholars believe that one can still detect the origin of many stories. Thus, the style, the genealogical interest, and the moral stance of the priestly school (P) are seen in Chapters 1; 2:1–4; 23; and 36. Chapters 3–4:24 are traced to J; Chapter 22 to E; and the Joseph cycle to the J/E tradition.

Most Jewish commentaries consider the patriarchal tales of Genesis to be very old. These stories were kept alive by an oral tradition until they could be written down many centuries later. Once written down, these stories were then subjected to further redaction and refinement before reaching what is today their accepted form. However, in its final redacted form certain seemingly obvious errors or contradictions were left in the text. These errors or contradictions remain out of respect for the various traditions which may have preferred slightly different versions of an ancient patriarchal tale. Thus, to give an example, while one source had God state that the descent into Egypt would last 430 years {see Exodus 12:40}[2], another would state that the time of servitude was 400 years {see Genesis 15:13}[3]. Such manifest contradictions were left standing side by side. This was done so that the ancient reader would understand that both traditions had come down through the centuries and that therefore both traditions need to be treated with reverence. Unlike the modern, the ancient reader did not feel compelled to say that both such traditions could not be true, that one or both of these traditions had to be

---

[2]Exodus 12:40 reads:

40 The length of time that the Israelites lived in Egypt was four hundred and thirty years;

[3]Genesis 15:13 reads:

13 And He said to Abram, "Know well that your offspring shall be strangers in a land not theirs, and they shall be enslaved and oppressed four hundred years;

false. For the ancient reader, the capacity to accept diverse traditions is a distinguishing feature of the biblical redactors and their times.

Genesis calls God by many names, but there is one appellation that is uniquely God's alone. That name is YHWH. The name YHWH first appears in Chapter 2 of Genesis. According to Genesis 4:26[4], YHWH is a name of long standing, but how ancient was its use, how it was developed, or even how it was pronounced were, and are, matters of scholarly dispute.

The name which describes God in Chapter 1 of Genesis is *Elohim*, and throughout the Bible this is a term for gods in general and Israel's God in particular. *Elohim* is a word with a plural ending (*im*). When it is used for pagan gods it commands a plural adjective or verb, but when denoting the God of Israel, the associated verb assumes the singular.

Elohim is an expanded form of the word *El,* a term current also in Canaanite religion. In Genesis, *El* appears always in connection with either another expanding term (*El Elyon*, "God on High"; *El Shaddai*, "God Almighty"), a place name (*El Beth-El*, "God of Beth-El"), or another identifying term (*El Avicha*, "God of Your Father"). Occasionally also, God is described by the relationship God has with humans (*Pachad*

Yitzchak, "Fear of Isaac"; *Abir Ya'acov,* "Strength of Jacob"). Such multiplicity of terms demonstrates the difficulty inherent with any human language which attempts to express the essentially inexpressible nature of the Divine.

The language of Genesis (and of the Torah in general)—relying originally on being heard rather than being read—is distinguished by key words and by word plays which are meant to denote inner relationships or, sometimes to serve as memory aids. Thus, the Jacob tale is distinguished by the repetition of the word "deceive." The word "deceive" is a constant reminder that deceptions punctuated the turning points in Jacob's life. At his father's blessing, his dealings with Laban, and the theft of Laban's household gods, Jacob deceives and is deceived in return.

In the Torah, word derivations may serve as memory devices or they may attempt to explain the name of a place or person. {For example, see Genesis 35:7[5] and 35:18[6].} Word plays also play a role. For instance, in the Joseph story, the same Hebrew word is used to convey three meanings: (1) to pardon, that is, to raise the chief butler to his former position; (2) to lift off the head of the chief baker, that is, to kill him; and (3) to single out or raise to prominence (Genesis 40:13, 19, 20[7]).

---

[4]Genesis 4:26 reads:

> *26 And to Seth, in turn, a son was born, and he named him Enosh. It was then that men began to invoke the LORD by name.*

[5]Genesis 35:7 reads:

> *7 There he built an altar and named the site El-bethel, for it was there that God had revealed Himself to him when he was fleeing from his brother.*

This verse is from the story of Jacob and the Hebrew term "El-bethel" means "the God of Bethel."

[6]Genesis 35:18 reads:

> *18 But as she breathed her last—for she was dying—she named him Ben-oni; but his father called him Benjamin. Thus Rachel died. She was buried on the road to Ephrath—now Bethlehem.*

[7]Genesis 40:12–22 reads:

> *12 Joseph said to him, "This is its interpretation: The three branches are three days.*

A somewhat related aspect of textual presentation involves the use of numbers, which also reflects an ancient belief that numbers relate to the inner nature of the subject that is numbered. Thus, in the Book of Numbers, one finds two census takings approved by God (see chapters 1 and 26), while, in 2 Samuel 24, a census which did not have divine approval was said to have caused a severe plague. It is more than evident that God is seen to be in charge of the secret of numbers. God literally is the one who "has our number," and only God may dispose of its use. Indeed, the lives of the Patriarchs are arranged in a numerical system. Thus, Abraham is 100 years old when Isaac is born, and he spends 100 years of his life in Canaan. Abraham "happens to be" 175 years old when he died. This number just "happens to be" the product of $7 \times 5 \times 5$. Isaac reaches 180 years. This number "happens to be" the product of $5 \times 6 \times 6$. And Jacob reached 147. This number "happens to be" the product of $3 \times 7 \times 7$. Obviously, with these three generations a descending/ascending numerical pattern was embedded in the lifespans of the patriarchs. This indicates that the lifespans of the patriarchs are probably more mathematical rather factual.

Similarly, there were ten generations from Adam to Noah, and the same number from Noah to Terah, Abraham's father. Joseph spends the first 17 years of his life as his father Jacob's ward, and Jacob lives his last 17 years as Joseph's ward in Egypt. The number 7 plays a great role—possibly because there were then seven observed planets; 10 and 12 are important numbers and so is 40—likely to represent a generation. The priestly source materials (P) places particular emphasis on recording names and ages; its archival interests reflect the important role of Southwest Asian and Egyptian record keeping.

In reading the Torah, it is helpful to keep in mind that the text of the Torah was composed in Hebrew and, therefore, partakes of the special thrust and meanings peculiar to the Hebrew language. No translation can ever fully capture the flavor of the original, and each translation is in itself a kind of interpretation. However skillfully created, however scholarly its renditions, the Genesis of the Torah is but an image of the master text, clear at times and blurred at others. Ultimately, the full quality of the biblical text can probably only be appreciated by reading and understanding it in Hebrew.

Ancient people, including the ancient Jews, considered the earth the center of the universe and natural law not as unalterable

---

13 In three days Pharaoh will pardon you and restore you to your post; you will place Pharaoh's cup in his hand, as was your custom formerly when you were his cupbearer. 14 But think of me when all is well with you again, and do me the kindness of mentioning me to Pharaoh, so as to free me from this place. 15 For in truth, I was kidnapped from the land of the Hebrews; nor have I done anything here that they should have put me in the dungeon." 16 When the chief baker saw how favorably he had interpreted, he said to Joseph, "In my dream, similarly, there were three openwork baskets on my head. 17 In the uppermost basket were all kinds of food for Pharaoh that a baker prepares; and the birds were eating it out of the basket above my head." 18 Joseph answered, "This is its interpretation: The three baskets are three days. 19 In three days Pharaoh will lift off your head and impale you upon a pole; and the birds will pick off your flesh." 20 On the third day—his birthday—Pharaoh made a banquet for all his officials, and he singled out his chief cupbearer and his chief baker from among his officials. 21 He restored the chief cupbearer to his cupbearing, and he placed the cup in Pharaoh's hand; 22 but the chief baker he impaled—just as Joseph had interpreted to them.

but as subservient to the will of God. This view is the basic principle underlying many stories, especially the opening chapters of the Book of Genesis which, in modern times, have become a formidable obstacle to the reading of the Bible. Why—it is asked—should we concern ourselves at all with stories of the six days of creation, with Adam and Eve, and the Garden of Eden? After all, these stories are deemed by most moderns to be unscientific, antiquated folklore, and therefore appear to be irrelevant.

In response to such criticism, many modern defenders of the Bible argue that while the Bible/Torah has little to tell about the scientific origins of the world and its inhabitants, it does have a great deal to tell about God's relationship to the created world and about human beings (especially the Jewish people) and their destiny. Since the Bible's scientific comprehension, they say, is limited to the world view of the ancients, just as ours is to that of our own time, it would be futile to look to the Bible for references to evolution or to suggest that "one day" in creation may correspond to millennia in scientific reckoning. This view, while it appears to rescue the Torah from the worst problems of an outmoded literalism, nonetheless does not do the book full justice because it approaches it with a facile sense of modern superiority. To be sure, from our modern perspective, it is presumed that our knowledge of science is vastly greater than that of the ancients. However, such a perspective is not necessarily accurate. Modern science, after all, constantly changes with new discoveries and often the new discoveries of tomorrow reduce our so-called advanced scientific insights of today to the same level as the outmoded ideas of the ancients.

Instead of looking for modern comparisons, it may prove to be more beneficial to approach the biblical text with a hum-

ble respect for the Torah's intellectual convictions and to understand that these are often expressed in metaphors which are framed in the vocabulary and understanding of antiquity. Thus, contemporary readers should restrain their inclination to totally discount or discredit the ancient notions of creation. Instead, modern readers should read the Torah for what it suggests about the nature of human history and the meaning of the existence and presence of God.

Within the last two centuries, the recovery of ancient Southwest Asian and Egyptian literature has radically transformed our understanding of the Bible, and especially our understanding of the book of Genesis. Only Psalms and Proverbs outnumber Genesis in the parallels suggested by the various translators. However, the parallels to Proverbs all come from the well-nigh universal tradition of preceptual epigrams, most of them Egyptian. Additionally, when it is remembered that the book of Psalms contains over 2,500 verses, compared to the 1,500 in Genesis, it would be seen that, proportionately, the first book of the Bible—the book of Genesis—is the book which most widely and most significantly parallels the ancient literature of Southwest Asia.

The reasons behind the numerous parallels are not difficult to find. Alone among the books of the Torah, the book of Genesis has the whole of ancient Southwest Asia and Egypt for its stage. The first eleven chapters of Genesis are set entirely in Babylonia while its last twelve are in Egypt. The intervening 27 chapters occupy the geographical terrain between Egypt and Babylonia.

The stories of Genesis tell of repeated semi-nomadic movements back and forth throughout the entire broad stretch of Syria-Palestine including both sides of the Euphrates and Jordan rivers. The presence of ancient Southwest Asian and Egyptian literary motifs in the tales of Genesis is thus no more startling than that of classical ones in Shakespeare's Greek and Roman dramas.

To "prove" the accuracy or validity of one literary text by another is, of course, at once the most difficult and the most heatedly debated task of scholars. Many have wanted to employ the discoveries of archaeology for such a purpose while many more have done so for the opposite reason. Ultimately, it must be acknowledged that unanimity is impossible to achieve. However, at least, we moderns can attempt to agree on what kind of questions it is desirable to prove.

With this as our perspective, it quickly becomes clear that we cannot gain greater confidence in the biblical version of creation simply because similar accounts have been found in the cuneiform sources of ancient Babylon. Nor, on the contrary, are the rather variant Egyptian and Sumerian versions of creation needed to "disprove" that of Genesis. From a modern Jewish perspective, whether Genesis accurately reports on these events is not the proper question. Instead, the more proper question is: Does the text of Genesis, as we know it today, accurately report what the ancient Hebrews believed to have happened?

It is today generally assumed that an extended period of oral transmission introduced distortions into the traditions which comprise the text of Genesis. It is also assumed that these distortions were aggravated by successive generations of scribes when the oral traditions were reduced to writing, and that their final canonization involved picking and choosing among the conflicting textual traditions on grounds other than that of their presumed antiquity or reliability.

On this premise, much modern criticism of Genesis has devoted itself to textual analysis and other attempts to recover a presumed original text. Such an "original text" is, however, unlikely ever to be found.

On the contrary, it may be that what exists today is the best text that could be derived from centuries of editing and amalgamation.

The history of other Southwest Asian literatures has shown that, at least in a literate environment, textual transmission was indeed subject to occasional periods of substantial change and adaptation. For example, reference may be made to the Mesopotamian versions of the story of the Flood. As an historical event and a chronological turning point, the concept of a great flood was an early and familiar fixture in Southwest Asian literature. The Sumerian King List teaches that kingship came down from heaven after the Flood and the idiom "before the Flood" (*lam abubi*) signified pristine time. The earliest literary treatments of the theme are in Sumerian, their hero is Ziusudra, ruler (or "son") of Shuruppak and last of the ante-diluvian dynasts. The first Akkadian flood story is associated with Atar-chasis whose epic is preserved in copies of the second and early first millennia B.C.T. Finally, the flood story was incorporated into the eleventh tablet of the Akkadian Gilgamesh Epic, where its hero is Uta-napishtim, who is variously equated with both Ziusudra and Atar-chasis.

The Gilgamesh Epic in its final written form cannot, as of now, be traced further back than circa 1100 B.C.T., and the extent to which it departed from its older Sumerian and Akkadian proto-types is evident even in translation. Certainly no Assyriologist would have ventured to reconstruct either of them from the canonical (later) version. Such an example inspires similar caution in current attempts to recover the original version or documents from which the canonical biblical text is presumed to have developed.

On the other hand, the recovery of the separate stages of many other ancient Southwest Asian texts has revealed, by the side of a certain amount of editorial revision, a rather tenacious faithfulness to many received texts which is at times astounding. Over widely scattered areas of cuneiform or hieroglyphic writing, and in periods separated by many centuries, certain canonical texts were copied verbatim and with an attention to detail not matched until the Alexandrian Greeks, or the Quranic specialists of the Righteous Caliphs, or the Tiberian Masoretes who codified the Bible, counting, vocalizing, and accentuating its every letter. To provide just one example: The Sumerian folktale of the warrior-god Ninurta probably was composed before the end of the third millennium; its first actual manuscripts date back to circa 1800 B.C.T., and it is known also in neo–Assyrian and neo–Babylonian copies beginning a thousand years later in which the Sumerian text is accompanied by an interlinear translation into Akkadian. However, for all the time interval, the differences between the earlier and later Sumerian versions are relatively minor. Such fidelity to a received textual tradition has led many biblical scholars to surmise that the received textual tradition associated with the Hebrew canon may be similarly reliable.

While some ancient Southwest Asian literary texts may have met with different fates in the course of their millennial transmission, in some cases adaptation and re-editing on a scale which defies prediction, in others extreme fidelity to the received text is evident. Ultimately, the experiences scholars have had with the Southwest Asian literary traditions lead them to the conclusion that, at present, we cannot hope to achieve certainty in recovering a more authentic text than that codified by the Masoretes after the Arab conquest. Even with the discoveries at Qumran and elsewhere, there are still far fewer extant pre–Masoretic manuscripts than the Masoretes themselves reviewed and disposed of, and the parsity of ancient texts makes it difficult to develop a conclusive methodology for choosing between conflicting readings.

Ultimately, from our modern Jewish perspective based upon the present state of biblical scholarship, today's scholars have come to accept that the Genesis stories are not verbatim transcripts of eyewitness accounts and that any attempt to place the stories on a pedestal above all criticism on theological grounds is counterproductive to a search for truth.

CREATION
{GENESIS 1:1–2:3}

BERESHIT[8, 9]

---

[8]The term "Genesis" is the Greek word for "origin" and goes back to the Greek translation of the Bible known as the Septuagint. However, for the Hebrew Bible, the name for the first book of the Bible is the same as the initial word in the book—*bereshit*.

[9]Hebrew is the original language of the Torah. However, by the time of the advent of Jesus of Nazareth, the Hebrew language of the Torah (and the Tanakh) lived on as a language of worship and of scholarship, but in everyday life it was largely displaced in Palestine, especially by Aramaic. This necessitated the translation of the Hebrew text into Aramaic (the so-called Targums). Outside Palestine, in the Hellenistic world, the spoken language for many Jews was Greek. In Alexandria (Egypt), home of the largest Jewish colony beyond the borders of the Holy Land, both the need to make the Bible accessible to Jewish believers who could no longer handle the Hebrew text and the desire to give an account of the Jewish religion to outsiders, interested or hostile, led to the production of the most influential of all translations of the Tanakh, the Greek Septuagint, so named because seventy-two translators were said to have worked on it, each coming up with an identical translation. The inclusion in the Septuagint of books that did not make it into the Palestinian canon led to the

CHAPTER 1   *1 When God began to create the heaven
                                          and the earth[11]*

            The First Day[10]   *2 the earth being unformed and void,*

---

ambiguous status of the deuterocanonical "Apocrypha," which, because Greek-speaking Christians adopted the Septuagint rather than the Hebrew version, became part of the Christian Bible. For a variety of reasons, the impulses within Judaism that had stimulated the creation of the Septuagint did not produce a continuing tradition of Jewish versions in different languages, and most of the translations of the Tanakh have been Christian.

[10]3760 B.C.T. of the Seder Olam Rabba Chronology. The Seder Olam Rabba Chronology is based upon a calculation made by Seder Olam Rabba which established 3760 B.C.T. as the year of Creation. In this book, the Seder Olam Rabba Chronology is being used only for discussion and comparison purposes. For the purposes of discussion and comparison, the Seder Olam Rabba Chronology used here was derived from the date of Creation calculated by Seder Olam Rabba and the dates set forth in the Ussher Chronology generated by the seventeenth century Irish theologian James Ussher. The dates given herein for the Seder Olam Rabba Chronology were obtained by subtracting 244 years from the dates given for the Ussher Chronology events. While neither the Ussher Chronology nor this Seder Olam Rabba Chronology can be deemed to be accurate based upon our measure of space-time, it is notable that of the two, the Seder Olam Rabba Chronology is deemed to be the more accurate with regards to identifying the time of the Jewish patriarchs. Nevertheless, as with the Ussher Chronology, the dates associated with the Seder Olam Rabba Chronology should not be relied upon as fact.

[11]This Jewish interpretation of the beginning of the Bible is slightly different from the rendition that appears in the King James Version of the Bible. Both translations are possible and acceptable. However, in the King James Version, the translation "In the beginning" was probably preferred as proof that God created out of nothing (*ex nihilo*). But, for the actual author, it is unlikely he was concerned with this problem.

It is noteworthy that beginning with the first sentence of Genesis, it is apparent that the existence of God is assumed. Nowhere is it doubted or argued; neither, however, is the existence of other gods ever questioned. In this regards, Genesis is radically different from the other books of the Torah and from the Prophets. Abraham, Isaac, and Jacob were distinguished in that they worshipped the One God and served God alone. However, the exclusive monotheism of later days was not theirs. Indeed, the great Jewish patriarchs may have even believed that the other gods of the time were real. Nevertheless, only One had made a covenant with them and to that One they committed their lives and the future of their offspring.

The God of the Jews appears in the pages of Genesis both as the Creator of the world and the Friend of the Patriarchs. In speaking of God, the book of Genesis has no difficulty in moving from universal to personal proportions and concerns. Modern man is likely to experience some problems with the personal nature of God reflected in Genesis because the relationship of modern man to God is not usually as intimately personal and direct as that of biblical man. To the ancients, God was not an abstract force, principle, or process. Instead, for the Jewish Patriarchs, God was Father, Friend, King—all of which implies a "person." Individuality was the highest expression of creation, and God the Creator could be spoken of only in such terms. It would not have occurred to the Patriarchs to speak of God in any way other than the way one speaks of a man. After all, man was created in God's image, and it was therefore most natural to think of God as speaking, seeing, regretting, and occasionally as walking just like any ordinary man. Additionally, even though God may have acted on a human level, for the ancients, the divinity and majesty of God would be no less diminished. It would not be until much later that human ascriptions of God (called anthropo-

with darkness over the surface of the deep[12] *and a wind from God*[13] *sweeping over the water*[14]—

3 God said,[15] *"Let there be light"; and there was light.*

4 God saw that the light was good, and God separated the light from the darkness.

5 God called the light Day, and the darkness He called Night. And there was evening and there was morning, a first day.

The Second Day

6 God said, "Let there be an expanse[16] *in the midst of the water, that it may separate water from water."*

7 God made the expanse, and it separated the water which was below the expanse from the water which was above the expanse. And it was so.

8 God called the expanse Sky. And there was evening and there was morning, a second day.

The Third Day

9 God said, "Let the water below the sky be gathered into one area, that the dry land may appear." And it was so.

10 God called the dry land Earth, and the gathering of waters He called Seas. And God saw that this was good.

11 And God said, "Let the earth sprout vegetation: seed-bearing plants, fruit trees of every kind on earth that bear fruit with the seed in it." And it was so.

12 The earth brought forth vegetation: seed-bearing plants of every kind, and trees of every kind bearing fruit with the seed in it. And God saw that this was good.

13 And there was evening and there was morning, a third day.

---

morphisms) began to create the kind of serious theological problems which are today experienced by the modern Bible reader.

Irrespective of the perspective of God that may prevail today, what appears to be clear is that there are three basic ideas which the modern Bible reader can glean from the book of Genesis. First, that God, as the Supreme Creative Force, provides all creation with purpose and that, therefore, to understand God means to understand one's own potential. Secondly, that God, as the Supreme Lawgiver, validates the principles of justice and righteousness which must govern the affairs of men. And third, that God, as the Grand Redeemer, guarantees the ultimate goals of existence and enables man to find meaning in his life.

Additionally, for practitioners of the Jewish faith, there exists another pervasive theme with far reaching theological and geopolitical implications. The basis of this theme is that it is through Abraham and Abraham's descendants that the realization of God's plan for humanity will not only be hastened but, in fact, made possible. The problem posed by this theme naturally being: Which set of Abraham's descendants may rightfully claim to be God's chosen people?

[12]The Hebrew word for *the deep* is *tehom*. The Hebrew *tehom* echoes the Mesopotamian creation story where it is told that heaven and earth were formed from the carcass of the sea dragon, Tiamat.

[13]The Hebrew word for *wind from God* is *ruach*. The word *ruach* can mean both "wind" and "spirit." Wind, however, provides a closer parallel to Babylonian texts than the traditional translation *spirit of God.*

[14]It is notable that here, as in other traditions, *the water* is given priority of existence.

[15]The appearance of the words *God said* in the text is as if God was addressing the universe.

[16]The Hebrew word for *an expanse* is *rakia*. The word *rakia* suggests a firm vault or dome over the earth. According to ancient belief, it was this vault which held the stars and which provided the boundary beyond which one would find the Divine.

The Fourth Day

14 God said, "Let there be lights in the expanse of the sky to separate day from night; they shall serve as signs for the set times—the days and the years;

15 and they shall serve as lights in the expanse of the sky to shine upon the earth."

16 God made the two great lights,[17] the greater light to dominate the day and the lesser light to dominate the night, and the stars.

17 And God set them in the expanse of the sky to shine upon the earth,

18 to dominate the day and the night, and to separate light from darkness. And God saw that this was good.

19 And there was evening and there was morning, a fourth day.

The Fifth Day

20 God said, "Let the waters bring forth swarms of living creatures, and birds that fly above the earth across the expanse of the sky."

21 God created the great sea monsters,[18] and all the living creatures of every kind that creep, which the waters brought forth in swarms; and all the winged birds of every kind. And God saw that this was good.

22 God blessed them, saying, "Be fertile and increase, fill the waters in the seas, and let the birds increase on the earth."

23 And there was evening and there was morning, a fifth day.

The Sixth Day

24 God said, "Let the earth bring forth every kind of living creature: cattle, creeping things, and wild beasts of every kind." And it was so.

25 God made wild beasts of every kind and cattle of every kind, and all kinds of creeping things of the earth. And God saw that this was good.

26 And God said, "Let us make man[19] in our image, after our likeness. They shall rule the fish of the sea, the birds of the sky, the cattle, the whole earth, and all the creeping things that creep on earth."

27 And God created man in His image, in the image of God He created him; male and female He created them.

---

[17]It is noteworthy that the *two great lights* referred to in the Biblical text are obviously the sun and the moon. However, here the sun and the moon are merely mentioned as part of creation unlike in other creation stories where they often have a divine or semi-divine status attributed to them.

[18]With regards to the reference to the *great sea monsters,* elsewhere the Bible reflects popular legends about certain forces of the deep that battled with God. Here they are simply listed with the other animals.

The sea monsters referred to in this verse are variously called Nahar, Yam, Leviathan, and Rahab. The latter especially recalls an ancient poetic tradition of a "lord of the sea."

[19]The reference in this verse to God's saying *Let us make man* is either a majestic plural or spoken to some kind of angelic or celestial court. The existence of this verse has historically been cited by Christian theologians as being evidence of the triune nature of God.

With regards to the creation of man, in the Jewish tradition it was said that God, the Master Architect, worked with a master plan of creation. This plan was the Torah, which provided that the world created by God would exist not merely for the sake of existing but for a moral purpose bound up with the creation of man.

Man is placed on the stage of creation after all else has been formed. He is represented as the crown of God's labors. In anticipation, the text of Genesis, Chapter 1, shifts into a slower gear. The words "God said" are not, as previously, directly followed by a creative act but by a further resolve, almost contemplative in nature: "Let us make man."

28 God blessed them and God said to them, "Be fertile and increase,[20] fill the earth and master it; and rule the fish of the sea, the birds of the sky, and all the living things that creep on earth."

29 God said, "See, I give you every seed-bearing plant that is upon all the earth, and every tree that has seed-bearing fruit; they shall be yours for food.

30 And to all the animals on land, to all the birds of the sky, and to everything that creeps on earth, in which there is the breath of life, I give all the green plants for food."[21] And it was so.

31 And God saw all that He had made, and found it very good. And there was evening and there was morning, the sixth day.[22]

The creature called man is formed in the image of God, in God's likeness. These words reflect the Torah's abiding wonder over man's special stature in creation, over man's unique intellectual capacity, which bears the imprint of the Creator. Marveling at man's powers, the Bible finds man to be "little less than divine."

This likeness also describes man's moral potential. Man's nature is radically different from God's, but man is capable of approaching God's actions: namely, God's love, God's mercy, and God's justice. Man becomes truly human as he attempts to do godly deeds.

Man's likeness to the Divine has a third and most important meaning: It stresses the essential holiness and, by implication, the dignity of all men, without any distinctions.

Above all demarcations of races and nations, castes and classes, oppressors and servants, givers and recipients, above all delineations even of gifts and talents stands one certainty: Man. Whoever bears this image is created and called to be a revelation of human dignity.

Six times the Bible says that God found the Creation "good"; after man was created God found it "very good." Being is better than nothingness, order superior to chaos, and man's existence—with all its difficulties—a blessing. But creation is never called perfect; it will in fact be man's task to assist the Creator in perfecting Creation—to become God's co-worker in the on-going creative process.

[20]Jewish tradition considers the use of the words *Be fertile and increase* to be the first of the Torah's 613 commandments. The *halachah*—the traditional Jewish law—derived from this commandment establishes man's duty to marry and have children. Extensive passages in the Talmud and the codes deal with the question whether this duty is imposed only upon the man or upon both the man and the woman. The prevailing opinion is that the duty is imposed only on the man and that the duty is incurred at the age of eighteen, while all other commandments are obligatory at age thirteen.

[21]The phrase *I give all the green plants for food* is of great significance for scholars. According to the biblical scheme, men and beasts apparently did not become carnivorous until after the Flood. {See Genesis 9:3.} At first, men and beasts had been vegetarians. According to Isaiah, in the messianic age man and beast would return to this original state of harmony so that the beasts will once again become vegetarians and the "lion will eat straw like the ox." {See Isaiah 11:7.}

[22]The Book of Genesis is a book of beginnings. Chapter 1 and the first three verses of Chapter 2 serve as the poetic prologue, setting the stage for the universal drama that is about to begin. Once this stage is set, once order has been brought out of chaos, once heaven and earth, plants and animals have been created, then the epic story of man can commence.

The prologue of the great story is cast in the form of a prose poem. It is written in terse, controlled phrases with rhythmic repetitions. In the prologue, the slow ascent of the cosmic drama culminates in the creation of man with the serene postscript describing the sanctification of the seventh day. In sparse, almost austere language, the prologue speaks of God, the world, and man in relationship with each other and reveals the basic and unalterable dependence of the world on the presence of God.

CHAPTER 2

1 The heaven and the earth were finished, and all their array.

The Sabbath

2 On the seventh day God finished the work which He had been doing, and He ceased[23] on the seventh day[24] from all the work which He had done.

3 And God blessed the seventh[25] day[26] and declared it holy, because on it God ceased from all the work of creation which He had done.

The Book of Genesis tells its story in a manner which at times may be difficult for contemporary readers to follow. Most contemporary readers are accustomed to following a story in a gradual evolutionary form, whereby man progressively learns, develops and grows. However, the Book of Genesis is a book which freely mixes devolution (descent from primal eminence) with evolution (ascent from a lower to a higher stage). In the Book of Genesis, religion and moral insight are not generally presented as a process of slow and painful moral growth. On the contrary, as evidenced by the Bible, religious genius appears repeatedly without traceable antecedents—as, for instance, in the case of Abraham. Ironically, just as modern evolutionary theory struggles with the role unpredictable mutations may have, so too in the Torah, one finds that mutations in the realm of the spiritual have occurred frequently in human experience, and the biblical record should in part be read as the record of such mutations. Indeed, the very creation of the people of Israel—of the Jewish people—is in and of itself a product of a spiritual mutation which deviated from and greatly advanced the spiritual progress and evolution of man.

[23]The use of the words *He ceased* is synonymous with the words *He rested*. Indeed, the Hebrew word *shavat* which appears in the text is related to the word which came to symbolize the seventh day—*Shabbat*—the Sabbath.

[24]Of particular interest for Hebrew scholars throughout the ages is the question raised by this verse. After all, if creation ceased "on" the seventh day, was this not, at least in part, another day of creating? This question has been much argued by the sages.

[25]The Hebrew Bible mentions the number seven more than 500 times. Some trace the concern with this number to the prominence of the sun, moon, and the five planets observed in antiquity. Others trace the fascination with seven to the fact that the lunar month falls roughly into four quarters of seven days each. Whatever the reason may be, it is evident that the number "seven" is the most prominent number in the Bible.

In addition to the weekly cycle, the Pesach festival is governed by seven; so are the seven weeks' period between Pesach and Shavuot and the sabbatical year. There are some scholars who suggest that the entire Book of Genesis and even the Torah itself are elaborately and ingeniously constructed around the sacred number "seven."

When and how the seventh day became the holy day of Israel has never been ascertained. A Babylonian division of the lunar month into four seven day periods and the designation of the day of the full moon as *shapattu* are possible links. Whatever the origins, in Genesis, the day becomes the divine seal of creation. And while it is not yet called the Sabbath, its significance is unmistakable. The seventh day is built into the very structure of the universe. It is God's holy time, and the Jewish people for ages to come will be called upon to make it the center of its existence, the mark of its covenant with God, "a memorial of the work of creation."

Thus, in a Jewish biblical view, creation, and history belong together. Creation is the foundation of a covenantal relationship between God and the world and, in a specific and important sense, between God and the Jews.

[26]In the Christian tradition, the seventh-day Sabbath was supplanted by a first-day Sabbath—the "Lord's Day"—in memory of the Resurrection of Jesus.

MAN IN EDEN
{GENESIS 2:4–24}

4 Such is the story of heaven and earth when they were created. When the Lord God made earth and heaven[27]—

5 when no shrub of the field was yet on earth and no grasses of the field had yet sprouted, because the Lord God[28] had not sent rain upon the earth and there was no man to till the soil,

6 but a flow would well up from the ground and water the whole surface of the earth—

---

[27]Genesis Chapter 2, Verse 4 begins the tale of "earth and heaven" and particularly the epic of man. The language and tone of the text changes here. Spare rhythms characterize Chapter 1, but in Chapter 2, a familiar, personal, and frankly human manner when speaking of God predominates. God is referred to as Lord God, while before God was merely called God.

The order of creation in Chapter 2 is changed from the order that appears in Chapter 1. In Chapter 1, humanity begins with male and female, while in Chapter 2 with male only. Where before man appeared in generic form, he now becomes concretely human. It is in Chapter 2 that man first speaks and feels.

Because of the differences between Chapters 1 and 2, most Jewish scholars generally agree that the two chapters come from two different traditions. Chapter 1 is usually assigned to the P-source, while Chapter 2 is assigned to the J-source. In the combination of the two (that is, in the text as we now have it), Chapter 1 may be seen as the ideal and Chapter 2 as the actual state of creation. Thus, the derivative origin of woman in Chapter 2 reflected the traditionally perceived prevailing social condition of the Southwest Asian woman, while ideally (as told in Chapter 1) men and women were created equal.

In the Genesis text of Chapter 2, verse 4 which appears here, the verse begins with the words "Such is the story..." The Hebrew words which comprise this phrase are elsewhere rendered as "These are the lines of..." This alternative interpretation of the Hebrew words stresses the genealogical aspects of the Genesis story, thereby making descent a keystone of Jewish biblical history.

[28]In the opening chapter of Genesis, the Creator is called "God" (*Elohim*). However, beginning in Chapter 2, God is referred to as "Lord God" (*Adonai Elohim*). This difference has been noted since ancient days and has been the starting point for many commentaries, as well as for modern biblical criticism. After all, it is the existence of such differences which provides clues for scholars to decipher the authorship of certain passages.

Elohim ("God" or "gods") is the generic term for divinity most frequently found in the Bible. It is used as a plural noun for gods of other nations and as a singular noun when applied to Israel's God. *Elohim* appears as an amplification of *Eloah*, a poetic form that does not occur in Genesis, and of *El*, which in Genesis occurs only in conjunction with other terms such as *El Elyon* ("God Most High"), *El Bethel* ("God of Bethel"), *El Shaddai* (usually rendered as "God Almighty"), and as a part of proper names such as Israel.

Adonai ("Lord") is the unique, personal name of God and the name most frequently used in the Bible. The Torah gives the meaning of the Hebrew script for *Yahweh* in Exodus 3:14, but that explanation is not clear. The original pronunciation of the Hebrew script for *Yahweh* (YHWH) was most likely *Yahweh*, but since Jewish tradition permitted the name to be voiced only by the High Priest it became customary, after the destruction of the Second Temple, to substitute the word *Adonai* (meaning "my Lord") when reading the Hebrew script for *Yahweh*.

The Masoretes who vocalized the Hebrew text therefore took the Hebrew vowels from the Hebrew script for the word *Adonai* and put them with the Hebrew script for *Yahweh* as a reminder to the reader to vocalize *Adonai* instead of *Yahweh*. This modification led the Christian writers of the sixteenth century—writers who were unaware of this substitution—

> *7 the Lord God formed man from the*   *the breath of life, and man became a living*
> *dust of the earth.*[29] *He blew into his nostrils*   *being.*[30, 31, 32, 33]

to transcribe the modified word as *Jehovah*. Today the term *Jehovah* has become quite prevalent in many Christian Bible translations, and has even spawned a particularly noted Christian sect—the Jehovah's Witnesses.

Jewish tradition interprets the names *Elohim* and *Adonai* as explanations of the two sides of the nature of God, the former representing the quality of justice, the latter reflecting the quality of mercy. The Midrash says that the world was originally created by God as *Elohim* {see Genesis 1}, but that afterward God is called *Adonai Elohim* {see Genesis 2} because God saw that without the added quality of mercy creation could not have endured.

[29]Man (*adam*) is formed from the earth (*adamah*). In modern terms, this is an assonance rather than correct etymology. Like sounding words were thought to hint at a special association of concepts. An English equivalent might be: God fashioned an earthling from the earth.

[30]In the text that appears here the verse ends with the phrase "living being" whereas in other translations the words "living soul" are used. The phrase "living being" is a better translation than the older "living soul" since the dichotomy between body and soul was of post-biblical origin.

[31]Adam is the name of the first human creature in the creation narratives found in the Hebrew scriptures—the Old Testament. The word *adam* may refer to the fact that this being was an "earthling" formed from the red-hued clay of the earth. Indeed, in Hebrew, *adom* means "red" and *adamah* means "earth." Significantly, this latter report is found only in Genesis 2:7, where the Creator enlivens Adam by blowing into his nostrils the breath of life.

[32]In Genesis 2, the first being is clearly a lone male, since the female was not yet formed from one of his ribs to be his helpmate. {See Genesis 2:21–23.} Ironically, in the earlier textual account of Genesis 1:1–24a, (which is generally considered to be a later version than that found in Genesis 2:4b–25, God first consulted with the divine retinue and then made an *adam* in his own "form and image": "in the form of God he created him; male and female he created them" {Genesis 1:27}. If the second clause is not simply a later qualification of a simultaneous creation of a male and a female both known as *adam* (see also Genesis 5:1), then we may have a trace of the creation of a primordial androgyne—a primordial being with both male and female characteristics.

Later ancient traditions responded to this version by speculating that the original unity was subsequently separated and that marriage is a social restitution of this polarity. Medieval Jewish Qabbalah, which took this expression "in the image of God" with the utmost seriousness, projected a vision of an *adam qadmon*, or "primordial Adam," as one of the configurations by which the emanation of divine potencies that constituted the simultaneous self-revelation of God and his creation could be imagined. And because Adam is both male and female according to spiritual authority, the qabbalists variously refer to a feminine aspect of the godhead that, like the feminine of the human world, must be reintegrated with its masculine counterpart through religious action and contemplation. Such a straight anthropomorphic reading of Genesis 1:27 was often specifically rejected by religious philosophers (both Jewish and Christian), and the language of scripture was interpreted to indicate that the quality which makes the human similar to the divine is the intellect or will. Various intermediate positions have been held, and even some modern Semiticists have preferred to understand the phrase "image of God" metaphorically; that is, as referring to man as a divine "viceroy," although such an understanding would appear to be in disregard of clearly opposing testimony in both Mesopotamian creation texts (like the *Enuma elish*) and the biblical language itself (compare to Genesis 5:1–3).

[33]According to the first scriptural narrative, Adam was the crown of creation. Adam was commissioned to rule over the non-human creations of the earth as a faithful steward (Genesis 1:29–2:9). In the second version (Genesis 2:7–4:1, where the specifying designation *ha-adam,* "the Adam," predominates), Adam is put into a divine garden (Eden) as its caretaker and told not to eat of the tree of the knowledge of good and evil under pain of death (Genesis 2:15–17). However, this prohibition was subsequently broken, with the result that death, pain of childbirth, and a blemished natural world were decreed for mankind (Genesis 3:14–19).

The original sin which resulted in the banishment of Adam and Eve from Eden and the subsequent propagation of the human species has been the subject of various treatments. The dominant rabbinic tradition is that the sin of Adam resulted in mortality for humankind and did not constitute a qualitative change in the nature of the species—in other words, the basic nature of humankind was not changed and humankind was not now set under the sign of sin as it proclaimed in the main Christian tradition, beginning with Paul and exemplified in the theologies of Augustine and John Calvin. Indeed, for Christian theology, the innate corruption of human nature that resulted from Adam's fall was restored by the atoning death of a new Adam—Jesus (1 Corinthians 15:22). In one Christian tradition, the redemptive blood of Christ flowed onto the grave of Adam, who was buried under Calvary in the Holy Sepulcher.

In contrast to the Christian theology, the role of Adam in Jewish tradition often focused on him as the prototype of humankind, *ab initio.* Thus, for Jews, the episode in Eden was read as exemplary or allegorical of an always extant human condition and an always existing propensity to sin. In this light, various spiritual, moral, or even legal consequences were also drawn, particularly with respect to the unity of the human race deriving from this "one father"—a race formed, according to one legend, from different colored clays found throughout the earth.

In addition, mystics, philosophical contemplatives, and gnostics of all times saw in the life of Adam a pattern for their own religious quest of life—as, for example, the idea that the world of the first Adam was one of heavenly luminosity, subsequently diminished; the idea that Adam was originally a spiritual being, subsequently transformed into a being of flesh—his body became his "garments of shame"; or even the idea that Adam in Eden was originally sunk in deep contemplation of the divine essence but that he subsequently became distracted, with the result that he became the prisoner of the phenomenal world. For many of these traditions, the spiritual ideal was to retrieve the lost spiritual or mystical harmony Adam originally had with God and all being.

Without question the story of Adam has had a fundamentally profound impact on the development of modern Western civilization. Apocryphal and intertestamental books about Adam and his life were produced in late antiquity up to the Middle Ages, and the theme of Adam and his life was also quite popular in Jewish and Christian iconography, in medieval morality plays, and in Renaissance art and literature. Well known among the latter is John Milton's *Paradise Lost,* illustrated by John Dryden. Michelangelo's great *Creation of Adam* in the Sistine Chapel, the Edenic world in the imagination of the modern painter Marc Chagall, and the agonies of loss, guilt, and punishment seen in the works of Franz Kafka demonstrate the continuing power of the theme of Adam's expulsion from Eden—of Adam's Fall from Grace.

8 The Lord God planted a garden in Eden,[34] in the east, and placed there the man whom He had formed.

9 And from the ground the Lord God caused to grow every tree that was pleasing to the sight and good for food, with the tree of life in the middle of the garden, and the tree of knowledge of good and bad.

10 A river issues from Eden to water the garden, and it then divides and becomes four branches.[35]

11 The name of the first is Pishon, the one that winds through the whole land of Havilah, where the gold is.

12 The gold of that land is good; bdellium is there, and lapis lazuli.[36]

13 The name of the second river is Gihon, the one that winds through the whole land of Cush.[37]

14 The name of the third river is Tigris, the one that flows east of Asshur. And the fourth river is the Euphrates.

15 The Lord God took the man and placed him in the garden of Eden, to till it and tend it.

16 And the Lord God commanded the man, saying, "Of every tree of the garden you are free to eat;

17 but as for the tree of knowledge of good and bad,[38] you must not eat of it; for as soon as you eat of it, you shall die."

18 The Lord God said, "It is not good for man to be alone; I will make a fitting helper for him."

19 And the Lord God formed out of the earth all the wild beasts and all the birds of the sky, and brought them to the man to see what he would call them; and whatever the man called each living creature, that would be its name.

20 And the man gave names to all the cattle and to the birds of the sky and to all the wild beasts; but for Adam no fitting helper was found.

21 So the Lord God cast a deep sleep upon the man; and, while he slept, He took one of his ribs[39] and closed up the flesh at that spot.

22 And the Lord God fashioned the rib that He had taken from the man into a woman[40]; and He brought her to the man.[41]

23 Then the man said, "This one at last/

---

[34]The place name of "Eden" is a word derived ultimately from the Sumerian, where it referred originally to a specific locale noted at first for its fertility but which subsequently became barren. The word then came to have the meaning of the uncultivated steppe or hinterland. In the Greek translation, Paradise, a Persian word meaning park, was used for Eden. In Jewish tradition, the Garden of Eden came to stand for the after-death abode of the righteous; it was no longer thought of as a geographic location on earth.

[35]The concept of a river dividing into four branches occurs also in other cultures, most notably in India and China.

[36]The reference to "lapis lazuli" is translated in other versions as "onyx." The precise Hebrew meaning of the word that appears in the text is uncertain.

[37]The reference to Cush usually refers to Ethiopia or Midian, but here it is most probably the land of the Kassites, in Babylonia.

[38]The reference to "good and bad" that appears here is also translated as "good and evil."

[39]With regards to the reference to "one of his ribs," some scholars suggest that this relates to a Sumerian story that knew of Nin-ti meaning either "Lady of the Rib" or "Lady of Life."

[40]Eve, or, in Hebrew, Havvah, was the first woman in the creation narratives of the Hebrew Bible. According to these narratives, Eve was formed from one of the ribs of Adam, the first man (Genesis 2:21–23). In this account, the Creator wished for Adam to have a mate and so brought all the beasts of the fold and birds of the sky before him to see what he would

call each one (Genesis 2:19). However, among these creatures the man found no one to be his companion (Genesis 2:20). Accordingly, this episode was not solely an etiology of the primal naming of all creatures by the male ancestor of the human race but an account of how this man (*ish*) found no helpmeet until a woman was formed from one of his ribs, whom he named "woman" (*ishshah*; Genesis 2:23). This account is juxtaposed with a comment that serves etiologically to establish the social institution of marriage wherein a male leaves his father and mother and cleaves to his wife so that they become "one flesh" together (Genesis 2:24). The matrimonial union is thus a re-union of a primordial situation when the woman was, literally and figuratively, flesh of man's flesh.

Such a version of the origin of the woman, as a special creation from Adam's body, stands in marked contrast to the creation tradition found in Genesis 1:27, where there is a hint that the primordial Adam was in fact androgynous. Alternatively, this latter half verse may have been concerned with correcting a tradition of an originally lone male by the statement that both male and female were simultaneously created as the first "Adam."

The mythic image of a male as the source of all human life (Genesis 2:21–22) reflects a male fantasy of self-sufficiency. The subsequent narrative introduces a more realistic perspective. Thus, after the woman has succumbed to the wiles of the snake, eaten of the tree of the knowledge of good and evil, and shared it with her husband, she is acknowledged as a source of new life—albeit with negative overtones, since the narrative stresses the punishment of pain that must be borne by Adam's mate and all her female descendants during pregnancy and childbirth. In recognition of her role as human ancestor, Adam gave to the woman a new name: she was henceforth called Eve—"for she was the mother of all life" (Genesis 2:19).

The new name, "Eve" (Hebrew, *Havvah*), is in fact a derivative of the word "life" (Hebrew, *hay*), since both *havvah* and *hay* allude to old Semitic words (in Aramaic, Phoenician, and Arabic) for "serpent." Another intriguing cross-cultural pun should be recalled, insofar as it may also underlie the key motifs of the biblical narrative. Thus, in a Sumerian tale, it is told that when Enki had a pain in his rib, Ninhursaga caused Nin-ti ("woman of the rib") to be created from him. Strikingly, the Sumerian logogram *ti* (in the goddess' name) stands for both "rib" and "life."

According to one rabbinic *midrash*, Eve was taken from the thirteenth rib of Adam's right side after Lilith, his first wife, had left him. Other legends, emphasize Eve's susceptibility to guile and persuasion. Christian traditions use the episode of Eve to encourage the submission of women to their husbands (see 2 Corinthians 11:3, 2 Timothy 2:22–25). Several church fathers compared Eve with Mary, the "new Eve" and mother of Jesus. The sinfulness and disobedience of the former were specifically contrasted with the latter. The temptation motif and the banishment of Eve and Adam are frequently found in medieval Jewish and Christian illuminated manuscripts and in Persian iconography. The theme is also found in medieval morality plays.

[41]Biblical man was undoubtedly aware of the pervasive bisexual pattern of nature and knew that in this regard humanity was not different from the rest of creation. However, the Torah gives this fact a special dimension by recognizing that man enters a fundamentally new state of life when he ceases to be alone. The words, "It is not good for man to be alone," speak about man's greatest need. The creation of woman becomes in effect the beginning of man's social history. Thereafter, man is able to fulfill his destiny completely only as a social being. Aloneness, in turn, is man's primary helplessness. Woman is more than man's female counterpart. Like his rib, the woman is part of the man, part of his structure, and without her he is essentially incomplete.

Nevertheless, despite the obvious importance of the woman, the Torah does not see the

Is bone of my bones/And flesh of my flesh./ This one shall be called Woman,[42]/For from man was she taken."

24 *Hence a man leaves his father and mother and clings to his wife,[43] so that they become one flesh.*

THE EXPULSION FROM EDEN
{GENESIS 2:25–3:24}

25 *The two of them were naked,[44] the man and his wife, yet they felt no shame.*

Chapter 3[45]

1 *Now the serpent[46] was the shrewdest of all the wild beasts that the Lord God had*

made. He said to the woman, "Did God really say: You shall not eat of any tree of the garden?"

2 *The woman replied to the serpent, "We may eat of the fruit of the other trees of the garden.*

3 *It is only about fruit of the tree in the middle of the garden that God said: You shall not eat of it or touch it, lest you die."*

4 *And the serpent said to the woman, "You are not going to die,*

5 *but God knows that as soon as you eat of it your eyes will be opened and you will be like divine beings[47] who know good and bad."*

6 *When the woman saw that the tree*

---

woman as the equal of the man. In the tradition of many Southwest Asian cultures, the Torah tradition is clearly male-oriented.

[42]The Hebrew word for "Woman" is derived from the Hebrew word for "man."

[43]The phrase "clings to his wife" may be more than simply a statement of personal relationship. It may reflect an ancient custom of having the man become part of the wife's family and household.

[44]In Hebrew, the word for "naked" is very similar to the printed word for "shrewd." Indeed, many scholars believe that verse 25 is actually the beginning of Chapter 3. However, most scholars consider verse 25 to actually be a bridge verse connecting Chapter 2 to Chapter 3.

[45]The first two chapters of Genesis tell of the origins of the world in an ideal condition. However, with Chapter 3, Genesis turns to growth, to man's actual condition, and to the problems man encounters in his humanness.

The underlying Southwest Asian traditions that shaped the Eden story have been radically altered to express the specific biblical (Jewish) view of God and man. In the Bible, the transcendent Creator of all creates man that he might freely do God's will. This contrasts with the Babylonian *Epic of Gilgamesh* in which the hero loses his immortality not only through weakness but also through accident, for in Gilgamesh the serpent steals the life-giving plant.

In another Southwest Asian tradition, the tale of "Adapa," immortality is lost by deliberate misrepresentation. In the Torah, the loss of Eden is ultimately traceable to man's own volition and action. Thus, if man fails to live up to his potential, man has no one to blame but himself.

[46]The association of serpents with guile is an old one. In Mesopotamian, Hurrian, and Ugaritic folktales, serpents oppose the will of the gods. Indeed, in ancient Hittite documents, the term "snake" was a recognizably derogatory term. Some scholars identify the serpent of Eden with Satan and say: "Through Satan's envy death entered the world." However, it has also been said that the serpent deceives in order to give man his humanity.

Serpents play an important part in two incidents in Israel's history. First, rods are turned into serpents by Moses and Egyptian magicians (see Exodus 4:3; 7:9–15). Secondly, serpents are agents of a plague in the wilderness (see Numbers 21:6–9).

[47]The reference to "like divine beings" in this text is derived from the word *elohim*. Elohim

was good for eating and a delight to the eyes, and that the tree was desirable as a source of wisdom, she took of its fruit[48] and ate. She also gave some to her husband, and he ate.

7 Then the eyes of both of them were opened and they perceived that they were naked[49]; and they sewed together fig leaves and made themselves loincloths.

8 They heard the sound of the Lord God[50] moving about in the garden at the breezy time of day; and the man and his wife hid from the Lord God among the trees of the garden.

9 The Lord God called out to the man and said to him, "Where are you?"

10 He replied, "I heard the sound of You in the garden, and I was afraid because I was naked, so I hid."

11 Then He asked, "Who told you that you were naked? Did you eat of the tree from which I had forbidden you to eat?"

12 The man said, "The woman You put at my side—she gave me of the tree, and I ate."

13 And the Lord God said to the woman, "What is this you have done!" The woman replied "The serpent duped me, and I ate."

14 Then the Lord God said to the serpent, "Because you did this,/More cursed shall you be/Than all cattle[51]/And all the wild beasts:/On your belly shall you crawl/And dirt shall you eat/All the days of your life./

---

usually means "God or gods" but at times also refers to celestial beings as in Genesis 6:4 or to divine beings as here. The word *elohim* also can refer to human judges or rulers. An alternative translation of Genesis 3:5 might be "*but God knows that as soon as you eat of it your eyes will be opened and you will be like God in telling good from bad.*"

[48]In the Jewish tradition the forbidden fruit was thought to be either wheat, grapes, fig, or citron, all of which are prominent Southwest Asian products. Some rabbis speculated that the forbidden fruit was the fig because it is the leaves from the fig tree which are subsequently mentioned in Genesis 3:7. Other rabbis advocate the grape because the abuse of the grape leads one to forget one's senses. Others support wheat because the Hebrew word for wheat, *chitah*, was seen as being related to the Hebrew word for sin, *chet*.

In the Christian tradition, the forbidden fruit is generally portrayed to be an apple. This distinction is generally attributable to the fact that the apple was a popular fruit in Europe and because the Latin translation of "bad" is *malum* which also means "apple."

[49]The Eden story may be read as the discovery not of man's ethical or intellectual knowledge but of his sexuality. This is suggested by the Hebrew word for "knowledge," which has the meaning of experience, especially of sexual experience. Note that the story of the expulsion from Eden begins with a discovery of nakedness and sexual shame {see Genesis 3:7}.

Reading the Eden tale in this light we see a link between the Tree of (Sexual) Knowledge and the Tree of Life. The latter, whose fruit would have bestowed earthly immortality, is no longer accessible. Man must now perpetuate his species through procreation, in the same way as other creatures do. But being man, his sexuality has a special dimension; his process of passing from childhood to adulthood, from innocence to maturity, is shot through with love and pain. Each man repeats in his person the journey from Eden into the world. As a child he lives in a garden of innocence; when he discovers his sexual impulse and grows up, he must leave the garden forever. And for many a man, most of the remainder of his life is spent in search of the garden of innocence which once was, but which now is lost.

[50]In this version of Genesis, God is depicted as being a corporeal being who, in human terms and form, inspects that which has been created.

[51]The reference to the cattle is meant to imply that the snake is lower than the cattle because at least cattle have legs to walk on.

15 I will put enmity/Between you and the woman,/And between your offspring and hers;/They shall strike at your head,/And you shall strike at their heel."

16 And to the woman He said, "I will make most severe/Your pangs in childbearing;/In pain shall you bear children.[52]/Yet your urge shall be for your husband,/And he shall rule over you."

17 To Adam He said, "Because you did as your wife said and ate of the tree about which I commanded you, "You shall not eat of it," Cursed be the ground because of you;[53]/ By toil shall you eat of it[54]/All the days of your life:/

18 Thorns and thistles shall it sprout for you. But your food shall be the grasses of the field;/

19 By the sweat of your brow/Shall you get bread to eat,/Until you return to the ground—/For from it you were taken./For dust you are,/And to dust you shall return."

20 The man named his wife Eve,[55] because she was the mother of all the living.

21 And the Lord God made garments of skins for Adam and his wife, and clothed them.

22 And the Lord God said, "Now that the man has become like one of us, knowing good and bad,[56] what if he should stretch out his hand and take also from the tree of life and eat, and live forever!"

23 So the Lord God banished him from the garden of Eden, to till the soil from which he was taken.[57, 58]

---

[52]This verse provides an explanation of the birth pangs endured by women during childbirth.

[53]The reference to "cursed be the ground" indicates that man and the earth are linked and that the earth is deemed to share in man's guilt. Accordingly, if man is corrupt so too will be the land.

[54]The reference to "by toil shall you eat" means that, pursuant to God's curse, man will need to work to live. However, some scholars have taken this to be a concession rather than a curse. These scholars contend that, by work, man is able to fend for and feed himself.

[55]The Hebrew script for the name Eve is translated as being the word *chavah* (*havvah*). The text of the Torah explains this name by connecting it with the Hebrew word for "living"— *chai* (*hay*). However, despite the scriptural connection, the true etymology—the true origin—of the name may be more obscure. It may be that the name Eve is a case of assonance. It may also be that the name Eve meaning "Mother of all the living" is an honorific title similar to the "Mother of all gods" title that appears in the Atrahasis epic of ancient Sumeria.

[56]In the Torah, the expression "good and bad" sometimes means "everything" {see Deuteronomy 1:39 and II Samuel 19:35–36} as when we say, "I know its good and its bad features," meaning that I know everything about it that can be known. The tale may therefore be understood to say that primal man ate of the Tree of Omniscience. Having tasted of the Tree of Omniscience, man forever after will attempt to know everything. Man will, in other words, forever after aspire to play the part of, and even to be, God.

This intellectual overreaching is what the Greeks called *hubris*—self-exaltation. Man strives to be godlike, but God will not permit him to become "like one of us." When man persists in deifying his own powers, God will call him to account and exact a terrible punishment. Like Adam, man will have to leave his Eden, his desire for divine power will always be turned back by the flaming sword at the gate of attainment.

[57]In Genesis, Adam and Eve are depicted as living in an environment of ease, free from pain and worry. Man's only task is to till and tend the garden, as a steward of God, the Creator. So idyllic is the depiction of Eden, that for many Eden is akin to being Paradise—to being Heaven.

The Genesis tale of the expulsion of Adam and Eve from Eden—the tale of "Paradise

Lost"—is perhaps the most compelling tale of the entire Torah. After all, it is this key story which relates how man came to forfeit his place in Paradise and which forms the basis for man's quest to return to Paradise. In other words, for much of Western society and culture, the Genesis tale forms the basis of Western theology and philosophy.

At the center of the story, as in the middle of the garden, stands the Tree of Knowledge. The tree is unique to biblical tradition, and three major interpretations have been offered to explain it.

Under the ethical interpretation, eating from the Tree of Knowledge of good and bad (or "good and evil" as many older translations render it) provided man with moral discrimination and thereby made him capable of committing sin. Yielding to the serpent's temptation and eating the fruit were two parts of the same act; once it was done, the relationship of man to God was essentially changed. Man's expulsion from Eden meant that he could never return to his former state of ethical indifference. In essence, man had become a being with the power of choice. Two radically different theologies developed from this interpretation:

Christianity, building on certain, largely sectarian Jewish teachings, taught that after Adam's transgression all men were inherently evil. In this interpretation the event has come to be known as "the fall of man," an expression absent from the Bible itself as well as from Jewish literature. "By one man, sin entered the world," said Paul in the Christian Scripture. For Christians, Adam's succumbing to temptation was man's original sin, a fatal flaw, from which man could be redeemed only after Jesus came into the world as the Christ. Without faith in Christ as the redemptive savior, men would live and die in their original sin. Over the course of centuries, the Christian doctrine of man's inherent sinfulness led to a thoroughly pessimistic view of man and a heavy emphasis on the right kind of faith.

However, from the Jewish perspective, the tale of Adam and Eve has a different significance. The mainstream of Judaism has refused to make the tale of Eden an important part of its world view and maintained that the only road to salvation was through godly deeds (*mitzvot*), rather than through belief in a savior. Additionally, from the Jewish perspective, while man tended to corruption, man was not basically a corrupt creature. Though man may be constantly exposed to the evil impulse, by carrying out God's commandments man can overcome or at least control the evil impulses and thereby develop counter impulses for good. For the Jews, the more closely man attends to godly deeds—to *mitzvot*—the greater would be man's protection from sin.

[58]The various interpretations of the story of expulsion of Adam and Eve from Eden,—the intellectual, ethical or sexual interpretations—are actually interwoven so that the fabric of the text exhibits not one theme but all, and each is discernible, depending on the light in which the text is viewed. This becomes particularly evident when one asks the questions: How did the storyteller view the intention of God? What did the storyteller believe God wanted man to be? Did the storyteller believe that God wanted man to be thoroughly obedient or potentially defiant; a moral automaton or a free spirit? Did God want man to stay in the garden or was God's purpose actually best served by man's expulsion? Finally, what was the punishment that was ultimately visited upon man? Is being condemned to be "human" really a punishment, or is it a great blessing in disguise?

These questions arise not only from the biblical text but also, in a wider sense, from the very creation of man. Man eats the tantalizing fruit, only to meet with disappointment and frustration. His is an act of disobedience and defiance, yet at the same time of growth and liberation. God appears to provide man with the possibility of remaining in Eden, but the very temptation of knowledge makes this impossible. God tempts man to be like God, but, when man yields, God rejects the attempt decisively.

Thus, the emergence of that contradictory creature called man is in itself a process of contradictions. Adam is free to defy God, at a price, but it is the theme of man's defiance which

24 He drove the man out, and stationed east of the garden of Eden the cherubim[59] and the fiery ever-turning sword, to guard the way to the tree of life.[60]

CAIN AND ABEL
{GENESIS 4:1–26}

Chapter 4

1 Now the man knew[61] his wife Eve, and she conceived and bore Cain,[62, 63] saying, "I have gained a male child with the help of the Lord."

2 She then bore his brother Abel.[64] Abel became a keeper of sheep, and Cain became a tiller of the soil.[65]

---

runs throughout much of the Bible and gives it its substance. After all, while man's freedom may be limited in so many respects, nevertheless, man must believe, and does believe, that toward God his freedom is limitless.

[59] The "cherubim" are the legendary winged beings who protect sacred places. The "fiery ever-turning sword" may represent bolts of lightning.

[60] Questions concerning immortality were of central concern to many ancient peoples, and it was widely believed that eating or drinking a sacred substance might bestow eternal life. Egyptian folklore spoke of a sycamore from which the gods obtained their immortality, the Greeks told of ambrosia, and the Indians of soma. Gilgamesh was promised access to a life-giving sea plant, and the "Adapa" tale spoke of magical bread and water. Some Christian sacraments, though they have long been spiritualized, still reflect their origins in the tree-of-life motif. The Bible, however, while retaining the symbolism of a life-endowing tree, gives it a minor role (which explains why no prohibition is issued to Adam in this respect) and shifts its main attention to the Tree of Knowledge. The latter, whatever meaning is assigned to its "knowledge," in effect became a Tree of Death, for eating of its fruit caused expulsion from Eden and the permanent inaccessibility of any magical fruit from the Tree of Life. By choosing "knowledge," man attained death. Immortality and knowledge are pictured as incompatible in the human sphere; man desires both but cannot have both. Since man chose knowledge, mortality is now built into the very structure of human life, ultimately distinguishing creature from Creator. By procreating, man can in part overcome death, but, like the rest of the creatures, he cannot become immortal—he cannot "be like God."

[61] The use of the word "knew" in this verse is based on the Hebrew word *yada* which in this context obviously means "had a sexual experience with."

[62] The name "Cain" is explained in the text by a play on the Hebrew words *kayin-kaniti*—"I have gained (or made) a male child with the help of the Lord." Some interpretations of this verse render this word play as "I have bought a male offspring from the Lord." This interpretation reflects the idea that the first-born belongs to God and must be bought from God.

Some commentators see in Cain the ancestor of the Kenites, the nomadic tribesmen in the Negev who earned their living as itinerant tinkers and smiths (*kenaya* in Aramaic, *kaynum* in Arabic). Thus, the lowly status of the Kenites in later days is seen as being explained by the curse put upon their progenitor—the curse of Cain.

[63] 3756 B.C.T. {Seder Olam Rabba Chronology}.

[64] The name of "Abel" is not explained in the Torah. However, in Hebrew, the name is usually interpreted as "breath" or "puff" or "vanity."

[65] The eviction of Adam and Eve from Eden and their subsequent mortality imply a transfer of important powers from God to man. Both the creation and termination of life now rest with man—the former "with the help of the Lord" (see Genesis 4:1), the latter in defiance of God (the killing of Abel). In the story of Cain and Abel, man's relationship with God is

3 In the course of time, Cain brought an offering to the Lord from the fruit of the soil;

4 and Abel, for his part, brought the choicest[66] of the firstlings of his flock. The Lord paid heed to Abel and his offering,

5 but to Cain and his offering He paid no heed. Cain was much distressed and his face fell.

6 And the Lord said to Cain, "Why are you distressed,/And why is your face fallen?/

7 Surely, if you do right,/there is uplift.[67]/But if you do not do right/Sin couches at the door[68];/Its urge is toward you,/Yet you can be its master."

8 Cain said to his brother Abel[69] ... and when they were in the field, Cain set upon his brother Abel and killed him.

9 The Lord said to Cain, "Where is your brother Abel?" And he said, "I do not know. Am I my brother's keeper?"[70]

10 Then He said, "What have you done?

---

explored in a social setting. It is in the context of human relationships that choices between good and evil will henceforth have to be made. And it is in this context that the interplay between human and divine responsibility must be viewed.

The story of Cain and Abel also introduces a secondary theme that will recur often in the Torah—the struggle between siblings. Time after time, the Bible reader's sympathies (and the blessings of God) are directed toward the younger sibling. The stories of Jacob and Esau and between Joseph and his brothers are indicative of this tendency, as are the fact that, in the Torah, such first-born as Ishmael, Reuben, and Aaron are often passed over. And, even when like Abel, the younger sibling dies, it is a still younger sibling (Seth) who provides the link with the future. This pattern may reflect a disinclination towards the institution of primogeniture—a biblical aversion to the rights of the first born.

[66]The reference to "choicest" is an idiomatic rendering of the Hebrew which literally means "the fat of."

[67]The reference to "there is uplift" means a relief from distress or from the descent into evil. The meaning of the Hebrew is not clear, and any translation is merely an educated guess.

[68]The reference to "sin couches at the door" is often translated as "sin is the demon at the door." This reference implies that Cain is free to choose good or evil.

[69]In the Torah, the text does not tell us what Cain said to Abel. However, in the Septuagint and Targum, Cain is said to have said, "Come, let us go out into the field." Nevertheless, it may be that the omission of what Cain said may be a purposeful ellipsis within the context of the Torah.

[70]Few phrases have been quoted more often than the bold counter-question that Cain poses to God. For many, the question of "Am I my brother's keeper?" has become the ultimate question the answer of which defines the foundation of the societies of man.

For many scholars, the question "Am I my brother's keeper?" implies the answer, for by posing his question to God Cain actually acknowledges a higher moral authority. There is someone to whom man must answer for his deeds and that someone is God.

The central theme of the story of Cain and Abel is human responsibility. God, by the punishment that God metes out, asserts that Cain was indeed his brother's keeper.

Cain's question is essentially defiant: "How would I know—or care?" With this retort, Cain, the first product of the post-Eden world, becomes a man who dares to openly defy God.

Some scholars have opined that when God asked Cain "Where is your brother Abel?" Cain answered "Am I my brother's keeper? No, You are. You have created man. It is Your task to watch him, not mine. If I ought not to have done what I did, You could have prevented me from doing it." Thus, Cain makes God responsible or at least co-responsible for Cain's actions.

Hark, your brother's blood cries out to Me from the ground!

11 Therefore, you shall be more cursed than the ground, which opened its mouth to receive your brother's blood from your hand.

12 If you till the soil, it shall no longer yield its strength to you. You shall become a ceaseless wanderer[71] on earth."

13 Cain said to the Lord, "My punishment is too great to bear!

14 Since You have banished me this day from the soil,[72] and I must avoid Your presence and become a restless wanderer on earth[73]—anyone[74] who meets me may kill me!"

15 The Lord said to him, "I promise,[75] if

It is important to note that God does not reply. The question, "Am I my brother's keeper?" remains unanswered and has remained so despite the questions of succeeding generations. Why is God silent when men kill each other? Where does God's power begin and where does it end? God can demand that man account for man's deeds, but can man likewise demand that God account for God's deeds? If I am my brother's keeper, are You not as well? If Abel's blood cries out against Cain, does it not also cry out against God?

Such an interpretation has a number of appealing nuances not only because it asks questions of great urgency today but also because it allows for a direct continuation of the Eden story. There, man's choice was essentially between life and death; now, in the post-Eden world, God offers man a new choice, the choice between good and evil. Cain chooses murder, the ultimate evil. And having granted man moral freedom, God, in a sense, shares in man's transgressions. But though man may ask where God was in the hour of violence, God's failure to answer does not reduce man's responsibility.

[71]The reference to a "ceaseless wanderer" seems a bit contradicted by the fact that Cain did settle in the land of Nod. However, the land of Nod is a land of "restlessness" and nowhere where Cain came to settle could he ever be at rest.

[72]Cain is punished by being exiled from his accustomed environment, from his occupation, and also from access to God. Human life, according to the Torah, is sacred. The wanton destruction of human life is seen as a crime against God.

[73]Much of Israel's early history is connected with shepherds, the nomadic life, and experiences encountered in traveling through desert lands. The Patriarchs were nomads or semi-nomads, and both Moses and David were shepherds. The nomad looked upon all settlers, urban as well as rural, with contempt: They were slaves to possessions and therefore prone to corruption and idolatry.

Cain is a farmer, a settler, and Abel is a shepherd. One reading of the Genesis story suggests that the brothers represent man's two original cultures in tension. It is interesting to note, however, that Cain is "condemned" to be a nomad. This is of interest because if the nomadic way of life was considered superior by Southwest Asian cultures, why would such a condemnation be deemed a form of punishment? Most probably, the farmer-shepherd theme contributed to the original story but was blurred in later generations. From time to time, the Bible returns to this theme, especially when the city is portrayed as an object of distrust.

Both Cain and Abel bring sacrifices to God but only Abel's is accepted. The biblical writer offers no explanation for God's choice. However, some commentators maintain that the key to God's preference may be found in the intent of the two worshipers. While Cain brings merely "an offering," Abel brings "the choicest" of his flock. In essence, under this interpretation, one son (Cain) only performs outward motions, while the other (Abel) offers the service of his heart.

However, another (and perhaps a better) interpretation is that God's rejection of Cain's offering is inexplicable in human terms. God acts in accordance with God's own wisdom (or

anyone kills Cain, sevenfold[76] vengeance shall be taken on him." And the Lord put a mark[77] on Cain, lest anyone who met him should kill him.

16 Cain left the presence of the Lord and settled in the land of Nod, east of Eden.

17 Cain knew his wife, and she conceived and bore Enoch. And he then founded a city, and named the city after his son Enoch.

18 To Enoch was born Irad, and Irad begot Mehujael, and Mehujael begot Methusael, and Methusael begot Lamech.

19 Lamech took to himself two wives: the name of the one was Adah, and the name of the other was Zillah.

20 Adah bore Jabal; he was ancestor of those who dwell in tents and amidst herds.

21 And the name of his brother was Jubal; he was the ancestor of all who play the lyre and the pipe.

22 As for Zillah, she bore Tubal-cain, who forged all implements of copper and iron. And the sister of Tubal-cain was Naamah.

23 And Lamech said to his wives, "Adah and Zillah, hear my voice;/O wives of Lamech, give ear to my speech./I have slain a man for wounding me,/And a lad for bruising me./

24 If Cain is avenged sevenfold,/Then Lamech seventy-sevenfold."[78]

25 Adam knew his wife again, and she bore a son[79] and named him Seth, meaning, "God has provided me with another offspring in place of Abel," for Cain had killed him.

---

capriciousness). God's reasons are unknown to man. The inexplicability of divine preferment marks Cain as an essentially tragic character. After all, ultimately, Cain reacts with a rather blind violence to a rejection he simply cannot comprehend.

[74]One of the great curiosities of the book of Genesis is how the world suddenly came to be filled with people, men and women of whom Cain was apparently afraid and who would come to build cities. The ancients tried to solve this difficulty by suggesting that twin sisters were born to Cain, Abel, and later Seth, and that, in this fashion, the earth was populated {see the Muslim Perspective, *infra*}. Modern Jewish scholars tend to discount the biblical silence on the method of the population of the world by saying that the Genesis story is not a history but rather a metaphorical explanation of man's spiritual state. Nevertheless, the biblical silence on the relatively rapid and somewhat incomprehensible populating of the earth does raise questions concerning the foundation of not only the Jewish but also the Christian and Muslim faiths.

[75]The Hebrew word for "promise" in the Torah script is *lachen*. When God says "lachen," it is a promise.

[76]The use of the word sevenfold means "many times" and not necessarily "seven times."

[77]In the context set forth here, the mark on Cain was not a mark of rejection but rather a sign of protection against blood revenge. However, some scholars interpret this passage to read, "And the Lord put Cain as a mark,.." Under this interpretation, Cain himself was the sign that warned men against murder. It is interesting to note that medieval Christianity justified the oppressive Jewish badge as a "mark of Cain."

[78]It is not clear why the Torah recorded this fragment. Lamech's song is possibly meant to relate his invention of weapons to his vengefulness or brutal arrogance. Lamech's life span of 777 years (see Genesis 5:31) is a sequence of the 7 and 77 of Genesis 4:24.

It has been suggested that verse 24 may be understood as "If Cain is avenged two times seven, then Lamech seventy-seven." This is based on the sequence of $2 \times 7 = (1 \times 1) + (2 \times 2) + (3 \times 3)$ while $77 = (4 \times 4) + (5 \times 5) + (6 \times 6)$, thus reflecting the pervasive numerology in Genesis.

[79]3630 B.C.T. {Seder Olam Rabba Chronology}

26 And to Seth, in turn, a son was born, and he named him Enosh.[80] It was then that men began to invoke the Lord by name.[81]

PRIMEVAL MAN
{GENESIS 5:1–6:8}

Chapter 5[82]

1 This is the record of Adam's line.— When God created man, He made him in the likeness of God;

2 male and female He created them. And when they were created, He blessed them and called them Man.—

3 When Adam had lived 130 years, he begot a son in his likeness after his image, and he named him Seth.

4 After the birth of Seth, Adam lived 800 years and begot sons and daughters.

5 All the days that Adam lived came to 930 years[83]; then he died.[84]

6 When Seth had lived 105 years, he begot Enosh.[85]

7 After the birth of Enosh, Seth lived 807 years and begot sons and daughters.

8 All the days of Seth came to 912 years; then he died.[86]

9 When Enosh had lived 90 years, he begot Kenan.[87]

10 After the birth of Kenan, Enosh lived 815 years and begot his sons and daughters.

11 All the days of Enosh came to 905 years; then he died.[88]

12 When Kenan had lived 70 years, he begot Mahalalel.[89]

13 After the birth of Mahalalel, Kenan lived 840 years and begot sons and daughters.

14 All the days of Kenan came to 910 years; then he died.[90]

15 When Mahalalel had lived 65 years, he begot Jared.[91]

16 After the birth of Jared, Mahalalel lived 830 years and begot sons and daughters.

17 All the days of Mahalalel came to 895 years; then he died.[92]

---

[80]"Enosh" is a poetic Hebrew term for "man."

[81]The use of the phrase "began to invoke the Lord by name" reflects the fact that antediluvian man is pictured as being close to God and of knowing God by name.

[82]With Chapter 5 of Genesis, the Torah presents the second of its genealogical lines. The first was that of heaven and earth (see Genesis 2:4), the second is the line of human progeny. The listing of names and the detailed accounts of legendary long lives find parallels in other ancient Southwest Asian traditional folktales. These extended genealogies bridge the gap between Adam and Noah, show the rise of civilization, and try to explain the present-day limitations of man's life expectancy.

[83]It is unknown whether the years attributed to the long lived patriarchs of Genesis had any symbolic or numerological meaning. In the Masoretic text, the years of the antediluvians add up to 1656 years; in the Samaritan version, 1307; and in the Septuagint, 2422.

[84]2830 B.C.T. {Seder Olam Rabba Chronology}.

[85]3525 B.C.T. {Seder Olam Rabba Chronology}.

[86]2718 B.C.T. {Seder Olam Rabba Chronology}.

[87]3435 B.C.T. {Seder Olam Rabba Chronology}.

[88]2620 B.C.T. {Seder Olam Rabba Chronology}.

[89]3365 B.C.T. {Seder Olam Rabba Chronology}.

[90]2525 B.C.T. {Seder Olam Rabba Chronology}.

[91]3300 B.C.T. {Seder Olam Rabba Chronology}.

[92]2473 B.C.T. {Seder Olam Rabba Chronology}.

18 When Jared had lived 162 years, he begot Enoch.[93]

19 After the birth of Enoch, Jared lived 800 years and begot sons and daughters.

20 All the days of Jared came to 962 years; then he died.[94]

21 When Enoch had lived 65 years, he begot Methuselah.[95]

22 After the birth of Methuselah, Enoch walked with God 300 years; and he begot sons and daughters.

23 All the days of Enoch came to 365 years.[96]

24 Enoch walked with God[97]; then he was no more, for God took him.[98]

25 When Methuselah had lived 187 years, he begot Lamech.[99]

26 After the birth of Lamech, Methuselah, lived 782 years and begot sons and daughters.

27 All the days of Methuselah came to 969 years, then he died.[100]

28 When Lamech had lived 182 years, he begot a son.[101]

29 And he named him Noah,[102] saying, "This one will provide us relief from our work and from the toil of our hands, out of the very soil which the Lord placed under a curse."

30 After the birth of Noah, Lamech lived 595 years and begot sons and daughters.

---

[93] 3138 B.C.T. {Seder Olam Rabba Chronology}.

[94] 2338 B.C.T. {Seder Olam Rabba Chronology}.

[95] 3073 B.C.T. {Seder Olam Rabba Chronology}.

[96] It must be noted that the number 365 is a schematic number which continues with the pervasive Genesis numerology and which is probably unrelated to the number of days in the year. After all, $365 = (10 \times 10) + (11 \times 11) + (12 \times 12)$.

[97] Like Noah later on, Enoch was deemed to be a righteous man and, like Moses and Elijah, Enoch died in a way befitting as one of God's intimates.

Many legends grew around Enoch, and the pseudepigraphical Book of Enoch (probably written around the first century of the Christian calendar) relates how Enoch was shown the mysteries of heaven along with the ushering in of the messianic era.

Islamic legend identifies Enoch with Idris ("the expounder of books") in the Qur'an.

[98] 2773 B.C.T. {Seder Olam Rabba Chronology}.

[99] 2886 B.C.T. {Seder Olam Rabba Chronology}.

[100] 2105 B.C.T. {Seder Olam Rabba Chronology}.

[101] 2704 B.C.T. {Seder Olam Rabba Chronology}.

[102] A comparison between the names of Cain's descendants {Genesis 4:17–22} and Seth's descendants {Genesis 5:6–29} reveals a startling similarity and some duplication:

Adam	1	Enosh
Cain	2	Kenan
Enoch	3	Mahalalel
Irad	4	Jared
Mehujael	5	Enoch
Methusael	6	Methuselah
Lamech	7	Lamech
Naamah	8	Noah

Adam and Enosh both mean "man." Other names in the two lists are like-sounding, and by exchanging the places of Enoch and Mehujael, one arrives at essentially the same (single) basic list,—a list which in rather customary biblical tradition is presented in two variants. The thrust of both of these genealogies is that mankind has one ancestor (Adam or Enosh) and only one line of descent. Noah appears when the seven generations of prehistoric man have run their course.

31 All the days of Lamech came to 777 years; then he died.[103]

32 When Noah had lived 500 years, Noah begot Shem, Ham and Japheth.

Chapter 6

1 When men began to increase on earth and daughters were born to them.

2 the divine beings[104] *saw how beauti-*

The inclusion of Seth's descendants and the change from Cain to Kenan was probably due to the understandable disinclination to have all men appear to be descended from a murderer. It is also suggested in the Jewish midrash that Naamah was actually Noah's wife.

There are strong parallels between these biblical genealogies and the Babylonian lists of antediluvian kings and their counselors. In both cases, these genealogies name "culture heroes" responsible for basic contributions to civilization, including the first cities. In both cases, the genealogies end with the protagonist of the Deluge story.

The Babylonian list of antediluvian kings is as follows:

1. Alulim   28,800 year reign
2. Alalgar   36,000 year reign
3. Enmenluanna   43,200 year reign
4. Enmengalanna   28,800 year reign
5. Dumuzi   36,000 year reign
6. Ensipazianna   28,800 year reign
7. Enmenduranna   21,000 year reign
8. Ubartutul   8,600 year reign

THE FLOOD

While the parallels between the biblical and Babylonian traditions are clearly visible, there are also significant differences. The Babylonians attached these traditions only to their king lists, but the Bible treats the antediluvians as ancestors of one another and, ultimately of all mankind. The Bible story is also notable in that it deals with men and not with semi-divine kings. Even the longevity attributed to Seth's line is more realistic when compared with that of the Babylonian antediluvian kings. The Babylonian kings were reputed to have lived for tens of thousands of years. However, none of the antediluvians of the Bible made it to even one thousand years of age.

The longevity of the antediluvians should, therefore, be seen in the context of such ancient traditions. To say that Methuselah's 969 years were meant as shorter units, such as months, merely subjects the Torah to artificial interpretation. The Bible presents the list of antediluvians and their long lives as an intermediate stage in man's development. Adam possessed potential immortality; his immediate descendants had, by our standards, very long life spans; the Jewish Patriarchs (Abraham, Isaac, and Jacob) along with Joseph, Moses and Joshua, all lived past the century mark. Thereafter, however, men have only the "normal" life span. In the biblical view, man's longevity is limited severely at some stage between prehistory and history, and only in the messianic days will man again reach the high ages of pre-Mosaic times {see Isaiah 65:20}.

[103] 2109 B.C.T. {Seder Olam Rabba Chronology}.

[104] The reference to "divine beings" in verse 2 is translated by others as "the sons of God." Hurrian, Phoenician, and Greek folklore told of Titans, supermen of great stature and strength, who were supposedly the offspring of unions between gods and men. One old understanding was that the "divine beings" were angels who had become fallen angels. Still another interpretation takes "divine beings" to refer to the descendants of Seth and takes "human daughters" to refer to the descendants of Cain. The phrase has also been taken as recording inter-class marital unions: sons of the aristocracy married daughters of the common folk. Despite the interpretative gymnastics, analytical scholars believe that the notation about

ful the daughters of men were and they took wives from among those that pleased them –

3 The LORD said, "My breath shall not abide in man forever, since he too is flesh; let the days allowed him be one hundred and twenty years."[105]—

4 It was then, and later too, that the Nephilim[106] *appeared on earth—when the divine beings cohabited with the daughters of men, who bore them offspring. They were the heroes of old, the men of renown.*

*5 The LORD saw how great was man's wickedness on earth, and how every plan de-*vised by his mind[107] has nothing but evil all the time.

6 And the LORD regretted[108] *that He had made man on earth, and His heart was saddened.*

7 The LORD said, "I will blot out from the earth the men whom I created—men together with beasts, creeping things, and birds of the sky; for I regret that I made them."[109]

8 But Noah found favor with the LORD.

---

the legendary "divine beings" and their giant offspring may be regarded as the one primitive theological fragment retained in Genesis. The question arises as to why this antiquated fragment was not excised? One possible explanation is that it was not excised because it served as an introduction to the Flood story and as such appeared to say: Men became giants, achieved renown in their time, and were heroes by their own values. However, when God evaluated human development, God looked neither at man's size nor at man's self-evaluation. Instead, God looked at man's heart.

According to Genesis, when God looked at man's heart, he found it corrupted by evil. Thus, God resolved to make a new start with Noah.

[105]The Hebrew meaning of the reference to the word "abide" that appears in this passage is uncertain. However, with regards to the reference to "one hundred and twenty years," this biblical reference appears to indicate that "one hundred and twenty years" is the "ideal" life span. Indeed, it would be Moses himself who would match this standard by living to be 120 years old. Although, for most men the expected age of man would be reduced to seventy years. As set forth in Psalms 90:10, "The days of our years are threescore years and ten." It is of interest to note that the number 120 happens to be the multiple of $1 \times 2 \times 3 \times 4 \times 5$. This "coincidental" multiple again probably reflects the biblical predilection for number symbolism.

[106]The word "Nephilim" appears to be a borrowed term or an archaic term. Some assert that the word "Nephilim" is related to the Hebrew word for "fall" (*nafal*). According to this assertion, the word "Nephilim" is best translated as "the fallen ones." The Septuagint translates the word as "giants."

The word "Nephilim" appears again in the Torah text in Numbers 13:33. There, when the spies whom Moses had sent returned, they reported that they had seen Nephilim in Canaan: "and we looked like grasshoppers to ourselves, and so we must have looked to them." In another view, the "heroes of old," not the Nephilim, were the result of the superhuman marriages.

[107]Some translations say "devised by his heart" since to many ancients the heart was believed to be the seat of thought. Additionally, the word "plan" is sometimes translated as "temperament."

[108]The Hebrew phrase for "the LORD regretted" can mean both "to change one's mind" and also "comfort," a word play referring to Genesis 5:29.

[109]Animals are included in the impending destruction because, according to the biblical view, they existed for the sake of man. As some have queried, what use would there be for animals if man ceased to exist?

THE FLOOD[110]
{GENESIS 6:9–8:14}[111]

9 This is the line of Noah. — Noah was a righteous man; he was blameless in his age; Noah walked with God. —

10 Noah begot three sons: Shem, Ham, and Japheth.

11 The earth became corrupt before God; the earth was filled with lawlessness.[112]

12 When God saw how corrupt the earth was, for all flesh had corrupted its ways on earth,

13 God said to Noah, "I have decided to put an end to all flesh, for the earth is filled with lawlessness because of them: I am about to destroy them with the earth.[113]

14 Make yourself an ark of gopher wood[114]; make it an ark with compartments, and cover it inside and out with pitch.

15 This is how you shall make it: the length of the ark shall be three hundred cubits, its width fifty cubits, and its height thirty cubits.[115]

16 Make an opening for daylight in the

---

[110]Many diverse cultures tell stories about a great flood. For many years, theologians suggested that these stories recall an earth-wide catastrophe brought on either by a terrestrial eruption or by a celestial collision, which may have resulted in a rise in sea level sufficient to cover all continents. More recent theories point to a global warming after the last ice age which may have caused the sea levels to rise fairly precipitously. Additionally, some recent scientific investigations have shown that, at some time near the transition between prehistory and history, flood waters from the Persian Gulf may have covered the southern section of the Mesopotamian valley. And perhaps most significantly with regards to the Genesis story, scientists have shown that some 7,000 years ago the Mediterranean Sea broke through a land barrier and flooded the Euxine Lake with millions of gallons of salt water to create what is today known as the Black Sea. These millions of gallons caused a catastrophic flooding which tremendously impacted the people of Asia Minor and Southwestern Asia. It now seems evident that a catastrophic flooding did occur and the human record of this event was left to reside in the memories of many ancient peoples of Southwest Asia.

With regards to the biblical story, it has long been contended that the Bible story is more than just prehistoric memory or a variant on an ancient folktale. For many, the Bible story is above all else a story with a moral. Its themes are sin, righteousness, and man's second opportunity to live in accordance with, rather than opposed to, the will of God.

There is agreement between the biblical and other Southwest Asian flood stories on many details—the ark, the raven, the dove—but there are fundamental differences in approach. In the Bible, it is human sin that causes the Flood while in the Babylonian-Akkadian epic of "Atrahasis," human boisterousness and noise disturb the sleep of the gods and cause them to react. In the Bible, Noah is saved so that he might begin the human voyage over again. In Gilgamesh, the flood hero is elevated to immortal status and thereby is removed from human history. Most importantly, in the Torah—in the Jewish Scriptures—God institutes law as the counteragent of human wickedness, while in other Southwest Asian traditions such a divine response is absent.

[111]In the Hebrew Bible, the first segment covering what is known as Genesis 1–6:8 is called *Bereshit*. The second segment covering what is known as Genesis 6:9–11:26 is called *Noach*.

[112]With regards to the use of the term "lawlessness," some translate the Hebrew term as meaning "violence."

[113]With regards to the use of the phrase "destroy them with the earth," some translate this as "destroy them from the earth."

[114]The "gopher wood" from which the ark was made is a species of wood which, as of the year 2000, had not been identified.

ark, and terminate it within a cubit of the top. Put the entrance to the ark in its side; make it with bottom, second, and third decks.

17 "For My part, I am about to bring the Flood—waters upon the earth—to destroy all flesh under the sky in which there is breath of life; everything on earth shall perish.

18 But I will establish My covenant with you, and you shall enter the ark, with your sons, your wife, and your sons' wives.

19 And of all that lives, of all flesh, you shall take two of each into the ark to keep alive with you; they shall be male and female.

20 From birds of every kind, cattle of every kind, every kind of creeping thing on earth, two of each shall come to you to stay alive.

21 For your part, take of everything that is eaten and store it away, to serve as food for you and for them."

22 Noah did so; just as God commanded him, so he did.

Chapter 7

1 Then the LORD said to Noah, "Go into the ark,[116] with all your household, for you alone have I found righteous before Me in this generation.

2 Of every clean animal[117] you shall take seven pairs, males and their mates, and of every animal which is not clean, two, a male and its mate;

3 of the birds of the sky also, seven pairs, male and female, to keep seed alive upon all the earth.

4 For in seven days' time I will make it rain upon the earth, forty days and forty nights, and I will blot out from the earth all existence that I created."

5 And Noah did just as the LORD commanded him.[118]

6 Noah was six hundred years old[119] when the Flood came, waters upon the earth.

7 Noah, with his sons, his wife, and his

---

[115]Assuming that a cubit is about eighteen inches long, the ark's tonnage was over 40,000 tons, or as large as a good-sized modern passenger ship. To ancient man, the mere thought of such dimensions must have evoked a sense of great awe.

[116]2105 B.C.T. {Seder Olam Rabba Chronology}.

[117]The reference here to "clean animal" means, in Torah terms, an animal fit for sacrifice.

[118]It is notable that nowhere does Noah show a feeling of sadness or remorse that an entire generation was to be lost, and the world destroyed; that men had lost their way of life and surrendered to their own sinful drives and passions. At no time, did a word of concern issue forth from Noah. It was as though Noah stood apart from the rest of the world. Nowhere was there an expression of tenderness, of regret that even though these men were wicked they would be lost—not only the men but also their wives and their children. Quite significantly, Noah did not leap forward with a plea for greater mercy. Never did Noah intercede on behalf of humanity.

It is said that Noah was a righteous man. It is said that Noah deserves to be in the circle of the great. But there was a fatal flaw in Noah as portrayed in the Bible. Noah was not the advocate for man and, as such, he would be incapable of becoming the father of a new religion, a new faith, and a new community. Ultimately, Noah lacked compassion and, because he lacked compassion, he forfeited the far greater place in history that might have been accorded to him but was instead accorded to Abraham. After all, Noah's fate is bound to "his generation," but Abraham's goes beyond his time, toward history. Abraham's faithfulness is God's hope—not because of what Abraham is "in his generation" but for what he will become for "future generations."

[119]According to the Bible, Methuselah died just before the Flood, and some commentators have noted that it was no coincidence that God waited until the mourning period for

sons' wives,[120] went into the ark because of the waters of the Flood.

8 Of the clean animals, of the animals that are not clean, of the birds, and of everything that creeps on the ground,

9 two of each, male and female, came to Noah into the ark, as God had commanded Noah.

10 And on the seventh day the waters of the Flood came upon the earth.

11 In the six hundredth year of Noah's life, in the second month,[121] on the seventeenth day of the month, on that day.

All the fountains of the great deep burst apart,

And the flood-gates of the sky broke open.

(12 The rain fell on the earth forty days and forty nights.)

13 That same day Noah and Noah's sons, Shem, Ham, and Japheth, went into the ark, with Noah's wife and the three wives of his sons—

14 they and all beasts of every kind, all cattle of every kind, all creatures of every kind that creep on the earth, and all birds of every kind, every bird, every winged thing.

15 They came to Noah into the ark, two each of all flesh in which there was breath of life.

16 Thus they that entered comprised male and female of all flesh, as God had commanded him. And the LORD shut him in.

17 The Flood continued forty days on the earth, and the waters increased and raised the ark so that it rose above the earth.

18 The waters swelled and increased greatly upon the earth, and the ark drifted upon the waters.

19 When the waters had swelled much more upon the earth, all the highest mountains every where under the sky were covered.

Methuselah had passed before sending the Flood. But what is obvious is that, except for Noah, the period of the antediluvians had run its course. Thus, the Flood closes the first era in man's post–Eden story. The Torah pictures this era as marked by devolution with the moral fibre of man deteriorated beyond hope of regeneration.

What was the monstrous evil that brought on God's wrath? The Bible does not specify it beyond calling it *chamas*—lawlessness. However, lawlessness (or violence, as some render it) is merely the manifestation of a social disease and not its cause. Certain Jewish literature speculates that it was unbounded affluence that caused men to become depraved, that wealth afforded them the leisure to discover new thrills and to commit sexual aberrations. Accompanying such material prosperity came an overbearing attitude toward God whom people judged to be incapable of hearing prayer and of enforcing moral standards.

Others have commented that the chief sin of the antediluvian generation lay in their refusal to beget children. Even Noah originally refused to marry and to have children. Indeed, Noah's first child was not born until Noah was 500 years old. This reluctance to procreate was in direct disobedience to God's commandment "Be fruitful and multiply."

In the Christian tradition, Noah and his generation prefigure the end of time: Only those who take refuge in faith will escape judgment. Similarly, the water of baptism represents salvation brought through flood water to Noah and his family.

[120]The Bible says that God chose to save Noah and his family from the Flood because he was "blameless in his age." However, it has been remarked that Noah was blameless only in his age. In other ages, he would not have been considered to be a righteous man. On the other hand, some have said that because Noah was righteous in his age, he would have been even more righteous in any other. Such debates have occurred for many years but the biblical fact is that for his time, Noah was the only man that God deemed to be righteous.

[121]The reference to the "second month" probably means the second month of the fall season when the rainy season begins in Southwest Asia.

20 *Fifteen cubits higher did the waters swell, as the mountains were covered.*

21 *And all flesh that stirred on earth perished—birds, cattle, beasts, and all the things that swarmed upon the earth, and all mankind.*

22 *All in whose nostrils was the merest breath of life, all that was on dry land, died.*

23 *All existence on earth was blotted out—man, cattle, creeping things, and birds of the sky; they were blotted out from the earth. Only Noah was left, and those with him in the ark.*[122]

24 *And when the waters had swelled on the earth one hundred and fifty days,*

Chapter 8

1 *God remembered*[123] *Noah and all the beasts and all the cattle that were with him in the ark, and God caused a wind to blow across the earth, and the waters subsided.*

2 *The fountains of the deep and the floodgates of the sky were stopped up, and the rain from the sky was held back;*

3 *the waters then receded steadily from the earth. At the end of one hundred and fifty days the water diminished.*

4 *so that in the seventh month, on the seventeenth day of the month, the ark came to rest on the mountains of Ararat.*[124, 125]

5 *The waters went on diminishing until the tenth month; in the tenth month, on the first of the month, the tops of the mountains became visible.*

---

[122]The occurrence of the Flood raises the question of how natural events can be understood as the judgments of God. Biblical man saw the hand of God in the Flood, just as he saw it working in other natural phenomena. Thus, the Flood is said to have lasted 364 days, to indicate that the very cycle of nature was interrupted until heaven and earth returned to their spheres a year later. While there are those whose faith still permits them to see a warning in every bolt of lightning and a retribution of the Divine in every natural disaster, most modern men do not believe in a God who arranges natural forces for the sake of man. In their view, the relevance of the Noah story is confined to its emphasis on God's moral judgment.

In considering the story as a homily on the consequences of man's corruption, lawlessness, and violence, modern man can affirm that such "sins" do bring on the judgment of God. We may experience it in man's social and moral conditions, or in nature's physical realm (as in our pollution of the atmosphere and water, or our disturbance of the ecological balance). God guarantees life and its laws. An offense against these is an offense against God and may occasion dire and unforeseen consequences.

[123]The Hebrew expression *va-yizkor*, referring to God remembering, occurs frequently in the Bible and consistently reflects a belief in moral continuity. What happened yesterday is not forgotten. It is stored up in divine memory and has a bearing on God's judgment in the future. The remembering God thus makes justice possible, even as among men there can be no ethical presence without ethical memories. Many prayers in the Jewish and Christian traditions ask God to remember. The Jewish memorial prayer begins with the words *yizkor Elohim*—"may God remember."

[124]Ararat is a district in Armenia, known in ancient history as Urartu. However, later traditions point to the Zagros mountains, east of the middle Tigris, as the resting place of Noah's ark. Attempts to find remains of Noah's ark have proven fruitless and are likely to remain so. But while the story of Noah may not be substantiated by any physical evidence, the evidence of a flood in the Asia Minor region is a scientific fact. {See 5,600 B.C.T.}

[125]2104 B.C.T. {Seder Olam Rabba Chronology}.

6 At the end of forty days, Noah opened the window of the ark that he had made

7 and sent out the raven[126]; it went to and fro until the waters had dried up from the earth.

8 Then he sent out the dove to see whether the waters had decreased from the surface of the ground.

9 But the dove could not find a resting place for its foot, and returned to him to the ark, for there was water over all the earth. So putting out his hand, he took it into the ark with him.

10 He waited another seven days, and again sent out the dove from the ark.

11 The dove came back to him toward evening, and there in its bill was a plucked-off olive leaf! Then Noah knew that the waters had decreased on the earth.

12 He waited still another seven days and sent the dove forth; and it did not return to him any more.[127]

13 In the six hundred and first year, in the first month, on the first of the month, the waters began to dry from the earth; and when Noah removed the covering of the ark, he saw that the surface of the ground was drying.

14 And in the second month, on the twenty-seventh day of the month, the earth was dry.

AFTER THE FLOOD
{GENESIS 8:15–9:29}

15 God spoke to Noah, saying,

16 "Come out of the ark, together with your wife, your sons, and your sons' wives.

17 Bring out with you every living thing of all flesh that is with you: birds, animals, and everything that creeps on earth; and let them swarm on the earth and be fertile and increase on earth."

18 So Noah came out, together with his sons, his wife, and his sons' wives.

19 Every animal, every creeping thing, and every bird, everything that stirs on earth came out of the ark by families.

20 Then Noah built an altar to the LORD and, taking of every clean animal and of every clean bird, he offered burnt offerings on the altar.

21 The LORD smelled the pleasing odor[128], and the LORD said to Himself: "Never again will I doom the earth because of man, since the devisings of man's mind are evil from his youth[129]; nor will I ever

---

[126]With regards to the reference to ravens, it is notable that birds were often used by ancient mariners as compasses. The Akkadian flood story also features a raven.

[127]The Flood story presents a particularly striking example of the confluence of two traditions in the Torah. Occasionally,—as in the first two chapters of Genesis and in the relation of the lines of Cain and Seth—the variant sources are fairly apparent. However, at other times, such as with the Noah story, the two traditions are so closely intertwined that at first glance they present a single strand.

While there is no consensus, scholars believe that the two sources—the J and P sources— can been seen in the following excerpts. For the J, the J source material can be seen in verses 6:5–6; 7:1–4, 10, 12; 8:8–12; and 8:20–22. For the P, the P source material can be seen in verses 6:12–13, 14, 20; 7:11, 24; 8:3, 7, 13, 18–19; 9:1–17.

[128]The Torah speaks of God in human terms. In its language, "smelled the pleasing odor" is equivalent to "accepted favorably." It is interesting to compare with a parallel incident in "Gilgamesh": "The gods smelled the savor,/The gods smelled the goodly savor,/The gods gathered like flies over the sacrificer."

[129]With regards to the reference "evil from his youth," this reference indicates that the Flood did not change the nature of man.

again destroy every living being,[130] *as I have done.*

22 So long as the earth endures,/Seed-time and harvest,/Cold and heat,/Summer and winter,/Day and night/Shall not cease."

Chapter 9

1 God blessed Noah and his sons, and said to them, "Be fertile and increase, and fill the earth.

2 The fear and the dread of you shall be upon all the beasts of the earth and upon all the birds of the sky—everything with which the earth is astir—and upon all the fish of the sea; they are given into your hand.

3 Every creature that lives shall be yours to eat[131]*; as with the green grasses, I give you all these.*

4 You must not, however, eat flesh with its life-blood in it.[132]

5 But for your own life-blood I will require a reckoning: I will require it of every beast[133]*; of man, too, will I require a reckoning for human life, of every man for that of his fellow man!*

6 Whoever sheds the blood of man,/By man shall his blood be shed;/For in His image/Did God make man.[134]

7 Be fertile, then, and increase; abound on the earth and increase on it."[135]

8 And God said to Noah and to his sons with him,

---

[130]With the Flood over, man began once more to face the problems of existence. Man is re-assured that God will not again "destroy every living being" and that there is immutable order that God himself will not abrogate. The rainbow is seen as God's signature to God's promise, and the sons of Noah set out to people the world.

[131]With regards to the reference to "yours to eat," it should be noted that Adam was restricted to a vegetarian diet {see Genesis 1:29}. However, Noah and his descendants are permitted to eat the flesh of animals.

[132]This prohibition reflects the conviction that blood has a sacred character.

[133]Animals, too, are held responsible for acts of violence against man: "When an ox gores a man or a woman to death, the ox shall be stoned" {see Exodus 21:28}.

[134]Several biblical passages in Genesis, Chapter 9 became the reference points for certain regulations of later Jewish law. For instance, the prohibition against consuming blood was based on "You must not, however, eat flesh with its life-blood in it" {see Genesis 9:4}. While this was taken to refer primarily to a limb from a living animal, it also became a foundation for many Jewish dietary and slaughtering regulations.

Similarly, the prohibition against self-injury and suicide was based on "for your own life-blood I will require a reckoning" {see Genesis 9:5}. It is important to note that in biblical times suicide was rare (except under stress of battle {see 1 Samuel 31:4 and 1 Kings 16:18}). Aside from the battle related suicides, the only other suicide recorded in the Jewish Scriptures is the death of Ahithopel {see 2 Samuel 17:23}.

The limits of self-defense were discussed in reference to Genesis 9:6 which forbids bloodshed because God made man in His image. Since one man's blood is not redder (or better) than another's, no man may take an innocent life even if this is the only way to save his own.

The prohibition against abortion was based on the same verse, but reading it in a different way, condemning: "Whoever sheds the blood of man in man."

The duty to have children was derived from "Be fertile and increase" {see Genesis 9:1 and 9:7}. When God first said that man should be fertile {see Genesis 1:28}, it was a blessing. But after God's experience with the antediluvians, this blessing became a commandment requiring man to father several children in order to comply with the desire of God.

[135]Even before the revelation made to Moses at Sinai there were certain laws that were binding on all men. While Jews were subject to the extensive provisions of the Torah, all non–Jews

9 "I now establish My covenant[136] with you and your offspring to come,

10 and with every living thing that is with you—birds, cattle, and every wild beast as well—all that have come out of the ark, every living thing on earth.

11 I will maintain My covenant with you: never again shall all flesh be cut off by the waters of a flood, and never again shall there be a flood to destroy the earth."

12 God further said, "This is the sign that I set for the covenant between Me and you, and every living creature with you, for all ages to come.

13 I have set My bow in the clouds,[137] and it shall serve as a sign of the covenant between Me and the earth.

14 When I bring clouds over the earth, and the bow appears in the clouds,

15 I will remember My covenant between Me and you and every living creature among all flesh, so that the waters shall never again become a flood to destroy all flesh.

16 When the bow is in the clouds, I will see it and remember the everlasting covenant between God and all living creatures, all flesh that is on earth.

17 That," God said to Noah, "shall be

(pre–Jews) were required to observe at least a number of fundamental precepts deemed essential for the maintenance of a decent society. These laws are called "Noahide" laws. The Noahide laws were believed to have been incumbent on the sons of Noah and therefore to have become obligatory for mankind, since from Noah's sons "the whole world branched out" {see Genesis 9:19.}

Jews believe that six basic laws applied to antediluvian man. These laws are: (1) Man may not worship idols; (2) Man may not blaspheme God; (3) Man must establish courts of justice; (4) Man may not kill; (5) Man may not commit adultery; and (6) Man may not steal. A seventh law—that man may not eat flesh cut from a living animal—was added after the Flood {see Genesis 9:4}. The implications of these laws is that every man—every person—can arrive at and must come to observe a minimum of religious and legal precepts.

Over time, Jews came to categorize non–Jews—Gentiles—according to their adherence to the Noahide laws. The *Nochri* (*Akkum*) were Gentiles who did not believe in the Noahide laws. The *Ben Noah* were Gentiles who did believe, and the *Ger Toshav* were Gentiles who officially declared before a court that they would observe the seven Noahide laws. For their pledge, the *Ger Toshav* would be given the privilege of becoming resident aliens in Israel. Of particular note, unlike Christianity, Judaism did not deny salvation to non–Jews. According to Jewish law, all non–Jews who observe the Noahide laws will participate in salvation and in the rewards of the world to come.

A question does arise however concerning the naming of these laws. After all, if most of these laws were already known to Adam, why were they named for Noah and not Adam? The answer appears to be that all law must be rooted in a covenant—a contract—, and before Noah there was no covenant between man and God. Only with God's covenant with Noah does it become possible to speak of law.

[136]With this statement, God now fulfills the promise that God made before the Flood {see Genesis 6:18}. The Hebrew term *berit* is often used with the Hebrew verb which translates as "cut." Thus, "to cut a *berit*" is idiomatic for "to conclude a covenant."

[137]In ancient folklore, a rainbow represented instruments used by gods in battle. The bows would be hung in the sky as symbols of victory. In Babylonian tradition, for example, the god Marduk suspended his bow in the heavens after he had defeated Tiamat, the goddess of the deep waters. The Bible has retained aspects of such folklore. The Hebrew word *keshet* means both "bow of war" and "rainbow," but as usual the Torah has assimilated the material to convey a deeper meaning.

The Torah forwards the belief that God is the proximate cause of all natural events and

the sign of the covenant that I have established between Me and all flesh that is on earth."

18 The sons of Noah who came out of the ark were Shem,[138] Ham, and Japheth— Ham being the father of Canaan.

19 These three were the sons of Noah, and from these the whole world branched out.

20 Noah, the tiller of the soil, was the first to plant a vineyard.[139]

21 He drank of the wine and became drunk, and he uncovered himself within his tent.

22 Ham, the father of Canaan, saw his father's nakedness and told his two brothers outside.[140]

23 But Shem and Japheth took a cloth, placed it against both their backs and, walking backwards, they covered their father's nakedness; their faces were turned the other way, so that they did not see their father's nakedness.

24 When Noah woke up from his wine and learned what his youngest son[141] had done to him,

25 he said, "Cursed be Canaan[142];/The

---

that manifestations of the natural order are invested with divine portent. Thunder, earthquakes, and floods fall under this rubric as does the rainbow. The Torah text sees the rainbow both as a sign of God's reign over the natural order and as God's permanent signature attesting to God's promise. The rainbow is thought to remind God of this promise and to remind man of the grace and forbearance of man's Creator.

[138]Shem is deemed to be the ancestor of all Semites. As for Ham, as far as the Torah is concerned, Ham's primary importance is in being the father of Canaan.

[139]Wine growing is represented as an ancient practice. Indeed, the Epic of Gilgamesh tells of Utnapishtim giving wine to his ark-building workmen.

[140]Some commentators believe that Noah was castrated by Ham, while others believe that Noah was sexually abused by Ham. These beliefs may seem absurd but there was precedent for such occurrences in the ancient folklore. For instance, in an old Canaanite story, the god El-Kronos emasculated his father. Additionally, a Hurrian legend tells of how Kumarbis severed the genitals of his father, the god Anu. In some Jewish literature, Ham is portrayed as laughing at his father, as does Kumarbis, and both Ham and Kumarbis are subsequently cursed for their deeds. It is important to remember that both the Canaanite and the Hurrian stories were known to the biblical writers and may have been incorporated into the story which has become associated with Genesis' Noah.

[141]Ham is here called the youngest. Elsewhere {see Genesis 9:18 and 10:1}, Ham is listed as the middle brother. Critics see two separate traditions here. Older commentators took "youngest" to mean "unworthy" as in Genesis 32:11.

[142]To some extent, the curse of Ham may be viewed as a bit of political propaganda. At the time of the Genesis writers, the tale of Ham and Noah may have been a not so subtle assertion that the Hamites (the Egyptians) and the Canaanites were the descendants of sexual deviates. As such, the crime of Ham most likely best belongs to the genre of polemics employed against Israel's nearest neighbors and most bitter enemies.

It is worth noting that the Bible assigned a prominent place to the theme of sexuality in the stories of both the first antediluvians (Adam and Eve) and the first postdiluvians (Noah and his offspring). Furthermore, the theme of sexual aberration linked to drunkenness occurs again in the story of Lot and his daughters—a story that ends by asserting that Moab and Ammon also were nations of indecent sexual background and that the Moabites and Ammonites were the products of sexual deviants. {See Genesis 19:32–38.}

Ultimately, it is most likely that the curse of Ham and the Canaanites along with the derogatory insinuation associated with the Moabites and Ammonites are examples of a form

lowest of slaves[143]*/Shall he be to his broth-ers.* "[144]

26 *And he said, "Blessed be the LORD/ The God of Shem*[145]*;/Let Canaan be a slave to them.*[146]*/*

27 *May God enlarge Japheth,/And let him dwell in the tents of Shem*[147]*;/And let Canaan be a slave to them."*

28 *Noah lived after the Flood 350 years.*

29 *And all the days of Noah came to 950 years; then he died.*[148]

THE NATIONS
{GENESIS 10:1–32}

Chapter 10[149]

1 *These are the lines of Shem, Ham, Japheth, the sons of Noah: sons were born to them after the Flood.*

2 *The descendants of Japheth: Gomer,*[150] *Magog,*[151] *Madai, Javan, Tubal, Meshech, and Tiras.*

---

of scurrilous religious political propaganda which over the course of time would come to haunt (and be used against) the Jewish people themselves.

[143]With regards to the use of the term "lowest of slaves," the actual Hebrew idiom is "slave of slaves."

[144]The punishment meted out to Ham seems harsh in the extreme, and this harshness suggests that the Bible was referring to a transgression far more serious than seeing one's father naked and in a drunken stupor. Uncovering a relative's nakedness was a biblical euphemism for sexual relations {see Leviticus 18}. The story of Ham and Noah, therefore, may be read as one of sexual perversion.

The brevity of the biblical story may be due to the expurgation of a more detailed version, but even in the condensed form the ancient Israelites doubtlessly understood its implication.

[145]Noah blesses not Shem but Shem's God, for blessing a person's divine protector represented or reinforced the blessing of the person himself. {See and compare with 1 Samuel 25:32.}

[146]With regards to the phrase "Let Canaan be a slave to them," it is notable that, historically, advocates for the enslavement of persons of African descent have relied upon this passage as forming the justification for the institution of African slavery. However, this passage has nothing whatsoever to do with race, and the notion that the Bible supported the perpetuation of the genocidal practice of enslaving Africans is perhaps the greatest blasphemy of all.

[147]Here Japheth most likely refers to the Philistines, while Shem refers to the Israelites. Genesis (unlike Judges and Samuel) envisions the Philistines and Israelites as living in harmony. The verse, therefore, probably means: "May God make room for the Philistines that they might dwell peacefully with Israel."

[148]1754 B.C.T. {Olam Rabba Chronology}.

[149]Chapter 10 is an overview of the nations known to biblical tradition. It belongs to the last segment of the book of Genesis in which the canvas becomes universal. Thereafter, the focus of Genesis contracts toward the major theme—the emergence of one family and the people who will descend from it. The table of nations is, therefore, more than a catalog of names—it is the background for the stories to follow.

[150]Some commentators believe that Gomer may have become the Cimmerians (from which today's Welsh derive their name Cymry).

[151]With regards to Magog, the land of Gog would be found in Armenia {see Ezekiel 38:2 and 39:6}.

3 The descendants of Gomer: Ashkenaz,[152] *Riphath, and Togarmah.*

4 The descendants of Javan: Elishah and Tarshish,[153] *the Kittim, and the Dodanim.*[154]

5 From these the maritime nations branched out. [These are the descendants of Japheth][155] *by their lands—each with its language—their clans and their nations.*

6 The descendants of Ham: Cush,[156] *Mizraim,*[157] *Put, and Canaan.*[158]

7 The descendants of Cush: Seba, Havilah, Sabtah, Raamah, and Sabteca. The descendants of Raamah: Sheba and Dedan.

8 Cush also begot Nimrod,[159] *who was the first man of might on earth.*

9 He was a mighty hunter[160] *by the grace of the LORD; hence the saying, "Like Nimrod a mighty hunter by the grace of the LORD."*

10 The mainstays of his kingdom were Babylon, Erech, Accad, and Calneh[161] *in the land of Shinar.*[162]

---

[152]Here "Ashkenaz" probably refers to the Scythians. In Medieval Hebrew, the term "Ashkenaz" was given to Germany, and Jews from Central and Eastern Europe were called Ashkenazim, in contrast to the Spanish and Asian Jews who were called Sephardim.

[153]Tarshish is best known as the place to which Jonah tried to flee. It is usually identified as Tartessos in Spain. However, since Spain appears to lie outside the geographic range mentioned in Genesis 10, this may refer to another place by the same name, perhaps Tarsus in Cilicia, Asia Minor.

[154]Dodanim, in 1 Chronicle 1:7, is called Rodanim, possibly referring to the people of Rhodes. Some translations say "Dordanim" instead of "Dodanim." If so, "Dordanim" would refer to Dardania, near Troy.

[155]The bracketed portion which appears here was probably omitted through scribal error.

[156]Cush refers either to Ethiopia or Midian (north of the Gulf of Akaba). In other contexts the name may refer to the Kassites, a people who ruled Babylonia from the sixteenth to the twelfth centuries B.C.T. and then retreated to the highlands east of the Tigris. That Cush may refer to Midian is evidenced by Exodus 2:16, 21 and Numbers 12:1 as well as by Egyptian execration texts which place Cush south of the Dead Sea.

[157]Most scholars agree that Mizraim means Egypt.

[158]The listing of Canaan as a descendant of Ham suggests an age in which Egypt's rule extended into Asia, Canaan, and beyond, before the invasions of the sea peoples (the Japhethites in the latter part of the second millennium B.C.T.) put an effective end to Egypt's Asiatic empire.

[159]The brief reference to Nimrod is probably a fragment from a large epic, well known in its time, which likely dealt with Tukulti-Ninurta I, who ruled Assyria from around 1244 to 1208 B.C.T. and who controlled both Babylonia and Assyria.

[160]Hunting was practiced in ancient Israel {see Leviticus 17:13} but apparently played only a small role in its largely agrarian and urban society. In later centuries, Jews would come to consider the hunt a cruel and therefore uncivilized sport.

[161]The presence of the phrase "and Calneh" is probably a case of faulty vocalization of the text. The original Hebrew manuscript was written without vowels, which were added more than a thousand years later. By changing the Hebrew script for *kalneh* to the Hebrew script for *kulanah*, the text comes to read: "The mainstays of his kingdom were Babylon, Erech, Accad, all of these [being] in the land of Shinar." {See Genesis 42:36.}

[162]Shinar was the biblical name for the area of Babylonia, and especially for Sumer.

11 From that land Asshur went forth and built Nineveh, Rehoboth-ir, Calah,[163]

12 and Resen between Nineveh and Calah, that is the great city.

13 And Mizraim begot[164] the Ludim, the Anamim, the Lehabim, the Naphtuhim,

14 the Pathrusim, the Casluhim, and the Caphtorim,[165] whence the Philistines came forth.

15 Canaan begot Sidon,[166] his first-born, and Heth[167];

16 and the Jebusites, the Amorites, the Girgashites,

17 the Hivites, the Arkites, the Sinites,

18 the Arvadites, the Zemarites, and the Hamathites. Afterward the clans of the Canaanites spread out,

19 (The [original] Canaanite territory extended from Sidon as far as Gerar, near Gaza, and as far as Sodom, Gomorrah, Admah, and Zeboiim, near Lasha.)

20 These are the descendants of Ham, according to their clans and language, by their lands and nations.

21 Sons were also born to Shem, ancestor of all the descendants of Eber[168] and older brother of Japheth.

22 The descendants of Shem: Elam,[169] Asshur, Arpachshad,[170] Lud, and Aram.[171]

23 The descendants of Aram: Uz, Hul, Gether, and Mash.

24 Arpachshad begot Shelah, and Shelah begot Eber.

25 Two sons were born to Eber: the name of the first was Peleg[172], for in his days the earth was divided; and the name of his brother was Joktan.

---

[163]Calah was a Mesopotamian city founded by Shalmaneser I (c.1274–1245 B.C.T.), which has been thoroughly explored by archaeologists. It was a "great city" in its day serving as one of the great capital cities of the neo-Assyrian kings from 880–615 B.C.T. Today, Calah is known as Nimrud.

[164]In biblical parlance, the term "begot" is meant to be understood as "was the ancestor of." Similarly, the expressions of "father" and "son" often mean ancestor and descendant.

[165]With regards to the phrase "and the Caphtorim," in the Hebrew text these words come at the end of the sentence. The transposition here is made because the Philistines came from Caphtor {see Amos 9:7}. The Caphtorim are usually identified as Cretans. However, no archaeological evidence has been found to make the identification certain.

[166]Sidon is located north of Acre.

[167]Heth is a reference to the "Neo-Hittites," who established themselves in northern Syria after the overthrow of the old Hittite (Hattia) empire in Anatolia, about 1200 B.C.T. Biblical references to Hittites are generally to the Neo-Hittites, some of whom drifted into Canaan {see Genesis 23:3}. {See also Deuteronomy 7:1.}

[168]The reference to Eber may actually be to "Abraham the Hebrew." {See Genesis 11:16.}

[169]Elam is a country mentioned frequently in the literature of antiquity. Its capital city was Susa (Shushan in Esther 1:2), located southeast of modern Luristan in Iran. The Christian Scriptures note that Elamites along with Parthians and Medes were found in Jerusalem on Shavuot—on Pentecost. {See Acts 2:9.}

[170]Arpachshad has been identified by some scholars as Ur-Casdim, the place of Abraham's origin.

[171]Aram is the ancestor of the Arameans whose script and language (Aramaic) began to spread in Southwest Asia before 1000 B.C.T. By the sixth century B.C.T., Aramaic was widely used in the area and after the Babylonian exile displaced Hebrew as the popular language in Palestine. Portions of the Books of Daniel and Ezra are in Aramaic, which is also the dominant language of the Talmud.

[172]During Peleg's lifetime, the people of the world branched out and became settled.

26 Joktan begot Almodad, Sheleph, Hazarmaveth, Jerah.

27 Hadoram, Uzal, Diklah,

28 Obal, Abimael, Sheba,

29 Ophir, Havilah, and Jobab; all these were the descendants of Joktan.

30 Their settlements extended from Mesha as far as Sephar, the hill country to the east.

31 These are the descendants of Shem according to their clans and languages, by their lands, according to their nations.

32 These are the groupings of Noah's descendants, according to their origins, by their nations; and from these the nations branched out over the earth after the Flood.[173]

THE TOWER OF BABEL
{GENESIS 11:1–26}

Chapter 11[174]

1 All the earth had the same language[175] *and the same words.*

---

[173]The geographic area covered by the biblical table reaches from the Caucasus mountains in the north to Ethiopia in the south, from the Aegean Sea in the west to the highlands of Iran in the east. Broadly speaking, Japheth refers to the peoples at the northern and western periphery of the Fertile Crescent, including the Medes, the Cypriots, the Scythians, and the Ionians. The offspring of Ham dwell about the Red Sea and include Ethiopians, Egyptians, and Canaanites. The descendants of Shem live in the heart of the Crescent itself and include Arabs, Arameans, and Assyrians.

Genesis Chapter 10 represents the combination of two separate traditions. The older one (Genesis 10:8–19, 21, 22–30) is concerned primarily with tribes and clans; the more recent one stresses the term *goy* or "nation" and is mainly a catalog of states and languages (as for instance, in verses 5, 20, 31, 32). The table of nations is remarkable for its wide scope and may be considered a pioneering effort among the ethnographic inquiries of antiquity. It is presented in a way which contrasts sharply with a comparable Babylonian list which states that "when kingship came down from heaven the kingdom was in Eridu."

It is, however, important to see the biblical list as more than ethnographic information. The list is an integral part of the story of God's promise to Noah. The list portrays the peoples of the earth, related through this promise, as one common humanity. The implicit theme of the text is the unity of man within the framework of apparent diversity.

No reference to "race" or skin color can be detected in this list. This is not to say that the Bible is without prejudices or preferences. Occasionally, the list reflects certain political animosities, and repeatedly it condemns various nations because of their immoral or idolatrous practices, but it is totally devoid of any notion of racial superiority. The dispassionate character of this chapter is indicative of the Bible's overall approach to the structure of humanity.

Quite notably, Israel is not listed in the catalog of nations. In fact, the text underplays the origins of the people to whom, after all, the Bible is devoted. Israel's origins are (like the stories of Eden and Noah) located outside Israelite territory, and just as in its territory there was no original distinction so there was none in its early ancestry. Its origins were seen as no different from those of any other nation. Only through its covenantal relationship with God would Israel pursue a special destiny.

Although Shem was the oldest of Noah's sons, he is listed last in the table of nations. Most probably this was done because his genealogy commands the Bible's eventual focus, and after the brief interruption occasioned by the Tower of Babel story, the text turns to a detailed description of Shem's line—the line that consists of the forebears of Abraham.

[174]Genesis, Chapter 11 relates the story of the Tower of Babel. The Tower of Babel story, interrupting the catalog of nations begun in Chapter 10 and continued in chapter 11, verse

2 And as men migrated from the east,[176] *they came upon a valley in the land of Shinar and settled there.*

3 They said to one another, "Come, let us make bricks and burn them hard."—Brick served them as stone, and bitumen served them as mortar.[177]*—*

4 And they said, "Come, let us build us a city, and a tower[178] *with its top in the sky, to make a name for ourselves; else we shall be scattered all over the world."*

5 The LORD came down[179] *to look at the city and tower which man had built,*

6 and the LORD said, "If, as one peo-

10, stands between the universal tableau of humanity and that specific list of families from which Terah, Abraham, and their line would spring.

The story of the Tower of Babel attempts to answer two questions: (1) Where did the variety of languages come from? and (2) How did man disperse and populate the world? These questions were not considered in chapter 10. By setting out to answer them, the Bible brings us a special tradition, one which must have existed independently from the table of nations. For the Babel story presents all mankind living undivided in one small area. This unity of language and living space ends because man's rebellious action once again brings down the judgment of God.

While there is a Sumerian story of the confounding of tongues, no parallel account has so far been found in Southwest Asian records that would afford us the kind of comparison and contrast through which the biblical purpose of the Flood tale is seen in high relief.

Biblical scholars generally believe that the opening section of Genesis which concludes here was originally separate from the patriarchal cycles which follow. The joining of prehistory and history (in its wider sense) affords the biblical editors the opportunity to show the rise of Abraham and his descendants in the full context of God's plan for mankind.

[175]Historically, the principal languages of Mesopotamia in the third millennium B.C.T. were Sumerian and Akkadian. The latter is a Semitic language related to Hebrew, though not as closely as are Amorite, Canaanite, and Aramaic. Today, the Semitic language most widely spoken in the area is Arabic.

[176]Apparently, men migrated from the east where they had settled after the Flood.

[177]The Bible means to explain that in Babylon brick and bitumen were used instead of stone and mortar as in Israel. Here, the entire story abounds in assonances and alliterations.

In comparison, in the *Enuma Elish,* the following description of the building of a shrine to Marduk appears: "The first year they molded bricks. When the second year arrived they raised high the head of Esagila, the counterpart of Apsu" (Apsu being a poetic term for the abyss). Herodotus describes the construction of a Mesopotamian moat as follows: "As fast as they dug the moat, the soil which they got from the cutting was made into bricks, and when a sufficient number were completed they baked the brick in kilns. Then they set to building, using hot bitumen throughout for their cement."

[178]A tower-like structure called a *zikurat* (ziggurat)—literally, "that which has been raised high"—was a distinctive feature of Babylonian temple complexes and may have served as the humanly constructed equivalent of the legendary holy mountain in Babylonian folklore. The *zikurat* (or ziggurat) called Etemenanki ("the house of the foundation of heaven and earth") was reported to have consisted of seven stories receding in pyramid like fashion toward a flat top and reaching a height of nearly 300 feet. Archeologists have uncovered the foundation of this *zikurat,* and its extent would seem to coincide with the reputed size of the Tower of Babel. Scholars have also confirmed the special use of hardened brick for such an enterprise.

The biblical writer's contempt for the paganism of Babylon determined not only his interpretation of the catastrophe that befell the city and its tower but also the style of the story,

ple with one language for all, this is how they have begun to act, then nothing that they may propose to do will be out of their reach.

7 let us, then, go down[180] and confound their speech there, so that they shall not understand one another's speech."

8 Thus the LORD scattered them[181] from there over the face of the whole earth; and they stopped building the city.

9 That is why it was called Babel,[182] because there the LORD confounded the speech of the whole earth; and from there the LORD

---

with its obvious overtones of sarcasm, its repeated word plays, and its explanation of Babel as a place of confusion.

[179]The reference to "the Lord came down" means that the Lord descended to earth in order to judge man. This expression is also used in telling the story of Sodom and Gomorrah. {See Genesis 18:21.}

[180]The use of the phrase "let us, then, go down" is either a majestic plural or is spoken to an angelic court. However, in Christian theology, the phrase is usually taken to indicate the triune nature of God. {See and compare with Genesis 1:26.}

[181]While we are told that God's judgment consisted of scattering the people of Babel and confounding their speech, their actual transgression is not specified. A city was built and in it a tower, and the builders hoped that its summit would reach high into the heavens. In viewing this activity, God said: "This is how they have begun to act" {see Genesis 11:6}. But what the word "this" refers to is not explained. A number of theories have been offered. One theory is that the people of Babylon were engaged in self-aggrandizement. According to the great majority of commentators, the tower represents man's tendency to reach too high, his attempt to equal if not displace God. Just as Adam desired to be like God and in consequence was driven from Eden, so in Babel, too, men exhibited excessive arrogance. They prided themselves on their accomplishments—they invented brick, knew how to use bitumen, and proceeded to build a large city with a skyscraping tower. Like the generation of the Flood, they were given to self-exaltation. Having a common dwelling place and a unified language encouraged their designs. Once these elements were removed, their rather pretentious enterprise collapsed.

Another theory behind God's possible concern was that the people of Babylon had rebelled against God. The sin of the generation of Babel may have consisted of their refusal to "fill the earth." They had been commanded to do so but still tried to defy the divine will. God's action, therefore, was not so much a punishment as a carrying out of God's plan. Confounding the human language was merely an assurance that the Babel incident would not be repeated. As the saying goes, "Man proposed, but God disposed."

A certain pathos adheres to the second theory. It senses in the generation of Babel not arrogance but anxiety, not a desire to reach the heavens so much as the need to press together on earth. Thus, the tale becomes a sort of condemnation of extreme centralization, the last consequence of which is one huge universal megalopolis which sees its final goal in bringing all men under One Tower or, as fundamentalist Christians warn against, bringing all men under one world government.

A third theory is that the city is a center of the account and all else is secondary. The tower is merely the embodiment of the city, and when the story closes it speaks only of the city. A brief notation reveals the whole purpose of the Babel story: "and they stopped building the city."

The third theory reflects most clearly a pervasive biblical motif. The city is the ultimate expression of man's presumption. Babel was the city, and, to the anti-urban tradition of the Bible, its downfall appeared as a proper divine judgment. Babel referred of course to Babylon, but it also symbolized all empire building, corruption, arrogance, craving to erect mon-

scattered them over the face of the whole earth.

10 This is the line of Shem. Shem was 100 years old when he begot Arpachshad, two years after the Flood.[183]

11 After the birth of Arpachshad, Shem lived 500 years[184] and begot sons and daughters.

12 When Arpachshad had lived 35 years, he begot Shelah.[185]

13 After the birth of Shelah, Arpachshad lived 403 years[186] and begot sons and daughters.

14 When Shelah had lived 30 years, he begot Eber.[187]

15 After the birth of Eber, Shelah lived 403 years[188] and begot sons and daughters.

16 When Eber[189] had lived 34 years, he begot Peleg.[190]

17 After the birth of Peleg, Eber lived 430 years[191] and begot sons and daughters.

18 When Peleg had lived 30 years, he begot Reu.[192]

19 After the birth of Reu, Peleg lived 209 years[193] and begot sons and daughters.

20 When Reu had lived 32 years, he begot Serug.[194]

21 After the birth of Serug, Reu lived 207 years[195] and begot sons and daughters.

22 When Serug had lived 30 years, he begot Nahor.[196]

23 After the birth of Nahor, Serug lived 200 years[197] and begot sons and daughters.

24 When Nahor had lived 29 years, he begot Terah.[198]

---

uments, desire for fame; it meant a turning away from what were considered the primary occupation of man—agriculture and the tending of flocks. Farmers and nomads "fill the earth"—they live close to the land and its creatures—while city-dwellers flee from the earth. Babel was an alienation of man from the simple life, and it is no accident that the Bible next turns to Abraham, a semi-nomad, as the source of all future blessings.

[182] While Babylonian tradition explained the name "Babel" to mean the "Gate of God," the biblical author substituted a satirical play on words: Babylon is only confusion. An English parallel might be Babel-babble.

[183] 2102 B.C.T. {Seder Olam Rabba Chronology}.

[184] 1602 B.C.T. {Seder Olam Rabba Chronology}.

[185] 2067 B.C.T. {Seder Olam Rabba Chronology}.

[186] 1637 B.C.T. {Seder Olam Rabba Chronology}.

[187] 2037 B.C.T. {Seder Olam Rabba Chronology}.

[188] 1634 B.C.T. {Seder Olam Rabba Chronology}.

[189] Eber is generally deemed to be the ancestor of the Hebrews.

[190] 2003 B.C.T. {Seder Olam Rabba Chronology}.

[191] 1573 B.C.T. {Seder Olam Rabba Chronology}.

[192] 1973 B.C.T. {Seder Olam Rabba Chronology}.

[193] 1764 B.C.T. {Seder Olam Rabba Chronology}.

[194] 1941 B.C.T. {Seder Olam Rabba Chronology}.

[195] 1734 B.C.T. {Seder Olam Rabba Chronology}.

[196] 1911 B.C.T. {Seder Olam Rabba Chronology}.

[197] 1711 B.C.T. {Seder Olam Rabba Chronology}.

[198] 1882 B.C.T. {Seder Olam Rabba Chronology}.

25 After the birth of Terah, Nahor lived 119 years[199] and begot sons and daughters.

26 When Terah[200] had lived seventy years,[201] he begot Abram, Nahor, and Haran.

Chapter 11 of Genesis is a transition from universal prehistory to a story of more limited scope—that of Abraham and his people. The Bible sees humanity's early history as a series of rebellions against the will of God. The rebellion of the people of Babel prompts God to look for a new chan-nel to man. To Abraham and his descendants God now entrusts the task of bringing blessings to all the nations of the earth. The remainder of the Torah is devoted to the story of this particular people and to the road they must follow in order to fulfill their universal responsibility. The Babel tale of divine displeasure and the subsequent genealogical list thus constitute both the conclusion of the prologue and the introduction to the first act of the main biblical drama.

---

[199]1763 B.C.T. {Seder Olam Rabba Chronology}.

[200]With the exception of Shem, all ancestral names down to Terah appear to reflect the names of cities in upper Mesopotamia, a district later called Aram-Naharaim and Paddan-Aram. Hence, it would appear that the Israelites considered themselves to be Arameans in origin {see Deuteronomy 26:5}.

Most of the pre–Patriarchs father their children at thirty years of age. Furthermore, note the round numbers 100 and 500 and that 403, like 30, occurs twice. Whether the system is based on multiples of six and seven, or of seven, ten, twelve, and forty is in doubt. However, that an underlying scheme exists appears certain despite the fact that the ancient versions differ somewhat in the numbers which appear. The symbolism must once have been comprehensible but became less so as time went on. Nevertheless, the numbers that do appear were later used to this end by the Seder Olam Rabba to arrive at 3760 B.C.T. as the year of creation. This date is not far from the archeologically suggested age for the emergence of civilization in Mesopotamia.

[201]1812 B.C.T. {Seder Olam Rabba Chronology}.

A Catholic Perspective

AN OVERVIEW

From a Catholic perspective, the Bible is not a single, unified book. It is, in fact, a collection of some 73 different works by different authors, using very different styles and perspectives, composed over a span of several centuries, in three different languages (Hebrew, Aramaic, and Greek). Most of the Old Testament (46 books) was written in Hebrew, but parts of the books of Daniel (Daniel 2:4 to 7:28); Ezra (Ezra 4:6 to 6:18 and 7:12–26); and one verse of Jeremiah (Jeremiah 10:11) were originally composed in Aramaic, a Southwest Asian language related to, but different from, Hebrew. All 27 of the New Testament books were composed in Greek.

The rich diversity of the Bible is one of its great assets and its great glories. This diversity allows the story of God's people to be told from various perspectives. It also presents a challenge to the reader who should be aware of the different cultural, historical, and literary contexts of each biblical book. However, from a Catholic perspective, there is a deeper unity to the Bible that binds together these individual pieces of literature. Through the many biblical books flows the continuing saga of God's love for Israel and for the community of Christians. Each of the biblical authors, no matter how much separated in time, culture, and literary style, shares a conviction that God's presence is felt in human history and that God invites the human family to respond with faith and integrity.

The creation of the Bible has been a long-term and difficult process. The Jewish or Hebrew canon ultimately recognizes 39 books, divided into three major categories:

1. The Law (sometimes referred to as the Pentateuch [in Hebrew *Torah*]) or the first five books of the Bible—namely, Genesis, Exodus, Leviticus, Numbers, and Deuteronomy.
2. The Prophets (in Hebrew *Nevi'im*) subdivided into the "Former Prophets" (Joshua, Judges, 1 and 2 Samuel, 1 and 2 Kings) and the "Latter Prophets" (Isaiah, Jeremiah, Ezekiel, and the "Twelve" [Hosea, Joel, Amos, Obadiah, Jonah, Micah, Nahum, Habakkuk, Zephaniah, Haggai, Zechariah, and Malachi]).
3. The Writings (in Hebrew *Kethuvim*): Psalms, Proverbs, Job, Song of Songs, Ruth, Lamentations, Ecclesiates, Esther, Daniel, Ezra, Nehemiah, and 1 and 2 Chronicles.

There are seven other books that Roman Catholics (and some Orthodox Christians) consider part of their Scriptures. Judaism reverences these books and considers them sacred, but they are not part of their "canon" or official list. These books are: Tobit, Judith, 1 and 2 Maccabees, Wisdom, Ecclesiasticus (or Sirach), and Baruch. There are also some additional passages in the books of Daniel and Esther.

Most Christians agree on the 27 books to be included in the New Testament. However there is a dispute about some of the books in the Old Testament. Roman Catholics and Orthodox Christians agree on the 46 books that make up the Old Testament (the Orthodox include additional books in their canon: 1 and 2 Esdras; the Prayer of Manasseh; Psalm 151; and 3 Maccabees). In contrast, Judaism and Protestant Christians hold to the shorter list of 39 books set forth in the Hebrew canon.

The reason for the divergence amongst the religious groups is that earliest Christianity used an ancient Greek translation of the Old Testament (called the Septuagint) as its Bible. This Greek version of the Bible included 46 books. Since most of the early Christians were Greek speaking, this is the Bible they preferred. However, when Judaism officially set out to determine its canon at the end of the first century, it drew up a shorter list of 39 books: those written in Hebrew. Subsequently, during the Reformation period, Protestants adopted the Hebrew canon—the 39 books—considering such to be more authentic.

From the beginning of its existence, the Bible has been the object of intense study, prayerful reading, and even heated debate. In many ways, the Bible took shape in prayer and reflection. The various biblical authors reflected on significant events in the history of the Jews, of Jesus, and of the early Christian Church. The biblical author's discovery of God's presence working within history gives the Bible its force. For most Christians, the Bible has unique authority as writings inspired by God's Spirit working within the Jewish and Christian communities. Indeed, for most Christians, it was God's Spirit which compelled the biblical writers to give expression in human words to their faith perspective.

For most of their history, the Jews have maintained a rich tradition of reflection on the Hebrew Scriptures. The rabbis lovingly studied every detail of the biblical text and saw an infinite possibility of applications to everyday life. For the Jews, the Hebrew Scriptures were deemed to be God's Word and thus took a central place within the prayer life of the synagogue.

Much of the tradition of Christianity has had a character akin to that of the Jews. Indeed, until the late Middle Ages, almost all of the church's theology and teaching was little more than an elaboration of the biblical text. Today, for most Christians, reading the Bible has a more modest, yet still important goal. Today's Christians turn to the Scriptures for inspiration in living out their life of faith.

The inspiration sought by so many Christians can be gained in many different ways. For some, the Scriptures are an important stimulant for prayer. The words of the Psalms, the challenge of the prophets, the compassionate mission of Jesus, the inspiring words of Paul—all of these give form and expression to the longing of our own hearts as we seek to establish our own relationship with God. Very often the biblical words are able to express the feelings and fears and hopes we could not put into words ourselves. Thus, by reaching out to the Bible, we unite ourselves with the faith of countless generations of believers who found the same solace and strength in the Scriptures.

For others, probing the Scriptures helps guide and illumine their daily life. Study of the biblical text and discussion of its meaning with other thoughtful persons can help us understand our own experience of faith and expand our perspective on what it means to be a believer in the modern world. This approach works best when the participant is not afraid to reflect on his or her own experience, and then relate that reflection to the ideas and images of the Bible. Very often the Bible opens its treasures when the reader brings to it questions and hopes that spring from the experiences of life. Then, in turn, for the believer, the biblical message can give new insight and sustenance to the believer's life of faith.

In reading the Scriptures, it is important to remember that the Scriptures are about human beings. The personalities of the Scriptures may have lived long ago and in a far distant place, but they shared many of the concerns and worries that continue to confront us today. After all, the characters of the Bible also had families. They had parents, children, brothers and sisters, aunts and uncles. They had families, and they had all the joys and problems that having families can bring.

The people of the Scriptures wondered about the world and their place in it, and tried to understand things as best they could. For the most part, the personalities of the Scriptures wanted people, rich and poor, to obey the law and act fairly. They wondered how to set up their society so that people would act according to the best parts of their nature. They had governments of which they could be proud, and other governments that they did not like. They worried about events in foreign countries, and how those events might affect their lives.

From a Catholic perspective, the Scriptures use human materials and human experiences to convey God's presence. God speaks to humanity from within the context of our human lives. Sometimes our lives, and the experiences that form a part of them, are less than we might hope they would be. The same is true of the people of the Bible. There are no characters in the Hebrew Scriptures, for instance, who receive more honor than Moses and David.

However, the Bible tells us the bad, as well as the good, about these great leaders. Moses killed a man in anger {see Exodus 2:11–14} and David committed adultery {see 2 Samuel 11 and 12}.

The lesson Catholics draw from such passages, and other difficult and painful episodes, is that all of life is involved in our understanding of God. The Bible does not try to gloss things over or pretend that they are better than they are. God uses it all, even the bad parts, to carry on the story.

From a Catholic perspective, the Bible, above all else, is a story. That does not mean that the Bible is fiction. Far from it. What it does mean is that whether reading the Old Testament or the New, in scripture one will find the features of good storytelling—plot, characters, and settings that help the reader to get caught up in the emotion and dynamic energy of the events being recounted.

This emphasis on story points to a great new biblical truth. People learn about God through the events of their lives. Many may have a notion that scripture relates a succession of "mountain top" events where God dictates laws and teachings to religious giants like Moses. But, except for the giving of the Ten Commandments, scripture narrates no such events. The usual way that the people of Israel discovered who God is and how God deals with people was through their life experience. Even when prophets raised their voices to deliver God's messages to the people, they were usually commenting on how the people were (or were not) living their lives. It was as though the prophets were saying: "Look at the mess you are in. God is speaking to you through the tragic events you are experiencing!"

The Jewish people's understanding of a "covenant" provides a fine example of understanding God through life experience. The covenant was first considered to be an eternal and unconditional pledge made by God to the people ("I am your God and you will always be my people whom I will protect"), but over the course of many years it came to be understood instead that it was conditioned on the people's behavior toward God and one another. If you are faithful to your part of the bargain—that is, love God and each other—then I will be faithful to mine. It took a lot of life experience to get to that realization,—a lot of paying the price for unfaithfulness—before the people realized that God would not be their divine warrior fighting on the side of Israel no matter what.

The lesson for all mankind is that God has made all of life holy, and it is in and through the events of our God-given lives that we will encounter and know our God. We must therefore pay close attention to the details of life, since it is there, on a daily basis, that God is revealed.

THE PENTATEUCH

In the United States, the Constitution, the Declaration of Independence, and the Bill of Rights stand as the foundational documents on which the democratic system of government is based. No matter what new laws are written or policies are made, every piece of legislation, every judicial decision is ultimately judged in light of those original documents.

The foundation documents for the people of Israel are the books we now commonly refer to as the Pentateuch, the first five books of the Bible. These books do more than introduce the rest of the Bible: they are the very foundation on which the rest of the scriptures stand. The Pentateuch serves as the blueprint or constitution by which all other scripture is interpreted. By understanding the special nature and special role of these first five books of the Old Testament, we will have a better understanding of the entire Bible.

The name "Pentateuch" means a five part writing. Accordingly, rather than five distinct books what we are really dealing with is one book in five volumes. Even in biblical times, the Pentateuch was considered a single work. Jewish tradition calls it "Torah," which is often translated as "law" but really means "teaching" or "instruction." In the Torah, one finds the basic teaching of the Jewish faith.

From a Catholic perspective, the Pentateuch is generally regarded as the source from which all the other books of the Old Testament flow. The teaching of the prophets and Israel's life experience both call the people back to fidelity to the teachings of the Pentateuch. In our own lives, we often have to face unpleasant consequences of our own actions. Often, these experiences remind us of the differences between right and wrong that we learned when we were younger. In the same way, Israel had both the words of the prophets and their own history to help them determine how well or how poorly they had lived out the message of the Pentateuch in their life as a nation. Even when they were deaf to the prophets' words, the morass they frequently found themselves in was sufficient to remind them that they had indeed been unfaithful to God and the law.

None of the books of the Bible got there by accident. Every decision about whether to include a certain book was carefully thought out, discussed, and probably hotly debated. The final decisions make a difference. When we read the books of the Bible we read them as part of a collection of books, and how we interpret the message of a book is determined, at least in part, by where that book stands in relation to other books.

Anywhere something of importance happens today newspaper and television reporters, photographers, and video cameras record every moment. We live in a world of instant replays where you do not have to wonder what someone said or did. You can even play it back in slow motion. In the ancient world, such technology, of course, was not available.

In a culture like ours, so dominated by science, we value exact observation and documentation for its own sake. We expect historians to prove the claims they make in their books with clear documentation. And we expect them to be unbiased reporters, not propaganda peddlers. That is a lot to ask in any age since even trained historians are never totally free of bias and have their own point of view that colors what they write. If modern historians are never entirely objective even when that is what is expected of them, then we certainly cannot hope for that kind of objectivity from ancient writers who never made it their goal.

Even if they had wanted to attain our modern standard of accuracy, ancient writers had no way to get much of the historical information. The reason that little or no information was preserved for its own sake was that history was seen not as a record of "what happened," but as a lesson people were to learn from. History was written to teach that one kind of behavior or attitude was more appropriate than another. It was written more like what we would call editorials, which take sides and argue for their favorite causes.

The bottom line is that ancient "history" was more interested in explaining why something happened than in what happened. It was more concerned with the meaning of events than in an accurate record of those events.

While the Pentateuch is a complete story, it is in no way a complete history. It picks and chooses the events and themes it wants to talk about. And it only talks about those things that will teach a religious les-

son. What we have here is a handbook or rule book for right living, a theology book much more than any real history of the people. That is why laws are so generously sprinkled in among the stories. The laws were part of the lesson the stories were meant to teach.

Clearly, many of the stories in the Pentateuch are not at all about ordinary time in history. Genesis 1–11, for example, does not fit the category of history telling because it treats the creation of the world and the first events of human existence without any historical concreteness. By trying to answer universal questions—questions like: Why did God make humans this way? Why do we sin? Why do we die? Why is it hard to obey God? Why are men and women different?—the stories of Genesis 1–11 fall into the literary genre of cultural folklore. Even the stories of the patriarchs and matriarchs in Genesis 12–50 are not like modern history. Though based on real history, they resemble folktale hero stories, and it is hard to pin them down to exact locations and events.

It is important to keep this in mind when reading the Scriptures especially when problems of logic are encountered. For example, in Genesis 4, Cain and Abel are the only two children of Adam and Eve. However, after killing Abel, Cain is banished and, we are told, Cain then has "relations with his wife." If this were a real history, we would have to ask how Cain could have a wife when Adam and Eve were, ostensibly, the only other living human beings at the time.

Obviously, the author's intent centers not on literal facts, but on a religious lesson, here concerning how the world came to be populated. Whether or not that lesson is consistent with what has previously been said does not concern the author. However, while it is important not to make the mistake of thinking that the Pentateuch is a record of history, it is also important not to think of it as just a clever story pulled from someone's imagination. It is a masterwork, a work of genius that makes God known to us. In beautiful language and powerful imagery it speaks of humanity's tendency toward sin, about the failure of most of the world to know God, and of God's choice of Israel to demonstrate to the world God's loving concern for humanity. The marvelous storytelling of the Pentateuch reveals God by focusing on a number of central events; the choice of the patriarchs, the giving of the Law, the making of a covenant, and the guidance through the wilderness to a promised land.

Good storytelling can give us pleasure, teach us about history, and give us philosophical and theological insights. As a great work of storytelling the Pentateuch is multi-layered. It tells history, but it does not allow us to question it too closely about exact descriptions. It presents religious and theological lessons, but warns us not to treat it like a catechism filled with lists of truths. Most of all it tells a story. The story teaches us by letting us compare our experience with that of the Hebrew people. As we read, we begin to discover that the story of the Hebrews and our story are intertwined, and that the God who was at work in the lives of the Hebrew people works in similar ways in our own lives.

Despite many difficulties, scholars are not completely in the dark when it comes to dating some of the events of the Pentateuch. Archaeological excavations in ancient sites have produced tablets and other records that offer a good idea of what each different period in the second millennium B.C.T. was like, so we can date the major events of the Pentateuch with a fair degree of confidence.

Accordingly, the patriarchal narratives fall somewhere between 2000 and 1500 B.C.T., the Exodus event between 1450 and 1250 B.C.T., and the invasion of the land of Palestine around 1250 to 1200 B.C.T. Non-biblical historical information makes some dates more likely than others. Since Egypt was governed by foreign rulers between 1750 and 1550 B.C.T. the story of how Joseph, a foreigner, rises to power best fits this time period. Exodus 1:11 says the enslaved Israelites constructed the cities of Pithom and Raamses, pointing to the reign of Sethi I as the period of enslavement and the reign of Ramesses II as the time of the Exodus.

For more than two thousand years, Moses was considered the author of the Pentateuch even though no book of the Bible specifically names him as the author. The Pentateuch was often called "the Book of Moses," and throughout the Bible there are frequent references to the "law of Moses." Indeed, Jesus, like most of his contemporaries, took for granted that Moses authored the Pentateuch.

However, even in the ancient world some questioned whether Moses could really have written the entire Pentateuch. How, for example, could Moses have written about his own death as in Deuteronomy 34:5–12? Additionally, many of the laws supposedly written by Moses deal with situations that occurred much later than the time when Moses led the people through the desert. Other evidence in the Bible leads scholars to believe the Pentateuch did not exist in its present state until approximately 450 B.C.T.—nearly 800 years after Moses' death.

No one can say for certain who did write the Pentateuch, but there is no question that Moses played a unique and important role in the events recorded in these books. Modern scholars do not attempt to prove that Moses directly authored the written books of the Pentateuch. From a Catholic perspective, the strongly held belief that the Bible is divinely inspired makes the identity of its human author an issue of limited importance. However, regardless of what is said or believed, it must be admitted that Moses must be regarded as one of the founders of the Jewish faith.

Studying the Scriptures is not an easy enterprise. Because it was written over many centuries by people living in cultures very different from our own, we cannot simply expect to pick up a Bible and be able to grasp its meaning in its entirety. On the other hand, we must not be intimidated by the amount of scholarly knowledge it takes to understand the Bible properly so that we start to feel it belongs only to some special educated caste. The reality lies somewhere in the middle.

Despite those who would argue for one over the other, it is clear that the Bible must be read on two levels at once. The first is the level of Scripture, that is, the word of God, God's authoritative and inspired communication to humanity which we read by the light of faith. For the second level, reading the Bible as the literature of a particular culture, we must draw on the insights of archaeology, history, ancient languages, and the many other fields that can open up the ancient world that produced these texts. Unless we are reading on both these levels, we will miss part of the Bible's message.

It is also important to remember that we cannot read on either level all by ourselves. We need the biblical scholar to interpret the text by means of scientific, linguistic, and cultural tools. And we need the theologians and religious leaders to interpret according to the traditions of our faith.

When we read the Bible we are looking for two things. First, we are looking at what the text meant to its original author and audience, and, secondly, we are looking at what it means now to us, its modern readers. We must be careful, however, not to let one meaning cancel out the other.

When we seek the original meaning of a text, we do not rule out the possibility that over the centuries a particular text may have taken on more meaning than even the author intended. So what it meant then and what it means now are not necessarily the same thing.

Some modern churchgoers have rejected scholarly theories and methods of study because they feel these have robbed the Bible of its status as God's inspired word and have turned it into an ordinary literary document. Why so negative a reaction? Maybe because some scholars approach the Bible with the assumption that they may not use God as the explanation for anything. While such scholars would not deny the possibility of miracles, they believe that what is called the critical method requires them to propose natural explanations whenever such explanations are plausible. Even discussions of inspiration are considered off-limits by some scholars. If one reads the Bible only on this level, one might think it would tell a person little of religious value.

However, and this is the heart of the matter, it is the critical method which helps us to unlock and clarify what is going on in a text. This is done in three ways. First, by connecting the text to historical events that we may have learned about through non-biblical sources. Second, by helping us understand unusual cultural customs. And third, by helping us understand special literary styles of expression that are no longer in use today.

Without scientific study we would not comprehend those things that are not part of our culture. When archaeologists dig up clay tablets that contain long lost information, biblical scholars become the bridge that connects that information with the Bible. They study how language works, how people hand down traditions, and how they record events and tell folk tales. All this helps us understand how biblical stories and laws were put together.

All religious writing is interpretation. The ancient authors interpreted what they thought God was communicating. Today the churches and synagogues interpret what these words of revelation mean for their congregations. Additionally, modern scholars and believing readers must also interpret and decide what relevance these long ago stories and events have for their lives. Everyone who reads the Bible asks "What does it mean?" But we can find a full answer only if our reading is illuminated by the twin lights of faith and scientific knowledge of the past. And nowhere in the Bible is this more crucial than in reading the Pentateuch.

The study of the Pentateuch has a long history that can be traced back even to the time of Jesus. In New Testament times, Jesus and the authors of various New Testament books referred to texts from the Bible, which at that time was simply the Hebrew Scriptures, what Christians now call the Old Testament. Usually they were referring to stories that were cited as proofs for something Jesus or one of the apostles was teaching. Some stories from the Pentateuch were treated as being predecessor representations in which an Old Testament figure is seen as a foreshadowing of a later character, like Abraham who is seen as a forerunner of the Christian believer, or Isaac who is seen as a foreshadowing of Jesus. The New Testament treats many passages from the Pentateuch, the prophets, and the psalms as a type of prophecy that predicts Jesus and helps explain his suffering, death, and resurrection. It would be fair to say that the New Testament uses the Hebrew Bible primarily to show the deep connection between Jesus and what went before him.

The early church (the community of believers during the four centuries after the death of the Apostles) saw the Bible operating on three levels of meaning. First there was the literal or historical meaning of the text. Then there was the spiritual or allegorical sense: a deep, often hidden, layer that went beyond the literal. The third level expressed the moral lesson the text meant to teach.

Level two, the spiritual level, was considered most important. Since scripture is inspired writing, pious believers thought it therefore must contain layers of meaning that even the author was not aware of. God, after all, was using the ancient author to point the way to Jesus. The meaning of a passage, then, could not be limited to what the author intended to say. The full meaning was much deeper, more spiritual, and not immediately obvious.

This perspective led to an almost total disregard for the literal meaning of the text. All the focus was on the so-called spiritual meaning intended by God. Because of the conviction that every word of scripture contained a prophecy about Jesus, and thus always said more than it seemed to say, the allegorical method flourished in the early church.

The medieval world was largely a period of love with the allegorical approach, and students of the Bible relied heavily on the opinions of the early church writers regarding each passage of scripture. However, the rise of scholasticism in the 12th and 13th centuries shifted the focus to a clear and literal interpretation of Bible texts. Medieval thinkers, however, lacked a knowledge of Hebrew and Greek with which to study the original words, and they still viewed the Bible as prophecy rather than as a history of a people's experience of God working in their lives. So they, too, read the Pentateuch more as a book about Christ and the church than about Israel.

The modern study of the Bible began with a French priest named Richard Simon who lived during the late 1600s. It was Simon who detected different literary styles within the Book of Genesis. He concluded that Moses did not write the Pentateuch from scratch, but probably was quoting sources that existed before him. This insight earned him church condemnation, but it also opened the door for further critical study.

In the 1700s, scholars began investigating the biblical passages that regularly call God by the proper name "Yahweh" (often rendered as "LORD" in certain biblical texts) and those that call God by the more generic term, "Elohim" (often rendered as "God" in most biblical texts). Even though the passages that use the two names are intermixed, they run through the entire Pentateuch (up to the Book of Numbers) as two complete, parallel stories.

New questions subsequently arose. Were these two separate written works that told the same history of Israel, or was one original story embellished and eventually turned into two different versions? The debate was intense. Then scholars began to notice that the so called "Elohist" passages really contained two separate accounts themselves. The one that was more narrative and interested in God's great interventions in history was called the Elohist strand, while the other, which was more concerned with priestly and ritual actions, was called the Priestly strand.

By the mid–1800s, scholars generally agreed that there were in fact three independent versions of the Pentateuchs's basic story, which could be labeled with the initials J (for German "Jahvist"), E (for Elohist), and P (for Priestly). The Book of Deuteronomy was considered a fourth and totally separate source of its own, and received the label "D."

Eventually a German scholar, Julius Wellhausen, proposed dates for the writing of each version and speculated on the historical situation that created the need for each different telling of the history. All this came to be known as the "four sources theory," and the method is called "source criticism." The scholars use the term "source" because it is uncertain as to who is responsible for each of the four identified traditions. It is unknown if it was a single author-editor or (most likely) a group of author-editors. What is clear is that each strand responds to a particular situation or need in the history of the Jewish people and incorporates the particular worldview of its author-editor.

Of the four sources, it is believed that the "J" source is the oldest. Scholars posit that the "J" (Yahwist) source materials were composed in the tenth or ninth century B.C.T. Written in Jerusalem, the "J" materials were designed to show that the promises to Abraham were fulfilled in the empire of David. The structure of the "J" verses indicate that the composer was a literary artist who loved stories. The "J" author focused on tales of the heart using earthy and frank language. The emphasis of the "J" text was on God's closeness with humanity. The "J" sources are identifiable by the noticeable use of the name "Yahweh" for "God." The name "Yahweh" was traditionally spelled "Jehovah," hence the label "J." The "J" materials favor strong leaders like David reflecting a view that pre-dominated in the Southern kingdom.

The "E" (Elohist) source materials were written around 900 B.C.T. The "E" materials were probably written after the division of the kingdom and were designed to provide the Northern kingdom's official account of the tradition. The "E" materials utilize Elohim for God's name. These materials stress the role of the prophet and exhibit a strong tone of challenge and stress on morality. The "E" materials emphasize the role of Jacob and the significance of the Northern kingdom ideas and places. The Northern tradition reflects an anti–Jerusalem view. Like the "D" (Deuteronomist) materials, the "E" materials stress that the covenant with Moses is more important than kingship.

Much of the "P" (Priestly) materials date to the eighth and seventh centuries B.C.T. However, some materials probably were written in the sixth century B.C.T. Some of the "P" materials reflect and respond to the needs of the exiles in the sixth century B.C.T. As such, there is a very strong interest in ritual and priesthood. There is less focus on story and more on religious symbols. The style of the materials is more formal. In the "P" texts, God is more distant, less intimately involved with human beings. The "P" materials stress obedience to law and permanence of God's blessing. The "P" source material is the most dominant tradition in the Pentateuch. The "P" materials reflect a Southern point of view. The "P" editors arranged the four sources into the present Pentateuch around 500 B.C.T.

The "D" (Deuteronomist) materials were written in the eighth and seventh centuries B.C.T. The "D" materials reassess the "J" and "E" traditions in light of pagan inroads and unfaithful kings. The "D" materials emphasize the role of family (parents) for instruction and fidelity to covenant. The "D" materials tend to be moralistic, stressing preaching and exhortation. The style of the "D" texts is eloquent with many oft repeated verbal formulas. The "D" materials emphasize Jerusalem as the sole place of worship. The "D" materials reflect a Northern tradition which stresses covenant over kingship.

The "J" and "E" source materials existed side by side while the two kingdoms lasted from 930 to 722 B.C.T. When the Northern kingdom fell, its "E" story was carried down to Judah by refugees, and there it was eventually combined (around 700 B.C.T.) with "J" into a single account. Still later, when Judah itself fell in 587 B.C.T. and during the Jewish exile, the "D" and "P" materials were combined with JE to form the final JEPD text which comprises the Pentateuch of today. Editors from the Priestly circles applied the final touches on the holy text.

All this speculation on sources led to even more research into the original units that made up each source. Where did the individual incidents, poems, stories, and laws come from? This search for the earliest and smallest units of the tradition gave birth to a new way of studying the Bible called "form criticism." By identifying the special form of a poem or hymn or law or narrative, scholars thought they could probably determine the cultural or historical situation from which it came.

Some scholars have also focused on the transmission history of a text, looking at how traditions get passed on and grow or change. Before reaching the final form they have today, original statements, stories, and laws went through a process of being combined with other units, and then combined again in still larger works. Study of how collections grew and how stories were sometimes arranged into a new order helps scholars to understand how the stories were used and the meaning they were given by different generations. For example, the story of Exodus was the story of escaping from an oppressive situation. However, later on, in the context of the law and the land, the story of Exodus became a story about the celebration of a feast year after year: the celebration of Passover. The bread, the lamb, and the bitter herbs all became parts of the yearly ritual Passover celebration.

THE THEMES OF THE PENTATEUCH

One of the most notable aspects concerning the text of the Pentateuch are the recurrent themes which are woven throughout the provisions of the books. Such themes as the demand for obedience to

God's will, which is seen as a sign of faith, and God's giving of the covenant, which is seen as a sign of God's love, are examples of the recurrent themes that appear throughout the Pentateuch.

In reading the Pentateuch it is important to remember that more than being a book *of* or *by* God, the Bible is actually a book *about* God. Through its many themes and stories, the Pentateuch reveals a God Israel has come to know as the one God, who acts in human history, and who has chosen Israel in a special way. All the themes of the Pentateuch reveal God's intimate relationship with people, emphasizing the need for humanity to respond to God's initiative.

From the Catholic perspective, there are ten central themes in the Pentateuch. The ten central themes are:

1. God Created a Good World

   When Genesis tells us God spoke the world into being, it means that creation was not an accident, but instead was part of a divine plan causing all things to work together in harmony. God judged all creation as being "very good" {Genesis 1:31}. Thus, no matter how bad things get, we must remember that the original blessing is never fully lost and that, ultimately, goodness will prevail.

2. God Has Blessed Human Life

   Twice Genesis tells us that God blessed the human race {Genesis 1:28 and 9:1}. If the world is good, so is all life within it.

3. Humanity Has a Tendency to Sin

   Much of the biblical story presents human beings as being disobedient and sinful, ignoring God's will. Many of the laws, therefore, center on atonement (particularly in Leviticus) and on the need to repent and turn back to God (Deuteronomy particularly).

4. God is a God of Mercy

   If humanity tends toward rebellion, God tends toward forgiveness and mercy. God spares Adam and Eve, Cain and Noah, and others in order to give the human race a new start each time after its sins. In the Exodus event, God is revealed above all else as a liberating God.

5. God Keeps Promises

   God promised Noah, Abraham, Isaac, Jacob, and Moses that they would become a great people, and repeatedly the Pentateuch stresses the fulfillment of that promise. Israel's God is a God of the future, not one patterned on the recurring cycles of nature. God inspires hope. Believers can expect that God can act in new and decisive ways.

6. The Covenant Binds God to Israel

   All people believe their god relates to them somehow, but only in Israel do we find a relationship based on love, permanent loyalty, and respect for the human partner. The covenant is the heart of the biblical faith because it expresses a unique bond between God and people.

7. The Law Expresses Israel's Bond to God

   The covenant establishes a relationship, but the laws of the Pentateuch show how that relationship can be lived out by the people. Laws are not restrictive rules; they are a joyful way of life that expresses faith in actions as well as words.

8. Worship is Praise is Thanksgiving

   An odd way to express a simple but important idea: To pray is to praise, and to praise is to thank God. The Pentateuch constantly reminds Israel of what God has done for them, and the laws express the need to rejoice and give thanks to God in everything.

9. Religious Life is Life in Community

God chose a people, not a lot of all-star individuals. Single hearts and voices can not know and praise God properly. Only human minds and voices joined together can do that. God's many faces can be seen only if we share our memories and relate to one another in love.

10. God Directs All History

The central conviction of Israel—that there is one, and only one, God—leads to recognition of God's lordship over all peoples and all events. God blesses and punishes, sets obstacles, and shows the way through them. All things are in God's hands, so the only thing that makes sense is to walk in the ways of the Lord.

From a Catholic perspective, in addition to the central themes of the Pentateuch, there are also ten theological themes of the Pentateuch. The theological themes of the Pentateuch have implications, and even imperatives, for the spiritual lives of any person who professes to be a disciple of God. The ten theological themes of the Pentateuch are:

1. All Things in Our Life Must Flow from Faith

The stories of the Pentateuch reveal that no part of life is outside of God's plan. Those who believe must live believing that God's will can be known and followed in all of life's situations.

2. Our Prayer and Our Daily Life Must Be One

A theological theme of the Pentateuch is that the believer's worship and prayer should relate to the real problems and decisions that the believer faces in daily life. The Bible speaks of wars and politics more than of anything else, and yet there is not a single area of life where God is not present.

3. We Must Respect God's Holiness

The Bible often speaks of God with beautiful human imagery, but it never allows us to forget that God is also the all powerful creator of the universe who cannot be represented by idols or treated like just another human being. The Pentateuch balances notions of God's closeness to the world with the clear recognition that our job is to do God's will,—not to make God do our will.

4. We Must Imitate God's Holiness

Since, according to the Bible, we are made in God's image and likeness, we have a responsibility to act like God. Thus, because God cares for the poor, the widow, the alien, and the orphan— so must we.

5. Holiness Must Be Translated into Compassion

Forgiveness is the hallmark of God's holiness. God claims to be a God who bestows "mercy down to the thousandth generation, on the children of those who love me" {see Exodus 20:6}. God even forgives "wickedness and crime and sin" {see Exodus 34:7}. Holiness is, thus, best expressed not in private prayer, but in our forgiving and merciful behavior toward each other.

6. Life is a Journey

Among the oldest of metaphors for human existence, the notion that life is a journey is an image which is deeply rooted in the Pentateuch itself. Abraham is called to a new land. Jacob must find God far from home. Joseph must go to Egypt, and Israel must cross the desert to find a Promised Land. The journey motif not only stresses the future to which we go, but even more, it emphasizes the value of the journey itself, for the God toward whom we move is already with us on the road.

7. Life's Journey Requires Trust in God

The most important thing to take along on one's journey in life is a trust in God. The Pentateuch asserts that God's guidance never fails even when the people turn from God's way. Keeping God's commandments builds our courage and confidence. The wise believer learns to trust in God's promises and to find peace therein.

8. We Are The People of The Land

The Promised Land dominates the stories of the Pentateuch. Israel was in love with her land and never lost her infatuation with it even when it was taken from her. Israel never wanted to be divorced from the concrete realities of everyday life and never embraced asceticism as an ideal. Its spirituality was hardheaded and included wrestling with the proper use of the land and its resources, working for justice in social settings, and molding politics and economics to the demands of God's law. Genesis says that we are from the earth and to the earth we shall return {see Genesis 3:19}. As such, believers must take the earth seriously and treat it with reverence and respect.

9. Faith is a Family Affair

Much of Israel's religious practice was centered in the home. The sabbath observance, Passover, prayer, teaching children the law are all home-centered religious practices which were narrated in the Pentateuch. Learning about these practices can teach believers much about how our own families can celebrate together, teach one another about God, and give concrete witness to what believers believe.

10. Prayer Must Fill Our Lives

The Pentateuch provides numerous examples both of public prayer and of the private prayers of great individuals responding to every experience of God's presence in their lives. Israel's need and ability to pray in all situations eventually gave birth to the Psalms, a collection of prayers and hymns that express the whole range of human feelings before God. Their boldness and yet humility provide modern believers with an example of how we can live our lives in prayer.

THE NATURE OF THE PENTATEUCH SOURCES

The Pentateuch, which consists of the first five books of the Bible (Genesis, Exodus, Leviticus, Numbers, and Deuteronomy), enjoys particular prestige among the Jews as the "Law," or "Torah," the concrete expression of God's will in their regard. It is more than a body of legal doctrine, even though such material occupies many chapters, for it contains the story of the formation of the Jewish people: Abraham and the patriarchs, Moses and the oppressed Hebrews in Egypt, the birth of Israel in the Sinai covenant, the journey to the threshold of the Promised Land, and the "discourses" of Moses.

The grandeur of this historic sweep is the result of a careful and complex joining of several historical traditions, or sources. These are primarily four: the so-called Yahwist, Elohist, Priestly and Deuteronomic strands that run through the Pentateuch. (They are conveniently abbreviated as J, E, P and D.) Each brings to the Torah its own characteristics, its own theological viewpoint—a rich variety of interpretation that the biblical scholar should take pains to appreciate. A superficial difference between two of these sources is responsible for their names: the Yahwist prefers the name *Yahweh* (represented in translations as "Lord") by which god revealed himself to Israel; the Elohist prefers the generic name for God, *Elohim*. The Yahwist is concrete, imaginative, using many anthropomorphisms in its theological approach, as seen, e.g., in the narrative of creation in Genesis, Chapter 2, compared with the Priestly version in Genesis, Chapter 1. The Elohist is more sober and moralistic. The Priestly strand, which emphasizes genealogies, is more severely theological in tone. The Deuteronomic approach is characterized by the intense hortatory style of Deuteronomy, Chapters 5–11, and by certain principles from which it works, such as the centralization of worship in the Jerusalem temple.

However, even the four-prong analysis of the Pentateuch is an over-simplification because it is not always possible to distinguish with certainty among the various sources. The fact is that each of these individual traditions incorporates much older material. The Yahwist was himself a collector and adapter. His narrative is made up of many disparate stories that have been reoriented, and given a meaning within the context in which they now stand; e.g., the story of Abraham and Isaac in Genesis 22. Within the J and P traditions one has to reckon with many individual units; these had their own history and life-setting before they were brought together into the present more or less connected narrative.

From a Catholic perspective, the four-prong scholarly analysis of Genesis should not be intended to deny the role of Moses in the development of the Pentateuch. It is true that modern Catholics do not conceive of Moses as the actual author of the books. But there is no reason to doubt that, in the events described in these traditions, Moses had an uniquely important role, especially as a lawgiver. Even the later laws which have been added in P and D are presented as a Mosaic heritage. Moses is the lawgiver *par excellence,* and, from a Catholic perspective, all later legislation is conceived in his spirit, and therefore attributed to him. Accordingly, a Catholic reader of the Scrip-

tures should not take the Scriptures literally when the Scriptures say, "the Lord said to Moses. Instead, the Catholic should keep in mind that the Pentateuch is the crystallization of Israel's age-old relationship with God.

In presenting the story of the genesis of the Jewish people, the Pentateuch looks back to the promises made to the patriarchs, and forward to the continuing fulfillment of these promises in later books of the Bible. The promises find their classic expression in Genesis 12:1 and following. There the "God of the Fathers" challenges Abraham to believe: the patriarch is to receive a people and a land, and through him the nations will somehow be blessed.

The mysterious and tortuous way in which this people is brought into being is described: Despite Sarah's sterility, Isaac is finally born—only then to be offered in sacrifice! The promises are renewed to him eventually, and also to the devious Jacob, as if to show that the divine design will be effected, with or without human cunning. The magnificent story of Joseph is highlighted by the theme of Providence; the promise of a people is taking shape.

Israel is not formed in a vacuum, but amid the age-old civilizations of Mesopotamia and the Nile. Oppression in Egypt provokes a striking intervention of God.

Yahweh reveals himself to Moses as a savior, and the epic story of deliverance is told in Exodus. This book also tells of the Sinai covenant, which is rightfully regarded as the key to the Old Testament. Through the covenant Israel becomes Yahweh's people, and Yahweh becomes Israel's God. This act of grace marks the fulfillment of the first promise: that Abraham will be the father of a great nation, God's special possession. The laws in Exodus and Leviticus (from the P tradition) are both early and late. They spell out the proper relationship of the federation of the Twelve tribes with

God. God is a jealous God, demanding exclusive allegiance. God cannot be imaged. God takes vengeance upon the wicked, and shows mercy to the good. Slowly God is revealed to the people and with remarkable honesty, Israel records the unsteady response—the murmurings and rebellions and infidelities through the desert wanderings up to the plain of Moab.

This sacred—this special—history was formed within the bosom of early Israel, guided by the spirit of God. This history was recited beside the desert campfires and it was commemorated in the liturgical feasts, such as Passover. This history was transmitted by word of mouth from generation to generation—until all was brought together in writing, around the sixth century B.C.T., when the literary formation of the Pentateuch came to an end.

The Book of Deuteronomy has a history quite peculiar to itself. Its old traditions and law code are put forth in the form of "discourses" of Moses before his death. The extraordinarily intense and hortatory tone fits the mood of a discourse. Deuteronomy contains possibly the preaching of the Levites in the northern kingdom of Israel before its fall in 721 B.C.T. If this book is situated in its proper historical perspective, its true impact is more vividly appreciated. It is the blueprint of the great "Deuteronomic" reform under King Josiah (640–609 B.C.T.) This was an attempt to galvanize the people into a wholehearted commitment to the covenant ideals, into an obedience motivated by the great commandment of love. Israel has yet another chance, if it obeys. The people are poised between life and death; and they are exhorted to choose life—today.

GENESIS

From a Catholic perspective, Genesis is not the first book of the Bible by accident. Everything it contains was intentionally chosen to set the stage for all that follows. While the fascinating stories of Genesis make great reading on their own, to fully understand the book's purpose a believer must also pay attention to its religious message and the key themes it develops.

Most often scholars divide Genesis into two parts: Chapters 1–11 and 12–50. While the parts seem to constitute a single, continuous story, there are actually significant differences between them in both subject matter and in the kind of literature they contain. The first eleven chapters, often referred to as the "primeval history," discuss the creation of the world and the first human beings—the ancestors of all humanity. The second part, on the other hand, describes the very specific ancestors of Israel itself. Genesis 1–11 falls into the literary category of "folklore" in which every story seems to model the proper relationship between God and humans. The stories of the latter part of Genesis, however, relate specific events in the life of what came to be a particular nation, Israel.

The characters and worlds of the two sections of Genesis are very different. The world of the primeval history bears little resemblance to the world we live in. In that world people lived incredibly long lives and spoke directly to God. In contrast, Abraham, Isaac, Jacob, and the other people described in Chapters 12–50, seem to live out their joys and struggles in a world like ours, making decisions that affect the whole history of the nation of Israel.

One way of organizing Genesis is to break it down into four blocs of material that focus on major characters. Such a division reveals the following:

Division of Genesis into Four Blocs of Material

1. Genesis 1–11

   The Prologue: primeval history of humankind's original blessing and failure through sin

2. Genesis 12–25

The story of Abraham: his call and response; his blessing and promise

3. Genesis 26–36

The stories of Abraham's son Isaac and grandson Jacob and how they carry on the blessing

4. Genesis 37–50

The story of Joseph in Egypt: preparation for God's great self-revelation in the Exodus

Genesis ends with Abraham's descendants living in Egypt instead of in the land of promise. But the book's ending reminds us that the story will continue: God's promise is not forgotten and Israel's future lies elsewhere.

THE TOLEDOTH LISTS

Genesis contains certain internal markers that help divide and organize the material. These markers are the genealogical lists, *toledoth*, that always begin "these are the descendants of …" These lists help make the point that while generations come and go, God's plan moves ahead no matter what. Sometimes appearing at the beginning and sometimes at the end of a section, the lists group together all the members of a family line or tribe to signal a break with the events that have just been recounted. The following provides a listing of the *toledoth* lists:

The Toledoth Lists

Genesis 2:4a	Begins the second story of creation
Genesis 5:1	Introduces the long break between the first family and the days of Noah
Genesis 6:9	Introduces the story of the flood

Genesis 10:1	Marks the great expansion of people all over the world
Genesis 11:10	Marks the addition of a new list of the nations of the world by the P source
Genesis 11:27	Begins the story of Abraham
Genesis 25:12	Closes off the life of Abraham's "other" family through Hagar and Ishmael
Genesis 25:19	Opens the story of Jacob's birth and destiny
Genesis 36:1	Ends the role of Jacob's twin, Esau, and directs us to Jacob's children, especially Joseph
Genesis 36:9	A repetition within the Esau list that marks its conclusion
Genesis 37:2	Marks the opening of the story of Joseph and his brothers that continues to the end of Genesis

THE BEGINNING OF GENESIS

From a Catholic perspective, there are four major points to keep in mind when reading the first eleven chapters of Genesis. These points are:

1. According to form criticism, the first eleven chapters are chiefly a combination of folklore and genealogical tables.

2. Source critics find in the first eleven chapters of Genesis a combination of the Yahwist (J) and Priestly (P) sources.

3. Similar, and older, versions of many of the Genesis stories have been found in the literature of ancient Southwest Asia.

4. The final masterpiece is unique. It is neither like the "J" or "P" accounts

taken by themselves, nor, in its purpose and beauty, like any other people's version.

The interweaving of the J and P sources in Genesis, Chapters 1 through 11, accounts for the fact that some stories seem to be told twice, with different details. For example, both J and P authors have a list of ancestors between Adam and Noah, a flood story (the two versions being now hopelessly intertwined into a single account), and a table of nations that also is interwoven into a single list.

The incidents chosen by the "J" author to tell the story of creation focus on the tension between God's goodness and human beings' disobedience. Adam and Eve, Cain and Abel, the wicked generation of the flood, the sons of Noah, and the builders of the tower of Babel all received plenty of evidence of God's love. Yet each generation chose to disobey by embracing one of the deadly vices: greed, envy, lust, pride.

The message conveyed by the "J" author is that because humanity repeatedly failed to respond to God's offering of intimate love, sin spread and contaminated all people. Now God must find a new way to demonstrate control over the earth and all of history, and to show love for humanity. As with Adam and Eve and Noah and his family, God begins this new round by again choosing a single family, Abraham's, and giving them a special revelation of divine goodness to share with the world.

If later Israelites had only the version of their history given in the "J" Source—sin, punishment, mercy, and the promise of being formed into a chosen people—they might have misunderstood it as promising absolute control over the land and great power for Abraham's descendants. However, by the time the Priestly writers were gathering their own accounts, Israel had already experienced military defeats and the loss of ten of the twelve tribes. Israel was wondering if God really was in control and would stand by them in hard times.

The Priestly writers apparently wanted to make sure the promises spoken in the creation stories would suggest two things: first, that God's control over world events was greater than any human power; and second, that it would be shown in ways besides Israel's political fortunes. In other words, Israel's misfortunes did not mean that God had lost control. The P source materials clearly state that humans are made in the image of God {see Genesis 1:27 and 9:6} to govern the earth and fill it, but P's stress is not on humanity's independent power; rather, an important element of being made in the image of God is humanity's responsibility to act as God would act.

The genealogies of Chapters 5 and 10–11 are also part of P's insistence that God has a plan that cannot be derailed by human whims, nor even upset by human sin. God is always in charge—even when we are experiencing just punishment. God's blessing can be relied on, all we must do is learn to trust. Indeed, we must learn trust! By stressing the goodness of creation and God's blessing of humanity, P's larger vision brought hope to Israel at a time when circumstances could have led it to despair.

CULTURAL INFLUENCES

Some critics note that there are similarities between the biblical creation stories and the folklore of ancient Southwest Asian and Egyptian people as a way of discrediting the biblical texts. These critics argue that since the biblical stories are derived from pagan folklore, the biblical stories have an unstable spiritual foundation and really that the stories have nothing more than a literary value. However, these critics miss the truism that just because a biblical writer may have borrowed from the folklore of neighboring cultures does not, in and of itself, diminish the theological value of the writing.

It is the biblical author's final product, not the original pagan story, which Catholics believe to be the inspired word of God, and which Muslims, Christians and Jews have canonized into the body of Scripture. Additionally, it is often evident that the final form developed by the biblical author differs significantly in purpose and theology from the pagan folklore. The differences indicate that the inspired writer not only may have borrowed, but perhaps was also trying to debunk the message of the pagan story with a more enlightened— a more inspired—message.

To take just two examples: The story of the creation of humanity and the story of the flood both have parallels among ancient Mesopotamian folklore. Many of the similarities are even quite striking. However, their overall messages are clearly different, especially in their presentation and understanding of God.

The Babylonian creation story called *Enuma Elish* presumes the existence of many gods who haphazardly created the world while fighting among themselves. Their creation is therefore partly good and partly evil, and human beings are nothing more than their slaves. Against this view of creation, the biblical writer presents a theology that asserts one, and only one, God who creates consciously and out of love. God's creation is all good and human beings are not slaves, but are made in God's own image and are given dominion over the earth.

The Noah flood story has a close parallel in the *Epic of Gilgamesh,* possibly the oldest of recorded human stories. In the *Epic of Gilgamesh,* Gilgamesh sets out to find an ancestor who has achieved immortality. The ancestor tells of having survived a great flood and of how he helped save humanity. In details, this flood account is surprisingly similar to the Genesis story. But the two versions present very different images of God.

The Babylonians believed there was an ongoing struggle between gods and humans. Their unpredictable gods found humans annoying and often erupted in hostility toward them. Human beings could never be sure of how to please their gods, nor of what would anger them. Genesis, on the other hand, presents a God who never changes. In Genesis, God is eternally just, yet loving and faithful. Israel's God punishes only when human beings have committed real wrong. However, even after punishing, the God of Genesis is always eager to forgive.

In sum, from a Catholic perspective, it is important to remember that being related to and derived from similar stories of ancient Southwest Asia and Egypt in no way compromises the religious truth or value of the stories we find in Genesis.

THE SIGNIFICANCE OF GENESIS

Genesis, the first book of the Bible, opens with the Hebrew word *bereshit* (*bereshith*), which means "in the beginning." The title "Genesis" was given to the Septuagint (Greek) translation of the book because of its concern with the origin of the world (Genesis 1:1–2:4), of the human race, and in particular, of the Hebrew people.

Eleven structural units (*toledoth*), of unequal length and importance, present the unity and purpose of the book in terms of God's universal sovereignty, his dealings with men, and his choice and formation of a special people to be the instrument of his plan of salvation.

The tracing of the direct descent from Adam to Jacob constitutes the major part of the book, while the genealogical tables of lateral branches are not so developed nor of such interest as those that pertain to the story of the Jewish people. In fact, these lateral branches gradually disappear from the narrative. And with the introduction of Abraham and his covenant with God, the history of humanity as such becomes contracted to the story of the descendants of Abraham through Isaac and Jacob—the chosen people.

Despite its unity of plan and purpose, Genesis is a complex work, not to be attributed to a single original author. Several sources, or literary traditions, that the final redactor used in his composition are discernible. These are the Yahwist (J), Elohist (E), and Priestly (P) sources, which in turn reflect older oral traditions.

In Genesis, the Yahwist source is the most important by reason of its teaching, its antiquity, and the continuity it gives the book. It constitutes a sacred history, continually drawing attention to the working out of God's design through his interventions in the affairs of men. The Elohist source, less well preserved, is found in fragmentary form only, depicting Gods' manifestation through visions and dreams rather than theophanies—rather than visual manifestations of a diety. Angels are God's intermediaries with men. Moreover, there is a solicitude for the divine transcendence and greater sensitivity toward the moral order. The Priestly source contains those elements—chronological data, lists, genealogies—that construct the framework of Genesis and bind its contents together. To the J and E sources it adds such legal institutions as the sabbath rest, circumcision and the alliances between God and Noah and God and Abraham.

Any astute reader of Genesis will recognize at once the distinct object that sets chapters 1–11 apart: these chapters recount the origin of the world and of man (primeval history). To make the truths contained in these chapters intelligible to the Hebrew people destined to preserve them, they needed to be expressed through elements prevailing among that people at that time. For this reason, the truths themselves must therefore be clearly distinguished from their literary garb and, perhaps, from their "racial" jingoism.

With the story of the patriarchs Abraham, Isaac and Jacob (Genesis 11:27–50: 26), the character of the narrative changes. While we do not view the account of the patriarchs as history in the strict sense, nevertheless certain of the matters recounted from the time of Abraham onward can be placed in the actual historical and social framework of Southwest Asia and Egypt in the early part of the second millennium B.C.T. (2000–1500), and documented by non-biblical sources.

Genesis contains many religious teachings of basic importance: the pre-existence and transcendence of God, God's wisdom and goodness, God's power through which all things are made and on which they all depend: the special creation of man in God's image and likeness, and of woman from the substance of man; the institution of marriage as the union of one man with one woman; man's original state of innocence; man's sin of pride and disobedience, and its consequences for the proto-parents and their posterity. Despite the severity of God's punishment, hope of reconciliation is offered by God through the first as well as the subsequent promises of salvation and blessing. Abraham is blessed for his faith and obedience, and he is to be a blessing for all nations through his offspring, Isaac, Jacob, and Jacob's sons {see Genesis 12:3, 18:18, 22:18}, of whom Jesus Christ, the Catholic/Christian Messiah, would eventually be born {see Galatians 3:8}.

THE FIRST STORY OF CREATION
{GENESIS 1:1–2:3}

1 *In the beginning, when God created*[202] *the heavens and the earth,*

2 *the earth was a formless wasteland, and darkness covered the abyss,*[203] *while a mighty wind*[204] *swept over the waters.*

3 *Then God said, "Let there be light," and there was light.*

4 *God saw how good the light was. God then separated the light from the darkness.*

5 *God called the light "day," and the darkness he called "night." Thus evening came, and morning followed—the first day.*[205]

6 *Then God said, "Let there be a dome in the middle of the waters, to separate one body of water from the other." And so it happened:*

7 *God made the dome, and it separated the water above the dome from the water below it.*

8 *God called the dome "the sky." Evening came, and morning followed—the second day.*

9 *Then God said, "Let the water under the sky be gathered into a single basin, so that the dry land may appear." And so it happened: the water under the sky was gathered into its basin, and the dry land appeared.*

10 *God called the dry land "the earth," and the basin of the water he called "the sea." God saw how good it was.*

11 *Then God said, "Let the earth bring forth vegetation: every kind of plant that bears fruit with its seed in it." And so it happened.*

12 *the earth brought forth every kind of plant that bears seed and every kind of fruit tree that bears fruit with its seed in it. God saw how good it was.*

13 *Evening came, and morning followed—the third day.*

14 *Then God said: "Let there be lights in*

---

[202]The great drama of creation opens with the affirmation that God did not have to "make" the universe by hand as a statue is made, but "created" (Hebrew *bara*') it by the unique divine power to will something and thereby achieve it {Genesis 1:1}. God works in this segment on unformed matter. The words describe the world as being empty and even chaotic and in the realm of darkness {Genesis 1:2}. This suggests that matter of itself is not subject to God "in whose light we find light" {see Psalms 36:10}, but was originally outside of divine control. Then the divine power began to act. The "mighty wind"—the "spirit of God" may mean God churning the waters in exercising control over their chaotic behavior or it may suggest a battle between the elements and God's purpose for them. In any event, the "spirit of God" does not mean merely a strong wind, for the wording echoes the *Enuma Elish*, the Babylonian creation story known to the Hebrews in exile, which described creation as a two-step process: first a battle between Marduk, the king of the gods, and Tiamat, the mother goddess (representing the ocean) who wished to destroy the gods of order. After Marduk's victory, he formed and ordered each part of the physical universe. The "abyss" or the "deep" (*tehom*) in verse 2 may well be intended to echo the sound of the name Tiamat.

[203]The reference to "the abyss" refers to the primordial ocean of the ancient Semitic cosmogony. After God's creative activity, part of this vast body forms the salt water seas; part of it is the fresh water under the earth which comes forth on the earth as springs and fountains; and part of it, the "upper water" is held up by the dome of the sky from which rain descends on the earth.

[204]The reference to "a mighty wind" actually literally means "a wind of God" or "a spirit of God."

[205]In ancient Israel a day was considered to begin at sunset. According to the highly artificial literary structure of Genesis 1:1–2:4, God's creative activity is divided into six days to teach the sacredness of the sabbath rest on the seventh day in the Jewish religion.

the dome of the sky, to separate day from night. Let them mark the fixed times, the days and the years,

15 and serve as luminaries in the dome of the sky, to shed light upon the earth." And so it happened:

16 God made the two great lights, the greater one to govern the day, and the lesser one to govern the night; and he made the stars.

17 God set them in the dome of the sky, to shed light upon the earth,

18 to govern the day and the night, and to separate the light from the darkness. God saw how good it was.

19 Evening came, and morning followed—the fourth day.

20 Then God said, "Let the water teem with an abundance of living creatures, and on the earth let birds fly beneath the dome of the sky." And so it happened:

21 God created the great sea monsters and all kinds of swimming creatures with which the water teems, and all kinds of winged birds. God saw how good it was,

22 and God blessed them, saying, "Be fertile, multiply, and fill the water of the seas; and let the birds multiply on the earth."

23 Evening came, and morning followed—the fifth day.

24 Then God said, "Let the earth bring forth all kinds of living creatures: cattle, creeping things, and wild animals of all kinds." And so it happened:

25 God made all kinds of wild animals, all kinds of cattle, and all kinds of creeping things of the earth. God saw how good it was.

26 Then God said: "Let us make man in our image, after our likeness.[206] Let them have dominion over the fish of the sea, the birds of the air, and the cattle, and over all the wild animals and all the creatures that crawl on the ground."

27 God created man in his image;
in the divine image he created him;
male and female he created them.

28 God blessed them, saying: "Be fertile and multiply; fill the earth and subdue it. Have dominion over the fish of the sea, the birds of the air, and all the living things that move on the earth."

29 God also said: "See, I give you every seed bearing plant all over the earth and every tree that has seed bearing fruit on it to be your food;

30 and to all the animals of the land, all the birds of the air, and all the living creatures that crawl on the ground, I give all the green plants for food." And so it happened.

31 God looked at everything he had made, and he found it very good.[207] Evening

---

[206]Man is presented here as the climax of God's creative activity. Here man is said to resemble God primarily because of the dominion God gives man over the rest of creation.

[207]Instead of a struggle to the death with Tiamat such as in the Babylonian creation story, the *Enuma Elish*, Genesis startles us with the miracle of a creation totally under God's guiding hand and completely organized so that chaos does not threaten. In this way, it counters the power of the Babylonian creation story to explain Marduk's superiority over the defeated and captured followers of YHWH. Instead God simply begins to speak and all things come to be. The power to create by the spoken word is not unique to Genesis. Examples occur in both Babylonian hymns and Egyptian creation stories. However, the sense of sublime wisdom and harmony created by the narrative finds no other ancient parallel. Israel's God has a plan and it unfolds steadily and awesomely in a carefully balanced sequence that matches all Marduk's works of creation. But in Genesis that order is organized as a single week with a single focus, the making of human beings in the divine image. It is formed in two panels. On the first three days, God makes the scenery and sets the staging; on days 4 to 6, the living actors are put in their proper places:

came, and morning followed—the sixth day."

Chapter 2

1 Thus the heavens and the earth and all their array were completed.

2 Since on the seventh day God was finished with the work he had been doing, he rested on the seventh day from all the work he had undertaken.[208]

3 So God blessed the seventh day and made it holy, because on it he rested from all the work he had done in creation.

4 Such is the story of the heavens and the earth at their creation.

Panel One: Day One
  The creation of light
Panel One: Day Two
  Water and air space are established
Panel One: Day Three
  The dry land and vegetation are arranged
Panel Two: Day Four
  The specific lights are made
Panel Two: Day Five
  Fish and birds fill the water and the air
Panel Two: Day Six
  Land creatures and humans populate the land

All of this is recited in the style of a liturgical profession of faith or creed. The formulas have a solemn and deliberate pace to them: "And God said ... and there was ... and God saw that it was good ... and God called it (___) ... and it was (___) ...." It should be noted that the implications of these repeated phrases, e.g., that created things were unhesitatingly obedient to God's word and performed exactly as they were intended to; that everything created is good both in its substance and in God's plan for it; that there is a close connection between God's creative word and the power to name things. The second creation story in Genesis 2:4–2:25 will take up these themes.

Finally, many scholars have pointed to the wisdom tradition at work in this chapter, particularly in the author's interests in different classifications of plant life and the ways humans are like God. We are seen to share God's likeness in the qualities of governing the world as a community of people who are fruitful and obedient and live in peace with all other creatures. Indeed, the first humans appear to have been prohibited from eating any animal life {see Genesis 1:29–30 and Genesis 9:3}. Many of these reflections echo concerns of the book of Proverbs {see Proverbs 3:19–26}. When all is finished, God looks over the whole of what has come to be and sees that it is very, very good.

[208]The great hymn of creation ends with a seventh day to fulfill the week. Symbolically the number seven (and thus, the week) signifies wholeness and completion. God's "resting" suggests two different conclusions: the first is that God can sit back and contemplate all of creation with joy and satisfaction, knowing nothing is lacking to it; and second, God will leave it alone because it is complete and adequate for the creatures in it, especially humankind. God will not keep changing the world or its ground rules, and humans will have a certain autonomy by which they can exercise their stewardship and freedom in the image and likeness of God. They will have not only the power to govern in God's name; they will also have the power to make decisions, both good and bad. In verse 3, God then blesses and sanctifies the Sabbath day. This would be read by any believing Hebrew as the basis for both the liturgical and personal observance of the Sabbath as commanded by the Law, especially as found in the ten commandments {see Exodus 20:8–11}.

THE SECOND STORY
OF CREATION
{GENESIS 2:4–2:25}[209]

At the time when the Lord God made the earth and the heavens—

5 while as yet there was no field shrub on earth and no grass of the field had sprouted, for the Lord God had sent no rain upon the earth and there was no man to till the soil,

6 but a stream was welling up out of the earth and was watering all the surface of the ground—

7 the Lord God formed man out of the clay[210] of the ground[211] and blew into his nostrils the breath of life, and so man became a living being.[212]

8 Then the Lord God planted a garden in Eden,[213] in the east, and he placed there the man whom he had formed.

9 Out of the ground the Lord God made various trees grow that were delightful to look at and good for food, with the tree of life in the middle of the garden and the tree of knowledge of good and bad.

10 A river rises[214] in Eden to water the garden; beyond there[215] it divides and becomes four branches.[216]

11 The name of the first is the Pishon; it is the one that winds through the whole land of Havilah, where there is gold.

12 The gold of that land is excellent; bdellium and lapis lazuli are also there.

13 The name of the second river is the Gihon; it is the one that winds all through the land of Cush.[217]

14 The name of the third river is the Tigris; it is the one that flows east of Asshur. The fourth river is the Euphrates.[218]

. 15 The Lord God then took the man and settled him in the garden of Eden, to cultivate and care for it.

16 The Lord God gave man this order: "You are free to eat from any of the trees of the garden

17 except the tree of knowledge of good and bad. From that tree you shall not eat; the moment you eat from it you are surely doomed to die.

18 The Lord God said: "It is not good for the man to be alone. I will make a suitable partner for him."

19 so the Lord God formed out of the

---

[209]This section is chiefly concerned with the creation of man. It is much older than the narrative of Genesis 1:1–2:4. Here God is depicted as creating man before the rest of his creatures, which are made for man's sake. {Compare with Genesis 1:25–26}.

[210]Here God is portrayed as though God was a potter molding man's body out of clay.

[211]Here there is a play on the Hebrew words *adam* ("man") and *adama* ("ground").

[212]The reference to "being" literally means "soul."

[213]Eden as used here is the name of a region in southern Mesopotamia. The term is derived from the Sumerian word "eden," meaning "fertile plain." A similar sounding Hebrew word means "delight." The garden in Eden could therefore be understood as the "garden of delight." Thus, through the Greek version, Eden is now known also as "paradise," literally, a "pleasure park."

[214]"A river rises" means that the river flooded and overflowed its banks.

[215]The reference to "beyond there" refers to as one travels upstream.

[216]Here the reference to "branches" literally means "headwaters."

[217]The land of Cush which is referred to in here and in Genesis 10:8 is not Ethiopia (Nubia) as it is elsewhere. Instead, here it refers to the region of the Kassites east of Mesopotamia.

[218]Geographically, the biblical Eden must have been located near the head of the Persian Gulf, where the Tigris and Euphrates join with two other streams to form a single river.

ground various wild animals and various birds of the air, and he brought them to the man to see what he would call them; whatever the man called each of them would be its name.

20 The man gave names to all the cattle, all the birds of the air, and all the wild animals; but none proved to be the suitable partner for the man.

21 So the Lord God cast a deep sleep on the man, and while he was asleep, he took out one of his ribs and closed up its place with flesh.

22 The Lord God then built up into a woman the rib that he had taken from the man. When he brought her to the man,

23 the man said: "This one, at last, is bone of my bones, and flesh of my flesh. This one shall be called 'woman,' for out of 'her man'[219] this one has been taken."

24 That is why a man leaves his father and mother and clings to his wife, and the two of them become one body.[220]

25 The man and his wife were both naked, yet they felt no shame.

THE FALL OF MAN
{GENESIS 3:1–3:24}

1 Now the serpent was the most cunning of all the animals that the Lord God had made. The serpent asked the woman "Did God really tell you not to eat from any of the trees in the garden?"

2 The woman answered the serpent: "We may eat of the fruit of the trees in the garden;

3 it is only about the fruit of the tree in the middle of the garden that God said, 'You shall not eat it or even touch it, lest you die.'"

4 But the serpent said to the woman: "You certainly will not die!

5 No, God knows well that the moment you eat of it your eyes will be opened and you will be like gods who know[221] what is good and what is bad."

6 The woman saw that the tree was good for food, pleasing to the eyes, and desirable for gaining wisdom. So she took some of its fruit and ate it; and she also gave some to her husband, who was with her and he ate it.

7 Then the eyes of both of them were opened, and they realized that they were naked; so they sewed fig leaves together and made loincloths for themselves.

8 When they heard the sound of the Lord God moving about in the garden at the breezy time of the day,[222] the man and his wife hid themselves from the Lord God among the trees of the garden.

9 The Lord God then called to the man and asked him, "Where are you?"

10 He answered, "I heard you in the garden; but I was afraid, because I was naked, so I hid myself."

11 Then he asked, "Who told you that you were naked? You have eaten, then, from the tree of which I had forbidden you to eat!"

12 The man replied, "The woman whom you put here with me—she gave me fruit from the tree, and so I ate it."

---

[219]In verse 23, there is a play on the similar sounding Hebrew words *ishsha* ("woman") and *ishah* ("her man, her husband").

[220]The reference to "one body" literally means "one flesh." The classical Hebrew has no specific word for "body." The sacred writer stresses the fact that the conjugal union is willed by God.

[221]The reference to "like gods who know" is also interpreted as "like God who knows."

[222]The reference to "breezy time of the day" may reflect the author's acquaintance with the weather of Palestine as opposed to the weather of Eden. On most days in Palestine a cooling breeze blows from the sea shortly before sunset.

13 The Lord God then asked the woman, "Why did you do such a thing?" The woman answered, "The serpent tricked me into it, so I ate it."

14 Then the Lord God said to the serpent: "Because you have done this, you shall be banned from all the animals and from all the wild creatures. On your belly shall you crawl, and dirt shall you eat all the days of your life.

15 I will put enmity between you and the woman, and between your offspring and hers. He will strike at your head, while you strike at his heel."[223]

16 To the woman he said: "I will intensify the pangs of your childbearing; in pain shall you bring forth children. Yet your urge shall be for your husband, and he shall be your master."

17 To the man he said: "Because you listened to your wife and ate from the tree of which I had forbidden you to eat, "Cursed be the ground because of you! In toil shall you eat its yield all the days of your life.

18 Thorns and thistles shall it bring forth to you, as you eat of the plants of the field.

19 By the sweat of your face shall you get bread to eat, until you return to the ground, from which you were taken; for you are dirt, and to dirt you shall return."

20 The Man called his wife Eve, because she became the mother of all the living.[224]

21 For the man and his wife the Lord God made leather garments, with which he clothed them.

22 Then the Lord God said: "See! The man has become like one of us, knowing what is good and what is bad! Therefore, he must not be allowed to put out his hand to take fruit from the tree of life also, and thus eat of it and live forever."

23 The Lord God therefore banished him from the garden of Eden, to till the ground from which he had been taken.

24 When He expelled the man, He settled him east of the garden of Eden; and He stationed the cherubim[225] and the fiery revolving sword, to guard the way to the tree of life.

CAIN AND ABEL
{GENESIS 4:1–4:16}

1 The man had relations with his wife Eve, and she conceived and bore Cain,[226] saying, "I have produced a man with the help of the Lord."

2 Next she bore his brother Abel. Abel became a keeper of flocks, and Cain a tiller of the soil.

3 In the course of time Cain brought an

---

[223]The reference to "He will strike ... at his heel" may not mean how it reads. Since the antecedent for he and his is the collective noun offspring, that is all the descendants of the woman, a more exact rendering of the sacred writer's words would be, "They will strike ... at their heels." However, later theology saw in this passage more than an unending hostility between snakes and men. The serpent was regarded as the devil whose eventual defeat seems implied in the contrast between head and heel. Because "the Son of God appeared that he might destroy the works of the devil {see 1 John 3:8}, this verse can be understood as the first promise of a Redeemer for fallen mankind. Accordingly, from a Catholic perspective, the woman's offspring then is primarily Jesus Christ.

[224]The Hebrew name *hawwa* ("Eve") is related to the Hebrew word *hay* ("living").

[225]The rendering of verse 24 which appears here is based on the ancient Greek version. However, the current Hebrew rendering is: "When He expelled the man, He settled east of the garden of Eden, the cherubim."

[226]The Hebrew name *qayin* ("Cain") and the Hebrew term *qaniti* ("I have produced") represent another fairly common play on words.

offering to the Lord from the fruit of the soil,

4 while Abel, for his part, brought one of the best firstlings of his flock. The Lord looked with favor on Abel and his offering,

5 but on Cain and his offering he did not. Cain greatly resented this and was crestfallen.

6 So the Lord said to Cain: "Why are you so resentful and crestfallen?

7 If you do well, you can hold up your head; but if not, sin is a demon lurking[227] at the door: his urge is toward you, yet you can be his master.

8 Cain said to his brother Abel, "Let us go out in the field." When they were in the field, Cain attacked his brother Abel and killed him.

9 Then the Lord asked Cain, "Where is your brother Abel?" He answered, "I do not know. Am I my brother's keeper?"

10 The Lord then said: "What have you done! Listen: Your brother's blood cries out to me from the soil!

11 Therefore you shall be banned from the soil that opened its mouth to receive your brother's blood from your hand.

12 If you till the soil, it shall no longer give you its produce. You shall become a restless wanderer on the earth."

13 Cain said to the Lord: "My punishment is too great to bear.

14 Since you have now banished me from the soil, and I must avoid your presence and become a restless wanderer on the earth, anyone may kill me at sight."

15 "Not so!" the Lord said to him. "If anyone kills Cain, Cain shall be avenged sevenfold." So the Lord put a mark[228] on Cain, lest anyone should kill him at sight.

16 Cain then left the Lord's presence and settled in the land of Nod,[229] east of Eden.

DESCENDANTS OF CAIN AND SETH {GENESIS 4:17–4:26}

17 Cain had relations with his wife, and she conceived and bore Enoch. Cain also became the founder of a city,[230] which he named after his son Enoch.

18 To Enoch was born Irad, and Irad became the father of Mehujael; Mehujael became the father of Methusael, and Methusael became the father of Lamech.

19 Lamech took two wives; the name of the first was Adah, and the name of the second Zillah.

20 Adah gave birth to Jabal, the ancestor of all who dwell in tents and keep cattle.

21 His brother's name was Jubal; he was the ancestor of all who play the lyre and the pipe.

22 Zillah, on her part, gave birth to Tubalcain, the ancestor of all who forge instruments of bronze and iron. The sister of Tubalcain was Naamah.

23 Lamech said to his wives:

---

[227]The phrase "demon lurking" is derived from the Hebrew term *robes* which literally means "croucher." The term *robes* is used here like the similar Akkadian term *rabisu*, to designate a certain kind of evil spirit.

[228]The "mark" referred to here is probably a tattoo. The use of tattooing for tribal marks has always been common among the nomads who roamed the deserts of Southwest Asia and Egypt.

[229]The "land of Nod" is not a definite geographic region. The term merely means "the land of nomads."

[230]In verses 12 through 16, Cain is depicted as the prototype of the nomads of Southwest Asia. However, in verse 17, Cain is depicted as the prototype of sedentary peoples with higher material culture.

"Adah and Zillah, hear my voice;
    wives of Lamech, listen to my ut-
terance:
    I have killed a man for wounding me,
        a boy for bruising me.
24 If Cain is avenged sevenfold,
        then Lamech seventy-sevenfold.
25 Adam again had relations with his wife, and she gave birth to a son whom she called Seth. "God has granted[231] me more offspring in place of Abel," she said, "because Cain slew him."
26 To Seth, in turn, a son was born, and he named him Enosh.[232]
At that time men began to invoke the Lord by name.[233]

THE GENERATIONS FROM ADAM TO NOAH {GENESIS 5:1–5:32}[234]

Chapter 5

1 This is the record of the descendants of Adam. When God created man, he made him in the likeness of God;
2 he created them male and female. When they were created, he blessed them and named them "man."
3 Adam was one hundred and thirty years old when he begot a son in his likeness, after his image; and he named him Seth.
4 Adam lived eight hundred years after the birth of Seth, and he had other sons and daughters.
5 The whole lifetime of Adam was nine hundred and thirty years; then he died.
6 When Seth was one hundred and five years old, he became the father of Enosh.
7 Seth lived eight hundred and seven years after the birth of Enosh, and he had other sons and daughters.
8 The whole lifetime of Seth was nine hundred and twelve years; then he died.
9 When Enosh was ninety years old, he became the father of Kenan.
10 Enosh lived eight hundred and fifteen years after the birth of Kenan, and he had other sons and daughters.
11 The whole lifetime of Enosh was nine hundred and five years; then he died.
12 When Kenan was seventy years old, he became the father of Mahalalel.
13 Kenan lived eight hundred and forty years after the birth of Mahalalel, and he had other sons and daughters.
14 The whole lifetime of Kenan was nine hundred and ten years; then he died.

---

[231] The phrase "has granted" is derived from the Hebrew word *shat* which in this context is a wordplay on the name *shet* ("Seth").

[232] The name "Enosh," in Hebrew, is a synonym of *adam* ("man").

[233] This sentence means that at that time men began to call God by God's personal name, Yahweh, which is rendered as "the Lord" in many biblical texts. The ancient, so-called Yahwist source used here employs the name Yahweh long before the time of Moses. Another ancient source, the Elohist (from its use of the term Elohim, "God," instead of Yahweh, "Lord," for the pre-Mosaic period), makes Moses the first to use Yahweh as the proper name of Israel's God, previously known by other names as well.

[234] Although this chapter, with its highly schematic form, belongs to the relatively late "P" source materials, it is based on very ancient traditions. Together with Genesis 11:10–26, the primary purpose of this chapter was to bridge the genealogical gap between Adam and Abraham. Adam's line is traced through Seth, but several names in the series are the same as, or similar to, certain names in Cain's line. {See Appendix 10.} The long lifespans attributed to these antediluvian patriarchs have a symbolic rather than a historical value. Babylonian tradition also recorded antediluvian kings with fantastically high ages who reigned successively before the flood. {See Appendix 3.}

15 When Mahalalel was sixty-five years old, he became the father of Jared.

16 Mahalalel lived eight hundred and thirty years after the birth of Jared, and he had other sons and daughters.

17 The whole lifetime of Mahalalel was eight hundred and ninety-five years; then he died.

18 When Jared was one hundred and sixty-two years old, he became the father of Enoch.

19 Jared lived eight hundred years after the birth of Enoch, and he had other sons and daughters.

20 The whole lifetime of Jared was nine hundred and sixty-two years; then he died.

21 When Enoch was sixty-five years old, he became the father of Methuselah.

22 Enoch lived three hundred years after the birth of Methuselah, and he had other sons and daughters.

23 The whole lifetime of Enoch was three hundred and sixty-five years.

24 Then Enoch walked with God, and he was no longer here, for God took him.[235]

25 When Methuselah was one hundred and eighty-seven years old, he became the father of Lamech.

26 Methuselah lived seven hundred and eighty-two years after the birth of Lamech, and he had other sons and daughters.

27 The whole lifetime of Methuselah was nine hundred and sixty-nine years; then he died.

28 When Lamech was one hundred and eighty-two years old, he begot a son

29 "and named him Noah,[236] saying, "Out of the very ground that the Lord has put under a curse, this one shall bring us relief from our work and the toil of our hands."

30 Lamech lived five hundred and ninety-five years after the birth of Noah, and he had other sons and daughters.

31 The whole lifetime of Lamech was seven hundred and seventy-seven years; then he died.

32 When Noah was five hundred years old, he became the father of Shem, Ham and Japheth.

ORIGIN OF THE NEPHILIM {GENESIS 6:1–6:4}[237]

Chapter 6

1 When men began to multiply on earth and daughters were born to them,

2 the sons of heaven[238] saw how beautiful the daughters of man were, and so they took for their wives as many of them as they chose.

3 Then the Lord said: "My spirit[239] shall not remain in man forever, since he is but

---

[235]In place of the usual formula, "Then he died," here the reader is told that "Enoch walked with God." This clearly implies that Enoch did not die but instead, like Elijah {see 2 Kings 2:11}, Enoch was taken alive to God's abode—to heaven.

[236]There is a similarity in sound between the Hebrew word *noah* and the verbal phrase *yenahamenu*, "he will bring us relief." The phrase *yenahamenu* refers both to the curse put on the soil because of the fall of man {see Genesis 3:17} and to Noah's success in agriculture, especially in raising grapes for wine {see Genesis 9:20}.

[237]Genesis 6:1–4 is apparently a fragment of an old legend. The author of this text incorporates the legend here, not only in order to account for the prehistoric giants of Palestine, whom the Hebrews called the Nephilim, but also to introduce the story of the flood with a moral orientation—the increasing wickedness of mankind.

[238]The reference to the "sons of heaven" actually means "the sons of the gods" or "the sons of God." In other words, these "sons of heaven" were celestial beings of an ancient folklore.

[239]The reference to "My spirit" is akin to the "the breath of life" referred to in Genesis 2:7.

flesh. His days[240] shall comprise one hundred and twenty years."

4 At that time the Nephilim appeared on earth (as well as later[241]), after the sons of heaven had intercourse with the daughters of man, who bore them sons. They were the heroes of old, the men of renown.

WARNING OF THE FLOOD[242]
{GENESIS 6:5–6:13}

5 When the Lord saw how great was man's wickedness on earth, and how no desire that his heart conceived was ever anything but evil,

6 he regretted that he had made man on the earth, and his heart was grieved.

7 So the Lord said: "I will wipe out from the earth the men whom I have created, and not only the men, but also the beasts and the creeping things and the birds of the air, for I am sorry that I made them."

8 But Noah found favor with the Lord.

9 These are the descendants of Noah. Noah, a good man and blameless in that age,

10 for he walked with God, begot three sons: Shem, Ham and Japheth.

11 In the eyes of God the earth was corrupt and full of lawlessness.

12 When God saw how corrupt the earth had become, since all mortals led depraved lives on earth,

13 he said to Noah: "I have decided to put an end to all mortals on earth; the earth is full of lawlessness because of them. So I will destroy them and all life on earth.

PREPARATION FOR THE FLOOD
{GENESIS 6:14–7:5}

14 Make yourself an ark of gopherwood,[243] put various compartments in it, and cover it inside and out with pitch.

15 This is how you shall build it: the length of the ark shall be three hundred cu-

---

[240]The sentence "His days shall comprise one hundred and twenty years" probably refers to the time God would still let men live on earth before destroying them with the flood, rather than the maximum span of life God would allot to individual men in the future.

[241]According to Numbers 13:33, when the Hebrews invaded Palestine and found there the tall aboriginal Anakim, they likened them to the Nephilim. {See also Deuteronomy 2:10.} Perhaps the huge megalithic structures in Palestine were thought to have been built by a race of giants, whose superhuman strength was attributed to semi-divine origin.

[242]The story of the great flood which is recorded in Genesis 6:5 through Genesis 8:22 is actually a composite narrative based on two separate sources interwoven into an intricate patchwork. To the Yahwist source,—the "J" source material—with some later editorial additions, are usually assigned Genesis 6:5–8; 7:1–5, 7–10, 12, 16, 17, 22–23; 8:2–3, 6–12, 13, 20–22. The other sections come from the "Priestly document"—the "P" source materials. The combination of the two source materials has produced certain duplications (compare Genesis 6:13–22 with Genesis 7:1–5). Additionally, certain inconsistencies are apparent, such as the number of the various animals taken into the ark (compare Genesis 6:19 and 7:14 [of the "P" source material] with Genesis 7:2 [of the "J" source material]), and the timetable of the flood (compare Genesis 8:3–5 and 13 [of the "P" source material] with Genesis 7:4, 10, 12, 17 and 8:6, 10, 12 [of the "J" source material]). Both the "P" and the "J" source materials go back ultimately to an ancient Mesopotamian story of a great flood, preserved in the eleventh tablet of the Gilgamesh Epic. The latter account, in some respects, remarkably similar to the biblical account, is in others very different from it.

[243]Gopherwood is an unidentified wood not mentioned elsewhere in the Bible.

bits, its width fifty cubits, and its height thirty cubits.[244]

16 Make an opening for daylight[245] in the ark, and finish the ark a cubit above it. Put an entrance in the side of the ark, which you shall make with bottom, second and third decks.

17 I, on my part, am about to bring the flood [waters] on the earth, to destroy everywhere all creatures in which there is the breath of life; everything on earth shall perish.

18 But with you I will establish my covenant; you and your sons, your wife and your sons' wives, shall go into the ark.

19 Of all other living creatures you shall bring two into the ark, one male and one female, that you may keep them alive with you.

20 Of all kinds of birds, of all kinds of beasts, and of all kinds of creeping things, two of each shall come into the ark with you, to stay alive,

21 Moreover, you are to provide yourself with all the food that is to be eaten, and store it away, that it may serve as provisions for you and for them."

22 This Noah did; he carried out all the commands that God gave him.

Chapter 7

1 Then the Lord said to Noah: "Go into the ark, you and all your household, for you alone in this age have I found to be truly just.

2 Of every clean animal, take with you seven pairs, a male and its mate; and of the unclean animals, one pair, a male and its mate;

3 likewise, of every clean bird of the air, seven pairs, a male and a female, and of all the unclean birds, one pair, a male and a female. Thus you will keep their issue alive over all the earth.

4 Seven days from now I will bring rain down on the earth for forty days and forty nights, and so I will wipe out from the surface of the earth every moving creature that I have made."

5 Noah did just as the Lord had commanded him.

THE GREAT FLOOD
{GENESIS 7:6–8:22}

6 Noah was six hundred years old when the flood waters came upon the earth.

7 Together with his sons, his wife, and his sons' wives, Noah went into the ark because of the waters of the flood.

8 Of the clean animals and the unclean, of the birds, and of everything that creeps on the ground,

9 [two by two] male and female entered the ark with Noah, just as the Lord had commanded him.

10 As soon as the seven days were over, the waters of the flood came upon the earth.

11 In the six hundredth year of Noah's life, in the second month, on the seventeenth day of the month: it was on that day that all the fountains of the great abyss[246] burst forth, and the floodgates of the sky were opened.

12 For forty days and forty nights heavy rain poured down on the earth.

[244]The dimensions of Noah's ark were approximately 440 × 73 × 44 feet since a cubit is a foot and a half (eighteen inches) long. In contrast, the ark of the Babylonian flood story was an exact cube, 120 cubits (180 feet) in length, width and height.

[245]The phrase "opening for daylight" appears to be a conjectural rendering of the Hebrew word *sohar*, occurring only here. The reference is probably to an open space on all sides near the top of the ark to admit light and air. The ark also had a window or hatch, which could be opened and closed. {See Genesis 8:6.}

[246]This reference to the great abyss refers to a subterranean ocean,—a remnant of the primordial ocean of the initial creation. {See Genesis 1:2.}

13 On the precise day named, Noah and his sons Shem, Ham and Japheth, and Noah's wife, and the three wives of Noah's sons had entered the ark,

14 together with every kind of wild beast, every kind of domestic animal, every kind of creeping thing of the earth, and every kind of bird.

15 Pairs of all creatures in which there was the breath of life entered the ark with Noah.

16 Those that entered were male and female, and of all species they came, as God had commanded Noah. Then the Lord shut him in.

17 The flood continued upon the earth for forty days. As the waters increased, they lifted the ark, so that it rose above the earth.

18 The swelling waters increased greatly, but the ark floated on the surface of the waters.

19 Higher and higher above the earth rose the waters, until all the highest mountains everywhere were submerged,

20 the crest rising fifteen cubits higher than the submerged mountains.

21 All creatures that stirred on earth perished: birds, cattle, wild animals, and all that swarmed on the earth, as well as all mankind.

22 Everything on dry land with the faintest breath of life in its nostrils died out.

23 The Lord wiped out every living thing on earth; man and cattle, the creeping things and the birds of the air; all were wiped out from the earth. Only Noah and those with him in the ark were left.

24 The waters maintained their crest

over the earth for one hundred and fifty days,[247]

Chapter 8

1 and then God remembered Noah and all the animals, wild and tame, that were with him in the ark. So God made a wind sweep over the earth, and the waters began to subside.

2 The fountains of the abyss and the floodgates of the sky were closed, and the downpour from the sky was held back.

3 Gradually the waters receded from the earth. At the end of one hundred and fifty days, the waters had so diminished

4 that, in the seventh month, on the seventeenth day of the month, the ark came to rest on the mountains of Ararat.[248]

5 The waters continued to diminish until the tenth month, and on the first day of the tenth month the tops of the mountains appeared.

6 At the end of forty days[249] *Noah opened the hatch he had made in the ark,*

7 and he sent out a raven, to see if the waters had lessened on the earth. It flew back and forth until the waters dried off from the earth.

8 Then he sent out a dove, to see if the waters had lessened on the earth.

9 But the dove could find no place to alight and perch, and it returned to him in the ark, for there was water all over the earth. Putting out his hand, he caught the dove and drew it back to him inside the ark.

10 He waited seven days more and again sent the dove out from the ark.

11 In the evening the dove came back to

---

[247]Some scholars assert that verse 24 is more properly connected to Chapter 8 as the introduction to the chapter.

[248]Ararat refers to ancient Urartu, north of the Mesopotamian plain, part of modern Armenia.

[249]In the original Yahwist ("J") source, from which verse 6 was taken, the forty days refer to the full period of the flood itself {see and compare with Genesis 7:4 and 17}. However, in the context in which it is used here, the forty days appears to refer to a period following the date just given in verse 5 which is from the Priestly ("P") source material.

him, and there in its bill was a plucked-off olive leaf! So Noah knew that the waters had lessened on the earth.

12 He waited still another seven days and then released the dove once more; and this time it did not come back.

13 In the six hundred and first year of Noah's life, in the first month, on the first day of the month, the water began to dry up on the earth. Noah then removed the covering of the ark and saw that the surface of the ground was drying up.

14 In the second month, on the twenty-seventh day of the month, the earth was dry.

15 Then God said to Noah:

16 "Go out of the ark, together with your wife and your sons and your sons' wives.

17 Bring out with you every living thing that is with you—all bodily creatures, be they birds or animals or creeping things of the earth—and let them abound on the earth, breeding and multiplying on it."

18 So Noah came out, together with his wife and his sons and his sons' wives;

19 and all the animals, wild and tame, all the birds, and all the creeping creatures of the earth left the ark, one kind after another.

20 Then Noah built an altar to the Lord, and choosing from every clean animal and every clean bird, he offered holocausts on the altar.

21 When the Lord smelled the sweet odor, he said to himself: "Never again will I doom the earth because of man, since the desires of man's heart are evil from the start[250];

nor will I ever again strike down all living beings, as I have done.

22 As long as the earth lasts, seedtime and harvest, cold and heat, summer and winter, and day and night shall not cease."

GOD'S COVENANT WITH NOAH {GENESIS 9:1–9:17}

Chapter 9

1 God blessed Noah and his sons and said to them: "Be fertile and multiply and fill the earth.

2 Dread fear of you shall come upon all the animals of the earth and all the birds of the air, upon all the creatures that move about on the ground and all the fishes of the sea; into your power they are delivered.

3 Every creature that is alive shall be yours to eat[251]; I give them all to you as I did the green plants.

4 Only flesh with its lifeblood still in it you shall not eat.[252]

5 For your own lifeblood, too, I will demand an accounting: from every animal I will demand it, and from man in regard to his fellow man I will demand an accounting for human life.

6 If anyone sheds the blood of man,
*   by man shall his blood be shed;*
For in the image of God
*   has man been made.*

7 Be fertile, then, and multiply; abound on earth and subdue it."

8 God said to Noah and to his sons with him:

---

[250]The reference to "from the start" means literally "from his youth." It is uncertain whether this means from the beginning of the human race or from the early years of each individual.

[251]Antediluvian creatures, including man, are depicted as vegetarians {see Genesis 1:29}. Only after the flood, did man become carnivorous.

[252]Because a living being dies when it loses most of its blood, the ancients regarded blood as the seat of life, and therefore as sacred. Although in itself the prohibition against eating meat with blood in it is comparable to the ritual laws of the Mosaic code, the Jews considered it binding on all men, because it was given by God to Noah, the new ancestor of all mankind. Therefore, the early Christian (Catholic) Church retained it for a time {see Acts 15:20 and 29}.

9 "See, I am now establishing my covenant with you and your descendants after you

10 and with every living creature that was with you: all the birds, and the various tame and wild animals that were with you and came out of the ark.

11 I will establish my covenant with you, that never again shall all bodily creatures be destroyed by the waters of a flood; there shall not be another flood to devastate the earth."

12 God added: "This is the sign that I am giving for all ages to come, of the covenant between me and you and every living creature with you:

13 I set my bow in the clouds to serve as a sign of the covenant between me and the earth.

14 When I bring clouds over the earth, and the bow appears in the clouds,

15 I will recall the covenant I have made between me and you and all living beings, so that the waters shall never again become a flood to destroy all mortal beings.

16 As the bow appears in the clouds, I will see it and recall the everlasting covenant that I have established between God and all living beings—all mortal creatures that are on earth."

17 God told Noah: "This is the sign of the covenant I have established between me and all mortal creatures that are on earth."

NOAH AND HIS SONS {GENESIS 9:18–9:29}[253]

18 The sons of Noah who came out of the ark were Shem, Ham and Japheth. (Ham was the father of Canaan.)

19 These three were the sons of Noah, and from them the whole earth was peopled.

20 Now Noah, a man of the soil, was the first to plant a vineyard.

21 When he drank some of the wine, he became drunk and lay naked inside his tent.

22 Ham, the father of Canaan, saw his father's nakedness, and he told his two brothers outside about it.

23 Shem and Japheth, however, took a robe, and holding it on their backs, they walked backward and covered their father's nakedness; since their faces were turned the other way, they did not see their father's nakedness.

24 When Noah woke up from his drunkenness and learned what his youngest son had done to him,

25 he said: "Cursed be Canaan! The lowest of slaves shall he be to his brothers."

26 He also said: "Blessed be the Lord, the God of Shem[254]! Let Canaan be his slave.

27 May God expand Japheth[255], so that he dwells among the tents of Shem; and let Canaan be his slave."

28 Noah lived three hundred and fifty years after the flood.

29 The whole lifetime of Noah was nine hundred and fifty years; then he died.

---

[253]The story of Noah and his sons seems to be a composite of two earlier accounts. In one, Ham was guilty, while in the other, it was Canaan. One purpose of the story is to justify the Israelites' enslavement of the Canaanites because of certain indecent sexual practices in the Canaanite religion. As such, the story offers no justification for enslaving sub-Saharan Africans, because the land of Canaan was a Southwest Asian land, a Semitic land, belonging to Hamitic Egypt at the time of the Israelite invasion.

[254]The text may have originally read: "Blessed of the Lord be Shem."

[255]In the Hebrew text, there is a play on the words with *yapt* ("expand") and *yepet* ("Japheth") appearing in alliteration.

TABLE OF NATIONS
{GENESIS 10:1–10:32}[256]

Chapter 10

1 These are the descendants of Noah's sons, Shem, Ham and Japheth, to whom sons were born after the flood.

2 The descendants of Japheth:

Gomer,[257] Magog, Madai,[258] Javan,[259] Tubal, Meshech and Tiras.

3 The descendants of Gomer: Ashkenaz,[260] Riphath and Togarmah.

4 The descendants of Javan: Elishah,[261] Tarshish, the Kittim[262] and the Rodanim.[263]

5 These are the descendants of Japheth, and from them sprang the maritime nations,

in their respective lands—each with its own language—by their clans within their nations.

6 The descendants of Ham: Cush,[264] Mizraim[265], Put[266] and Canaan.

7 The descendants of Cush: Seba, Havilah, Sabtah, Raamah and Sabteca. The descendants of Raamah:

Sheba and Dedan.

8 Cush[267] became the father of Nimrod,[268] who was the first potentate on earth.

9 He was a mighty hunter by the grace of the Lord; hence the saying, "Like Nimrod, a mighty hunter by the grace of the Lord."

10 The chief cities of his kingdom were

---

[256]This chapter presents a remarkably good classification of the various peoples known to the ancient Jews. It is theologically important as stressing the basic family unity of all men on earth. The relationship between the various peoples is based partly on linguistic, partly on geographic, and partly on political grounds according to their languages, lands and nations. In general, the descendants of Japheth (verses 2–5) are the peoples of the Indo-European languages to the north and west of Mesopotamia and Syria; the descendants of Ham (verses 6–20) are the Hamitic speaking peoples of northern Africa; and the descendants of Shem (verses 21–31) are the Semitic speaking peoples of Mesopotamia, Syria and Arabia. But there are many exceptions to this rule; the Semitic speaking peoples of Canaan, for instance, are considered descendants of Ham, because at the time they were subject to Hamitic Egypt (verses 6 and 15–19). This chapter is a composite from the Yahwist ("J") source materials (verses 8–19, 21, and 24–30) of about the ninth century B.C.T., and the Priestly ("P") source materials (verses 1–7, 20, 22, and 31) of a few centuries later. That is why certain tribes of Arabia are listed under both Ham (verse 7) and Shem (verses 26–28).

[257]"Gomer" probably refers to the Cimmerians.

[258]"Madai" probably refers to the Medes.

[259]"Javan" probably refers to the Greeks.

[260]"Ashkenaz" probably refers to the Scythians.

[261]"Elishah" probably refers to Cyprus.

[262]"Kittim" probably refers to certain inhabitants of Cyprus.

[263]"Rodanim" probably refers to the inhabitants of Rhodes.

[264]"Cush" probably refers to biblical Ethiopia or Nubia.

[265]"Mizraim" probably refers to Egypt.

[266]"Put" probably refers to either Punt in East Africa or Libya.

[267]Here the reference to "Cush" probably refers to the Kassites. The Kassites inhabited a region to the east of Mesopotamia.

[268]The reference to Nimrod is probably actually to Tukulti-Ninurta I, the thirteenth century B.C.T. Assyrian ruler who was the first Assyrian conqueror of Babylonia.

Babylon, Erech and Accad, all of them in the land of Shinar.[269]

11 From that land he went forth to Asshur,[270] where he built Nineveh, Rehoboth-Ir[271] and Calah,[272]

12 as well as Resen, between Nineveh and Calah, the latter being the principal city.

13 Mizraim became the father of the Ludim, the Anamim, the Lehabim, the Naphtuhim,

14 the Pathrusim,[273] the Casluhim, and the Caphtorim[274] from whom the Philistines sprang.

15 Canaan became the father of Sidon, his first born, and of Heth[275];

16 also of the Jebusites, the Amorites, the Girgashites,

17 the Hivites, the Arkites, the Sinites,

18 the Arvadites, the Zemarites and the Hamathites. Afterward, the clans of the Canaanites spread out,

19 so that the Canaanite borders extended from Sidon all the way to Gerar, near Gaza, and all the way to Sodom, Gomorrah, Admah and Zeboiim, near Lasha.[276]

20 These are the descendants of Ham, according to their clans and languages, by their lands and nations.

21 To Shem also, Japheth's oldest brother and the ancestor of all the children of Eber, sons were born.

22 The descendants of Shem:
Elam, Asshur, Arpachshad, Lud and Aram:

23 The descendants of Aram:
Uz, Hul, Gether and Mash.

24 Arpachshad became the father of Shelah, and Shelah became the father of Eber.

25 To Eber two sons were born: the name of the first was Peleg, for in his time the world was divided[277]; and the name of his brother was Joktan.

26 Joktan became the father of Almodad, Sheleph, Hazarmaveth, Jerah,

27 Hadoram, Uzal, Diklah,

28 Obal, Abimael, Sheba

29 Ophir, Havilah and Jobab. All these were descendants of Joktan.

30 Their settlements extended all the way to Sephar, the eastern hill country.

31 These are the descendants of Shem, according to their clans and languages, by their lands and nations.

32 These are the groupings of Noah's sons, according to their origins and by their nations. From these the other nations of the earth branched out after the flood.

---

[269]"Shinar" probably refers to ancient Sumer in southern Mesopotamia, mentioned also in Genesis 11:2 and 14:1.

[270]"Asshur" probably refers to Assyria.

[271]"Rehoboth-Ir" literally means "wide streets city." This name was probably not the name of another city but rather an epithet for Nineveh {see Jonah 3:3}.

[272]"Calah" probably refers to the Assyrian Kalhu, the capital of Assyria in the ninth century B.C.T.

[273]The Pathrusim were the people of upper (southern) Egypt.

[274]"Caphtorim" probably refers to Crete and it is believed that Caphtor was the place of origin of the Philistines.

[275]"Heth" refers to the biblical Hittites.

[276]The reading of the name "Lasha" is a bit uncertain. It may be that the name "Bela" is the better rendering.

[277]In the Hebrew text, there is a play on words between the name "Peleg" and the word *ni-plega* which means "was divided."

THE TOWER OF BABEL
{GENESIS 11:1–11:9}[278]

Chapter 11

1 The whole world spoke the same language, using the same words.

2 While men were migrating in the east, they came upon a valley in the land of Shinar and settled there.

3 They said to one another, "Come, let us mold bricks and harden them with fire." They used bricks for stone, and bitumen for mortar.

4 Then they said, "Come, let us build ourselves a city and a tower with its top in the sky,[279] and so make a name for ourselves; otherwise we shall be scattered all over the earth."

5 The Lord came down to see the city and the tower that the men had built.

6 Then the Lord said: "If now, while they are one people, all speaking the same language, they have started to do this, nothing will later stop them from doing whatever they presume to do.

7 Let us then go down and there confuse their language, so that one will not understand what another says."

8 Thus the Lord scattered them from there all over the earth, and they stopped building the city.

9 That is why it was called Babel,[280] because there the Lord confused the speech of all the world. It was from that place that he scattered them all over the earth.

THE LINE FROM SHEM TO ABRAHAM
{GENESIS 11:10–26}[281]

10 This is the record of the descendants of Shem. When Shem was one hundred years old, he became the father of Arpachshad, two years after the flood.

11 Shem lived five hundred years after the birth of Arpachshad, and he had other sons and daughters.

12 When Arpachshad was thirty-five years old, he became the father of Shelah.[282]

13 Arpachshad lived four hundred and three years after the birth of Shelah, and he had other sons and daughters.

---

[278]The story of the Tower of Babel is based on traditions about the temple towers or ziggurats of Babylonia. This story is used by the author primarily to illustrate man's increasing wickedness, shown here as man's presumptuous effort to create an urban culture apart from God. The secondary motive in the story is to present an imaginative origin of the diversity of the languages among the various peoples inhabiting the earth, as well as an artificial explanation of the name "Babylon."

[279]The reference to the "tower with its top in the sky" is a direct reference to the chief ziggurat of Babylon, the E-sag-ila—"the house that raises high its head." Babylonian ziggurats were the earliest skyscrapers.

[280]The name "Babel" is the Hebrew form of the name "Babylon." The indigenous name "Babili" means "gate of the gods." The Hebrew word *balil*—"he confused"—has a similar sound. Apparently, the name referred originally only to a certain part of the city, the district near the gate that led to the temple area.

[281]The genealogy set forth in Genesis 11:10–26 is a continuation of the genealogical record given in Genesis 5:1–32. Although the ages of the patriarchs in this list are much lower than those of the antediluvian patriarchs, they are still artificial and devoid of historical value. The ages given here are from the current Hebrew text; the Samaritan and Greek texts have divergent sets of numbers in most cases.

[282]The Greek text has a certain Kenan between Arpachshad and Shelah. The Greek text is subsequently followed in Luke 3:36.

14 When Shelah was thirty years old, he became the father of Eber.[283]

15 Shelah lived four hundred and three years after the birth of Eber, and he had other sons and daughters.

16 When Eber was thirty-four years old, he became the father of Peleg.

17 Eber lived four hundred and thirty years after the birth of Peleg, and he had other sons and daughters.

18 When Peleg was thirty years old, he became the father of Reu.

19 Peleg lived two hundred and nine years after the birth of Reu, and he had other sons and daughters.

20 When Reu was thirty-two years old, he became the father of Serug.

21 Reu lived two hundred and seven years after the birth of Serug, and he had other sons and daughters.

22 When Serug was thirty years old, he became the father of Nahor.

23 Serug lived two hundred years after the birth of Nahor, and he had other sons and daughters.

24 When Nahor was twenty-nine years old, he became the father of Terah.

25 Nahor lived one hundred and nineteen years after the birth of Terah, and he had other sons and daughters.

26 When Terah was seventy years old, he became the father of Abram, Nahor and Haran.

---

[283]Eber is the eponymous ancestor of the Hebrews, who are known as the "descendants of Eber."

A Protestant Perspective

THE BIBLE

The word "Bible" is derived from the Greek word *biblia* which is the plural form of the singular noun *biblion,* which means "little book." Accordingly, the word "Bible" literally means "little books." In Latin, which took the word over from the Greek, the word "Bible" came to be regarded as a singular noun, having the same form, meaning "book." As a singular noun, the word was adopted early on into the language of the Western Christian Church, and as such it is used even today in modern European languages as the Bible—the Book. This use of the word Bible as a singular noun is responsible for much misapprehension, because the Bible can never be rightly appreciated unless it is borne in mind that it is not so much one book as it is a library consisting of many books, written by different authors at different times, in different places, from different points of view, and reflecting different stages of religious, moral, social, and political development. Altogether, in most modern Protestant Bibles, there are sixty-six separate writings in the collection known as the Bible.

There are two great divisions in the Bible used by Christians, called respectively the "Old Testament" and the "New Testament," the former containing thirty-nine books, the latter twenty-seven. The designation "Testament" is somewhat mislead-ing. A more accurate rendering would be "Covenant." Indeed, some of the early church Fathers speak of "the divine Scriptures, the so-called Old and New Covenants." The Old Testament includes books reflecting the religious life and experience of the Hebrews which originated during the period when the national covenant between Jehovah and the people of Israel, believed to have been mediated through Moses, was held to be in force. Similarly, the New Testament contains books reflecting the early Christian movement, interpreted as marking the establishment of a new and universal covenant between God and men through Jesus Christ.

The thirty-nine books of the Old Testament are arranged in a four-fold grouping, which, with some modifications, has been recognized for many centuries—since the Greek translation known as the Septuagint was made, before the beginning of Christian time. The four fold grouping of the Old Testament is as follows:

1. *The Law— The Pentateuch (5 books):*
   Genesis, Exodus, Leviticus, Numbers, and Deuteronomy

2. *The History (12 books):*
   Joshua, Judges, Ruth, First and Second Samuel, First and Second Kings, First and Second Chronicles, Ezra, Nehemiah and Esther

211

3. *Poetry (5 books):*
   Job, Psalms, Proverbs, Ecclesiates, and Song of Songs

4. *Prophecy (17 books):*
   (a) *The Major Prophets (5 books):*
   Isaiah, Jeremiah, Lamentations, Ezekiel, and Daniel

   (b) *The Minor Prophets (12 books):*
   Hosea, Joel, Amos, Obadiah, Jonah, Micah, Nahum, Habakkuk, Zephaniah, Haggai, Zechariah, and Malachi

The twenty-seven books of the New Testament may be arranged in three groups. The three fold grouping of the New Testament is as follows:

1. *The Historical Books (5 books):*
   (a) *The Gospels (4 books):*
   Matthew, Mark, Luke, and John

   (b) The Acts *(1 book)*

2. *The Epistles or Doctrinal Books (21 books):*
   Romans; First and Second Corinthians; Galatians; Ephesians; Philippians; Colossians; First and Second Thessalonians; First and Second Timothy; Titus; Philemon; Hebrews; James; First and Second Peter; First, Second and Third John; and Jude

3. *The Apocalyptic (1 book):*
   Revelation

The Pentateuch

According to the arrangement in the Hebrew Bible, the Old Testament consists of three parts,—the Law, the Prophets and the Writings. In Hebrew these three parts are known as *Torah, Nebhiim,* and *Kethubhim.*

The first division—the Torah—is so-called because it embodies practically the entire legal system of the Hebrews. The Torah is sometimes called "The Five Books of Moses." The early rabbis speak of the Torah as "the Five-fifths of the Law," an indication that the fivefold division was introduced at a very early date. The early church Fathers, beginning with Tertullian, employ the term, still in common use, "the Pentateuch."

The full form of the name of the Torah in Greek would be *pentateuchos biblos,* the "fiveroll book." Strictly speaking teuchos denotes not the book or roll itself, but rather the box or chest in which it was kept. Symmachus, an early translator of the Old Testament uses it as the equivalent of the Hebrew word *megillah,* or roll.

The five books in the Pentateuch are: Genesis, Exodus, Leviticus, Numbers, Deuteronomy. Even the casual reader can see that Genesis forms a book by itself, and so does Deuteronomy. The general contents and characteristics of Leviticus separate it from the books on either side, while the opening words of Exodus {see Exodus 1:1–7} and the closing words of Numbers {see Numbers 36:13} clearly show that these two books are also considered complete in themselves.

All the material in the five books, varied as it is, may be arranged under two headings: history and law. Under the heading of history, the historical portions of the Pentateuch cover the period beginning with the creation of the world and ending with the encampment of the Israelite tribes in the plain of Moab. This period may be divided as follows: (1) the beginning of all things {see Genesis 1:1–11:9}; (2) the Hebrew patriarchs {see Genesis 11:10–50:26}; and (3) the Exodus from Egypt and the organization of Israel into a more or less compact national unit, with a national consciousness.

It is important to note that in the Pentateuch, no attempt is made by the authors to furnish a complete history. Many events of considerable importance from the point of view of the historian are treated only briefly or are ignored. Nevertheless, the stream of history is never wholly interrupted, and though at time it almost disappears, it always reappears and flows on to the end.

The early readers focused their attention upon the legal elements in the Pentateuch. Consequently, the books came to be known as the Law or the Torah. Leviticus consists entirely of legal material while Exodus and Numbers are a mixture of law and history. Deuteronomy consists mainly of addresses embodying law. Genesis, which is chiefly narrative, mentions the laws of marriage and of the Sabbath as given in primeval times, gives regulations concerning food in the days of Noah, and relates the institution of circumcision in the time of Abraham.

It is customary among some scholars to group together not only the first five books and call the collection the Pentateuch, but also to add Joshua and designate the whole as the Hexateuch—the "six-fold" book. Joshua is added because its contents and its literary structure indicate that it is intimately connected with the Pentateuch and describes the final stage in the history of the origins of the Hebrew people. After all, the divine promise that the descendants of Abraham should occupy Canaan, which is repeatedly made in Genesis, only attains its full realization in Joshua. It would appear that Joshua was separated from the Pentateuch because (1) Moses could not be connected with this material as its author and (2) the contents of Joshua made it impossible to link it with the books of the Pentateuch as an authoritative rule of life.

In much of the Old Testament, it is assumed that the Law—the Torah—is the work of Moses. {See Ezra 3:2 and 7:6 and 2 Chronicles 34:14.} However, it is by no means clear that in these passages "Torah" is used to refer to the entire Pentateuch. It may refer simply to the legal system embodied in the Pentateuch, or, possibly, to only a part of this system. However, whatever the significance of these and similar Old Testament passages may be, Philo of Alexandria, and Josephus, and many early biblical scholars proceeded on the assumption that Moses wrote the entire Pentateuch.

With regards to Mosaic authorship of the Torah, the Babylonian Talmud, embodying early official Jewish tradition, makes the definite claim: "Moses wrote his own book, the section about Balaam and Job." Only the closing verses of Deuteronomy are ascribed to Joshua, on the reasonable assumption that Moses could not have written during his lifetime the statement, "And he died there." {See Deuteronomy 34:5.} However, a commentary on this verse in the Gemara assigns even these verses to Moses, stating that he wrote them "with weeping."

The view that Moses wrote the entire Pentateuch, with the possible exception of the closing verses, was the predominate view until the time of the Reformation. During the Renaissance and Reformation periods, conditions changed and questions began to be posed. Over time, increasing numbers of biblical scholars became convinced that Moses could not be the author of the Pentateuch in anywhere near its present form.

On the other hand, arguments in favor of the Mosaic authorship have been put forward with much skill by those who still defend the traditional view. These arguments generally fall within four groups. First, the pro-Moses advocates note that there is indirect evidence of Moses' authorship. This indirect evidence includes such considerations as the lack of unanimity among those who deny the Mosaic authorship; the manner of the literary composition practiced among the ancients; and the unity of theme and plan in the Pentateuch texts.

Secondly, external evidence is found in New Testament statements, especially in the words of Jesus; in the traditions current among Jews and Christians; and in the testimony of Old Testament books other than the Pentateuch.

Thirdly, there is direct internal evidence which consists of statements in the books of the Pentateuch themselves that Moses wrote something.

And fourth, greatest reliance is placed on what may be called indirect internal evidence, i.e., evidence found in the contents of the books apart from definite statements which point to Moses as the author.

What is the weight and value of these arguments? If it were possible to limit consideration to the facts and phenomena emphasized by the defenders of Mosaic authorship, and if the conclusions reached by them could be accepted without question, the arguments might appear quite formidable, if not overwhelming. However, it may be well to keep in mind some rather important considerations:

(1) One cannot escape the conviction that the method followed by the defenders of the fundamentalist view is neither fair nor scientific. Only the facts that can be interpreted in favor of Mosaic authorship are usually taken into account while contradictory facts are passed over lightly or are entirely ignored.

(2) The only argument that has anything to do directly with the writing of the Pentateuch is the linguistic argument; but this has proved so unsatisfactory that it is now rarely used by those who know Hebrew, for the simple reason that further study has disproved the high antiquity of the alleged archaic words and forms.

(3) The student of the Hebrew legal system as a whole, not of a few well-chosen examples apart from the larger context, finds it exceedingly difficult to believe that the desert wanderings furnished an opportunity for framing the intricate criminal, civil, moral, and ceremonial codes embodied in the Pentateuch.

Ultimately, all that the facts presented may prove is that the Pentateuch may contain some elements which originated in Mosaic times, but even so, these facts cannot prove that these elements were ever presented in a written form during those Mosaic times. Nor is it possible to point out definitely any of these Mosaic elements, for they may have undergone in the course of transmission either accidental or intentional alterations. The only conclusion warranted by the facts may be briefly expressed in these words: Whatever may be the time of the final composition or compilation of the Pentateuch, it contains elements, both historical and legal, which may have originated in the days of Moses.

Any elements which may have originated in Mosaic times undoubtedly underwent modification which, theoretically, were done in the spirit of Moses. The result of these modifications, continuing through several centuries, is today embodied in the Pentateuch. If there were no evidence to the contrary, it might be legitimate to take a further step and ascribe the entire work to Moses. But if such a step is taken, it is in the nature of an inference and nothing more.

THE PENTATEUCH AUTHORS

Few questions based on the careful examination of facts were raised regarding the Mosaic authorship of the Pentateuch prior to the Reformation. Around the eleventh century of the Christian calendar, a

Spanish Jew, Rabbi Isaac ben Jasos, pointed out that Genesis 36:31[284] must have been written later than the founding of the Hebrew monarchy since there were no Hebrew monarchs during the time of Moses. In the twelfth century of the Christian calendar, Ibn Ezra also called attention to certain passages which he found difficult to harmonize with belief in Mosaic authorship.

The Renaissance and Reformation caused a marked change. The Renaissance aroused men's interest in literature and science; the Reformation aroused their interest in religion as a personal experience. In the Renaissance, men began to think for themselves in matters of science and literature; in the Reformation they began to think for themselves in matters of religion. It was inevitable that the awakening of thought and the substitution of reason for authority in science, secular literature and secular history would ultimately affect biblical literature and biblical history as well. At any rate, some of the leaders in the Reformation movement, like Martin Luther, did not hesitate to express independent judgments with reference to the Mosaic authorship of the Pentateuch. Similarly, Andreas Masius, a learned Roman Catholic, maintained that the Pentateuch received its final form from Ezra or some other man of God.

The general church, both Catholic and Protestant, did not adopt the liberal attitude of the Reformation iconoclasts. Instead these institutions continued to regard belief in the Mosaic authorship of the Pentateuch an essential article of faith. Nevertheless, the facts to which earlier writers had called attention continued to assert themselves, and new facts came to be discovered. Thus, it was not so unexpected

that scholars within and without the church continued to insist that the belief in Mosaic authorship was not well founded. Scholars such as Spinoza and Hobbes began to propose various theories in explanation of the facts. The value of the discussions generated by these proposals lies not necessarily in the conclusions reached by the scholars but rather by the continued insistence that the facts—the indisputable facts—should be considered and explained.

Jean Astruc, a physician in the court of France's King Louis XIV and a professor of medicine in Paris, gave new direction to the whole scholarly study of the Pentateuch. Astruc did not deny the Mosaic authorship, instead he maintained that Moses used several literary sources which Moses then incorporated into the Pentateuch. On the basis of Astruc's discovery that in some sections of Genesis the divine name *Elohim* (God) was used, while in others *Yahweh* (Jehovah) was used, Astruc divided the book of Genesis into two principal sources— the Elohistic and the Jehovistic—admitting at the same time the presence of smaller sections from nine or ten minor sources. Having compiled Genesis in this manner, Astruc opined that Moses then wrote the remaining four books of the Pentateuch. Astruc set forth this hypothesis in a book entitled *Conjectures* which was published in 1753.

The investigations begun by Astruc were continued by scholars during the latter part of the eighteenth and the first half of the nineteenth century. In the course of these and later investigations, various theories were proposed to account for the complicated facts discovered by the investigators. These theories include:

(1) *The Fragment Theory* which looked upon the Pentateuch as an agglomera-

---

[284]Genesis 36:31 reads:

> *And these are the kings that reigned in the land of Edom, before there reigned any king over the children of Israel.*

tion of longer and shorter fragments, between which no threads of continuous connection could be traced. The arguments in support of this theory were drawn chiefly from the middle books of the Pentateuch in which, because of the presence of extensive legal sections, the transitions are frequently quite abrupt.

(2) *The Supplement Theory* which is based on a better appreciation of a common plan and purpose running through the entire Pentateuch. According to this theory, the Elohistic portion of the Pentateuch was the oldest; subsequently this was revised by the Jehovist, who annotated the older work and added to it a considerable number of new and independent sections.

(3) *The Document Theory* which is a modification of the Supplement theory made necessary by advances along two lines: (a) the discovery in 1853 of a second Elohim source; and (b) a better understanding of the interrelation of the different literary layers in the Pentateuch. The Document Theory owes its name to the fact that, by those who accept it, the Pentateuch, in its present form, is thought to be the result of the compilation of material coming from at least four documents, each of which is thought to have had originally an independent existence. Though over the course of time various symbols have been used to designate the four documents, and though even now complete uniformity is lacking, at present the four documents are generally known as J, E, D, P. The first, called J, uses in the sections narrating events prior to the call of Moses the divine name *Jehovah*; E, the Elohistic document, uses in the corresponding sections the divine name *Elohim*; D, the Deuteronomic Code, furnishes the heart of the present book of Deuteronomy; P, the Priestly Code, is a document combining both history and law, which owes its name to the perception that it is written from a distinctively priestly point of view. These four documents in turn are thought to embody material taken from still earlier sources which had an independent existence in written or oral form.

Today the Document Theory is the prevailing theory, but not in the form in which it was first presented. After undergoing various transformations, the Document Theory emerged in a form now commonly known as the Graf-Wellhausen Theory, or the Development Theory, and it is in this form that it is most widely accepted. The Graf-Wellhausen Theory derives its name from the fact that two of its most convincing exponents were K. H. Graf and Julius Wellhausen. Their special contribution to the theory of biblical research was the determination of the chronological order and of the dates of the several documents. The four documents are thought to have originated in the order of J, E, D, P and their dates, not considering later amendments, were fixed as follows:

(1) For the "J" source materials, about 850 B.C.T.;

(2) For the "E" source materials, about 750 B.C.T.;

(3) For the "D" source materials, about 650 B.C.T.; and

(4) For the "P" source materials, between 500 and 350 B.C.T.

Most modern scholars have adopted the Graf-Wellhausen order and dates for these Pentateuchal source documents.

The modern critical view of the origin and development of the Pentateuch includes the following items:

(1) The Pentateuch is a relatively late compilation of material taken from written sources, all of which reached their final form significantly after the time of Moses.

(2) The compiler depended chiefly upon four documents: "J," traces of which are found throughout the entire Pentateuch; "E," closely interwoven with "J" and, like it, found throughout the Pentateuch; "D," found chiefly in the book of Deuteronomy, though traces of it are found also elsewhere; and "P," which served as the groundwork for the entire compilation.

(3) "D" is identical with the Book of the Law that served as the basis of Josiah's reform in 621 B.C.T. It was in existence separately at that time; hence the Pentateuch in its final form cannot be older than that date, though some of the material embodied in it may be much older.

(4) "J" and "E" are both older than "D," and, according to most investigators, "D" is older than "P."

(5) The several documents show such striking differences that, on the whole, it is quite easy to separate them.

Any adequate discussion of the modern view must therefore include at least four points:

(1) The Pentateuch is a compilation of material from different documents written at different times.

(2) The Pentateuch contains some material that originated subsequently to the time of Moses.

(3) The Book of the Law found in the days of Josiah was not the Pentateuch in its final form but the Deuteronomic Code.

(4) The Pentateuch in its present form is the result of gradual growth during several centuries following the age of Moses.

In support of the claim that the Pentateuch is a compilation of material taken from different sources, attention is called to the following facts:

(1) The peculiar use of the divine names *Jehovah* (*Yahweh*) and *Elohim* in narratives of events prior to the call and commission of Moses. There are large sections of Genesis and of the opening chapters of Exodus which systematically use the name *Jehovah*, while others with equal consistency use *Elohim*. Thus, in Genesis 1:1–2:4 (the first account of creation) one can find *Elohim* being used thirty-five times while *Jehovah* is not present at all. However, in Genesis 2:4–2:25 (the second account of creation) the *Jehovah-Elohim* combination is used exclusively. Then again, in Genesis 12–16, *Jehovah* is used twenty-seven times and *Elohim* is not to be found. But in Genesis 33–50, *Jehovah* occurs but once, while *El* or *Elohim* is found fifty-seven times.

(2) The presence of repetitions and discrepancies both in the narrative and the legal portions of the Pentateuch. Scholars believe that it is unlikely that such duplications would have occurred if the Pentateuch had been the work of a single author. These repetitions and discrepancies include:

(a) In the *narrative* portions, the repetitions and discrepancies, which are found appear in large numbers and are of three kinds:

(1) In some instances the duplicate narratives appear side by side, as in the case of the story of creation {see and compare Genesis 1:1–2:4 with Genesis 2:4–2:25}. While attempts have been made to deny the presence of parallel accounts, as a matter of fact these two chapters cannot be satisfactorily explained except on the assumption that we are face to face with two distinct accounts, which must be traced to two different authors.

(2) In other cases, it may seem to the casual reader that he is dealing with a single continuous

story; and yet closer study reveals the presence of repetitions and even discrepancies which show that the narrative in its present form is the result of compilation. Thus a careful reading of the narrative of the Flood (Genesis 6–9) reveals two accounts of man's corruption and God's consequent displeasure. Also, one can find repetitions in the statements concerning the entering into the ark, the rising of the water, the perishing of all living creatures and the drying of the earth. Additionally, some passages speak of one pair of every kind of animals being taken into the ark, while others distinguish between clean and unclean animals and state that of the former seven pairs of each were preserved. According to some verses, the Flood continued for forty days, according to others, one hundred and fifty.

(3) There are, in addition, to these cases pointing in the direction of compilation, some parallel accounts of the same events, not placed side by side, but found in different parts of the Pentateuch. Under this heading may be mentioned duplicate accounts of the origin of names like Beersheba {see and compare Genesis 21:31 with Genesis 26:32–33}; Bethel {see and compare Genesis 28:18–19 with Genesis 35:15}, Israel {see and compare Genesis 32:28 with Genesis 35:10}. Additionally, there are two accounts of the promise of a son to Abraham {see and compare Genesis 17:16–19 with Genesis 18:9–15}; there is the father-in-law of Moses who bears two different names {see and compare Exodus 2:18 with Exodus 3:1}; and there are two accounts of the sending of manna and quails {see and compare Exodus 16 with Numbers 11}.

(b) In the legal portions of the Pentateuch, the repetitions and discrepancies are equally numerous, but again only a few typical illustrations may be given:

(1) Particular attention may be called to the differences in the legislation concerning the place of sacrifice. According to the Book of the Covenant, Jehovah could be worshiped in different places and the altar could be built of earth or unhewn stone {see Exodus 20:24–25). However, the Deuteronomic Code repeatedly and emphatically prohibited the worship of Jehovah at local sanctuaries, and insisted that the worship of Jehovah be centered in one, and only one, place {see Deuteronomy 12:2–7 and see and compare with Deuteronomy 14:23; 16:2; 16:6–7}. Additionally, the Priestly Code specified that the same altar which, according Exodus 20:24–25, was to be made of earth or unhewn stone, should actually be constructed with acacia wood {see Exodus 27:1}.

(2) Similar differences may be seen in the laws with reference to the priesthood. The Book of the Covenant knows no priestly race. It agrees with the earlier historical records, which assume that the priests may be taken from any tribe, and that the heads of families may offer sacrifice {see Judges 13:19; 1 Samuel 7:17; 1 Samuel 20:29; and 1 Kings 18:30}. However, in stark contrast, Deuteronomy clearly recognizes a priestly tribe—the Levites {see Deuteronomy 17:9; 17:18; 18:1; and 21:5}. This implies that the priesthood was limited to the

members of the tribe of Levi and, conversely, that all the members of the tribe of Levi were priests. Further still, the Priestly Code expresses a different view, namely, that the priesthood is limited to a particular family within the tribe of Levi, the sons of Aaron. The Priestly Code also assigns to other members of the tribe the lower offices and tasks connected with the sanctuary {see Exodus 28:1; Numbers 3:5–10; 18:1–7}.

(3) Within the Pentateuch, there are also many apparent differences in theological conception, style, and vocabulary. These differences support the supposition that the Pentateuch was a multi-source compilation as opposed to a single author composition. The differences are most apparent in the two stories of creation {Genesis 1:1–2:4 and Genesis 2:4–2:25}. For example, for the primitive God concept reflected in the second creation account, "Jehovah-Elohim" is said to "form" or "fashion" man and the animals, and to "breathe" into man's nostrils the breath of life. Here, God "takes" a rib from the man's body, "closes up" the opening, and "builds" the rib into a woman. God also "plants" the garden, "takes" man and "sets him down" in it. It is generally conceded that the second account of creation is the earlier (more ancient) account. It also generally conceded that the second account is more primitive. Thus, it should require no extraordinary powers of observation to see that the conception of God in the first account (Genesis 1:1–2:4) moves on a much higher, more spiritual, and more ethical plane. Additionally, even the English reader of the Genesis stories can appreciate certain striking differences in vocabulary. Then when we remember that the same differences characterize the rest of the Pentateuch it becomes virtually impossible to deny that whoever may have been responsible for putting the Pentateuch together in its present form most certainly must have relied on material which was drawn from different literary sources composed by different authors.

Given the fact that most contemporary biblical scholars believe that the Pentateuch is a compilation, the question arises as to whether it can be determined as to the chronological order of the source materials which came to become components of the composite Pentateuch. Scholars have sought to find an answer to this inquiry by studying the documents along the following lines: (1) the historical situation reflected in the documents; (2) the theological standpoint expressed or implied; (3) the relation of the Pentateuchal documents to other Old Testament writings; (4) peculiarities of vocabulary and style; (5) the relation of the documents to each other.

The conclusions reached by the scholars may be summarized as follows:

(1) "J" and "E" reflect the historical situation of the period of the Judges and of the early monarchy; "D" that of the later monarchy, especially conditions reflected in the account of Josiah's reforms in 621 B.C.T. and in the utterances of Jeremiah; "P" that of the later exilic and the post-exilic period, especially the age of Ezra and Nehemiah.

(2) In the case of each of the four documents, the theological standpoint agrees with what is known of Hebrew theological thinking during the period to which it is assigned on the basis

of the historical situation reflected in it.

(3) "J" and "E" have points of contact with Old Testament writings known to have originated before 650 B.C.T. (e.g., the prophetic books of the eighth century); "D" with the literature that originated between 650 B.C.T. and the Exile (e.g., Kings and Jeremiah); "P" with that of the post-exilic period (e.g., Malachi, Ezra, Nehemiah, Chronicles). "D" seems to have been unknown prior to the seventh century, "P" was unknown before the Exile.

(4) The style and vocabulary of each document are what they might be expected to be if the documents were actually written during the periods to which the historical background assigns them.

(5) In their legal, as in their historical sections, "JE," "D," and "P" represent three successive stages of development—"P" implies the prior existence of "D," "D" the prior existence of "J" and "E."

(6) Certain evidence points to the following approximate dates for the documents which comprise the Pentateuch: "J" belongs to the early centuries of the monarchy, perhaps about 850 B.C.T.; "E" originated not long before the appearance of the eighth century prophets around 750 B.C.T.; "D" presupposes the activity of the eighth century prophets and may have been written during the reactionary reign of Manasseh, around 650 B.C.T.; "P" originated among the descendants of the exiles in Babylonia, around 500 to 450 B.C.T. and was completed in Palestine in the days of Ezra-Nehemiah, before 400 B.C.T.

THE CREATION STORY

As is most evident from any perusal of the pertinent literature, the biblical accounts of the creation of the world have their background in ancient Southwest Asian folklore. In this folklore, creation was often depicted as the deity's victory over the forces of chaos, represented by threatening waters, as a result of which a god is established as a supreme being. A large number of references (e.g., Psalms 74:12–17 and Psalms 89:9–13) show that this concept was well known in Israel also.

The immediate source of the Creation story was probably Canaanite folklore. Amongst the Jews, Creation was particularly associated with the Jerusalem Temple, where it seems likely that God's victory over primeval chaos and God's subsequent royal enthronement were celebrated in a great annual festival.

Since the extended descriptions of creation in the first chapters of Genesis similarly reflect this background, they are not to be viewed as providing a scientific account of the origin of the universe. They are religious statements, designed to show God's glory and greatness, the result of theological reflection by which the older folklore was radically transformed to express Israel's distinctive faith.

The two accounts found in the first two chapters of Genesis at Genesis 1:1–2:4 and Genesis 2:4–25 both tell of the creation of the physical world and the creation of humanity.

The first account of Creation which appears at Genesis 1:1–2:4 is generally considered to be from the hand of a sixth-century B.C.T. priestly writer (P) who, however, depended on a much older tradition. In form it is a poem or a hymn, as the repeated refrain indicates, and its seven-day structure may be due to its having been recited during the period of the annual festival mentioned above. Although the watery chaos is still there, there is no conflict between it and God. In Genesis 1:1–2:4, God creates, in unfettered freedom, by his word or command, and creation is brought about by the separation of the elements of the universe, which thereby produces an ordered and habitable world. Thus, Creation is not so much dealing with absolute beginning, creation from nothing (although this idea appeared later in 2 Maccabees 7:28) as it does with the creation of a world of order as perceived by human beings.

An originally separate account of the creation of humankind (Genesis 1:26–30) appears to have been added to the Creation story. This separate emphasis indicates that the creation of human beings was the crowning moment of creation. Humanity too was created by separation into male and female made in the image of God, a much discussed expression that probably means that God makes beings with whom he can communicate and who can respond, because, in contrast to the rest of nature, human beings are spiritual beings in a temporary corporeal form.

Because mankind is created in the likeness of God, humanity receives the divine blessing and is given the role of God's vice-regent, in language drawn from kingship vocabulary, to have dominion or control over the future course of the world. The final verses, which tell of God's seeing all he has made and his rest on the Sabbath, emphasize the completeness and perfection of the created order.

The perspective of the second creation account (generally attributed to J) is essentially similar but its form is very different. Genesis 2:4–25 is older and it is a folktale, reflecting the concerns and interests of a peasant society. In this tale, God is described in human terms; but behind this apparent naïveté lies profound insights. The second account of creation deals primarily with the creation of humanity, while the creation of the world is directed to providing a suitable agricultural environment for human beings.

In the second Genesis account of Creation, God molds the first man (Adam) from the dust of the ground, an idea found in many other cultures. Adam is deemed to be part of the natural order, but he is given a unique status when God breathes into him the divine breath and Adam becomes not just a living being but a spiritual one as well.

Adam's naming of the animals means that he appropriates them, corresponding to the notion of dominion in Genesis 1, and the command about the trees in the garden implies responsibility toward his maker, which is part of what is meant by humanity as the image of God. No doubt the fact that woman (Eve) is created secondarily from man corresponds to the position of the male in a patriarchal society. However, even more strongly the story stresses the unity of the sexes and their mutual, contemporary need. Thus, the first creation account, with its cultic background, ends with the religious institution of the Sabbath; the second, which is directed to humankind in community, with the social institution of marriage.

Explicit references to the Creation may appear to be comparatively rare in the Bible. However, the Creation accounts in Genesis are the starting point for the history that follows and are inseparably linked with it in the biblical narrative. The prophets and the wisdom literature also both presuppose a comprehensive world order to which they summon men and women to conform. There are, however, two particular developments in later texts to which special attention may be directed.

First, the idea grows that the goal of history is to spawn a new creation—a creation which returns to the beginning when the Creator's original intention, frustrated by human sin and rebellion, will be fulfilled. The visions of the end of time are pictured in terms of the first things. Such is a dominant theme in the later chapters of Isaiah (see Isaiah 65:17 and Isaiah 66:22) and in other apocalyptic literature.

Secondly, in certain parts of the wisdom tradition, Wisdom comes to be represented as already existing before the creation of the world and, parallel to the divine word in Genesis 1, the means of God's creative activity (see Job 28:12–27). Wisdom can be strongly personified and viewed as God's personal agent in creation (see Proverbs 8:22–31). In Sirach 24:3,[285] the figure of Wisdom is identified both with the word of Genesis 1 and the primary act of creation in Genesis 2:6.

It is these two developments that determine the way in which the idea of Creation is transposed into a new key in the New Testament. The New Testament writers inherited the Jewish belief in the creation of the world by the one God and frequently appeal to the ordering of the world and human life that God established at the beginning (see Mark 10:6[286] and Romans 1:20[287]). However, the advent of Christ inaugurates the long awaited new Creation (Revelations 21:1–4[288]), both of the universe (Romans 8:19–21[289]) and of humanity (2 Corinthians 5:17[290]). This comes about because, from the Christian perspective, Jesus recapitulates the former creation. Jesus is the new Adam (1 Corinthians 15:45[291]), and the image and likeness

---

[285]Sirach 24:3 reads:

3 "I am the word spoken by the Most High; it was I who covered the earth like a mist."

[286]Mark 10:6 reads:

6 But from the beginning of the creation God made them male and female.

[287]Romans 1:20 reads:

20 For the invisible things of him from the creation of the world are clearly seen, being understood by the things that are made, even his eternal power and Godhead; so that they are without excuse.

[288]Revelations 21:1–4 reads:

1 And I saw a new heaven and a new earth: for the first heaven and the first earth were passed away; and there was no more sea. 2 And I John saw the holy city, new Jerusalem, coming down from God out of heaven, prepared as a bride adorned for her husband. 3 And I heard a great voice out of heaven saying, Behold, the tabernacle of God is with men, and he will dwell with them, and they shall be his people, and God himself shall be with them, and be their God. 4 And God shall wipe away all tears from their eyes; and there shall be no more death, neither sorrow, nor crying, neither shall there be any more pain: for the former things are passed away.

[289]Romans 8:19–21 reads:

19 For the earnest expectation of the creature waiteth for the manifestation of the sons of God. 20 For the creature was made subject to vanity, not willingly, but by reason of him who hath subjected the same in hope. 21 Because the creature itself also shall be delivered from the bondage of corruption into the glorious liberty of the children of God.

[290]2 Corinthians 5:17 reads:

17 Therefore if any man be in Christ, he is a new creature: old things are passed away; behold, all things are become new.

[291]1 Corinthians 15:45 reads:

45 And so it is written, The first man Adam was made a living soul; the last Adam was made a quickening spirit.

of God (Colossians 1:15[292] and 2 Corinthians 4:4[293]).

At the same time that Jesus is perceived as the recapitulation of the new Creation, he is also perceived as the agent and sustainer of all Creation (Colossians 1:16[294]) and is described as the word of God (Revelations 19:13[295]) and the wisdom of God. However, it is the figure of creative Wisdom which seems to have been most influential for the understanding of Jesus. Thus, like Wisdom, Jesus is preexistent (Colossians 1:17[296]) and the reflection of God's glory (Hebrews 1:3[297]).

Most striking is the first chapter of John's gospel, the opening words of which echo the beginning of Genesis, with its picture of Jesus as the Logos. This term unites the concept of the creative word of the Hebrew Bible and, from its use in Greek philosophy, the concept of Wisdom as the mediator in Creation.

THE FIRST ACCOUNT OF CREATION {GENESIS 1:1–2:4}

Chapter 1

In the beginning God created the heaven and the earth.[298]

2 And the earth was without form, and void; and darkness was upon the face of the deep. And the Spirit of God moved upon the face of the waters.[299]

3 And God said, Let there be light: and there was light.

---

[292]Colossians 1:15 reads:

15 Who is the image of the invisible God, the firstborn of every creature:

[293]2 Corinthians 4:4 reads:

4 In whom the god of this world hath blinded the minds of them which believe not, lest the light of the glorious gospel of Christ, who is the image of God, should shine unto them.

[294]Colossians 1:16 reads:

16 For by him were all things created, that are in heaven, and that are in earth, visible and invisible, whether they be thrones, or dominions, or principalities, or powers: all things were created by him, and for him:

[295]Revelations 19:13 reads:

13 And he was clothed with a vesture dipped in blood: and his name is called The Word of God.

[296]Colossians 1:17 reads:

17 And he is before all things, and by him all things consist.

[297]Hebrews 1:3 reads:

3 Who being the brightness of his glory, and the express image of his person, and upholding all things by the word of his power, when he had by himself purged our sins, sat down on the right hand of the Majesty on high;

[298]In 1650 C.C., the Irish theologian James Ussher, would calculate that Creation began on Sunday, October 23 of the year 4004 B.C.T. The full biblical chronology developed by Ussher—the Ussher Chronology—was considered for centuries to be an accurate and factual history, but today the vast majority of historians and theologians consider Ussher's Chronology to be historically inaccurate and to be factually deficient. In this book, the Ussher Chronology is being used only for discussion and comparison purposes. Accordingly, the dates associated with the Ussher Chronology should not be relied upon as fact.

[299]There is no order, no shape, no distinction between solid and liquid in this narrative. There is nothing but a confused indiscriminate mixture, and, hovering above, as a bird over its nest, is the Breath—the Spirit—of God.

4 *And God saw the light, that it was good: and God divided the light from the darkness.*

5 *And God called the light Day, and the darkness he called Night. And the evening and the morning were the first day.*[300, 301]

6 *And God said, Let there be a firmament in the midst of the waters, and let it divide the waters from the waters.*

7 *And God made the firmament, and divided the waters which were under the firmament from the waters which were above the firmament: and it was so.*

8 *And God called the firmament Heaven. And the evening and the morning were the second day.*[302, 303]

9 *And God said, Let the waters under the heaven be gathered together unto one place, and let the dry land appear: and it was so.*

10 *And God called the dry land Earth; and the gathering together of the waters called he Seas: and God saw that it was good.*

11 *And God said, Let the earth bring forth grass, the herb yielding seed, and the fruit tree yielding fruit after his kind, whose seed is in itself, upon the earth: and it was so.*

12 *And the earth brought forth grass, and herb yielding seed after his kind, and the tree yielding fruit, whose seed was in itself, after his kind: and God saw that it was good.*

13 *And the evening and the morning were the third day.*[304, 305]

14 *And God said, Let there be lights in the firmament of the heaven to divide the day from the night; and let them be for signs, and for seasons, and for days, and years:*

15 *And let them be for lights in the firmament of the heaven to give light upon the earth: and it was so.*

16 *And God made two great lights; the greater light to rule the day, and the lesser light to rule the night: he made the stars also.*

17 *And God set them in the firmament of the heaven to give light upon the earth,*

18 *And to rule over the day and over the night, and to divide the light from the darkness: and God saw that it was good.*

---

[300]Sunday, October 23 {Ussher Chronology}.

[301]In formulae which persist throughout the first chapter of Genesis, the "making" of light is described. It is, to the Hebrew mind, independent of luminaries, which are rather concentrated masses of the pervading substance. According to Genesis, the light created by God is in eternal contrast and opposition to the darkness.

[302]Monday, October 24 {Ussher Chronology}.

[303]The process of creation continued with the making of a *firmament*—a plate of hard material, probably envisioned as being dome-shaped. Here the narrative gives a needed point of departure, a fixed spot in the midst of the chaos from which a start can be made. This done, the second day ends, with the prospect that the organization of the earth will follow.

[304]Tuesday, October 25 {Ussher Chronology}.

[305]According to the biblical narrative, the third day was given to the "making" of the earth as man knows it. The account starts from the "firmament," which is surrounded on all sides by the half-liquid, half-solid matter of the chaos. At the divine command, this recedes from below the firmament, and an empty space (air and other gaseous substances are not recognized as material) is left under the plate of hard material—the dome. The pressure is so great that it separates the solid from the liquid elements, and the latter are collected to form the sea, while the former become the dry land. From the ground thus formed sprang the natural vegetable products of the soil, which, though not endowed with life as the Hebrews understood that term, yet grow and yield their fruits, and God sees that all is good.

19 And the evening and the morning were the fourth day.[306, 307]

20 And God said, Let the waters bring forth abundantly the moving creature that hath life, and fowl that may fly above the earth in the open firmament of heaven.

21 And God created great whales, and every living creature that moveth, which the waters brought forth abundantly, after their kind, and every winged fowl after his kind: and God saw that it was good.

22 And God blessed them, saying, Be fruitful, and multiply, and fill the waters in the seas, and let fowl multiply in the earth.

23 And the evening and the morning were the fifth day.[308, 309]

24 And God said, Let the earth bring forth the living creature after his kind, cattle, and creeping thing, and beast of the earth after his kind: and it was so.

25 And God made the beast of the earth after his kind, and cattle after their kind, and every thing that creepeth upon the earth after his kind: and God saw that it was good.

26 And God said, Let us make man in our image, after our likeness: and let them have dominion over the fish of the sea, and over the fowl of the air, and over the cattle, and over all the earth, and over every creeping thing that creepeth upon the earth.

27 So God created man in his own image, in the image of God created he him; male and female created he them.

28 And God blessed them, and God said unto them, Be fruitful, and multiply, and replenish the earth, and subdue it: and have dominion over the fish of the sea, and over the fowl of the air, and over every living thing that moveth upon the earth.

29 And God said, Behold, I have given you every herb bearing seed, which is upon the face of all the earth, and every tree, in the which is the fruit of a tree yielding seed; to you it shall be for meat.

30 And to every beast of the earth, and to every fowl of the air, and to every thing that creepeth upon the earth, wherein there

---

[306]Wednesday, October 26 {Ussher Chronology}.

[307]At this point in the biblical creation narrative, the sky above the completed earth is still empty, and the fourth day is occupied with the making of bright radiant objects. These objects are not merely celestial ornaments; their purpose is to indicate time. These celestial objects mark day from night. They also tell human beings when the seasons change and when the festal occasions are due. The sacred times are deemed to be older than man, and they exist independently from man. When man is later formed, he becomes obligated to observe the sacred times which preceded him. The presence of the heavenly bodies would leave man without any excuse. These celestial bodies are all that man needs for his religious duty and they are all that God intends.

[308]Thursday, October 27 {Ussher Chronology}.

[309]In this account of creation, on the fifth day a new element is introduced—the concept of corporeal life. In the creation of animal life, there is a factor for which there was no existing basis in matter or in its products. Here God must step in and fashion something entirely new. Accordingly, the waters came to swarm with life, manifested first in the creatures of the seas and oceans, then in the winged things that fly in the empty space between the earth and the heavens. However, this time it is not enough that God should merely pronounce them good. He has a special relation to these beings in whom there is implanted a second grade of his creative power. He blesses them and bids them multiply. This is significant because the reproduction of plants, their seed and fruit production is automatic, whereas that of the animal kingdom is due to conscious acts and needs both divine authority and divine command to initiate.

is life, I have given every green herb for meat: and it was so.

31 And God saw every thing that he had made, and, behold, it was very good. And the evening and the morning were the sixth day.[310, 311]

Chapter 2

Thus the heavens and the earth were finished, and all the host of them.

2 And on the seventh day God ended his work which he had made; and he rested on the seventh day from all his work which he had made.

3 And God blessed the seventh day,[312] *and sanctified it: because that in it he had rested from all his work which God created and made.*[313]

---

[310]Friday, October 28 {Ussher Chronology}.

[311]On the sixth day, the final two acts of creation occurred. The first of these was the production of the terrestrial animals, who were drawn from the earth as the fish have been drawn from the sea. Linked in a certain way with them, through the elements which compose his physical frame, comes man. God is represented as consulting with some other beings (*Let us make man in our image*) as to the formation of humanity. This language suggests that this segment of Genesis reflects a relic of the old polytheistic phraseology which had escaped a careful editing by the biblical writer. Additionally, a further hint of a lower theological position has been seen by some in the repeated phrase *in our image, in his image, in the image of God,* which is thought to point to a time when men believed that God had a material frame like that which man possesses. Yet it is more probable that the expression *in the image of God* has no physical implications, but is meant to suggest that man differs from all the rest of the creation in the possession of self-conscious personality and that it is this possession of self-conscious personality which makes man the only creature to resemble God.

In verse 27 for the third time, the word *create* is used. Again the use of this word coincides with the introduction of a new element. Previous acts of creation will not account for the creation of man. Man shares in the physical nature of the universe, and in the life found in fish and bird and beast. But these two factors alone do not account for him. Man is created in the image of God, and, unlike any other being, has something possessed by the Creator and not merely by creation.

Man is thus the crown and supreme glory of the whole universe—just because man is greater than the universe. Physically inferior than many of the animals, man is, nevertheless, the lord of the animal kingdom. In this narrative of the creation, the reader is left with a picture of a natural kingdom, with no internal warfare, but with a monarch. All live at peace with one another, since the vegetable world supplies all needed food. Above all, as God's viceregent, stands the one being who really resembles the Creator. Above all, stands man.

[312]The first Sabbath, Saturday, October 29 {Ussher Chronology}.

[313]The biblical story of creation reaches a climax with an item of ritual which would become fundamental to pious Jews and Christians alike. God's work had occupied six "days," and God took the seventh day as a day of rest. The fact that God rested on the seventh day created a "tabu" on it. The seventh day became "holy"—a day which should be set apart from the affairs of ordinary life. Such a seventh day festival appears to have been customary in Mesopotamia. Parallels observed in the Old Testament and elsewhere have suggested that originally the "Sabbath" of the western Semites occurred not once a week but at the full moon only. The transference of the name to a weekly festival would then have taken place under Babylonian influence, possibly during the Exile.

It must be stressed that no one has ever supposed the narrative of Genesis 1 and 2 to have been the free invention of the exilic or post-exilic period. These portions undoubtedly con-

A Second Account of Creation
{Genesis 2:4–2:25}[314]

4 These are the generations of the heavens and of the earth when they were created,

---

tain and are based upon far older material. However, this does not exclude the possibility that it was only at a comparatively late period that the form of Genesis 1:1 through 2:3 which we have in our Bibles was derived.

[314]A careful examination of the narratives contained in the Book of Genesis reveals that these narratives are not consistent and that the narratives come from many disparate sources. There are traditions contained in the narratives which clearly come down from ages far older than Israel, snatches of song relating to peoples of whom all other traces have long been lost, racial memories which, because they became enshrined in language, would never die.

Within the narratives, there are stories which are the common heritage of many peoples, finding parallels in the lore of other portions of the world, particularly of ancient Southwest Asia. In reading the narratives of Genesis, and in comparing them to the foreign narratives from which they may be derived, it is fascinating to see how the Jewish writers modified, purified and frequently ennobled the original stories.

It must be remembered that the narratives of Genesis are essentially stories that were told for generation after generation. One can imagine that for centuries these stories main existence was when they were told round the shepherds' campfires. Only later would they become sacred stories of the famous centers of worship, in which every visitor must have been instructed by the attendant priesthood. Additionally, some of the stories are obviously connected to genealogies which must have been tenaciously preserved in the memories of essentially unlettered peoples. Finally, occasionally local traditions would explain how a certain spot or locale came by its name and its importance. These traditions would also be orally transmitted from generation to generation.

In constructing the Genesis narratives, every available source of information appears to have been utilized. After being assembled, the materials that were collected were woven into a single whole but with some peculiarities.

A scientific study of the Genesis narratives shows that they fall into several fairly well-marked groups. Two of these are similar to one another, and but for the fact that these disparate narratives are sometimes interwoven with one another, the reader might have remained oblivious to the distinction between the two. However, there are some significant differences between stories derived from these two groups. One of them seems to show greater interest in southern Israel than in the north, and prefers to use the personal divine name "Jehovah"—hence it is known as J. The other seems to have been current in the north. The "Ephraim" narratives in Genesis prefer the more general word for God which in Hebrew was "Elohim." Accordingly, the stories derived from this source are generally cited by the symbol E.

It is often held that each group once formed an independent book; and if this opinion is correct, it is clear that the writers were drawing on material far older than their own day, sometimes older than Israel itself.

A third group of narratives stands widely apart from these two, and bears all the marks of coming from a different age. The "J" and "E" narratives, in the form in which they were embodied in Genesis, were practically contemporaries, reflecting the same general cycle of ideas and the same level of cultural and religious development. However, this third class of passages differs widely from both.

In Genesis, the third class of narratives, like the "E" narratives, prefers to use the divine name "Elohim" instead of "Yahweh" (a word which appears in the King James version as "Jehovah" or "the LORD God"). But there was little else in which this third class of passages resembles either of the others. The whole tone is loftier, and reflects the thought and feeling of a much more advanced age.

The conception of God in the third class of narratives is less material and more spiritual, and while there is comparatively little narrative to be included under this head, what there is bears the impress of a very striking style. Additionally, in the third class of narratives, genealogy is a favorite theme. Indeed, some have said that in the third class of narratives are genealogy narratives with a bit of historical narrative thrown in.

It is worth noting that in the third class of narratives, there is an evident fondness for exact figures, and that where events, as distinct from mere names, are recorded, they always have in them a legal element, and point to the establishment of some principle well recognized in the later Law.

Because of these characteristics, the third class of narratives have been described as being "priestly" narratives and are indicated by the letter "P." These narratives are believed to have been taken from a long comprehensive work, which included not only an outline history of Israel down to the end of the wanderings, but also the great mass of the Law as it appears in Exodus, Leviticus, and Numbers. However, the long comprehensive work appears to have been lost. What remains is what we read.

In putting together the patchwork narratives which now comprise the text of the Old Testament, it is clear that the narratives which are grouped under the letter P have been used as a kind of framework into which the "J" and "E" narratives are frequently woven. For the most part, the "P" framework consists of genealogies with the bare mention of one of two outstanding events in the lives of the more important persons named. There are, however, some half a dozen more extended narratives with the characteristics of "P," each of which is clearly introduced with a special purpose, to which the same treatment is given as to narratives derived from other groups. Each is inserted in its place in the life of the person to whom it refers. Usually the narratives are simply placed side by side, but where similar accounts are derived from different groups, they are woven together, sentences or paragraphs from the one being inserted alternately with those drawn from the other. It is usually a simple matter to discern where this occurs because it is through discrepancies in the passage that attention is called to its composite structure.

One can most clearly see the composite nature of the Old Testament text by examining the first two chapters of Genesis. The first two chapters of Genesis both provide accounts of creation but with significant differences in structure and style.

In the first account of creation (the account set forth in Genesis 1:1–2:3), one notices that the passages possessed a certain dignity and are written in a lofty tone. The whole narrative is arranged under a series of days, and to each day are assigned portions of the universe. The events are fitted into a framework which consists of certain formula, repeated at the beginning and end of each separate act. Throughout the narrative there is a definite and progressive order. The theology is relatively advanced. In this narrative, God needs no physical means or material agency. God's word alone suffices.

In this narrative—this "P" narrative—there is an expression of the supreme truth that God is the author of the universe and this expression is made in a form that is suited to a people of high intelligence, developed culture, and profound religious thinking.

The priestly narrative of Genesis 1:1–2:3 contrasts sharply with the "J" narrative of Genesis 2:4–2:25. In the "J" account of creation, there is no true cosmogony—no true creation of the universe or our world. Except for the absence of rain (which is not mentioned in any "J" passage until the story of the Great Flood), the world in this narrative is simply assumed. The order of events in the second creation narrative is different. In the second narrative, man is the first object created and woman is the last. Additionally, the creation of woman appears to be due to man's spiritual need for companionship, not to the need for reproduction.

in the day that the LORD God made the earth and the heavens,[315]

5 And every plant of the field before it was in the earth, and every herb of the field before it was in the earth, and every herb of the field before it grew: for the LORD God had not caused it to rain upon the earth, and there was not a man to till the ground.

6 But there went up a mist from the earth, and watered the whole face of the ground.

7 And the LORD God formed man of the dust of the ground, and breathed into his nostrils the breath of life; and man became a living soul.

8 And the LORD God planted a garden eastward in Eden; and there he put the man whom he had formed.

9 And out of the ground made the LORD God to grow every tree that is pleasant to the sight, and good for food; the tree of life also in the midst of the garden, and the tree of knowledge of good and evil.

10 And a river went out of Eden to water the garden; and from thence it was parted, and became into four heads.

11 The name of the first is Pison: that is it which compasseth the whole land of Havilah, where there is gold;

12 And the gold of that land is good: there is bdellium and the onyx stone.

13 And the name of the second river is Gihon: the same is it that compasseth the whole land of Ethiopia.

14 And the name of the third river is Hiddekel: that is it which goeth toward the east of Assyria. And the fourth river is Euphrates.

15 And the LORD God took the man, and put him into the Garden of Eden to dress it and to keep it.

16 And the LORD God commanded the man, saying, Of every tree of the garden thou mayest freely eat:

17 But of the tree of the knowledge of good and evil, thou shalt not eat of it: for in the day that thou eatest thereof thou shalt surely die.

18 And the LORD God said, It is not good that the man should be alone; I will make him an help meet for him.

19 And out of the ground the LORD

There is some odd geography in the second account of creation. The rivers Pison, Gihon (Nile), Hiddekel (Tigris), and Euphrates are said to have a common source, a seemingly obvious geographic error.

In the second account of creation, the conception of Jehovah appears to be extremely primitive. In comparison to the first account of creation, the second account, with all its beauty, appears to be intended for an audience that was intellectually and spiritually immature.

[315]In the second account of creation which begins at Genesis 2:4, Jehovah, finding the clay moistened by the heavy mist, models a man. This might have been done by any skilled potter, but Jehovah does more. Jehovah breathes into this figure and thus man comes to life, not merely as a toy or an animal but as a living soul.

At the time of man's creation, there is as yet no suitable home for him, but the need is met by the planting of a garden. In this garden trees are made to grow out of the ground. The garden is situated in Eden, to the east, and its produce includes trees good for food, ornamental plants, and two others with special qualities, the tree of knowledge and the tree of life.

In the garden, the man is beset with a double duty to perform. First, he has to be the servant of the ground, rendering to it those offices which it would naturally reward with its fruits. Secondly, the man has to protect the garden against unnamed enemies.

In the garden, the man is told that he may enjoy the fruits of his work except that the tree bearing fruit containing the knowledge of good and evil was forbidden. The sanction for eating of this tree was to be death.

God formed every beast of the field, and every fowl of the air; and brought them unto Adam to see what he would call them: and whatsoever Adam called every living creature, that was the name thereof.

20 And Adam gave names to all cattle, and to the fowl of the air, and to every beast of the field; but for Adam there was not found an help meet for him.[316]

21 And the LORD God caused a deep sleep to fall upon Adam, and he slept: and he took one of his ribs, and closed up the flesh instead thereof;

22 And the rib, which the LORD God had taken from man, made he a woman, and brought her unto the man.

23 And Adam said, This is now bone of my bones, and flesh of my flesh: she shall be called Woman, because she was taken out of Man.[317]

24 Therefore shall a man leave his father and his mother, and shall cleave unto his wife: and they shall be one flesh.

25 And they were both naked, the man and his wife, and were not ashamed.[318]

---

[316]In verses 18–20, it is evident that Jehovah was concerned with the well-being of man. As part of this concern, Jehovah observes the loneliness of man. However, seemingly at first Jehovah does not appear to know how the man's need should be met. In an attempt to address the loneliness of man, Jehovah first constructs other creatures in the same way that he has made man except that Jehovah does not breathe into these creatures. In order to find out whether the experiment is successful, Jehovah brings the animals to man. As each beast comes before him, the man utters an exclamation. Based upon what is uttered, Jehovah judges whether the particular animal is suitable or not.

As each creature appears, the man utters a sound. This sound becomes the name of the creature. This naming of the creatures bears a striking similarity to the Hebrew practice of naming the newly born with the first exclamation that comes forth from the parent. This is why so many Hebrew names are derived from prayers.

Despite the vast variety of creatures which are presented to the man, none of the creatures appear to satisfy the needs of the man. Something more is needed. The man needs a mate.

[317]Jehovah's first experiments with finding a companion for the man failed. Having failed, Jehovah tries something else.

Instead of creating something from the earth, Jehovah causes the man to enter into a deep anesthetic sleep, such as that which a divine power may always use when it seeks to work on man. Although the man seems to know what is happening, without hurting the man, Jehovah takes a rib from the man's side. After taking the rib, Jehovah closes up the hole left in the man.

Using the man's rib, Jehovah builds up a new creature. Jehovah then brings the new creature to the man and is greeted with an exclamation which indicates that this time the experiment is a success.

As expressed by the Scriptures, the reason for Jehovah's success is that the new creature was made from the very substance of the man himself. Thus, the exclamation for—the name of—the new creature shall be "Wo-man" for the new creature is "from-man."

The writer of these verses adds a note to the effect that this explains why men leave their parents but not their wives and why they make new homes for themselves with their wives.

[318]Many Bible scholars today acknowledge that the creation narratives of Genesis 1 and 2 are not history and are not science. These scholars call the Genesis creation narratives folklore and note that such Hebraic folklore has parallels in the early stories of other peoples. Many of these same scholars stress the fact that each age, with each grade of intellectual and social development, has its own special method of instruction. Thus, what may have been an appropriate method of instruction in 600 B.C.T. may not be appropriate for today. Never-

MAN'S TEMPTATION AND FALL {GENESIS 3:1–3:24}

Chapter 3[319]

Now the serpent was more subtil than any beast of the field which the LORD God had made. And he said unto the woman,

Yea, hath God said, Ye shall not eat of every tree of the garden?

2 And the woman said unto the serpent, We may eat of the fruit of the trees of the garden:

3 But of the fruit of the tree which is in the midst of the garden, God hath said, Ye

---

theless, for the time of ancient Judea and the ancient Judeans, the folklore set forth in Genesis 1 and 2 may have provided the best way, and perhaps the only way, of conveying the Truth—the Truth being that man owes his origin and his existence to God.

[319]Chapter 3 of the Book of Genesis is really the story of the way in which man lost his chance for immortality. A story with the same general purpose was current in Babylonia, though, as usual in such cases, the details are widely different from what we find in Genesis. The Mesopotamian tradition sent a man, in despair at the common lot of death, to search for the fruit of immortality, and explained how he was cheated by one of the gods into eating the fruit of death.

In the Genesis narrative, the crafty enemy of man is the snake. The snake is the cleverest of all the beasts that Jehovah made. However, strikingly, this snake stands erect and speaks with a human voice. Clearly this snake is not the same kind of snake of which we know today. However, while the serpent of Genesis 3 is not the serpent of today neither is it the Devil, even though it does attempt to deceive man to do evil.

The conversation between the snake and the woman suggests with extraordinary psychological fidelity the main features of normal temptation. There is first the casting of doubt on God. The snake slyly contradicts God by essentially telling the woman that God has forbidden her from eating from the tree in the midst of the garden because God is afraid that if the humans eat of the forbidden tree they will become as good and as great as God. Indeed, if the humans eat from the forbidden tree, they will themselves become gods.

The serpent prefaces this observation with a direct contradiction of God's warning by saying that if the humans do eat from the forbidden tree, they will surely not suffer the consequences which God said would happen.

Oddly, in this narrative, it is the serpent which appears to be telling the truth. Indeed, from all appearances, the record of this narrative seems clear that the serpent is accurately stating the facts as they were known to him.

As the narrative unfolds, all that the snake has said comes true. The humans, after eating the fruit from the forbidden tree, do not immediately die and the humans, after eating the fruit, do attain a knowledge of good and evil. However, while the serpent is clever, he is not omniscient—he does not know all. For instance, the serpent apparently does not know—or at least he does not inform the woman—what the first effect of the acquisition of knowledge will be. The woman, and the man, are therefore somewhat surprised by the shame they feel upon seeing their nakedness. This was but the first of the unpleasant surprises that woman and man would encounter in the passages to come.

However, before leaving this section it must be noted that the aversion to personal nudity highlighted in Genesis 3 is a peculiarly Semitic trait. There are many races who have no objection to nakedness and for whom nudity does not awaken or evoke improper feelings. However, among Semitic peoples, the attitude expressed in Genesis 3 appears to be almost universal, and in Semitic societies nudity is considered a terrible thing. In the Genesis narrative, even the aprons of fig-leaves (which, perhaps, gave rise to the eastern tradition that the tree of knowledge was a fig-tree) do not give the humans an adequate sense of protection in the presence of Jehovah.

shall not eat of it, neither shall ye touch it, lest ye die.

4 And the serpent said unto the woman, Ye shall not surely die:

5 For God doth know that in the day ye eat thereof, then your eyes shall be opened, ye shall be as gods, knowing good and evil.

6 And when the woman saw that the tree was good for food, and that it was pleasant to the eyes, and a tree to be desired to make one wise, she took of the fruit thereof, and did eat, and gave also unto her husband with her; and he did eat.

7 And the eyes of them both were opened, and they knew that they were naked; and they sewed fig leaves together, and made themselves aprons.

8 And they heard the voice of the LORD God walking in the garden[320] in the cool of the day: and Adam and his wife hid them-

---

[320]According to this narrative, it would appear that Jehovah delights in walking in the garden when the morning or evening breeze is blowing cool, and to enjoy the company and the conversation of his living toys. However, after the man and the woman had eaten of the forbidden fruit, they hid from God. According to the narrative, God could not find them and had to call them.

The man and woman eventually respond to God's call. However, when God sees them they are filled with shame. Although it appears that in this narrative God is not omniscient, God nevertheless, is far wiser than the man or the snake, and God knows that this new shyness can have only one cause. The man and the woman have denied God's edict and eaten of the forbidden tree.

The man's defense is a rather sly defense. The man does not blame the woman but instead blames God. The man says, in effect, that since God gave the woman to the man then the man assumed that anything she brought to him was brought with God's blessing.

God, of course, does not buy this defense. Both the man and the woman are free agents with free will. Accordingly, the actions of the man or the woman are their own individual acts and should not be attributable to God.

When God next turns to the woman for an explanation, the woman essentially says that the snake bewitched her into disobeying God's command.

God's judgment is then delivered without the snake even being invited to make a defense. After all, the snake's guilt is obvious. For its transgressions, the snake is punished. The snake loses its erect posture, and is forbidden the vegetable food which it had hitherto shared with man and all other animals. Instead of eating vegetables, the snake is consigned to eating dirt. Additionally, God ordains that there is to be endless hostility between snakes and men, the one crushing the head of the other whenever opportunity arises, and the snake striking at the heel of man.

Of course, this passage of the Old Testament is erroneous. While snakes do burrow into the earth, they do not eat dirt for their sustenance. This passage of the Old Testament reflects an ancient notion of zoology which has long since been dispelled. However, it is certainly true that many snakebites are inflicted on the foot. This Genesis narrative attributes this propensity to the "curse" or doom laid on the creature for having misled the woman. Modern zoologists contend otherwise.

The details of the woman's punishment are not certain, but it is clear that we have here an explanation of a societal fact, namely the social inferiority of women which has long existed in Southwestern Asia. Indeed, there are references to the sex life, and, in particular, to the pains of childbirth, to which Hebrew women seem to have been more subject than others in the ancient world.

Jehovah God then deals with the man. Although the man did not procure the fruit, he did partake of it even though God had commanded him not to. Accordingly, the man must be punished as well.

selves from the presence of the LORD God amongst the trees of the garden.

9 And the LORD God called unto Adam, and said unto him, Where art thou?

10 And he said, I heard thy voice in the garden, and I was afraid, because I was naked; and I hid myself.

11 And he said, Who told thee that thou wast naked? Hast thou eaten of the tree, whereof I commanded thee that thou shouldest not eat?

12 And the man said, The woman whom thou gavest to be with me, she gave me of the tree, and I did eat.

13 And the LORD God said unto the woman, What is this that thou hast done? And the woman said, The serpent beguiled me, and I did eat.

14 And the LORD God said unto the serpent, Because thou hast done this, thou art cursed above all cattle, and above every beast of the field; upon thy belly shalt thou go, and dust shalt thou eat all the days of thy life:

15 And I will put enmity between thee and the woman, and between thy seed and her seed; it shall bruise thy head, and thou shalt bruise his heel.

16 Unto the woman he said, I will greatly multiply thy sorrow and thy conception; in sorrow thou shalt bring forth chil-

dren; and thy desire shall be to thy husband, and he shall rule over thee.

17 And unto Adam he said, Because thou hast hearkened unto the voice of thy wife, and hast eaten of the tree, of which I commanded thee, saying, Thou shalt not eat of it: cursed is the ground for thy sake; in sorrow shalt thou eat of it all the days of thy life;

18 Thorns also and thistles shall it bring forth to thee; and thou shalt eat the herb of the field;

19 In the sweat of thy face shalt thou eat bread, till thou return unto the ground; for out of it wast thou taken: for dust thou art, and unto dust shalt thou return.

20 And Adam called his wife's name Eve, because she was the mother of all living.

21 Unto Adam also and to his wife did the Lord God make coats of skins, and clothed them.

22 And the LORD God said, Behold, the man is become as one of us, to know good and evil: and now, lest he put forth his hand, and take also of the tree of life, and eat, and live for ever:

23 Therefore the LORD God sent him forth from the garden of Eden, to till the ground from whence he was taken.

24 So he drove out the man; and he placed at the east of the garden of Eden Cherubims[321], and a flaming sword which

---

As his punishment, the man is told the ground shall be cursed. Although the man has always had to work, previously his labors had been productive and comparatively painless. In the future, the efforts of the man in working the soil were to be exhausting and, at times, futile. It is not the work that is the punishment, but the uncertain and grim struggle against hostile nature which is the punishment.

At the close of this segment, the narrator appends two notes, one explaining the name ("Eve") the man gave to his wife and the other describing Jehovah's method of clothing the man and his wife. The man and the woman are allowed to wear skins, though there is no hint as to the way in which these skins were procured. Probably neither the narrator nor his first hearers speculated as to whether any animals were killed, and, if not, whence the skins were derived.

[321]As for the Cherubim mentioned in Genesis 3:24, Cherubim, in name as well as in concept, were Assyrian or Akkadian in origin. The word "cherubim," in Akkadian, is *karibu* and means "one who prays" or "one who intercedes," although Dionysius declared the word to mean knowledge. In ancient Assyrian art, the cherubim were pictured as huge, winged crea-

turned every way, to keep the way of the tree of life.[322]

CAIN AND ABEL
{GENESIS 4:1–4:16}

tures with leonine or human faces, bodies of bulls or sphinxes, eagles, etc. The cherubim were usually placed at entrances to palaces or temples as guardian spirits. An ivory from the collection of a king of Megiddo, circa 1200 B.C.T., shows a Canaanite ruler seated on a throne, "supported by winged lions with human heads." These figures, scholars assert, are the imaginary, composite beings which the Israelites called cherubim. As winged beasts with human heads, two cherubim are also shown supporting the throne of Hiram, king of ancient Byblos.

In early Canaanitish lore, the cherubim were not conceived of as angels. Indeed, Theodorus, Bishop of Heracleaa, declared "these cherubims not to be any Angelicall powers, but rather some horrible visions of Beasts, which might terrifie Adam from the entrance of paradise." It was only later that the cherubim began to be regarded as heavenly spirits.

To Philo, the cherubim symbolized God's highest and chiefest potencies, sovereignty, and goodness. The cherubim are the first angels to be mentioned (and to be construed as angels) in the Old Testament. The cherubim guarded with flaming sword the Tree of Life and Eden, hence their designation as the "flame of whirling swords."

In Exodus 25:18 one finds two cherubim "of gold," one on either side of the Ark. In Ezekiel (10:14), four cherubim, each with four faces and four wings, appear at the river Chebar where the Hebrew prophet glimpses them. In 1 Kings 6:23, the two cherubim in Solomon's temple are carved out of olive wood. In rabbinic and occult lore, the cherubim are prevailingly thought of as charioteers of God, bearers of God's throne, and personifications of the winds. In Revelation (4:8), the cherubim are living creatures who render unceasing praise to their Maker. In Revelation, John refers to the cherubim as beasts (holy, divine beasts), six-winged and "full of eyes within."

John of Damascus in his *Exposition of the Orthodox Faith* also speaks of the cherubim as "many-eyed." In the Talmud, the cherubim are equated with the order ophanim (wheels or chariots) or the order hayyoth (holy beasts) and are said to reside in the sixth or seventh Heaven. In the Dionysian scheme, the cherubim rank second in the nine choir hierarchy and are guardians of the fixed stars. Chief rulers, as listed in most occult works, include Ophaniel, Rikbiel, Cherubiel, Raphael, Gabriel, Zophiel, and—before his fall—Satan, who was, the supreme angel in the choir of cherubim.

In early traditions of Muslim lore, it is claimed that the cherubim were formed from the tears Michael shed over the sins of the faithful. In secular stories, the cherubim have been called "black cherubim" (Dante), "young-eyed cherubim" (Shakespeare), and "helmed cherubim" (Milton). Blake describes Satan as the "covering cherub" and turns the Ezekiel vision of the four creatures into his own *Four Zoas*. In the latter, the cherubim sound the four trumpets heralding the apocalypse.

As angels of light, glory, and keepers of the celestial records, the cherubim excel in knowledge. The notion of winged, multiple-headed beasts serving as guardians of temples and palaces must have been general in many southwest Asian countries, for in addition to appearing in Assyrian-Chaldean-Babylonian art and writings (where the authors of Isaiah and Ezekiel doubtlessly first came upon them), they appear in Canaanitish lore. It was with this Canaanitish lore that the ancient Israelites were most familiar and which, therefore, influenced the accounts of the cherubim which appear in Genesis and other Old Testament books.

[322]The snake's promises were thus fulfilled, but with seemingly disastrous further consequences. The man attained the knowledge of good and evil, but was not immediately put to

Chapter 4

And Adam knew Eve his wife; and she conceived, and bare Cain[323], and said, I have gotten a man from the LORD.

2 And she again bare his brother Abel. And Abel was a keeper of sheep, but Cain was a tiller of the ground.

3 And in process of time it came to pass, that Cain brought of the fruit of the ground an offering unto the LORD.

4 And Abel, he also brought of the firstlings of his flock and of the fat thereof.

And the LORD had respect unto Abel and to his offering:

5 But unto Cain and to his offering he had not respect. And Cain was very wroth, and his countenance fell.

6 And the LORD said unto Cain, Why art thou wroth? and why is thy countenance fallen?

7 If thou does well, shalt thou not be accepted? and if thou doest not well, sin lieth at the door. And unto thee shall be his desire, and thou shalt rule over him.

---

death. However, death most certainly would one day come to the man. Additionally, the man was condemned to a life of struggle. Thus, while the man gained knowledge, he lost the trust and confidence of God.

But even more than the loss of trust and confidence of God, the man evoked a new emotion from God. With man's acquisition of knowledge, God became afraid that the man would no longer be satisfied with what he was. God became apprehensive that man might find and eat the fruit from another tree in the garden—the tree of life—and that, if the man had done so, then God's remaining hold over the man would be gone forever. Thus, in addition to the penalty already imposed, the man and the woman—Adam and Eve—were driven out of the garden and the exiled pair were forced to till the soil outside the primordial paradise.

To prevent Adam's return to Eden, God places guards over the way. God places Cherubims at the entrance. Frequently, in ancient folklore from southwestern Asia, strange beings who were half human and half animal, would be placed at the doors of palaces and of temples. It is clear that these strange beings represent guardian spirits, and, to judge from the description given by Ezekiel, and from other references, these beings were known by the name of Cherubim.

With the expulsion of Adam and Eve from Eden, God stations the Cherubim to the east of the garden, and (apparently in addition) a whirling sword of living flame keeps the way to the tree of life. According to this narrative of creation, man, because of his disobedience to God, forever lost his last chance for immortality.

It is of interest to note that this narrative provides a presentation of God and of God's character, an ideal of religion, which are typical of a certain stage in the development of Israel, and, perhaps, of other nations as well. In this narrative, Jehovah insists on his own superiority as compared with the man whom God has created. God's only command is that the man shall not eat the fruit of the tree of knowledge, for to acquire what that food will give him will help to raise the man to the level of God. When that command is broken a further danger is imminent, that the man would attain to immortality, and there would be no difference at all in powers and in status between the Creator and the creature. This must be prevented at all costs, and the final act in the passage secures the permanent inferiority of man. Religion must consist of the reverent submission of the inferior to the superior, and in the recognition and maintenance of the supremacy of God over man. Friendship and affectionate association are certainly not excluded, but their basis must be the condescension of God and the humility of man. The basis for this relationship would form the outstanding feature of the religious thought of the Jews throughout their history.

[323]4000 B.C.T. {Ussher Chronology}.

8 And Cain talked with Abel his brother: and it came to pass, when they were in the field, that Cain rose up against Abel his brother, and slew him.

9 And the LORD said unto Cain, Where is Abel they brother? And he said, I know not: Am I my brother's keeper?

10 And he said, What hast thou done? the voice of thy brother's blood crieth unto me from the ground.

11 And now art thou cursed from the earth, which hath opened her mouth to receive thy brother's blood from thy hand;

12 When thou tillest the ground, it shall not henceforth yield unto thee her strength; a fugitive and a vagabond shalt thou be in the earth.

13 And Cain said unto the LORD, My punishment is greater than I can bear.

14 Behold, thou hast driven me out this day from the face of the earth; and from thy face shall I be hid; and I shall be a fugitive and a vagabond in the earth; and it shall come to pass, that every one that findeth me shall slay me.

15 And the LORD said unto him, Therefore whosoever slayeth Cain, vengeance shall be taken on him sevenfold. And the Lord set a mark upon Cain, lest any finding him should kill him.

16 And Cain went out from the presence of the LORD, and dwelt in the land of Nod, on the east of Eden.[324]

LAMECH AND HIS SONG {GENESIS 4:17–4:26}

17 And Cain knew his wife; and she conceived, and bare Enoch: and he builded a

---

[324]Many scholars believe that the story of Cain and Abel is not really a story about two individuals but rather a story about two types of people who inhabited Southwest Asia in the third millennium B.C.T. There existed in ancient Southwest Asia a distinct social order with two categories of people. On the one hand, there was the shepherd who was usually a nomad. On the other hand, there was the farmer, whose sedentary lifestyle required a settled home.

There is always antagonism between the nomad and the farmer. In the Genesis narrative, this antagonism is manifested in the conflict between the first two brothers, Cain and Abel. Cain, the older son, is a farmer, while Abel, the younger son, is a shepherd. Ironically, the professions adopted by these two brothers run counter to the usually accepted historical order of the professions. History generally indicates that shepherds came before farmers.

However, despite their differences, the great contrast between Cain and Abel seemingly lies dormant until the time when both Cain and Abel take an offering to God. God took a liking to the offering of Abel, and Cain took offense at the slight. Cain became jealous of Abel.

Cain met with Abel, talked with him, and slew him. Abel's blood spills onto the ground, and this blood being the chief seat of life in the body takes on a personality of its own which cries out to God.

God is the guardian of the blood and is compelled to seek justice. God confronts Cain. Cain denies knowing the whereabouts of his brother, but this denial is futile because God has the evidence of the blood before him, and passes on to give sentence.

It is worth noting that God does not impose an arbitrary penalty on Cain. God merely states the inevitable effect of his crime. The ground has been compelled to receive a draught of that which it loathes—the ground has been compelled to receive Abel's blood. Accordingly, the ground has become angered against the person who has forced this upon it, and the ground would no longer cooperate with Cain in readily producing fruit for his labors. Instead, Cain is forced to abandon his profession and to become a wanderer,—a person without home and without kin.

Apparently by this time, the world was well populated with men and women. Thus, an

city, and called the name of the city, after the name of his son, Enoch.[325]

18 And unto Enoch was born Irad: and Irad begat Mehujael: and Mehujael begat Methusael: and Methusael begat Lamech.

19 And Lamech took unto him two wives: the name of the one was Adah, and the name of the other Zillah.

20 And Adah bare Jabal: he was the father of such as dwell in tents, and of such as have cattle.

21 And his brother's name was Jubal: he was the father of all such as handle the harp and organ.

22 And Zillah, she also bare Tubal-cain, an instructer of every artificer in brass and iron: and the sister of Tubal-cain was Naamah.

23 And Lamech said unto his wives, Adah and Zillah, Hear my voice; ye wives of Lamech, hearken unto my speech: for I have slain a man to my wounding, and a young man to my hurt.

24 If Cain shall be avenged sevenfold, truly Lamech seventy and sevenfold.

25 And Adam knew his wife again; and she bare a son, and called his name Seth: For God, said she, hath appointed me another seed instead of Abel, whom Cain slew.

26 And to Seth, to him also there was born a son; and he called his name Enos: then began men to call upon the name of the LORD.

ANTEDILUVIAN MAN
{GENESIS 5:1–6:4}

unprotected and isolated stranger with neither kindred nor God to avenge him had only a small chance of escaping disaster. God, however, has no animus against Cain. In order to protect Cain while Cain is far away, God sets a mark on Cain.

From that time on, Cain is no longer merely an individual. Cain is a clan whose members are distinguished by some special mark which they bear. Anyone who sees that mark knows that the man who carries it belongs to a fierce and terrible people. Normally, if a member of a tribe is killed, the survivors exact a life for a life, but for each man killed, the tribe of Cain will demand seven lives from the tribe of the offender.

This story explains the history of the Cainites (Kenites). Although the Cainites no longer dwelled in the land which God is thought to hold as God's own, God's power can still reach beyond God's land and fiercely avenge transgressions against God's people wherever they may be.

[325]Verse 17 of Genesis, Chapter 4 begins with a short genealogy, which differs markedly from those so frequent in the group which we call "P" (priestly). The purpose of this genealogy seems to be to connect Cain with Lamech, and there is a note of the building of a city called Enoch, so named after a son of Cain. There seems to have been some error in the transmission of the text, and probably Enoch himself was the founder of the city in question. The genealogy is carried to a generation beyond Lamech, and gives the origin of the tent-dweller, the musician, and the smith—all, curiously enough, features of life found among the nomads.

This genealogy also serves to introduce the very ancient song of Lamech, clearly a tribal saying. The men of the tribe are represented as telling their wives how savagely they avenge injuries. For an actual wound they are ready to take the life of a man, and even for a blow they will kill a boy. They compare themselves with the tribe of Cain, and claim that they are eleven times as bloodthirsty as the bloodthirsty Cainite tribe.

Chapter 4 of Genesis ends with a note concerning the birth of Seth and of his son. The name of Seth's son was Enos (Enosh)—another word for "man"—and the remark is made that it was during Enos' lifetime that the worship of God was first introduced {then began men to call upon the name of the LORD}.

Chapter 5[326]

This is the book of the generations of Adam. In the day that God created man, in the likeness of God made he him;

2 Male and female created he them; and blessed them, and called their name Adam, in the day when they were created.

3 And Adam lived an hundred and thirty years,[327] and begat a son in his own likeness, after his image; and called his name Seth:

4 And the days of Adam after he had begotten Seth were eight hundred years: and he begat sons and daughters:

5 And all the days that Adam lived were nine hundred and thirty years: and he died.[328]

6 And Seth lived an hundred and five years,[329] and begat Enos:

7 And Seth lived after he begat Enos eight hundred and seven years, and begat sons and daughters:

8 And all the days of Seth were nine hundred and twelve years: and he died.[330]

9 And Enos lived ninety years,[331] and begat Cainan:

10 And Enos lived after he begat Cainan eight hundred and fifteen years, and begat sons and daughters:

---

[326]The genealogy set forth in Genesis, Chapter 5 is derived from the priestly ("P") narratives. The genealogy set forth in Chapter 5 traces man through Seth, the third son of Adam. In Chapter 5, the word "Adam" is used for the first time as a proper name.

It is interesting to compare the Seth genealogy of Chapter 5 with the Cain genealogy of Chapter 4. {See Genesis 4:17–18} The Cain genealogy is derived from "J" narratives while the Seth genealogy is derived from "P" narratives. The Cain genealogy has six generations while the Seth genealogy has nine.

What is striking about the Cain and Seth genealogies is that two of the names—Enoch and Lamech—are identical in both narratives. This striking coincidence has led some commentators to suggest that what is occurring here is two versions of the same genealogy, diverging at an early period and yet both springing from the same source.

The names that are contained in the Seth genealogy convey very little information. The names have been compared to the traditional lists of Babylonian antediluvian kings, but while the names have much in common with Babylonian names, the length of the reigns (the length of the lifespans) actually coincides better with those assigned to Mesopotamian monarchs. In any event, if the source material for the Seth genealogy does go back to a common source, it underwent significant revision at the hands of the Hebrew writers.

Methuselah is remembered as the man who lived the longest on earth, and the span of his life suggests that in the end he perished in the Flood. Except for Adam and Noah, of the long life men, Enoch alone stands out as a real personality. Of Enoch we have the simple statement that Enoch walked with God, and he was not, for God took him. Enoch's life is by far the shortest life in the list, and the explanation of this fact is that Enoch made himself the familiar companion of God. Thus, God conferred upon Enoch the gift of immortality, taking him to dwell with himself. It is natural enough that legends should have grown about his name, and he became in later Judaism the center of a large eschatological literature.

[327]3874 B.C.T. {Ussher Chronology}.

[328]3074 B.C.T. {Ussher Chronology}.

[329]3769 B.C.T. {Ussher Chronology}.

[330]2962 B.C.T. {Ussher Chronology}.

[331]3679 B.C.T. {Ussher Chronology}.

11 And all the days of Enos were nine hundred and five years: and he died.[332]

12 And Cainan lived seventy years,[333] *and begat Mahalaleel:*

13 And Cainan lived after he begat Mahalaleel eight hundred and forty years, and begat sons and daughters:

14 And all the days of Cainan were nine hundred and ten years: and he died.[334]

15 And Mahalaleel lived sixty and five years,[335] *and begat Jared:*

16 And Mahalaleel lived after he begat Jared eight hundred and thirty years, and begat sons and daughters:

17 And all the days of Mahalaleel were eight hundred ninety and five years: and he died.[336]

18 And Jared lived an hundred sixty and two years,[337] *and he begat Enoch:*

19 And Jared lived after he begat Enoch eight hundred years, and begat sons and daughters:

20 And all the days of Jared were nine hundred sixty and two years: and he died.[338]

21 And Enoch lived sixty and five years,[339] *and begat Methuselah:*

22 And Enoch walked with God after he begat Methuselah three hundred years,[340] *and begat sons and daughters:*

23 And all the days of Enoch were three hundred sixty and five years:

24 And Enoch walked with God: and he was not; for God took him.

25 And Methuselah lived an hundred eighty and seven years,[341] *and begat Lamech:*

26 And Methuselah lived after he begat Lamech seven hundred eighty and two years, and begat sons and daughters:

27 And all the days of Methuselah were nine hundred sixty and nine years: and he died.[342]

28 And Lamech lived an hundred eighty and two years,[343] *and begat a son:*

29 And he called his name Noah saying, This same shall comfort us concerning our work and toil of our hands, because of the ground which the LORD hath cursed.

30 And Lamech lived after he begat Noah five hundred ninety and five years, and begat sons and daughters:

31 And all the days of Lamech were seven hundred seventy and seven years: and he died.[344]

---

[332] 2864 B.C.T. {Ussher Chronology}.

[333] 3609 B.C.T. {Ussher Chronology}.

[334] 2769 B.C.T. {Ussher Chronology}.

[335] 3544 B.C.T. {Ussher Chronology}.

[336] 2717 B.C.T. {Ussher Chronology}.

[337] 3382 B.C.T. {Ussher Chronology}.

[338] 2582 B.C.T. {Ussher Chronology}.

[339] 3317 B.C.T. {Ussher Chronology}.

[340] 3017 B.C.T. {Ussher Chronology}.

[341] 3130 B.C.T. {Ussher Chronology}.

[342] 2349 B.C.T. {Ussher Chronology}. According to the Ussher Chronology, Methusaleh may have died in the Flood. Methuselah, who was 969 years old at the time of his death, was the last of the long life men (except, of course, for Noah).

[343] 2948 B.C.T. {Ussher Chronology}.

[344] 2353 B.C.T. {Ussher Chronology}.

32 And Noah was five hundred years old: and Noah begat Shem,[345] Ham, and Japheth.[346]

Chapter 6

And it came to pass, when men began to multiply on the face of the earth, and daughters were born unto them.

2 That the sons of God saw the daughters of men that they were fair; and they took them wives of all which they chose.

3 And the LORD said, My spirit shall not always strive with man, for that he also is flesh: yet his days shall be an hundred and twenty years.

4 There were giants in the earth in those days; and also after that, when the sons of

God came in unto the daughters of men, and they bare children to them, the same became mighty men which were of old, men of renown.[347, 348]

THE FLOOD
{GENESIS 6:5–9:29}

5 And GOD saw that the wickedness of man was great in the earth, and that every imagination of the thoughts of his heart was only evil continually.

6 And it repented the LORD that he had made man on the earth, and it grieved him at his heart.

7 And the Lord said, I will destroy man whom I have created from the face of the

---

[345]2446 B.C.T. {Ussher Chronology}.

[346]2448 B.C.T. {Ussher Chronology}. Although the biblical sequence obviously has Japheth being listed last and seemingly being born last, Ussher lists Japheth as having been born first. Ussher's reverse listing of birth order seems to be validated and repeated by the listing of the sons of Terah which occurs in Genesis chapter 11.

[347]In the passages from Genesis 6:1–4, the Bible reader is introduced to a rather strange old story which has largely escaped the modifications which a later theology might have made. Many explanations have been forwarded. One such explanation has the beings identified as the sons of God as being angels, who because of their sins were driven from their heavenly abode. Evidently we have here a narrative which originated in days so early that men still believed in the existence of a multitude of deities. Alongside of—almost compared with— the "gods" of verses 2 and 4 there is the Jehovah—the LORD—of verse 3. The reader is led to believe that at the time Jehovah was only one of a number of beings of the same order and species, although Jehovah may be superior to the rest.

The other divine beings identified in Genesis 6:1–4 regard the daughters of men as suitable mates for themselves, and from their marriages sprang forth the famous heroes and giants of whom ancient legend told. Jehovah, on the other hand, looks on them as Jehovah's creatures, and sees to it that Jehovah's Spirit,—that power which at the first gave man life,— shall not dwell for unlimited periods in man. In ancient Hebrew thought, man was an animated body, and when the spirit was withdrawn, man ceased to live. According to the Scriptures, the spirit of man had been bestowed by Jehovah. It was a power almost personal in nature, and it could be recalled by Jehovah whenever Jehovah pleased.

It is notable that in verse 3 the life span of man was limited to a hundred twenty years. This was ostensibly done to prevent man from living long enough to encroach upon the prerogatives of God.

[348]The passages of Genesis 5:1 through 6:4 form a link between the story of creation and the next important point, the Flood. These passages illustrate the desire of the Biblical historian to narrow the range of interest until it centers on the immediate ancestors of Israel. Following Adam, Noah, the hero of the Flood, would be the outstanding character. The passages of Genesis 5:1 through 6:4 explain Noah's antecedents and the reasons for the Flood.

earth; both man, and beast, and the creeping thing, and the fowls of the air; for it repenteth me that I have made them.

8 But Noah found grace in the eyes of the Lord.

9 These are the generations of Noah: Noah was a just man and perfect in his generations, and Noah walked with God.

10 And Noah begat three sons, Shem, Ham, and Japheth.

11 The earth also was corrupt before God, and the earth was filled with violence.

12 And God looked upon the earth, and, behold, it was corrupt; for all flesh had corrupted his way upon the earth.

13 And God said unto Noah, The end of all flesh is come before me; for the earth is filled with violence through them; and, behold, I will destroy them with the earth.

14 Make thee an ark of gopher wood; rooms shalt thou make in the ark, and shalt pitch it within and without with pitch.

15 And this is the fashion which thou shalt make it of: The length of the ark shall be three hundred cubits, the breadth of it fifty cubits, and the height of it thirty cubits.

16 A window shalt thou make to the ark, and in a cubit shalt thou finish it above; and the door of the ark shalt thou set in the side thereof: with lower, second, and third stories shalt thou make it.

17 And, behold, I, even I, do bring a flood of waters upon the earth, to destroy all flesh, wherein is the breath of life, from under heaven; and every thing that is in the earth shall die.

18 But with thee will I establish my covenant; and thou shalt come into the ark,

thou, and thy sons, and thy wife, and thy sons' wives with thee.

19 And of every living thing of all flesh, two of every sort shalt thou bring into the ark, to keep them alive with thee; they shall be male and female.

20 Of fowls after their kind, and of cattle after their kind, of every creeping thing of the earth after his kind, two of every sort shall come unto thee, to keep them alive.

21 And take thou unto thee of all food that is eaten, and thou shalt gather it to thee; and it shall be for food for thee, and for them.

22 Thus did Noah; according to all that God commanded him, so did he.

Chapter 7

And the LORD said unto Noah, Come thou and all thy house into the ark[349]; for thee have I seen righteous before me in this generation.

2 Of every clean beast thou shalt take to thee by sevens, the male and his female: and of beasts that are not clean by two, the male and his female.

3 Of fowls also of the air by sevens, the male and the female,: to keep seed alive upon the face of all the earth.

4 For yet seven days, and I will cause it to rain upon the earth forty days and forty nights; and every living substance that I have made will I destroy from off the face of the earth.

5 And Noah did according unto all that the LORD commanded him.

6 And Noah was six hundred years old when the flood of waters was upon the earth.[350]

7 And Noah went in, and his sons, and

---

[349]Sunday, November 30, 2349 B.C.T. {Ussher Chronology}.

[350]Today, as in the past, catastrophic floods are experienced universally, and stories about them are often ingrained in our memories. The flood stories share many features: land is submerged, multitudes are drowned, and survivors survive by living in a boat. People living in basically similar ways in separate places will react similarly. Thus, common features in flood stories are predictable and are not proof that all such ancient stories refer to one great flood. {But see 13,600 B.C.T. and 5,600 B.C.T. of Part One: A Secular Perspective.}

his wife, and his sons' wives with him, into the ark,[351] because of the waters of the flood.

8 Of clean beasts, and of beasts that are not clean, and of fowls, and of everything that creepeth upon the earth,

9 There went in two and two unto Noah into the ark, the male and the female, as God had commanded Noah.

10 And it came to pass after seven days, that the waters of the flood were upon the earth.

11 In the six hundredth year of Noah's life, in the second month, the seventeenth day of the month, the same day were all the fountains of the great deep broken up, and the windows of heaven were opened.

12 And the rain was upon the earth forty days and forty nights.

13 In the selfsame day entered Noah, and Shem, and Ham, and Japheth, the sons of Noah, and Noah's wife, and the three wives of his sons with them, into the ark;

14 They, and every beast after his kind, and all the cattle after their kind, and every creeping thing that creepeth upon the earth after his kind, and every fowl after his kind, every bird of every sort.

15 And they went in unto Noah into the ark, two and two of all flesh, wherein is the breath of life.

16 And they that went in, went in male and female of all flesh, as God had commanded him: and the LORD shut him in.

17 And the flood was forty days upon the earth; and the waters increase, and bare up the ark, and it was lift up above the earth.

Nevertheless, the Babylonian and Hebrew stories concerning a great flood share so much in common that a connection between them can hardly be denied. Surviving copies of the Babylonian story come from the seventeenth and seventh centuries B.C.T. (The Epic of Atrahasis and the Epic of Gilgamesh, respectively) while the age of the Hebrew account in Genesis 6–9 is debated. Both narratives have a pious hero warned by his god to build a great ship—an ark—and to load it with his family and selected animals in order to escape the coming deluge. Once all others have perished, the ship grounds on a mountain in Armenia (Mount Ararat), a sacrifice pleases the god, and a divine oath follows never to send another flood. The later Babylonian version (Gilgamesh) even describes the hero releasing birds to seek vegetation. However, the clay tablets on which the earlier text is recorded have been damaged where that episode might have occurred.

Both the older Babylonian account (Atrahasis) and the Hebrew account (Genesis) belong to larger compositions passing from the creation of human beings to later history, the flood, and its aftermath. Other Babylonian records show a wider tradition preserving names of kings from the beginning of the human race onward, interrupted by the flood. Genesis 5 and 11 present comparable lists in a comparable context. All these similarities indicate a close connection between the Babylonian and Hebrew stories.

Scholars often claim that the Hebrew flood story depends on the Babylonian, with modifications in the interest of Israel's monotheistic faith. Consideration of certain differences, however, makes it more likely that both depend upon a common original story from an as yet undetermined source.

Whether such a flood occurred, or not, is impossible to prove. Archaeologists finding layers of silt in three Babylonian cities associated them with the flood, but each was confined to one place and they were not contemporary.

What physical traces such a flood would leave may be debatable. Although the Genesis tale does imply a global flood, such may not be the case because the Hebrew word translated in Genesis as the "earth" can also mean the "land" or the "country." Thus, the Genesis narrative could be read to be limited to record a limited deluge confined to the Genesis writer's own world. {But again see 13,600 B.C.T. and 5,600 B.C.T. of the Secular Perspective.}

[351]Sunday, December 7, 2349 B.C.T. {Ussher Chronology}.

18 And the waters prevailed, and were increased greatly upon the earth; and the ark went upon the face of the waters.

19 And the waters prevailed exceedingly upon the earth; and all the high hills, that were under the whole heaven, were uncovered.

20 Fifteen cubits upward did the waters prevail; and the mountains were covered.

21 And all flesh died that moved upon the earth, both of fowl, and of cattle, and of beast, and of every creeping thing that creepeth upon the earth, and every man:

22 All in whose nostrils was the breath of life, of all that was in the dry land, died.

23 And every living substance was destroyed which was upon the face of the ground, both man, and cattle, and the creeping things, and the fowl of the heaven; and they were destroyed from the earth: and Noah only remained alive, and they that were with him in the ark.

24 And the waters prevailed upon the earth an hundred and fifty days.

Chapter 8

And God remembered Noah, and every living thing, and all the cattle that was with him in the ark: and God made a wind to pass over the earth, and the waters assuaged;

2 The fountains also of the deep and the windows of heaven were stopped, and the rain from heaven was restrained;

3 And the waters returned from off the earth continually: and after the end of the hundred and fifty days the waters were abated.

4 And the ark rested in the seventh month, on the seventeenth day of the month, upon the mountains of Ararat.[352]

5 And the waters decreased continually until the tenth month: in the tenth month, on the first day of the month, were the tops of the mountains seen.[353]

6 And it came to pass at the end of forty days, that Noah opened the window of the ark which he had made:

7 And he sent forth a raven,[354] which went forth to and fro, until the waters were dried up from off the earth.

8 Also he sent forth a dove[355] from him, to see if the waters were abated from off the face of the ground;

9 But the dove found no rest for the sole of her foot, and she returned unto him into the ark, for the waters were on the face of the whole earth: then he put forth his hand, and took her, and pulled her in unto him into the ark.

10 And he stayed yet other seven days; and again he sent forth the dove out of the ark:

11 and the dove came in to him in the evening; and, lo, in her mouth was an olive leaf pluckt off: so Noah knew that the waters were abated from off the earth.

12 And he stayed yet other seven days; and sent forth the dove; which returned not again unto him any more.

13 And it came to pass in the six hundredth and first year, in the first month, the

---

[352]According to the Ussher Chronology, the Ark came to rest on one of the mountains of Ararat, on Wednesday, May 6, 2348 B.C.T.

[353]According to the Ussher Chronology, the tops of the mountains appeared above the water on Sunday, July 19, 2348 B.C.T.

[354]According to the Ussher Chronology, Noah opened the window of the Ark and sent forth a raven on Friday, August 28, 2348 B.C.T.

[355]According to the Ussher Chronology, Noah sent forth a dove on Friday, September 4, 2348 B.C.T.

first day of the month, the waters were dried up from off the earth: and Noah removed the covering of the ark, and looked, and, behold, the face of the ground was dry.[356]

14 And in the second month, on the seven and twentieth day of the month, was the earth dried.

15 And God spake unto Noah saying,

16 Go forth of the ark, thou, and thy wife, and thy sons, and thy sons' wives with thee.

17 Bring forth with thee every living thing that is with thee, of all flesh, both of fowl, and of cattle, and of every creeping thing that creepeth upon the earth; that they may breed abundantly in the earth, and be fruitful, and multiply upon the earth.

18 And Noah went forth, and his sons, and his wife, and his sons' wives with him:[357]

19 Every beast, every creeping thing, and every fowl, and whatsoever creepeth upon the earth, after their kinds, went forth out of the ark.

20 And Noah builded an altar unto the LORD; and took of every clean beast, and of every clean fowl, and offered burnt offerings on the altar.

21 And the LORD smelled a sweet savour; and the LORD said in his heart, I will not again curse the ground any more for man's sake; for the imagination of man's heart is evil from his youth; neither will I again smite any more every thing living, as I have done.

22 While the earth remaineth, seedtime and harvest, and cold and heat, and summer and winter, and day and night shall not cease.[358]

---

[356]According to the Ussher Chronology, Noah took off the covering of the Ark on Friday, October 23, 2348 B.C.T.—the 1656th anniversary of the First Day of Creation.

[357]According to the Ussher Chronology, Noah disembarked on Thursday, December 18, 2348 B.C.T. It is notable that immediately after the flood the years of a biblical man's life were made half-shorter.

[358]The story of a universal Flood which destroyed nearly every living thing is found in the folklore of many peoples. These traditions differ in details very widely, though occasionally we find resemblances which suggest a common origin. Whether all go back to a single catastrophe {see 5600 B.C.T.}, or whether similar events took place in different parts of the world {see 13,600 B.C.T.}, is a question which is still the subject of significant debate. The two traditions—taken from "J" and "P"—preserved in Genesis are not dissimilar, but are yet different enough to make it advisable to look at them separately.

Throughout the "J" story, the reader may note the relatively naive outlook of the narrator, and his very elementary theology. Jehovah is described in anthropomorphic terms. In the "J" story, God shuts Noah into the ark and uses the waters of nature, though in an unnatural quantity, to produce a catastrophe. As the catastrophe worsens, God is so affected by the smell of sacrifice that God realizes that perhaps a mistake has been made in destroying man.

From the perspective of God of the "J" narrative {Genesis 6:1–8, 7:1–11}, the destruction of man was warranted because of the wickedness of man. However, Noah's high character appeals to God and because of this, God decides to warn Noah and to spare him.

It should also be noted that, in the "J" narrative, God leaves Noah to find out by his own experiment when the earth is dry enough for him to come out of the ark.

In the "P" narrative, the atmosphere is different although the facts are the same. In the "P" narrative, the reader is given the same ethical basis for the actions of God and the same recognition of Noah's goodness. After all, Noah, like Enoch, "walked with God." {Genesis 6:9–22} In the "P" narrative, we have the exact details of the ark and the dates of the stages of the Flood itself. The catastrophe is not produced simply by rain, but by a temporary col-

Chapter 9

And God blessed Noah and his sons, and said unto them, Be fruitful and multiply, and replenish the earth.

2 And the fear of you and the dread of you shall be upon every beast of the earth, and upon every fowl of the air, upon all that moveth upon the earth, and upon all the fishes of the sea; into your hand are they delivered.

3 Every moving thing that liveth shall be meat for you; even as the green herb have I given you all things.

4 But flesh with the life thereof, which is the blood thereof, shall ye not eat.

5 And surely your blood of your lives will I require; at the hand of every beast will I require it, and at the hand of man; at the hand of every man's brother will I require the life of man.

6 Whoso sheddeth man's blood, by man shall his blood be shed: for in the image of God made he man.

7 And you, be ye fruitful, and multiply; bring forth abundantly in the earth, and multiply therein.[359]

8 And God spake unto Noah, and to his sons with him, saying,

9 And I, behold, I establish my covenant with you, and with your seed after you;[360]

10 And with every living creature that is with you, of the fowl, of the cattle, and of every beast of the earth with you; from all that go out of the ark, to every beast of the earth.

11 And I will establish my covenant with you; neither shall all flesh be cut off any more by the waters of a flood; neither shall there any more be a flood to destroy the earth.

12 And God said, This is the token of the covenant which I make between me and you and every living creature that is with you, for perpetual generations:

13 I do set my bow in the cloud, and it shall be for a token of a covenant between me and the earth.

14 And it shall come to pass, when I bring a cloud over the earth, that the bow shall be seen in the cloud:

15 And I will remember my covenant, which is between me and you and every living creature of all flesh; and the waters shall no more become a flood to destroy all flesh.

16 And the bow shall be in the cloud; and I will look upon it, that I may remember the everlasting covenant between God and every living creature of all flesh that is upon the earth.

---

lapse of the structure of the cosmos, through which water streams in above and below from the chaos outside. {Genesis 8:2} The conditions are maintained for a hundred and fifty days {Genesis 7:24 and 8:3} and the whole duration of the Flood is at least a year {Genesis 8:13}.

[359]Following the Flood the story of humanity begins anew. Just as the first human pair were ordered to increase and fill the earth, so the survivors of the Flood are instructed to re-populate it. The authority originally conferred over all the lower orders of being is confirmed, and one new element is introduced into life—the flesh of animals may in the future be used as food. To this permission, however, a restriction is added. The sanctity of blood must be maintained, and under no circumstances whatever must it be eaten. The same principle will apply to man as to the beasts; whoever sheds the blood of another must submit to the law of blood-revenge, for the blood is a living, almost a personal, entity {see Genesis 4:10}, and will not be satisfied until it has been appeased by the blood of the slayer himself. Finally, God proclaims God to be the vindicator against the aggression both of man and of beast.

[360]According to Genesis 9:8–11, God promised never again to send "a flood to destroy the earth." The covenant with Noah (Genesis 9:12–17) sets human society on a basis of individual responsibility, and Genesis goes on to trace this concept in the special revelation that God ostensibly gave to the Jews.

17 And God said unto Noah, This is the token of the covenant, which I have established between me and all flesh that is upon the earth.[361]

18 And the sons of Noah, that went forth of the ark, were Shem, and Ham, and Japheth: and Ham is the father of Canaan.

19 These are the three sons of Noah: and of them was the whole earth overspread.

20 And Noah began to be an husbandman, and he planted a vineyard:

21 And he drank of the wine, and was drunken: and he was uncovered within his tent.

22 And Ham, the father of Canaan, saw the nakedness of his father, and told his two brethren without.

23 And Shem and Japheth took a garment, and laid it upon both their shoulders, and went backward, and covered the naked-ness of their father; and their faces were backward, and they saw not their father's naked-ness.

24 And Noah awoke from his wine, and knew what his younger son had done unto him.

25 And he said, Cursed be Canaan; a servant of servants shall he be unto his brethren.

26 And he said, Blessed be the LORD God of Shem; and Canaan shall be his servant.

27 God shall enlarge Japheth, and he shall dwell in the tents of Shem; and Canaan shall be his servant.

28 And Noah lived after the flood three hundred and fifty years.

29 And all the days of Noah were nine hundred and fifty years: and he died.[362, 363]

---

[361]Lest man should have to live in constant dread of a repetition of the disaster which has thus ended the first age of biblical history, God makes a promise and a covenant. As part of God's covenant, God promises that never again would God bring such a Flood over the earth. As a sign of this covenant, to reassure men when they are fearful in time of rain, God calls attention to the bow in the cloud—the rainbow. It is not suggested that there had been no rainbow before the Flood, but simply that the rainbow thereafter would have a new function in the life of the world, and men are to remember that the God who created the rainbow would keep the covenant.

The story of the rainbow is a story common in its broader outlines to many peoples. The forms in which it has come down to us clearly did not originate in Palestine, but in some country of wide level plains such as Mesopotamia, and the story which shows the closest resemblances is that which we know from Babylonian sources. However, again, the differences are more significant than the resemblances because the Jewish revision of the Babylonian story makes this story play a new part in the history of not only religion but also of human development.

The story of the flood and the rainbow marks a fresh stage in that human order whose basis, to the mind of the writer, is the relation of man to God, and dwells not merely on the power of God, but also on God's fidelity. Some scholars would call this biblical story folklore; if so, once more, over time, it became consecrated folklore.

[362]1998 B.C.T. {Ussher Chronology}.

[363]The narrative set forth in Genesis 9:18–29 presents the reader with a new picture of Noah, the first cultivator of the vine and the first man to suffer from drunkenness. This story also includes a very ancient curse on Canaan and a blessing on Japheth. These last two must be very ancient indeed, and belong to the early days of the Semitic race. The story of Noah is difficult to reconcile with the presentation given in the Flood narrative, and probably comes from a different cycle, though, as it stands, it belongs to the same general group of passages.

It seems that two different themes have been combined in this segment of narrative. In

THE RECOVERY OF MAN AND THE REPOPULATION OF THE EARTH
{GENESIS 10:1–11:9}

Chapter 10

Now these are the generations of the sons of Noah, Shem, Ham, and Japheth: and unto them were sons born after the flood.

2 The sons of Japheth; Gomer, and Magog, and Madai, and Javan, and Tubal, and Meshech, and Tiras.

3 And the sons of Gomer; Ashkenaz, and Riphath, and Togarmah.

4 And the sons of Javan; Elishah, and Tarshish, Kittim, and Dodanim.

5 By these were isles of the Gentiles divided in their lands; every one after his tongue, after their families, in their nations.

6 And the sons of Ham: Cush and Mizraim, and Phut, and Canaan.[364]

7 And the sons of Cush; Seba, and Havilah, and Sabtah, and Raamah, and Sabtechah: and the sons of Raamah; Sheba, and Dedan.

8 And Cush begat Nimrod: he began to be a mighty one in the earth.

9 He was a mighty hunter before the LORD: wherefore it is said, Even as Nimrod the mighty hunter before the LORD.

10 And the beginning of his kingdom was Babel, and Erech, and Accad, and Calneh, in the land of Shinar.

11 Out of that land went forth Asshur, and builded Nineveh, and the city Rehoboth, and Calah,

12 And Resen between Nineveh and Calah: the same is a great city.

13 And Mizraim begat Ludim, and Anamim, and Lehabim, and Naphtuhim,

14 And Pathrusim, and Casluhim, (out of whom came Philistim,) and Caphtorim.

15 And Canaan begat Sidon his firstborn, and Heth,

16 And the Jebusite, and the Amorite, and the Girgasite,

17 And the Hivite, and the Arkite, and the Sinite,

18 And the Arvadite, and the Zemarite,

---

the first place we have the sin of Ham, and in the second the curse of Canaan. Although the latter is introduced as the son of Ham, it seems more likely that the curse was of an independent origin reflecting the writer's familiarity with Israel's subsequent struggles with the more senior inhabitants of Palestine.

It is interesting to note that, in this narrative, Ham and Canaan are linked. This is interesting because the Canaanites were a people of true Semitic stock who spoke Hebrew, a language akin to the Aramaic of the ancestors of Israel. However, because they were frequent rivals of the Hebrews, this narrative places upon them a curse. Likewise, the other Hamites—the other accursed people—were all African. This curse also may reflect the author's familiarity with the subjugation of Palestine by Egypt. {See Psalms 105:27.}

Thus, the "curse" of Ham, from a perspective in a biblical analysis, would appear to be more of a political curse rather than a spiritual one.

It must be noted that Noah's drunkenness, the mockery of Ham, and the modest piety of Shem and Japheth bring out strongly the Hebrew sense of shame. None but a drunken man would allow himself to be exposed, and apparently the worst insult that one man could put on another was that which Ham offered his father. {See Genesis 3:7.}

[364]According to the chronology set forth by the theologian James Ussher, Ham (Cham), the son of Noah, carried his colony into Egypt in 2188 B.C.T.

As most historians note, Egypt is in Africa, and both the Bible and the early Greek and Roman explorers and historians viewed this great civilization of the Nile as African. Before the modern idea of race and color prejudice, the distinctions noted in antiquity between the brown Egyptians and their darker hued neighbors to the south did not contain the racial and cultural connotations that exist today.

and the Hamathite: and afterward were the families of the Canaanites spread abroad.

19 And the border of the Canaanites was from Sidon, as thou comest to Gerar unto Gaza; as thou goest, unto Sodom and Gomorrah, and Admah, and Zeboim, even unto Lasha.

20 These are the sons of Ham, after their families, after their tongues, in their countries, and in their nations.

21 Unto Shem also, the father of all the children of Eber, the brother of Japheth the elder, even to him were children born.

22 The children of Shem; Elam, and Asshur, and Arphaxad, and Lud, and Aram.

23 And the children of Aram; Uz, and Hul, and Gether, and Mash.

24 And Arphaxad begat Salah; and Salah begat Eber.

25 And unto Eber were born two sons: the name of one was Peleg; for in his days

was the earth divided; and his brother's name was Joktan.

26 And Joktan begat Almodad, and Sheleph, and Hazarmaveth, and Jerah,

27 And Hadoram, and Uzal, and Diklah,

28 And Obal, and Abimael, and Sheba,

29 And Ophir, and Havilah, and Jobab: all these were the sons of Joktan.

30 And their dwelling was from Mesha, as thou goest unto Sephar a mount of the east.

31 These are the sons of Shem, after their families, after their tongues, in their lands, after their nations.

32 These are the families of the sons of Noah, after their generations, in their nations: and by these were the nations divided in the earth after the flood.[365]

---

[365]The genealogy in Genesis, Chapter 10 is clearly composite. One element connecting itself with the type of genealogy that can be found in Chapter 5 ("P"), the other, with its occasional personal notes, belonging to "J." Both seem to proceed on the same general principle—that of describing racial and geographical affinities as though they were family relationships. This was a familiar method in the ancient East, and even the Greeks used it in describing the main divisions of their people.

The arrangement in the "P" narrative is comparatively simple. There are three main groups of peoples, northern, southern, and eastern. The first are derived from Japheth, the second from Ham, and the third from Shem. Most of the names in the first group are familiar to us from other sources and all except the Medes belong to Asia Minor or the Mediterranean coastal lands. The geographical knowledge of the day evidently did not extend as far as continental European Greece, although the islands mentioned may include the Greek settlements in the Aegean.

Most of the peoples in the second group also are referred to elsewhere in ancient records. They are not all African, for Seba was a district in southern Arabia and Canaan, a land inhabited by Semitic Canaanites, was only linked, through Ham, to Hamitic Egypt.

The third table includes the chief races of Mesopotamia, although it is interesting to find that there is no mention of the Babylonians. It has been conjectured that this list of races was compiled at a later time when Babylon was subject to Assyria and therefore was not thought worthy of separate mention.

The other table of nations (in the "J" portion of the narrative) begins with the mention of Cush. {Genesis 10:8}. However, the Cush mentioned in verse 8 is probably not the same Cush who is the descendant of Ham mentioned in verses 6 and 7. Instead, the Cush of verse 8 appears to be the eponymous ancestor of an entirely different group—the inhabitants of lands of Mesopotamia. Notable among these names is that of Nimrod, who is not a people but an individual, regarded as the first man who attempted to form a great empire.

No name resembling the name of Nimrod has yet been found among the early

Chapter 11

And the whole earth was of one language, and of one speech.

2 And it came to pass, as they journeyed from the east, that they found a plain in the land of Shinar; and they dwelt there.

3 And they said one to another, Go to, let us make brick, and burn them throughly. And they had brick for stone, and slime had they for mortar.

4 And they said, Go to, let us build us a city and a tower whose top may reach unto heaven; and let us make us a name, lest we be scattered abroad upon the face of the whole earth.

5 And the LORD came down to see the city and the tower, which the children of men builded.

6 And the LORD said, Behold, the people is one, and they have all one language; and this they begin to do; and now nothing will be restrained from them, which they have imagined to do.

7 Go to, let us go down, and there confound their language, that they may not understand one another's speech.

8 So the LORD scattered them abroad from thence upon the face of all the earth: and they left off to build the city.

9 Therefore is the name of it called Babel; because the LORD did there confound the language[366] of all the earth: and from thence did the LORD scatter them abroad upon the face of all the earth.

Mesopotamian monarchs. However, the depiction of the great king who was also a mighty hunter is one with which scholars have become familiar in Assyrian sculpture and records.

The distribution of the "sons" of Egypt reflects the political situation of the second half of the second millennium B.C.T., with nominal Egyptian control over Palestine and Phoenicia, and with Hittites and Philistines in the country, though neither was dominant. The name "Shem" is here used simply to cover the descendants of Eber, the eponymous ancestor of the Hebrews, and it is interesting to note that most of the tribes under this head which can be identified at all seem to come from southern Arabia—from the area which is generally assigned to Ham.

[366]It was always unintelligible to primitive peoples that there were differences in speech between the various tribes and nations. Many early peoples have stories which were intended to explain this fact. Israelite tradition connected the differences with the building of Babylon or of one of the great temple-towers or ziggurats, characteristic of Babylonian temples. The name "Babel" (of which "Babylon" is a later Greek form) means literally "gate of god." However, the word as used in this narrative is connected with a Hebrew word *balal* meaning "to mix or confuse." To a certain extent, the modern word "babble" conveys the effect rather than the cause which is conveyed by the original term.

The brief narrative in Genesis 11:1–9 explains how there could exist a variety of languages among the earth's people. The understanding that the earliest humans shared a common language is found in the Sumerian *Enmerkar Epic*. Genesis 11:1–9 tells how Noah's descendants wandered to the plain of Shinar (Babylonia) where they perfected the techniques for monumental brick architecture and built the renowned tower of Babel. Building the tower is interpreted as an act of arrogance, and human history is here understood to take a decisive turn from a common thread to many strands as God descends to confuse human speech and scatter the people all over the earth.

Mesopotamian theology held that the true home of the gods was in a mountain, far north of Babylonia, and to make a suitable home it was necessary to imitate this mountain home as far as possible. Hence the temples always had great towers, with successive stories of decreasing height. These towers were built, as the biblical narrative correctly states, mainly of

THE GENEALOGY OF ABRAHAM {GENESIS 11:10–11:26}

10 These are the generations of Shem: Shem was an hundred years old, and begat Arphaxad two years after the flood[367]:

11 And Shem lived after he begat Arphaxad five hundred years,[368] *and begat sons and daughters.*

12 And Arphaxad lived five and thirty years, and begat Salah[369]:

13 And Arphaxad lived after he begat Salah four hundred and three years,[370] *and begat sons and daughters.*

14 And Salah lived thirty years, and begat Eber[371]:

15 And Salah lived after he begat Eber four hundred and three years,[372] *and begat sons and daughters.*

16 And Eber lived four and thirty years, and begat Peleg[373]:

17 And Eber lived after he begat Peleg

---

unburned bricks, albeit faced with harder material. This was necessitated by the fact that there was very little building stone in southern Babylonia.

In the narrative, one notices the relatively naive and elementary theology which is observed elsewhere in much of the Genesis narrative. The building of the tower is interpreted as an attempt to invade the sky, the home of Jehovah, although the reason is ostensibly that the tower may be a central rallying point for all mankind. Jehovah becomes alarmed by the tower and its invasion of God's privileges. Thus, in response, Jehovah takes action to defend God's prerogatives.

The enormous ziggurats of Mesopotamia could easily have symbolized the presumptuousness of the Mesopotamian urban elite, and likewise the ruination of these ziggurats symbolizes the judgment of God. Even as ruins, the massive dimensions of the ziggurats would have been striking. The Sumerian temple tower of the moon god Nanna ta Ur could have been the model for the tower of Babel. This huge terraced mountain of brick, with the god's temple on top, at least seventy feet (21 meters) above ground level, was built around 2100 B.C.T. Of similar construction, the great temple of Marduk in Babylon, the E-sagila, is possibly the model for the Genesis narrative. According to the Babylonian epic *Enuma Elish*, it took a year just to make the bricks for this colossally high structure.

With the scattering of man, and the creation of "babble," the first epoch in the biblical history of man comes to an end. Here, the human race has been brought into being, in a world especially prepared, and the interest has gradually narrowed until it rests on a single family. One great critical event, the Flood, stands half-way down the story, and a minor occurrence, the building of Babel and the scattering of the nations, has been mentioned. All that has happened is the work of a single power—Jehovah; Jehovah has been preparing the way for God's people. Jehovah made the world, Jehovah created man, Jehovah eliminated the hopelessly sinful, and Jehovah scattered men throughout the world. In everything that has taken place Jehovah's will has been manifest. Nothing has been done without a reason. After long preparation the stage is now ready for Jehovah's particular action upon those who are to be the ancestors of the Jews

[367]2346 B.C.T. {Ussher Chronology}.

[368]1846 B.C.T. {Ussher Chronology}.

[369]2311 B.C.T. {Ussher Chronology}.

[370]1881 B.C.T. {Ussher Chronology}. {See also footnote 357.}

[371]2281 B.C.T. {Ussher Chronology}.

[372]1878 B.C.T. {Ussher Chronology}.

[373]2247 B.C.T. {Ussher Chronology}. It is also notable that, beginning with Peleg, the years of a biblical man's life appear to once again be made half-shorter.

four hundred and thirty years,[374] *and begat sons and daughters.*

18 And Peleg lived thirty years, and begat Reu[375]*:*

19 And Peleg lived after he begat Reu two hundred and nine years,[376] *and begat sons and daughters.*

20 And Reu lived two and thirty years, and begat Serug[377]*:*

21 And Reu lived after he begat Serug two hundred and seven years,[378] *and begat sons and daughters.*

22 And Serug lived thirty years, and begat Nahor[379]*:*

23 And Serug lived after he begat Nahor two hundred years,[380] *and begat sons and daughters.*

24 And Nahor lived nine and twenty years, and begat Terah[381]*:*

25 And Nahor lived after he begat Terah an hundred and nineteen years,[382] *and begat sons and daughters.*

26 And Terah lived seventy years,[383] *and begat Abram, Nahor, and Haran.*[384]

27 Now these are the generations of Terah: Terah begat Abram,[385] *Nahor, and Haran; and Haran begat Lot.*

28 And Haran died before his father Terah in the land of his nativity, in Ur of the Chaldees.

29 And Abram and Nahor took them wives: the name of Abram's wife was Sarai; and the name of Nahor's wife, Milcah, the daughter of Haran, the father of Milcah, and the father of Iscah.

30 But Sarai was barren; she had no child.

31 And Terah took Abram his son, and Lot the son of Haran his son's son, and Sarai his daughter in law, his son Abram's wife; and they went forth with them from Ur of the Chaldees to go into the land of Canaan; and they came unto Haran, and dwelt there.

32 And the days of Terah were two hundred and five years[386]*: and Terah died in Haran.*[387]

---

[374]1817 B.C.T. {Ussher Chronology}.

[375]2217 B.C.T. {Ussher Chronology}.

[376]2008 B.C.T. {Ussher Chronology}.

[377]2185 B.C.T. {Ussher Chronology}.

[378]1978 B.C.T. {Ussher Chronology}.

[379]2155 B.C.T. {Ussher Chronology}.

[380]1955 B.C.T. {Ussher Chronology}.

[381]2126 B.C.T. {Ussher Chronology}.

[382]2007 B.C.T. {Ussher Chronology}.

[383]2056 B.C.T. {Ussher Chronology}.

[384]The genealogy set forth in Genesis 11 is attributed to the "P"—the priestly—narrative. It is a simple genealogy which bridges the period from Noah to Abraham.

[385]According to the Ussher Chronology, Abram was born in 1996 B.C.T. Like the ordering of the sons of Noah, it may be that the youngest son is set forth first. This ordering may also account for the fact that Terah's first son would have been born in 2056 B.C.T., sixty years before the birth of Abram.

[386]1921 B.C.T. {Ussher Chronology}.

[387]As it is to Abraham (Abram) that later Israel would look as the real founder of the nation, this portion of Genesis provides Abraham's genealogy. It is believed that the source for this

material is the priestly narrative. Here it is explained how Abraham came to be in western Asia. Abraham's father, Terah, is represented as moving from southern Babylonia—from Ur of the Chaldees—at an advanced age, after one of his sons had died. Since it is expected that the sons would survive the father, a special note is taken of the fact that Haran, the son, dies before the father, Terah.

In leaving Ur, Terah took with him his remaining two sons, Nahor and Abram, and his grandson, Lot, the son of the dead Haran. The names of the wives of Abram and Nahor are given. It is interesting that Nahor's wife appears to be his niece, since Milcah is stated to be the daughter of Haran. Additionally, it is noted that, at this point in the narrative, Sarai (Sarah) had borne Abram no children.

The migration of Terah and his children proceeds and terminates at a placed called, ironically, or in tribute, Haran, the same name as Terah's deceased child. This Haran was evidently an important center roughly midway between Mesopotamia and Palestine. It was in Haran that Terah died, perhaps both physically and metaphorically.

A Fundamentalist Christian Perspective

GENESIS

Genesis appropriately stands as the first book of the Old Testament and serves as an essential introduction to the whole Bible. The book's title in Hebrew is derived from the first word of the book, *bereshith* ("in the beginning"). "Genesis," the title in our English language Bibles is the Greek translation of the Hebrew title and means "the origin, source, creation, or beginning of something." Genesis is "the book of beginnings."

The author of Genesis is nowhere designated in the book itself. The testimony of the rest of the Bible, however, is that Moses was the author of the entire Pentateuch (the first five books of the Old Testament) and thus of Genesis.[388] Also, ancient Jewish writers and the early church fathers unanimously testify that Moses was the author/editor of Genesis. Finally, from the fundamentalist Christian perspective, it is important to note that Jesus refers to Moses as an author of Scripture {see Luke 16:31 and 24:44 and John 5:46, 47}.

Insofar as the entire history of Genesis predates Moses' life, his role in writing Genesis was largely to integrate, under the inspiration of the Holy Spirit, all the available written and oral records from Adam to the death of Joseph that are now preserved in Genesis. Perhaps an indication of the historical records used by Moses when writing Genesis is found in the eleven occurrences of the phrase, "these are the generations of" (in Hebrew, *'elleh toledoth*), which also may be translated as "these are the histories by."[389]

From a Fundamentalist Christian perspective, Genesis accurately records creation, the beginnings of human history, and the origin of the Hebrew people and God's covenant with them through Abraham and the other patriarchs. The historical reliability of Genesis as inspired Scripture is certified in the New Testament by Jesus[390] and by the apostles.[391] Additionally, Moses was remarkably prepared by education {see Acts 7:22} and by God to write this unique first book of the Bible.

[388]See 1 Kings 2:3; 2 Kings 14:6; Ezra 6:18; Nehemiah 13:1; Daniel 9:11–13; Malachi 4:4; Mark 12:26; Luke 16:29, 31; John 7:19–23; Acts 26:22; 1 Corinthians 9:9; and 2 Corinthians 3:15.}

[389]See Genesis 2:4; 5:1; 6:9; 10:1; 11:10,27; 25:12,19; 36:1, 9; and 37:2.

[390]See Matthew 19:4–6; 24:37–39; Luke 11:51; 17:26–32; John 7:21–23; and 8:56–58.

[391]See Romans 4; 1 Corinthians 15:21–22; 45–47; 2 Corinthians 11:3; Galatians 3:8; 4:22–24, 28; 1 Timothy 2:13–14; Hebrews 11:4–22; 2 Peter 3:4–6; and Jude 7, 11.

Genesis provides an essential foundation for the remainder of the Pentateuch and all subsequent Biblical revelation. From a fundamentalist Christian perspective, it preserves the only trustworthy record about the beginnings of the universe, humankind, marriage, sin, cities, languages, nations, Israel, and redemptive history. It was written in accordance with God's purpose to give God's covenant people in both the Old Testament and New Testament a foundational understanding of God, creation, the human race, the fall, death, judgment, covenant, and the promise of redemption through the seed of Abraham. {See Genesis 12:1–3, Matthew 1:17, and Galatians 3:6–9, 29.}

Genesis divides naturally into two major parts:

(A) Chapters 1–11 provide an overview of human beginnings from Adam to Abraham and focus on five epochal events

    (1) Creation {Genesis 1–2}
    God created all things, including Adam and Eve whom God placed in the Garden of Eden.

    (2) The Fall {Genesis 3}
    Adam and Eve, by their transgression, introduced the curse of sin and death into human history.

    (3) Cain and Abel {Genesis 4–5}
    This tragedy set in motion the two basic streams of history: humanistic civilization and a redemptive remnant.

    (4) The Great Flood {Genesis 6–10}
    The ancient world had become so evil by the time of Noah's generation that God destroyed it by a universal flood, sparing only righteous Noah and his family as a remnant.

    (5) Tower of Babel {Genesis 11}
    When the post-flood world unified in idolatry and rebellion, God dispersed it by fragmenting language and culture and by scattering the human race throughout the earth.

(B) Chapters 12–50 record the beginnings of the Hebrew people and focus on God's ongoing redemptive purpose through the lives of Israel's four great patriarchs—Abraham, Isaac, Jacob, and Joseph. God's call of Abraham (Chapter 12) and God's covenantal dealings with Abraham and Abraham's seed form the pivotal beginning of the outworking of God's purpose concerning a Redeemer and redemption in history. Genesis concludes with the death of Joseph and the impending bondage of Israel in Egypt.

Seven major features characterize Genesis:

(1) It was the first book of the Bible written (with the possible exception of Job) and records the beginning of human history, sin, the Hebrew people, and redemption.

(2) The history in Genesis spans a larger period of time than the rest of the Bible combined, beginning with the first human couple, broadening to pre-flood world history, and then narrowing the Hebrew history as the redemptive stream that is traced throughout the remainder of the Old Testament.

(3) Genesis reveals that the material universe and life on earth are distinctly God's work and not an independent process of nature. Fifty times in chapters 1–2 God is the subject of verbs showing what God did as Creator.

(4) Genesis is a book of firsts—recording the first marriage, first family, first birth, first sin, first murder, first polygamist, first musical instruments, first promise of redemption, and the like.

(5) The covenant of God with Abraham, which began with Abraham's call {see Genesis 12:1–3}, was made formal in chapter 15, and was ratified in chapter 17, is central to all of Scripture.

(6) Genesis alone explains the origin of the twelve tribes of Israel.

(7) Genesis reveals how the descendants of Abraham ended up in Egypt (for 430 years) and thus sets the stage for the exodus, the central redemptive event in the Old Testament.

Genesis reveals the prophetic history of redemption and a Redeemer as coming through the seed of the woman {see Genesis 3:15} through the line of Seth {see Genesis 12:3}. The New Testament applies Genesis 12:3 directly to God's provision of redemption in Jesus Christ {see Galatians 3:16, 29}. Numerous persons and events from Genesis are mentioned in the New Testament in relation to faith and righteousness {e.g., Romans 4 and Hebrews 11:1–22}, God's judgment {e.g., Luke 17:26–29, 32; 2 Peter 3:6; and Jude 7, 11} and the person of Christ {e.g., Matthew 1:1; John 8:58; and Hebrew 7}.

THE CHRONOLOGY OF GENESIS

While many fundamentalist Christians still adhere to the Ussher Chronology {see footnote 298}, some fundamentalist Christians today acknowledge that the Ussher Chronology—or the chronology that one often finds in the marginal notes of many of the older Bibles (notably the Authorized Version of King James)—is not a part of the Bible itself and is not accurate. These dissenting fundamentalist Christians note that Archbishop Ussher arrived at the date of 4004 B.C.T. by using his calculations of the years in the patriarchal genealogies in Genesis, Chapters 5 and 11. However, the dissenting fundamentalist Christians assert that a comparison of these genealogies with those in the Gospels reveals that biblical genealogies are not necessarily complete by design nor were they given to allow us to calculate the span of time between various events in the early history of man. These genealogies present certain significant names and omit others. Therefore, they cannot be used to establish the date of creation. The earliest times from which we can calculate calendar years with approximate accuracy is the time of Abraham. For the dissenting fundamentalist Christians, the age which one prescribes for the earth is extremely dependent on one's view of creation. In essence, the age of the earth is a relative quantity.

The dissenting fundamentalist Christians assert that there are five major theories on the interpretation of the six days of creation. The pictorial day theory claims that the six days mentioned in Genesis are the six days during which God revealed to Moses the events of creation. However, the Bible relates the creation as clearly, simply, and historically as it does any other events. To interpret the text in this manner requires the abandonment of all analytical principles.

The gap view claims that Genesis 1:1 describes an original creation which was followed by the fall of Satan and great judgment. Genesis 1:2 is then supposed to be a description of the re-creation or restoration that took place. However, Exodus 20:11 teaches that all the universe, including the heavens and the earth (Genesis 1:1), was created in the six day period mentioned in the first chapter of Genesis and implies that the six days of Creation were consecutive.

The intermittent day view claims that the days mentioned are literal days, but that they are separated by long periods of time. However, unless all the creative activity is limited to the literal days, this view is in direct contradiction to Exodus 20:11.

The day-age theory claims that the word *yom,* which is the Hebrew word for "day," is used to refer to periods of indefinite length, not to literal days. While this is a viable meaning of the word {see Leviticus 14:2, 9, and 10}, it is not the common meaning, nor is the meaning of the word sufficient foundation for the theory.

The literal day theory accepts the clear meaning of the text: the universe was created in six literal days. For the literal day theorist, the various attempts to join together the biblical account of creation and evolution are not supportable even by the various gap theories because the order of creation is in direct opposition to the views

of modern science (e.g., the creation of trees before light). Thus, for the literalist—the fundamentalist,—the phrase "evening and morning" indicates a literal day and the creation that is set forth in Genesis is the creation that was.

THE CREATION {GENESIS 1:1–2:3}

Chapter 1

1 In the beginning God created[392] *the heaven and the earth.*[393]

2 And the earth was[394] *without form, and void*[395]*; and darkness was upon the face of the deep. And the spirit of God moved upon the face of the waters.*

3 And God said, Let there be light[396]*: and there was light.*

---

[392]The opening phrase of Genesis "In the beginning God created" is emphatic and draws attention to the fact of an auspicious beginning. Many other ancient religions, when speaking of creation, indicate that creation came about out of something that was already there. Some of these religions see history as occurring forever in cycles. In contrast, the Bible looks at history in a linear way, with a God given goal. From the fundamentalist Christian perspective, God had a plan in creation and God will carry it out.

Several implications flow from the truth contained in the first verse of the Bible. First, since God is the source of all that exists, human beings and nature are not self-existent, but rather owe their being and continuance to God. Secondly, all existence and life is good if it is related rightly to God and dependent upon God. Thirdly, all life and creation can be eternally meaningful and purposeful. And fourthly, God has sovereign rights over all creation by virtue of being its Creator. In a fallen world, God lays claim to those rights through redemption.

[393]God, by God's own free will and by God's absolute power called the universe into being, creating it out of nothing. When one acknowledges the absolute power of God, one must accept God's power to create and destroy as stated in the Scriptures. There are many concepts such as this in Scripture which the finite mind cannot completely grasp. The believer must accept those things by faith.

[394]The Old Scofield Bible maintains that the condition of the earth in Genesis 1:2 is the result of judgment, and therefore interprets the Hebrew verb *hayah* ("was") as "became." However, the Hebrew construction of Genesis 1:2 is disjunctive, describing the result of the creation described in verse one.

[395]Genesis 1:2 describes not only the process God used in creating but also the role of the Holy Spirit in creation. It is interesting to note that the phrase "without form and void" is often misunderstood because of the rendering in Genesis 1:2. These words are found only in a few other places. {See Isaiah 34:11 and 45:18 and Jeremiah 4:23.} These words do not describe chaos, but rather emptiness. A better translation might be "unformed and unfilled."

[396]The Hebrew word for "light" is *'or* which refers to the initial waves of light energy coming upon the earth. Later God placed "lights" (Hebrew *ma'or*—the "lightbearers") in the

4 And God saw the light, that it was good: and God divided the light from the darkness.

5 And God called the light Day, and the darkness he called Night. And the evening and the morning were the first day.[397]

6 And God said, Let there be a firmament in the midst of the waters, and let it divide the waters from the waters.

7 And God made the firmament, and divided the waters which were under the firmament from the waters which were above the firmament[398]*: and it was so.*

8 And God called the firmament Heaven. And the evening and the morning were the second day.

9 And God said, Let the waters under the heaven be gathered together unto one place, and let the dry land appear: and it was so.

10 And God called the dry land Earth; and the gathering together of the waters called he Seas: and God saw that it was good.[399]

11 And God said, Let the earth bring forth grass, the herb yielding seed, and the fruit tree yielding fruit after his kind, whose seed is in itself, upon the earth: and it was so.

12 And the earth brought forth grass, and herb yielding seed after his kind, and the tree yielding fruit, whose seed was in itself, after his kind: and God saw that it was good.

13 And the evening and the morning were the third day.

14 And God said, Let there be lights in the firmament of the heaven to divide the day from the night; and let them be for signs,[400] *and for seasons, and for days, and years:*

15 And let them be for lights in the firmament of the heaven to give light upon the earth: and it was so.

16 And God made two great lights; the greater light to rule the day, and the lesser light to rule the night: he made the stars also.

17 And God set them in the firmament of the heaven to give light upon the earth.

18 And to rule over the day and over the

---

heavens as permanent generators and reflectors of light waves. {See Genesis 1:14.} The primary purpose of these light-bearers was to serve for signs and seasons, and to mark days and years.

[397]The phrase "And the evening and the morning were the day" is repeated six times in Genesis, Chapter 1. {See Genesis 1:5, 8, 13, 19, 23, and 31.} The Hebrew word for day is *yom*. The word *yom* normally means a twenty-four hour day, or the daylight portion of the twenty-four hours ("day" as distinct from "night"). However, it also can refer to a time period of undetermined length (e.g., a "time of harvest" {see Proverbs 25:13}). It is interesting to note that Genesis 2:4 appears to lump all six creation days together as "the day." Many fundamentalist Christians believe that the creation days were twenty-four hour days because they are described as consisting of an "evening" and a "morning." Other fundamentalists believe the "evening" and "morning" simply mean that a particular evening brought an end to that step of creation and the next morning brought a new beginning.

[398]The "firmament" refers to the atmosphere between the water on earth and the clouds above.

[399]Seven times God states that what God created was "good." {See Genesis 1:4, 10, 12, 18, 21, 25, and 31.} Each part of God's creation completely fulfilled God's will and intended purpose. God created the world to reflect God's glory and to be a place where humankind could share in God's joy and love.

[400]From a fundamentalist perspective, God intended that the sun, moon, and stars serve as signs that point to God as well as mark the advancing days, seasons, and years. Astrology has twisted these intended purposes for the stars by proposing instead the false theory that the stars and planets guide the lives of people.

night, and to divide the light from the darkness: and God saw that it was good.

19 And the evening and the morning were the fourth day.

20 And God said, Let the waters bring forth abundantly the moving creature that hath life, and fowl that may fly above the earth in the open firmament of heaven.

21 And God created great whales, and every living creature that moveth, which the waters brought forth abundantly, after their kind, and every winged fowl after his kind: and God saw that it was good.

22 And God blessed them,[401] *saying, Be fruitful, and multiply, and fill the waters in the seas, and let fowl multiply in the earth.*

23 And the evening and the morning were the fifth day.

24 And God said, Let the earth bring forth the living creature after his kind, cattle, and creeping thing, and beast of the earth after his kind: and it was so.

25 And God made the beast of the earth after his kind, and cattle after their kind, and every thing that creepeth upon the earth after his kind: and God saw that it was good.

26 And God said, Let us[402] *make man in*

---

[401]God blessed living creatures and declared nature and animals good. God delighted in that which had been created and valued it for itself. Likewise, the fundamentalist believer should regard nature and its beauty and animals as good, something to be enjoyed, and of immense value. Although nature is now marred by sin, it still has great value as an expression of God's glory and love for humankind. Fundamentalist believers should pray for the complete liberation of creation from its bondage to sin and decay.

[402]The expression "let us" is an early implication of the triune God. The use of the plural "us" suggests that God has a certain plurality. Revelation of the tri-unity of God does not become clear, however, until the New Testament. {See Matthew 3:17.}

Questions concerning the triune nature of God have long existed. Some Scriptures imply that God is a singular entity {see Deuteronomy 6:4 and 32:39; Isaiah 45:5 and 6; John 17:3 and 1 Corinthians 8:6}. Other Scripture suggest that God is a plural entity {see Genesis 3.22, 11:7 and 18:1–3; Isaiah 6:8 and 48:16; John 10:30 and John 17.2}. The Hebrew word for God is '*Elohim*, a plural noun. In Genesis 1:1, the word for God is used in grammatical agreement with a singular verb *bara'* ("created"). When plural pronouns are used, "Let us make man in our image after our likeness," does it denote a plural of number or the concept of excellence or majesty which may be indicated in such a way in Hebrew? Could God be speaking to the angels, the earth, or nature thus denoting God's relationship to one of these? Or is this a hint of a distinction in the divine personality? Genesis is not clear, but irrespective of the lack of biblical clarity, for fundamentalist Christians, not until Jesus came onto the scene, was the essential (internal) unity of the Godhead understood to any great extent, even though it had been previously intimated.

From a fundamentalist Christian perspective, God is essentially Spirit. Therefore, man, who is similar to God, possesses an immortal spirit. Men resemble God in certain respects without being equal with God. Man's likeness to God is what truly distinguishes him from the rest of creation. Man is a personal being with the power to think, feel, and decide. Man has the ability to make moral choices and the capacity for spiritual growth or decline. In the beginning, man loved God and was a holy creature. The Fall changed this. Man's spirit was so altered by sin that he fled from God and now loves evil more than righteousness. After Adam's time, only those who lived uprightly before God were considered to be God's offspring. Man is no longer in the perfect state of innocence as at the time of his creation. Therefore, man does not have the same spiritual, God-like attributes and qualities of that original state. Jesus, the second Adam, came to undo Satan's works and to restore a spiritual likeness to God.

our image, after our likeness: and let them have dominion over the fish of the sea, and over the fowl of the air, and over the cattle, and over all the earth, and over every creeping thing that creepeth upon the earth.

27 So God created man in his own image, in the image of God created he him; male and female created he them.

28 And God blessed them, and God said unto them, Be fruitful, and multiply, and replenish the earth,[403] and subdue it: and have dominion over the fish of the sea, and over the fowl of the air, and over every living thing that moveth upon the earth.[404]

29 And God said, Behold, I have given you every herb bearing seed, which is upon the face of all the earth, and every tree, in which is the fruit of a tree yielding seed; to you it shall be for meat.

30 And to every beast of the earth, and to every fowl of the air, and to every thing that creepeth upon the earth, wherein there

---

[403]Man and woman were charged with being fruitful and with ruling over the earth and animal kingdom. From this charge, fundamentalist Christians have derived the following:

(1) Man and woman were created to form family relationships. This stated purpose of God in creation indicates that God considers a godly family and the raising of children of utmost priority in the world.
(2) God expected man and woman to consecrate all things in the earth and to manage it in a God-glorifying way, fulfilling the divine purpose.
(3) The future of the earth was placed under the dominion of man and woman. When man and woman sinned, they brought ruin, futility, and suffering to God's creation.
(4) It is the work of Jesus alone to restore the earth to its perfect place and function at Jesus' coming at the end of this age.

[404]In Genesis 1:26–28, the Bible tells of the creation of human beings. Genesis 2:4–25 gives more specific details about their creation and environment. These two accounts are complementary and teach several things. First, both man and woman were a special creation of God, not a product of evolution.

Second, man and woman were both created in the "image" and "likeness" of God. On the basis of this image, they could respond to and have fellowship with God and uniquely reflect God's love, glory, and holiness. They were to do this by knowing, and obeying, God. {See Genesis 2:15–17.}

It is important to understand that man and woman possessed a "moral" likeness to God, for they were sinless and holy, possessing wisdom, a heart of love, and the will to do right. Man and woman lived in a personal fellowship with God that involved moral obedience and intimate communion. {See Genesis 2:16–17.} When Adam and Eve sinned, their moral likeness to God was corrupted. In redemption, believers must be renewed to the original moral likeness.

Adam and Eve possessed a natural likeness to God. They were created personal beings with spirit, mind, emotions, self-consciousness, and the power of choice.

In a rather unique sense, man and woman's physical makeup is in God's image in a way not true of animals. God gave to human beings the image in which God was to appear visibly to them and the form that God's Son (Jesus) would one day assume.

A third teaching of the Genesis creation stories is that although human beings were made in the image of God, this does not mean that human beings are divine. Human beings have been created on a lower order and are dependent on God.

Finally, a fourth teaching of the Genesis creation stories is that all human life is derived initially from Adam and Eve.

is life, I have given every green herb for meat: and it was so.

31 And God saw every thing that he had made, and, behold, it was very good.[405] *And the evening and the morning were the sixth day.*

Chapter 2

1 Thus the heavens and the earth were finished, and all the host of them.

2 And on the seventh day God ended his work which he had made; and he rested on

---

[405]God is revealed in the Bible as an infinite, eternal, self-existent Being Who is the First Cause of all that is. Never was there a moment when God did not exist. God existed eternally and infinitely before creating the finite universe. God is above, independent of, and prior to all that has been created in heaven and on earth.

God is revealed as a personal Being who created Adam and Eve "in his own image." {See Genesis 1:27.} Because Adam and Eve were created in God's image, they could respond to and have fellowship with God in a loving and personal way.

God is also revealed as a moral Being Who created everything good and therefore without sin. After God had finished creating and was surveying what had been made, God observed that it was "very good." {See Genesis 1:31.} Since Adam and Eve were created in God's image and likeness, they also were initially without sin. Sin entered human existence when Eve was tempted by the serpent, or Satan. {See Genesis 3.}

God created all things in "the heaven and the earth." {See Genesis 1:1.} The Hebrew word for "created" is *bara'*. The word *bara'* is used exclusively for an activity that only God can do. It means that at a specific moment God called into existence matter and substance which had no prior existence.

The Bible describes God's creation as formless, empty, and covered with darkness. {See Genesis 1:2.} At that time the universe and the world did not have the ordered form it has now. It was empty, barren of all living creatures, and void of all light. After this initial stage, God created light to dispel the darkness {see Genesis 1:3–5}, gave form to the universe {see Genesis 1:6–13}, and filled the earth with living things {see Genesis 1:20–28}.

The method God used in creation was the power of the Word. Over and over it is stated, "And God said …" {See Genesis 1:3, 6, 9, 11, 14, 20, 24 and 26.} Quite literally, God spoke the heavens and earth into being. Before God's creative Word went forth, they had no prior existence.

From a fundamentalist Christian perspective, the entire Trinity, not just God the Father, had a role in creation. Jesus, the Son of God, himself is the powerful Word through whom God created all things. In the prologue to John's Gospel, Jesus is revealed as the eternal Word of God. {See John 1:1.} "All things were made by him; and without him was not any thing made that was made" {see John 1:3}. Likewise, the apostle Paul affirms that by Jesus "were all things created, that are in heaven, and that are in earth, visible and invisible .. all things were created by him, and for him." {See Colossians 1:16.} Finally, the author of the letter to the Hebrews asserts emphatically that by Jesus, God made the worlds. {See Hebrews 1:2.}

Like Jesus, the Holy Spirit also had an active role in the work of creation. God is pictured as "moving" over the creation, preserving and preparing it for God's further creative activity. The Hebrew word for "Spirit" (*ruah*) may also be translated as "wind" and "breath." Thus, the psalmist affirms the role of the Holy Spirit when the psalmist states: "By the word of the Lord were the heavens made; and all the host of them by the breath (*ruah*) of his mouth." {See Psalms 33:6.}

God had specific reasons for creating the world. First, God created the heavens and the earth as a manifestation of God's glory, majesty, and power. By looking at the entire created cosmos—from the immense expanse of the created universe to the beauty and order of nature—we cannot help but stand in awe of the majesty of the Lord God, our Creator.

Secondly, God created the heavens and the earth in order to receive back the glory and honor that God was due. All the elements of nature—e.g., sun and moon, trees of the forest, rain and snow, rivers and streams, hills and mountains, animals and birds—shout out praise to the God who made them. How much more God desires and expects to receive glory and praise from human beings!

Thirdly, God created the earth in order to provide a place where God's purpose and goals for humankind might be fulfilled. God created Adam and Eve in God's own image so that God could have a loving, personal relationship for all eternity. God designed humankind as a triune being (body, soul, and spirit), possessing mind, emotion, and will with which they can respond to God freely as Lord and worship and serve God out of faith, loyalty, and gratitude. God so desired this intimate relationship with the human race that, when Satan succeeded in tempting Adam and Eve to rebel against and disobey God's command, God promised to send a Savior to redeem humankind from sin's consequences. In this way, God would have a people for God's own possession who would enjoy God, glorify God, and live in righteousness and holiness before God. The culmination of God's purpose in creation is recorded in the book of Revelation, where John describes the end of history with these words: "He will dwell with them, and they shall be his people, and God himself shall be with them, and be their God." {See Revelation 21:3.}

Evolution is the predominant view regarding the origin of life and the universe proposed in the scientific and educational community of the contemporary world. Bible believing—fundamentalist—Christians should consider these four observations about evolution. First, from a fundamentalist Christian perspective, evolution is a naturalistic effort to account for the origin and development of the universe. This view begins with the assumption that there is no personal, divine Creator who made and fashioned the world; but rather, everything came into existence by a series of chance happenings that occurred over billions of years.

Secondly, the teaching of evolution is not truly scientific. According to the scientific method, all conclusions must be based on indisputable evidence gathered from experiments that can be duplicated in any laboratory. However, no experiments have been or can be devised to test and substantiate theories about the origin of matter from their simplest to their most complex form. Consequently, evolution is a hypothesis without scientific "evidence." Therefore, to accept it one must have faith in a human theory. The faith of God's people, in contrast, is in the Lord and in God's inspired revelation, which states that God is the one who made all things out of nothing. {See Hebrews 11:3.}

Thirdly, it is undeniable that change and development within various species of living things occur. For example, some varieties of species are becoming extinct; on the other hand, we occasionally see new strains forming within species. However, there is no evidence, not even in the geologic record, which supports the theory that one "kind" of living thing ever evolved from another "kind." Rather, existing evidence supports the Bible's declaration that God created each living creature "after his kind." {See Genesis 1:21, 24–25.}

Finally, Bible-believing—fundamentalist—Christians must also reject the theory of theistic evolution. This theory adopts most of the conclusions of naturalistic evolution, adding only that God started the evolutionary process. Such a theory denies the Biblical revelation that ascribes to God an active role in all aspects of creation. For example, every main verb in Genesis, Chapter 1, has God as its subject, except for Genesis 1:12 (which fulfills the command of God in verse 11) and the recurring phrase "there was evening and there was morning." God is not a passive supervisor of an evolutionary process; rather, God is the active Creator of all things.

the seventh day from all his work which he had made.[406]

3 And God blessed the seventh day,[407] *and sanctified it: because that in it he had rested from all his work which God created and made.*

ADAM AND EVE {GENESIS 2:4–25}[408]

4 These are the generations of the heavens and of the earth when they were created, in the day that the Lord God[409] *made the earth and the heavens,*

---

[406]According to the Book of Genesis, God created the world and all that is in it in six days. Then God declared it all to be "very good." The Creator rested on the seventh day.

While there were other "creation stories" among the pagan nations of the ancient world, the biblical account is unique in that God existed before creation and called the physical world into being from nothing. These pagan nations, particularly the Babylonians, believed the material universe was eternal and that it brought their gods into being. However, Genesis describes a God who is clearly superior to the physical world.

God began organizing a shapeless and barren earth, providing light, and separating land from water. The creation of plant and animal life followed, including creatures of the sea, air, and land. Man and woman were created on the sixth day, before the Creator's Sabbath rest.

Scholars disagree about the length of the creation "days." Some believe that these days were actually twenty-four hour days, while others believe they were periods of undetermined length. Regardless of the length of these days, the biblical writer is declaring that God created the world in orderly fashion as part of a master plan. The world did not just evolve on its own or by accident.

The "gap" theory, advanced to reconcile the biblical account of creation with geology, holds that creation in Genesis 1:1 was followed by catastrophe, then succeeded by God's re-creation or reshaping of the physical world. But this theory reduces God to a weak being with little control over that which had been created. The all-powerful God who created the world also presides over its destiny.

Man and woman are the crowning achievements of God's creative work. As free moral beings who bear the image of God, they were assigned dominion over the natural world. They alone among the living creatures of the world are equipped for fellowship with their Creator.

[407]God blessed the seventh day (i.e., Sabbath) and designated it both as a sacred and special day of rest and as a memorial to the completion of all God's created work. God later made the Sabbath a day of blessing for God's faithful people. God designed it as a day of rest, service, and communion with God.

[408]It is well known that there seem to be two different accounts of creation in the first two chapters of Genesis, but this need not cause us to conclude that they are incompatible, as some have suggested. The two sections actually complement each other. Genesis 1:1–2:3 presents a wide-angle view of all seven days of creation and deals with the creation of man and woman as a single act. Then in Genesis 2:4–2:24 the author focuses on the sixth day, giving details which were not mentioned in the overview in chapter one. The separate origins of man and woman are brought into sharp focus. Therefore, chapters one and two are not in chronological sequence.

The second account of creation contained in Genesis 2:4–25 is not contradictory to the first account which is contained in Genesis 1:1–2:3. The second account just explains in greater detail the creation of man and woman, their environment, and their probation. The second account of creation gives details in a topical fashion while the first account concentrates on telling the creation story in chronological order.

[409]Another name for God is introduced in Genesis 2:4, the name "Lord" (Hebrew *YHWH* or *Yahweh* or *Jehovah*). Whereas *Elohim* is the general name for God, emphasizing God's

5 And every plant of the field before it was in the earth, and every herb of the field before it grew: for the Lord God had not caused it to rain upon the earth, and there was not a man to till the ground.

6 But there went up a mist from the earth, and watered the whole face of the ground.

7 And the Lord God formed man of the dust of the ground, and breathed into his nostrils the breath of life; and man became a living soul.[410]

8 And the Lord God planted a garden eastward in Eden[411]; and there he put the man whom he had formed.[412]

9 And out of the ground made the Lord

---

greatness and power, "Lord" is the personal and covenant name by which God is revealed to God's people. Inherent in the revelation of God's covenant name is God's loving kindness. God's redemptive concern for the human race, and God's nearness to and faithful presence with God's people. This personal name is used in situations where God is seen in direct relationship to God's people or nature. Where the words "Lord God" are coupled together, it points to God as the all-powerful Creator who has entered into a caring covenant relationship with humankind.

[410]The term "soul" has been used in a variety of senses by different writers in the Bible. The Old Testament Hebrew word is *nephesh* which means "that which breathes." It corresponds to the Greek word *psuche* in the New Testament, which is usually translated "soul" or "life." The term "living soul" does not refer to Adam's spirit as immortal, but simply to the fact that he was a living, physical being. The same term is used in Genesis 1:20, 21 with reference to flying and swimming creatures. It merely signifies that Adam became alive; it denies the possibility of theistic evolution (the soul being breathed into a living animal form).

The giving of life to human beings is described as the result of a special act of God in distinction from the creation of all other living things. God specifically imparted life and breath to the first man, indicating that human life stands higher and in a different category from all other forms of life and that there is a unique relationship of divine life to human life. God, after all, is the ultimate source of human life.

[411]The Garden of Eden was located near the Tigris (called Hiddekel in this version of Genesis) and Euphrates flood plain. Some believe that the Garden of Eden was located in what is now known as southern Iraq. Others maintain that there is not sufficient data given in the Biblical account to determine a specific location.

[412]The Garden of Eden was the first home of Adam and Eve, the first man and woman. Eden is a translation of a Hebrew word which means "Delight," suggesting a "Garden of Delight." The garden contained many beautiful and fruitbearing trees, including the "tree of life" and the "tree of the knowledge of good and evil."

Pinpointing the exact location of the Garden of Eden is difficult, although the best theory places it near the source of the Tigris and Euphrates rivers in the Armenian highlands. A major catastrophe, perhaps the Flood of Noah's time, may have wiped out all traces of the other two rivers mentioned—the Pishon and the Havilah. However, modern space photography has produced evidence that two rivers, now dry beds, could have flowed through the area centuries ago.

God commanded Adam and Eve not to eat of the tree of the knowledge of good and evil. They fell from their original state of innocence when Satan approached Eve through the serpent and tempted her to eat of the forbidden fruit. She ate the fruit and also gave it to her husband to eat. Their disobedience plunged them and all of the human race into a state of sin and corruption.

Because of their unbelief and rebellion, they were driven from the garden. Other consequences of their sin were loss of their innocence, pain in childbearing and submission of the

God to grow every tree that is pleasant to the sight, and good for food; the tree of life[413] also in the midst of the garden, and the tree of knowledge of good and evil.

10 And a river went out of Eden to water the garden; and from thence it was parted, and became into four heads.

11 The name of the first is Pison: that is it which compasseth the whole land of Havilah, where there is gold;

12 And the gold of that land is good: there is bdellium and the onyx stone.

13 And the name of the second river is Gihon: the same is that compasseth the whole land of Ethiopia.

14 And the name of the third river is Hiddekel: that is it which goeth toward the east of Assyria. And the fourth river is Euphrates.

15 And the Lord God took the man, and put him into the garden of Eden[414] to dress it and to keep it.[415]

16 And the Lord God commanded the man,[416] saying, Of every tree of the garden thou mayest freely eat:

17 But of the tree of the knowledge of

---

wife to her husband, the cursing of the ground and the resultant hard labor for man, and separation from God.

The apostle Paul thought of Jesus as the Second Adam who would save the old sinful Adam through God's plan of redemption and salvation. *As in Adam all die, even so in Christ all shall be made alive.* {See 1 Corinthians 15:22.}

[413]Two trees in the Garden of Eden had special importance. First, the "tree of life" was probably intended to make physical death impossible. Fundamentalist Christians believe that God's people will have access to the tree of life in the new heaven and new earth. The second tree was the "tree of knowledge of good and evil." This tree was apparently designed to test Adam's faith and his obedience to God and God's Word. God created humans as moral beings with the ability to choose freely to love and obey their Creator, or to disobey God and rebel against God's Will.

[414]Fundamentalist Christians believe that, at this time, Adam, as the first man, was holy, free from sin, and in perfect communion with God. Adam was the pinnacle of God's creation and was given the responsibility of working under the direction of God in caring for God's creation. This harmonious relationship between God and the human race was lost because of Adam and Eve's disobedience.

[415]Man was always meant to accomplish work, but God intended man to enjoy it. Work only became drudgery after the Fall {see Genesis 3:17–19}. Is it possible for anyone to live sinlessly as Adam did prior to the Fall? The Bible explicitly pronounces all human beings to be sinners {see Psalms 14:1–3 and Romans 3:9–23 and 5:12–15}, and cites the origin of their sin in Adam. Because of Adam's disobedience, all men are made sinners. But how is the sin of Adam imputed to the rest of mankind? Some people say that Adam's state of corruption and guilt is transmitted to his descendants. Others feel that Adam acted as the sole representative of the human race {see Romans 5:12–20 and 10:5}. The fact remains that all humans are now hopelessly lost and in need of a Savior. That is why Jesus came {see Luke 19:10}.

[416]It is a tenet of fundamental Christianity that from the very beginning of history the human race has been bound to God through belief in and obedience to God's Word as absolute truth. Life through faith and obedience is presented as the governing principle in Adam's relationship to God in Eden. Adam was warned that he would die if he transgressed God's will and partook of the tree of the knowledge of good and evil. This threat of death had to be accepted by faith based on what God said, since Adam had not yet seen human death. The command of God was given to Adam as a moral test. It placed before him a conscious, deliberate choice to believe and obey, or to disbelieve and disobey the Creator's will. As long

good and evil, thou shalt not eat of it: for in the day that thou eatest thereof thou shalt surely die.[417]

18 And the Lord God said, it is not good that the man should be alone; I will make him an help meet for him.[418]

19 And out of the ground the Lord God formed every beast of the field, and every fowl of the air; and brought them unto Adam to see what he would call them: and whatsoever Adam called every living creature, that was the name thereof.

20 And Adam gave names to all cattle, and to the fowl of the air, and to every beast of the field; but for Adam there was not found an help meet for him.

21 And the Lord God caused a deep sleep to fall upon Adam, and he slept: and he took one of his ribs, and closed up the flesh instead thereof;

22 And the rib, which the Lord God had taken from man, made he a woman, and brought her unto the man.

23 And Adam said, This is now bone of my bones, and flesh of my flesh: she shall be called Woman, because she was taken out of Man.

24 Therefore shall a man leave his father and his mother,[419] and shall cleave unto his wife: and they shall be one flesh.[420]

25 And they were both naked, the man and his wife, and were not ashamed[421, 422]

THE FALL OF MAN
{GENESIS 3:1–24}

as Adam believed God's word and obeyed, he would continue in eternal life and in blessed fellowship with God. If he sinned by disobeying, he would reap moral disaster and a harvest of death.

[417]Verses 15 through 17 of Genesis, Chapter 2, contains what fundamentalist Christians call the Edenic Covenant. The covenant in Eden is the first of the general or universal covenants. In it, Adam is charged to: (1) populate the earth; (2) subdue the earth; (3) exercise dominion over the animal creation; (4) care for the garden of Eden and enjoy its fruit; and (5) refrain from eating the fruit of the tree of the knowledge of good and evil, under penalty of death. The Edenic Covenant was terminated by man's disobedience, when Adam and Eve ate of the fruit of the tree of the knowledge of good and evil, resulting in their spiritual and physical deaths. This failure necessitated the establishment of the covenant with Adam.

[418]Woman was created to be a loving companion for man and a helper for him. As such, woman was to share his responsibility and cooperate with him in fulfilling God's purpose for his life and the life of their family.

[419]God in the beginning ordained marriage and the family unit as the first and most important institution on earth. God's plan for marriage consists of one male and one female who become "one flesh." This instruction excludes adultery, polygamy, homosexuality, immoral living, and unscriptural divorce.

[420]Monogamy for a lifetime was and is God's original plan. Jesus re-emphasizes this principle in Matthew 19:3–9.

[421]There was no shame before sin entered into the world. Only after Adam and Eve sinned did they become self-conscious of their naked bodies. God intends for intimate, sexual joys to be fulfilled only within the bonds of marriage, and there without shame {see Hebrews 13:4}.

[422]Verses 18 through 25 of Genesis, Chapter 2 fill in the details which surrounds the simple statement in Genesis 1:27: *Male and female He created them.*" The account in these verses particularly amplify the "and female" part of the statement and shows how woman was created. Three observations can be made on the passage that will help us to understand how the family began:

Chapter 3

1 Now the serpent[423] *was more subtle than any beast of the field which the Lord God had made. And he said unto the woman, Yea, hath God said, Ye shall not eat of every tree of the garden?*[424]

2 And the woman said unto the serpent, We may eat of the fruit of the trees of the garden:

3 But of the fruit of the tree which is in the midst of the garden, God hath said, Ye shall not eat of it, neither shall ye touch it, lest ye die.

4 And the serpent said unto the woman, Ye shall not surely die[425]:

(1) There was a need for the woman. The woman of Genesis, Chapter 2, is absolutely essential in God's plan. It was God who observed, *It is not good that man should be alone,* and determined to make a "helper" for Adam. Woman's role in the will of God was to be a "helper" who was suitable to man in every particular mental, spiritual, emotional, social, and physical need. God undertook an orientation program to show man the need that God alone had observed. God brought to man the birds and beasts God had created, so that man should exercise his dominion over them and name them. However, in verse 20, it is noted that for Adam there was no "helper" similar to himself.

(2) The provision of the woman was for the man. God caused Adam to go to sleep, and God removed one of Adam's "ribs." Exactly what God removed is not known, but it was adequate for God's purpose. God made a woman whom Adam recognized as being his equal, as being "bone of my bones and flesh of my flesh." This resulted in what has become known as the universal law of marriage in which it can be seen that (a) the responsibility for marriage is on the man's shoulders; (b) the responsibility for keeping the union together is on the man's shoulders; and (c) the union is indissoluble—the man and woman shall become one.

(3) The initial state of the first man and woman was a natural state. From the beginning, the man and the woman were "naked" in each other's presence and "were not ashamed." There is no shame in nudity when it occurs within the right context—within the context of the marital union. Genesis 2:25 clearly teaches that (a) sex was God's idea and is not sinful; (b) sex came before the Fall, and if the Fall had never taken place there still would be sexual relations between a man and his wife; and (c) the propagation of the species is one, but not the exclusive, purpose for sex. The Bible gives two other reasons for sex: (a) to promote love between the husband and wife {see Hebrews 13:4} and (b) to prevent fornication—the unlawful satisfaction of the God-given sexual desire {see 1 Corinthians 7:2}.

[423]In the story of the temptation, the serpent attacks God through God's great creation. The serpent stated that what God had said to Adam was not true; he ultimately caused God to curse God's creation, including the human race whom God had made in God's image. The "serpent" is later identified with Satan or the devil. Satan evidently took control of the serpent and used it as an instrument in his work of temptation.

[424]Satan's temptation of Eve begins by planting the seed of doubt, "Yea, hath God said ..?" Notice how Satan negatively restates the prohibition that God made in Genesis 2:16 and 2:17. And Eve belies her desire for the fruit and her hatred of God's command by adding the phrase "neither shall ye touch it" to God's prohibition.

[425]Satan did not attempt to explain why "Ye shall not surely die," he merely affirmed it! He said it so convincingly that Eve believed it. Then the serpent went on to slander God's motives. He claimed God was keeping something from them. Once Eve "accepted" these assumptions, her desire for the fruit grew until she took of the tree and ate.

5 For God doth know that in the day ye eat thereof, then your eyes shall be opened, and ye shall be as gods,[426] *knowing good and evil.*

6 And when the woman saw that the tree was good for food, and that it was pleasant to the eyes, and a tree to be desired to make one wise, she took of the fruit[427] *thereof, and did eat, and gave also unto her husband with her*[428]*; and he did eat.*

7 And the eyes of them both were opened, and they knew that they were naked[429]*; and they sewed fig leaves together, and made themselves aprons.*[430]

The human race is bound to God by faith in God's word as absolute truth. Because Satan knew this, he sought to destroy the woman's faith in what God had said by raising doubts about that word. Satan suggested that God did not really mean what God said. In other words, the first lie proposed by Satan was a form of denial—denying the judgment of death for sin and apostasy. One of the basic sins of humankind is unbelief in God's word. It is believing that somehow God does not really mean what God says about salvation, righteousness, sin, judgment, and death. Satan's most persistent lie is that unrepentant, deliberate sin and rebellion against God will not necessarily bring separation from God and eternal condemnation.

[426]Fundamentalist Christians believe that Satan, from the beginning of the human race, has tempted humans to believe that they can be like God and decide for themselves what is good and what is evil. Humanity, in seeking to be "as gods," became independent from God Almighty and as such became false gods. Humans now seek to derive moral knowledge and ethical discernment from their own minds and desire independence from God's word. Nevertheless, only God has the right to determine what is good and evil. The Scripture declares that all who seek to be gods "shall perish from the earth, and from under these heavens." This will likewise be the fate of the anti-christ, who will claim "that he is God."

[427]The idea that the fruit mentioned in this passage was an apple could have come from the similarity of the Latin words *malam* ("apple") and *malum* ("evil"). Whatever the fruit was, eating it was a clear violation of the divine prohibition. The seriousness of the offense lies in Adam and Eve's deliberate, willful rejection of God's explicit command.

[428]When Adam and Eve sinned, moral and spiritual death came immediately, while physical death came later. God had said, "In the day that thou eatest thereof thou shalt surely die." Thus, spiritual and moral death occurred at once when they sinned. Moral death consisted of the death of God's life in the man and woman and their nature becoming sinful; spiritual death meant that their former relationship to God was destroyed. Since the sin of Adam and Eve, every person born comes into the world with a sinful nature. This corruption of human nature involves the innate desire to go one's own selfish way without concern for God or others, and is passed on to all human beings. It should be noted, however, that nowhere does Scripture teach that all sinned when Adam sinned, or that his guilt was imputed to the whole human race. The Bible does teach that Adam introduced the law of sin and death to the whole human race.

[429]When Adam and Eve lived in moral innocence, nakedness was not wrong nor did it bring a feeling of shame. However, after they sinned, the awareness of nakedness became associated with sin and the fallen and depraved condition of humankind. Because of the evil that nakedness would cause in the world, God made garments and clothed Adam and Eve, and now God commands all people to dress discreetly and modestly.

[430]Adam's sin does not seem to be a very great sin from man's perspective. All Adam did was take a bite of some fruit. However, Adam's sin was serious because the fruit that he ate was fruit from the tree of knowledge of good and evil, and God had said that Adam was not to

8 And they heard the voice of the Lord God walking in the garden in the cool of the day: and Adam and his wife hid themselves[431] from the presence of the Lord God[432] amongst the trees of the garden.

9 And the Lord God called unto Adam, and said unto him, Where art thou?

10 And he said, I heard thy voice in the garden, and I was afraid, because I was naked; and I hid myself.

11 And he said, Who told thee that thou wast naked? Hast thou eaten of the tree, whereof I commanded them that thou shouldest not eat?

12 And the man said, The woman whom thou gavest to be with me, she gave me of the tree, and I did eat.

13 And the Lord God said unto the woman, What is this that thou hast done? And the woman said, The serpent beguiled me,[433] and I did eat.

14 And the Lord God said unto the serpent, Because thou hast done this, thou are cursed above all cattle, and above every beast of the field; upon thy belly shalt thou go, and dust shalt thou eat all the days of thy life.

15 And I will put enmity between thee and the woman, and between thy seed and

---

eat from the tree under penalty of death. Up to this time Adam was morally innocent. When he sinned, he, by nature, became a sinner. As such, Adam died. He died spiritually immediately and began to die physically. Adam was the first man ever to live upon the face of the earth. From Adam and Eve come every other human being who ever has lived upon the face of the earth. Thus, Adam is the "federal head" from whom every other man came. Like begets like. Apples begat apples. Dogs begat dogs. Human beings begat human beings. Since Adam became a sinner before Eve conceived a child, every human being descended from Adam is a sinner just like him except, of course, Jesus. Because of Adam's sin, death entered into the human race and now every human being needs to have a new life—to be born again.

[431]The guilt and consciousness of sin caused Adam and Eve to shun God. Adam and Eve felt afraid and uncomfortable in God's presence, knowing that they were sinful and under God's displeasure. In this condition, they found it impossible to draw near to God with confidence. In our sinful condition, we too are like Adam and Eve. However, God has provided us a way to cleanse our guilty conscience, free us from sin, and restore us to divine fellowship. The "way" is called Jesus. Through the redemption God provided in Jesus, we can draw near to God in order to receive God's love, mercy, grace, and help in time of need.

[432]In this instance, the presence of God from which Adam and Eve fled was the visible and special manifestation to them at that time. These manifestations are called "theophanies,"—appearances of God in human form. Theophanies are instances where God became man to relate to human weaknesses so that he might communicate with man in a more personal way. However, God is not a man, and God does not look like man or think like man. God is a personal being who seeks to fellowship with man, like a loving parent.

[433]From a fundamentalist Christian perspective, Satan caused the downfall of the human race through deception. This is one of Satan's chief methods for leading people away from God's way and truth. For fundamentalist Christians, the Bible teaches that Satan deceives and blinds the minds of the unbelieving of this world in order that they may not understand the gospel. According to Paul, it is through Satan's deception that some within the church will believe they can live immoral lives and still inherit the kingdom of God. Deception will be Satan's chief means of leading many into rebellion against God at history's end. All Christians must be prepared for, and committed to, a continuous life-and-death struggle against the deception of Satan as it relates to their personal lives, marriages, families, schools, churches, and work.

her seed; it shall bruise thy head, and thou shalt bruise his heel.[434]

16 Unto the woman he said, I will greatly multiply thy sorrow[435] *and thy conception; in sorrow thou shalt bring forth children; and thy desire shall be to thy husband, and he shall rule over thee.*

17 And unto Adam he said, Because thou hast hearkened unto the voice of thy wife, and hast eaten of the tree, of which I commanded thee, saying, Thou shalt not eat of it: cursed is the ground for thy sake: in sorrow shalt thou eat of it all the days of thy life:

18 Thorns also and thistles shall it bring forth to thee; and thou shalt eat the herb of the field;

19 In the sweat of thy face shalt thou eat bread, till thou return unto the ground, for out of it wast thou taken: for dust thou art, and unto dust shalt thou return.[436]

---

[434]Genesis 3:15 contains the first implicit promise of God's plan of redemption for the world. It predicts the ultimate victory for humankind and God over Satan and evil by prophesying of a spiritual conflict between the "seed" of the woman (i.e., the Lord Jesus Christ) and the "seed" of the serpent (i.e., Satan and his followers). God promised here that Jesus would be born of a woman and would be "bruised" through Jesus' crucifixion. Yet, Jesus would rise from the dead to completely destroy (i.e., to "bruise") Satan, sin and death for the sake of the salvation of the human race.

[435]The punishment placed upon man and woman, as well as the effect of sin upon nature, were meant to remind humankind of the terrible consequences of sin and cause them to depend upon God in faith and obedience. God intended the present condition of the human race on earth to be redemptive. Eve's attempt to liberate herself from God and act independently from her husband would be counteracted by a strong desire for her husband. Her deep attraction towards Adam and his headship over her would bring trouble and suffering along with joy and blessing. Because of God's curse upon nature, Adam and Eve would experience physical hardships, toil, struggle, and eventually death for themselves and all their offspring.

[436]The covenant with Adam that is set forth in Genesis 3:14–19 is the second general or universal covenant and is known as the Adamic Covenant. This covenant could also be called the covenant with mankind, for it sets forth the conditions which will hold sway until the curse of sin is lifted. According to the covenant, the conditions which will prevail are:

(1) The serpent, the tool used by Satan to effect the fall of man, is cursed. The curse affects not only the instrument, the serpent, but also the in-dwelling energizer, Satan. Great physical changes took place in the serpent. Apparently, it was, at first, upright; but after the curse it was consigned to move about on its belly (verse 14). Originally, the serpent was the most desirable animal of the animal creation; now it is the most loathsome. The sight or thought of a snake should be an effective reminder of the devastating effects of sin.

(2) Satan is judged—he will enjoy limited success ("you shall bruise his heel"), but ultimately he will be judged ("He shall bruise your head") (verse 15).

(3) The first prophecy of the coming Messiah is given (verse 15).

(4) There will be a multiplication of conception, necessitated by the introduction of death into the human race (verse 16).

(5) There will be pain in childbirth (verse 16).

(6) The woman is made subject to her husband (verse 16).

(7) The ground is cursed and will bring forth weeds among the food which man must eat for his existence (verses 17–19).

(8) Physical change takes place in man; he will perspire when he works. He will have to work all his life long (verse 19).

20 And Adam called his wife's name Eve[437]; because she was the mother of all living.

21 Unto Adam also and to his wife did the Lord God make coats of skins, and clothed them.

22 And the Lord God said, Behold, the man is become as one of us, to know good and evil[438]: and now, lest he put forth his hand, and take also of the tree of life, and eat, and live for ever:

23 Therefore the Lord God sent him forth from the garden of Eden, to till the ground from whence he was taken.

24 So he drove out the man[439]; and he placed at the east of the garden of Eden Cherubims, and a flaming sword which turned every way, to keep the way of the tree of life.

CAIN AND ABEL
{GENESIS 4:1–26}

Chapter 4

1 And Adam knew Eve his wife[440]; and she conceived, and bare Cain, and said, I have gotten a man from the Lord.

2 And she again bare his brother Abel.[441] And Abel was a keeper of sheep, but Cain was a tiller of the ground.

3 And in process of time it came to pass, that Cain brought of the fruit of the ground an offering unto the Lord.[442]

4 And Abel, he also brought of the

---

(9) In sinning, man dies spiritually, and ultimately will die physically. Man's flesh will decay until it returns to the dust from which it was originally taken (verse 19).

[437]Adam called his wife "Eve," meaning "life," because she was the first mother of all humanity of all generations. The name "Eve" (in Hebrew *chawwah*) means "life." The fact that "Eve" is a Hebrew name does not mean that Hebrew was the original language. As thoughts were conveyed from one language to another, proper nouns were adjusted to carry their original meaning.

[438]Adam and Eve had attempted to set themselves up as God's equal and to determine their own standards. Through their fall, human beings became to some extent independent of God and began to distinguish for themselves between good and evil. In this world, imperfect and perverted human judgment often decides what is good or evil. This was never God's will, for God intended us to know only good in dependence on God and God's word. All who confess Jesus as Lord return to God's original purpose for humankind. They rely on God's word to determine what is good.

[439]Adam's perfect relationship to God had been lost. He was now driven from the garden, and a life of dependence on God in the midst of trials began. In addition, Satan in some sense gained power over the world through the fall of Adam and Eve, for the New Testament speaks of Satan as being "the prince of this world." {See John 14:30.} However, God so loved the human race that God determined to conquer Satan by reconciling them and the world to God at the cost of the life of Jesus, who Christians believe to have been the Son of God.

[440]The Hebrew word *yada'* indicates the most intimate relationship between a man and a woman, the sexual bond. Its basic meaning is "to know," but it could be translated "and Adam experienced Eve." The word "knew" is commonly used in the Bible for marital and sexual intimacy. It should be noted that when Eve gave birth to her son, she gave sincere praise to the Lord for the child. Eve was seeking to be rightly related to God in thankfulness for God's love, forgiveness, and help.

[441]Cain and Abel may have been twins since Eve's conception is only mentioned once.

[442]The Lord accepted the offering of Abel because he came before God in true faith and dedication to righteousness. Cain's offering was rejected because he lacked a sincerely obedient

firstlings of his flock and of the fat thereof. And the Lord had respect[443] *unto Abel and to his offering:*

5 But unto Cain and to his offering he had not respect. And Cain was very wroth, and his countenance fell.

6 And the Lord said unto Cain, Why art thou wroth? And why is thy countenance fallen?

7 If thou doest well, shalt thou not be accepted? and if thou doest not well, sin lieth at the door. And unto thee shall be his desire[444]*, and thou shalt rule over him.*

8 And Cain talked with Abel his brother[445]*: and it came to pass, when they were in the field, that Cain rose up against Abel his brother, and slew him.*

9 And the Lord said unto Cain, Where is Abel thy brother? And he said I know not: Am I my brother's keeper?

10 And he said, What hast thou done? the voice of thy brother's blood crieth unto me from the ground.[446]

11 And now art thou cursed[447] *from the earth, which hath opened her mouth to receive thy brother's blood from thy hand;*

12 When thou tillest the ground, it shall not henceforth yield unto thee her strength; a fugitive and a vagabond shalt thou be in the earth.

13 And Cain said unto the Lord, My punishment is greater than I can bear.

14 Behold, thou hast driven me out this day from the face of the earth; and from thy

---

faith and because his deeds were evil. God takes pleasure in our offerings and thanksgivings only when we are striving to live a righteous life according to God's will.

[443]Is God a respecter of persons {see Exodus 2:25; Leviticus 26:9; 2 Kings 13:23; Psalms 138:6}, or is God completely impartial {see Deuteronomy 10:17; 2 Chronicles 19:7; Acts 10:34; Romans 2:11; Galatians 2:6; Ephesians 6:9; and 1 Peter 1:17}? The first series of texts implies a righteous and benevolent "respect" based on a proper discrimination as to character which God exercises toward man. The second series of biblical references denotes a "respect" which is partial, arising out of selfish and unworthy considerations which God does not exercise because God is impartial.

That God accepted Abel's sacrifice and rejected Cain's was not based on the fact that Cain's sacrifice was bloodless. Many of the required Old Testament offerings were bloodless (as meal and meat offerings). The difference was in the hearts of the two men. Abel offered in faith {see Hebrews 11:4}, while Cain did not. This basic difference is indicated by the wording of the passage: God "had respect unto Abel and to his offering; but unto Cain and to his offering he had not respect." Only when they are offered in faith do the sacrifices and service of men please God {see Isaiah 1:11–17 and Ephesians 6:5–7}.

[444]A better translation of Genesis 4:7 might be: "Sin is crouching at the door; its desire is to possess you, but you must master it." God pictures sin as a tempting force or power which, like a wild beast or demon, is ready to attack and to devour. Yet God also ascribes to human beings the capacity to overcome and resist sin by submitting to God's word, with the assistance of God's grace. It is their choice whether they will yield to sin or will conquer it.

[445]The Septuagint, the Samaritan Pentateuch, and the Syriac Version add the phrase, "Let us go out to the field," after the phrase "And Cain talked with Abel his brother."

[446]The death of Abel and God's concern for him show that God throughout the ages cares for all who suffer because of their commitment to righteousness. Their suffering is known to God, and God will one day act on their behalf to render justice and destroy all evil.

[447]Cain was cursed by God in the sense that God would no longer bless his efforts to gain his living from the ground. Evidently Cain did not humble himself in godly sorrow and repentance, for he separated himself from the Lord and sought to live without God's help.

face shall I be hid; and I shall be a fugitive and a vagabond in the earth; and it shall come to pass, that every one that findeth me shall slay me.[448]

15 And the Lord said unto him, Therefore whosoever slayeth Cain, vengeance shall be taken on him sevenfold. And the Lord set a mark upon Cain,[449] *lest any finding him should kill him.*

16 And Cain went out from the presence of the Lord,[450] *and dwelt in the land of Nod, on the east of Eden.*

17 And Cain knew his wife[451]*; and she conceived, and bare Enoch: and he builded a city, and called the name of the city, after the name of his son, Enoch.*

18 And unto Enoch was born Irad: and Irad begat Mehujael: and Mehujael begat Methusael: and Methusael begat Lamech.

19 And Lamech took unto him two wives[452]*: the name of the one was Adah, and the name of the other Zillah.*

20 And Adah bare Jabal: he was the father of such as dwell in tents, and of such as have cattle.

21 And his brother's name was Jabal: he was the father of all such as handle the harp and organ.

22 And Zillah, she also bare Tubal-cain, an instructor of every artificer in brass and iron: and the sister of Tubal-cain was Naamah.

23 And Lamech said unto his wives, Adah and Zillah, Hear my voice; ye wives of Lamech, hearken unto my speech: for I have slain a man to my wounding, and a young man to my hurt.[453]

24 If Cain shall be avenged sevenfold, truly Lamech seventy and sevenfold.

25 And Adam knew his wife again; and she bare a son, and called his name Seth: For God, said she, hath appointed me another seed instead of Abel, whom Cain slew.

26 And to Seth, to him also there was

---

[448]Cain's cry was one of remorse, not true repentance. Cain was overwhelmed by the severity of the sentence, but he was not sorry for his crime. There was no plea for pardon or expression of sorrow or regret. Cain was a selfish person who was about to be deprived of all material belongings and driven into the wilderness. Cain was afraid that some of the relatives of Abel would find him and kill him in revenge. Thus, it is logical to assume that the population of the world had already multiplied considerably since the expulsion of Adam and Eve from the garden of Eden.

[449]This should probably be understood in the sense of a sign given to Cain to assure him of God's promise. The death penalty was not carried out on Cain. Capital punishment came later when the wickedness and violence of humankind became very great on the earth. {See Genesis 6:5–7, 11 and 9:6.}

[450]Cain and his descendants were the pioneers of God-estranged human civilization. A basic motivation in all humanistic societies is the attempt to overcome the curse, find pleasure, and regain "Paradise" without submission to God. In other words, the world's system is founded upon the principle of self-redemption for the human race in its revolt against God.

[451]Adam and Eve had other sons and daughters. {See Genesis 5:4.} Hence, Cain must have married one of his sisters. Such a relationship was necessary in the beginning. Later, because the results of the fall increased and inter-family marriages multiplied the biological weaknesses in the children, this type of marriage was forbidden.

[452]Lamech was the first to reject God's ordained principle of monogamy. {See Genesis 2:21–24.} Inherited depravity was progressively manifesting itself in the home and family.

[453]The outburst of Lamech which appears in Genesis 4:23 shows a proud and presumptuous self-confidence. This was the boast of a bold, bad man who was elated with the possession of arms which his son Tubal-cain had invented. He felt he could take a human life at will.

born a son; and he called his name Enos: then began men to call upon the name of the Lord.[454]

THE DESCENDANTS OF ADAM {GENESIS 5:1–32}[455]

Chapter 5

1 This is the book of the generations of Adam.[456] In the day that God created man, in the likeness of God made he him;

2 Male and female created he them; and blessed them, and called their name Adam, in the day when they were created.

3 And Adam lived an hundred and thirty years, and begat a son in his own likeness, after his image; and called his name Seth:

4 And the days of Adam after he had begotten Seth were eight hundred years: and he begat sons and daughters:

5 And all the days that Adam lived were nine hundred and thirty years: and he died.[457]

6 And Seth lived an hundred and five years, and begat[458] Enos:

7 And Seth lived after he begat Enos eight hundred and seven years, and begat sons and daughters:

---

[454]Under the encouragement of Enos, public prayer and worship began. The ungodly family of Cain developed and centered their lives around the secular arts and business, establishing a way of self-reliance. The family of Seth, in contrast, called "upon the name of the Lord" in order to express their dependence upon God. Thus, two fundamentally different family groups were developing on the earth—the godly people and the ungodly.

[455]Genesis, Chapter 5 gives a list of the descendants of Adam down to the time of the Flood. The names reflect the godly line who stood for God in an increasingly corrupt age. Hebrews, Chapter 11, of the New Testament, selects two individuals (Abel and Enoch) for special mention from this period of time as being among those few who pleased God by their faith. {See Hebrews 11:4–5.} These two were among the remnant, the faithful few who refused to go the way of Cain. By the time of the flood the hearts of nearly everyone were evil; only eight individuals remained who were saved. {See Genesis 6:5, 11, 18 and 7:1, 7}. There will always be some, at times only a few, who will worship God, remain faithful to God, follow God's word, and wait for God's promises. These people will be a minority. However, God marks their names as God did the people of Genesis, Chapter 5. Today, if believers feel that they are standing alone in their faith in God and in God's word, the believers need only remember that they are never alone. God still has thousands of fellow believers throughout the earth who remain faithful to God and to God's cause.

[456]For fundamentalist Christians, in this chapter of Genesis, Moses gives a ten person genealogy of the people of the pre-flood era, and in chapter eleven there is a similar listing of ten post-flood persons which ended with Terah, Abraham's father. In both lists, the longevity of these men is far beyond anything in our own day. Yet fundamentalist Christians believe that Moses himself lived to be 120 years of age {see Deuteronomy 34:7}, and that Moses intended that the figures listed be taken literally. For fundamentalist Christians, this was a time when men were capable of procreation at 182 years of age {see Genesis 5:28}. Since it is impossible to accurately assess past conditions based upon existing conditions, these statements should be taken literally.

[457]The reason that humankind lived a great number of years may be because sin had only just begun to work its corrupting influence upon the environment and one's physical body. By Abraham's time life expectancy had fallen to less than two hundred years.

[458]The word "begat" can also mean "became the ancestor of." Thus, the genealogies of Genesis, like other genealogies in the Bible, were not intended to name every individual in the actual line of descent.

8 *And all the days of Seth were nine hundred and twelve years: and he died.*

9 *And Enos lived ninety years, and begat Cainan:*

10 *And Enos lived after he begat Cainan eight hundred and fifteen years, and begat sons and daughters:*

11 *And all the days of Enos were nine hundred and five years: and he died.*

12 *And Cainan lived seventy years, and begat Mahalaleel:*

13 *And Cainan lived after he begat Mahalaleel eight hundred and forty years, and begat sons and daughters:*

14 *And all the days of Cainan were nine hundred and ten years: and he died.*

15 *And Mahalaleel lived sixty and five years, and begat Jared:*

16 *And Mahalaleel lived after he begat Jared eight hundred and thirty years, and begat sons and daughters:*

17 *And all the days of Mahalaleel were eight hundred ninety and five years: and he died.*

18 *And Jared lived an hundred sixty and two years, and he begat Enoch:*

19 *And Jared lived after he begat Enoch eight hundred years, and begat sons and daughters:*

20 *And all the days of Jared were nine hundred sixty and two years: and he died.*

21 *And Enoch lived sixty and five years, and begat Methuselah:*

22 *And Enoch walked with God*[459] *after he begat Methuselah three hundred years, and begat sons and daughters:*

23 *And all the days of Enoch were three hundred sixty and five years:*

24 *And Enoch walked with God*[460]: *and he was not; for God took him.*[461]

25 *And Methuselah lived after he begat*

---

[459]Enoch undoubtedly excelled in godliness. Indeed, this godliness is amply verified in other biblical passages where we are told that Enoch "walked with God" (Genesis 5:22 and 24) meaning that he lived by faith in God, trusted in God's word and promises {see Hebrews 11:5–6}; endeavored to live a holy life {see and compare with 1 John 1:5–7}; and embraced God's ways {see and compare with Amos 3:3}, while standing firm against the ungodliness of his generation {see Jude 14–15}.

Enoch was a preacher of righteousness who denounced sin and the unrighteous lifestyle of his generation. Referring to Enoch, Jude 14–15 tell us that Enoch cried out against ungodliness and immorality by warning people of God's coming judgment to punish men and women for their ungodly deeds: *And Enoch also, the seventh from Adam, prophesied of these, saying, Behold, the Lord cometh with ten thousands of his saints, to execute judgment upon all, and to convince all that are ungodly among them of all their ungodly deeds which they have ungodly committed, and of all their hard speeches which ungodly sinners have spoken against him.*

Enoch pleased God. His life, message, and sympathy with God so pleased God that the Lord honored Enoch by taking him away from the earth to be in God's presence forever without experiencing death.

For fundamentalist Christians, it would be wise to ponder the life of Enoch as an example, especially since it is generally believed that we live in an evil and ungodly generation. Thus, it is incumbent upon Christian believers to walk with God by living in true holiness, by denouncing sin, and by warning people to flee the wrath to come.

[460]It is notable that in both verse 22 and verse 24, the original Hebrew adds the definite article before "God" in both of these verses. Perhaps this is an indication that idolatry was emerging, but Enoch lived in accordance with the will of the true God. By so doing, Enoch became known in the biblical record as one who pleased God {see Hebrews 11:5}.

[461]Enoch's being taken directly to heaven without experiencing death implies that righteous men and women who preceded Abraham also possessed a hope for future life with God. Verse

Lamech seven hundred eighty and two years, and begat sons and daughters:

27 And all the days of Methuselah were nine hundred sixty and nine years: and he died.

28 And Lamech lived an hundred eighty and two years, and begat a son:

29 And he called his name Noah, saying, This same shall comfort us concerning our work and toil of our hands, because of the ground which the Lord hath cursed.

30 And Lamech lived after he begat Noah five hundred ninety and five years, and begat sons and daughters:

31 And all the days of Lamech were seven hundred seventy and seven years: and he died.

32 And Noah was five hundred years old: and Noah begat Shem, Ham, and Japheth.

THE FLOOD
{GENESIS 6:1–8:22}

1 And it came to pass, when men began to multiply on the face of the earth, and daughters were born unto them,

2 That the sons of God[462] saw the daughters of men that they were fair; and they took them wives of all which they chose.

3 And the Lord said, My spirit shall not always strive with man, for that he also is flesh: yet his days shall be an hundred and twenty years.

4 There were giants in the earth in those days; and also after that, when the sons of God[463] came in unto the daughters of men,

---

24 also puts forth one of the first hints of the belief in immortality for the righteous. In the Old Testament, the bodies of both Enoch and Elijah {see 2 Kings 2:11} were doubtless transformed {see 1 Corinthians 15:51 and 52}. Enoch and Elijah may have been given spiritual bodies similar to that of the resurrected Jesus {see Luke 24:38–43 and John 20:19}. Enoch is also the speaker of a prophecy {see Jude 1:14–15}. The reference to Enoch in the New Testament is said to have been a part of an apocryphal book containing various prophecies given by Enoch. It is more likely that Enoch merely spoke these words and the Lord preserved them through Jude.

[462]The "sons of God" most likely refer to men who were descendants of the godly line of Seth. These "sons of God" began to intermarry with the "daughters of men" (i.e., women from the ungodly family of Cain. The theory that the "sons of God" were angels is less likely in view of Jesus' words that angels do not marry. {See Matthew 22:30 and Mark 12:25.} This union of the godly with the unrighteous led to "wickedness" (i.e., the godly became preoccupied with evil). As a result the earth became corrupt and filled with violence.

[463]The identity of the "sons of God" is uncertain. Three main theories are advanced to identify the "sons of God" and the "daughters of men." The first theory is that the "sons of God" are fallen angels and the "daughters of men" are mortals. The wickedness for which they are condemned is the unlawful marriage between those who are supernatural and those who are mortal. This ancient viewpoint hinges in part on the assumption that Jude 1:6, 7 refer to these angels. The proponents of this view insist, perhaps with some Scriptural backing, that the term "sons of God" refers only to angels {see Job 1:6–12}. However, there is no precedent at this point from which we can conclude this idea. And if this sin is, at least to a large extent, the fault of the angels, why is man punished by the Flood? When the proponents of this theory are reminded of the fact that Jesus {in Matthew 22:30} says that angels do not marry, the theorists answer that Jesus only said that they do not, not that they could not or did not. However, there is considerable theological difficulty with the existence of human beings who are, at least in part, not descended from Adam {see Acts 17:26}.

The second theory as to their identity is the one most often held to within conservative scholarship. The "sons of God" are reckoned to be the godly line of Seth while the "daugh-

and they bare children to them, the same became mighty men which were of old, men of renown.

5 And God saw that the wickedness of man was great[464] in the earth, and that every imagination of the thoughts of his heart was only evil continually.

6 And it repented the Lord[465] that he had made man on the earth, and it grieved him at his heart.

7 And the Lord said, I will destroy man whom I have created from the face of the earth; both man, and beast, and the creeping

---

ters of men" are of the line of Cain. Thus the sin with which they are charged is one which is common to the whole of Scripture, and especially of the Pentateuch: the intermarriage of the chosen people of God (the believers) with those who are unholy. How can these men be considered holy when the Bible states that only Noah was holy {see Genesis 6:8 and 9}? And why is the term "sons of God" not used with this meaning in any other place? Other people also question why only sons and not daughters are associated with the line of Seth.

The last theory is one that is becoming preferred amongst many fundamentalist Christians. Fundamentalist Christians point to recent archaeological evidence which suggests that the phrase "sons of God" was sometimes used to describe kings {see Exodus 21:6; 22:8 and Psalms 82:6, 7}. Therefore, the "sons of God" are immoral human kings who use their power to take as many women and whatever women they choose. It must be noted that the Scripture never describes human rulers as deities. This theory rests upon the conjecture that the "giants" of verse four are the children of the union described in the preceding verses. The word "giant" comes from the Septuagint rendering of the Hebrew *nephilim* ("the fallen ones") which comes from *naphal*—"to fall." It is often associated with violence, and so translated "overthrow, fall upon." The term emphasizes their violence and lack of respect for others. However, neither the text nor the fact that they were "giants" supports the idea that they are the result of a union between angels and human beings. No one believes that because the children of Anak, Goliath and his brothers, were giants that they were necessarily the offspring of some supernatural union.

[464]In Noah's day the character of human sin was blatantly manifested in two primary ways: sexual lust and violence. From a fundamentalist Christian perspective, human depravity has not changed; it is still through lust and violence that evil finds unrestrained expression. Today immorality, ungodliness, pornography, and violence, dominate our societies.

[465]God is revealed in these early chapters of the Bible as a God who deals with people personally and is capable of emotion, disappointment, and reaction against the willful sin and rebellion of humankind. The word "repented" indicates that because of the tragic sin of the human race, God's disposition was changed towards them; God's attitude of mercy and longsuffering turned to one of judgment. Although God's existence, character, and ultimate purposes remain changeless, God remains open and responsive in God's dealings with humans. God does alter God's feelings, attitudes, actions and mind in accordance with a changing response to God's will. This revelation of God as a God who can have regret and grief makes clear that God exists in a personal and intimate relationship to creation. God possesses an intense love for human beings and a divine attentiveness to the plight of the human race. (For some fundamentalist Christians, Genesis 6:6 has puzzled students of the Bible for many years. Contrary to the immediately preceding explanation, for many fundamentalist Christians, the phrase "it repented the Lord" does not mean that God changed {see Numbers 23:19; 1 Samuel 15:29; Malachi 3:6; and James 1:17}, nor does it mean that God is affected by sorrow or other feelings which are common to humanity. From the perspective of these fundamentalist Christians, the use of the word "repented" was necessary because the inspired biblical writers needed to use terms which were comprehensible to the minds of human beings. Most people cannot conceive of God except in human terms and concepts.)

thing, and the fowls of the air; for it repen-
teth me that I have made them.

9 These are the generations of Noah:
Noah was a just man and perfect in his gen-
erations,[466] *and Noah walked with God.*

10 And Noah begat three sons, Shem,
Ham, and Japheth.

11 The earth also was corrupt before
God, and the earth was filled with vio-
lence.

12 And God looked upon the earth, and,

behold, it was corrupt; for all flesh had cor-
rupted his way upon the earth.

13 And God said unto Noah, The end
of all flesh is come before me; for the earth
is filled with violence through them; and,
behold, I will destroy them with the earth.

14 Make thee an ark[467, 468] *of gopher*
wood; rooms shalt thou make in the ark,
and shalt pitch it within and without with
pitch.

15 And this is the fashion which thou

---

[466]Amidst the widespread wickedness and evil of pre-Flood days, God found in Noah one man who still sought communion with God and who was a righteous man. The reference to "perfect in his generations" indicates that he kept himself separate from the moral evil of the society around him. Because Noah was a righteous man who feared God and set his face against popular public opinion and conduct, Noah found favor with God. This righteousness in Noah's life came by God's grace, through Noah's faith and walk with God. Salvation in the New Testament era must be found in exactly the same way, namely, by God's mercy and grace received through a faith so vital that it results in a sincere effort to walk with God and remain separated from a perverse generation. Hebrews 11:7 states that Noah "became heir of the righteousness which is by faith." The New Testament also states that Noah was not only a just man, but also a preacher of righteousness. In this he is an example of what preachers ought to be.

[467]The Hebrew word for "ark" means a vessel for floating and occurs only in the story of the Flood and in Exodus 2:3, 5 where it is used on the basket in which the baby Moses was placed. The ark resembled a barge, but not necessarily with square corners. Its dimensions are given in "cubits." An ancient cubit equaled about eighteen inches. Thus, the ark was approximately 450 feet long, seventy-five feet wide, and forty-five feet high. Its carrying capacity was equal to more than 300 railroad stock cars. It is calculated that the ark could hold some 7,000 kinds of animals. Hebrews 11:7 suggests that the ark is a type of Christ, for the ark is also a means of the believer's salvation from judgment and death.

[468]The ark was a vessel built by Noah to save himself, his family, and animals from the Flood sent by God. The ark was about 450 feet long, 75 feet wide, and 45 feet high, with three decks. Scholars have calculated that a vessel of this size would hold more than 43,000 tons.

After almost a year on the water, the ark came to rest on Mount Ararat in what is now Turkey. Numerous attempts across the centuries to find the remains of the ark have proven futile. Shifting glaciers, avalanches, hidden crevices, and sudden storms make mountain climbing in the area extremely dangerous.

The ark reveals both the judgment and mercy of God. God's righteous judgment is seen in the destruction of the wicked, but God's mercy and care are demonstrated in God's preservation of Noah, and, through him, of the human race. The ark is striking illustration of Jesus, who preserves us from the flood of divine judgment through God's graces.

From the ancient world there are several other flood stories that are remarkably similar to the biblical account in many details. In the most famous of these, Utnapishti, the Babylonian "Noah," constructed a boat, which was about 180 feet long, 180 feet wide, and 180 feet high—hardly a seaworthy design. In stark contrast to these stories, the Book of Genesis presents a holy and righteous God who sends the flood in judgment against sin and yet mercifully saves Noah and his family because of their righteousness.

shalt make it of: The length of the ark shall be three hundred cubits, the breadth of it fifty cubits, and the height of it thirty cubits.[469]

16 A window shalt thou make to the ark, and in a cubit shalt thou finish it above; and the door of the ark shalt thou set in the side thereof; with lower, second, and third stories shalt thou make it.

17 And behold, I, even I, do bring a flood of waters upon the earth, to destroy all flesh, wherein is the breath of life, from under heaven; and every thing that is in the earth shall die.

18 But with thee will I establish my covenant[470]; and thou shalt come into the ark, thou, and thy sons, and thy wife, and thy sons' wives with thee.

19 And of every living thing of all flesh, two of every sort shalt thou bring into the ark, to keep them alive with thee; they shall be male and female.

20 Of fowls after their kind, and of cattle after their kind, of every creeping thing of the earth after his kind, two of every sort shall come unto thee, to keep them alive.

21 And take thou unto thee of all food that is eaten, and thou shalt gather it to thee; and it shall be for food for thee, and for them.

22 Thus did Noah; according to all that God commanded him, so did he.

Chapter 7

1 And the Lord said unto Noah, Come thou and all thy house into the ark; for thee have I seen righteous before me in this generation.

2 Of every clean beast thou shalt take to thee by sevens, the male and his female: and of beasts that are not clean by two, the male and his female.

3 Of fowls also of the air by sevens, the male and the female; to keep seed alive upon the face of all the earth.

4 For yet seven days, and I will cause it to rain upon the earth forty days and forty nights; and every living substance that I have made will I destroy from off the face of the earth.

5 And Noah did according unto all that the Lord commanded him.

6 And Noah was six hundred years old when the flood of waters was upon the earth.[471]

7 And Noah went in, and his sons, and his wife, and his sons' wives with him, into the ark, because of the waters of the flood.

8 Of clean beasts, and of beasts that are

In the New Testament, Jesus spoke of the Flood and Noah and the ark, comparing "the days of Noah," with the time of "the coming of the Son of Man."

[469]The dimensions of the ark present an interesting contrast when set beside the Sumerian account of the flood. In the longest and most famous of these accounts, the Akkadian Epic of Gilgamesh, the ark was a perfect cube, 200 feet long on each side. In contrast, the relative dimensions of Noah's ark are not only seaworthy, but that of modern ships are very similar.

[470]Through this covenant, God promised Noah that he would be saved from the judgment to be meted out through the Flood. Noah responded to God's covenant by believing in God and God's word. Noah's faith was demonstrated by being "moved with fear" and by preparing and entering the ark.

[471]The flood was God's universal judgment upon an ungodly and unrepentant world. The apostle Peter refers to the flood to remind his readers that God will again judge the whole world at the end of time, then by fire. {See 2 Peter 3:10.} That judgment will involve the outpouring of God's wrath upon the ungodly in a way unequaled in history. God calls believers today, as God did Noah of old, to warn the unsaved about this terrible day and to call them to repent of their sins, turn to God through Christ, and be saved.

not clean, and of fowls, and of every thing that creepeth upon the earth.

9 There went in two and two unto Noah into the ark, the male and female, as God had commanded Noah.

10 And it came to pass after seven days, that the waters of the flood were upon the earth.

11 In the six hundredth year of Noah's life, in the second month, the seventeenth day of the month, the same day were all the fountains of the great deep broken up,[472] *and the windows of heaven were opened.*

12 And the rain was upon the earth forty[473] *days and forty nights.*

13 In the selfsame day entered Noah, and Shem, and Ham, and Japheth, the sons of Noah, and Noah's wife, and the three wives of his sons with them, into the ark;

14 They, and every beast after his kind, and all the cattle after their kind, and every creeping thing that creepeth upon the earth after his kind, and every fowl after his kind, every bird of every sort.

15 And they went in unto Noah into the ark, two and two of all flesh, wherein is the breath of life.

16 And they that went in, went in male and female of all flesh, as God had commanded him: and the Lord shut him in.

17 And the flood was forty days upon the earth; and the waters increased, and bare up the ark, and it was lift up above the earth.

18 And the waters prevailed, and were increased greatly upon the earth; and the ark went upon the face of the waters.

19 And the waters prevailed exceedingly upon the earth; and all the high hills, that were under the whole heaven, were covered.

20 Fifteen cubits upward did the waters prevail; and the mountains were covered.

21 And all flesh died that moved upon the earth, both of fowl, and of cattle, and of beast, and of every creeping thing that creepeth upon the earth, and every man:

22 All in whose nostrils was the breath of life, of all that was in the dry land, died.

23 And every living substance was destroyed which was upon the face of the ground, both man, and cattle, and the creeping things, and the fowl of the heaven; and they were destroyed from the earth: and Noah only remained alive,[474] *and they that were with him in the ark.*

---

[472]Two cataclysmic events precipitated the Flood. First, the eruption of great reservoirs of subterranean waters, perhaps caused by earthquakes with subsequent great tidal waves from the oceans, and second, the torrential rains which fell on the earth for forty days. Thus, all living creatures outside the ark who normally lived on dry land died, both human and animal life. Water rose to such height that it covered all the high hills, that were under the whole heaven (i.e., the entire earth was covered with water). This indicates a universal flood and not simply a local one confined to a small portion of earth. The water began to recede only after 150 days. Noah's ark finally came to rest on one of the mountains of Ararat (Armenia), 500 miles from where it started. After the earth dried up, Noah left the ark 377 days after the flood began. The apostle Peter states that the pre-flood world "perished" This suggests that due to the enormous topographical upheaval, the pre-flood earth changed radically, both physically and geologically, into the earth that now exists.

[473]The number forty is not merely an arbitrary period nor a rounded figure of the period during which it rained. The number forty is used repeatedly in Scripture to signify periods of testing, sometimes of judgmental testing. Other prominent references involving the number forty are: Noah's waiting after the tops of the mountains appeared {see Genesis 8:6}; Moses' forty days on Mount Sinai {see Exodus 24:18 and Deuteronomy 19:9}; the spies forty days searching out Canaan {see Numbers 13:25}; the forty years in the wilderness {see Numbers 14:33}; the forty days Nineveh was given until judgment {see Jonah 3:4}.

[474]The flood story tells of both judgment and salvation. The flood with its total destruction

24 And the waters prevailed upon the earth an hundred and fifty days.

Chapter 8

1 And God remembered Noah,[475] and every living thing, and all the cattle that was with him in the ark: and God made a wind to pass over the earth, and the waters assuaged;

2 The fountains also of the deep and the windows of heaven were stopped, and the rain from heaven was restrained.

3 And the waters returned from off the earth continually: and after the end of the hundred and fifty days the waters were abated.

4 And the ark rested in the seventh month, on the seventeenth day of the month, upon the mountains of Ararat.

5 And the waters decreased continually until the tenth month: in the tenth month, on the first day of the month, were the tops of the mountains seen.

6 And it came to pass at the end of forty days, that Noah opened the window of the ark which he had made:

7 And he sent forth a raven, which went forth to and fro, until the waters were dried up from off the earth.

8 Also he sent forth a dove from him, to see if the waters were abated from off the face of the ground;

9 But the dove found no rest for sole of her foot, and she returned unto him in the ark, for the waters were on the face of the whole earth: then he put forth his hand, and took her, and pulled her in unto him into the ark.

10 And he stayed yet other seven days; and again he sent forth the dove out of the ark;

11 And the dove came in to him in the evening; and, lo, in her mouth was an olive leaf plucked off: so Noah knew that the waters were abated from off the earth.

12 And he stayed yet other seven days; and sent forth the dove; which returned not again unto him any more.

13 And it came to pass in the six hundredth and first year, in the first month, the first day of the month, the waters were dried up from off the earth: and Noah removed the covering of the ark, and looked, and, behold, the face of the ground was dry.

14 And in the second month, on the seven and twentieth day of the month, was the earth dried.

15 And God spake unto Noah, saying,

16 Go forth of the ark, thou, and thy wife, and thy sons, and thy sons' wives with thee.

17 Bring forth with thee every living thing that is with thee, of all flesh, both of fowl, and of cattle, and of every creeping thing that creepeth upon the earth; that they may breed abundantly in the earth, and be fruitful, and multiply upon the earth.

18 And Noah went forth, and his sons, and his wife, and his sons' wives with him:

19 Every beast, every creeping thing, and

---

of all human life outside the ark was necessary in order to blot out the extreme moral corruption of men and women and to give the human race a new chance for fellowship with God. The apostle Peter states that Christian baptism corresponds to Noah's salvation through the flood waters.

[475]Noah had not heard from God for 150 days. Noah's faith was being tested, for he had no idea when the waters would subside or when God would intervene again. Then God acted out of concern and love for Noah and his family. God's dealings with Noah are recorded to give all God's faithful people hope and trust in God's ways. Fundamentalist Christians believe that if God has not acted in your life for a long time, you can be confident that God will act again and manifest a loving care toward you. At the present time, the believer's task is to draw near to the Lord and continue in faithful obedience to God's word and Spirit.

every fowl, and whatsoever creepeth upon the earth, after their kinds, went forth out of the ark.

20 And Noah builded an altar unto the Lord; and took of every clean beast, and of every clean fowl, and offered burnt offerings on the altar.

21 And the Lord smelled a sweet savour; and the Lord said in his heart, I will not again curse the ground any more for man's sake, for the imagination of man's heart is evil from his youth[476]; neither will I again smite any more every thing living, as I have done.

22 While the earth remaineth,[477] seed-time and harvest, and cold and heat, and summer and winter, and day and night shall not cease.

GOD'S COVENANT WITH NOAH {GENESIS 9:1–9:19}

Chapter 9

1 And God blessed Noah and his sons, and said unto them, Be fruitful, and multiply, and replenish the earth.

2 And the fear of you and the dread of you shall be upon every beast of the earth, and upon every fowl of the air, upon all that moveth upon the earth, and upon all the fishes of the sea; into your hand are they delivered.

3 Every moving thing that liveth shall be meat for you; even as the green herb have I given you all things.

4 But flesh with the life thereof, which is the blood thereof, shall ye not eat.

5 And surely your blood of your lives will I require; at the hand of every beast will I require it, and at the hand of man; at the hand of every man's brother will I require the life of man.[478]

6 Whoso sheddeth man's blood, by man shall his blood be shed[479]: for in the image of God made he man.

7 And you, be ye fruitful, and multiply;

---

[476]The Lord states the truth about the corruption and depravity of human nature. The tendency toward evil is innate in a person from birth and is expressed early in childhood or youth.

[477]Contained in the phrase "while the earth remaineth" is a promise that is easy to miss. Day, night, and the seasons will continue. However, the earth was not intended by God to be eternal. Its final destruction is described in Psalms 102:26 {quoted in Hebrews 1:11, 12}. The most graphic account of the end of the world, indeed of the entire physical universe, is found in 2 Peter 3:10.

[478]It has been assumed that human government was officially instituted after the Great Flood in Genesis 9. However, some form of law and order undoubtedly existed prior to this period. This is strongly suggested by both Jesus and Jude. Jesus in Luke 17:26 and 27 says that prior to the Flood in Noah's day people conducted their affairs in much the same manner as we do today. Jude gives us the text of a message Enoch preached to sinners prior to the Flood {see Jude 14 and 15}. One of the main factors which brought about the Flood was man's disobedience to the revealed law of God.

At any rate, there is certainly no doubt concerning the source of human government. God is its divine author. Two individuals give testimony to this fact. Daniel reminds King Nebuchadnezzar that "the Most High rules in the kingdom of men, and gives it to whomever He chooses." The apostle Paul exhorts Christians to be subject to the laws of human government because all earthly powers exist through God's divine permission.

If one rightly understands the origin of human government, then the conclusion is reached that lawless anarchy is not only rebellion against human authority, but actual blasphemy against the divine Creator.

[479]Because of the desire for violence and bloodshed that arises within the human heart, God sought to guard the sanctity of human life by restraining murder in society. God did this in

bring forth abundantly in the earth, and multiply therein.

8 And God spake unto Noah, and to his sons with him, saying,

9 And I, behold, I establish my covenant[480] *with you, and with your seed after you;*

10 And with every living creature that is with you, of the fowl, of the cattle, and of every beast of the earth with you; from all that go out of the ark, to every beast of the earth.

11 And I will establish my covenant with you; neither shall all flesh be cut off any more by the waters of a flood; neither shall there any more be a flood to destroy the earth.

12 And God said, This the token of the covenant which I make between me and you and every living creature that is with you, for perpetual generations:

13 I do set my bow in the cloud,[481] *and it shall be for a token of a covenant between me and the earth.*

14 And it shall come to pass, when I bring a cloud over the earth, that the bow shall be seen in the cloud:

15 And I will remember my covenant, which is between me and you and every living creature of all flesh; and the waters shall no more become a flood to destroy all flesh.

16 And the bow shall be in the cloud; and I will look upon it, that I may remember the everlasting covenant between God and every living creature of all flesh that is upon the earth.

17 And God said unto Noah, This is the token of the covenant,[482] *which I have established between me and all flesh that is upon the earth.*[483]

18 And the sons of Noah, that went forth

---

two ways. First, by emphasizing that humans have been created in God's image and that their lives are sacred in God's sight. Secondly, by instituting capital punishment, commanding that every murderer be punished with death. The authority of governments to use the "sword" for capital punishment is reaffirmed in the New Testament. {See Acts 25:11 and Romans 13:4.}

[480]Verses 9 through 17 of Genesis, Chapter 9, speak of God's covenant with humanity and nature, in which God promised never again to destroy the earth and all living creatures with a flood.

[481]The rainbow was God's sign and ongoing reminder of God's promise never again to destroy all inhabitants on the earth by a flood. The rainbow should remind us of God's mercy and God's faithfulness to God's word.

[482]Throughout history, God has dealt with man through covenants or agreements. Later, the Jews regarded this covenant between God and Noah as the basis of the relationship between God and all mankind, but the covenants with Abraham {see Genesis, Chapter 15} and with Moses at Mount Sinai were seen as forming the basis of God's special relationship with Israel. Some believe that the stipulations laid on the Gentiles in Acts 15:20, 29 find validity here in the covenant between God and Noah. In spite of the fact that the distinction between clean and unclean animals existed {see Genesis 7:2}, God allowed the eating of any plant or animal. The only restriction was the eating of animal blood, for that is where the life of the animal resided {see Genesis 9:4}. Later, Israel was forbidden to eat not only blood but also the flesh of certain animals. The Lord removed the clean-unclean distinction from food altogether under the New Covenant {see Mark 7:15; Acts 10:15; 1 Timothy 4:4 and 5; and Titus 1:15}.

[483]God's covenant with Noah which appears at Genesis 9:1–17 is the third general or universal covenant. In Genesis 9, Noah had just passed through the universal flood in which all the world's population had been wiped out. Only Noah, his wife, his three sons, and their wives—eight people—constitute the world's population. Noah might have thought that the

of the ark, were Shem, and Ham, and Japheth: and Ham is the father of Canaan.

19 These are the three sons of Noah: and of them was the whole earth overspread.

THE CURSE OF CANAAN {GENESIS 9:20–9:29}

20 And Noah began to be an husbandman, and he planted a vineyard:

21 And he drank of the wine, and was drunken[484]; and he was uncovered within his tent.

22 And Ham, the father of Canaan, saw the nakedness[485] of his father, and told his two brethren without.[486]

23 And Shem and Japheth took a garment, and laid it upon both their shoulders, and went backward, and covered the nakedness of their father; and their faces were backward, and they saw not their father's nakedness.

24 And Noah awoke from his wine, and knew what his younger son had done unto him.

25 And he said, Cursed be Canaan[487]; a servant of servants shall he be unto his brethren.

26 And he said, Blessed be the Lord God of Shem; and Canaan shall be his servant.

27 God shall enlarge Japheth, and he

---

things provided by the covenant with Adam had now been changed. However, God gives the Noahic Covenant so that Noah and all the human race to follow might know that the provisions made in the Adamic Covenant remain in effect with one notable addition: the principle of human government which includes the responsibility of suppressing the outbreak of sin and violence, so that it will not be necessary to destroy the earth again by a flood. The provisions of the covenant are:

(1) The responsibility to populate the earth is reaffirmed (verse 1).
(2) The subjection of the animal kingdom to man is reaffirmed (verse 2).
(3) Man is permitted to eat the flesh of animals. However, he is to refrain from eating blood (verses 3 and 4).
(4) The sacredness of human life is established. Whatever sheds man's blood, whether man or beast, must be put to death (verses 5 and 6).
(5) The Noahic Covenant is confirmed not only with Noah but also with all mankind, and every living creature on the face of the earth (verses 9 and 10).
(6) The promise is given never to destroy the earth again by a universal flood (verse 11). The next time God destroys the earth, the means will be fire.
(7) The rainbow is designated as a testimony of the existence of the Noahic Covenant and the promise never to destroy the earth by flood. As long as we can see the rainbow we will know that the Noahic Covenant is in existence (verses 12–17).

[484]The first mention of wine in Scripture is connected with drunkenness, sin, shame, and a curse. Because of the accompanying evils of intoxicating beverages, God has made total abstinence the high standard for God's people.

[485]The Hebrew word for "nakedness," *'erwah*, actually means "shameful nakedness" and is often used to describe immoral behavior. A different word *'eyrom* is used to describe simple nakedness or bareness.

[486]Ham's sin consisted in his failure to honor and respect his father; rather than covering him, Ham exposed Noah's shameful condition.

[487]When Noah learned of Ham's shameful action, he pronounced a curse on Ham's son Canaan (though not on Ham himself). Perhaps Canaan was in some way involved in Ham's sin or possessed the same character faults of his father. The curse indicated that Canaan's

shall dwell in the tents of Shem; and Canaan shall be his servant.

28 And Noah lived after the flood three hundred and fifty years.

29 And all the days of Noah were nine hundred and fifty years: and he died.

The Descendants of Noah's Sons
{Genesis 10:1–10:32}

Chapter 10

1 Now these are the generations of the sons of Noah,[488] *Shem, Ham, and Japheth: and unto them were sons born after the flood.*

2 The sons of Japheth[489]*; Gomer, and Magog, and Madai, and Javan, and Tubal, and Meshech, and Tiras.*

3 And the sons of Gomer; Ashkenaz, and Riphath, and Togarmah.

4 And the sons of Javan; Elishah, and Tarshish, Kittim, and Dodanim.

5 By these were the isles of the Gentiles divided in their lands; every one after his tongue, after their families, in their nations.

6 And the sons of Ham[490]*; Cush, and Mizraim, and Phut, and Canaan.*

7 And the sons of Cush; Seba, and Havilah, and Sabtah, and Raamah, and Sabtecha: and the sons of Raamah; Sheba, and Dedan.

8 And Cush begat Nimrod: he began to be a mighty one in the earth.

9 He was a mighty hunter before the Lord: wherefore it is said, Even as Nimrod the mighty hunter before the Lord.

10 And the beginning of his kingdom was Babel, and Erech, and Accad, and Calneh, in the land of Shinar.

11 Out of that land went forth Asshur, and builded Nineveh, and the city Rehoboth, and Calah,

12 And Resen between Nineveh and Calah: the same is a great city.

13 And Mizraim begat Ludim, and Anamim, and Lehabim, and Naphtuhim,

14 And Pathrusim, and Casluhim, (out of whom came Philistim,) and Caphtorim.

15 And Canaan begat Sidon his firstborn, and Heth,

16 And the Jebusite, and Amorite, and the Girgasite,

17 And the Hivite,[491] *and the Arkite, and the Sinite,*

---

descendants (who were not black) would be oppressed and under the control of other nations. In contrast, Shem and Japheth's descendants would be blessed by God. This prophecy of Noah was conditional for all concerned. Any descendants of Canaan who turned to God would also receive the blessing of Shem, while any descendants of Shem and Japheth who departed from God would experience the curse of Canaan. (The prophecy of Noah was to a large extent fulfilled when the Canaanites became "hewers of wood and drawers of water" for the Israelites {see Joshua 9:23}.)

[488]The purpose of Genesis, Chapter 10 was to reveal how all the nations and people of the earth stemmed from Noah and his sons after the flood.

[489]Verses 2 through 5 of Genesis, Chapter 10, list the descendants of Japheth, who went north and settled around the coast lands of the Black and Caspian Seas. The sons of Japheth became the progenitors of the Medes, Greeks, and the Caucasian races of Europe and Asia.

[490]Verses 6 through 20 of Genesis, Chapter 10 list the descendants of Ham, who settled in southern Arabia, southern Egypt, and the east shore of the Mediterranean, and north coast of Africa. Canaan's descendants settled in a territory that was given the name of Canaan, a territory that was later to become the home of the Jewish people.

[491]The Hivites were one of the seven nations descended from Canaan {see Genesis 10:17 and Deuteronomy 7:1}. They were present in Shechem, Gibeon, and Lebanon {see Genesis 34:2 Joshua 9:3–7; and Judges 3:3}. Israel was commanded to destroy them, but they failed to obey, and some were still present in Solomon's day {see 1 Kings 9:20 and 21}.

18 And the Arvadite, and Zemarite, and the Hamathite: and afterward were the families of the Canaanites spread abroad.

19 And the border of the Canaanites was from Sidon, as thou comest to Gerar, unto Gaza; as thou goest, unto Sodom, and Gomorrah, and Admah, and Zeboim, even unto Lasha.

20 These are the sons of Ham, after their families, after their tongues, in their countries, and in their nations.

21 Unto Shem[492] also, the father of all the children of Eber, the brother of Japheth the elder, even to him were children born.

22 The children of Shem; Elam, and Asshur, and Arphaxad, and Lud, and Aram.

23 And the children of Aram; Uz, and Hul, and Gether, and Mash.

24 And Arphaxad begat Salah; and Salah begat Eber.

25 And unto Eber were born two sons: the name of one was Peleg; for in his days was the earth divided; and his brother's name was Joktan.

26 And Joktan begat Almodad, and Sheleph, and Hazarmaveth, and Jerah,

27 And Hadoram, and Uzal, and Diklah,

28 And Obal, and Abimael, and Sheba,

29 And Ophir, and Havilah, and Jobab: all these were the sons of Joktan.

30 And their dwelling was from Mesha, as thou goest unto Sephar a mount of the east.

31 These are the sons of Shem, after their families, after their tongues, in their lands, after their nations.

32 These are the families of the sons of Noah, after their generations, in their nations: and by these were the nations divided in the earth after the flood.

THE TOWER OF BABEL {GENESIS 11:1–11:9}

Chapter 11

1 And the whole earth was of one language, and of one speech.

2 And it came to pass, as they journeyed from the east, that they found a plain in the land of Shinar[493]; and they dwelt there.

3 And they said one to another, Go to, let us make brick, and burn them thoroughly. And they had brick for stone, and slime had they for mortar.

4 And they said, Go to, let us build us a city and a tower[494], whose top may reach

---

[492]Verses 21 through 31 of Genesis, Chapter 10, list the descendants of Shem, who settled in Arabia and the Southwest Asian Valley. They include Jews, Assyrians, Syrians, and Elamites.

[493]The land of Shinar is the Old Testament name for the territory of ancient Sumer and later of Babylonia or Mesopotamia.

[494]The Tower of Babel was built on the plain of Shinar, a site probably in ancient Babylonia in southern Mesopotamia, some time after the great flood of Noah's time. A symbol of man's sinful pride and rebellion, the structure was built to satisfy the people's vanity: "Let us make a name for ourselves" {Genesis 11:4}.

The pyramid-like tower was expected to reach heaven. These people were trying to approach God on their own self-serving terms, but they learned that the gates of heaven cannot be stormed. Men and women must approach the holy God in reverence and humility.

This tower was built of bricks and mortar, since no stones were available on the flat plains of southern Mesopotamia. The Babel Tower appears to be similar to the ziggurats the ancient inhabitants of southern Mesopotamia built as places for the worship of their gods. Both Assyrian and Babylonian kings prided themselves on the height of these pagan temples, boasting of building them as high as heaven.

One such tower, built in Ur, Abraham's ancestral city in southern Mesopotamia, about 2100 B.C.T., was a pyramid consisting of three terraces of diminishing size. The temple was

unto heaven; and let us make us a name,[495] *lest we be scattered abroad upon the face of the whole earth.*

5 And the Lord came down to see the city and the tower, which the children of men builded.

6 And the Lord said, Behold, "the people is one, and they have all one language; and this they begin to do: and now nothing will be restrained from them, which they have imagined to do.

7 Go to, let us go down, and there confound their language, that they may not understand one another's speech.

8 So the Lord scattered them abroad from thence upon the face of all the earth: and they left off to build the city.

9 Therefore is the name of it called Babel[496]*; because the Lord did there confound the language of all the earth: and from thence did the Lord scatter them abroad upon the face of all the earth.*

THE DESCENDANTS OF SHEM {GENESIS 11:10–11:26}

10 These are the generations of Shem: Shem was an hundred years old, and begat Arphaxad two years after the flood:

11 And Shem lived after he begat Arphaxad five hundred years, and begat sons and daughters.

12 And Arphaxad lived five and thirty years, and begat Salah:

13 And Arphaxad lived after he begat Salah four hundred and three years, and begat sons and daughters.

14 And Salah lived thirty years, and begat Eber:

15 And Salah lived after he begat Eber four hundred and three years, and begat sons and daughters.

16 And Eber lived four and thirty years, and begat Peleg:

17 And Eber lived after he begat Peleg four hundred and thirty years, and begat sons and daughters.

18 And Peleg lived thirty years, and begat Reu:

19 And Peleg lived after he begat Reu two hundred and nine years, and begat sons and daughters.

---

climbed by converging stairways. The uppermost part of the tower was an altar devoted to pagan worship.

God intervened to prevent the builders of Babel from partaking of the power and glory that belongs only to God. The language of the builders was confused so they could no longer communicate with one another. In their frustration, they abandoned the project. Then the prideful builders were scattered abroad. How small and weak this tower was in comparison to God's power! Humankind's misguided efforts at self-glorification brought on confusion and frustration and their dispersion throughout the world.

[495]The sin of the people in the land of Shinar was the desire to dominate the world and their own destiny apart from God through man-centered organizational unity, power, and great accomplishments. This purpose was based on pride and rebellion against God. God destroyed this effort by multiplying languages so that some could no longer communicate with others. This explains the diversity of race and language in the world. At this time the human race turned from God to idolatry, sorcery, and astrology. As a result, God gave them up to the impurity of their own hearts, and God turned to Abram to begin a way of salvation for humanity.

[496]Josephus, the Jewish historian, places Babel in the days of Nimrod. Babel was a pointed rejection of God's instruction to "replenish the earth" {Genesis 9:1}. It was a flagrant example of the corporate pride and willfulness of man. The intent of the tower may not have been to reach heaven; the expression can refer to a tower with an idolatrous "temple for heaven" on its top.

20 And Reu lived two and thirty years, and begat Serug:

21 And Reu lived after he begat Serug two hundred and seven years, and begat sons and daughters.

22 And Serug lived thirty years, and begat Nahor:

23 And Serug lived after he begat Nahor two hundred years, and begat sons and daughters.

24 And Nahor lived nine and twenty years, and begat Terah:

25 And Nahor lived after he begat Terah an hundred and nineteen years[497], and begat sons and daughters.

26 And Terah lived seventy years, and begat Abram, Nahor, and Haran.

---

[497]Note the steadily decreasing lifespans of the descendants of Shem and compare with the lifespans of the descendants of Seth {see Genesis 5:1–32}

A Muslim Perspective

An Overview

In the year 610 of the Christian calendar, Muhammad received the first revelations during the night while on Mount Hira (Ramadan/March 26–27). This night came to be known as "The Night of Destiny" (*layla al-qadar*) and is commemorated every year. Muhammad's revelations became the basis for the *Qur'an*, and the *Qur'an* came to be the collection of revelations that Muslims believe God vouchsafed to Muhammad via the angel Gabriel. The *Qur'an* is one of the main sources of Islamic law, literature, and culture. The *Qur'an* is also known as the "Koran."

Muhammad and the Qur'an

Muhammad seems to have followed the customs of his contemporaries, and, if some Western analyses of Qur'anic passages are to be relied on, he looked first to the religious traditions of his clan and tribe for answers to his spiritual quest. Muhammad seems not to have been alone in this search. *Hadith* tell of at least four other contemporaries of Muhammad who broke with polytheism and adopted a form of monotheism. In addition, the presence of a thriving Jewish community along with several Christian denominations actively engaged in missionary efforts in and around Arabia was bound to have an effect on the religious climate.

Muhammad followed the custom of religious withdrawal and devotion for a month every year. This custom may have been influenced by Christian practices, but it is said to have been the practice of the Quraysh before the rise of Islam. It was during one of these devotional retreats on Hira, a mountain near Mecca, that Muhammad had his first religious experience. Opinions differ about which Sura represents the first revelation, a minority giving Sura 74 that position, and the rest holding that Sura 96:1–5 was the first. In any event, the revelations came on Muhammad suddenly and frightened him. Muhammad even contemplated suicide so as not to be thought a *kahin*—an ecstatic seer or lunatic—an epithet which would later be lodged against him by his detractors.

Muhammad was dissuaded from the notion of self-delusion by a vision of a figure which has generally been identified as the Angel Gabriel. Gabriel is believed to have been the bearer of God's revelations to Muhammad. The first of these revelations were generally in the form of inspiration—*wahy*—rather than visions. Sometimes Muhammad would wrap himself in a cloak, possibly an inducement for the reception of revelation, but he was not in control or able to predict when revela-

288

tions would come to him. When they did come, Muhammad would undergo physical changes apparent to those around him, such as shaking and profuse sweating, even on cold days. This led his detractors to charge that he had fits or epilepsy, a charge which persisted among Western writers for many centuries.

The first messages of the Qur'an emphasize Muhammad's relationship to God, what he received from God, God's goodness, and Muhammad's obligations for that goodness. Then, by extension, these messages were applied to the rest of the Quraysh and, ultimately, to all Arabs. There is, however, no agreement about the order of the chapters and sections of the Qur'an, and many arguments about some aspect of Muhammad's early spiritual life are based on arrangements of the pieces of the Qur'an to fit the argument.

There is general agreement that Muhammad's spiritual awareness began with the realization of his good fortune, partly through his participation in the Meccan trade and partly through his association with Khadija. Allah is represented as being a good, giving God, Who created all people, Who provides for all of creation. Human response to these actions of God should ideally be a sense of gratitude and humility, a recognition of the position of being a creature with respect to the creator and benefactor. Unfortunately, humans are usually ungrateful. Each is *kafir*, a term which came to mean "unbeliever" because of the denial of the obligations of Allah's munificence.

Humans also have obligations to other people—to God's other creatures. One should not oppress the weak, and should be generous with that which God has given. Many see Muhammad's early experiences in this social message. There is more than just the responsibility of the individual. God is seen as having given wealth to the tribe of Quraysh through their commercial activities, in return for which they are expected to give proper worship. Failure to show gratitude was to invite calamity in this world, and the next. Thus, Muhammad believed he was sent to remind his fellow humans of God's gifts to them and their obligations.

These themes form the basis of the earliest message of Islam. Muhammad, the warner, is made aware of what he had received from God, and is told of his obligations to God and to his fellow man. These obligations apply to all Arabs who received God's blessing. Failure to heed the warnings would result in dire consequences on the Day of Judgment or even before. While it is not explicitly stated that Muhammad believed his early mission had universal applicability, there is nothing in the early Qur'anic passages to prevent such an interpretation.

THE *QUR'AN*

At the time of his death in 632 of the Christian calendar, the revelations of Muhammad had not been codified. It was not until the year 653 that 'Uthman, the Muslim caliph—or successor to Muhammad—established the standard version of the *Qur'an*. The actual text of the *Qur'an*, or Vulgate, was established by Zayd ibn Thabit.

It was in the *Qur'an* that the teachings of Islam's founder Muhammad were collected. These teachings are believed by Muslims to be divinely revealed. The *Qur'an* is thus the sacred text of Islam.

Qur'an is an Arabic word meaning "reciting, recitation, or reading." The term *Qur'an* refers to the collected revelations received by Muhammad. In the *Qur'an*—in this "reciting" in the Arabic language—, Muslims hear God speaking in his own words: it is God's speech (*kalam* Allah) and self-revelation in much the way that Christ, the Divine Logos, is for Christians. The "revealing"—the *wahy*—of God's word through Muhammad has been and is the unique, inimitable miracle (*mu'jizah*) for Muslims, providing them with a guide for all aspects of living, a scripture for constant "remembrance" (*dhikr*) of God, a shaping determinant of individual and collective thinking, and a comprehensive vision of history and destiny.

The collected revelations are normally referred to as "The Noble Qur'an" (*al-Qur'an al-karim*), or simply "The Book" (*al-Kitab*), although the terms for God's word in the revelations themselves and in Muslim tradition are numerous. The whole Qur'an is almost the length of the Christian New Testament and consists of 114 main divisions, or *suras*, which range in length in a common printed text from slightly over two lines (Sura 108) to some 710 (Sura 2).

The suras are numbered and arranged in approximate descending order of length, albeit with notable exceptions, the prime being Sura 1, "The Opening," (*al-Fatihah*), with only seven ayahs. In Muslim usage, each sura is referred to not by number but by name—this usually taken from one of the initial words (e.g., 92, "Night") or some striking passage or phrase (e.g., 2, "The Cow") in the sura. Although very old, the names are evidently not part of the Divine Word, since some suras have more than one name (e.g., 112, "Pure Devotion" or "Unity").

There is no unanimity about the precise chronological order in which the separate revelations came to Muhammad, but texts of the *Qur'an* traditionally list every sura as either "Meccan," "Medinan," or a combination of the two according to whether its contents were sent down during Muhammad's prophetic career in Mecca or Medina. In all schemes, Muslim and non–Muslim, there is general agreement that the preponderance of early (Meccan) material is to be found in the short, dramatic suras and ayahs of the final portion of the collected *Qur'an*, and most of the later (Medinan) material in the longer, generally less intense passages of the first part of the text.

The contents of the *Qur'an* take the form of words from God addressed alternately to all mankind, to the faithful, to the unbelievers, or to Muhammad alone. The language of the revelations is in prose, but a generally dramatic and poetic, often rhyming, prose that is anything but "prosaic." The power of the language, especially in some of the shorter, more lyrical passages, is overwhelming and all but impossible to capture in translation. The content ranges widely and includes paeans of praise for the One God and his myriad "signs" in the natural world, sharp warnings about the final Day of Resurrection and Judgment, exhortations to piety and good works, reminders of the history of God's dealing with mankind through the long series of previous prophets and revelations, commands concerning personal morality and social intercourse, and statements about particular events contemporary with the revelations themselves. Any or all of these and other themes recur repeatedly, often in the same sura, giving the whole a mosaic effect in which the unity of the discrete parts lies not in narrative development so much as stylistic and thematic repetition. The marked repetitiveness of the Qur'an is indicative of the "recitative" nature of the revelations, a quality underscored by the fact that in daily use the sura divides for purposes of recitation alone: (1) into thirty roughly equal "parts," each of these further halved to yield sixty "portions," and each "portion" subdivided into quarters to give 240 short recitations; (2) into thirds {see Suras 1–9, 10–30, 31–114}; and (3) into sevenths. While the latter two kinds of division are not normally indicated in printed texts, the 30-60-240 divisions are usually marked for the reader.

The early sources recount in some detail how the process of "revealing" to Muhammad went on over a long period, perhaps more than twenty years if one dates the first revelation—traditionally the first five ayahs of Sura 96—around 610 C.C., as most scholars do. Muslim sources treat in detail the "occasions of revelation," i.e., the historical circumstances in which particular ayahs or suras were given the Prophet, and the "modes of revelation," or different ways in which revelations were given—e.g., through the angel Gabriel in waking or in dream, or as an auditory experience. Muhammad seems to have distinguished clearly between what was direct divine word intended for "reciting" (*qur'an*) and what was inspiration for his own words and acts. The revelations likely received some editing and arrangement in Medina at his hands; certainly some of them were written down, and the names of several "scribes of the Revealing" are preserved. Nevertheless, at Muhammad's death there was no *Qur'an* as a single, codified book. The *Qur'an*, at that time, was still primarily an oral reality for the Muslims, the Arabic "recitations" from the Divine Book in Heaven were not yet a single text "between two boards."

Whether the traditions about early attempts under Abu Bakr (the first caliph) and especially 'Umar (the second caliph) to collect the "recitations" and organize them are accurate or not, it is clear that under the auspices of the third caliph, 'Uthman, a largely successful effort was made to compile an "authoritative" text from the variant "readings" (*qira'at*) of the best reciters from among the Companions of Muhammad. Carried out by Zayd ibn Thabit and other Companions who "had" the revelation "by heart," the 'Uthmanic recension was an attempt to eliminate divergent arrangements of the Qur'anic material, to prevent errors and interpolations, and to provide a single text for ritual and educational use in the rapidly expanding Islamic community.

Variant readings, such as those of Ibn Mas'ud, did persist long after 'Uthman, but these are of relatively minor import and have not been a crucial issue in Muslim life. Recitative variants have even been classified according to seven accepted systems. There has been little discord among Muslims over the integrity of the basic 'Uthmanic text, although some among the Shi'a have made charges of omissions concerning Ali and his descendants.

While a few non–Muslim scholars have questioned the antiquity of the received text, these scholars have found little acceptance for their ideas, and the *Qur'an* remains of all major scriptures the one with the clearest textual history. This is largely due to the voluminous records and scholarship of the Muslims from early times. They have always recognized (even in some measure when literalist concepts of God's revelation and speech have prevailed) that the faultless preservation and transmission (*tawatur*) of God's Word must be assured by the community and its consensus. The Divine Speech had to be preserved in human hearts, recited on human tongues, and written by human hands. The Muslims themselves, collectively, through every generation, are the bondsmen for the inviolate integrity of the Divine Word; to understand this is to understand in good part the close identification of the Muslim *umma*—the Muslim community—with the *Qur'an*'s scriptural revelation.

The religious significance of the *Qur'an* is reflected in Muslim attitudes toward, and treatment of, the *Qur'an* across the centuries and around the globe. In the *Qur'an*, Muslims find the quintessential expression of God's Eternal Word, which is with God on a "preserved tablet," "The Mother of the Book," or simply "The Book." From a Muslim perspective, the *Qur'an* sums up, corrects, and completes the revelations given earlier prophets such as Moses and Jesus, and in it Muslims find the basic source for social order, personal ethics, devotion, liturgy, salvation history, eschatology, and the life of faith.

Of all Muslim religious sciences, the noblest is the study of God's Word—its meaning, proper reading, and practical application. Qur'anic interpretation in particular has been prolific and important in every age, normally taking the form of detailed exegesis with historical, grammatical, and theological explanation of every line. Memorization of the entire *Qur'an* has been and remains the mark of learning and piety, carrying with it the honored title of Hafiz—one who "guards" the Book in the heart.

Every performance of prayer—of *salat*—involves recitation from the *Qur'an*, and non–Arab Muslims who know no other words of Arabic know enough of it to recite segments in worship. To touch the *Qur'an*, one must be ritually pure; to copy it is a sacred task; to give it is to give the finest gift.

Mystics have chanted and sung, meditated upon, and esoterically interpreted the *Qur'an*; grammarians have based rules for Arabic on it; theologians have formulated guidelines for all of life in light of it; artists have embellished almost all Islamic buildings and artifacts with its words in elaborate calligraphy; conservators of the status quo have claimed it as their authority; reformers have built movements around a return to its preaching; and ordinary people have patterned their lives as well as their speech after its words. The *Qur'an* stands at the core of Islamic faith as the active communication of the divine will for humankind.[498]

THE *HADITH*

While the *Qur'an* is at the core of Islamic faith, it is not the only source for Islamic religious beliefs.

After the reign of 'Abd al-Malik came to an end in 705 C.C., there were legal, ascetic, and philosophical movements that exerted some influence on Muslim thought. None of them, however, adequately interpreted the nature of Islamic corporate identity. The creed of Abu Hanifa did emphasize the importance of knowing God and publicly professing faith in him, but it was probably not widely accepted before 750 C.C. What needed to emerge to provide a genuine basis for solidarity was a scriptural authority complementary to the *Qur'an* but more specific in detail, avowedly Arab in content yet also Islamic in tone.

Toward the end of the Umayyad dynasty in 750 C.C., a group of pious Muslims emerged who began to develop a core of Muslim thought which advanced the principle of *jama'a*. These pious Muslims were known as *Qur'an* reciters. They were trained to intone the scriptural core of Islamic faith on ritual, public occasions. They also circulated among themselves reports about what the Prophet and his companions had said or done that would be relevant for those attempting to lead a fully pious Islamic life.

The reports that were circulated by the *Qur'an* reciters soon became a body of literature that is today known as the *hadith*. These reports, with their text and verifiable line of transmitters, became the basis for constructing the biography of Muhammad. Some of the reports provided background information for the occasions on which

---

[498]As an historical aside, because the Arabic language in which the *Qur'an* came to be written is considered sacred, and because Islamic law forbade most kinds of representational images, beginning in the 600s, great attention was paid in Islamic art to calligraphy—to handwriting—as an expression of faith and of beauty.

passages in the *Qur'an* had been revealed to Muhammad. Others described the Prophet's reaction to skirmishes and battles in which Muhammad had participated. These reports—these *hadith*—thus became supplementary to the *Qur'an* in detail and complementary to the *Qur'an* in authority.

However, the original *hadith* were not immediately evaluated, arranged, and compiled as independent books of particular importance for Islamic jurisprudence—for *fiqh*. The potential of the *hadith* for defining Muslim corporate and private modes of conduct was still unrealized. Extraordinary fluidity in range of material and scope of interpretation continued to characterize legal, doctrinal, ascetic, and philosophical issues to the end of the Umayyad period.

THE *SIRAH*

In addition to the *Qur'an* and the *hadith*, Muslims have also come to rely upon commentaries which were composed during the early days of the religion.

With regards to Islamic biblical commentaries on Genesis, the most notable Islamic commentary on Genesis is Ibn Ishaq's *Sirah*. Ibn Ishaq's *Sirah* is the earliest full biography of Muhammad. It is also a study of Ibn Ishaq's vision of Islam as a universal religion, the *Qur'an* as God's word, and Muhammad as the ultimate prophet. By means of the reconstructed text we can examine an early attempt to shape Muslim self-perceptions and understandings.

It is important to understand that as Islam spread after the death of Muhammad, Muslims encountered and conquered the oldest portions of the Judeo-Christian world, along with a population well schooled by long centuries of sectarian conflict to meet the challenge of Muslim missionaries. When Muhammad had encountered the Jews of Medina, he had used scriptural arguments against them. Some of those arguments were recorded in the *Qur'an* and the *Sirah*. The *Qur'an*, however, was not a complete guide for understanding Jewish and Christian Scriptures, and one of the goals of early Muslim scholars was to make adequate sense of the "biblical" references in the *Qur'an* through the use of Jewish and Christian Scriptures and other literature derived from the *ahl al-kitab*,—the People of the Book.[499]

As a result of this quest for understanding, many of Muhammad's contemporaries relied upon Jewish and Christian traditions and texts. Abu Hurayrah had extensive knowledge of the Torah; Abu Dharr, who had been a monotheist in the pre–Islamic period, was influenced by Jewish thought; and the great trio of Muhammad, Abu Bakr, and 'Umar all made visits to the Bet Midrash in Medina. Additionally, converted Jews such as 'Ubayy bin Ka'b, transmitted much information originally derived from rabbinic traditions found in the Talmud and Midrashim. The same can be said of Ka'b al-Ahbar, the Yemenite Jew who converted under the caliphate of Abu Bakr and was the author of numerous works on biblical matters.

---

[499]Some of the literature of the *ahl al-kitab* which undoubtedly influenced Muslim perceptions of the Scriptures was the intertestamental literature which abounded in Southwest Asia. A brief discussion and presentation of the scope of the intertestamental literature appears in Appendices 21 through 23 of this book. However, a fuller understanding of the role that the intertestamental literature played in the development of Muslim, Christian, and Jewish thought is crucial in understanding how these faiths came to be and, God willing, the intertestamental literature will be presented and discussed at length in the succeeding volumes of *The Creation*.

However, the primary credit for assimilating biblical traditions into Islam must be attributed to Ibn 'Abbas. Ibn 'Abbas was the ultimate authority for many of the *hadith* reports found in Ibn Ishaq's *Kitab al-Mubtada'*. Ibn 'Abbas was so important for the development of *Qur'an* commentary, particularly the type called *Isra'iliyat*, that subsequent generations, confronted with the necessity of assigning attribution and authority to already accepted anonymously derived *hadith* reports, chose his name as the one figure who would not be controverted.

The generation after Muhammad continued the practice of seeking extra–Islamic material for *Qur'an* commentary, biography of prophets, and for personal devotion. For example, Abu Jald of Basrah was accustomed to reading both the *Qur'an* and the Torah in his devotionals, claiming that divine mercy derived from reading both of them. Ultimately, Ibn Ishaq, as an inheritor of this tradition, augmented reliance upon both Jewish and Christian sources in developing his *Sirah*.

When Ibn Ishaq wrote the *Sirah*, sometime before 767 C.C., Muhammad, the founder of Islam, had been dead for over a century. During that first Islamic century, Muslim conquerors and settlers had established themselves from southern France and the Iberian peninsula in the west to the Indus valley in the east. Arab Muslims seized the empire of the Persian Sassanids and took over the major eastern territories of the Byzantine empire. The conquering forces from Arabia became the rulers of Alexandria, Antioch, Ctesiphon, Damascus, Jerusalem, and similar major centers of religion and power. However, Muslim political control did not mean that the population instantly converted to Islam. The population in the newly acquired Islamic lands changed religions only very slowly, even though they acknowledged the Muslims as masters. It is estimated that by the middle of the eighth century of the Christian calendar only about eight percent of the population of Persia (Iran) had become Muslim. Similar rates of conversion can be assumed for the other areas conquered by Muslim forces. Ibn Ishaq lived and wrote in a world where Christians, Jews, and Zoroastrians vastly outnumbered Muslims.

The dynamic first century of the Muslim diaspora was also a period of internal contention and conflict about the nature of the new religion of Islam and the nature of Islamic society. When Muslims began writing histories of the beginnings of Islam, most of which date no earlier than the end of the 700s, members of the Islamic community were depicted as agreeing on some fundamental assumptions about their religious heritage. For example, it was agreed that Muhammad had founded a new religion called Islam; that God had spoken to the world through Muhammad; that the record of God's message was the *Qur'an*; that the *Qur'an* was complete in Muhammad's lifetime; and that Islam was the natural and proper heir to the prophetic traditions of Judaism and Christianity. However, the development of foundation stories in Islam covered over political and doctrinal disputes in ways similar to the role played by foundation stories in Christianity or Judaism.

Two of the most important topics of discussion in the first centuries of the Muslim diaspora were the nature of the Qur'anic canon and the source of the authority in Islam. A close examination of the historical record shows that there was very little agreement about these fundamental areas of religious discourse. Indeed, the first centuries of the Muslim diaspora were marked by a proliferation of rival groups, each with a religious and political message. Civil wars, the rise of the Kharijites, the beginnings of the *Shi'i*, and dynastic revolutions were all part of the early social and intellectual discourse.

It was in this context that Ibn Ishaq composed his biography of Muhammad, not as a neutral, dispassionate piece of scholarship but as an active voice in the vocal debate. Ibn Ishaq's purpose was to write a "salvation history," an apostolic proclamation preaching the religious message of Muhammad. In the *Sirah*, Ibn Ishaq helped form an image of Muhammad that accounted for the rise of Islam. In doing so, Ibn Ishaq also explained the course of the history of the world, established the primacy of the Quranic text as scripture, and installed Muhammad as the central religious authority for Muslims. The effect of the *Sirah* was to begin the formalization of the image of Muhammad.

Ibn Ishaq set an ambitious plan for his biography of Muhammad, a plan that went well beyond the events of Muhammad's life and political career. The *Sirah* began with creation, described the lives of all the prophets mentioned in the *Qur'an*—and some who were not mentioned—and ended with Muhammad. The form was universal history; the content was a mixture of Jewish Haggadah, Arab folklore, and Christian martyrology. In the *Sirah*, characteristic features associated with earlier prophets became attached to the description of Muhammad. According to Ibn Ishaq, Adam founded God's worship in Mecca, Abraham restored both the worship and the shrine, and Muhammad, by cleansing the Ka'ba and restoring God's worship, became the new Adam and the new Abraham. Islam, by extension, was cast as the new dispensation, a theological parallel to growing Muslim hegemony over Jews and Christians in the conquered territories.

There are three sections of the *Sirah*: the *Kitab al-Mubtada'*, the *Kitab al-Mab'ath*, and the *Kitab al-Maghazi*. Each of these sections is distinguished by subject and, to some extent, by source material. The *Kitab al-Mubtada'*,—the first section—, covers the period from Creation up to the beginning of Arabian pre–Islamic history. It includes the Arabian prophets Hud and Salih as well as the Arabian interests of Adam, Abraham, Solomon, and Bilqis. However, the primary focus of the *Kitab al-Mubtada'* is on the ancient history of God's revelations to the world. Accordingly, the *Kitab al-Mubtada'*, can justly be translated as "The Book of Beginnings" or "The Book of Genesis."

The *Kitab al-Mab'ath* starts with Arabian events that lead directly to the stories of the birth and early life of Muhammad. The scope is first of all Arabia. However, as the chronological presentation comes closer to Muhammad's birth, the focus is on the Hijaz, and finally on Mecca. There are tales of Jews, Christians, and pagans foretelling the coming of Muhammad and his prophetic mission. The *Kitab al-Mab'ath* is "The Book of the Sending Forth" or "The Book of the Advent."

The *Kitab al-Maghazi* covers Muhammad's career as a prophet, community leader, and military commander. This is the section of the Sirah that is most biographical in the modern, Western sense of the term. The *Kitab al-Maghazi*—the "Book of Military Campaigns"—is the political and military history of the formation of the community of Islam up to Muhammad's death in 632 C.C.

Ibn Ishaq includes or refers to passages from the *Qur'an* in all three sections of the *Sirah*, although the *Sirah* cannot, and should not, be primarily considered as a *Qur'an* commentary. Each of the stories in the *Sirah* assumes a certain knowledge of the *Qur'an*. Short references usually suffice to tie the passage to a particular verse in Scripture, and only occasionally is the *Qur'an* cited *in extenso*. However, there is some question about the state and completeness of the canon of the *Qur'an* at the time that Ibn Ishaq was writing. Both the image of Muhammad and the nature of the *Qur'an* appear to have been in flux. Insofar as the *Sirah* supplies material that locates the occasion of the revelation of a Qur'anic passage within the history of Muhammad's career or supplies auxiliary material for understanding the meaning of a particular passage, Ibn Ishaq helped form a view of the *Qur'an* that became part of the Islamic community's understanding of the canon.

Ibn Ishaq had an inclusive view of what sources could be used to set the life of Muhammad into a world history context. Ibn Ishaq drew on a wide variety of material available to him: Arab legends, oral reports from converts to Islam, recollections by older women, and assorted books and inscriptions. Among the materials which Ibn Ishaq used in the *Sirah* was a body of stories called in Arabic *Isra'iliyat* (Judaica). These were stories about and usually derived from Jews and Christians. The *Isra'iliyat* were used most extensively in the first part of the biography, the *Kitab al-Mubtada'* and the *Kitab al-Mab'ath*, although they are scattered throughout the *Sirah*. In their Jewish or Christian contexts, the literary sources for *Isra'iliyat* are haggadic and midrashic treatises {see pages 123–124} which explicated Scripture. One effect of Ibn Ishaq's use of *Isra'iliyat* is to link the *Sirah* and the *Qur'an* to previous Scripture through the *Sirah* stories. The *Sirah*, particularly the *Kitab al-Mubtada'*, is a commentary on the Bible as well as a commentary on the *Qur'an*. In telling its stories, the *Sirah* also fosters the Muslim claim that Islam is the heir to Judaism and Christianity.

IBN ISHAQ

Ibn Ishaq (c.704-c.767) started collecting information for the *Sirah* in Arabia, in his native city of Medina. Ibn Ishaq was the grandson of a Persian war captive who had converted to Islam. He was educated by his father and his uncle, who were themselves collectors of stories about Muhammad.

Ibn Ishaq made at least one trip to Egypt to research the biography among the descendants of the Companions of Muhammad who had moved there. However, there are good reasons to believe that only the *Kitab al-Maghazi*—the political and military history of the community—was composed at this period of his life. With the rise of the Abbasids around 750 C.C., Ibn Ishaq left Medina and journeyed to the Abbasid center of power in Iraq, where he became attached to the court of the caliph al-Mansur (v. 754–775) at his palace in the new city of Baghdad. Ibn Ishaq became the court tutor for al-Mansur's heir, Muhammad bin 'Abdullah al-Mahdi (v. 775–785). Although we know little of his duties, Ibn Ishaq's *Sirah* appears to have been part of the instructional material for the future caliph.

In the generation after Ibn Ishaq, the use of extra–Islamic sources fell into disrepute. Use of *Isra'iliyat* was frowned upon by many Muslims and banned by the most scrupulous scholars. In that climate, a summarized version of the *Sirah* was made by the Egyptian scholar Ibn Hisham (c.834 C.C.). Ibn Hisham's shortened version disposed of most of the *Isra'iliyat*. Ibn Hisham's summary eliminated almost all of the *Kitab al-Mubtada'* and some portions of the *Kitab al-Mab'ath* as well. Ibn Hisham's version of the *Sirah* began with a genealogy that linked Muhammad to the biblical past while concentrating on the Prophet's mission and the history of the founding of the *umma*—the Islamic community. Ibn Ishaq's world history perspective and catholic methodology was excised. Ibn Hisham's version of the *Sirah* became the popular one, and is the one which survives mostly intact to this day.

Nevertheless, the material of Ibn Ishaq's *Kitab al-Mubtada'* was able to garner a rather wide and favorable circulation among *Qur'an* commentators, purveyors of stories of the prophets, and historians. In particular, the famous historian Muhammad bin Jarir at-Tabari (839–923 C.C.) quoted Ibn Ishaq's *Sirah* extensively in his monumental history, *Kitab Ta'rikh ar Rusul wa-l-Muluk*, and his *Qur'an* commentary, *Jami' al-Bayan 'an Ta'wil al-Quran*. Accordingly, Ibn Ishaq's vision of world history set the pattern not only for at-Tabari's scholarship but also for the many scholars who followed after him.

IBN HISHAM

As far as we know, no manuscript of the entire *Sirah* survives. What does survive is a summary of it composed by Abu Muhammad 'Abd al-Malik bin Hisham, known to history as Ibn Hisham. Ibn Hisham was an Egyptian scholar who died around 833 C.C., a little more than half a century after Ibn Ishaq. This is the work that is known in the Muslim world as the *Sirah*. In the *Sirah*, most of the *Kitab al-Mubtada'* and some of the *Kitab al-Mab'ath* were eliminated. Ibn Ishaq represented the end of an era of open scholarly inquiry into Jewish and Christian knowledge, and Ibn Hisham's summary marked a closing of the doors of such open investigation. The closing of those doors coincided with, and was part of, the formation of a new Islamic self-image. Ironically, Ibn Ishaq's *Sirah*, notwithstanding its wide vision, was one of the instruments that crafted a more self-contained Islamic self-image. By concentrating on Muhammad and raising Muhammad above the other prophets, Ibn Ishaq helped make Islamic scholarship independent of Jewish and Christian sources.

CREATION, ADAM AND EVE

The *Qur'an* does not give a complete narrative of the sequence of creation. Indeed, the passages that do appear in the *Qur'an* concerning creation are often fragmentary. It is the stories that Ibn Ishaq collected in his *Sirah* which fill the spaces and gaps that are evident in the Qur'anic material. The following are edited and codified (in biblical mode) excerpts from Ibn Hisham's version of Ibn Ishaq's *Sirah* on the subject of the Creation.

IN THE NAME OF GOD, THE MERCIFUL AND THE COMPASSIONATE[500]

1 *Concerning God's saying, "And He was the One who created the heavens and the earth in six days; and His throne was upon the water" [Q 11:7]*[501]

2 *Ibn Ishaq said: "It was as the Blessed*

---

[500]For the footnotes which appear in this section and which quote Sura passages, the first half footnote is taken from A. J. Arberry's *The Koran Interpreted*, while the second half footnote is taken from Ahmed Ali's Qur'an translation which comprises *Sacred Writings: Islam: The Qur'an*.

[501]Sura 11:7 reads:

And it is He who created the heavens and the earth in six days, and His Throne was upon the waters—that He might try you, which one of you is fairer in works. And if thou sayest, "You shall surely be raised up after death," the unbelievers will say, "This is naught but a manifest sorcery."

[It is He who created the heavens and the earth in six spans, and has control over the waters (of life) so that he may bring out the best that everyone of you could do. Yet if you said to them: "You shall certainly be raised from the dead," the unbelievers will say: "This will be nothing but sorcery."]

and Most High described Himself: There was nothing but water upon which was the throne, which possessed might, power, and authority.

3 The first thing that God created was light and darkness.[502] Then He separated the two of them, and He made the darkness into night, black and murky. He made the light into day, bright and sight-giving.

4 Then He vaulted the seven heavens out of smoke. Some say that it was out of steam, but God knows best.

Thus they stood by themselves.

5 God had not yet set orbits for the stars, and He made night dark in the lowest heaven and doused its light.

6 Night and day coursed through it, but it was still without a sun or a moon or stars.

7 Then God spread out the earth and anchored it with mountains. He assigned nourishment for the earth and put what creatures He pleased on it.

8 And in four days, He completed the earth and the nourishment He had decreed."

9 Then He turned to the heavens, which were smoke, as was said, and He gave them their courses.

10 He fixed the sun, the moon, and the stars in the lowest heaven, and He imparted rule to each heaven.

11 He completed their creation in two days and finished the creation of the heavens and the earth in six days.

12 On the seventh day, He mounted His heavens.

13 He said to the heavens and the earth, "Come, willingly or unwillingly'; do as I wish, and be calmed willingly or unwillingly."

14 Both of them said, "We come willingly." [Q 41:11][503]

15 The People of the Torah say that He began the Creation on Sunday and finished it on the Sabbath, and He made it a festival for His servants, making it great, honored, and noble.

16 The People of the Gospels say that the beginning was on Monday and that the end was on Sunday.

17 Muslims say that the beginning of creation was on the Sabbath and the completion was on Friday, for Friday is called the Day of Congregation on account of the coming together of creation on that day.

18 The People of the Book claim that God created the angels from fire. Fire and light are the same here in the sense of refined light.

---

[502]In only one place is Ibn Ishaq's *Sirah* in stark variance with the Qur'an. This appears in Ibn Ishaq's report that light and darkness were the first creations, after which Allah distinguished between the two of them, making night and day. Many Islamic scholars prefer the traditions derived from Ibn 'Abbas. In these traditions, it is contended that God was seated on his throne above the heavenly waters before creation and that the first thing that God created was the pen. However, it is evident that Ibn Ishaq adheres more closely to the biblical account, probably because his sources were the *ahl al-kitab*—the People of the Book. Nevertheless, the notion that the pen was the first creation persists in large part because of Sura 96:3–5 which states: *Recite: And thy Lord is the Most Generous, who taught by the Pen, taught Man that he knew not. [Read, for your Lord is the most beneficent, Who taught by the Pen, taught Man what he did not know.]* Additionally, there is the notion that the pen is an extension of the Divine Logos—the Word of God.

[503]Sura 41:11 actually reads:

Then He lifted Himself to heaven when it was smoke, and said to it and to the earth, "Come willingly, or unwillingly!" They said, "We come willingly."

[Then He turned to the heavens, and it was smoke. So He said to it and the earth: "Come with willing obedience or perforce." They said: "We come willingly."]

19 Ibn Ishaq said...: "Before Iblis[504] fomented rebellion among the angels, his name was Azazil. He dwelt on earth and was the most diligent and the most knowledgeable of the angels. That is what led to his pride. He was of a race called the Jinn."[505]

20 When God wished to use His power to create Adam as an obedience test of Adam, the angels, and all of creation, God assembled the heavenly and earthly angels and said, "I am going to put a viceroy on earth [Q 2:30],[506] an inhabitant or dweller who will live in it and populate it with creatures other than you."

21 Having told them about His plan, God said, "They will act corruptly on the earth, shed blood, and foment rebellion."

21 Together the angels said, "Will you put there one who will act corruptly and shed blood while we sing praises to you and sanctify you? [Q 2:30] We do not disobey nor do we do anything which you hate."

22 God said, "I know what you do not. I have more knowledge than you. There is no other way but for them to be rebellious, corrupt, shedders of blood, and doers on the earth of what I hate,...."

23 God said to the angels, "...I will create a mortal of clay, and when I have fashioned him and breathed my spirit into him, fall down prostrating to him." [Q 38:72][507]

24 The angels heeded His admonition and took the words to heart.

25 All agreed to obey Him except Iblis, the Enemy of God. He kept silent because of the envy, covetousness, and pride in his soul.

26 God created Adam from earth out of sticky clay which He shaped with His hand, giving him honor and making him great by His command.

---

[504]Roughly speaking, Iblis is the Arabic equivalent of the Christian Satan. As an angel in good standing, Iblis was once treasurer of the heavenly Paradise. Indeed, before his fall, Iblis was called Azazil (Azazel). But when Adam was created, God commanded all the angels to worship Adam. Iblis refused and, as his punishment, God turned Iblis into a devil and, thereafter, Iblis became the father of devils. In the Qur'an, Iblis is deemed to be a jinn rather than an angel or a fallen angel. The Arabs have three categories of spirits: angels, jinn (good and evil) and demons.

[505]In Muslim theology, the jinn were created 2,000 years before Adam. They were originally of a high estate, equal to the angels, with Iblis being chief among them. But when Iblis refused to worship Adam and was cast out of Heaven, the jinn were cast out with him. These jinn subsequently became demons.

[506]Sura 2:30 reads:

> And when thy Lord said to the angels, "I am setting in the earth a viceroy." They said, "What, wilt Thou set therein one who will do corruption there, and shed blood, while We proclaim Thy praise and call Thee Holy?" He said, "Assuredly I know that you know not."

> [Remember, when your Lord said to the angels: "I have to place a trustee on the earth," they said: "Will You place one there who would create disorder and shed blood, while we intone Your litanies and sanctify Your name?" And God said: "I know what you do not know."]

[507]Sura 38:71–72 reads:

> 71 When thy Lord said to the angels, "See, I am creating a mortal of a clay. 72 When I have shaped him, and breathed My spirit in him, fall you down, bowing before him!"

> [71 When your Lord said to the angels: "I am going to create a man from clay; 72 And when I have made him and have breathed into him of My spirit, fall down in homage before him."]

27 It is said, and God knows best, that God created Adam and then put him aside for forty days before he breathed the spirit in him so that he became dry clay like pottery untouched by fire.

28 His creation was on Friday at the last hour. That is because of God's words, "Has there come upon man a time when he was a thing not remembered?" [Q 76:1][508]

29 The People of the Torah give an exegesis that God created Adam in His image when He wished to give Adam dominion over the earth and what is in it.

30 It is said, and God knows best, that when the spirit got into his head, he sneezed and said, "Praise be to God," and his Lord said to him, "God bless you."

31 When Adam stood up, the angels fell down prostrating to him, remembering God's admonition, obeying His order.

32 The Enemy of God, Iblis, stood among them, and he did not prostrate himself out of pride, desire, and envy.

33 He said to him, "O Iblis, what prevents you from prostrating to what I created with my hands ... I will fill Hell with you and those who follow you." [Q 38:76–86][509]

34 When God finished censuring Iblis and he still refused to do anything but rebel, God cast a curse on him and expelled him from the Garden.

35 Then He went to Adam and taught him all names. He said "O Adam, inform them of their names ... up to His words ... You are the Knower, the Wise." [Q 2:31–32][510]

---

[508]Sura 76:1 reads:

Has there come on man a while of time when he was a thing unremembered?

[Was there not a time in the life of man when he was not even a mentionable thing?]

[509]Sura 38:76–88 reads:

76 Said he, "I am better than he; Thou createdst me of fire, and him Thou createdst of clay." 77 Said He, "Then go thou forth hence; thou are accursed. 78 Upon thee shall rest My curse, till the Day of Doom." 79 Said he, "My Lord, respite me till the day they shall be raised." 80 Said He, "Thou art among the ones that are respited 81 until the day of the known time." 82 Said he, "Now, by Thy glory, I shall pervert them all together, 83 excepting those Thy servants among them that are sincere." 84 Said He, "This is the truth, and the truth I say; 85 I shall assuredly fill Gehenna with thee, and with whosoever of them follows thee, all together." 86 Say: "I ask of you no wage for it, neither am I of those who take things upon themselves. 87 It is nothing but a reminder unto all beings, 88 and you shall surely know its tiding after a while."

[76 He said: "I am better than he. You created me from fire, and him from clay. 77 (God) said: "Then go hence, ostracised. 78 Upon you will be My damnation till the Day of Doom." 79 He said: "O Lord, give me respite till the day the dead rise from their graves." 80 (God) said: "You have the respite 81 Till the appointed day." 82 He said: "By Your authority, I will lead them astray, 83 Other than the chosen ones among Your creatures." 84 (God) said: "This is right by Me, and what I say is right. 85 I will fill up Hell with you together with those who follow you." 86 Say: "I do not ask any compensation of you for it, nor am I a specious pretender. 87 This is only a warning for mankind. 88 You will come to know its truth in time."]

[510]Sura 2:31–32 reads:

31 And He taught Adam the names, all of them; then He presented them unto the angels and said, "Now tell Me the names of these, if you speak truly." 32 They said, "Glory be to Thee! We know not save what Thou hast taught us. Surely Thou art the All-knowing, the All-wise."

36 Adam walked upright, and there was no other animal on the earth walking like him.

37 The Eagle came to the sea and said to the Fish, "I have seen a creature walking on his hind feet. It has two hands to attack with, and on each hand are five fingers."

38 The Fish said, "It is my opinion that you are describing a creature that will not leave you alone in the height of the air nor leave me alone in the depth of the sea."

39 'Abdullah bin al-'Abbas reported on the authority of the People of Scripture, the People of the Torah, and other scholars that God cast a sleep over Adam.

40 He took one of his ribs from an opening in his left side and repaired the place with flesh while Adam slept, not waking from his slumber.

41 Then God created Eve from his rib as a mate for him. He made her a woman so that Adam would find her a comfort.

42 When sleep was lifted from him, and he awoke from his slumber, he saw her at his side, and he said, according to what they say, and God knows best, "My flesh and my blood and my mate."

43 So he was comforted by her.

44 Now that God had made a mate for Adam and gave him comfort, He said to him, "Enter, O Adam, you and your mate; dwell in the garden and eat what is pleasant there. But do not come near this tree, for you will be among the sinners." [Q 2:35][511]

45 Ibn 'Abbas used to say on the authority of a scholar who got it from Mujahid

that the tree which Adam was forbidden was the wheat tree.

46 Some of the people of the Yemen, on the authority of Wahb bin Munabbih the Yemenite, used to say that it was the wheat tree, but the fruit from it in the Garden was like the kidneys of the cow, softer than butter and sweeter than honey.

47 The People of the Torah would say that it was the wheat tree.

48 Ya'qub bin 'Utbah related that it was the tree which the angels used to touch in order to live forever.

49 On the authority of Layth bin Abu Sulaym, who got it from Taus the Yamanite, Ibn 'Abbas said that the Enemy of God, Iblis, presented himself to the animals of the world to see which one of them would carry him into the Garden to talk with Adam and his wife.

50 All of the animals refused until he talked with the serpent.

51 He said to her, "I will protect you from the children of Adam; you will be under my protection if you get me into the Garden."

52 So she placed him between her two fangs. Then she went in with him, and the two of them spoke from her mouth.

53 She was graceful, walking up on all fours, but God, the Most High, afflicted her and made her walk on her belly.

54 Ibn 'Abbas used to say, "Kill her wherever you find her, and watch out for the protection of the Enemy of God over her."

55 Some scholars said that when Adam, peace be unto him, entered the Garden, saw

---

[31 Then He gave Adam knowledge of the nature and reality of all things and every thing, and set them before the angels and said: "Tell Me the names of these if you are truthful." 32 And they said: "Glory to You (O Lord), knowledge we have none except what You have given us, for You are all-knowing and all-wise."]

[511]Sura 2:35 reads:

And We said, "Adam, dwell thou, and thy wife, in the Garden, and eat thereof easefully where you desire; but draw not nigh this tree, lest you be evildoers."

[And We said to Adam: "Both you and your spouse live in the Garden, eat freely to your fill whereever you like, but approach not this tree or you will become transgressors."]

the noble things in it and what God had given him out of it, he said, "If only we could live forever."

56 When the Devil heard that from him, he discovered his weakness and came to him offering eternal life.

57 The first of the Devil's plots against Adam and Eve was that he wept over them, mourning them.

58 When they heard it, they said to him, "What makes you to weep?"

59 He said, "I weep for the two of you, because you will die and leave the pleasure and honor you are in."

60 That struck their very souls.

61 Then the Devil came to them and whispered to them, saying, "O Adam, Shall I lead you to the tree of eternal life and the power of not growing old?" [Q 20:120][512]

62 "Your Lord did not keep you from this tree except that you would become two angels or that you would become immortal."

63 And, he swore to the two of them: "I am one of the well-wishers for you [Q 7:20–21],[513] that is, you two will become angels or you will live forever. Even if you are not two angels, you will not die while in the pleasure of the Garden."

64 This is according to God's words, "He led them with vanities." [Q 7:22][514]

65 Sa'id bin al-Mussayib said on the authority of Yazid bin 'Abdullah bin Qusayt, "I heard him swear by God that there was no doubt that Adam did not eat from the tree while he had all his senses.

66 "Eve plied him with an intoxicating beverage. When he became drunk, she led him to the tree, and he ate of it.

67 "When Adam and Eve sinned, God expelled them from the Garden and denied them the pleasure and honor which they had.

68 "He flung them down and caused enmity on the earth between them, Iblis, and the serpent.

---

[512]Sura 20:120 reads:

Then Satan whispered to him saying, "Adam, shall I point thee to the Tree of Eternity, and a Kingdom that decays not?"

[But then Satan tempted him by saying: "O Adam, should I show you the tree of immortality, and a kingdom that will never know any wane?"]

[513]Sura 7:20–21 reads:

20 Then Satan whispered to them, to reveal to them that which was hidden from them of their shameful parts. He said, "Your Lord has only prohibited you from this tree lest you become immortals." 21 And he swore to them, "Truly, I am for you a sincere adviser."

[20 But Satan suggested (evil) to them, in order to reveal their hidden parts of which they were not aware (till then), and said: "Your Lord has forbidden you (to go near) this tree that you may not become angels or immortal." 21 Then he said to them on oath: "I am your sincere friend;"]

[514]Sura 7:22 reads:

So he led them on by delusion; and when they tasted the tree, their shameful parts revealed to them, so they took to stitching upon themselves leaves of the Garden. And their Lord called to them, "Did not I prohibit you from this tree, and say to you, 'Verily Satan is for you a manifest foe'?"

[And led them (to the tree) by deceit. When they tasted (the fruit) of the tree their disgrace became exposed to them; and they patched the leaves of the Garden to hide it. And the Lord said to them: "Did I not forbid you this tree? And I told you that Satan was your open enemy."]

69 "Their Lord said to them, Go down as enemies, some of you against the other."

70 Ibn 'Abbas and the People of the Torah said that the Devil came to Adam and his wife with God's authority, which He had given to him, to test Adam and his progeny and that he comes to the son of Adam in his sleep, while awake, and in every state.

71 The Devil comes to call him to rebellion and put lust in his soul, but he is not seen.

72 God said, "The Devil whispered to the two of them and caused them to go out of what they were in." [Q 7:20]515

73 And He said, "O Children of Adam, do not let Satan seduce you as he expelled your parents from the Garden and tore their clothes off of them to show them their shame.

74 "He sees you, he and his tribe, from whence you see them not. We have made dev-ils protectors to those who do not believe." [Q 7:27]516

75 God said to His Prophet, upon him be prayers and peace, "Say, I seek refuge in the Lord of the people, the King of the people ... up to the end of the chapter." [Q 114:1–6]517

76 Then he mentioned the account which was transmitted about the Prophet, the prayers and peace of God be upon him, that the Devil flows in mankind's bloodstream.

77 Ibn Ishaq said, "The son of Adam was instructed about what was between him and the Enemy of God just as it was commanded between him and Adam.

78 God said, "Go down from it; it is not for you to show pride here; so go out; you are of the debased" [Q 7:13]518

79 Then the Devil went to Adam and

515Sura 7:20 reads:

Then Satan whispered to them, to reveal to them that which was hidden from them of their shameful parts. He said, "Your Lord has only prohibited you from this tree lest you become angels, or lest you become immortals."

[But Satan suggested (evil) to them, in order to reveal their hidden parts of which they were not aware (till then), and said: "Your Lord has forbidden you (to go near) this tree that you may not become angels or immortal."]

517Sura 7:27 reads:

Children of Adam! Let not Satan tempt you as he brought your parents out of the Garden, stripping them of their garments to show them their shameful parts. Surely he sees you, he and his tribe, from where you see them not. We have made the Satans the friends of those who do not believe.

[O sons of Adam, let not Satan beguile you as he did your parents out of Eden, and made them disrobe to expose their disgrace to them. For he and his host can see you from where you cannot see them. We have made the devils the friends of those who do not believe.]

517Sura 114:1–6 reads:

1 Say: "I take refuge with the Lord of men, 2 the King of men, 3 the God of men, 4 from the evil of the slinking whisperer 5 who whispers in the breasts of men 6 of jinn and men."

[1 Say: "I seek refuge with the Lord of men, 2 The King of men, 3 The God of men, 4 From the evil of him who breathes temptations into the minds of men, 5 Who suggests evil thoughts to the hearts of men—6 From among the jinns and men.]

518Sura 7:13 reads:

Said He, "Get thee down out of it; it is not for thee to wax proud here, so go thou forth; surely thou art among the humbled."

his wife to talk with them, as God told us in their story: "The Devil whispered to him, saying, O Adam, shall I lead you to the tree of eternity and the power of not growing old?" [Q 20:120][519]

80 The Devil went to them as he has gone to Adam's offspring ever since, they unable to see him.

81 And, God knows best, they repented to their Lord.

82 The People of the Torah said, Adam fell down in India on a mountain called Wasim in a valley called Bahil between ad-Dahnaj and al-Mandal, two areas in the land of India.

83 Eve fell to Jiddah in the land of Mecca.

84 Adam fell on the mountain, and with him were leaves from the Garden. He spread them on that mountain, and from them was the root of all good things and all fruit found nowhere but India.

85 When Adam, upon him be peace, was cast down to the earth, he grieved about missing what he used to see and hear of God's worship in the Garden.

86 So God gave him a place to live in the Holy House and commanded him to travel to it.

87 He journeyed to it, never making camp without God's providing a spring of water for him, until he came to Mecca.

88 He remained there worshiping God at that house and circumambulating it, and it did not cease to be his home until God buried him there.

89 It reached me that Iblis, after he was expelled from the Garden, married the serpent whose mouth he entered when he spoke to Adam, upon him be peace, and they had offspring.

CAIN AND ABEL

1 According to some scholars of the People of the First Book, Adam, upon him be peace, had been having sexual intercourse with Eve in the Garden before the sin, and she bore him Cain, the son of Adam, and his twin sister.

2 She did not crave certain foods during pregnancy, nor was she uncomfortable, nor did she experience labor pains when she bore the two of them.

3 And she did not menstruate because of the purity of the Garden.

4 After the two of them ate from the tree, rebelled, fell to the earth, settled down and had intercourse, she bore Abel and his twin sister.

5 With the two of them, she craved certain foods and experienced discomfort.

6 She had labor pains when she bore them, and she saw blood with them.

7 And Eve, according to what they say, never bore any children except twins, one a male and one a female.

8 Eve bore Adam forty children, male and female, in twenty pregnancies.

9 There was a man who wished to marry no one but his twin who was born with him, but she was not licit to him.

10 That was because there was not a woman at the time except their sisters and their mother Eve.

11 On the authority of some of the scholars of the First Book, Adam commanded his son Cain to marry the twin of Abel, and he ordered Abel to marry the twin of Cain.

12 Abel agreed to that and was pleased, but Cain refused, hated to show generosity to Abel's sister, and loathed to have his own sister with Abel.

[So God said: "Descend, You have no right to be insolent here. Go, and away; you are one of the damned."]

[519]Sura 20:120 reads:

Then Satan whispered to him saying, "Adam, shall I point thee to the Tree of Eternity, and a Kingdom that decays not?" [But then Satan tempted him by saying: "O Adam, should I show you the tree of immortality, and a kingdom that will never know thy wane?"]

13 He said, "We are Children of Paradise, and they are Children of the Earth; I have more right to my sister."

14 Some of the scholars of the First Book say that, on the contrary, Cain's sister was one of the most beautiful people, and he begrudged her to his brother and wanted her for himself, and God knows which is so.

15 His father said to him, "O my son, she is not licit for you."

16 But Cain refused to accept that on his father's authority, so his father said to him, "O my son, offer a sacrifice, and your brother Abel will offer a sacrifice.

17 "Which of the two of your sacrifices God accepts, he has the greater right to her."

18 Cain was a sower of the earth, and Abel a tender of flocks; Cain offered wheat, and Abel offered the firstlings of his sheep and goats, and some say he even sacrificed a cow.

19 God, the Mighty and the Powerful, sent a white fire which consumed Abel's sacrifice, leaving the sacrifice of Cain.

20 That was how God, the Mighty and the Powerful, accepted sacrifices.

21 When God accepted Abel's sacrifice, judging in his favor about Cain's sister, Cain became angry.

22 Pride vanquished him, and the Devil urged him on.

23 So he followed his brother Abel while he was out walking and killed him.

24 They are the two about whom God told Muhammad, may the prayers and peace of God be upon him, in the Qur'an.

25 He said, "Tell them," that is, the People of the Book, "the account of the two sons of Adam in truth, when they offered sacrifices, and it was accepted from one of them ... to the end of the story." [Q 5:27][520]

---

[520]Sura 5:27–32 reads:

27 And recite thou to them the story of the two sons of Adam truthfully, when they offered a sacrifice, and it was accepted of one of them, and not accepted of the other. "I will surely slay thee," said one. "God accepts only of the godfearing," said the other. 28 "Yet if thou stretchest out thy hand against me, to slay me, I will not stretch out my hand against thee, to slay thee; I fear God, the Lord of all Being. 29 I desire that thou shouldest be laden with my sin and thy sin, and so become an inhabitant of the Fire; that is the recompense of the evildoers." 30 Then his soul prompted him to slay his brother, and he slew him, and became one of the losers. 31 Then God sent forth a raven, scratching into the earth, to show him how he might conceal the vile body of his brother. He said, "Woe is me! Am I unable to be as this raven, and so conceal my brother's vile body?" And he became one of the remorseful. 32 Therefore We prescribed for the Children of Israel that whoso slays a soul not to retaliate for a soul slain, nor for corruption done in the land, shall be as if he had slain mankind altogether; and whoso gives life to a soul, shall be as if he had given life to mankind altogether. Our Messengers have already come to them with the clear signs; then many of them thereafter commit excesses in the earth.

[27 Narrate to them exactly the tale of the two sons of Adam. When each of them offered a sacrifice (to God), that of one was accepted, and that of the other was not. Said (the one): "I will murder you," and the other replied: "God only accepts from those who are upright and preserve themselves from evil. 28 If you raise your hand to kill me, I will raise not mine to kill you, for I fear God, the Lord of all the worlds; 29 I would rather you suffered the punishment for sinning against me, and for your own sin, and became an inmate of Hell. And that is the requital for the unjust." 30 Then the other was induced by his passion to murder his brother, and he killed him, and became one of the damned. 31 Then God sent a raven which scratched the ground in order to show him how to hide the nakedness of his brother. "Alas, the woe," said he, "that I could not be even like the raven and hide the nakedness of my brother," and was filled with remorse. 32 That is why We decreed for the children of

26 When Abel fell before Cain, Cain did not know how to conceal him. According to what is asserted, that is because this was the first killing among Adam's children.

27 So God sent a raven to dig up the earth to show him how to hide the genitals of his brother.

28 He said, "Woe is me. I am not able to be as this raven and hide the genitals of my brother." ...

29 Then many of them after that became prodigals on the earth. [Q 5:31–32][521]

30 The People of the Torah assert that God said to Cain when he killed his brother Abel, "Where is your brother Abel?"

31 He said, "I do not know; I am not his guardian."

32 And God said to him, "The voice of the blood of your brother calls to me even now. You are cursed on the earth which opened its mouth and received the blood of your brother from your hand.

33 "Since you did this on the earth, it will not yield its tilth to you, so that you will become frightened and lost on the earth."

34 Cain said, "My sin has become so great that you cannot forgive it, for you have expelled me today from the face of the earth, from your presence, and I will be frightened and lost on the earth. Anyone who meets me will kill me."

35 And God, the Mighty and the Powerful, said, "That will not be so. It will not be that everyone who kills will be recompensed by seven for that one, but he who kills Cain will be accounted for by seven."

36 And God placed a sign on Cain lest anyone who found him would kill him.

37 So Cain went out from the presence of God, the Mighty and the Powerful, from the east of the Garden of Eden.

THE CHILDREN OF ADAM AND EVE

1 The total number of children that Eve bore Adam was forty males and females in twenty pregnancies.

2 The names of some of them have reached us, and some have not reached us.

3 The names of those which reached us are fifteen men and four women, among them Cain, Abel, Liyudha, Ashuth, the daughter of Adam and her twin brother, Seth and his twin sister, Hazurah and her twin brother, born when Adam was one hundred and thirty years of age.

4 Then Iyad, and his twin sister, Jaligh and his twin sister, Ithathi and his twin sister, Tubah and his twin sister, Bunan and his twin sister, Hayyan and his twin sister, Darabis and his twin sister, Hadhar and his twin sister, Sandal and his twin sister, and the Bariz and his twin sister.

5 Each man of them had a woman born with him in the same pregnancy in which he was carried.

6 On the authority of Daud bin al-Husayn, who got it from 'Ikrimah, Ibn 'Abbas said, "Eve bore children to Adam, and he devoted them to the service of God, the Mighty and the Powerful.

7 "He named them 'Abdullah [the Servant of God] and 'Ubaydallah [the Servant of God], and so on like that, and they died.

8 "So Iblis came to her and to Adam, upon him be peace, and said, 'If the two of you would name them other than what you named them, they would live.'

9 'So she bore him a boy, and the two of them named him 'Abdu-l-Harith [the servant of al-Harith]."

10 God, the Mighty and the Powerful,

Israel that whosoever kills a human being, except (as punishment) for murder or for spreading corruption in the land, it shall be like killing all humanity; and whosoever saves a life, saves the entire human race. Our apostles brought clear proofs to them; but even after that most of them committed excesses in the land.]

[521]See immediately preceding footnote for text of Sura 5: 31–32.

sent down a message about this: "He is the one who created you from one soul … up to His words … the two of them ascribed partners to Him in what He had given them … to the end of the verse." [Q 7:189–190]⁵²²

THE DEATH OF ADAM

1 According to what they allege, and God knows best, when Adam's death was near, he called his son Seth, entrusted him with his legacy, taught him the hours of the night and day, and instructed him in the worship of the Creator in every hour of them.

2 He told him that every hour has a particular characteristic for His worship.

3 He said to him, "O my son, the Flood will be upon the earth, lasting for seven years."

4 Then he wrote his will, and Seth, according to what is mentioned, was the executor of the estate of his father Adam, upon him be peace.

5 The leading position went to Seth after the death of Adam.

6 According to what is transmitted on the authority of the Messenger of God, may the prayers and peace of God be upon him, God sent down fifty sheets to him.

7 After Adam, the prayers of God be upon him, wrote his will, he died, and the angels gathered around him because he was a friend of the Merciful.

8 The angels, Seth and his brothers buried him east of Paradise in a village which was the first village on the earth.

9 The sun and the moon were eclipsed seven days and nights on account of him.

10 When the angels gathered around him, the will was taken and placed on a ladder along with the horn which our father Adam took from Paradise in order not to neglect the mention of God, the Mighty and the Powerful.

11 Yahya bin 'Abaad, who got it from his father, said, I heard him say that when Adam died, upon him be peace, God sent material from the Garden to enshroud him and embalm him.

12 Then the angels came to his grave and buried him so that the earth covered him.

13 On the authority of al-Hasan bin Dhakwan, who heard it from al-Hasan bin Abu-Hasan, Ubayy bin Ka'b said, the Messenger of God, may the prayers and peace of God be upon him, said that your father Adam, may the prayers and peace of God be upon him, was as tall as a tall palm tree, sixty cubits, and very hairy, covering his genitals.

14 When the sin touched him, his shame became apparent to him, and he fled in the Garden. A tree grabbed him and took hold of his forelock.

15 His Lord called to him, "Do you flee from me, O Adam?"

---

⁵²²Sura 7:189–190 reads:

189 It is He who created you out of one living soul, and made of him his spouse that he might rest in her. Then, when he covered her, she bore a light burden and passed by with it; but when it became heavy they cried to God their Lord, "If Thou givest us a righteous son, we indeed shall be of the thankful." 190 Thereafter, when He gave them a righteous son, they assigned Him associates in that He had given them; but God is high exalted above that they associate.

[189 It is He who created you from a single cell, and from it created its mate, that you may live as companions. When the man covered the woman she conceived a light burden and carried it about. And when she was heavy (with child) they prayed together to their Lord: "If You bestow a healthy son on us we shall truly be grateful." 190 But when they were given a healthy son, they started ascribing to other powers a share in what God had bestowed on them. But God is above what they ascribe to Him.]

16 He said, "No, by God, O Lord, except out of shame before you for what I have done."

17 So God cast him down to the earth.

18 But when his time of death came, God sent him the materials from Paradise to embalm and enshroud him.

19 When Eve saw the angels, she tried to go in to Adam without them.

20 He said, "Go away from me and the messengers of my Lord. I would not have encountered what I encountered except for you, and what happened to me would not have happened except for you."

21 When he died, they washed him with the leaves of the lote and water separately, and wrapped him in a single garment.

22 Then they dug a grave for him and buried him.

23 Then they said, "This is the precedent for the children of Adam after him."

THE DESCENDANTS OF SETH AND CAIN

1 Seth married his sister Hazurah, the daughter of Adam.

2 She bore him Enosh, (the son of Seth) and Ni'mah (the daughter of Seth).

3 Seth was at this time one hundred and five.

4 He lived beyond the time he sired Enosh eight hundred and seven years.

5 Enosh, the son of Seth, married his sister Ni'mah, the daughter of Seth, and she bore him Cainan when he was ninety years old.

6 Enosh lived after he sired Cainan eight hundred and fifteen years, and he sired sons and daughters.

7 And the lifespan of Enosh was nine hundred and five years.

8 Then Cainan, the son of Enosh, at the age of seventy married Dinah, the daughter of Barakil, the son of Mahuil, the son of Enoch, the son of Cain.

9 She (Dinah) bore … Mahalail, the son of Cainan.

10 And Cainan lived eight hundred and forty years after he sired Mahalail.

11 The lifespan of Cainan was nine hundred and ten years.

12 At the age of sixty-five, Mahalail, the son of Cainan, married his maternal aunt, Sim'an, the daughter of Barakil, who was the son of Mahuil, the son of Enoch, the son of Cain, the son of Adam.

13 She (Sim'an) bore him (Mahalail) Yarad at eight hundred and thirty; and sons and daughters were born to him.

14 The lifespan of Mahalail was eight hundred and ninety-five years, and then he died.

15 Cain married his sister Ashuth, the daughter of Adam, and she bore him men and women, Enoch (the son of Cain) and Eden (the daughter of Cain).

16 Enoch, the son of Cain, married his sister, the daughter of Cain, and she bore him men and women: 'Irad, the son of Enoch, Mahuil, the son of Enoch, Abushil, the son of Enoch, Mawlith, the daughter of Enoch.

17 Abushil, the son of Enoch, married Mawlith, the daughter of Enoch, and she bore to Abushil a man whose name was Lamech.

18 Lamech married two women: The name of the first was 'Ada, and the name of the second was Sala.

19 'Ada bore him (Lamech) Tulin, the son of Lamech, and he (Tulin) was the first to dwell in a structure with a cupola and acquire property, and Tuyish, and he was the first to play the cymbals.

20 And she bore him a son whose name was Tubalcain, and he was the first to work copper and iron.

21 Their children were giants and tyrants, and they had been given great size, so that a man, according to what they allege, would be thirty cubits.

22 Now the children of Cain died out, and they only left a few after them.

23 And all of the genealogies of Adam's descendants are unknown, and their line has

been cut off, except what was from Seth, the son of Adam.

24 From him is the line and the genealogy of all the people today, excluding his father, Adam, who is really the father of mankind.

25 The People of the Torah say that Cain married Ashuth, and she bore him Enoch, and Irad was born to Enoch, and Irad sired Mahuil, and Mahuil sired Abushil, and Abushil sired Lamech, and Lamech married 'Ada and Sala, and the two of them bore him (Lamech) the ones (previously) mentioned,…

26 Then at the age of one hundred and twenty-six, Yarad married Barkana, the daughter of ad-Darmasil, the son of Mahuil, the son of Enoch, the son of Cain.

27 She bore him Akhnukh, the son of Yarad, and Akhnukh was Idris, the prophet.

28 He was the first of the children of Adam who was given prophethood, and he wrote with the pen.

29 Yarad lived after Akhnukh was born to him eight hundred years and sons and daughters were born to him.

30 The lifespan of Yarad was nine hundred sixty-two years; then he died.

31 Then Akhnukh, the son of Yarad, married Hadanah, and, it is said, Adalah, the daughter of Bawil, the son of Mahuil, the son of Enoch, the son of Cain, the son of Adam.

32 He was sixty-five years old when Methuselah, the son of Akhnukh was born to him.

33 He lived three hundred years after Methuselah was born to him, and he sired sons and daughters.

34 The lifespan of Akhnukh was three hundred sixty-five years; then he died.

35 Then according to what Ibn Ishaq said, Methuselah married Araba, the daughter of Azrail, the son of Abushil, the son of Khanukh, the son of Cain, the son of Adam, when he was one hundred thirty-seven years old.

36 Lamech, the son of Methuselah, was born to him and he lived seven hundred years after Lamech was born, and sons and daughters were born to him.

37 The lifespan of Methuselah was nine hundred and nineteen years; then he died.

38 Lamech, the son of Methuselah, married Cainush, the daughter of Barakil, the son of Mahuil, the son of Enoch, the son of Cain, the son of Adam, upon him be peace.

39 He was one hundred eighty-seven years old when Noah, the prophet, may the prayers and peace of God be upon him, was born to him.

40 Lamech lived five hundred and ninety-five years after Noah was born to him, and his lifespan was seven hundred and eighty years; then he died.

41 Noah, the son of Lamech, married Amrurah, the daughter of Barakil, the son of Mahuil, the son of Enoch, the son of Cain, the son of Adam, and he was five hundred years old when his sons Shem, Ham, and Japheth were born to him.

NOAH AND THE FLOOD

The *Sirah* story of Noah follows the *Qur'an* closely, utilizing extensive quotations and references to this popular Islamic prophet. As has been observed by both Muslim and non–Muslim scholars, the figure of Noah is conceived as a pre-figuration of Muhammad. This is because Noah is understood as a new Adam, ushering in a new age, a view of Noah that Muslims share with Christians and Jews.

It should be noted that there are similarities between the rabbinic (Jewish) version and the Islamic version of the Noah story. This is particularly noticeable for the story of Noah's son, Yam, the son who was left behind. Additionally, the figure of Og ('Uj) in the Islamic version of the Noah story also appears in the Jewish stories about this giant. Og is supposed to have been born before the flood and survived by riding on the ark.

The Qur'anic passage "We opened the gates of heaven with pouring water and we caused the earth to gush forth springs, and the waters met according to a preordained command" [Q 54:11–12][523] presupposes the notion of the undoing of the original act of creation as described in Genesis, when the waters were divided. Here, the primordial waters come together, and only a few humans survive. On the number of passengers on the ark, Ibn Ishaq lists Noah, his wife, Shem, Ham, and Japheth, their wives, and six more believers. In various Muslim versions of the Noah story, the number varies between seven and eighty people. However, in Ibn Ishaq's variation, the passenger manifest lists enough humans for a *minyan*—a Jewish religious quorum.

The stories of the Devil's trick to enter the ark and the etiological stories of the first cats and the first pigs are similar in type to those told by early Muslim street preachers, the *Qass*. The early Muslim street preachers began to appear around the time of the caliph 'Umar I (634–644 C.C.), preaching on street corners and in mosques. The *Qass* soon acquired considerable popular followings and sometimes had more authority among the Muslim rank and file than the learned scholars. It appears that the *Qass* were purveyors of a wide variety of stories, some of which appear in Jewish literature. The popularity of the preachers helped assimilate these stories into general use in sermons and *Qur'an* commentaries.

Other details to note in the Muslim version of the Noah story are the extensions of the genealogies and the system of chronology beyond the usual biblical parameters. By including the pre–Islamic ancestors of the Arabs, Ibn Ishaq attempted to integrate the Arabs into the biblical panorama. It is this panorama that appropriates, in a distinctly Islamic key, successive periods of reckoning human history that end with the era of Muhammad. Thus, by this device, Ibn Ishaq underscores the emergence of Islam as the result of an inevitable historical progression.

1 In the name of God, the Merciful and the Compassionate

2 [It is said that the people of Noah's time would attack Noah.]

3 [They] would choke him until he would pass out.

4 When he would recover, he would say, "O Lord, forgive my people for they are unknowing."

5 This went on until they spread rebellion, and sin became great on the earth because of them.

6 He waited for son after son, but every age was more wicked than the one before, until it was the last.

7 All the while he would say, "This madness was with our fathers and our uncles."

8 Noah's people would not accept anything from him, so Noah complained about their situation to God, the Mighty and the Powerful.

9 He said, as God, the Mighty and the Powerful, told us in His Book, "Lord, I have called my people night and day, but my calling does not add anything but defection" … up to the end of the story … when he said, "Do not leave one of the unbelievers on the earth, for if You leave them, they will lead

---

[523]Sura 54:11–12 reads:

11 Then We opened the gates of heaven unto water torrential, 12 and made the earth to gush with fountains, and the waters met for a matter decreed.

[11 And We opened up the flood gates of the sky with water pouring down in torrents, 12 And we opened up the springs of the earth; and the waters met for a decreed end.]

Your servants astray, and I will sire not ... up to the end of the story." [Q 71:5–27][524]
10 *When Noah complained about them* this way to his Lord, and asked His help against them, God, the Mighty and the Powerful, inspired him, "Build a ship under our

---

[524]Sura 71 reads:

1 We sent Noah to his people, saying, "Warn thy people, ere there come on them a painful chastisement." 2 He said, "O my people, I am unto you a clear warner, saying, 3 'Serve God, and fear Him, and obey you me, 4 and He will forgive you your sins, and defer you to a stated term; God's term, when it comes, cannot be deferred, did you but know.'" 5 He said, "My Lord, I have called my people by night and by day, 6 but my calling has only increased them in flight. 7 And whenever I called them, that Thou mightest forgive them, they put their fingers in their ears, and wrapped them in their garments, and persisted, and waxed very proud. 8 Then indeed I called them openly; 9 then indeed I spoke publicly unto them, and I spoke unto them secretly, 10 and I said, 'Ask you forgiveness of your Lord; surely He is ever All-forgiving, 11 and He will loose heaven upon you in torrents 12 and will succour you with wealth and sons, and will appoint for you gardens, and will appoint for you rivers. 13 What ails you, that you look not for majesty in God, 14 seeing He created you by stages? 15 Have you not regarded how God created seven heavens one upon another, 16 and set the moon therein for a light and the sun for a lamp? 17 And God caused you to grow out of the earth, 18 then He shall return you into it, and bring you forth. 19 And God has laid the earth for you as a carpet, 20 that thereof you may thread ways, ravines.'" 21 Noah said, "My Lord, they have rebelled against me, and followed him whose wealth and children increase him only in loss, 22 and have devised a mighty device and have said, 23 'Do not leave your gods, and do not leave Wadd, nor Suwa', Yaghuth, Ya'uq, neither Nasr.' 24 And they have led many astray. Increase Thou not the evildoers save in error!" 25 And because of their transgressions they were drowned, and admitted into a Fire, for they found not, apart from God, any to help them. 26 And Noah said, "My Lord, leave not upon the earth of the unbelievers even one. 27 Surely, if Thou leavest them, they will lead Thy servants astray, and will beget none but unbelieving libertines. 28 My Lord, forgive me and my parents and whosoever enters my house as a believer, and the believers, men and women alike; and do Thou not increase the evildoers save in ruin!"

[1 We sent Noah to his people to warn them before the painful punishment came upon them. 2 He said: "O my people, I warn you clearly 3 That you should worship God and fear Him, and follow me 4 That He may forgive some of your sins and prolong your term till an appointed time. Surely when God's appointed time is come it will not be put off, if only you knew! 5 He said: "O Lord, I called my people night and day, 6 But the more I called they only ran the farther away. 7 And every time I called them that You may forgive them, they thrust their fingers into their ears, and covered themselves with their garments, and became wayward, and behaved with downright insolence. 8 Then I called them loudly and more openly, 9 And declared to them in public and in private, 10 And I told them: 'Ask your Lord to forgive you. He is verily forgiving. 11 He will send you abundant rain from the sky, 12 And will give you increase of wealth and sons, and give you gardens and springs of water. 13 What has come upon you that you do not fear the majesty of God, 14 Knowing that He has created you by various stages? 15 Do you not see how God has fashioned seven skies one above the other, 16 And has placed the moon therein, an illumination, and has placed the sun, a lighted lamp? 17 God produced you from the earth like a vegetable growth; 18 He will then return you back to it, and bring you out again. 19 God has made the earth for you a spreading, 20 So that you may walk upon its spacious paths.' 21 But they did not listen to me," Noah said, " and followed him whose wealth and children only added to his ruin. 22 And they contrived a plot of great magnitude, 23 And said: 'Do not abandon your gods, and

eyes and inspiration, and do not preach to me about those who sin, for they are drowned." [Q 11:37][525]

11 So Noah accepted the building of the ship and renounced his people.

12 He began cutting the wood and beating the iron and arranging the tackle of the ship with pitch and other things which no one could do well except him.

13 His people began passing by him while he was working, scoffing at him and deriding him.

14 He [Noah] would say, "Though you mock us, we mock you as you are mocking, and you will know to whom a punishment which will debase him will come and upon whom a punishment which will undo him will be set." [Q 11:38–39][526]

15 And they would say, according to

what reached us, "O Noah, have you become a carpenter after being a prophet?"

16 So, God closed the wombs of the women [of the generation of the Flood], and they did not bear.

17 The People of the Torah assert that God, the Mighty and Powerful, commanded him to build the ship of teak; that he make it curved; and that he coat it with pitch inside and out; that he make its length eighty cubits, its width fifty cubits, and its height thirty cubits; that he make it with three decks, a lower, a middle, and a top; and that he put a window in it.

18 So Noah did as God, the Mighty and the Powerful, commanded him, until he finished it.

19 God promised him, "When our command comes and the oven gushes forth water,

---

do not abandon Wadda or Suwa', or Yaghuth, Ya'uq or Nasr.' 24 And they misled many. So do not give the evil-doers increase but in error." 25 They were drowned because of their habitual sinfulness, and sent to Hell, and did not find any helper other than God. 26 Noah said: "O Lord, do not leave a single habitation of unbelievers on the earth. 27 If you leave them, they will lead Your creatures astray, and beget but iniquitous and ungrateful offspring . 28 O Lord, forgive me, my parents, and any one who enters my house as a believer, and all believing men and women, and do not give the evil-doers increase save in ruin."]

[525]Sura 11:36–37 reads:

36 And it was revealed to Noah, saying, "None of thy people shall believe but he who has already believed; so be thou not distressed by that they may be doing. 37 Make thou the Ark under Our eyes, and as We reveal; and address Me not concerning those who have done evil; they shall be drowned."

[36 And Noah was informed through revelation: "Apart from those who have come to believe already not one of your people is going to believe. 37 Build an ark under Our eye and as We instruct. Do not plead for those who have been wicked, for they shall certainly be drowned."]

[526]Sura 11:38–39 reads:

38 So he was making the Ark; and whenever a council of his people passed by him they scoffed at him. He said, "If you scoff at us, we shall surely scoff at you, as you scoff, 39 and you shall know to whom will come a chastisement degrading him, and upon whom there shall alight a lasting chastisement."

[38 So he built the ark; and when groups of his people passed by him, they scoffed at him. He said to them: "Though you laugh at us (now), we shall laugh at you, as you are laughing at us. 39 You will soon come to know who suffers the punishment that would put him to shame, and who suffers lasting torment."]

then load it with two of every kind, a pair, and your household, except him to whom the word has gone forth already, and those who believe," and no one believed except a few. [Q 11:40][527]

20 The oven was set as a sign between them.

21 He said, "When the command comes, then load it with two of every kind, a pair, and depart.

22 When the oven gushed forth water, Noah took into the ship the ones whom God had ordered, and they were few, as He said.

23 And he took in it a pair of every kind, animal and vegetable, male and female.

24 He took his three sons, Shem, Ham, and Japheth, and their wives, and six who believed in him.

25 They were ten people, Noah, his sons plus their wives.

26 Then he took aboard what beasts God commanded him.

27 But he left behind his son Yam, who was an unbeliever.

28 [The] first animal Noah took on board the ship was the ant and the last was the ass.

29 When the ass entered and got its breast in, Iblis, may God curse him, grabbed on its tail, and it could not pick up its feet.

30 Noah began to say, "Woe unto you, enter, even if the Devil is with you."

31 The words slipped from his tongue.

32 When Noah said it, the Devil let the ass go on its way, and it entered, and the Devil entered with it.

33 Noah said to him, "What caused you to come on board with me, O Enemy of God?"

34 He [the Devil] said, "Did you not say Enter, even if the Devil is with you?"

35 He [Noah] said, "Depart from me, O Enemy of God."

36 The Devil said, "There is no way out for you but to carry me, and he was, according to what they assert, in the back of the boat."

37 When Noah had provisioned the ship and put in it all who believed in him—and that was in the month of the year after the six-hundredth year of his life, in the seventeenth night of the month—and when he entered and took with him whom he took, the springs began to pour forth water in a great flood.

38 The gates of heaven opened, as God said to His prophet, may the prayers and peace of God be upon him: "We opened the gates of heaven with pouring water and we caused the earth to gush forth springs, and the waters met according to a preordained command," [Q 54:11–12][528]

39 Noah and those with him entered the ship and concealed themselves on the decks.

40 Between the time God sent the water and when the water bore the ship away were forty days and forty nights.

---

[527]Sura 11:40 reads:

40 Until, when Our command came, and the Oven boiled, We said, "Embark in it two of every kind, and thy family—except for him against whom the word has already been spoken—and whosoever believes." And there believed not with him except a few.

[40 When Our command was issued and the waters gushed forth from the source, We said: "Take into (the ark) a pair of every species, and members of your family other than those against whom the sentence has been passed already, and those who come to believe." But only a few believed to him.]

[528]Sura 54:11–12 reads:

11 Then We opened the gates of heaven unto water torrential, 12 and made the earth to gush with fountains, and the waters met for a matter decreed.

41 Then the water rose up, just as the People of the Torah assert, and became great and strong and raised up, according to the saying of God, the Mighty and the Powerful, to His prophet, Muhammad, may the prayers and peace of God be upon him: "We carried him on a thing of planks and nails which ran by our sight as a recompense for him who was ungrateful." [Q 54:14][529]

42 And the word for nail means peg, pegs of iron.

43 The ship was made to go with him and those with him on a wave like a mountain.

44 Noah called his son who was destroyed along with those who were destroyed while he was in seclusion.

45 When Noah saw what he saw of the truth of the promise of his Lord, he said, "O my son, ride with us and do not be among the ungrateful."

46 He was a rogue who harbored ingratitude in his heart.

47 He replied, "I will go to a mountain which will protect me from the water."

48 It had been the duty of the mountains to be a protection against the rain, and he thought it was as it had been.

49 Noah said, "There is no protection today against the command of God, except out of mercy."

50 The waves came between them, and he was among the drowned.

51 The water increased and raged and raised up over the mountains, as the People of the Torah assert, fifteen cubits, so the creatures on the face of the earth, everything animal and vegetable, perished.

52 No creatures remained except Noah and those with him in the ship except 'Uj bin A'naq, according to what the People of the Book assert.

53 Between the time God sent the flood and the recession of the water was six months and ten nights.

54 ...[When] the people's waste offended Noah on the ship, he was commanded to stroke the tail of the elephant.

55 So he stroked it, and two pigs came forth from it, and he was freed from it [because they ate it].

56 The mouse gave birth on the ship, and when they troubled him, he [Noah] was commanded to order the lion to sneeze, and two cats came forth from the nostrils which ate the mice.

57 God, the Blessed and Most High, sent the flood in the six-hundredth year of Noah's life, and Noah lived, according to the People of the Torah, after he disembarked from the ship, three hundred forty-eight years.

58 Noah's total lifespan was one thousand years less fifty when God made him die.

59 ...[When] Adam fell from the Garden, and his children spread out, his descendants reckoned dating from the Fall of Adam.

60 That was the system of dating until God sent Noah.

61 Then they dated from the advent of Noah until the flood, and those were destroyed who were destoyed on the face of the earth.

62 The dating was then from the flood to the fire of Abraham, and from the fire of Abraham to the advent of Joseph, and from the advent of Joseph to the coming of Moses, and from the advent of Moses to the kingdom of Solomon, and from the rule of

[11 And We opened up the flood gates of the sky with water pouring down in torrents, 12 And We opened up the springs of the earth; and the waters met for a decreed end.]

[529]Sura 54:14 reads:

14 And We bore him upon a well-planked vessel well-caulked running before Our eyes—a recompense for him denied.

[14 Which sailed right under Our eyes: A recompense for him who had been denied.]

Solomon to the advent of Jesus, and from the advent of Jesus the son of Mary to the time of the advent of the Prophet of God, may the prayers and peace of God be upon him.

THE DESCENDANTS OF NOAH

1 When Noah and his offspring and all who were in the ship went down onto the land, he divided the land among his sons in thirds.

2 He gave Shem the middle third of the earth, and in it is the Holy Temple, the Nile, the Euphrates, the Tigris, Sihan, Jihan, and Fishun, and what is between the Fishun to the east of the Nile, and what is between the origin of the south wind to the origin of the north.

3 He gave Ham his portion west of the Nile and what is behind it to the origin of the west wind. He assigned Japheth the portion in the Fishun and what is behind it to the origin of the east wind.

4 Gomer, the son of Japheth, was, according to Ibn Ishaq, the father of Gog and Magog, Marih, Wail, Hawan, Tubil, Hushil, Taras, and Shabkah, his daughter.

5 Among the sons of Japheth were Gog and Magog, the Slavs and the Turks, according to what they assert.

6 The wife of Ham, the son of Noah, was Yahlab, the daughter of Marib, the son of ad-Darmasil, the son of Mahuil, the son of Enoch, the son of Cain, the son of Adam.

7 She bore him three sons, Cush, the son of Ham, Qut, the son of Ham, and Canaan, the son of Ham. Cush, the son of Ham, the son of Noah, married Qarnabil, the daughter of Batawil, the Son of Tarnas, the son of Japheth, the son of Noah, and she bore him Copt, and Copt is Egypt according to what they say.

8 Canaan, the son of Ham, the son of Noah, married Arsal, the daughter of Batawil, the son of Taras, the son of Japheth, the son of Noah, and she bore him black Nubia, Fazzan, Zanj, as-Zaghawah, and all the people of the Sudan.

9 ...[The] People of the Torah assert that this was ... so because of a curse Noah called down on his son Ham.

10 That was because Noah slept, and his private parts were uncovered, and Ham saw them and did not cover them.

11 Shem and Japheth saw them and threw a cloak over them and covered his private parts.

12 So, when he awoke from his sleep, he knew what Ham, Shem, and Japheth had done.

13 He said, "Cursed is Canaan, the son of Ham; as a slave he will be to his brothers."

14 And he said, "May God, my Lord, bless Shem, and may Ham be a servant to his two brothers.

15 "And may God advance Japheth and allow him the dwelling places of Shem, and Ham will be a servant to them."

16 The wife of Shem, the son of Noah, was Saliha, the daughter of Batawil, the son of Mahuil, the son of Enoch, the son of Cain, the son of Adam. She bore him sons: Arpakhshad, Ashudh, Laudh, and 'Awilam, the sons of Shem. And Aram was of Shem.

17 I do not know whether Aram belongs to Arpakhshad and his brothers or not.

18 Laudh, the son of Shem, the son of Noah, married Sabakah, the daughter of Japheth, the son of Noah, and she bore him Fars and Jurjan, and the people of Persia.

19 Along with Fars, Tasm and 'Amaliq were born to Laudh, and I do not know whether he is of the mother of Fars or not.

20 'Amaliq is the father of the Amalekites, all of them, a people scattered over the land. The people of the East and the people of Oman and the people of the Hijaz and the people of Syria and the people of Egypt are of them.

21 And from them are the giants in Syria who were called Canaanites.

22 From them are the pharaohs of Egypt, the people of Bahrein and Oman, a people called Jasim.

23 They used to inhabit Medina.

24 Of them are Bin Haff, Sa'd bin Hazzan, the Bin Matr, and the Bin al-Azraq.

25 The people of Nejd are of them, and Badil, Rahil, Ghaffar, and the people of Teima are of them.

26 The king of the Hijaz, whose name was al-Arqam, was one of them, and they were inhabitants of Najd.

27 The inhabitants of at-Taif were the Bin 'Abd bin Dakhm, a tribe of the 'Abbas al-Awal.

28 The sons of Umaym, the son of Laudh, the son of Shem, the son of Noah, were the people of Wabar in the land of ar-Raml, and Raml of 'Alij.

29 They became many and prosperous there.

30 And God took vengeance on them because of frowardness, and they were destroyed.

31 Only a remnant remained called an-Nusnas.

32 Tasam, the son of Laudh, dwelt in al-Yamamah and its environs, and they became many and prosperous, extending as far as Bahrein.

33 Tasam and the Amalekites and Umaym and Jasim were an Arab people in language who were born into the Arabic language.

34 Fars was of the people of the East of the land of Persia who spoke Persian.

35 Aram, the son of Shem, the son of Noah, sired 'Aws, ..., and Ghathir, ..., and Huil, ...

36 Ghathir, the son of Aram, sired Thamud, ..., and Judays, ...

37 They were an Arab-speaking people speaking the language of Mudar.

38 The Arabs used to call these people true Arabs because of their language into which they were born, and they used to call the descendants of Ismail, the son of Abraham, arabicized Arabs because they only spoke the language of these people when they dwelt in their midst.

39 'Ad, Thamud, the Amalekites, Umaym, Jasim, Jadis, and Tasam were Arab.

40 'Ad was in this country as far as Hadramaut and all the Yemen.

41 Thamud was in al-Hijr, between al-Hijar and Syria to Wadi al-Qura and environs.

42 Jadis clove to Tasam and was with them in al-Yamamah and environs to Bahrein.

43 The name of al-Yamamah was Jaww.

44 Jasim dwelt in Oman.

Epilogue

In this volume, a number of perspectives on the Creation have been presented. But it is important to remember that only a rather limited number of perspectives have been presented. There are many more perspectives and many more facets to explore.

For instance, there is still much to discuss concerning the ancient cultures and societies which existed at the time that the scriptural account of the Creation was composed. As alluded to in this volume, those cultures had Creation stories of their own. To fully understand our Creation, it is important to understand those cultures, their histories and their Creation stories if we are to ascertain the contributions that they made to the Creation story we know so well.

Additionally, the secular story of the Creation and the biblical version of the Creation are not the only versions of the Creation. Creation stories abound throughout the world. Stories from China and India, stories from the Maya and the Aborigines of Australia, stories from Africa and Oceania, stories from ancient Europe and from the Indigenous people of the Americas, all give an account of how we came to be. If we are to begin to understand how we came to be what we are, it behooves us to understand these stories.

Furthermore, even amongst the Muslims, Christians, and Jews, variations on the Creation stories abounded and influenced the shaping of our theology. To fully understand the development of our relationship with God, it is important to understand the scope and substance of the other Creation stories which, for centuries, were circulated amongst the Muslims, the Christians, and the Jews.

Finally, no understanding of our Creation would be complete without a critical examination of the Creation theories forwarded by contemporary secular and scriptural contingents. The seemingly conflicting concepts of "evolution" and "divine creation," along with the contemporary rise of such concepts as "creation science" and "intelligent design," need to be discussed.

God willing, in the succeeding volumes of *The Creation*, these subjects, and many more, will be explored. After all, a few perspectives, broad though they may be, are really quite limited. There is so much more we need to know if we are to begin to truly appreciate the infinite facets of God.

Appendix 1.
Geological Time Scale

[The standard block numbers are taken from McGraw-Hill's Encyclopedia of Science & Technology, Eighth Edition, *while the italicized time periods are taken from the* Smithsonian Timelines of the Ancient World.*]*

A.	Hadean Eon	(4.65–3.8 Billion B.C.T.)
B.	Archaen Eon*	(3.8–2.5 Billion B.C.T.)
C.	Proterozoic Eon*	(2.5–0.57 Billion B.C.T.)
D.	Phanerozoic Eon	(570 Million B.C.T. to Present)

    1. Paleozoic Era   (570–245 Million B.C.T.)

       a. Cambrian Period   (570–505 Million B.C.T.)
(570–510 Million B.C.T.)

       b. Ordovician Period   (505–438 Million B.C.T.)
(510–440 Million B.C.T.)

       c. Silurian Period   (438–408 Million B.C.T.)
(440–410 Million B.C.T.)

       d. Devonian Period   (408–360 Million B.C.T.)
(410–360 Million B.C.T.)

       e. Mississippian Period†   (360–320 Million B.C.T.)

       f. Pennsylvanian Period†   (320–286 Million B.C.T.)
(320–290 Million B.C.T.)

       g. Permian Period   (286–245 Million B.C.T.)
(290–245 Million B.C.T.)

    2. Mesozoic Era   (245–65 Million B.C.T.)

       a. Triassic Period   (245–208 Million B.C.T.)

       b. Jurassic Period   (208–146 Million B.C.T.)

       c. Cretaceous Period   (146–65 Million B.C.T.)

---

*The Proterozoic Eon combined with the Archean Eon may alternatively be designated as the Precambrian Eon.

†The Mississippian Period combined with the Pennsylvanian Period may alternatively be designated as the Carboniferous Period.

3. Cenozoic Era   (65 Million B.C.T. to Present)

  a. Tertiary Period   (65–1.6 Million B.C.T.)

     i. Paleocene Epoch   (65–57.8 Million B.C.T.)
(65–56.5 Million B.C.T.)

     ii. Eocene Epoch   (57.8–36.6 Million B.C.T.)
(56.5–35.4 Million B.C.T.)

     iii. Oligocene Epoch   (36.6–23.7 Million B.C.T.)
(35.4–23.3 Million B.C.T.)

     iv. Miocene Epoch   (23.7–5.3 Million B.C.T.)
(23.3–5.2 Million B.C.T.)

     v. Pliocene Epoch   (5.3–1.6 Million B.C.T.)
(5.2–1.6 Million B.C.T.)

  b. Quaternary Period   (1.6 Million B.C.T. to Present)

     i. Pleistocene Epoch   (1.6–0.01 Million B.C.T.)

     ii. Holocene Epoch   (10,000 B.C.T. to Present)

Appendix 2.
The Archaeological Ages for Southwest Asia

Lower Paleolithic Period	1.5 Million to 250,000 B.C.T.
Middle Paleolithic Period	250,000 to 45000 B.C.T.
Upper Paleolithic Period	45000 to 18000 B.C.T.
Epi-Paleolithic Period	18000 to 8300 B.C.T.
Pre-Pottery Neolithic Period	8300 to 5500 B.C.T.
Neolithic Period	5500 to 4500 B.C.T.
Chalcolithic Period	4500 to 3500 B.C.T.
Early Bronze Age	3500 to 2200 B.C.T.
Middle Bronze Age	2200 to 1550 B.C.T.
Late Bronze Age	1550 to 1200 B.C.T.
Iron Age	1200 to 332 B.C.T.
Early Iron Age	1200 to 800 B.C.T.
Assyrian Period	800 to 650 B.C.T.
Neo-Babylonian Period	650 to 539 B.C.T.
Persian Period	539 to 332 B.C.T.
Hellenistic Period	332 to 60 B.C.T.
Roman Period	60 B.C.T. to 640 C.C.
Early Roman Period	60 B.C.T. to 70 C.C.
Roman Imperial Period	70 to 324 C.C.
Byzantine Period	324 to 640 C.C.
Early Islamic Period	623 to 900 C.C.
Conquest Period	623 to 661 C.C.
Umayyad Period	661 to 750 C.C.
Early Abbasid Period	749 to 900 C.C.
Middle Ages	900 to 1517 C.C.
Fatimid Period (Egypt and Palestine)	909 to 1100 C.C.
Seljuk Period (Iraq, Syria, Turkey)	1000 to 1200 C.C.
Crusader Period (Palestine)	1099 to 1291 C.C.

Ayyubid Period (Egypt, Syria)	1169 to 1260 C.C.
Late Abbasid Period (Iraq)	900 to 1258 C.C.
Ikhanid Period (Iran, Iraq)	1256 to 1336 C.C.
Mamluk Period (Egypt, Syria)	1250 to 1517 C.C.
Ottoman Empire	1517 to 1917 C.C.
Modern Period	1917 to present

Appendix 3.
The Babylonian List
of Antediluvian Kings

The Babylonian list of antediluvian (pre–Flood) kings is as follows:

1. Alulim   28,800 year reign
2. Alalgar   36,000 year reign
3. Enmenluanna   43,200 year reign
4. Enmengalanna   28,800 year reign
5. Dumuzi   36,000 year reign
6. Ensipazianna   28,800 year reign
7. Enmenduranna   21,000 year reign
8. Ubartutul   8,600 year reign
   THE FLOOD

Appendix 4.
The Family of Languages
of the Family of Man

Languages are classified genetically if they are descendants of a common ancestral language. The conservative genetic classification of languages into a language family is based on an abundance of cognates (related words) in the member languages. Using these terms, one may treat the languages of the world according to the following principal geographic divisions: Africa, Southwest Asia, South Asia, Southeast Asia (including Austronesian), East Asia, North Asia, Europe, and the Americas.

AFRICA

Although, in many parts of Africa, European languages imported with 19th century colonialism are spoken and utilized as national languages, the indigenous African language families are the Afro-Asiatic (formerly known as the Hamito-Semitic), Nilo-Saharan, Niger-Congo, and Khoisan families. The Afro-Asiatic languages are spoken across North Africa from Mauritania to Somalia and beyond into southern Asia. The Nilo-Saharan languages are spoken in central interior Africa. The Niger-Congo languages, of which there are almost 900, are spoken from Mauritania to Kenya and south into South Africa. The Khoisan languages consist of about 50 languages spoken in southern Africa and Tanzania.

SOUTHWEST ASIA

In Southwest Asia, the languages spoken are either Indo-European, Turkic, Caucasian, or Semitic. Of the Indo-European languages, almost all the Iranian languages, including Persian, Pashto, Kurdish, and Balochi, are spoken in Iran. Armenian is spoken in Armenia and Georgia. The Turkic language Turkish is spoken in Turkey, and other Turkic languages are spoken in the Caucasus, where more than 30 Caucasian languages are spoken. Of the Semitic languages spoken in Southwest Asia, Arabic is spoken in Israel, and West Aramaic dialects are spoken in Lebanon and Syria.

SOUTH ASIA

In South Asia, the languages of India, Bangladesh, Pakistan, and the border states are genetically classified into the Indo-Aryan and Iranian subgroups of the Indo-Aryan branch

324

of Indo-European. There are more than 20 members of the Indo-Aryan subgroup and many more dialects, but the most widely spoken are Bengali-Assamese, West Hindi, Bihari, and East Hindi. The languages of the Iranian subgroup have fewer speakers in South Asia than the Indo-Aryan languages: Kashmiri and Shina, the most widely spoken Iranian languages in South Asia, are spoken only in Jammu and Kashmir. A few indigenous languages, such as the Dravidian languages of Telugu and Tamil, are spoken in South Asia, as are a few Sino-Tibetan languages. In many parts of post-colonial South Asia, English is still spoken as an interstate and international language.

SOUTHEAST ASIA

Southeast Asia is composed of a mainland sub-region south of China and east of India, insular Malaysia, Indonesia, and the Philippines, and the name of the language generally corresponds to the name of the country. The languages on the mainland belong to the Austroasiatic, Tai, and Sino-Tibetan language groups, while the insular languages are all members of the Austronesian family. More than 50 Austroasiatic languages, such as Khmer in Cambodia, Mon in Thailand, and Vietnamese in Vietnam, are spoken on the mainland of Southeast Asia. The Tai and Sino-Tibetan families are represented by Thai in Thailand, Lao in Laos and Cambodia, and Burmese in Myanmar (Burma). In insular Southeast Asia, more that 500 Austronesian languages are spoken, the largest group of which is the Western Indonesian subgroup, which includes Tagalog, the basis for Pilipino, and 100 other languages spoken in the Philippines. While New Guinea and Australia may be said to belong to insular Southeast Asia, they contain only non–Austronesian languages, predominantly the Papuan languages of New Guinea and the more than 200 Australian Aboriginal languages.

EAST ASIA

In East Asia, the languages spoken are largely Chinese languages (or dialects) in China, Japanese in Japan, and Korean in Korea, although the Altaic group is represented in China by Uighur, a Turkic language, and Manchu, a Manchu-Tungus language. Of the Chinese languages, Mandarin, Wu, and Cantonese are the most widely spoken. Mandarin, the native language of 70 percent of the Chinese, has more native speakers than any other language in the world. Tai and Miao-Yao languages are spoken in south-central China, Vietnam, Laos, and Thailand.

NORTH ASIA

The languages of North Asia are those spoken from the Arctic Ocean on the north to South Asia and China on the south and from the Caspian Sea and Ural Mountains in the west to the Pacific Ocean in the east. These languages are genetically classified into either the Uralic family, the Altaic group, the Indo-European family, or the Paleo-Siberian group. Although speakers of the Uralic languages are few in number, many speakers of Altaic languages are found in Iran, Afghanistan, and the Kansu province of China. Most Indo-European languages, such as Iranian, have been introduced into North Asia only recently. The Paleo-Siberian languages are not genetically linked to each other or to the other languages of North Asia and are spoken largely in northeasternmost Siberia.

EUROPE

The languages of Europe and of regions inhabited by descendants of Europeans (e.g., the English, French, Portuguese and Spanish speaking peoples of the Americas) are primarily of the Indo-European and Uralic, or, more specifically, Finno-Ugric, language families. In the Indo-European family, Portuguese, Spanish, Catalan, French, Romansh, Ladin, Friulian, Italian, and Romanian constitute the Romance subgroup of the Italic branch. The extant Germanic language groups spoken are English, Frisian, Netherlandic-German, Insular Scandinavian, and Continental Scandinavian, with these groups dividing further on national criteria (e.g., Continental Scandinavian divides into Norwegian, Danish, and Swedish). The Celtic branch of Indo-European is composed of Welsh, Breton, Irish Gaelic, and Scottish Gaelic. The literary languages within the Slavic branch of Indo-European may be divided into three geographic zones: East Slavic, West Slavic, and South Slavic, of which zones Russian, Polish, and Serbo-Croatian are respective examples. The three remaining branches of Indo-European are Baltic, Greek, and Albanian. Languages of the Finno-Ugric family, such as languages of the Sami (Lapp) and Baltic-Finno groups (e.g., Sami, Finnish, and Livonian), are spoken in parts of Norway, Sweden, Finland, and Russia. Hungarian is also a member of the Finno-Ugric family.

THE AMERICAS

In the Americas, European languages such as Spanish, English, Portuguese, and French predominate. English is the language of most of North America, while Spanish and Portuguese are the dominant languages in South and Central America. The Western Hemisphere's indigenous languages, which came from Asia and the ancestors of the American Indians, are classified into the North and Central American Indian language families and the South American Indian language families. The North and Central American Indian language family is in part composed of the 20 Athabascan languages, the only North American Indian language group successfully traced into South America. The South American Indian languages are much more numerous: the Andean-Equatorial group, for example, includes 14 families and almost 200 languages spoken from French Guiana to Colombia and south to Paraguay, as well as along the Amazon.

Appendix 5.
The Ussher Chronology

The Ussher Chronology is based upon a history written by the Irish theologian James Ussher around 1650 C.C. While Ussher's chronology was considered for centuries to be an accurate and factual history, today the vast majority of historians and theologians consider Ussher's Chronology to be chronologically inaccurate and to be factually deficient. In this book, the Ussher Chronology is being used only for discussion and comparison purposes. Accordingly, the dates associated with the Ussher Chronology should not be relied upon as fact.

4004 B.C.T.

Sunday, October 23: God created the light. {Genesis 1:3–5}

Monday, October 24: God created the firmament known as Heaven. {Genesis 1:6–8}

Tuesday, October 25: God created the dry land known as the Earth. {Genesis 1:9–13}

Wednesday, October 26: God created the sun and the moon and the stars. {Genesis 1:14–19}

Thursday, October 27: God created the living creatures of the Earth. {Genesis 1:20–23}

Friday, October 28: God created human beings. {Genesis 1:26–28} (Adam and Eve were created. {Genesis 2:18–25})

Saturday, October 29: God rested. {Genesis 2:2}

4000 B.C.T.

Cain and Abel were born. {Genesis 4}

3874 B.C.T.

Seth, the son of Adam and Eve, was born. {Genesis 5:3}

3769 B.C.T.

Enos was born. {Genesis 5:3–6}

3679 B.C.T.

Cainan was born. {Genesis 5:3–9}

3609 B.C.T.

Mahalaleel was born. {Genesis 5:3–12}

3544 B.C.T.

Jared was born. {Genesis 5:3–15}

3382 B.C.T.

Enoch was born. {Genesis 5:3–18}

3317 B.C.T.

Methuselah was born. {Genesis 5:3–21}

3130 B.C.T.

Lamech was born. {Genesis 5:25}

3074 B.C.T.

Adam died. {Genesis 5:3–5}

3017 B.C.T.

Enoch was translated. {Genesis 5:22–24}

2962 B.C.T.

Seth died. {Genesis 5:3–8}

2948 B.C.T.

Noah was born. {Genesis 5:3–29}

2864 B.C.T.

Enos died. {Genesis 5:3–11}

2769 B.C.T.

Cainan died. {Genesis 5:3–14}

2717 B.C.T.

Mahalaleel died. {Genesis 5:3–17}

2582 B.C.T.

Jared died. {Genesis 5:3–20}

2469 B.C.T.

God sent Noah out to preach to the wicked to plead with them to repent.

2448 B.C.T.

Noah's son Japheth was born (Genesis 10:21).

2446 B.C.T.

Shem was born (Genesis 10:11).

2353 B.C.T.

Lamech died at age 777. {Genesis 5:3–31}

2349 B.C.T.

Methusaleh died, perhaps in the Flood. Methusaleh was 969 years old and was the last (except for Noah) of the long life men. {Genesis 5:3–27}

On Sunday, November 30, 2349 B.C.T., God commanded Noah to enter the Ark. {Genesis 7:1–4}

On Sunday, December 7, Noah entered the Ark and the flood began. {Genesis 7:4–10}

2348 B.C.T.

On Wednesday, May 6, the Ark came to rest on one of the mountains of Ararat. {Genesis 8:4}

On Sunday, July 19, the tops of the mountains appeared above the water. {Genesis 8:5}

On Friday, August 28, Noah opened the window of the Ark and sent forth a raven. {Genesis 8:6–7}

On Friday, September 4, Noah sent forth a dove. {Genesis 8:8–9}

On Friday, October 23, Noah took off the covering of the Ark. {Genesis 8:13}

On Thursday, December 18, Noah disembarked. {Genesis 8:15–18}

In this year, the years of a man's life were made half-shorter.

2346 B.C.T.

Arphaxad was born. {Genesis 11:11}

2311 B.C.T.

Salah was born. {Genesis 11:12}

2281 B.C.T.

Eber (Heber) was born. {Genesis 11:14}

2247 B.C.T.

Peleg (Phaleg) was born {Genesis 11:16}

In this year, the years of a man's life appear once again to have been made half-shorter.

2217 B.C.T.

Reu (Rehu) was born. {Genesis 11:18}

2188 B.C.T.

Ham (Cham) carried his colony into Egypt.

2185 B.C.T.

Serug was born. {Genesis 11:20}

2155 B.C.T.

Nahor (Nachor) was born. {Genesis 11:22}

2126 B.C.T.

Terah (Terach) was born. {Genesis 11:24}

2056 B.C.T.

Terah's oldest son was born. {Genesis 11:26}

2008 B.C.T.

Peleg (Phaleg) died. {Genesis 11:19}

2007 B.C.T.

Nahor (Nachor) died. {Genesis 11:25}

1998 B.C.T.

Noah died. He was 950 years old. Noah died 350 years after the Flood came to an end. {Genesis 9:28–29}

1996 B.C.T.

Abram (Abraham) was born. {Genesis 11:32}

Appendix 6.
The Seder Olam Rabba Chronology

The Seder Olam Rabba Chronology is based upon a calculation made by Seder Olam Rabba which established 3760 B.C.T. as the year of Creation. In this book, the Seder Olam Rabba Chronology is being used only for discussion and comparison purposes. For the purposes of discussion and comparison, the Seder Olam Rabba Chronology used here was derived from the date of Creation calculated by Seder Olam Rabba and the dates set forth in the Ussher Chronology generated by the seventeenth century Irish theologian James Ussher. The dates given herein for the Seder Olam Rabba Chronology were obtained by subtracting 244 years from the dates given for the Ussher Chronology events. While neither the Ussher Chronology nor this Seder Olam Rabba Chronology can be deemed to be accurate based upon our measure of space-time, it is notable that of the two, the Seder Olam Rabba Chronology is deemed to be the more accurate with regards to identifying the time of the Jewish patriarchs. Nevertheless, as with the Ussher Chronology, the dates associated with the Seder Olam Rabba Chronology should not be relied upon as fact.

3760 B.C.T.

The First Day: God created the light. {Genesis 1:3–5}

The Second Day: God created the firmament known as Heaven. {Genesis 1:6–8}

The Third Day: God created the dry land known as the Earth. {Genesis 1:9–13}

The Fourth Day: God created the sun and the moon and the stars. {Genesis 1:14–19}

The Fifth Day: God created the living creatures of the Earth. {Genesis 1:20–23}

The Sixth Day: God created human beings. {Genesis 1:26–28} (Adam and Eve were created. {Genesis 2:18–25})

The Sabbath: God rested. {Genesis 2:2}

3756 B.C.T.

Cain and Abel were born. {Genesis 4}

3630 B.C.T.

Seth, the son of Adam and Eve, was born. {Genesis 5:3}

3525 B.C.T.

Enos was born. {Genesis 5:3–6}

3435 B.C.T.

Cainan was born. {Genesis 5:3–9}

3365 B.C.T.

Mahalaleel was born. {Genesis 5:3–12}

3300 B.C.T.

Jared was born. {Genesis 5:3–15}

3138 B.C.T.

Enoch was born. {Genesis 5:3–18}

3073 B.C.T.

Methuselah was born. {Genesis 5:3–21}

2886 B.C.T.

Lamech was born. {Genesis 5:25}

2830 B.C.T.

Adam died. {Genesis 5:3–5}

2773 B.C.T.

Enoch was translated. {Genesis 5:22–24}

2718 B.C.T.

Seth died. {Genesis 5:3–8}

2704 B.C.T.

Noah was born. {Genesis 5:3–29}

2620 B.C.T.

Enos died. {Genesis 5:3–11}

2525 B.C.T.

Cainan died. {Genesis 5:3–14}

2473 B.C.T.

Mahalaleel died. {Genesis 5:3–17}

2338 B.C.T.

Jared died. {Genesis 5:3–20}

2225 B.C.T.

God sent Noah out to preach to the wicked to plead with them to repent.

2204 B.C.T.

Noah's son Japheth was born (Genesis 10:21).

2202 B.C.T.

Shem was born (Genesis 10:11).

2109 B.C.T.

Lamech died at age 777. {Genesis 5:3–31}

2105 B.C.T.

Methusaleh died, perhaps in the Flood. Methusaleh was 969 years old and was the last (except for Noah) of the long life men. {Genesis 5:3–27}

God commanded Noah to enter the Ark. {Genesis 7:1–4}

Noah entered the Ark and the flood began. {Genesis 7:4–10}

2104 B.C.T.

The Ark came to rest on one of the mountains of Ararat. {Genesis 8:4}

The tops of the mountains appeared above the water. {Genesis 8:5}

Noah opened the window of the Ark and sent forth a raven. {Genesis 8:6–7}

Noah sent forth a dove. {Genesis 8:8–9}

Noah took off the covering of the Ark. {Genesis 8:13}

Noah disembarked. {Genesis 8:15–18}

In this year, the years of a man's life were made half-shorter.

2102 B.C.T.

Arphaxad was born. {Genesis 11:11}

2067 B.C.T.

Salah was born. {Genesis 11:12}

2037 B.C.T.

Eber (Heber) was born. {Genesis 11:14}

2003 B.C.T.

Peleg (Phaleg) was born {Genesis 11:16}

In this year, the years of a man's life appear once again to have been made half-shorter.

1973 B.C.T.

Reu (Rehu) was born. {Genesis 11:18}

1944 B.C.T.

Ham (Cham) carried his colony into Egypt.

1941 B.C.T.

Serug was born. {Genesis 11:20}

1911 B.C.T.

Nahor (Nachor) was born. {Genesis 11:22}

1882 B.C.T.

Terah (Terach) was born. {Genesis 11:24}

1812 B.C.T.

Terah's oldest son was born. {Genesis 11:26}

1764 B.C.T.

Peleg (Phaleg) died. {Genesis 11:19}

1763 B.C.T.

Nahor (Nachor) died. {Genesis 11:25}

1754 B.C.T.

Noah died. He was 950 years old. Noah died 350 years after the Flood came to an end. {Genesis 9:28–29}

1752 B.C.T.

Abram (Abraham) was born. {Genesis 11:32}

Appendix 7.
A Chronology of Pentateuch Source Materials

The modern critical view of the origin and development of the Pentateuch includes the following items:

(1) The Pentateuch is a relatively late compilation of material taken from written sources, all of which reached their final form significantly after the time of Moses.

(2) The compiler of the Pentateuch depended chiefly upon four documents: "J", traces of which are found throughout the entire Pentateuch; "E", closely interwoven with "J" and, like it, found throughout the Pentateuch; "D", found chiefly in the book of Deuteronomy, though traces of it are found also elsewhere; and "P", which served as the groundwork for the entire compilation.

(3) "D" is identical with the Book of the Law that served as the basis of Josiah's reform in 621 B.C.T. It was in existence separately at that time; hence the Pentateuch in its final form cannot be older than that date, though some of the material embodied in it may be much older.

(4) "J" and "E" are both older than "D", and, according to most investigators, "D" is older than "P".

(5) The several documents show such striking differences that, on the whole, it is quite easy to separate them.

(6) "J" and "E" reflect the historical situation of the period of the Judges and of the early monarchy; "D" that of the later monarchy, especially conditions reflected in the account of Josiah's reforms in 621 B.C.T. and in the utterances of Jeremiah; "P" that of the later exilic and the post-exilic period, especially the age of Ezra and Nehemiah.

(7) In the case of each of the four documents, the theological standpoint agrees with what is known of Hebrew theological thinking during the period to which it is assigned on the basis of the historical situation reflected in it.

(8) "J" and "E" have points of contact with Old Testament writings known to have originated before 650 B.C.T. (e.g., the prophetic books of the eighth century); "D" with the literature that originated between 650 B.C.T. and the Exile (e.g., Kings and Jeremiah); "P" with that of the post-exilic period (e.g., Malachi, Ezra, Nehemiah, Chronicles). "D" seems to have been unknown prior to the seventh century, "P" was unknown before the Exile.

(9) The style and vocabulary of each document are what they might be expected to be if the documents were actually written during the periods to which the historical background assigns them.

(10) In their legal, as in their historical sections, "JE", "D", and "P" represent three suc-
       cessive stages of development – "P" implies the prior existence of "D", and "D" the
       prior existence of "J" and "E".

(11) Accordingly, certain evidence points to the following approximate dates for the doc-
       uments which comprise the Pentateuch:

       (A) "J" belongs to the early centuries of the monarchy, perhaps about 850 B.C.T.;

       (B) "E" originated not long before the appearance of the eighth century prophets
            around 750 B.C.T.;

       (C) "D" presupposes the activity of the eighth century prophets and may have been
            written during the reactionary reign of Manasseh, around 650 B.C.T.;

       (D) "P" originated among the descendants of the exiles in Babylonia, around 500 to
            450 B.C.T. and was completed in Palestine in the days of Ezra-Nehemiah, before
            400 B.C.T.

Appendix 8.
Provisions of the Pentateuch Associated with Specific Source Materials

Some scholars have been able to link specific verses of the Pentateuch to specific source materials. A listing of the specific source materials for verses of the Pentateuch follows:

Abbreviation Key: Yahwist .... (J)
Elohist .... (E)
Priestly .... (P)
Redactor {an unknown editor} .... (R)
Deuteronomist 1 .... (D1)
Deuteronomist 2 .... (D2)
Other .... (O)

GENESIS

1:1–2:3	(P)	8:2b–8:3a	(J)
2:4a	(R)	8:3b–8:5	(P)
2:4b–4:26	(J)	8:6	(J)
5:1–5:28	(R)	8:7	(P)
5:29	(J)	8:8–8:12	(J)
5:30–5:32	(R)	8:13a	(P)
6:1–7:5	(J)	8:13b	(J)
7:6	(R)	8:14–8:19	(P)
7:7	(J)	8:20–8:22	(J)
7:8–7:9	(P)	9:1–9:17	(P)
7:10	(J)	9:18–9:27	(J)
7:11	(P)	9:28–10:1a	(R)
7:12	(J)	10:1b–10:7	(P)
7:13–7:16a	(P)	10:8–10:19	(J)
7:16b–7:20	(J)	10:20	(P)
7:21	(P)	10:21	(J)
7:22–7:23	(J)	10:22–10:23	(P)
7:24–8:2a	(P)	10:24–10:30	(J)
		10:31–10:32	(P)
		11:1–11:9	(J)

11:10–11:27a	(R)		28:19	(J)
11:27b–11:31	(P)		28:20–28:22	(E)
11:32	(R)		29:1–35	(J)
12:1–12:4a	(J)		30:1–30:24a	(E)
12:4b–12:5	(P)		30:24b–30:43	(J)
12:6–13:5	(J)		31:1–31:2	(E)
13:6	(P)		31:3	(J)
13:7–13:11a	(J)		31:4–31:16	(E)
13:11b–13:12a	(P)		31:17–31:18a	(J)
13:12b–16:2	(J)		31:18b	(P)
16:3	(P)		31:19–32:13	(E)
16:4–16:14	(J)		32:14–32:24	(J)
16:15–17:27	(P)		32:25–33:20	(E)
18:1–19:28	(J)		34:1–34:31	(J)
19:29	(P)		35:1–35:8	(E)
19:30–19:38	(J)		35:9–35:15	(P)
20:1–20:18	(E)		35:16–35:20	(E)
21:1a	(J)		35:21–35:22	(J)
21:1b	(P)		35:23–35:29	(P)
21:2a	(J)		36:1	(R)
21:2b–21:5	(P)		36:2–36:30	(P)
21:6	(E)		36:31–36:43	(J)
21:7	(J)		37:1	(P)
21:8–22:10	(E)		37:2a	(R)
22:11–22:16a	(R)		37:2b	(J)
22:16b–22:19	(E)		37:3a	(E)
22:20–22:24	(J)		37:3b	(J)
23:1–23:20	(P)		37:4	(E)
24:1–24:67	(J)		37:5–37:11	(J)
25:1–25:4	(E)		37:12–37:18	(E)
25:5–25:6	(J)		37:19–37:20	(J)
25:7–25:11a	(P)		37:21–37:22	(E)
25:11b	(J)		37:23	(J)
25:12	(R)		37:24–37:25a	(E)
25:13–25:18	(P)		37:25b–37:27	(J)
25:19	(R)		37:28a	(E)
25:20	(P)		37:28b	(J)
25:21–26:33	(J)		37:29–37:30	(E)
26:34–26:35	(P)		37:31–37:35	(J)
27:1–27:45	(J)		37:36	(E)
27:46–28:9	(P)		38:1–40:23	(J)
28:10–28:11a	(J)		41:1–41:45a	(E)
28:11b–28:12	(E)		41:45b–41:46a	(P)
28:13–28:16	(J)		41:46b–41:57	(E)
28:17–28:18	(E)		42:1–42:4	(J)

42:5–42:7	(E)		4:18	(E)
42:8–42:20	(J)		4:19–4:20a	(J)
42:21–42:25	(E)		4:20b	(E)
42:26–42:34	(J)		4:21a	(J)
42:35–42:37	(E)		4:21b	(R)
42:38–43:13	(J)		4:22–6:1	(J)
43:14	(E)		6:2–6:12	(P)
43:15–45:2	(J)		6:13	(R)
45:3	(E)		6:14–6:25	(P)
45:4–45:28	(J)		6:26–6:30	(R)
46:1–46:5a	(E)		7:1–7:13	(P)
46:5b	(J)		7:14–7:18	(J)
46:6–46:27	(P)		7:19–7:20a	(P)
46:28–47:27a	(J)		7:20b–7:25	(J)
47:27b–47:28	(P)		8:1–8:3a	(P)
47:29–47:31	(J)		8:3b–8:11a	(J)
48:1–48:2	(E)		8:11b	(R)
48:3–48:6	(P)		8:12–8:15	(P)
48:7	(R)		8:16–9:7	(J)
48:8–48:22	(E)		9:8–9:12	(P)
49:1–49:27	(J)		9:13–9:34	(J)
49:28	(R)		9:35	(R)
49:29–49:33	(P)		10:1–10:19	(J)
50:1–50:11	(J)		10:20	(R)
50:12–50:13	(P)		10:21–10:26	(J)
50:14–50:22	(J)		10:27	(R)
50:23–50:26	(E)		10:28–11:8	(J)
			11:9–11:10	(R)
			12:1–12:20	(P)
EXODUS			12:21–12:23	(J)
			12:24–12:27	(E)
1:1–1:5	(R)		12:28	(P)
1:6–1:7	(P)		12:29–12:36	(E)
1:8–1:12	(E)		12:37a	(R)
1:13–1:14	(P)		12:37b–12:39	(E)
1:15–1:21	(E)		12:40–12:49	(P)
1:22–2:23a	(J)		12:50–12:51	(R)
2:23b–2:25	(P)		13:1–13:19	(E)
3:1	(E)		13:20	(R)
3:2–3:4a	(J)		13:21–14:4	(P)
3:4b	(E)		14:5–14:7	(J)
3:5	(J)		14:8	(P)
3:6	(E)		14:9a	(J)
3:7–3:8	(J)		14:9b–14:10a	(P)
3:9–3:15	(E)		14:10b	(J)
3:16–4:17	(J)			

14:10c	(P)		34:2–34:28	(J)
14:11–14:12	(E)		34:29–40:38	(P)
14:13–14:14	(J)			
14:15–14:18	(P)		**LEVITICUS**	
14:19a	(E)		1:1–23:38	(P)
14:19b	(J)		23:39–23:44	(R)
14:20a	(E)		24:1–26:38	(P)
14:20b	(J)		26:39–26:46	(R)
14:21a	(P)		27:1–27:34	(P)
14:21b	(J)			
14:21c–14:23	(P)		**NUMBERS**	
14:24	(J)			
14:25a	(E)		1:1–2:34	(P)
14:25b	(J)		3:1	(R)
14:26–14:27a	(P)		3:2–9:14	(P)
14:27b	(J)		9:15–9:23	(R)
14:28–14:29	(P)		10:1–10:12	(P)
14:30–15:18	(J)		10:13	(R)
15:19	(R)		10:14–10:27	(P)
15:20–15:21	(E)		10:28	(R)
15:22a	(R)		10:29–10:36	(J)
15:22b–15:25a	(J)		11:1–12:16	(E)
15:25b–15:26	(E)		13:1–13:16	(P)
15:27–16:1	(R)		13:17–13:20	(J)
16:2–16:3	(P)		13:21	(P)
16:4–16:5	(E)		13:22–13:24	(J)
16:6–16:35a	(P)		13:25–13:26	(P)
16:35b	(E)		13:27–13:31	(J)
16:36	(P)		13:32	(P)
17:1	(R)		13:33	(J)
17:2–18:27	(E)		14:1a	(P)
19:1	(P)		14:1b	(J)
19:2a	(R)		14:2–14:3	(P)
19:2b–19:9	(E)		14:4	(J)
19:10–19:16a	(J)		14:5–14:10	(P)
19:16b–19:17	(E)		14:11–14:25	(J)
19:18	(J)		14:26–14:39	(P)
19:19	(E)		14:39–14:45	(J)
19:20–19:25	(J)		15:1–15:31	(R)
20:1–20:17	(P)		15:32–16:1a	(P)
20:18–24:15a	(E)		16:1b–16:2a	(J)
24:15b–31:18	(P)		16:2b–16:11	(P)
32:1–33:23	(E)		16:12–16:14	(J)
34:1a	(J)		16:15–16:24	(P)
34:1b	(R)		16:25–16:26	(J)
			16:27a	(P)

16:27b–16:32a	(J)	4:32–8:18	(D1)
16:32b	(P)	8:19–8:20	(D2)
16:33–16:34	(J)	9:1–11:32	(D1)
16:35–19:22	(P)	12:1–26:15	(O)
20:1a	(R)	26:16–28:35	(D1)
20:1b–20:13	(P)	28:36–28:37	(D2)
20:14–20:21	(J)	28:38–28:62	(D1)
20:22	(R)	28:63–28:68	(D2)
20:23–20:29	(P)	29:1–29:20	(D1)
21:1–21:3	(J)	29:21–29:27	(D2)
21:4a	(R)	29:28–29:29	(D1)
21:4b–21:9	(E)	30:1–30:10	(D2)
21:10–21:20	(R)	30:11–30:13	(D1)
21:21–21:35	(J)	30:14–30:20	(D2)
22:1	(R)	31:1–31:13	(D1)
22:2–24:25	(E)	31:14–31:15	(E)
25:1–25:5	(J)	31:16–31:22	(D2)
25:6–26:8	(P)	31:23	(E)
26:9–26:11	(R)	31:24–31:27	(D1)
26:12–27:23	(P)	31:28–31:30	(D2)
28:1–29:39	(R)	32:1–32:43	(O)
30:1–32:42	(P)	32:44	(D2)
33:1–33:49	(R)	32:45–32:47	(D1)
33:50–36:13	(P)	32:48–32:52	(O)
		33:1	(E)
		33:2–33:29	(O)

DEUTERONOMY

		34:1–34:6	(E)
1:1–4:24	(D1)	34:7–34:9	(P)
4:25–4:31	(D2)	34:10–12	(D1)

Appendix 9.
A Chronology of
Old Testament Composition

The following chronology connects the time of composition of certain portions of Old Testament literature with important contemporary events in the history of the Jewish people. The dates are all B.C.T. However, please note that for any given date there may still be a considerable amount of scholarly debate. Accordingly, caution is advised.

I

THE FIRST PERIOD
{1200–1013 B.C.T.}

A. Jewish Historical Events: Israel (Before the Division), Through the Reign of Saul

1200–1028 B.C.T.	Period of Invasion and Conquest
1150 B.C.T.	Battle of Barak against Canaanites under Sisera
1155–1080 B.C.T.	Eli
1100 B.C.T.	Gideon and Abimelech
1100–1020 B.C.T.	Samuel
1080–1028 B.C.T.	Philistine domination
1065–1013 B.C.T.	Saul
1028–1013 B.C.T.	Saul's reign

B. Related Historical Events

1195 B.C.T.	Settlement of the Philistines in Palestine
1100 B.C.T.	Report of Wen-amon

C. Fragments of Old Testament Literature Written Before 1000 B.C.T.

Song of Lamech {Genesis 4:23–24}
Song of Miriam {Exodus 15:21}
The Ritual of the Ark {Numbers 10:35f}
The Oath Concerning Amalek {Exodus 17:16}

340

The Song of Satire on the Amorites {Numbers 21:27–30}

The Song of the Well {Numbers 21:17f}

A Fragmentary Station List from the Book of the Wars of Jehovah {Numbers 21:14f}

A Fragment from the Book of Jashar {Joshua 10:12f}

The Song of Deborah {Judges 5}

A Proverb "of the ancients" quoted by David {1 Samuel 24:13}

Two Riddles and a Triumph Song of Samson {Judges 14:14; 14:18; 15:16}

The Fable of Jotham {Judges 9:7–15}

The Curse and Blessing of Noah {Genesis 9:25–27}

The Blessing (a summary of tribal history) of Jacob {Genesis 49}

The Oracles of Balaam, the Seer {Numbers 23–24}

II

THE SECOND PERIOD
{1013–933 B.C.T.}

A. Jewish Historical Events: Israel (Before the Division), Through the Reign of Solomon

    1050–973 B.C.T.   David lived

    1013–973 B.C.T.   David's reign

    973–933 B.C.T.   Solomon's reign

B. Related Historical Events

    1000 B.C.T.   The Aramaean occupation of Syria

    969–936 B.C.T.   Hiram of Tyre

    950 B.C.T.   Rezin founded the Aramaean kingdom of Damascus. His successors were Hezion and Tabrimmon

C. Fragments of Old Testament Literature from the Times of David and Solomon

A song celebrating the prowess of David {1 Samuel 18:7, 21:11, 29:5}

The Benjamite Battle Cry {2 Samuel 20:1}

David's Lament over Saul and Jonathan {2 Samuel 1:19–27}

David's Lament over Abner {2 Samuel 3:33f}

The Parable of Nathan {2 Samuel 12:1–4}

The Blessing (a summary of tribal history) of Moses {Deuteronomy 33}

The Book of the Wars of Jehovah

The Book of Jashar (of the Valiant?)

The early strand of narrative in Samuel {1 Samuel 9, etc.}

The Court History of David {2 Samuel 9–1 Kings 2}

The Book of the Acts of Solomon

The kernel of the Temple narratives

The Code of the Covenant {Exodus 20:23–23:19}

The so-called "J" Decalogue {Exodus 34}

III

THE THIRD PERIOD
{933–843 B.C.T.}

A. Jewish Historical Events

  1. The Northern Kingdom: Israel from Jeroboam I to the Revolution of Jehu

933–912 B.C.T.	Jeroboam I
912–911 B.C.T.	Nadab
911–888 B.C.T.	Baasha
888–887 B.C.T.	Elah
887 B.C.T.	Zimri
887–876 B.C.T.	Omri
880 B.C.T.	Omri conquered Moab
876–854 B.C.T.	Ahab and the Prophetic activity of Elijah
858 B.C.T.	First War between Israel and the Aramaeans
857 B.C.T.	Second War between Israel and the Aramaeans
854 B.C.T.	Third War between Israel and the Aramaeans
854 B.C.T.	Ahab allied with Benhadad II of Damascus against Shalmaneser in the battle of Qarqar (Karkar)
854–853 B.C.T.	Ahaziah
853–842 B.C.T.	Joram and the Wars against Benhadad II of Syria
850 B.C.T.	Mesha threw off the Israelite yoke (Inscription of Mesha)
850 B.C.T.	Prophetic activity of Elisha in Israel

  2. The Southern Kingdom: Judah from Rehoboam's Accession to 843 B.C.T.

933–917 B.C.T.	Rehoboam
917–915 B.C.T.	Abijam
915–875 B.C.T.	Asa
875–851 B.C.T.	Jehoshaphat
851–844 B.C.T.	Joram
844–843 B.C.T.	Ahaziah

B. Related Historical Events

954–924 B.C.T.	Sheshonk I (Shishak) of Egypt campaigned against Israel and Judah
900 B.C.T.	Benhadad I of Damascus conducted a war against Israel
884–860 B.C.T.	Ashurnazirpal of Assyria approached Hebrew territory
859–825 B.C.T.	Shalmaneser III of Assyria
849 B.C.T.	First Assyrian campaign against Damascus and allies
846 B.C.T.	Second Assyrian campaign against Damascus and allies
845 B.C.T.	Hazael of Damascus warred against Israel

C. Old Testament Literature

  The core of the Elijah narratives {1 Kings 17–19, 21, and 2 Kings 1 and 2}

  The core of the Elisha narratives {2 Kings 2–8 and 13:14–21}

  The revolution of Jehu {2 Kings 9 and 10}

Chronicles of the Kings of Israel, similar to the Book of the Acts of Solomon
Chronicles of the Kings of Judah, similar to the Book of the Acts of Solomon
The "J" Document (around 850 B.C.T.)

IV

THE FOURTH PERIOD
{843–722 B.C.T.}

A. Jewish Historical Events
  1. The Northern Kingdom: Israel from Jehu to the Fall of Samaria

843–816 B.C.T.	Jehu
842 B.C.T.	Jehu paid tribute to Shalmaneser III of Assyria
816–800 B.C.T.	Jehoahaz
800–785 B.C.T.	Joash
785–745 B.C.T.	Jeroboam II
760 B.C.T.	Prophetic ministry of Amos
750–735 B.C.T.	Prophetic ministry of Hosea
744 B.C.T.	Zechariah
744 B.C.T.	Shallum
743–737 B.C.T.	Menahem
738 B.C.T.	Menahem paid tribute to Tiglathpileser III (Pul)
737–736 B.C.T.	Pekahiah
736–734 B.C.T.	Pekah
734 B.C.T.	Syro-Ephraimitic war. Rezin (Damascus) and Pekah (Israel) against Ahaz (Judah)
733–732 B.C.T.	Tiglathpileser placed Hoshea on the throne of Israel
733–722 B.C.T.	Hoshea
722 B.C.T.	Sargon captured Samaria. Israel fell.

  2. The Southern Kingdom: Judah from Queen Athaliah to Micah

843–837 B.C.T.	Athaliah
837–798 B.C.T.	Joash
798–780 B.C.T.	Amaziah
780–740 B.C.T.	Azariah (Uzziah)
740–735 B.C.T.	Jotham
740–701 B.C.T.	Prophetic activity of Isaiah
735–720 B.C.T.	Ahaz
725–690? B.C.T.	Prophetic activity Micah

B. Related Historical Events: Assyrian History

842 B.C.T.	Shalmaneser III initiated his fourth campaign against Damascus
810–782 B.C.T.	Adadnirari III conquered the west including Israel ("the land of Omri"), Phoenicia, Edom, Damascus, but not Judah

745–727 B.C.T.   Tiglathpileser III of Assyria
738 B.C.T.   Tiglathpileser's first western campaign
733–732 B.C.T.   Tiglathpileser III began another campaign against the west
732 B.C.T.   Fall of Damascus
727–722 B.C.T.   Shalmaneser V
722–705 B.C.T.   Sargon of Assyria
722 B.C.T.   Sargon carried 27,290 Israelite prisoners into captivity

C. Old Testament Literature
 Continuation of Chronicles of the Kings of Israel
 Continuation of Chronicles of the Kings of Judah
 The Writings of Amos
 The Writings of Hosea
 The Writings of Isaiah 1–39 (excluding 13:1–14:23; 21; 24–27; 34; and 35)
 The Writings of Micah {725–690 B.C.T.}
 The "E" document (around 750 B.C.T.)

V

THE FIFTH PERIOD
{722–538 B.C.T.}

A. Jewish Historical Events: Judah from the Fall of Israel (the Northern Kingdom) and the History of the Jewish Exiles (after 597 B.C.T) to the Return

720–692 B.C.T.   Hezekiah
711 B.C.T.   Judah "punished" by Sargon
701 B.C.T.   Sennacherib besieged Hezekiah, who became his tributary
692–638 B.C.T.   Manasseh, a vassal of Esarhaddon
638 B.C.T.   Amon
638–608 B.C.T.   Josiah
627 B.C.T.   Prophetic activity of Zephaniah
626–585 B.C.T.   Prophetic activity of Jeremiah
621 B.C.T.   The discovery of Deuteronomy and the Deuteronomic reform
615 B.C.T.   Prophetic activity of Nahum
612 B.C.T.   The fall of Nineveh
608 B.C.T.   The Battle of Megiddo and the death of Josiah
608–597 B.C.T.   Jehoiakim
605 B.C.T.   Battle of Carchemish
600 B.C.T.   Prophetic activity of Habakkuk
597 B.C.T.   Jehoiachin and the first captivity.
597–586 B.C.T.   Zedekiah
592–570 B.C.T.   Prophetic activity of Ezekiel (in Babylonia)
586 B.C.T.   The destruction of Jerusalem and the second captivity

561 B.C.T.	The release of Jehoiachim by Evil-Merodach
540 B.C.T.	Prophetic activity of Deutero-Isaiah {see Isaiah 40–55}
538 B.C.T.	Cyrus gave the Jewish exiles permission to return

B. Related Historical Events

1. Assyrian and Babylonian Historical Events

722–710 B.C.T.	Merodach-Baladan of Babylon struggled for the mastery of Assyria
711 B.C.T.	Sargon's expedition against Azuri of Ashdod
705–681 B.C.T.	Sennacherib of Assyria
703 B.C.T.	Sennacherib's expedition against Merodach-Baladan of Babylon
701 B.C.T.	Sennacherib's campaign against the west. Sennacherib confines Hezekiah "like a caged bird" in Jerusalem while carrying away 200,150 captives along with a large quantity of booty.
681–668 B.C.T.	Esarhaddon of Assyria
668–626 B.C.T.	Ashurbanipal of Assyria
625–604 B.C.T.	Nabopolassar of Babylon founded the Chaldean kingdom
612 B.C.T.	Fall of Assyria to Nabopolassar, Medes and Scythians
605 B.C.T.	Nebuchadnezzar of Babylon defeated Necho at Carchemish
562–560 B.C.T.	Amel-Marduk (Evil-Merodach)
560–556 B.C.T.	Neriglissar
556–538 B.C.T.	Nabonidus
553–529 B.C.T.	Cyrus of Persia mastered Media, Lydia and Asia Minor and at length, by 539 B.C.T, Babylon

2. Egyptian Historical Events

712–700 B.C.T.	Sabaka
700–689 B.C.T.	Shabataka
689–664 B.C.T.	Taharka
664–661 B.C.T.	Tanutamon
663 B.C.T.	Destruction of Thebes by Ashurbanipal
663–609 B.C.T.	Psammetichus I
609–593 B.C.T.	Necho
605 B.C.T.	Necho was defeated at Carchemish
593–588 B.C.T.	Psammetichus II placed a Jewish garrison at Elephantine
588–566 B.C.T.	Apries (Hophra)

C. Old Testament Literature

Combination of "J" and "E" Documents

Deuteronomy was written around 650 B.C.T. and introduced around 621 B.C.T.

Zephaniah {627 B.C.T.}

Jeremiah {626–585 B.C.T.}

Nahum {615 B.C.T.}

Habakkuk {600 B.C.T.}

Ezekiel {592–570 B.C.T.}

Portions of Lamentations {586–570 B.C.T.}

Code of Holiness [Leviticus 17–26] {560 B.C.T.}

Combination of "J", "E" and "D" {560 B.C.T.}

The Deuteronomic editing and the exilic re-editing (around 550 B.C.T.) of the Book of Kings

Deuteronomic narratives of Joshua, Judges, and Samuel

The Song of Moses [Deuteronomy 32]

Isaiah 13:1–14:23 and 21

Deutero-Isaiah {Isaiah 40–55}

VI

THE SIXTH PERIOD
{538–323 B.C.T.}

A. Jewish Historical Events: From the Return of the Jews to the Death of Alexander the Great: Judah Restored

538 B.C.T.	Return of a band of exiles under Sheshbazzar
537 B.C.T.	The altar for burnt-offerings was rebuilt
536 B.C.T.	The foundation of the temple was laid
520–518 B.C.T.	Prophetic activity of Haggai and Zechariah
520–516 B.C.T.	The rebuilding of the temple under Zerubbabel and Joshua
460 B.C.T.	Prophetic activity of Malachi
444–432 B.C.T.	Nehemiah's first and second visits to Jerusalem. The wall was rebuilt. Eliashib became high priest.
411 B.C.T.	Jehohanan became the high priest at Jerusalem
407 B.C.T.	Bagoas became governor or Judah (Elephantine papyri)
397(?) B.C.T.	The time of Ezra and the Introduction of the Priestly Code
351 B.C.T.	Jaddua became high priest
350 B.C.T.	Jerusalem was taken by Artaxerxes III
335 B.C.T.	A Samaritan schism occurred. The Samaritan temple was constructed on Mount Gerizim.
331 B.C.T.	Syria and Palestine were conquered by Alexander the Great
323 B.C.T.	Alexander the Great died and his empire was partitioned.

B. Related Historical Events

    1. Persian Historical Events

538 B.C.T.	Cyrus seized control in Babylon
529–522 B.C.T.	Cambyses
525 B.C.T.	The Egyptian expedition of Cambyses
522–521 B.C.T.	Gaumata
521–485 B.C.T.	Darius I

485–464 B.C.T.   Xerxes I

464–424 B.C.T.   Artaxerxes I

408–358 B.C.T.   Artaxerxes II (Mnemon)

358–337 B.C.T.   Artaxerxes III   (Ochus)

337–331 B.C.T.   Darius III

2. Egyptian Historical Events

525 B.C.T.   Cambyses conquered Egypt. The Jewish temple at Elephantine was left unharmed.

411 B.C.T.   The Jewish temple at Elephantine was destroyed

C. Old Testament Literature

Isaiah 63:7–64:12 {538–520 B.C.T}

Haggai and Zechariah 1–8 {520–518 B.C.T.}

Majority of the Psalms were collected, many pre-exilic in origin

Malachi {460 B.C.T.}

Obadiah {460 B.C.T.}

Trito-Isaiah 56–66 (excluding 63:7–64:12) {460–450 B.C.T.}

Isaiah 34 and 35 {450 B.C.T.}

Job {450–400 B.C.T.}

The Priestly Code and the Priestly redaction of the Pentateuch (the "P" document) {500–400 B.C.T.}

Memoirs of Nehemiah {444–432 B.C.T.}

Memoirs of Ezra(?) {after 397 B.C.T.}

Ruth {400 B.C.T.}

Joel {400 B.C.T.}

The "Little Apocalypse"—Isaiah 24–27 {340–332 B.C.T.}

VII

THE SEVENTH PERIOD
{323–150 B.C.T.}

A. Jewish Historical Events: From the Death of Alexander the Great to the End of the Old Testament

323–198 B.C.T.   Palestine under the (Egyptian) Ptolemies

321 B.C.T.   Ptolemy captured Jerusalem

198–164 B.C.T.   Palestine under the (Syrian) Seleucids. Onias III became the high priest, contemporary with Seleucus IV

175 B.C.T.   Jason became the high priest, contemporary with Antiochus IV

171 B.C.T.   Menelaus secured the high priesthood

168 B.C.T.   Antiochus attempted to suppress the Jewish religion

168–163 B.C.T.   The Maccabean era

168–160 B.C.T.   Judas Maccabeus

165 B.C.T.   The rededication of the altar

161 B.C.T.	Alcimos became the high priest and leader of a Hellenistic faction
160–142 B.C.T.	Jonathan became the ruler
153 B.C.T.	Jonathan became the high priest
142 B.C.T.	Jews under Simon (142–135 B.C.T.) gained political independence

B. Related Historical Events

  1. Syrian Historical Events

323 B.C.T.	Seleucus I Nikator of Babylon
316 B.C.T.	Seleucus was driven out by Antigonus
312 B.C.T.	Seleucus founded the Seleucid (Syrian) dynasty
312–280 B.C.T.	Seleucus I (Nikator)
279–261 B.C.T.	Antiochus I (Soter)
261–246 B.C.T.	Antiochus II (Theos)
246–226 B.C.T.	Seleucus II (Callinicus)
226–223 B.C.T.	Seleucus III (Ceraunos)
223–187 B.C.T.	Antiochus III the Great
187–176 B.C.T.	Seleucus IV (Philopator)
175–164 B.C.T.	Antiochus IV (Epiphanes)

  2. Egyptian Historical Events

323–285 B.C.T.	Ptolemy I (Soter)
285–247 B.C.T.	Ptolemy II (Philadelphus)
247–222 B.C.T.	Ptolemy III (Energetes)
222–205 B.C.T.	Ptolemy IV (Philopator)
205–182 B.C.T.	Ptolemy V (Epiphanes)
182–164 B.C.T.	Ptolemy VI (Philometor)
170–164 B.C.T.	Ptolemy VII (Euergetes) [jointly with Ptolemy VI}
164–146 B.C.T.	Ptolemy VII (Euergetes) [alone]

C. Old Testament Literature

Jonah {300 B.C.T.}

Song of Songs {300 B.C.T.}

Zechariah 9–14 {300–250 B.C.T.}

Proverbs compiled {300–250 B.C.T.} although many were very old in origin

Chronicles, Ezra and Nehemiah {300–250 B.C.T.}

Beginnings of the Greek translation of the Old Testament (the Septuagint—LXX) {250 B.C.T.}

Ecclesiastes {250–200 B.C.T.}

Daniel {167 B.C.T.}

Esther {150 B.C.T.}

Psalms [final edition] {shortly after 150 B.C.T.}

Appendix 10.
The Descendants
of Cain and Seth

A comparison between the names of Cain's descendants {Genesis 4:17–22} and Seth's descendants {Genesis 5:6–29} reveals a startling similarity and some duplication:

Adam	1	Enosh
Cain	2	Kenan
Enoch	3	Mahalalel
Irad	4	Jared
Mehujael	5	Enoch
Methusael	6	Methuselah
Lamech	7	Lamech
Naamah	8	Noah

Adam and Enosh both mean "man." Other names in the two lists are like-sounding, and by exchanging the places of Enoch and Mehujael, one arrives at essentially the same (single) basic list—a list which in rather customary biblical tradition is presented in two variants. The thrust of both of these genealogies is that mankind has one ancestor (Adam or Enosh) and only one line of descent. Noah appears when the seven generations of prehistoric man have run their course.

Appendix 11.
The Table of Contents of the Tanakh (The Jewish Scriptures)

Torah (The Five Books of Moses)

> Genesis
> Exodus
> Leviticus
> Numbers
> Deuteronomy

Nevi'im (The Prophets)

> Joshua
> Judges
> 1 Samuel
> 2 Samuel
> 1 Kings
> 2 Kings
> Isaiah
> Jeremiah
> Ezekiel

(The Twelve Minor Prophets)

> Hosea
> Joel
> Amos
> Obadiah

> Jonah
> Micah
> Nahum
> Habakkuk
> Zephaniah
> Haggai
> Zechariah
> Malachi

Kethuvim (The Writings)

> Psalms
> Proverbs
> Job
> The Song of Songs
> Ruth
> Lamentations
> Ecclesiastes
> Esther
> Daniel
> Ezra
> Nehemiah
> 1 Chronicles
> 2 Chronicles

Appendix 12.
The Table of Contents of the Old Testament of the Catholic Bible

The Pentateuch*

Genesis
Exodus
Leviticus
Numbers
Deuteronomy
Joshua
Judges
Ruth

The Historical Books

1 Samuel
2 Samuel
1 Kings
2 Kings
1 Chronicles
2 Chronicles
Ezra

Nehemiah
Tobit
Judith
Esther
1 Maccabees
2 Maccabees

The Wisdom Books

Job
Psalms
Proverbs
Ecclesiastes
Song of Songs
Wisdom
Sirach (Ecclesiasticus)

The Prophetic Books

Isaiah

Jeremiah
Lamentations
Baruch
Ezekiel
Daniel
Hosea
Joel
Amos
Obadiah
Jonah
Micah
Nahum
Habukkuk
Zephaniah
Haggai
Zechariah
Malachi

*The Table of Contents of the Catholic Bible lists eight books under the heading "Pentateuch" and groups the books of the Old Testament into four categories: The Pentateuch, the Historical Books, the Wisdom Books, and the Prophetic Books.

Appendix 13.
A Catholic Overview
of the Pentateuch

GENESIS: Origins: Creation and stories of primeval times. Abraham, Isaac, Jacob, Joseph: The great ancestors of the Jewish people.

EXODUS: God chooses Moses to deliver Israelites from slavery in Egypt. The giving of the Law at Mount Sinai. Many laws regarding daily life and religious practice.

LEVITICUS: Laws for the people of God relating to sacrifice, priesthood, and religious feasts. Recurring call to be "holy" as God is holy.

NUMBERS: More laws. Desert wanderings and military exploits on the way to the Promised Land. Repeated acts of unfaithfulness to God and Moses extend the wandering to forty years.

DEUTERONOMY: A "second law" that sums up the significance of the Exodus. Moses' farewell speech delivered at the borders of the Promised Land in which Moses warns people that they must obey the covenant or risk losing the land.

Appendix 14.
A Catholic Perspective on the Jewish Divisions of the Bible

The Law (Torah)

    Genesis
    Exodus
    Leviticus
    Numbers
    Deuteronomy

The Prophets

    Former Prophets
    Joshua
    Judges
    1 Samuel
    2 Samuel
    1 Kings
    2 Kings

    Latter Prophets
    Isaiah

Jeremiah
Ezekiel
The Book of the Twelve

The Writings

    Psalms
    Job
    Proverbs
    Ruth
    Song of Songs
    Ecclesiastes
    Lamentations
    Esther
    Daniel
    Ezra
    Nehemiah
    1 Chronicles
    2 Chronicles

Appendix 15.
A Catholic Perspective on How the Bible Has Been Read Throughout the Passage of Time

NEW TESTAMENT TIMES: Scripture viewed as prophecy of Jesus, and used to show connection between Jesus and what went before him.

EARLY CHURCH TIMES: Scripture read allegorically. Literal meaning rejected because Bible contains deeper meanings put there (inspired) by God. Therefore, Bible always says more than the author intended to say.

MEDIEVAL PERIOD: Allegorical reading still predominates. Growing respect for literal meaning of text. But much of Old Testament still viewed as prediction of Jesus.

MODERN TIMES: Critical study of texts. Four sources theory and source criticism developed. Development of form criticism, the search for literary genres and the earliest and smallest literary units of tradition, and transmission history, the account of how the current texts came to be.

Appendix 16.
A Catholic Perspective on the Four Sources and the Four "Ps"

Who	What	How
Yahwist (J)	Emphasizes role of *Poet*	Storytelling
Elohist (E)	Emphasizes role of *Prophet*	Challenging
Priestly (P)	Emphasizes role of *Priest*	Legislating
Deuteronomist (D)	Emphasizes role of *Parents*	Exhorting

Appendix 17.
A Catholic Perspective on the Differences Between the Two Major Divisions of Genesis

Topic	Genesis 1–11	Genesis 12–50
TIME	Set in time before human history	Set in historical times well known to ancient records
PLACE	Locations vague: Somewhere to the East and northern	Locations exact: Palestine and Egypt Mesopotamia
PERSONS	Characters seem like symbols, little is known of their lives	Characters have names and behave like typical people of second millennium B.C.T.
STORIES	Many stories can be classified as as folklore; they resemble those known from Mesopotamia	Sagalike stories and epic history narratives similar to oral lore of tribal groups
EVENTS	Most events seem to have supernatural quality	Major events resemble normal human experience
PURPOSE	Describes the origins of humanity long before Israel's time	Traces the direct tribal ancestors of Israel itself

Appendix 18.
A Catholic Perspective on the Division of Genesis Into Four Blocs of Material

1. Genesis 1–11

   The Prologue: primeval history of humankind's original blessing and failure through sin

2. Genesis 12–25

   The story of Abraham: his call and response; his blessing and promise

3. Genesis 26–36

   The stories of Abraham's son Isaac and grandson Jacob and how they carry on the blessing

4. Genesis 37–50

   The story of Joseph in Egypt: preparation for God's great self-revelation in the Exodus

Appendix 19.
A Catholic Perspective on the Toledoth Lists

Genesis contains certain internal markers that help divide and organize the material. These markers are the genealogical lists, *toledoth,* that always begin "these are the descendants of …" These lists help make the point that while generations come and go, God's plan moves ahead no matter what. Sometimes appearing at the beginning and sometimes at the end of a section, the lists group together all the members of a family line or tribe to signal a break with the events that have just been recounted. The following provides a listing of the *toledoth* lists:

Genesis 2:4a   Begins the second story of creation

Genesis 5:1   Introduces the long break between the first family and the days of Noah

Genesis 6:9   Introduces the story of the flood

Genesis 10:1   Marks the great expansion of people all over the world

Genesis 11:10   Marks the addition of a new list of the nations of the world by the P source

Genesis 11:27   Begins the story of Abraham

Genesis 25:12   Closes off the life of Abraham's "other" family through Hagar and Ishmael

Genesis 25:19   Opens the story of Jacob's birth and destiny

Genesis 36:1   Ends the role of Jacob's twin, Esau, and directs us to Jacob's children, especially Joseph

Genesis 36:9   A repetition within the Esau list that marks its conclusion

Genesis 37:2   Marks the opening of the story of Joseph and his brothers that continues to the end of Genesis

Appendix 20.
A Protestant Perspective
on the Divisions of the Bible

The thirty-nine books of the Old Testament are arranged in a four-fold grouping, which, with some modifications, has been recognized for many centuries—since the Greek translation known as the Septuagint was made, before the beginning of Christian time. The four fold grouping of the Old Testament is as follows:

(4) *The Law—The Pentateuch (5 books):* Genesis, Exodus, Leviticus, Numbers, and Deuteronomy

(5) *The History (12 books):* Joshua, Judges, Ruth, First and Second Samuel, First and Second Kings, First and Second Chronicles, Ezra, Nehemiah, and Esther

(6) *Poetry (5 books):* Job, Psalms, Proverbs, Ecclesiastes, and Song of Songs

(7) *Prophecy (17 books):*

  (a) *The Major Prophets (5 books):* Isaiah, Jeremiah, Lamentations, Ezekiel, and Daniel

  (b) *The Minor Prophets (12 books):* Hosea, Joel, Amos, Obadiah, Jonah, Micah, Nahum, Habakkuk, Zephaniah, Haggai, Zechariah, and Malachi

The twenty-seven books of the New Testament may be arranged in three groups. The three fold grouping of the New Testament is as follows:

(1) *The Historical Books (5 books):*

  (a) *The Gospels (4 books):* Matthew, Mark, Luke, and John

  (b) The Acts *(1 book)*

(2) *The Epistles or Doctrinal Books (21 books):* Romans; First and Second Corinthians; Galatians; Ephesians; Philippians; Colossians; First and Second Thessalonians; First and Second Timothy; Titus; Philemon; Hebrews; James; First and Second Peter; First, Second and Third John; and Jude

(3) *The Apocalyptic (1 book):* Revelation

Appendix 21.
The Intertestamental Literature

In many of the Bibles that have been circulated for many years, the period of time between the Old Testament and the New Testament receives little, if any, attention. Indeed, for much of Christianity, the intertestamental period is deemed to be a "period of silence" and the centuries separating the Old Testament and the New Testament are deemed to be "The Silent Centuries." These designations are based upon a perception held by many Christian scholars that from the time when the last Old Testament book was written to the period of the writing of the first New Testament book, the voice of inspired prophecy was silent, there were no other worthy mouthpieces of God, and as a result of this dearth not a single page of literary material worthy of consideration was handed down.

However, for Catholics and for many modern Christian scholars, there is merit to the literature of the intertestamental period. Indeed, for Catholics there was so much merit associated with the literature that eleven of the so called "apocryphal" or "hidden" books were declared to be canonical in 1546 C.C. by the Roman Catholic Church and have appeared in the Catholic editions of the Scriptures ever since.

Nevertheless, for most of the Protestant Church the apocryphal books have never been accepted as being canonical. The objections to their inclusion in the Bible were based on four reasons:

(1) The apocryphal books were never quoted by Jesus, and it is doubtful if they were ever alluded to by the apostles.
(2) Most of the early Church Fathers regarded the apocryphal books as being uninspired.
(3) The apocryphal books did not appear in the Ancient Hebrew canon.
(4) The inferior quality of most of the writings as compared with the canonical books, marks them as being unworthy of a place in the sacred Scriptures.

While recognizing the objections raised by the Protestant Church, in this book the intertestamentary literature is deemed to be very important for a number of reasons.

First of all, the intertestamentary literature provides us with insights into the important events which form the background for the advent and life of Jesus and for the theology propounded by Muhammad. For two hundred years after the captivity, the Province of Judea remained under Persian rule. The conquest of Alexander the Great in 330 B.C.T., not only brought the Jews under Grecian dominion, but also introduced the Greek language and ideas throughout the ancient world. After the death of Alexander, his kingdom was divided, and there came on a struggle between the Ptolemies of Egypt and the monarchs of Syria, which resulted first in the overlordship of Egypt in Judea, and later on of Syrian rule.

The period of Syrian rule was a dark period in Jewish history, especially during the reign of Antiochus Epiphanes, the Syrian king, who committed many outrages against the Jews, sought to establish idolatry in Jerusalem, and defiled the temple. The wickedness of Antiochus Epiphanes led to the Maccabean revolt in 166 B.C.T., in which the priest Matthias and his sons defeated the Syrians in a series of battles, which secured the independence of the Province of Judea. The independence of Judea then became the foundation of the Asmonaean Dynasty, which reigned from 166–63 B.C.T.

This history is important because recent scholarship has indicated that some of the "canonical" books of the Bible were actually written during the intertestamental period themselves. Until modern times, it was assumed that the last book of the Old Testament — the Book of Malachi — was the last book to be written and that it was written around 450 B.C.T. Based upon this assumption, it was posited that the "period of silence" lasted from 450 B.C.T. to about 50 C.C., the time of the first written records of the New Testament. However, modern scholarship has revealed that several books of the Old Testament (such as Job, Ruth, Jonah and a number of the Psalms) were probably written in the fourth century B.C.T. or even later, and two books of the Old Testament (Ecclesiastes and Esther) may not have been written until as late as the second century B.C.T. Thus, in some cases, the intertestamentary literature may actually pre-date the books of the Old Testament and may have influenced the writers of those books.[1,2]

A better appreciation of the history of religion, especially the religion of Israel, is another factor responsible for the rehabilitation of this period. The complete story of the religion of Israel cannot be told with the Old Testament as its only source. Much essential information is secured from the study of the languages and literatures, as well as the religious, social, and political organizations, of contemporary peoples, and such a study can only be thorough if the literature of the intertestamental period is examined and understood as well.

Finally, the importance of the intertestamental period literature for the student of the Old Testament, the New Testament and the Qur'an, is a fuller understanding of the

---

[1]While not directly referring to the intertestamental literature discussed herein, it is important to note that non-canonical sources did influence the authors of the Old Testament. Unfortunately, most of those non-canonical sources are no longer in existence. Nevertheless, the biblical record indicates that, once upon a time, there existed the following documents: The Book of the Wars of Yahweh (Numbers 21:14); the Book of the Just (Joshua 10:13, 2 Samuel 1:18); the Book of the Acts of Solomon (1 Kings 11:41); the Book of the Annals of the Kings of Israel (1 Kings 14:19, 2 Chronicles 33:18); the Book of the Annals of the Kings of Judah (1 Kings 14:29, 15:7); the Annals of Samuel the Seer (1 Chronicles 29:29); the History of Nathan the Prophet (2 Chronicles 9:29); the Annals of Shemaiah the Prophet and of Iddo the Seer (2 Chronicles12:15), the Annals of Jehu, Son of Hanani (2 Chronicles 20:34); the Annals of Hozai (2 Chronicles 33:18); and a Lament for Josiah (2 Chronicles 35:25).

[2]It is notable that one canonical book of the Christian Bible, the Epistle of Jude, does directly refer, at least twice, to the language of the intertestamental book we call 1 Enoch and in a third instance quotes it in an authoritative manner as prophetic. Jude also refers to a legend about the body of Moses known to us as the book called the Assumption of Moses.

entire Hellenistic and Roman world during the "Silent Centuries." The New Testament, and even the Qur'an, cannot be fully understood without some knowledge of the Palestinian, Alexandrian, and even Roman Judaism.

Thus, in modern times, the study of the intertestamentary literature has taken on new prominence.

The historical occasions for literary activity in the intertestamental period are varied. Perhaps the most significant occasion furnishing incentives for literary endeavor was the Dispersion of the Jews to every large center within the Mediterranean basin. The literature of the Jewish Diaspora was motivated by three objectives: (1) to control and retain racial identity; (2) to demonstrate the antiquity and priority of the Jewish Law; and (3) to construct a synthesis of Jewish and Greek thought that would be attractive to both Jew and Gentile. The occasions for literary activity in Palestine were the Maccabean Rebellion, the glories and triumphs of the Maccabean rulers, the party strife of the Pharisees and the Sadducees, the oppression under the Romans, and the Fall of Jerusalem. These occasions were periods of war, civil discord, persecution, foreign domination, and destruction of nationality. As a result, much of the literature carries a note of cynicism and pessimism.

The Jewish literature of the intertestamental period falls naturally into two large groups, the Apocrypha proper and the Pseudepigrapha. The term "Apocrypha" is derived from a Greek word meaning "something hidden." Originally it was used in a laudatory sense of literature hidden from the eyes of the uninitiated, and intended only for the wise. Later the term came to be used in a derogatory sense and was applied to literature of secondary value. Later still, in the days of Origen and Jerome, it was applied to literature considered false and heretical. There are those today who accept the last mentioned meaning. However, generally speaking, the modern use of the term does not involve such unfavorable judgment; it is used simply as a convenient designation of the non-canonical literature closely related to the Old Testament and the New Testament. In its broadest sense the term Apocrypha includes the Old Testament Apocrypha, the New Testament Apocrypha and various other Jewish writings of a pseudepigraphal and apocalyptic character. In a narrower sense the term is restricted to the Old Testament Apocrypha or the New Testament Apocrypha.

The term "Pseudepigrapha" means "writings under assumed names" and is applied in a narrower sense than the term Apocrypha. Generally, the term "Pseudepigrapha" is applied to all Jewish literature of the intertestamental period outside of the Old Testament Apocrypha proper. However, as the term suggests, it is really intended to cover all the Jewish writings written under assumed names, such as Enoch, the Twelve Sons of Jacob, Moses, Ezra, etc. Indeed, there are some books of a pseudepigraphal nature in the Apocrypha itself, such as 1 Baruch, the Epistle of Jeremy, and 2 Esdras.

The books listed as Old Testament Apocrypha proper are as follows: 1 and 2 Esdras (1 and 2 Ezra), Tobit, Judith, additions to Esther, the Wisdom of Solomon, Ecclesiasticus (Sirach), 1 Baruch, the Epistle of Jeremy (the Letter of Jeremiah), the Prayer of Azariah and Song of the Three Children, Susanna, Bel and the Dragon, Prayer of Manasses (Prayer of Manasseh), 1 and 2 Maccabees. Generally speaking, these books represent the success of the Alexandrian canon of the Old Testament over the Palestinian or Hebrew canon. The Alexandrian canon is in Greek and is known from the early Greek translation called the Septuagint. Some manuscripts of the Septuagint contain also the Books of 3 and 4

Maccabees. At the Council of Trent, in 1546, the Roman Catholic Church declared all the books of the Apocrypha proper canonical, with the exception of 1 and 2 Esdras and the Prayer of Manasses.

For many years, the books of the Pseudepigrapha were listed as follows: 3 and 4 Maccabees, Enoch, the Testaments of the Twelve Patriarchs, Jubilees, the Letter of Aristeas, Sibylline Oracles, Psalms of Solomon, Zadokite Fragments, Assumption of Moses, 2 Enoch, 2 Baruch, 3 Baruch, Martyrdom of Isaiah, and the Books of Adam and Eve.[3] However, due to modern scholarship, the list has been greatly expanded to a point where a contemporary listing would include the following:

Apocalypse of Abraham	Hecataeus of Abdera
Testament of Abraham	Pseudo-Hecataeus
Apocalypse of Adam	Hellenistic Synagogal Prayers
Testament of Adam	Testament of Hezekiah
Life of Adam and Eve	Fragments of Historical Works
Ahiqar	Testament of Isaac
An Anonymous Samaritan Text	Martyrdom and Ascension of Isaiah
Letter of Aristeas	Vision of Isaiah
Aristeas the Exegete	Ladder of Jacob
Aristobulus	Prayer of Jacob
Artapanus	Testament of Jacob
2 Baruch	Jannes and Jambres
3 Baruch	Testament of Job
4 Baruch	Joseph and Aseneth
Cave of Treasures	History of Joseph
Cleodemus Malchus	Prayer of Joseph
Apocalypse of Daniel	Jubilees
More Psalms of David	*Liber Antiquitatum Biblicarum*
Demetrius the Chronographer	The Lost Tribes
Eldad and Modad	3 Maccabees
Apocalypse of Elijah	4 Maccabees
1 Enoch	5 Maccabees
2 Enoch	Prayer of Manasseh
3 Enoch	Syriac Menander
Eupolemus	Apocalypse of Moses
Pseudo-Eupolemus	Assumption of Moses
Apocalypse of Ezekiel	Prayer of Moses
Apocryphon of Ezekiel	Testament of Moses
Ezekiel the Tragedian	Book of Noah
Fourth Book of Ezra	Orphica
Greek Apocalypse of Ezra	*Paraleipomena Jeremiou*
Questions of Ezra	Philo the Epic Poet
Revelation of Ezra	Pseudo-Philo
Vision of Ezra	Pseudo-Phocylides
Fragments of Pseudo-Greek Poets	Fragments of Poetical Works

---

[3] 4 Ezra, which is the same as 2 Esdras 3-14, is frequently classified among the Pseudepigrapha.

The Lives of the Prophets
History of the Rechabites
Apocalypse of Sedrach
Treatise of Shem
Sibylline Oracles
Odes of Solomon
Psalms of Solomon
Testament of Solomon
Five Apocryphal Syriac Psalms
Thallus
Theodotus
Testaments of the Three Patriarchs
Testaments of the Twelve Patriarchs
    Testament of Reuben

Testament of Simeon
Testament of Levi
Testament of Judah
Testament of Issachar
Testament of Zebulun
Testament of Dan
Testament of Naphtali
Testament of Gad
Testament of Asher
Testament of Joseph
Testament of Benjamin
Vita Adae et Evae
Apocalypse of Zephaniah
Apocalypse of Zosimus

The great expanse of Pseudepigrapha points to the wealth of literature which was at the disposal of many of the authors of the New Testament and also, possibly in some oral form, to Muhammad, the revealer of the Qur'an. Consequently, a study of, and understanding of, these texts has become increasingly important for our understanding of the basis for the Christian and Muslim faiths.

Appendix 22.
The Date of Composition
of the Traditional
Intertestamental Literature

Much of the literature of the traditional Intertestamental literature may be arranged according to the century and date of origin. However, some caution should be used since many of the books are composites with each portion being written at different dates. The dates provided here are in round numbers and can be regarded only as approximate.

(1) Second Century B.C.T. (200–100 B.C.T.)
  General: Tobit (200 B.C.T.)
            Ecclesiasticus (180 B.C.T.)
            Judith (150 B.C.T.)
            Jubilees (110 B.C.T.)
            Sibylline Oracles 3 (125–100 B.C.T.)
  Apocalyptic: Enoch 1–36, 83–90, 106–107 (200–160 B.C.T.)
            Enoch 72–82 (125–100 B.C.T.)
            Testaments of the Twelve Patriarchs (125–100 B.C.T.)
(2) First Century B.C.T. (100–1 B.C.T.)
  General: 1, 2, 3 Maccabees (100 B.C.T.)
            1 Esdras (100 B.C.T.)
            Prayer of Manasses (100 B.C.T.)
            Epistle of Jeremy (100 B.C.T.)
            Prayer of Azariah and Song of the Three Children (100 B.C.T.)
            Susanna (100 B.C.T.)
            Bel and the Dragon (100 B.C.T.)
            Additions to Esther (100 B.C.T.)
            Letter of Aristeas (100 B.C.T.)
            Wisdom of Solomon (50 B.C.T.)
            4 Maccabees (50 B.C.T.)
            Psalms of Solomon (50 B.C.T.)
            Zadokite Fragments (50 B.C.T.)

      Apocalyptic: Enoch 37–71 (105–91 B.C.T.)

                  Enoch 108 (100–75 B.C.T.)

(3) First Century C.C. (1–100 C.C.)

    General: 1 Baruch (100 C.C.)

               Martyrdom of Isaiah (100 C.C.)

               The Books of Adam and Eve (100 C.C.)

               Sibylline Oracles 4, 5 (80–130 C.C.)

    Apocalyptic: Assumption of Moses (1–30 C.C.)

               2 Enoch (50 C.C.)

               2 Baruch (50–90 C.C.)

               3 Baruch (100 C.C.)

               4 Ezra (60–120 C.C.)

Appendix 23.
The Character of the Traditional Intertestamental Literature

The literature traditionally associated with the intertestamental period may be classified under certain descriptive titles indicating the general types or kinds of literature.

(1) *History:* 1, 2, and 3 Maccabees and the Zadokite Fragments

Not all these books are history in any strict sense of the word. Indeed, 1 Maccabees is the only book of the group that measures up to modern historical standards. 2 and 3 Maccabees are only semi-historical. The Zadokite Fragments are classed here only because they furnish the history and covenant of the Zadokite Sect.

(2) *Recensions of and Additions to Old Testament Stories:* Jubilees, Prayer of Manasses, Epistle of Jeremy, Prayer of Azariah and Song of the Three Children, Susanna, Bel and the Dragon, Additions to Esther, 1 Esdras, and 1 Baruch

Most of this material represents enlargements of Old Testament narratives, sometimes the additions are appended to the canonical books, at other times they are inserted in the midst of the narratives, as is done, for example, in Daniel and Esther. The book of Jubilees contains an apocalyptic reinterpretation of the book of Genesis from the standpoint of the later concepts of the Law.

(3) *Stories and Homilies:* Tobit, Judith, Letter of Aristeas, 4 Maccabees, the Books of Adam and Eve, and the Martyrdom of Isaiah

The books in this group are considered to be largely works of fiction. Their purpose appears to be to glorify Jewish customs and institutions.

(4) *Wisdom Literature:* Ecclesiasticus, Wisdom of Solomon, Psalms of Solomon, and the Sibylline Oracles

The wisdom literature is modeled on the wisdom literature of the Old Testament, such as Proverbs and some of the Psalms. The Sibylline Oracles contain some apocalyptic material. They are cast in the form of short verses and epigrammatic statements.

(5) *Apocalyptic Literature:* Enoch, Testaments of the Twelve Patriarchs, Assumption of Moses, 2 Enoch, 2 and 3 Baruch, and 4 Ezra (same as 2 Esdras 3–14)

Appendix 24.
The Lost Documents
of the Old Testament

The biblical record indicates that, once upon a time, there existed the following documents:

The Book of the Wars of Yahweh
    (Numbers 21:14)

The Book of the Just
    (Joshua 10:13, 2 Samuel 1:18)

The Book of the Acts of Solomon
    (1 Kings 11:41)

The Book of the Annals of the Kings
of Israel
    (1 Kings 14:19, 2 Chronicles 33:18)

The Book of the Annals of the Kings
of Judah
    (1 Kings 14:29, 15:7)

The Annals of Samuel the Seer
    (1 Chronicles 29:29)

The History of Nathan the Prophet
    (2 Chronicles 9:29)

The Annals of Shemaiah the Prophet
and of Iddo the Seer
    (2 Chronicles 12:15)

The Annals of Jehu, Son of Hanani
    (2 Chronicles 20:34)

An Untitled Writing of Isaiah
    (2 Chronicles 26:22)

The Annals of Hozai
    (2 Chronicles 33:18)

A Lament for Josiah
    (2 Chronicles 35:25)

Appendix 25.
The Table of Contents of the Qur'an

For the double listings which appear in this table, the first listing is taken from A. J. Arberry's *The Koran Interpreted*, while the second listing is taken from Ahmed Ali's Qur'an translation which comprises *Sacred Writings: Islam: The Qur'an*.

Sura		
1	The Opening	
	The Prologue	*Al-Fatihah*
2	The Cow	
	The Cow	*Al-Baqarah*
3	The House of Imran	
	The Family of Imran	*Al-'Imran*
4	Women	
	The Women	*An-Nisa*
5	The Table	
	The Feast	*Al-Ma'idah*
6	Cattle	
	The Cattle	*Al-An'am*
7	The Battlements	
	Wall Between Heaven and Hell	*Al-A'raf*
8	The Spoils	
	Spoils of War	*Al-Anfal*
9	Repentance	
	Repentance	*At-Taubah*
10	Jonah	
	Jonah	*Yunus*

11	Hood	
	Hud	*Hud*
12	Joseph	
	Joseph	*Yusuf*
13	Thunder	
	Thunder	*Ar-Ra'd*
14	Abraham	
	Abraham	*Ibrahim*
15	El-Hijr	
	Al-Hijr	*Al-Hijr*
16	The Bee	
	The Bees	*An-Nahl*
17	The Night Journey	
	The Children of Israel	*Bani Isra'il*
18	The Cave	
	The Cave	*Al-Kahf*
19	Mary	
	Mary	*Maryam*
20	Ta Ha	
	Ta Ha	*Ta Ha*
21	The Prophets	
	The Prophets	*Al-Anbiya*
22	The Pilgrimage	
	The Pilgrimage	*Al-Hajj*
23	The Believers	
	The True Believers	*Al-Mu'minun*
24	Light	
	The Light	*An-Nur*
25	Salvation	
	The Criterion	*Al-Furqan*
26	The Poets	
	The Poets	*Ash-Shu'ara'*
27	The Ant	
	An-Naml	*An-Naml*
28	The Story	
	The History	*Al-Qasas*

47	Muhammad Muhammad	*Muhammad*
48	Victory Victory	*Al-Fath*
49	The Companies Apartments	*Al-Hujurat*
50	Qaf Qaf	*Qaf*
51	The Scatterers The Dispersing	*Adh-Dhariyat*
52	The Mount The Mount	*At-Tur*
53	The Star The Star	*An-Najm*
54	The Moon The Moon	*Al-Qamar*
55	The All-Merciful Ar-Rahman	*Ar-Rahman*
56	The Terror The Inevitable	*Al-Waqi'ah*
57	Iron Iron	*Al-Hadid*
58	The Disputer The Disputant	*Al-Mujadilah*
59	The Mustering Confrontation	*Al-Hashr*
60	The Woman Tested The Woman Tried	*Al-Mumtahanah*
61	The Ranks Formations	*As-Saff*
62	Congregation The Congregation	*Al-Jumu'ah*
63	The Hypocrites The Hypocrites	*Al-Munafiqun*
64	Mutual Fraud Exposition	*At-Taghabun*

83	The Stinters The Defrauders	*Al-Mutaffifin*
84	The Rending The Cleaving	*Al-Inshiqaq*
85	The Constellations Signs of the Zodiac	*Al-Buruj*
86	The Night-Star The Night Star	*At-Tariq*
87	The Most High The Most High	*Al-A'la*
88	The Enveloper The Overpowering	*Al-Ghashiyah*
89	The Dawn The Dawn	*Al-Fajr*
90	The Land The Earth	*Al-Balad*
91	The Sun The Sun	*Ash-Shams*
92	The Night The Night	*Al-Lail*
93	The Forenoon Early Hours of Morning	*Ad-Duha*
94	The Expanding The Opening Up	*Al-Inshirah*
95	The Fig The Fig	*At-Tin*
96	The Blood-Clot The Embryo	*Al-'Alaq*
97	Power Determination	*Al-Qadr*
98	The Clear Sign The Clear Proof	*Al-Bayyinah*
99	The Earthquake The Earthquake	*Al-Zilzal*
100	The Chargers The Chargers	*Al-'Adiyat*

Appendix 26.
References to Genesis Themes in the Qur'an

For the listings which appear below, the first number refers to the number of the Sura, while the second set of numbers refer to the range of lines of the Sura where the specific reference may be found. A range of lines is provided because not all translations of the Qur'an are the same.

ADAM
2:25–35
3:30–35
3:50–60
7:10–30
19:55–60

    worshipped by the angels
    2:25–35
    7:10–15
    15:25–45
    17:60–65
    18:45–55
    20:115–120
    38:70–80

    expelled from Paradise
    2:25–35
    7:20–30
    20:120–125

    children of Adam
    7:25–35
    7:170–175
    17:70–75
    36:60–65

ANGELS
2:25–35
2:90–95
2:170–175
2:285–290
3:120–125
4:95–100
4:160–165
6:60–65
6:110–115
7:10–15
8:5–10
15:5–10
16:1–5
16:30–40
25:20–30
35
53:25–30
66:5–10
74:30–35
78:35–40

ARK, NOAH'S
7:60–65
10:70–75
11:35–40
23:25–30
54:10–15
69:10–15

Bibliography

Ahmed Ali, translator. *Sacred Writings: Islam: The Qur'an.* New York: Book-of-the-Month Club, 1992.

Arberry, Arthur J., translator. *The Koran Interpreted.* New York: Macmillan Publishing Company, Inc., 1955.

Armstrong, Karen. *A History of God: The 4,000 Year Quest of Judaism, Christianity and Islam.* New York: Ballantine Books, 1993.

Asher, R. E., editor-in-chief. *The Encyclopedia of Language and Linguistics.* Tarrytown, New York: Pergamon Press, Inc., 1994.

Ayto, John. *Dictionary of Word Origins.* New York: Arcade Publishing, 1990.

Azim A. Nanji, ed. *The Muslim Almanac: A Reference Work on the History, Faith, Culture, and Peoples of Islam.* Detroit: Gale Research, Inc., 1996.

Ball, Philip. "Earth Feature: Snowball Fight." *Nature: Science Update*, April 6, 2000.

_____. "Space: Barren Galaxies." *Nature: Science Update,* April 10, 2000.

Barnes-Svarney, Patricia, editorial director. *The New York Public Library Science Desk Reference.* New York: Macmillan, Inc., 1995.

Bartlett, John (Justin Kaplan, ed.). *Bartlett's Familiar Quotations.* Boston: Little, Brown and Company, 1992.

"A Billion Years of Stability." *Discover,* Vol. 19, No. 9 (September 1998).

Blomfield, Adrian. "Scientists discover second genus of early human." *Contra Costa Times,* March 21, 2001.

Boyd, Robert S. "Report gives hellish view of dinosaurs' last days." *The West County Times,* June 6, 2000.

Bunch, Bryan, and Hellemans, Alexander. *The Timetables of Technology: A Chronology of the Most Important People and Events in the History of Technology.* New York: Simon and Schuster, 1993.

Charlesworth, James H., editor. *The Old Testament Pseudepigrapha.* New York: Doubleday, 1983.

Clayton, Peter A. *Chronicle of the Pharaohs: The Reign-by-Reign Record of the Rulers and Dynasties of Ancient Egypt.* London: Thames and Hudson, Ltd., 1994.

"The Colorful Cambrian." *Discover,* Vol. 19, No. 12 (December 1998).

Continents Adrift. San Francisco: W. H. Freeman and Company, 1970.

Coogan, Michael D., editor. *The Oxford History of the Biblical World.* New York: Oxford University Press, 1998.

Crim, Keith, editor. *Dictionary of World Religions.* San Francisco: Harper & Row. 1989.

Davidson, Gustav. *A Dictionary of Angels.* New York: The Free Press, 1967.

Dunham, Will. "Mars calamity may have created conditions for life." *Contra Costa Times*, Thursday, March 15, 2001.

Eiselen, Frederick Carl; Lewis, Edwin; and Downey, David G., editors. *The Abingdon Bible Commentary.* Garden City, New York: The Abingdon Press, 1929.

Eliade, Mircea, ed. *The Encyclopedia of Religion.* New York: Macmillan Publishing Company, 1987.

Encyclopedia Americana. New York: Grolier Incorporated, 1998.

Encyclopaedia Britannica

Encyclopaedia Britannica, Inc. *Great Books of the Western World.* Chicago: Encyclopaedia Britannica, Inc., 1971.

Encyclopedia of Science and Technology, Eighth Edition. New York: McGraw-Hill, 1997.

"End of an Ice Age, Onset of a Cold Spell." *National Geographic,* Vol. 197, No. 2 (February 2000).

The Extinction Files. British Broadcasting Company website: www.bbc.co.uk/education/darwin/exfiles.

Fagan, Brian M., editor. *The Oxford Companion to Archaeology.* New York: Oxford University Press, 1996.

Farmer, William R., editor. *The International Bible Commentary: A Catholic and Ecumenical Commentary for the Twenty-First Century.* Collegeville, Minnesota: The Liturgical Press, 1998.

Felsenfeld, Peter. "Supernova gives insight on unfolding of universe." *Contra Costa Times,* April 3, 2001.

Ferris, Timothy. *Galaxies.* New York: Harrison House, 1987.

Freeman-Grenville, G. S. P. *The Chronology of World History.* Totowa, New Jersey: Rowman and Littlefield, 1978.

Friedman, Richard Elliott. *Who Wrote the Bible?* New York: Summit Books, 1987.

Funk & Wagnalls New Encyclopedia (1983).

"A Global Winter's Tale." *Discover,* Vol. 19, No. 12 (December 1998).

Gonen, Amiram, editor. *The Encyclopedia of the Peoples of the World.* New York: Henry Holt and Company, 1993.

Greenspan, Karen. *The Timetables of Women's History: A Chronology of the Most Important People and Events in Women's History.* New York: Simon & Schuster, 1994.

Gribetz, Judah. *The Timetables of Jewish History: A Chronology of the Most Important People and Events in Jewish History.* New York: Simon & Schuster, 1993.

Hellemans, Alexander, and Bunch, Bryan. *The Timetables of Science: A Chronology of the Most Important People and Events in the History of Science.* New York: Simon & Schuster, 1988.

Hiesberger, Jean Marie, general editor. *The Catholic Bible.* New York: Oxford University Press, 1995.

Hotz, Robert Lee. "Researchers unearth new human ancestor." *Contra Costa Times,* March 22, 2001.

Jackson, Guida M. *Women Who Ruled.* New York: Barnes & Noble, Inc., 1990.

Jenkins, Everett, Jr. *The Muslim Diaspora: A Comprehensive Reference to the Spread of Islam in Asia, Africa, Europe and the Americas, 570–1500.* Jefferson, North Carolina: McFarland & Company, 1999.

Jones, C. H. W., translator. *The Oldest Code of Laws in the World: The Code of Laws Promulgated by Hammurabi, King of Babylon, B.C. 2285–2242.* Edinburgh: T. & T. Clark, 1905.

Koeberl, Christian, and Sharpton, Virgil L. *Terrestrial Impact Crater Slide Set.* Lunar and Planetary Institute.

Krisciunas, Kevin, and Yenne, Bill. *The Pictorial Atlas of the Universe.* Brompton Books Corporation, 1989.

Lapidus, Ira M. *A History of Islamic Societies.* New York: Cambridge University Press, 1988.

Lemley, Brad. "Why is there life?" *Discover,* November 2000.

Lemonick, Michael D. "The Riddle of Time." *Time,* Vol. 154, No. 26 (December 27, 1999).

Long, Charles H. *Alpha: The Myths of Creation.* Atlanta: Scholars Press, 1963.

The Lost Books of the Bible and the Forgotten Books of Eden. World Bible Publishers, 1926 and 1927.

Mantran, Robert, ed. *Great Dates in Islamic*

History. New York: Facts on File, Inc., 1996.

Maran, Stephen P. *How the Moon Was Born.* Chicago: World Book, Inc., 1999.

"Mars Revealed: A New Look at Forces That Shape the Desert Planet." National Geographic Society. National Geographic Maps, February 2001.

Mason, Anthony; Mahon, Anne; and Currie, Andrew. *World Facts and Place.* London: Tiger Books International, 1993.

McLean, Dewey. "Dinosaur Extinction: The Volcano-Greenhouse Theory." McLean website: filebox.vt.edu/artsci/geology/mclean/Dinosaur_Volcano_Extinction/

Merriam Webster's Geographical Dictionary. Third Edition. Springfield, Massachusetts: Merriam-Webster, Inc., 1997.

Metzger, Bruce M., and Coogan, Michael D., editors. *The Oxford Companion to the Bible.* New York: Oxford University Press, 1993.

Naeye, Robert. "Moon of Our Delight." *Discover,* Volume 15, Number 1 (January, 1994).

The New Open Bible: Study Edition. Nashville: Thomas Nelson Publishers, 1990.

Newby, Gordon Darnell. *The Making of the Last Prophet: A Reconstruction of the Earliest Biography of Muhammad.* Columbia: University of South Carolina Press, 1989.

Norell, Mark A.; Gaffney, Eugene S.; and Dingus, Lowell. *Discovering Dinosaurs.* New York: Alfred A. Knopf, 1995.

Ochoa, George, and Corey, Melinda. *The Timeline Book of Arts.* New York: The Stonesong Press, Inc., 1995.

_____. *The Timeline Book of Science.* New York: The Stonesong Press, Inc., 1995.

Parfit, Michael. "Australia—A Harsh Awakening." *National Geographic,* July 2000.

Parfitt, Tudor. *Journey to the Vanished City: The Search for a Lost Tribe of Israel.* New York: Saint Martin's Press, 1993.

Parise, Frank, ed. *The Book of Calendars.* New York: Facts on File, Inc., 1982.

Parker, Geoffrey, ed. *The World: An Illustrated History.* New York, Harper & Row, 1986.

"Passover and the Plague." *Discover,* Vol. 19, No. 8 (August 1998).

Perlman, David. "Crystal Hints at Life on Mars: But not all scientists see it as evidence of ancient organism." *San Francisco Chronicle,* Tuesday, February 27, 2001.

Powell, Corey S. "Before Stonehenge." *Discover,* Vol. 19, No. 7 (July, 1998).

_____. "Twenty Ways the World Could End." *Discover,* Vol. 21, No. 10 (October 2000).

"Report: skin color a regional adaptation." *Daily Republic,* August 27, 2000.

Ross, Emma. "Europeans tracked to a few African ancestors." *Contra Costa Times,* April 21, 2001.

Ryan, William, and Pitman, Walter. *Noah's Flood: The Scientific Discoveries About the Event That Changed History.* New York: Simon & Schuster, 1998.

Sacred Writings: Christianity: The Apocrypha and the New Testament. New York: Book-of-the-Month Club, 1992.

Sacred Writings: Islam: The Qur'an. New York: Book-of-the-Month Club, 1992.

Sacred Writings: Judaism: The Tanakh. New York: Book-of-the-Month Club, 1992.

Sawyer, Kathy. "Unveiling the Universe." *National Geographic,* Volume 196, No. 4 (October 1999).

Scarre, Chris, editor-in-chief. *Smithsonian Timelines of the Ancient World.* London: Dorling Kindersley, Inc., 1993.

Stamps, Donald C., general editor. *The Full Life Study Bible: An International Study Bible for Spirit-Filled Christians.* Grand Rapids, Michigan: Zondervan Publishing House, 1992.

Thompson, Frank Charles, editor. *The New Chain-Reference Bible.* Indianapolis: B. B. Kirkbride Bible Company, Inc., 1964.

Trager, James. *The People's Chronology: A Year-by-Year Record of Human Events from Prehistory to the Present.* New York: Henry Holt and Company, Inc., 1992.

_____. *The Women's Chronology: A Year-by-Year Record, from Prehistory to the Present.*

New York: Henry Holt and Company, Inc., 1994.

Ussher, James. *The Annals of the World.* London: E. Tyler for J. Crook and G. Bedell, 1658.

Watson, Jane Werner. *The Giant Golden Book of Dinosaurs and Other Prehistoric Reptiles.* Racine, Wisconsin: Western Publishing Company, Inc., 1960.

Webster's New Collegiate Dictionary. Springfield, Massachusetts: G. & C. Merriam Company, 1981.

Webster's New World Encyclopedia. New York: Simon & Schuster, 1992.

Weekes, Richard V., ed. *Muslim Peoples: A World Ethnographic Survey.* Westport, Connecticut: Greenwood Press, 1984.

Weiner, Jonathan. *Planet Earth.* New York: Bantam Books, Inc., 1986.

Wilford, John Noble. "Faint Objects Found in Cosmic X-rays." *The New York Times,* January 14, 2000.

World Book Dictionary

World Book Encyclopedia

World Book Encyclopedia Yearbook

World Book Encyclopedia Science Yearbook

Zabarenko, Deborah. "Distant supernova hints at dark, repulsive energy." *Contra Costa Times,* April 2, 2001.

Zodhiates, Spiros, executive editor. *Hebrew-Greek Key Word Study Bible.* Chattanooga, Tennessee: AMG Publishers, 1991.

Index